Sisson's
Word and Expression
Locater

Sisson's

Word and Expression

Locater

A. F. Sisson

Parker Publishing Company, Inc.
West Nyack, N.Y.

Third Printing......June, 1967

© 1966 by Parker Publishing Company, Inc.
West Nyack, N.Y.

Library of Congress Catalog Card Number: 66-10390
Printed in the United States of America

81067   B&P

How to Use This Book

This volume is a type of thesaurus, containing a most complete word and expression index and the more important synonyms or words of related connotation. It is thus an *index verborum* and a *synonymicon*. In fact, it is an index to the unabridged dictionary and to other sources of the more obscure and unusual words and phrases useful in English construction. It may seem paradoxical that there should be a need for a word index, since all standard dictionaries have their items arranged in alphabetical order. Nevertheless, a person may be unable to locate a word or expression unless he has a reasonable idea of the spelling of the word, or unless he can remember at least the initial portion of the expression he wishes to use.

Suppose one cannot recall the Latin expression meaning "there is no accounting for tastes." In this book, such expression (*de gustibus non est disputandum*) will be found, together with a French phrase of similar meaning, indexed under "taste." A person may wish to know the term for the religious ascetic who sits and gazes at his navel, or the name of this practice. Both can be located in this book under "navel," whereas unless one knows "hesychast," "omphalopsychite," or "omphaloskepsis" he would be unlikely to find these words in a dictionary. Perhaps one may want the name of the primitive practice of making a small crude model of a person who is to be harmed by sticking the model with pins or otherwise mistreating it. This word cannot be found under "model" or "magic" in any dictionary or other word book, but it can in this volume, which also contains hundreds of words and expressions that *cannot* be found in the unabridged dictionary.

Other unusual words made easy to locate include that for hater of tobacco smoke (misocapnist, **q.v. under** "tobacco") ; mania for holding public office (empleomania, **indexed under** "public") ; a novel, often biographical, developing a character from childhood to maturity (entwicklungsroman, **listed under** "novel") ; computing time by counting tree rings (dendrochronology, **q.v. under** "time" **and** "tree") ; having beautiful and shapely buttocks (callipygian, **indexed under** "buttocks") ; pretentious use of recondite words and phrases (lexiphanticism, **see under** "word") ; use of long words such as these (sesquipedalianism **or** polysyllabism, **also indexed under** "word") ; an uncontrollable obsession for words (verbo-onomatomania, **see under** "word") ; stretching when drowsy upon awakening (pandiculation, **q.v. under** "stretching") ; a description of rivers (potamography, **listed under** "river") ; the right of the strongest (*le droit du plus fort,* **see** "strong") ; practice of transposition of letters, words, etc., in reading or writing (metathesis **or** strephosymbolia, **q.v. under** "letter," "transposition" **or** "word") ; unintentional repetition of letters or words (dittography, **see under** "repetition") ; an unconscious use of a word or words other than that intended (heterophemy **or** *lapsus linguae,* **see under** ("word") ; speech that puts one asleep (*discours as-*

soupissant, **indexed under** "speech"); an insignificant anonymous writer (anony-muncule, **listed under** "writer"); a person who is self-taught (autodidact, **see under** "self"); a supplement to a book containing matters not included in the text (paralipomena, **q.v. under** "supplement"); a novel with real persons, events, etc., disguised (*roman à clef,* **listed under** "novel"); a person who is mentally defective but brilliant in some field (idiot savant, **listed under** "person"); false and spurious writings (anagignoskomena, apocrypha, **or** pseudepigrapha, **q.v. under** "falsely" **or** "writing"); use of a man's name by a woman writer, as George Eliot (pseu-dandry, **listed under** "name" **or** "writer"); use of a woman's name by a man writer (pseudogyny, **similarly listed**); complete works of a writer (*opera omnia,* **q.v. under** "writer"); mania for writing (*cacoethes scribendi* **or** *furor scribendi,* **listed under** "writing"); a pompous person (Aldibrontiphoscophornio, **indexed under** "person"); and thousands of others.

From the foregoing, it will be observed that this book enables one not only to locate, from the thought involved, unusual and unfamiliar terminology, but also to help recall to mind a word or phrase which may have been temporarily for-gotten. It is thus a locater, an aid to memory (*aide-memoire* **which expression will be found under** "memory"), and an aid to vocabulary enhancement.

This is, in some respects, a dictionary in reverse. Instead of supplying the mean-ing of a word, it furnishes the word from its meaning. As an indication of its comprehensiveness, one need only to examine such entries as "word" (136 entries and 309 definitions), "person" (137 entries and 413 definitions); "stubborn" (56 synonyms or related meanings), and such other items as "fear," "food," "knowl-edge," "language," "name," "self," "time," to name only a few.

Sisson's Word and Expression Locater has been prepared for persons who seek to express their thoughts with precision and effectiveness, and who desire to have access to an alphabetized listing of words and phrases useful in their work or studies. Business executives, advertising copywriters, authors, journalists, and others who prepare literature for public perusal will find among the synonyms and related terms a wellspring of variable choices to overcome bromidic and stereo-typical words and expressions so often encountered, thus making it possible to add scintillation and a cachet of originality to their literary efforts. For example, in this book one finds after the entry "attractive" (with cross-reference to "alluring") the following choices: arresting, beguiling, bewitching, bonny, captivating, Cir-cean, comely decorative, decorous, enticing, fascinating, intriguing, magnetic, mes-meric, personable, persuasive, prepossessing, psychagogic and seductive. Many other classifications are even more extensive, there being 56 synonyms for "stub-born" 34 for "change," 34 for "secret," 26 for "trick," and 23 for "gaiety" to cite but a few.

This volume will be of invaluable assistance to college and high-school students in the preparation of term papers, theses, and other monographs, or as a vocabu-lary builder. Any educated adult who wishes to enhance his vocabulary, or to locate a word or expression which has escaped his memory, will find this book very useful.

How to Use This Book

Many ordinary words, those a person of average schooling would be presumed to know, have not been included, nor is the book loaded with scientific or technical terms, there being listed only those which have some general application. In this way, and in many other respects, it differs from all previous synonymicons, thesauri, word finders, and other books dealing with vocabulary.

All polysyllabic words found in English writing are not in this book. For example, the following are taken from *Gargantua* by Rabelais, Chapter XV:

disincornifistibulated his nether shoulder blade

morrambouzevezengouzequoquemorgasacbaquevezinemaffreliding my poor eyes

mocrocastebezasteverestegrigeligoscopapopondrillated us in all our upper members

trepignemanpenillorifrizonoufresterfumbledtumbled and squeezed her.

And from Shakespeare's *Love's Labor Lost* (Act V, Scene I):

honorificabilitudinitatibus.

I have made a careful edit of the manuscript copy of *Sisson's Word and Expression Locater* by Dr. A. F. Sisson, and I should like to say that I have been deeply impressed by the contents of this most remarkable book. In my forty-one years as a teacher of English language and literature at the University of Maryland, I have examined many books dealing with vocabulary and linguistic studies and with words and their ways and uses in the development of the English language, and I can certify that no book with which I am familiar shows as much thoroughness and as much real scholarship as the *Word and Expression Locater*.

Any person interested in expanding his vocabulary or in finding unusual expressions for familiar and trite terminology is certain to be rewarded by referring to this remarkable text. Teachers, editors, critics, linguists and especially writers of scholarly texts should own and use Dr. A. F. Sisson's *Word and Expression Locater*. Its use is certain to be rewarding.

Susan E. Harman, Ph. D.
Professor Emeritus
English Language and Literature
University of Maryland

Explanation of Abbreviations
and Signs Used in This Book

Phrases and expressions relating to aspects of subject words appear in italics under subject words. For example, *great* and *lack of* and *one having great diversity of* are indexed under ABILITY, with definitions provided.

a. .... adjective	**mus.** .... music *or* musical
abb. .... abbreviated	**n.** .... noun
acct. .... account	**opp.** .... opposite
adv. .... adverb	**part.** .... particularly
bet. .... between	**pert.** .... pertaining
cond. ...... condition	**pl.** .... plural
conj. .... conjunction	**prep.** ...... preposition
dir. .... direction	**q.v.** .... which see
esp. .... especially	**rel.** .... relating *or* relative
fem. .... feminine *or* female	**sing.** .... singular
int. .... interjection	**usu.** .... usually
lit. .... literature *or* literary	**v.** .... verb
misc. ...... miscellaneous	**w/o.** .... without

A

ABANDON: **v.** abdicate; abjure; apostatize; jettison; recant; relinquish; renounce; repudiate; surcease; surrender; vacate; **n.** ABANDONMENT: abdication; abjuration; apostasy; defection; recantation; relinquishment; renunciation; **a.** ABANDONED: apostate; apostatic; derelict; renunciative; renunciatory

ABASH: **v.** chagrin; daunt; discomfit; discompose; disconcert; humble; humiliate; mortify; **n.** ABASHMENT: (**see** "embarrassment") humiliation; mortification

ABBREVIATE: **v.** abridge; curtail; diminish; epitomize; synopsize; truncate; **n.** ABBREVIATION: **see** "summary"

ABDOMEN: **n.** paunch; pleon; tharm; venter
  contents of: **n.** viscus; (**pl.** viscera); **a.** alvine; c(o)eliac; intestinal; splanchnic; visceral
  having large: **a.** abdominous; ventripotent
  pain in (esp. stomach): **n.** gastralgia
  pert. to: **a.** abdominous; alvine; c(o)eliac; intestinal; splanchnic; visceral

ABERRATION: **see** "deviation"

ABET: **v.** advocate; countenance; espouse; foment; instigate; sanction; subscribe; subsidize; succor; **a.** (**see** "aiding") adjuvant; ancillary; contributory; subsidiary; **n.** ABETMENT: (**see** "help") adjuvancy; **n.** ABETTOR: **see** "accessory"

ABHORRENCE, *object or person of:* **n.** abomination; *bête noire;* execration; odium

ABILITY (or ABILITIES): **n.** adroitness; (ambi)dexterity; aptitude; attainment; caliber; capability; capacity; competence; *dynamis;* dynamism; endowment; faculty; ingeniosity; ingenuity; panurgy; potency; proficiency; talent; versatility
  great: **n.** expertise; virtuosity
  lack of: **n.** incapacitation; incompetence
  one having great diversity of: (**see** "jack-of-all-trades") **n.** Proteus; **n.** (ambi)dexterity

ABJECT: (**see** "base") **a.** contemptible; despicable; grovel(l)ing; ignoble

ABLE: (**see** "competent") **a.** dextrous; ingenious; proficient; versatile

ABNORMAL: **a.** aberrant; adventitious; anomalistic; anomalous; atypical; bizarre; eccentric; exceptional; extraordinary; grotesque; heteroclite; heterodox; idiosyncratic; pathological; phenomenal; preternatural; prodigious; supernatural; teratogenic; unconventional; unorthodox; **n.** ABNORMALITY: aberration; anomalism; anomaly; deviant; deviate; foible; heterodox(y); idiosyncrasy; imperfection; irregularity; macula; mannerism; phenomenality; phenom(enon); singularity; stigma
  person or thing: **n.** aberrant; anomaly; atypical; deviant; deviate; heteroclite; heterodox; mutation; phenomenality; phenom(enon); prodigy; *rara avis;* sport

ABODE: (**see** "house") **n.** aerie; caravansary; domicile; habitat(ion); hearthstone; ingleside; rookery; xenodochium; a domiciliary

ABOLISH: (**see** "eliminate") **v.** abrogate; annihilate; deracinate; disestablish; eradicate; expunge; exterminate; extirpate; invalidate; vitiate

ABOMINABLE: **see** "accursed"

ABOUT: **prep.** anent; *circa; circiter; in re*
  -face: (**see** "reversal") **n.** *volte-face*

1

ABOVE: **a.** superior; superadjacent; supernal
  as: **adv.** *ut supra*
  being or coming from: **a.** celestial; supernal
  -board: **adv.** *cartes sur table*
  mentioned, where: **adv.** *ubi supra*

ABRADE: **see** "annoy"

ABREAST: **see** "up-to-date"

ABRIDGE: **see** "abbreviate" **and** "abstract"

ABRIDGEMENT: (**see** "summary") **n.** *précis;* schema

ABRUPT: (**see** "rude") **a.** brusque; impetuous; instantaneous; precipitant; precipitate; precipitous; staccato; subitaneous; tumultuous; unceremonious; **n.** ABRUPTNESS: (**see** "haste") brusqueness; brusquerie; impetuosity; impulsivity; instantaneity; precipitancy

ABSENCE: **n.** absentation
  during: **adv.** *durante absentia*
  in: **adv.** *in absentia*
  of mind: **see** "absent-mindedness"
  to be conspicuous by: **adv.** *briller par son absence*

ABSENT: **a.** absentaneous; abstracted
  in state of being: **adv.** *in absentia*
  -minded: **a.** abstracted; distrait; distraught; inattentive; oblivious; preoccupied
  -mindness: **n.** *absence d'esprit;* abstraction; heedlessness; preoccupation; reverie

ABSOLUTE: (**see** "inclusive" **and** "out-and-out") **a.** arbitrary; arrant; authentic; authoritative; autocratic; categorical; despotic; exhaustive; imprescriptible; inalienable; indefeasible; indubitable; invincible; irrefutable; mathematical; official; peremptory; plenary; plenipotent(ial); plenipotentiary; *pur et simple;* sweeping; thorough-going; unalienable; unequivocal; unmitigated; unqualified; unquestionable; unswerving; wholehearted
  possession or control: **n.** monopolization; monopoly; **a.** monopolistic
  rule: **n.** tyrannis; tyranny; **a.** tyrannic(al)

ABSORB: **v.** assimilate; consume; engulf; imbibe; incorporate; osmose; metabolize; monopolize; **a.** ABSORBENT: assimilative; assimilatory; bibulous; imbibitional; monopolistic; osmotic

ABSORPTION: **n.** assimilation; bibulosity; consumption; inhibition; incorporation; metabolism; monopolization; osmosis
  agent increasing: **n.** absorbefacient
  not capable of: **a.** inabsorbable

ABSTRACT: **v.** (**see** "remove") abridge; condense; epitomize; purloin; **a.** abstruse; acroamatic; esoteric; hermetic(al); inconcrete; incorporeal; metaphysical; nebulous; recondite; stratospheric(al); supernatural; theoretical; transcendental; **n.** abbrieviature; abridgement; capsulation; compendium; conspectus; epitome; lexicon; *precis; résumé;* summary; syllabus; synopsis
  entity (as "whiteness" or "virtue"): **n.** abstractum; (**pl.** abstracta); subsistent
  in the: **adv.** *in abstracta*
  quality or state of being: **n.** transcendentality
  rel. to or dealing w/ the: **a.** nomothetic; theoretic(al)
  scheme or plan: **n.** architectonic(s)

ABSTRACTED: **see** "absent-minded"

ABSTRACTION: **n.** abbreviature; abridgement; abstrusity; immateriality; incorporeality; incorporeity; nebulosity
  mental: **n.** brown study; cogitation; lucubration; preoccupation; reverie

ABSTRUSE: **see** "abstract" **and** "abstraction"
  something which is, or quality of being: **n.** abstrusity; immateriality; incorporeality; incorporeity; nebulosity; profundity

ABSURD: (**see** "funny") **a.** ad absurdum; asinine; baroque; bizarre; chimerical; daedalic; egregious; fantastic; fatuous; grotesque; impracticable; inane; infeasable; insuperable; laputan; ludicrous; macaronic; monstrous; preposterous; ridiculous; unbelievable; unrealistic
  too (absurd) for belief: **adv.** *ab absurdo; ad absurdum*

ABSURDITY: **n.** asininity; *bêtise;* bizarrerie; grotesqueness; grotesquerie; inanity; incredibility; ineptitude; irrationality; *non sequitur;* ridiculosity; **a. see** "absurd"

imaginary creature regarded as absolute
(*absurdity*) : **n.** coquecigrue
proof of opposite by showing: **n.** *reductio
ad absurdum*
argument by this method: **n.** apagoge;
a. apagogic(al)
stupid: **n.** maggotry
to the point of: **adv.** *ad absurdum*

ABUNDANCE: **n.** affluence; amplitude;
copiosity; copiousness; cornucopia; lavishness; luxuriance; magnitude; opulence;
opulency; plen(t)itude; pleonasm; plethora; prodigality; profusion; repletion;
satiety; sumptuosity; superfluity; **a.**
ABUNDANT: abounding; affluent; ample; copious; cornucopian; exhaustless;
exuberant; feracious; inexhaustible; lavish; lush; luxuriant; opulent; plenteous;
plen(t)itudinous; plethoric; profuse; prolific; replete; teeming
of words: **n.** affluence; circumlocution;
copia verborum; facundity; loquaciousness; loquacity; periphrasis; tautology

ABUSE: (**see** "censure") **v.** blaspheme;
defame; disparage; malign; maltreat; revile; traduce; vituperate; **n.** (**see** "sassiness") abusiveness; animadversion; billingsgate; calumny; castigation; condemnation; contumely; defamation; excoriation; execration; expostulation; humiliation; infamy; maltreatment; objurgation;
obloquy; philippic; reprehension; scurrility; villification; vituperation
language of: **n.** billingsgate; vituperation

ABUSIVE: **a.** captious; castigatory; caustic; censorious; clamorous; condemnatory;
contemptuous; contumelious; damnatory;
defamatory; denunciatory; despicable; disparaging; infamous; malign; objurgatory;
opprobrious; reproachful; reprobative;
sarcastic; sardonic; satirical; scurrilous;
trenchant; vituperative; vituperous
and loud: **a.** scurrilous; thersitical
speech or writing: **n.** diatribe; jeremiad;
philippic; tirade

ACADEMIC: **a.** collegiate; conjectural; didactic; doctrinaire; doctrinal; hypothetical; literary; pedantic; Platonic; postulatory; propaedeutic(al); quodlibetic(al);
scholarly; scholastic; speculative; suppositional; supposititious; theoretical
environment: **n.** academe; academia

expression: **n.** scholasm

ACCENT: **n.** cadence; emphasis; ictus; inflection; intonation; stress

ACCEPT: *as own or as equal, or give full
validity to:* **v.** nostrificate; **n.** nostrification
for want of anything better: **adv.** *faute
de mieux;* **n.** Hobson's choice

ACCEPTED: (**see** "conventional") **a.** according to Hoyle; canonical; conformable;
orthodox; prevalent, sanctioned; traditional; **n.** ACCEPTANCE: acceptation;
canonicity; orthodoxy
in social usage: **a.** *comme il faut*
moral standards or behavior: **n. pl.** (the)
amenities; canons of propriety; (the) civilities; convenances; conventions; (the)
proprieties
standards, conforming to: (**see** "proper"
and "standards") **a.** canonical; ethical;
orthodox

ACCESS: **n.** approach; channel; *entrée*

ACCESSORY: (**see** "adjunct") **n.** accomplice; addendum; appurtenance; auxiliary;
coadjutor; collaborator; collaborateur;
colleague; complementary; confederate;
confrère; incidental; satellite; subordinate;
succenturiate; **a.** (**see** "subsidiary") auxiliary; complementary; incidental; succenturiate
in crime: **n.** confederate; *particeps
criminis; socius criminis*
something which is: **n.** appurtenance;
parergon; (**pl.** parerga); satellite

ACCIDENT: **n.** calamity; casualty; contingency; contretemps; fortuity; inadvertence; inadvertency; misadventure; mischance; mishap
inevitable or unavoidable: **n.** act of God;
casus fortuitus; force majeure; vis major
loss from: **n.** *damnum fatale*
unlucky: **n.** contretemps

ACCIDENTAL: (**see** "involuntary") **a.**
adjective; adventitious; casual; contingent; extraneous; fortuitous; inadvertent;
incidental; serendipitous; unfortunate; un
intentional; unmotivated; unpremeditated;
untoward; unwitting
discovery: **n.** serendipity; **a.** serendipitous
quality or state of being: **n.** accidentality; extraneity; fortuity; inadvertency

ACCLAIM: (see "honor" and "fame") n. *éclat;* homage; plaudit

ACCLIMATE: see "accustom"

ACCOMMODATE: see "adapt"

ACCOMPANIMENT: n. circumstantiality; collaboration; complement; concomitance; noncomitancy; concomitant; corollary; obbligato
w/o musical: a. or adv. *a capella*

ACCOMPANYING: (see "at same time" and "secondary") a. adventitious; circumstantial; concomitant; incidental

ACCOMPLICE: see "accessory"

ACCOMPLISH: (see "complete") v. actualize; consummate; effectuate; execute; fulfill; implement; perpetrate; realize; a. (see "done") implementary

ACCOMPLISHMENT: n. achievement; actuality; actualization; consummation; effectuation; entelechy; fulfillment; implementation; realization; talent
one's special: n. forte; *métier; tour de force*

ACCORD: (see "agreement") n. assonance; compatibility; congruity; consentience; consonance; correspondence; harmony; unanimity; unity
in: a. concordant; consentaneous; consentient; consonant; *en rapport;* harmonious; unanimous

ACCORDING *to custom:* adv. *ad usum* (abb. ad us.) ; *comme il faut; ex more*
to rule: adv. *ad amussim; ad usum* (abb. ad us.) ; *en règle;* a. consuetudinary; conventional; *de règle; de rigueur; selon les règles;* traditional
to value: adv. *ad valorem*

ACCUMULATE: v. agglutinate; aggregate; conglomerate; pyramid; n. ACCUMULATION: accretion; acervation; agglutination; aggregation; cache; congeries; conglomeration; incrustation; pyramid; superfetation; a. ACCUMULATIVE: accumulatable; augmentative; cumulative; pyramidal

ACCURATE: (see "correct" and "precise") a. authentic; authoritative; author-

ized; definitive; trustworthy; unflattering; veracious; n. ACCURACY: authenticity; correctitude; correctness; definitude; exactitude; fidelity; pnuctuality; veracity

ACCURSED: (see "bad") a. abominable; detestable; execrable; inimical; maledictive; maledictory; malefic
greed of gold: n. *auri sacra fames*

ACCUSATION: n. arraignment; ascription; attribution; crimination; delation; denouncement; impeachment; imputation; incrimination; inculpation
central part of: n. gravaman
counter: n. recrimination; v. recriminate; a. recriminative; recriminatory

ACCUSE: v. impeach; impute; (in)criminate; inculpate; indict; reproach; a. ACCUSATORY: accusative; imputable; imputational; (in)criminative; inculpative; inculpatory

ACCUSER: n. accusant; (fem. accusatrix); delator; denunciator; informer; plaintiff; prosecutor

ACCUSTOM: v. acclimate; acclimatize; discipline; familiarize; habituate; inure; naturalize; orientate; season; n. acclimation; acclimatization; habituation; inurement; orientation

ACID: a. acescent; acidulated; acidulent; acidulous; acrimonious; caustic; corrosive; penetrating; trenchant; vinegary; n. ACIDITY: acerbity; acor, acrimony; causticity
containing or yielding: a. acidiferous
convert into: v. acidify; n. acidification

ACME: n. apex; apogee; climacteric; climacterium; climax; consummation; culmination; meridian; *nec plus ultra;* pinnacle; sublimity; ultimate; vertex; zenith; a. (see "greatest") climacteric

ACQUAINTED: (see "familiar") a. *au courant; au fait;* cognizant; (con)versant

ACQUIRE: see "get"

ACQUITTAL: n. absolution; deliverance; emancipation; exculpation; justification; vindication; a. absolutory; justificatory; vindicatory

ACRIMONY: **n.** acerbity; acridity; asperity; causticity; irascibility; malevolence; virulence

ACT(S): (**see** "action") **n.** exploit; gest(e); gymnastic(s); gyration; performance; **v.** function; officiate; operate
  bold: **n.** bravura; (**pl.** audacities)
  caught in the: **adv.** *in actu; in flagrante delicto;* red-handed
  courteous or graceful: **n. pl.** civilities; convenances; (the) amenities; (the) proprieties; urbanities
  evil or unlawful: **n.** felony; malefaction; malfeasance; misdemeanor; **a.** felonious; malfeasant
  interval or short program bet.: **n.** *entr'acte*
  justified by result: **n.** *exitus acta probat*
  "of God": **n.** *casus fortuitus; force majeure; vis major*
  pathological repetition of those of others: **n.** echopraxia
  thoughtless: **n.** *étourderie*

ACTING *for a principal:* **a.** delegated; substitutionary; vicarious; **n.** *locum tenens*
  or actors, pert. to: **a.** histrionic(al); (melo)dramatic; operatic; theatrical; tragicomic; **n.** histrionic; theatricality; (**pl.** histrionics; theatrics)
  second-rate (playing to audience): **n.** cabotinage; theatricality

ACTION(S): (**see** "act(s)" **and** "conduct") **n.** accomplishment; achievement; liveliness; sprightliness; vivacity
  initiator of: **see** "stimulator"
  not free (theory): **n.** determinism; fatalism; predestination
  out of (action): **adv.** *hors de combat;* **a.** emerited; emeritus; superannuated
  ready for: **a.** *en garde*
  remote, or w/o contact: **n.** *actio ad distans*
  repetition, pathological, of those of others: **n.** echomimia; echopraxia
  shameless or vainglorious: **n. pl.** heroics; histrionics; theatricalities; theatrics
  sudden and successful: (**see** "stroke") **n.** coup
  symbolic: **n.** charade

ACTIVATOR: **see** "stimulator"

ACTIVE: (**see** "busy") **a.** animated; athletic; dynamic(al); indefatigable; kinetic; operose; sedulous; spirited; sprite; sthenic; vivacious

ACTIVITY: (**see** "energy") **n.** agility; animation; celerity; gambit; liveliness; nimbleness; operosity; ploy; pursuit; sprightliness; vivacity
  center of: **n.** tempest; vortex
  feverish: **n.** alarums and excursions
  muscular, abnormally increased: **n.** hyperkinesia; **a.** hyperkinetic

ACTOR(S): (**see** "acting") **n.** barnstormer; facient; histrio(n); participant; thespian; tragedian; (**fem.** tragedienne); trouper; (**pl.** *corps dramatique; dramatis personae; personae*)
  beginner (fem.): **n.** ingenue; soubrette
  extra, or w/ small part: **n.** supernumerary
  goddess of: **n.** Minerva
  leading or star: **n.** protagonist; (**fem.** *première*)
  next to star: **n.** deuteragonist
  of third importance in play: **n.** tritagonist
  pert. to: **see under** "acting"
  silent: **n.** *persona muta*

ACTRESS, *young:* **n.** ingenue; soubrette

ACTUAL: (**see** "real") **a.** authentic; concrete; *de facto;* existent; legitimate; official; substantial; unadulterated; veritable
  assume to be or treat as: **v.** hypostatize

ACTUALITY: (**see** "accomplishment") **n.** entity; existent; objectivity, verity
  complete: **n.** entelechy; *factum est; fait accompli*

ACUTE: **a.** critical; crucial; discerning; exigent; extreme; penetrating; penetrative; poignant; trenchant

ADAGE: (**see** "maxim") **n.** aphorism; apothegm; bromide; saw; truism; **a.** aphoristic; apothegmatic(al); bromidic

ADAPT: (**see** "accustom") **v.** acclimate; acclimatize; accommodate; conform; habituate; harmonize; naturalize; orientate; reconcile; **a.** ADAPTABLE: (**see** "teachable") adaptational; amenable; flexuous; labile; malleable; plastic; tractable
  to a situation: **v.** temporize; **n.** conformation; habituation; inurement; orientation; temporization

ADAPTATION : **n.** accommodation; adjustment; conformation; habituation; inurement; lability; orientation
as lit. or mus. work: **n.** rifacimento
to situation or environment: **see under** "adapt"

ADD : **v.** aggrandize; aggravate; augment; enhance; exacerbate; intensify; introduce; magnify; (super)impose; **a.** ADDED : **see** "additional"

ADDICT : **n.** buff; devotee; enthusiast; habituate; *habitué*

ADDITION : **n.** accessory; addendum; additament; adjunct(ion); ap(p)anage; appendage; augmentation; (super)imposition; **a.** ADDITIONAL : (**see** "supplementary") **n.** *au reste*
gradual: **n.** accrescence; accretion; agglutination; concretion

ADDRESS : (**see** "skill") **n.** adroitness; bearing; deportment; dexterity; ingenuity
in speech or writing: (**see** "speech") **n.** allocution; apostrophe; salutation; **a.** apostrophic; salutational; salutatory; **v.** apostrophize
to person usu. not present, or to something personified for rhetorical purpose: **n.** apostrophe; **v.** apostrophize

ADEQUATE : (**see** "equivalent") **a.** condign; commensurate; competent; **n.** ADEQUACY : abundance; adequation; amplitude; competence; competency; copiosity; copiousness; equivalence; plentitude; sufficiency

ADHERE : **v.** (ag)glutinate; cohere; persevere; **n.** ADHERENT : **see** "follower"; **a.** adhesive; agglutinative; cohesive; glutinous; mucillaginous; tenacious; viscid; viscous
closely (adhering): **a.** adhesive; cohesive; osculant; tenacious

ADJACENT (or ADJOINING) : **a.** abutting; co(n)terminous; contiguous; juxtaposed; juxtapositional; limitrophe; satellite; tangent; **n.** ADJACENCY : contiguity; immediacy; tangency

ADJOURNMENT, *final:* **adv.** *sine die*

ADJUNCT : (**see** "accessory") **n.** addendum; additament; ap(p)anage; appendage; appurtenance; auxiliary; endowment; perquisite

ADJUST : (**see** "adapt") **v.** accommodate; concinnate; equalize; equate; harmonize; methodize; pacify; rectify; resolve; synchronize; systematize; **a.** ADJUSTABLE : adaptable; adjustmental; amenable; fictile; malleable; modificatory; modulatory; plastic; pliable; **n.** ADJUSTABLITY : adaptability; amenability; modulability; plasticity

ADJUSTMENT : **n.** acclimation; acclimatization; accommodation; concinnity; equilibration; equilibrium; harmonization; orientation; synchronization
to line of sight: **n.** collimation; **v.** collimate

ADMIRE : **v.** adulate; apotheosize; canonize; deify; eulogize; idolize; panegyrize; venerate; **n.** ADMIRATION : adoration; adulation; approbation; canonization; deification; idolatry; idolization; **a.** ADMIRING : adulatory; complimentary; encomiastic; eulogistic; idolatric; idolatrous; laudatory; panegyrical

ADMIT : **v.** acknowledge; acquiesce; adhibit; concede; divulge; intromit; **n.** ADMITTANCE (or ADMISSION) : acknowledg(e)ment; acquiescence; concession; *entrée;* intromission; reception

ADO : (**see** "commotion" **and** "turmoil") **n.** agitation; brouhaha; coil; hullabaloo; imbroglio

ADORN : **v.** bedizen; caparison; diamondize; embellish; enrich; garnish; lard; **n.** ADORNMENT : bedizenment; caparison; *drap d'or;* embellishment; garnishment; ornamentation

ADROIT : (**see** "skillful") **a.** dexterous; **n.** ADROITNESS : address; dexterity; *savoir-faire*

ADULTERY : **n.** infidelity; unfaithfulness

ADULT(HOOD) : **n.** majority; maturity
approaching: **a.** maturescent; **n.** maturation; maturescence
garment to symbolize (anc. Rome): **n.** *toga virilis*
maintaining stable social conds. among (adults): **n.** homeostasis

rites at attaining (*Heb.*) : **n.** bar mitz-vah ; (**fem.** bath [**or** bas] mitzvah)

ADVANCE : **v.** aggrandize ; aggravate ; augment ; enhance ; escalate ; exacerbate ; graduate ; progress ; **n.** ADVANCE-MENT : aggrandizement ; aggravation ; anabasis ; augmentation ; development ; enhancement ; escalation ; evolution ; exacerbation ; graduation ; overture ; preferment ; progression ; tender
sensational: **n.** breakthrough

ADVANTAGE : **n.** opportunity ; precedence ; preference ; preferment ; superiority ; **a.** ADVANTAGEOUS : (**see** "beneficial") auspicious ; expedient ; opportune ; preferent(ial) ; profitable ; propitious ; remunerative ; strategic(al) ; strategetic ; tactical

ADVENTURE : **n.** escapade ; gambade ; gambado ; gest(e) ; ploy ; **a.** ADVENTUROUS (**or** ADVENTURESOME) : cavalier ; Icarian ; incautious ; picaresque ; precarious ; precipitate ; quixotic ; risky ; speculative ; temerarious ; uncalculating ; venturesome

ADVERSARY : **n.** antagonist ; competitor ; disputant ; opponent

ADVERSE : (**see** "stubborn") **a.** adversative ; antagonistic ; antipathetic(al) ; antipathic ; antithetical ; calamitous ; counteractive ; deplorable ; derogatory ; detrimental ; disadvantageous ; disparaging ; inimical ; ominous ; portentous ; prejudicial ; repellant ; repugnant ; repulsive ; sinister ; unpropitious ; untoward

ADVERSITY, *friends proved by: amici probantur rebus adversis*

ADVERTISE : **v.** disseminate ; exploit ; promulgate ; publicize ; ventilate ; **n.** ADVERTISING : dissemination ; exploitation ; promotion ; promulgation ; propaganda ; publicity ; **a.** exploitative ; promotional ; propagandistic

ADVICE : **n.** adhortation ; admonition ; counsel ; exhortation ; expostulation ; intelligence ; recommendation ; **a. see** "advisable" **and** "advisory"
willing to follow: **a.** amenable ; cordial ; docile ; facile ; fictile ; genial ; gracious ; **n.** amenability ; docility ; malleability ; plasticity ; tractability

ADVISABLE : **a.** expedient ; opportune ; politic ; provident ; prudent(ial) ; seemly

ADVISER, *disinterested:* **n.** *amicus curiae* (friend of the court)
woman: **n.** Egeria

ADVISORY : **a.** admonitory ; consultative ; consultatory ; (ex)hortative ; (ex)hortatory ; expedient ; expostulatory ; recommendatory

ADVOCACY : **n.** commendation ; desiration ; espousal ; patronage ; subscription

ADVOCATE : (**see** "agent") **n.** barrister ; champion ; counselor ; exemplifier ; exponent ; hierophant ; paladin ; paraclete ; paranymph ; partisan ; propugnator ; protagonist ; **v.** commend ; desiderate ; espouse
devil's: **n.** *advocatus diaboli*
leading: **n.** hierophant

AFFABLE : (**see** "courteous") **a.** benign ; complacent ; complaisant ; conversable ; cordial ; gallant ; gracious ; hospitable ; ingratiating ; suave ; urbane

AFFECTATION : (**see** "pretense") **n.** artificiality ; hypocrisy ; mannerism ; *minauderie ;* pietism ; pretension
esp. in language: **n.** grandiloquence ; preciosity

AFFECTED : **a.** affectational ; artificial ; *distingué ;* histrionic ; hypocritical ; (melo)-dramatic ; pedantic ; pietistic ; *précieuse ; précieux ;* pretentious ; puritanical ; staged ; theatrical
or artificial style in lang.: **n.** euphuism ; grandiloquence ; preciosity ; **a.** aureate ; euphuistic(al) ; grandiloquent
person: **n.** poseur ; (**fem.** *poseuse*) ; *précieuse*

AFFIRM : **v.** asseverate ; confirm ; predicate ; ratify ; validate ; **n.** AFFIRMATION : asseveration ; declaration ; predication ; ratification ; validation

AFFIRMATIVE : **a.** declarative ; positive
implication: **n.** negative pregnant

AFFLICTION : (**see** "disease") **n.** anguish ; calamity ; plague ; scourge ; tribulation ; visitation

AFFRONT : **n.** humiliation ; indignity ; provocation

7

to position or authority: **n.** *infra dignitatem* (**abb.** infra dig.) ; *lese majesty*

AFRAID : (**see** "timid") **a.** apprehensive; awestricken ; timorous

AFRESH : **adv.** *de integro; de novo*

AFTER : **a.** posteriad ; posterior ; postlimin(i)ary ; subsequent ; succedent
  death: **a.** posthumous ; post-mortem
  me (or us) the flood: après moi (**or** *nous*) *le déluge*
  meals: **a.** postprandial
  sadness, gladness: post nubila, jubila
  this: **adv.** *post hoc*
  this, therefore because of this: **adv.** *post hoc, ergo propter hoc*
  -word: **n.** epilogue

AFTERNOON, *pert. to:* **a.** postmeridian ; post meridiem

AGAIN : **see** "afresh"

AGAINST : **see** "opposed"

AGE : (**see** "aged") **v.** decline ; maturate ; mature ; mellow ; senesce ; **n.** caducity ; decrepitude ; dotage ; longevity ; maturation ; primogeniture ; saeculum ; senescence ; senility ; seniority ; *siècle;* superannuation
  advanced: **n.** (anec)dotage ; caducity ; senectude ; superannuation
  evidence of by tone or coating: **n.** patina
  old: **see under** "old"
  old, study of: **see under** "aged"
  respect for: **n.** veneration
  under legal: **n.** infancy ; juniority ; nonage

AGED : (**see** "old") **a.** aet. ; aetat. ; anile ; antediluvian ; antiquated ; decrepit ; Nestorian ; patriarchal ; senescent ; superannuated ; venerable
  government by: **n.** gerontocracy
  love of or attraction to: **n.** gerontophilia ; **a.** gerontophilic
  middle-: **see** "middle"
  study of diseases and problems of: **n.** geriatrics ; gerontology ; nostology
  worship of: **see under** "old"

AGENT : (**see** "advocate") **n.** dragoman ; facient ; factor ; factotum ; fiduciary ; mandatary ; minister ; plenipotentiary ; proxy ; representative
  joint: **n.** coefficient

secret: **n.** (agent) provocateur
w/ or by authority of an: **adv.** by proxy ; *per procuration; per procurantionem*

AGGRAVATE : **v.** aggrandize ; enhance ; exacerbate ; exaggerate ; exasperate ; infuriate ; intensify ; irritate ; magnify ; provoke ; stimulate ; **a.** AGGRAVATING : **see** "annoying" ; **n.** AGGRAVATION : exacerbation ; exacerbescence ; infuriation ; provocation ; vexation

AGGRESSIVE : (**see** "hostile") **a.** assertive ; bellicose ; belligerent ; combative ; contentious ; enterprising ; gladiatorial ; martial ; militant ; provocative ; pugilistic ; pugnacious ; self-asserting ; taurine ; truculent ; warlike ; **n.** AGGRESSIVENESS : (**see** "hostility") bellicosity ; belligerency ; combativeness ; pugnacity ; truculency

AGILE : (**see** "brisk") **a.** acrobatic ; adroit ; lissome

AGILITY, *mental or physical:* **n.** address ; adeptness ; adroitness ; dexterity ; legerity ; lissomeness

AGITATED : **a.** activated ; cyclonic ; demoniacal ; distracted ; febrile ; fervid ; feverish ; foaming ; fuming ; maniac(al) ; overwrought ; perturbed ; seething ; tumultuary

AGITATION : (**see** "ado") **n.** chemistry ; hatemongering ; instigation ; jactation ; jactitation ; perturbation ; turmoil

AGITATOR : (**see** "stimulator") **n.** (agent) provocateur ; firebrand ; hatemonger ; hothead ; hotspur ; incendiary ; instigator ; prompter

AGO : **see** "aged" **and** "old"

AGOG : **see** "eager"

AGONY : (**see** "anguish" **and** "distress") **n.** *angoisse;* excruciation ; travail ; tribulation
  scene or occasion of: **n.** Gethsemane

AGREE : **v.** coincide ; correspond ; harmonize ; homologate ; synchronize ; syncretize ; **a.** AGREED : *d'accord; en rapport;* **n.** **see** "agreement"

AGREEABLE : (**see** "pleasing") **a.** apolaustic ; appetizing ; compatible ; com-

plaisant; concordant; congruous; consentaneous; consentient; consistent; consonant; delectable; dulcet; gemutlich; halcyon; harmonious; palatable; plausible; sapid; savory
and disagreeable, rel. to both: **a.** algedonic

AGREEABLENESS: **n.** agreeability; amenity; compatibility; complaisance; congeniality; delectation; docility; tractability; unanimity

AGREEING: **a.** acquiescent; assentatious; consentaneous; consentient; *d'accord; en rapport;* unanimous; **adv.** *una voce*
in rate or speed: **n.** synchroneity; synchronicity; synchronism; **a.** synchronous; **v.** synchronize

AGREEMENT: **n.** assentation; assonance; commensality; communion; concord-(ance); congeniality; congruence; congruity; consentience; consonance; correspondence; *entente;* harmony; rapport; solidarity; unanimity
as bet. states: **n.** *entente*
friendly: **n.** *entente cordiale*

AGRICULTURE: **n.** agronomics; agronomy; geoponics; horticulture; husbandry; **a.** AGRICULTURAL: agrarian; agrestic; agronomical; horticultural
goddess of: **n.** Ceres

AHEAD: see "premature"
of times: **n.** *avant-garde; avant-gardism; avant-gardist(e);* vanguard(ism)

AID(E): (**see** "accessory," "assistant" **and** "helper") **n.** adjuvant; adminicle; ancillary; coadjutor; cohort; facilitation; handmaid(en); secours; **v.** (**see** "help") succor
financial: **n.** endowment; largess(e); subvention

AIDING: (**see** "supplemental") **a.** accessory; adjuvant; adminicular; benevolent; contributory; ministrant; subsidiary

AIM: (**see** "purpose") **n.** ambition; aspiration; intendment, philosophy; significance
having a purposeful: **a.** tendentious

AIMLESS: **a.** capricious; chaotic; desultory; haphazard; indiscriminate; random; tumultuary; unpremeditated; **n.** AIM-

LESSNESS: (**see** "idleness" **and** "idling") indirection

AIR: (**see** "atmosphere") **v.** publicize; ventilate; **n.** aura; demeanor; deportment; mien; nimbus; (**pl.**) *minauderie*
bad or contaminated: **n.** miasma; **a.** miasmic
containing or conveying: **a.** aeriferous; pneumatic
expired in breathing: **n.** exhalation; expiration; flatus
in open: **a.** *à la belle étiole; al fresco;* hypaethral; *sub Jove;* upaithric
letting or sucking in: **n.** implosion; **a.** implosive
originating in: **a.** atmogenic
pert. to, moved or worked by: **a.** pneumatic
w/ superior or condescending: **a. or adv.** *de haut en bas*

AIRTIGHT: **a.** hermetic(al); impenetrable; impervious

AIRY: **a.** aerial; animated; atmospheric; blithesome; buoyant; debonair; ethereal; frolicsome; riant; sprightly; vivacious; zephyrean; zephyrous; **n.** AIRINESS: aeriality; buoyancy; ethereality; sprightliness

AKIN: (**see** "related") **a.** affiliated; agnate; cognate; collateral; congeneric; consanguineous; fraternal; germane; propinquitous; **n.** agnation; consanguinity; propinquity

ALARM: (**see** "apprehension") **n.** tocsin

ALCOHOL: **n.** *aqua vitae;* ethanol; ethyl hydroxide; (**pl.** ardent spirits; spiritous liquors)
pert. to: **a.** bacchanalian; spiritous; vinic; vinous; **n.** spirituosity
total abstinence fr.: **n.** nephalism; nephalist; teetotaler; teetotalism; teetotalist

ALCOHOLIC: **n.** (**see** "drunkard") bacchanalian; bacchante; dipsomaniac; dramdrinker; oenophilist; winebibber; **a.** intoxicating; liquorish; liquorous; liquory; spiritous; vinic; vinous

ALCOHOLISM: **n.** bibacity; bibation; bibulosity; crapulence; dipsomania; ebriosity; inebriation; inebriety; insobriety; in-

9

temperance; oenophlygia; temulence; winebibbing
   pert. to: (**see** "drunken") **a.** dipsomaniacal

ALERT: **see** "prompt," "observant" **and** "watchful"

ALIEN: (**see** "foreign") **a.** adventitious; contradictory; estranged; extraneous; extrinsic; impertinent; inappropriate; inconsistent; irrelevant; unsympathetic; **n.** auslander; outlander; tramontane
   resident: **n.** peregrine
   to: **prep.** *dehors*

ALIGN: (**see** "adjust") **v.** collimate; hierarchize; regiment; **n.** ALIGNMENT: collimation; hierarchization; regimentation

ALIKE: (**see** "uniform") **a.** analogical; analogous; congruent; homogeneous; homologous; homonymous; parallel; synonymous; **n.** ALIKENESS: **see** "uniformity"
   in form and size: **a.** congruent; homomorphic
   in nature or character: **a.** concordant; unisonant; unisonous

ALIVE: **a.** animated; pullulant; spirited; teeming; vital; vivacious

ALL: **adv.** *in toto;* **n.** (**see** "allness") totality
   -comprehensive: **a.** encyclopedic(al); omnigenous; unabridged; universal; **n.** mutuality; omneity; omnitude; totality; unanimity; universality
   -creating: **a.** omnific; omnificent; **n.** omnificence
   -devouring: **a.** omniverous
   -inclusive: (**see** "universal") **a.** (en)-cyclopedic(al); omniferous; omnivorous; **n.** catholicity; catholicon; comprehensibility; comprehensiveness; universality
   is vanity: **n.** *omnia vanitas*
   -knowing: **a.** omniscient; pansophic(al); **n.** omniscience; pansophism
   -or-nothing: **adv.** *tout bien ou rien*
   -powerful: (**see** "almighty") **a.** multipotent; omnipotent; **n.** omnipotence
   -present: **a.** omnipresent; ubiquitous; **n.** omnipresence; ubiquity
   -seeing: **a.** panoptic
   taking or occupying (all): **a.** monopolistic; **n.** monopolization; monopoly
   the more: **adv.** *a fortiori*

the world: **n.** *tout le monde*
   together: (**see** "unanimous") **adv.** *en masse;* holus-bolus

ALLEGIANCE: **see** "loyalty"

ALLEGORY: (**see** "fable") **n.** apologue; symbolization; **a.** ALLEGORICAL: parabolic(al)
   make into: **v.** allegorize; **n.** allegorization

ALLIANCE: (**see** "union") **n.** affinity; confederation; consociation; consortion; consortium; monopolization; monopoly

ALLIED: **a.** agnate; analogous; cognate

ALLNESS: **n.** catholicity; entirety; omneity; omnitude; totality; universality

ALLOT: **v.** allocate; apportion; appropriate; parcel; ration

ALLOW: **v.** acknowledge; acquiesce; authorize; concede; countenance; empower; franchise; sanction; suffer; **a.** ALLOWED (or ALLOWABLE): (**see** "permissive") authorized; dispensable; franchised; legitimate; licensed; licit
   graciously: **v.** vouchsafe
   not (allowable): **a.** impermissible; **n.** impermissibility

ALLOWANCE: **n.** authorization; complement; emolument; honorarium; indulgence; mileage; permission; perquisite; sanction; stipend(ium); sufferance; tolerance; **a.** stipendiary
   additional, as for injured feelings: **n.** solatium
   with some: **adv.** *cum grano salis*

ALLUDE: **see** "hint"

ALLURE: **v.** beckon; beguile; cajole; captivate; enamor; ensorcel(l); enthral(l); entice; fascinate; instigate; inveigle; mesmerize; prompt; provoke; seduce; stimulate; tantalize; **n.** ALLUREMENT: blandishment(s); cajolery; persuasion

ALLURING: **a.** *aguichant;* (**fem.** *aguichante*); arresting; captivating; Circean; enticing; fascinating; magnetic; mesmeric; persuasive; provocative; seductive; sirenic(al); tantalizing; tempting
   appeal: **n.** siren song

ALLUSION: (see "hint") **n.** inference; innuendo; intimation

ALLY: see "assistant"

ALMIGHTY: **a.** multipotent; omnipotent; puissant; **n.** ALMIGHTINESS: omnipotence; puissance
ruler: **n.** Pantocrator

ALMOST: (see "near") **adv.** quasi

ALONE: (see "aloof") **a.** exclusive; immanent; incomparable; individual; isolated; lorn; sequestered; solitary; solus; unaccompanied; un(at)tended; unique
abnormal fear of being: **n.** autophobia; monophobia
all (alone): **adv.** *tout seul;* (**fem.** *toute seule)*
capable of standing, as sentence structure or logical idea: **a.** categorematic
not capable of: **a.** syncategorematic
one who enjoys being: (see "hermit") **n.** solitudinarian

ALONGSIDE: **a.** attingent; contiguous; juxtaposed; tangent
to place: **v.** appose; collocate; juxtapose; **n.** collocation; juxtaposition

ALOOF: (see "alone") **a.** cautious; circumspect; delitescent; detached; indifferent; remote; secluded; sequestered; unsociable; **n.** ALOOFNESS: delitescence; delitescency; detachment; indifference; remoteness

ALOUD: **adv.** *à haute voix;* audible

ALPHABET: **n.pl.** rudiments
book of the: **n.** abecedarium; primer
learner or student of: **n.** alphabetarian
pert. to: **a.** abecedarian; alphabetical; alphabetiform; rudimentary
teacher of: **n.** abecedarian

ALPHABETICAL *order, in:* (see "order") **adv.** *alphabétiquement; par ordre alphabétique*
order, initial letters of poem or writing in: **n.** abecedarius

ALTER: (see "change") **v.** castrate; commute; diversify; emasculate; metamorphose; metastasize, modulate; spay; swerve; tamper; transfigure; transform; transmogrify; transmute; **n.** ALTER-

ATION: conversion; deformation; deviation; diversion; emendation; metastasis; modulation; (per)mutation; reciprocity; transfiguration; transformation; transmogrification; transmutation; **a.** ALTERATIVE: emendatory

ALTERCATION: see "quarrel"

ALTERNATIVE: (see "choice") **n.** alternant; horns of a dilemma; option; preference; **a.** alternant; oscillative; reciprocative; synal(l)agmatic

ALTITUDE: **n.** elevation; loftiness; stature
pert. to or at greatest: (see "acme") **a.** altitudinous; culminant

ALTOGETHER: **adv.** collectively; *en banc; en bloc; en masse; en toto; tout ensemble;* unanimously

ALTRUISTIC: see "unselfish"

ALWAYS: (see "everlasting") **adv.** habitually; *in adfinitum; in aeternum; in perpetuity; in perpetuum; in saecula saeculorum;* invariably; perpetually; unceasingly; uniformly

AMASS: see "accumulate"

AMATEUR: (see "devotee") **n.** catechumen(ate); dilettante; initiate; neophyte; novice; proselyte; tyro; votary; **a.** AMATEURISH: dilettantish; non-professional

AMATIVE: **a.** affectionate; amatory; amorous; anacreontic; enamored; erotic; fervent; impassioned; **n.** amorosity; amorousness

AMAZE: (see "astonish") **v.** flabbergast; paralyze; petrify; **n.** AMAZEMENT: astonishment; consternation; perturbation; petrifaction; stupefaction; **a.** AMAZING: astonishing; astounding; incredible; ineffable; monstrous; portentous; preposterous; prodigious; stupendous; unspeakable

AMBIGUITY: (see "doubt") **n.** amphibology; double entendre; double entente; dubiosity; paradox

AMBIGUOUS: (see "vague") **a.** amphibolic; amphibological; amphibolous; cabalistic; Delphian; Delphic; dubious; enigmatic(al); equivocal; homonymous;

indeterminate; obscure; paradoxical; sibylline; unintelligible
   construction or phrase: **n.** amphibologism; amphibology; verbal fallacy

AMBITION: **n.** aspiration; initiation; initiative; intendment; **a.** AMBITIOUS: ardent; aspirant; aspiring; elaborate; emulous; extensive; fervent; impetuous; pretentious (**see** "showy"); rapacious; sedulous; solicitous

AMENDS, *make or making:* **v.** expiate; rectify; redress; **a.** compensative; compensatory; expiatory; reparative; **n.** atonement; expiation; indemnity; redress; reparation; retribution

AMENITIES: **see** "proprieties"

AMIABLE: (**see** "affable") **a.** benignant; complaisant; cordial; gracious; hospitable; indulgent; neighborly; obliging; winsome

AMONG *other persons:* **adv.** *inter alios*
   other things: **adv.** *inter alia*
   ourselves: **adv.** *entre nous; inter nos*

AMOROUS: **see** "amative" **and** "loving"

AMOUNT: (**see** "sum") **n.** aggregate; amplitude; magnitude; portion; quantum; (**pl.** quanta); totality

AMPLE: **a.** boundless; capacious; commodious; copious; expansive; prolix; replete; spacious; verbose; voluminous

AMUSE: **v.** beguile; divert; entertain; recreate; tit(t)ivate; **n.** AMUSEMENT: distraction; diversion; divertissement; entertainment; facetiosity; joviality; recreation; tit(t)ivation; **a.** AMUSING: diverting; divertive; entertaining; facetious; farcical; jocose; jocular; ludicrous; recreative; risible; whimsical

ANAL *region:* **n.** breech; perineum; podex; pudendum

ANALOGOUS: (**see** "alike" **and** "similar") **a.** homeopathic; homogeneous; synonymous

ANALYSIS: **n.** anatomy; critique; exegesis; exposition; hermeneutics; interpretation; synopsis; titration
   by separation: **n.** dialysis; **a.** dialytic

ANALYZE: **v.** anatomize; dissect; parse; **a.** ANALYTIC(AL): exegetic(al); expositive; expository; hermeneutic; interpretative

ANATOMICAL *material, substance or tissue:* **n.** substantia

ANATOMY: **n.** anthropotomy
   specialist in (anatomist): **n.** anthropotomist

ANCESTOR(S): **n.** antecedent; ascendant; forebear; forefather; forerunner; precursor; primogenitor; procreator; progenitor; (**fem.** progenitress; progenitrix); prototype
   after the manner of one's: **adv.** *more majorum*
   from many: **a. or n.** polyphyletic
   from single: **a. or n.** monophyletic
   having same: **a.** agnate; cognate; consanguineous
   immediate: **n.** ascendant
   in direct line: **n.** progenitor
   list or record of: **n.** genealogy; pedigree
   resemblance to remote: **n.** atavism; **a.** atavistic
   veneration or worship of: **n.** ancestor cult; manism; **a.** manistic
   worship of spirits of: **n.** manism; **a.** manistic

ANCESTRAL: (**see** "hereditary") **a.** ancestorial; primogenitive; progenitorial

ANCESTRY: **n.** extraction; genealogy; lineage; paternity; pedigree; stemma
   pert. to: **a.** ancestral; ancestorial; atavic; atavistic; genealogical; hereditary; progenitive; progenitorial

ANCHOR *of hope:* **n.** *anchora spei*
   of salvation or safety: **n.** *anchora salutis*

ANCIENT: (**see** "aged" **and** "old") **a.** antediluvial; antediluvian; antemundane; antiquated; antique; archaic; archaistic; immemorable; immemorial; Neanderthal(ian); Ogygian; paleolithic; paleozoic; patriarchial; preadamite; prehistoric; primeval; protohistoric; venerable; **n.** ANCIENTNESS: ancientry; antiquity; venerability
   one attached to opns. or practices of the: **n.** antiquarian
   worship of what is: **n.** archaeolatry; archaicism; archaism

writing(s): **n.** or **a.** cuneiform; hieroglyphic

AND *elsewhere:* **adv.** *et alii* (**abb.** *et al*)
others: **adv.** *et alii* (**abb.** *et al*)
so forth: **adv.** *et cetera* (**abb.** etc.) ; *und so weiter* (**abb.** u.s.w.)
symbol for (*&*) : **n.** ampersand
the following: **adv.** *et sequens* (**abb.** *et seq.*) ; (**pl.** *et sequentes; et sequentia*)

ANEMIA : **n.** emptiness; lifelessness
in young: **n.** chlorosis
local area: **n.** ischemia

ANEW : **adv.** *de novo; de integro*

ANGELIC : **a.** beatific; celestial; cherubic; heavenly; saintly; seraphic; sublime

ANGELS *and saints, homage to:* **n.** dulia
belief concerning: **n.** angeology

ANGER : (**see** "fury") **n.** acrimony; animosity; animus; asperity; choler; dudgeon; ebullition; exasperation; incensement; indignation; irascibility; malice; malignity; petulance; pique; resentment; turbulence; vexation; virulence; umbrage; **a.** ANGRY: (**see** "mad") acrimonious; choleric; indignant; iracund; irascible; irate; ireful; piqued; provoked; rancorous; wrathful
tending to incite: **a.** ignescent; incendiary; inflammatory; phlogistic; provocative; seditious; **v.** alienate; inflame; pique; provoke
will or powerful force (angry), effect or expression of: **n.** terribilita

ANGERED, *easily:* (**see** "contentious" **and** "hostile") **a.** choleric; iracund; irascible

ANGLES, *having equal:* **a.** equiangular; isagonal; isagonic
having many: **a.** mult(i)angular

ANGUISH : (**see** "distress") **n.** affliction; *angoisse;* angst; bereavement; consternation; (ex)cruciation; travail
place of: **n.** Gethsemane

ANIMAL(S) : **n.** mammal(i)an; quadruped; vertebrate; (**pl.** animalia; mammalia; vertebrata) ; **a.** carnal; gross; mammalian; mammality; zoological
abnormal fear of: **n.** zoophobia

and plant life, regional: **n.** biota; fauna and flora
and plants, science of development of: **n.** biology; **a.** biological
and plants, science of distribution of: **n.** biogeography
behavior, study of: **n.** ethology; **n.** ethologist; **a.** ethological
caused by or associated w/: **a.** mammalogical; zoogenic; zoogenous; zoological
characteristics, attribute to inanimate objects: **n.** animalism; animism; theriomorphism
characteristics, attribute to man: **n.** theriomorphism
fond of: **n.** philotherianism; **a.** philotherian; zoophilic; zoophilous
form, having: **a.** theriomorphic; zoomorphic; **n.** theriomorph
form, symbolic, in art or lit.: **n.** zoomorphism; **a.** zoomorphic; **v.** zoomorphize
happier than humans, theory: **n.** animalitarianism
human characteristics attributed to: **n.** anthropomorphism; anthropopathism; **a.** anthropomorphic; anthropopathic
life: **n.** fauna
loving of: **a.** philotherian; zoophilic; zoophilous
nature: **n.** animality; mammality
object shaped like: **n.** theriomorph; theriomorphic; **a.** theriomorphism
of or rel. to: **a.** animalic; animalistic; mammalian; zoic; zoological; **n.** animality; mammality
state of being an (or animal life) : **n.** animality; mammality
study of: **n.** zoology
very small: **n.** animalcule; animalculum; (**pl.** animalcula; animalculae)
Wild, utilization or exploitation of: **n.** besticulture; domestication

ANIMATE : (**see** "incite") **v.** ensoul; invigorate; motivate; prompt; quicken; suscitate; vitalize; vivificate; vivify; **a.** ANIMATED: see "lively"

ANIMATION : **n.** ebullience; effervescence; exhilaration; exuberance; intoxication; invigoration; liveliness; sprightliness; suscitation; vivacity; vivaciousness
suspended: **n.** anabiosis; catalepsy; hibernation; **a.** cataleptic

ANIMATING *and stirring, as a song:* **a.** proceleusmatic

ANNIHILATE: (see "abolish") v. decimate; demolish; deracinate; eradicate; expunge; exterminate; extinguish; extirpate; obliterate; pulverize

ANNOTATION(S): n. scholium; (pl. scholia)
  marginal: n. postil; scholium; (pl. marginalia; scholia)

ANNOTATOR: n. glossarist; scholiast; a. scholiast

ANNOUNCEMENT: n. annunciation; declamation; manifesto; proclamation; pronunciation; a. declamatory; proclamatory

ANNOUNCING: a. annunciatory; declamatory; declaratory; enunciative; proclamatory; pronunciative

ANNOY: v. abrade; chafe; discomfit; discommode; disconcert; gall; harass; importune; molest; pique; provoke; n. ANNOYANCE: discomfiture; harassment; irritation; molestation; nuisance; pique; provocation; umbrage; vexation; a. ANNOYING: abhorrent; aggravating; calamitous; discommodious; disconcerting; execrable; excruciating; galling; invidious; mortifying; nettlesome; pestiferous; pestilent; plaguing; provocative; repellant; repulsive

ANNUAL: a. etesian
  state of occurring (annually): n. annularity

ANNUL: v. abrogate; countermand; disclaim; neutralize; nullify; obliterate; quash; recant; repeal; rescind; revoke; a. ANNULLING: recissory; revocative; revocatory; n. ANNULMENT: abrogation; cassation; defeasance; disaffirmance; disaffirmation; nullification; recision; rescission; revocation
  not capable of (annulment): a. inalienable; indefeasible

ANOINTING, *act of:* n. unction

ANOMALOUS: see "abnormal"

ANOTHER *self:* n. alter ego

ANSWER: (see "reply") v. rejoin; replicate; respond; retort; n. antiphon; counterstatement; rebuttal; rejoinder; replica-

tion; *réplique;* response; responsion; retort
  negative: n. negation

ANTAGONISM: (see "hostility") n. antipathy; friction; a. ANTAGONISTIC: (see "contrary") ambivalent; dissident; dissonant; inimical; schizoid

ANTICIPATION: see "expectation"; a. ANTICIPATORY: intuitive; prevenient
  of needs of others: n. *prévenance;* prevenience

ANTICLIMAX: n. bathos; disappointment; a. ANTICLIMACTICAL: bathetic

ANTS, *family of:* n.pl. formicidae
  feeding on: a. formicivorous
  study of: n. myrmecology
  study of, specialist in: n. formicologist; myrmecologist

ANXIETY: (see "uneasiness") n. angst; anxiousness; apprehension; disquiet (ude); dyspathy; dysphoria; inquietude; malaise; solicitude; trepidation; uneasiness
  generalized or indefinite: n. dysphoria; panophobia

ANXIOUS: (see "impatient") a. apprehensive; expectant; solicitous; solicitudinous
  care or desire: n. solicitude; a. solicitous; solicitudinous

APART: see "alone" **and** "aloof"

APATHETIC: a. adiaphorous; *blasé; dégagé;* detached; dispirited; hebetudinous; impassive; imperturbable; impervious; indifferent; insipid; lackadaisical; languid; languorous; Laodicean; lethargic; pachydermatous; phlegmatic; pococurante; spiritless; stoical; supine; torpid; unenthusiastic; unfeeling
  person: n. Laodicean; pococurante

APATHY: (see "inaction") n. acedia; adiaphoria; anhedonia; detachment; doldrums; hebetude; immobility; impassiveness; impassivity; inappetency; indifference; inertia; inertness; lackadaisy; languor; lassitude; lethargy; listlessness; *minauderie;* nonchalance; phlegm; stoicism; supineness; supinity; tenuity; torpor; unconcern; unfeelingness
  religious: n. adiaphoria; adiaphorism;

adiaphorist; Laodicean; **a.** adiaphoristic; adiaphorous; Laodicean

APE *or monkey:* **n.** anthropoid; primate; simian; **a.** anthropoidal; simian; simious
   resembling: **a.** pithecomorphic; **n.** simianity
   study of: **n.** pithecology

APERTURE: (**see** "opening") **n.** fenestration; orifice; os; ostiole
   having wide or spreading: **a.** patulous

APEX: **n.** acme; apogee; cacumen; culmination; meridian; perihelion; pinnacle; sublimity; zenith

APOLOGY: **n.** apologia; **a.** APOLOGETIC: excusatory
   for error: **n.** *amende honorable*
   formal: **n.** apologetic
   one who makes: **n.** apologete; apologist

APOSTLE: (**see** "follower") **n.** disciple; harbinger; messenger

APPARATUS: **n.** armamentarium; mechanism; (**pl.** accoutrements; appurtenances; armamentaria; *matériel;* paraphernalia)

APPAREL: **see** "clothing"
   showy or sumptuous: **n.** caparison

APPARENT: (**see** "evident") **a.** conspicuous; demonstrable; discernible; exoteric; explicit; illusory; indubitable; manifest; obvious; ostensible; ostensive; palpable; patent; perceivable; perceptible; phanic; presumable; presumptive; *prima facie;* seeming; self-evident; unconcealed; unobstructed

APPEAL: **n.** attraction; attractiveness; enchantment; entreaty; imploration; invocation; popularity; supplication; **a.** APPEALING: (**see** "alluring") invocative; invocatory; provocative; provocatory; supplicative
   alluring: **n.** siren song; **a.** Circean; sirenic(al)
   to ignorance of facts: **n.** or **adv.** (*argumentum*) *ad ignorantiam*
   to mind or reason: **a.** cogent; compelling; convincing; **n.** cogency
   to modesty: **n.** or **adv.** (*argumentum*) *ad verecundiam*
   to penalties: **n.** or **adv.** (*argumentum*) *ad baculum*

to pity or compassion: **n.** or **adv.** (*argumentum*) *ad misericordiam*
   to please the crowd: **n.** or **adv.** (*argumentum*) *ad captandum* (*vulgus*)
   to popular passion and prejudice: **n.** or **adv.** (*argumentum*) *ad populum*
   to prejudices: **n.** or **adv.** (*argumentum*) *ad hominem*
   to reason: **n.** *argumentum;* argumentation
   to selfish interests: **n.** or **adv.** (*argumentum*) *ad hominem*
   to the people: **n.** or **adv.** (*argumentum*) *ad populum*
   to the purse: **n.** or **adv.** (*argumentum*) *ad crumenam*
   to the rod: **n.** or **adv.** (*argumentum*) *ad baculum*

APPEAR: (**see** "emerge") **v.** materialize; **a. see** "apparent" **and** "seeming"

APPEARANCE: (**see** "aspect") **n.** attendance; color; debut; debutant(e); development; habitus; manifestation; ostent; perspective; phantasmagoria; phenomenon; prospect; semblance; simulacrum
   bodily: **n.** countenance; feature; habitus; lineament; mien; profile; physiognomy; physique; visage
   do not trust: **adv.** *ne fronti credi*
   general or external: **n.** facies; superficies
   having diseased: **a.** cachectic; cadaverous; scrofulous
   trust not overmuch to: **adv.** *nimium ne credi colori*
   ungainly: **n.** angularity

APPEARING: **see** "apparent" **and** "seeming"

APPEASE: **v.** allay; alleviate; assuage; conciliate; dulcify; lenify; mitigate; moderate; mollify; propitiate; soothe; temper; tranquilize; **a.** APPEASING: (**see** "peaceful") expiatory; mitigatory; piacular; propitiative; propritiatory; **n.** APPEASEMENT: atonement; conciliation; expiation; mitigation; pacification; propitiation

APPEASED, *incapable of being:* **a.** avenging; immitigable; implacable; inappeasable; inflexible; intractable; irreconcilable; rancorous; relentless; remorseless; ruthless; unappeasable; unassuageable; unmitigable; untamable; unyielding; vindicative

15

APPENDAGES, *having:* **a.** appendiculate(d)

APPETITE: (**see** "taste") **n.** appetition; edacity; orexis; voracity
appealing to the: **see** "appetizing"
causing loss of (as drug. etc.): **a.** anorexigenic; **n.** anorexia; anorexic
depraved or perverted: **n.** allotriogeustia; allotriophagia; geophagy; parorexia
excessive or abnormal: **n.** (**see** "glutton") acoria; ad(d)ephagia; bulimia; gluttony; gulosity; hyperorexia; phagomania; polyphagia; **a.** (**see** "gluttonous") bulimic; polyphagous
increasing: (**see** "appetizing") **a.** orexigenic
lack or loss of: **n.** anorexia; inappetence; **a.** anore(c)tic; anorexic
person devoted to gratification of: **n.** bon vivant; epicure; gastronome(r); gourmet; hedonist; sybarite; **a.** epicurean; hedonistic; Sybaritic; **n.** hedonics; hedonism
pleasures of: **n. pl.** *abdominis voluptates*
rel. to: **a.** appetible; appetitive; epithumetic; orectic
sensual or sexual: (**see** "sensual") **n.** concupiscence; **a.** concupiscent; concupiscible; epithumetic
stimulator of: (**see** "appetizer") **n. or a.** apertive
without: (**see** "lack or loss of" *above*) **a.** anorectic

APPETIZER: **n.** *apéritif;* apertive; *canapé; hors d'oeuvre*

APPETIZING: **a.** ambrosial; appetible; appetitious; appetitive; delectable; gustable; gustatory; gustful; luscious; nectareous; orexigenic; palatable; piquant; sapid; saporous; savory; toothsome; **n.** sapidity; sapor; saporosity; piquance; piquancy

APPLAUD, *one hired to:* **n.** claqueur
persons hired to: **n.** claque

APPLAUSE: (**see** *"approval"*) **n.** acclamation; commendation; *éclat;* encomium; eulogy; laudation; plaudit; **a.** commendatory; laudatory; plauditory
eagerness for: **n.** captation; esurience

APPLES, *of or rel. to:* **a.** pomaceous

APPLICABLE: **a.** adaptable; apposite; appropriate; commensurate; congruent; germane; pertinent; proportional

APPOINTMENT: **n.** consultation; engagement; rendezvous; tryst; (**pl.** accoutrements)
secret: **n.** assignation; rendezvous; tryst

APPORTION: **v.** admeasure; allocate; appropriate; mete; parcel; ration; **n.** APPORTIONMENT: appropriation

APPRECIABLE: **a.** measurable; palpable; perceptible; ponderable; recognizable

APPREHENDED, *not readily:* **a.** impalpable

APPREHENSION: **n.** cognition; cognizance; disquiet(ude); foreboding; forewarning; inquietude; intellection; misgiving; perception; prehension; premonition; presentiment; understanding; **a.** APPREHENSIVE: anticipative; conscious; discerning; knowing; premonitory; presentient
instantaneous: **n.** intuition; **a.** intuitional; intuitive

APPROPRIATE: (**see** "apportion") **v.** accroach; arrogate; commandeer; confiscate; impound; preempt; sequester; **a.** apposite; apropos; *comme il faut;* concordant; condign; decorous; felicitous; germane; idoneous; opportune; pertinent; seemly; **n.** APPROPRIATENESS: (**see** "fitness") aproposity; idoneity; relativity
yet untrue: **a.** ben trovato

APPROVAL: (**see** "applause") **n.** acclaim; acclamation; accolade; accreditation; approbation; bravissimo; bravo; commendation; *éclat;* endorsement; imprimatur; plaudit; ratification; ratihabition; sanction; subscription; sufferage; sufferance; unanimity
expressive of: **a.** acclamatory; adulatory; affirmatory; approbatory; commendable; commendatory; laudable; laudatory; plauditory; sanctionative; **adv.** *à la bonne heure*
sign or mark of: **n.** cachet; *forensis strepitus* (clamor of the forum); hallmark; imprimatur

APPROVE: **v.** accredit; approbate; commend; compliment; endorse; homologate; ratify; sanctify; sanction; subscribe
not (approved): **see** "unauthorized"

APPROXIMATION: (**see** "nearness") **n.** *circa*

APT: (see "appropriate" **and** "knowing")
a. apropos; decorous; poignant; seemly;
n. APTNESS: appropriateness; aproposity; towardliness
expression: (**see** "witticism") **n.** bijouterie; *bon mot;* epigram.

ARBITRARY: (**see** "arrogant") **a.** ab-
solutist(ic); bigoted; capricious; captious;
despotic; determinate; dogmatic; imperious; inexorable; positive; preferential;
thetic(al); tyrannical
statement(s): **n.** dictum; (**pl.** dicta);
dogmatism; *ipse dixit;* ipsedixism

ARCH: **a.** picaresque; roguish; **n.** arcuation; concameration; incurvation

ARCHDEACON, *like a:* **a.** archidiaconal

ARCHED: **a.** archated; arcuated; cam-
bered; concamerated
body: **n.** opisthotonos

ARCHER: **n.** sagittarius; sagittary; toxophilite; **n.** ARCHERY: toxophily
pert. to (or archery): **a.** toxophilite;
toxophilitic

ARCHITECTURAL *figure:* **n.** antic (*grotesque*); caratid (**fem.**); telamon (**male**)

ARCHITECT(URE), *pert. to:* **a.** (archi)-
tectonic

ARDENT: (**see** "eager") **a.** crusading; devoted; dithyrambic; ebullient; enraptured;
enthusiastic; evangelical; evangelistic; fervent; glowing; igneus; impassioned; passionate, (per)fervid; plutonic; rapturous;
volcanic

ARDOR: (**see** "zeal") **n.** calenture; ebullience; ebulliency; ebullition; *empressement;* enthusiasm; fervidity; fervor; fidelity; incalescence; intensity; loyalty;
passion; rapture
increasing in: **a.** incalescent

ARDUOUS: (**see** "laborious") **a.** exacting;
rigorous; strenuous; **n.** strenuosity

AREA: (**see** "region") **n.** arena; environment; environ(s); milieu
*containing things of obscure classifica-
tion:* **n.** penumbra
occurring or taking place in same: **a.**
sympatric

ARGUE: **v.** contend; ergotize; expostulate;
maintain
for argument's sake: **v.** ratiocinate; **n.**
ratiocination; speciosity

ARGUMENT: (**see** "appeal" **and** "reasoning") **n.** argumentation; argumentum;
(**pl.** argumenta); dialectic(s); disputation; enthymeme; expostulation; polemic;
quodlibet; syllogism; **a. see** "argumentative"
art of: **n.** dialectic(s); forensic(s);
polemic(s)
by induction: **see** "induction"
clever and plausible but fallacious: **n.**
casuistry; philosophism; pilpul; sophism;
sophistry; speciosity; **a.** casuistic; quodlibetic; specious; sophistical
hater or hatred of: **n.** misologist; mis-
ology; **a.** misopolemical
last or final: **n.** *ultimo ratio*
on subtle or debatable point: **n.** quodlibet; **a.** quodlibetic

ARGUMENTATIVE: **a.** agonistic; contentious; controversial; debatable; dialectic; discursory; disputatious; disputative;
eristic; forensic; polemic(al); presumptive

ARGUMENTUM: **see** "appeal"

ARID: (**see** "dry") **a.** anhydrous; jejune;
monotonous; sterile; unproductive

ARISING: **a.** ascendant; assurgent; emergent
spontaneously: **a.** abiogenic; idiogenetic;
idiopathic
unexpectantly: **a. or n.** emergent

ARISTOCRAT: (**see** "elite") **n.** *bas bleu;*
Brahmin; grand signeur; grandee; patrician (**pl.** aristoi)

ARISTOCRATIC: **a.** hierarchic(al); patrician
class: **n.pl.** aristoi; **n.** patriciate

ARISTOTLE('S) *dictum:* **n.** *dictum de
omni et nullo* (what may be affirmed or
denied of a class may be affirmed or denied
of every member thereof)
follower of: **n.** Aristotelian; Peripatetic;
Peripateticism; **a.** Peripatetic

ARM(S): **n.** accouterment(s); arma-
ment(s); armamentarium; arsenal; ord-

nance; tentacles; weaponry; (**pl.** armamentaria; *matériel*); **a.** tentacular
by force of: **adv.** *vi et armis*
call to: aux armes!
having: **a.** brachiate; tentaculate
w/ open: **adv.** *à bras ouverts*

ARMOR, *complete suit of:* **n.** panoply

ARMPIT: **n.** axilla; (**pl.** axillae)

AROUND: **prep.** *circa; circiter;* **adv.** approximately

AROUSE: (**see** "incite") **v.** fillip; stimulate; **a.** AROUSING: (**see** "stimulating") galvanic

ARRANGE: **v.** alphabetize; catalogue; categorize; classify; collate; collicate; compartmentalize; concinnate; dispose; improvisate; improvise; marshal; methodize; mobilize; orchestrate; predetermine; synthesize; systematize; tabulate
for: **v.** bespeak

ARRANGED: **a.** alphabetized; categorized; compartmentalized; concinnate; orchestrated; schematic; stratified; synthesized; systematized; tabulated
in layers or strata: **a.** stratose

ARRANGEMENT: (**see** "plan") **n.** collation; collocation; combination; concinnity; contrivance; disposition; improvisation; permutation
clear: **n.** *lucidus ordo*
in layers, classes, castes, etc.: **n.** compartmentalization; hierarchization; stratification; **a.** stratose
of parts to form lit. style: **n.** concinnity
systematic: **n.** alphabetization; categorization; orchestration; schema; (**pl.** schemata); subordination; **a.** (**see** "arranged") schematic

ARRAY: (**see** "arrange" and "adorn") **v.** marshal; **n.** ARRAY(MENT): battery; display; gamut; rainbow; spectrum
complete or magnificent: **n.** panoply

ARREST: **v.** apprehend; restrain; retard; thwart; **n.** arrestation; arrestment

ARROGANCE: **n.** audacity; effrontery; haughtiness; hauteur; hubris; insolence; lordliness; presumption; superbity; **a.** ARROGANT: (**see** "haughty") audacious;

autocratic; cavalier; commanding; compelling; dictatorial; dogmatic; domineering; fastuous; hubristic; imperative; imperious; impudent; lordly; magisterial; masterful; misproud, overbearing; preemptory

ARROWHEAD, *shaped like:* **a.** sagitatte

ART(S): (**see** "skill") **n.** (a)esthetic(s); dexterity; expertise; finesse; techne; virtuosity
early work of: **n.** incunabulum
for art's sake: **adv.** *ars gratia artis*
four liberal: **n.** quadrivium
goddess of: **n.** Athena; Muse
irrationality in: **n.** Dadism; Dadist
is long, life is short: ars longa, vita brevis
lost: **n.pl.** *artes perditae*
morbid or scandalous creation in: **n.** *fleur du mal*
one having taste for: **n.** connoisseur; esthete; virtuoso
patron or benefactor of: **n.** Maecenas
pert. to: **a.** (a)esthetic(al); artistic
the fine: **n.** *beaux-arts*
three liberal: **n.** trivium
work of: **n.** *objet d'art; ouvrage d'art*

ARTERIES, *hardening of:* **n.** arteriosclerosis; **a.** arteriosclerotic

ARTFUL: **see** "crafty"

ARTIFICE: (**see** "deception" and "trick") **n.** astucity; astuteness; contrivance; finesse; gambit; imposture; ingenuity; intrigue; inventiveness; machination; maneuver; stratagem; subterfuge; subtlety

ARTIFICIAL: (**see** "false") **a.** affected; artifactitious; Brummagem; conventional(ized); counterfeit; ersatz; fabricated; factitious; feigned; fictitious; histrionic; melodramatic; *papier-mâché;* postiche; pseudo; shallow; simulated; spurious; supposititious; synthetic(al); theatrical; **n.** ARTIFICIALITY: affectation; artifact; simulation; theatricality
limb or other body substitute: **n.** prosthesis; **a.** prosthetic
to make: **v.** artificialize

ARTIFICIALLY *made or produced:* **a.** (arti)factitious; ersatz; *papier-mâché;* synthetic; (**n.pl.** *fructus industriales*)

ARTIST, *greatest work of:* **n.** *chef-d'oeuvre; magnum opus;* maestro; *meisterwerk; pièce de résistance*
   studio of: **n.** atelier

ARTISTIC: **a.** (a)esthetic(al); Bohemian; **n.** (a)estheticism; Bohemianism

ARTLESS: **a.** candid; ignorant; inartistic; *ingénu;* ingenuous; naive; unaffected; unauspicious; uncultured; unskillful; unsophisticated; **n.** ARTLESSNESS; *naïveté;* simplicity; unsophistication

AS *above:* **adv.** *ut supra* (**abb.** u.s.)
   below: **adv.** *ut infra* (**abb.** u.i.)
   circumstances require: **adv.** *pro re nata* (**abb.** p.r.n.)
   far as this: **adv.** *quod hoc*
   if: **adv.** qua; quasi
   (in the capacity of): **adv.** qua
   it should be: **adv.** *comme il faut*
   occasion requires, or need occurs: **see** "circumstances require" *above*
   usual: **adv.** *à l'ordinaire; comme à l'ordinaire; comme d'ordinaire*

ASCENDANCY: (**see** "prevalence") **n.** paramountcy; precedence; sovereignty; supremacy

ASCETIC: **n.** anchoret; anchorite; ascesis; Essene; heautontimorumenas; hermit; recluse; sabbatarian; Simeon Stylites; solitudinarian; **a.** austere; Essenic; Essenian; self-denying; self-disciplined; self-mortifying
   extreme: **n.pl.** Cathari; perfecti
   practice: **n.** ascesis; asceticism; austerity; self-denial; self-discipline; self-mortification

ASCRIBE: **v.** accredit; arrogate; attribute; impute

ASEXUAL *reproduction:* **n.** abiogenesis; agamogenesis; parthenogenesis; **a.** abiogenetic(al); agamic; agamous

ASHES, *like or color of (ashen):* **a.** cineraceous; cinerous

ASIDE: **adv.** *en aparté*

ASLEEP: **a.** comatose; dormant; hypnotic; inactive; latent; lethargic; quiescent; somniferous; somnolent; torpescent; **n.** see "sleep"

cond. of limb due to pressure: **n.** obdormition

ASPECT(S): **n.** angle; countenance; facet; ostent; semblance
   general or external: **n.** facies; habitus; mien; physique; superficies (**also pl.**)
   having many: **a.** heterogeneous; multifarious; multiphasic; multivarious; omnifarious

ASPERSE: **see** "slander"

ASPIRIN: **n.** acetylsalicylic acid

ASS *at the lyre:* **n.** *asinus ad lyram*

ASSAIL: **v.** censure; **n.** ASSAILMENT: castigation; oppugnation

ASSEMBLE: **v.** categorize; collimate; conglomerate; congregate; convene; convoke; correlate; muster; rendezvous; synthesize; **n.** ASSEMBLAGE: agglomeration; aggregation; conglomeration; convocation; ensemble

ASSENT: **v.** accede; acquiesce; sanction; **n.** ASSENTATION: acquiescence; approbation; concurrence; sanction; **a.** ASSENTATIOUS: acquiescent; approbative; compliant

ASSERTION: **see** "statement"

ASSERTIVE: (**see** "positive") **a.** affirmative; articulate; declaratory; peremptory; pronunciative

ASSETS *on hand:* **n.pl.** *valeurs disponibles*

ASSIGNEE: **n.** cessionary

ASSIGNMENT: **n.** allotment; appointment; appropriation; assignation; designation

ASSIST: **see** "help"; **n.** ASSISTANCE; (**see** "aid[e]") abetment; coadjuvancy; cooperation; encouragement; furtherance; patronage; secours; subvention; succor

ASSISTANT: (**see** "helper") **n.** abettor; acolyte; adjutant; adjuvant; aide-de-camp; ancillary; associate; auxiliary; coadjutor; confederate; *confrère; collaborateur;* collaborator; colleague; handmaid(en); subaltern(ate); subordinate;

subsidiary; (**fem.** coadjutress; coadjutrix) *in religious ceremony:* **n.** acolyte

ASSOCIATE(S): (**see** "assistant") **n.** affiliate; affiliation; *confrère;* cohort; colleague; companion; concomitant; consort; socius; supporter; **v.** affiliate; fraternize
  close: **n.** *alter ego;* compeer
  group of: **n.** claque; clique; mieny
  in crime: **n.** accessory; *particeps criminis; socius criminis*

ASSOCIATED: **a.** affiliated; appendant; corollary

ASSOCIATION: (**see** "alliance" **and** "brotherhood") **n.** companionship; congress; conjunction; consortium; fraternity; partnership
  existence in: **n.** concomitance; concomitancy; **a.** concomitant
  for common or mutually pleasing purposes: **n.** comity
  harmful: **n.** antibiosis; **a.** inimical

ASSORTED: **a.** heterogeneous; miscellaneous; **n.** ASSORTMENT: (**see** "variety") heterogeneity; hodgepodge; miscellaneity; miscellany; (**pl.** miscellanea); multiformity; olla-podrida

ASSUAGE: see "ease"

ASSUME: **v.** appropriate; arrogate; ascribe; attribute; conjecture; hypothecate; hypothesize; posit; postulate; presume; theorize; undertake; **a.** ASSUMED: academic; appropriated; assumptious; assumptive; conjectural; counterfeit; factitious; feigned; fictitious; gratuitous; hypothesized; hypothetical; inferred; postulated; postulatory; simulated; *soi-disant;* speculated; speculative; spurious; supposititious; theoretical; usurped; **adv.** *sub silentio*

ASSUMPTION: **n.** adoption; appropriation; arrogance; hypothesis; incorporation; postulate; postulation; (**pl.** postulata); presumption; supposition; susception
  basic: **n.** constantation
  involving: **a.** hypothetical; officious; postulatory; presumptuous; supposititious

ASSURANCE: **n.** arrogance; audacity; certitude; confidence; effrontery; guaran-

tee: impudence; infallibility; self-possession; *savoir faire;* self-reliance; surety
  lack of: **n.** inferiority complex; timidity
  with: **n.** *à plomb;* aplomb; certitude; confidence; self-possession

ASSUREDLY: **adv.** certes; indubitably; verily

ASTONISH: **v.** affright; astound; amaze; flabbergast; paralyze; petrify; **n.** ASTONISHMENT: amazement; petrifaction; petrification

ASTONISHING *occurrence:* **n.** *coup de foudre*

ASTRAY: (**see** "roaming") **a.** *dépaysé*

ASTRONOMY, *muse of:* **n.** Urania

ASYLUM: **see** "sanctuary"

AT *any price:* **adv.** *à tout prix*
  first sight or view: **a.** *prima facie*
  full length: **a.** *in extenso*
  hand: **a.** calamitous; imminent; impending; threatening; **n.** immanence
  home: **a.** or **adv.** *en famille*
  last: **adv.** *en fin;* ultimately
  once, all: **adv.** *tout à coup;* holus-bolus
  pleasure: **adv.** *a bene placito; ad libitum* (**abb.** ad lib.); *à volonté*
  random: **adv.** *à l'abandon; à tort et à travers;* **a.** stochastic
  same time: **a.** conjugate; contemporaneous; contemporary; simultaneous; synchronic(al); synchronous; **adv.** or **a.** *pari passu;* **n.** contemporaneity; simultaneity
  this time: **adv.** *hoc tempore*
  whatever the cost: **adv.** *à tout prix*
  will: (**see** "at random" *above*) **adv.** *ad arbitrium; à discrétion*

ATHLETE: **n.** gladiator
  weaned from another school: **n.** or **v.** proselyte

ATHLETICS, *intense interest or participation in:* **n.** athleticism

ATMOSPHERE: (**see** "air") **n.** aura; decor; environment; fascination; glamor; nimbus; ornamentation
  encompassing or pervading: **n.** ambiance; ambience; ambiente; **a.** ambient
  heavy or pervasive; **n.** miasma; **a.** miasmal; miasmatic; miasmic; noxious

originating in: **a.** atmogenic
outer layers of, in order: **n.** stratosphere; ionosphere; mesosphere; exosphere
unhealthful: **see** "heavy" *above*

ATOMIC: **a.** Democritean; infinitesimal; molecular

ATONE: **v.** expiate; harmonize; reconcile; **a.** expiatory; piacular; propitiative; propitiatory; **n.** ATONEMENT: expiation; propitiation; reconciliation; satisfaction
incapable of being (atoned): **a.** inexpiable
means of (atonement): **n.** expiation; purgatory

ATTACK: (**see** "criticize") **v.** assail; bombard; **n.** ambuscade; assailment; oppugnation
adapted for: **a.** expugnatory
bitter or violent: **n.** denunciation; diatribe; invective; philippic; tirade; vituperation; **a.** denunciatory; invective; vituperative; **v.** inveigh
literary: **n.** *coup de plume*
nervous: **n.** *une attaque de nerfs*
not open to: **a.** impregnable; indubitable; inexpugnable; invincible; irrefutable
open to: **a.** exposed; expugnable; surmountable; vincible; vulnerable
person rather than issue(s): **adv.** (*argumentum*) *ad hominem*
(rape or attempted rape): **n.** indecent assault
ready for: **adv.** *en garde*
sudden: **n.** coup; paroxysm; seizure; **a.** paroxysmal
sudden surprise: **n.** *coup d'état; coup de main*
verbal: **n.** polemic; tirade

ATTAIN: **see** "get"; ATTAINMENT: **see** "endowment"

ATTEMPT: (**see** "endeavor") **v. or n.** essay; **n.** conatus; undertaking
act of making: **n.** conation; endeavor; **a.** conative
at first: **n.** *coup d'essai*

ATTENDANT(S): **n.** accompaniment, appendant; auxiliary; concomitant; corollary; entourage; retinue
loyal: **n.** hireling; mercenary; minion; myrmidon
uniformed: **n.** chasseur

ATTENTION(S): (**see** "diligence" **and** "heed") **n.** advertence; advertency; application; assiduity; (**pl.** assiduities); attentiveness; circumspection; concentration; consideration; diligence; intendence; perception; **a. see** "attentive"
draw to: **see** "allure"
drawing away from: **a.** digressive; distractive; diversionary
lack of: **n.** detachment; ignoration; inattention; laches
little: **n.pl.** assiduities; *petits soins*
paying of no: **see** "lack of" *above*

ATTENTIVE: **a.** advertent; assiduous; circumspect; diligent; heedful; inspective; perceptive; sedulous; **a. or adv.** *arrectis auribus*
to needs of others: **n.** complaisance; *prévenance;* prevenience

ATTIRE: (**see** "dress") **n.** accoutrement(s); array; caparison; equipage; habiliment; (in)vestment; toilette; vesture
formal or fashionable: **n.** toilette
of office: **n.pl.** pontificalibus

ATTITUDE: (**see** "behavior") **n.** attitudinization; disposition; posture
strike an: **v.** attitudinize; **a.** attitudinal; **n.** attitudinarianism
one who does: **n.** attitudinarian

ATTORNEY: **n.** barrister; counselor; solicitor
w/o help of: **adv.** *in propria persona*

ATTRACT: **v. see** "allure"; **a.** ATTRACTIVE: (**see** "alluring") arresting; beguiling; bewitching; bonny; captivating; Circean; comely; decorative; decorous; enticing; fascinating; intriguing; magnetic; mesmeric; personable; persuasive; prepossessing; psychagogic; seductive; **n.** ATTRACTION: **see** "appeal"

ATTRIBUTE: (**see** "characteristic") **n.** ap(p)anage; appendage; cachet; endowment; essence; perquisite; property; proprium; quality

AUCTION, *act of offering for sale or bidding at:* **n.** licitation

AUDACITY: (**see** "gall") **n.** arrogance; effrontery; hubris; impertinence; impetuosity; intrepidity; temerity

AUDIENCE, *playing to the:* **n.** cabotinage; Sardoodledom; theatricality

AUGMENT: (**see** "increase") **v.** aggrandize; enhance; exacerbate

AUGUR: (**see** "foretell") **v.** auspicate; **a.** auspicatory

AUSPICES: (**see** "protection") **n.** (a)egis; patronage; tutelage
under bad: **adv. or n.** *malis avibus*
under better: **adv. or n.** *melioribus auspiciis*
under good: **adv. or n.** *bonis avibus*

AUSTERE: (**see** "strict") **a.** acrimonious; ascetic; Draconian; extortionate; imperative; inexorable; inflexible; inquisitorial; obdurate; procrustean; rigorous; ruthless; Spartan(ic); stringent; uncompromising; unembellished; unrelenting; **n.** AUSTERITY: ascesis; inflexibility; Spartanism; stringency
person: **see** "disciplinarian"

AUTHENTIC: (**see** "authoritative") **a.** authorized; *bona fide;* legitimate; official; original; trustworthy; veritable

AUTHOR(S): (**see** "authorship" **and** "writer") **n.** ancestor; creator; originator; procreator; **a.** auctorial; authorial
complete works of an: **n.pl.** *opera omnia*
in handwriting of: **a.** holographic; onomastic; **n.** holograph
insignificant anonymous: **n.** anonymuncule
unknown: **n.** anonym(e); pseudonym; **a.** anonymous; pseudonymous; **n.** pseudonymity
written by several: a. polygraphic

AUTHORITARIAN: (**see** "dictatorial") **a.** autocratic; hierarchic(al); totalitarian; **n.** autocrat; despot; tyrant

AUTHORITATIVE: **a.** absolute; apostolic(al); authentic; canonical; cathedral; cathedratic; certified; classic; conclusive; convincing; dictatorial; documented; dogmatic; *ex cathedra;* magistral; magisterial; magistratical; official; orthodox; pompous; preemptory; **n.** AUTHORITATIVENESS: apostolicity; officiality; orthodoxy
group or tribunal: **n.** areopagus; areophagite; **a.** areophagitic; **n.** apostolicism

passage (in writing[s]): **n.** *locus classicus*
pronouncement, saying, etc.: **n.** allocution; dictum

AUTHORIZED: **see** "authoritative"

AUTHORITY: **n.** ascendency; authorization; autonomy; canonicity; dominion; influence; jurisdiction; magisteriality; officiality; prerogative; sovereignty; suzerainty
assumed, exaggerated: **v.** pontificate
beyond prescribed or permitted: **adv.** *ultra vires*
blind submission to: **n.** authoritarianism
by what?: **adv.** *quo warranto?*
exceeding legal or proper: **adv.** *ultra vires*
full: (**see** "unlimited" *below*) **a. or n.** *carte blanche;* **adv.** *pleno jure*
of another, subject to: **a.** *aleni juris*
of office, etc.: **n.** attribution; **a.** attributive
on any subject: **n.** pundit
range or limit of: **n.** dominion; jurisdiction; purview
to transact business: **n.** plenipotence; **a.** plenipotent
unlimited: **n.** *carte blanche; lettre de cache;* multipotence; omnipotence; **adv.** *pleno jure*
unlimited, having: **a.** multipotent; omnipotent; plenipotent(iary)
with: **see** "authoritative"
within prescribed or permitted: **adv.** *intra vires*
w/o prescribed or permitted: **adv.** *ultra vires*

AUTHORSHIP: **n.** instigation; paternity
study of writing(s) to determine authenticity of: **n.** bibliotics

AUTOBIOGRAPHY: (**see** "biography") **n.pl.** anamnesis; memoirs; recollections; reminiscences

AUTOCRATIC: **see** "authoritarian"

AUTOMATIC: (**see** "involuntary") **a.** automatous; mechanical; reflex; self-regulating; spontaneous; **n.** AUTOMATION: automatism; mechanization; spontaneity
to make: **v.** automate; automatize; mechanize; robotize

AUTOMATON: **n.** android; golem; robot

AUXILIARY: (see "assistant") **n.** adjunct; adminicle; **a.** (see "subsidiary") adminicular; supplementary
as in sentence construction: **a.** syncategorematic; synsemantic

AVAILABLE: **a.** accessible; attainable; dispensable; expendable; obtainable; remittable; utilizable

AVARICE: **n.** covetousness; cupidity; greediness; parsimony; rapaciousness; rapacity; venality

AVENGER *of wrong:* **n.** Nemesis; *vindex injuriae*

AVERSE: see "unwilling"

AVERSION: (see "dislike) **n.** animosity; antipathy; reluctation; repugnance; revulsion; unwillingness; **a.** AVERSIVE: reluctant; repugnant; repulsive
having natural or constitutional: **a.** antipathetic(al); antipathic
special: **n.** *bête noire*
to society: **n.** anthropophobia; apanthropia; apanthropy; **a.** anthropohobic; apanthropic

AVOID: **v.** abjure; bypass; eschew; evade; sidestep; **n.** AVOIDANCE: abjuration; annulment; eschewal; evasion

AVOWEDLY: **adv.** *ex professo*

AWAKENING: **n.** burgeoning; disenchantment; disillusionment; quickening; realization; recognition

AWARD: **v.** adjudge; apportion; bestow; **n.** accolade; guerdon
highest: **n.** *cordon bleu; grand prix*

AWARE: (see "knowing) **a.** apprised; cognizant; conscious; mindful; observant; sensible; sensitive; sentient; vigilant; watchful; **n.** AWARENESS: apprehension; cognition; cognizance; consciousness; discernment; insight; intuition; observation; orientation; perception; percipience; sentience; sentiency; vigilance
capable of being: **a.** cognizable; cognoscible; cognoscitative

AWE-*inspiring:* **a.** august; awesome; doughty; formidable; illustrious; redoubtable
religious: **n.** (the) numinous

AWFUL: (see "outrageous") **a.** appalling; awe-inspiring; awesome; ghastly; horrendous; horrific; indescribable; ineffable; ominous; portentous; redoubtable

AWKWARD: (see "clumsy") **a.** bungling; elephantine; gauche; inapt; inept; inexpert; infelicitous; inopportune; loutish; lumbering; maladroit; ponderous; uncouth; ungainly; unwield(l)y
incident: **n.** contretemps; gaucherie

AWKWARDNESS: **n.** clumsiness; embarrassment; gaucherie; inaptitude; inelegance; ineptitude; maladroitness
of manner(s): **n.** gaucherie; rusticity

AXIOM: **n.** see "maxim"; **a.** AXIOMATIC: (see "self-evident") aphoristic; hypothetico-deductive; postulational

B

BABBLE: **n.** babblement; bavardage; galimatias; gibberish; harangue; jargon; stultiloquence; stultiloquy; **a.** stultiloquent (ial)

BABY-*talk:* **n.** hypocorism; **n. or a.** hypocoristic

BACHELOR: **n.** agamist; celibate; coelebs; misogynist; **n.** BACHELORHOOD: bachelorism; celibacy; **a.** agamous; celibatarian

BACK: (**see** "support") **n.** dorsum; posteriority; tergum; **a.** dorsal; posterior; tergal
    bending: **n.** retroflexion
    farthest: **a.** posteriormost
    lying on: **a.** supine; **n.** decubation; dorsal decubitus; reclination; recumbency; supinity
    out: **v.** renege
    turning: **a.** recessive; regressive; retrocessive; retrogradatory; retrograde; retroverse; **n.** recession; recidivism; regression; retrocession; retrogradation; retrogression; retroversion; reversion

BACKGROUND: **n.** heredity; history; lineage; milieu; *mise-en-scène;* pedigree
    pert. to: **a.** circumstantial; employmental; environmental; situational

BACKER: (**see** "supporter") **n.** abettor; cohort; colleague; constituent; corroborator

BACKSLIDE: **v.** recidivate; regress; relapse; renege; retrogress; **n.** recidivation; recidivism; retrogression

BACKSLIDER: **n.** apostate; recidivant; recidivist; renegade; turncoat

BACKWARD: **a.** *à reculons;* backwoodsy; behindhand; diffident; reactionary; reluc-
tant; unprogressive; **n.** BACKWARDNESS: barbarism; barbarity; regression; retrocession; retrogradation; retrogression

BACKWARDS, *moving or directed:* **a.** *à reculons;* retrograde; **n.** retrogression
    name written: **n.** ananym
    sentence or word reading same as forward: **n.** palindrome

BACTERIA, *agent destroying:* **a. or n.** antibiotic; antiseptic

BAD: (**see** "adverse" **and** "wicked") **a.** abominable; base; damnable; deficient; delinquent; delitescent; demeritorious; despicable; detestable; dilapidated; disagreeable; diseased; disobedient; displeasing; egregious; execrable; faulty; flagrant; harmful; intractable; malignant; mischievous; notorious; pernicious; regrettable; sinister; substandard; unhealthy; viperous
    because prohibited or unlawful: **adv. or n.** *malum prohibitum*
    blood: **n.** *mauvais sang*
    boy or person: (**see** "person, base and despicable") **n.** *enfant terrible*
    custom or habit: **n.** cacoethes
    faith, in: **adv.** *malâ fide*
    in itself, or inherently: **adv. or n.** *malum in se*
    manner, in a: **adv.** *malo modo*
    mood, in a: **see** "irritable"
    situation: **n.** *mauvais pas;* plight
    smelling: **see** "stinking"
    taste: **n.** *mauvais goût;* **a.** egregious
    -tempered: **see** "irritable"
    -tempered person: **n.** curmudgeon

BADNESS: **n.** abomination; depravity; malevolence; malignancy; sinisterity; virulence

BAFFLE: **v.** checkmate; circumvent; counteract; disconcert; frustrate; obfuscate;

thwart; **a.** BAFFLED: nonplussed; perplexed; **n.** BAFFLEMENT: confusion; obfuscation; perplexity; **a.** BAFFLING: enigmatic(al); inexplicable; obfuscatory; obscure

BAGGAGE (see "equipment") **n.** luggage; (**pl.** impedimenta)

BAILOR: **n.** adpromissor

BALANCE: **v.** equalize; equate; equilibrate; equilibrize; equiponderate; librate; neutralize; stabilize; **n.** composure; equanimity; equilibrium; equipoise; equipollence; equiponderance; equiponderation; harmony; libration; poise; proportion; serenity; stability; stabilization; symmetry
lack of: **n.** astasia; disequilibration; disequilibrium; imbalance; instability
mental: **n.** composure; equanimity; homeostasis; serenity; **a.** Apollonian; Apollonistic; Apollonic; equanimous
serving to: **a.** compensative; compensatory; equipollent; equiponderant
with: **adv.** *aequo animo*

BALANCED: (see "level") **a.** Apollonian; equalized; harmonious; neutralized; stabilized

BALANCING: **a.** compensative; compensatory; equilibrant; (equi)libratory; equipollent; equiponderant; isonomic

BALD: **a.** alopecic; epilated; glabrate; glabrescent; glabrous; outright; palpable; patent; unadorned; undisguised
head, or bald-headed person: **n.** pilgarlic

BALDNESS: **n.** acomia; alopecia; atrichia; atrichosis; calvities; phalacrosis
front of head: **n.** anaphalantiasis

BALK: **v.** demur; frustrate; impede; thwart; **n.** demur; hindrance; **a.** BALKY: (see "contrary") recalcitrant; restive

BALL, *formed into or shaped like:* **a.** conglobate; conglomerate; globular; orbicular; spheroid(al); **n.** conglomeration; spheroid; **v.** conglobe

BALLET, *art of:* **n.** choreography; **a.** choreographic(al)
dancer, esp. a star (fem.): **n.** *coryphée*
rel. to or suitable for: **a.** balletic
teacher: **n.** choreographer

BALMY: **a.** anodyne; anodynous; aromatic; balsamic; favonian; lenitive; mitigative; temperate

BAN: **v.** anathematize; execrate; interdict; prohibit; proscribe; **n.** anathema; execration; interdiction; prohibition; proscription; **a.** interdictive; interdictory; proscribed; proscriptive
temporary: **n.** armistice; moratorium

BANAL: (see "trite") **a.** asinine; insipid; pedestrian; platitudinous; **n.** BANALITY: pedestrianism

BANISH: **v.** deport; dispossess; eject; exile; expatriate; extradite; ostracize; proscribe; relegate; **n.** BANISHMENT: expatriation; expulsion; extradition; ostracism; relegation

BANKRUPT: (see "poor") **a.** depleted; deprived; destitute; exhausted; impecunious; impoverished; insolvent; **n.** BANKRUPTCY: depletion; destitution; impoverishment; insolvency

BANNED, *list of what is:* (see **under** "book(s)") **n.** *index expurgatorius*

BANNER, *of battle, or one inspiring devotion:* **n.** oriflame
symbolical: **n.** labrum

BANQUET: **n.** convivium; symposium
pert. to: **a.** convivial; epulary; festive

BANQUETER: **n.** symposiarch; symposiast

BANTER: **n.** asteism; badinage; persiflage; raillery; sarcasm; **v.** persiflate
one who engages in: **n.** persifleur; railleur

BAPTISM, *spiritual:* **n.** consolamentum

BARBARIC: (see "cruel" and "wild") **a.** atrocious; barbaresque; barbarous; feral; ferocious; inhuman; philistinic; philistinish; procrustean; tramontane; tyrannical; uncivilized; **n.** BARBARITY: barbarousness; barbarism; ferity; inhumanity; philistinism; savagery

BARE: (see "naked") **a.** exposed; manifest; minimum
to lay: **v.** denude; denudate; **a.** denudate; denudative; **n.** denudation

26

BARGAIN : (see "barter") **v.** haggle ; negotiate
at a: **adv.** *à bon marché; à vil prix* (dirt cheap)

BARK, *remove:* (see "peel") **v.** decorticate ; **n.** decortication

BARREL, *shaped like:* **a.** doliform

BARREN : **a.** acarpous ; fruitless ; hardscrabble ; immature ; infecund ; infertile ; inhospitable ; jejune ; juvenile ; nonparous ; nulliparous ; sterile ; unfructuous ; unfruitful ; unprofitable ; **n.** BARRENNESS : desolation ; infecundity ; infertility ; sterility

BARTENDER(ING) : **n.** mixologist ; mixology

BARTER : (see "bargain") **v.** commute ; reciprocate ; **n.** commutation ; *quid pro quo*

BASE : (see "wicked") **a.** contemptible ; counterfeit ; degenerate ; degraded ; degrading ; despicable ; dishonorable ; ignoble ; infamous ; inferior ; low-minded ; mean-spirited ; menial ; plebeian ; proletarian ; substratal ; substrative ; unworthy ; **n.** foundation ; fundament(um) ; groundwork ; pedestal ; plinth ; principium ; substratum
attached at: **a.** sessile
of operations; **n.** *pou sto*
particularly military: **n.** *point d'appui*
rel. to or situated at: **a.** basal ; basic ; basilar ; fundamental

BASENESS : (see "wickedness") **n.** degeneration ; degradation ; terpitude

BASHFUL : (see "shy") **a.** coy ; Daphnean ; demure ; diffident ; self-conscious ; timorous ; verecund ; **n.** BASHFULNESS : coyness ; diffidence ; *mauvaise honte;* timidity ; timorousness ; verecundity

BASIC : **a.** abecedarian ; abecedary ; alkaline ; basal ; basilar ; canonical ; constitutional ; elementary ; essential ; fundamental ; indispensable ; ingrained ; inherent ; innate ; intrinsic ; irreducible ; orthodox ; primary ; primitive ; primeval ; substrate ; **adv.** BASICALLY : *au fond;* essentially ; fundamentally ; intrinsically ; **n.** BASICNESS : essentiality ; fundamentality ; primality ; quintessence ; ultimacy
law: **n.** canon ; constitution ; decalogue ; magna c(h)arta

principle: **n.** fundament(um) ; postulate ; tenet

BASIS : (see "base") **n.** authority ; foundation ; frame of reference ; fundament(um) ; philosophy ; *point d'appui; pou sto;* principium ; theory

BASK *in sun:* **v.** apricate ; **n.** aprication

BASTARD : **n.** *filius nullis; filius populi;* hybrid ; illegitimate ; mongrel ; **a.** counterfeit ; debased ; illegitimate ; sinister ; spurious
fact or cond. of being: **n.** bar sinister

BAT : **n.** chiropter ; *fledermaus;* Vespertilio ; (**pl.** Vespertilionidae) ; **a.** chiropteran ; vespertilian ; vesptertine

BATH(S) : **n.** ablution ; balneation ; **n.** BATHING : balneology ; **a.** ablutionary ; balneal ; balneary
treatment by: **n.** balneo-therapeutics ; balneo-therapy ; hydrotherapy

BATTLE : **n.** collision ; conflict ; encounter ; engagement ; skirmish
flag or standard: **n.** oriflamme
great and decisive: **n.** Armageddon

BATTLEFIELD : **n.** aceldama ; Armageddon ; battleground

BAUBLE : see "trifle"

BE *what you seem to be: esto quod esse videris*

BEAK : (see "nose") **n.** proboscis
hooked type: **a.** aduncous ; aquiline

BEAN, *pert. to or like:* **a.** fabaceous
shaped like: **a.** fabiform

BEAR *or bear family, pert. to:* **a.** arctoid ; (**pl.** arctoidea) ; ursine

BEARD(S), *cultivation or growing of:* **n.** pogonotrophy
study of or treatise on: **n.** pogonology
trimming: **n.** pogonotomy

BEARDED : **a.** aristate ; awned ; barbate ; pogoniate

BEARING : **n.** address ; application ; behavior ; carriage ; démarche ; demeanor ;

deportment; direction; mien; poise; posture; prestance; purport; relation; significance
  live beings: **a.** proligerous; viviparous
  noble: **n.** *démarche noble*

BEARINGS, *loss of:* **n.** disorientation

BEAST: (**see** "animal") **n.** behemoth; quadruped
  one believing himself to be (mental disorder): **n.** lycanthropy; zoanthropia; zoanthropy

BEAT: (**see** "accent") **n.** arsis; ictus; intonation; palpitation; pulsation; thesis
  as w/ stick: **v.** castigate; cudgel; flagellate; fustigate; lambaste
  or stress, recurring: **n.** ictus pulsation
  rapidly: **v.** palpitate; **a.** palpitant; **n.** palpitation; tachycardia (*heart*)

BEAUTIFUL: (**see** "attractive") **a.** (a)esthetic(al); beauteous; captivating; comely; delectable; excellent; *fait a peindre;* pulchritudinous; tempean
  form: **n.** *belle tournure*
  love of the: **n.** (a)esthetics; philocaly; **a.** (a)esthetic(al); philocalic

BEAUTY: (**see** "glory") **n.** beauteousness; comeliness; excellence; felinity; magnificence; pulchritude; radiance; splendor; symmetry; **v.** BEAUTIFY: (**see** "adorn") adonize; embellish
  and art, pert to: **a.** (a)esthetic(al); artistic
  goddess of: **n.** Aphrodite; Venus
  ideal or perfect: **n.** *beau idéal; beauté achevée, une beauté accomplie*
  paragon of: **n.** phoenix
  physical: **n.** comeliness; pulchritude; **a.** comely; pulchritudinous
  place of great natural (beauty) or charm: **n.** Tempe; **a.** tempean
  science of: **n.** (a)esthetics
  worshipper of: **n.** (a)esthete; connoisseur

BECAUSE *of this:* **adv.** *propter hoc*

BECKON: **see** "allure"

BECLOUD (or BEDIM): **see** "obscure"

BED: **n.** foundation; framework; matrix
  -chamber, small: **n.** cubiculum
  -wetting: **n.** nocturnal enuresis

BEDECK: (**see** "adorn") **v.** caparison; lard

BEFORE: (**see** "previous") **prep.** awaiting; confronting; **adv.** anterior
  as: **adv.** *sicut ante; status quo ante*
  feeling of having been somewhere (before): **n.** *déjà vu(e)*; paramnesia
  going: (**see** "preliminary") **a.** antecedent; antecedental; premundane; **n. see** "forerunner"
  state of being; **n.** antecedence; anteriority; precedence; **a.** antecedaneous; antecedent; anterior; precedent; premundane; prevenient

BEG: (**see** "beseech" **and** "pray") **v.** adjure; importune; solicit

BEGET: **v.** procreate; (pro)generate; propagate; reproduce; **n.** BEGETTING: procreation; **a.** procreant; procreative; reproductive

BEGGAR: **n.** cadger; gaberlunzie; mendicant; pariah; petitioner; suppliant; **a.** BEGGARLY: contemptible; sordid; tatterdemalion

BEGGING: **a.** beseeching; importunate; mendicant; precative; precatory; soliciting; solicitous; supplicatory; **n.** mendicancy; mendicity
  the question (assuming what is to be proved): **n.** *petitio principii*

BEGIN: **v.** actuate; generate; germinate; inaugurate; initiate; institute; motivate; originate; **n.** BEGINNER: (**see** "learner") abecedarian; actuator; amateur; apprentice; catalyst; catechumen; founder; neophyte; novice; novitiate; originator; postulate

BEGINNING: (**see** "origin") **n.** actuation; commencement; exordium; foundation; genesis; impulsion; inauguration; inception; incipience; incipiency; inconabulum; (**pl.** inconabula); initiation; investiture; nascency; *premier pas;* primordium; principium; **a.** aborning; alpha; catechumenical; elementary; embryonic; genetic; germinal; inchoate; incipient; inconabular; *in fieri;* initiatory; nascent; parturient; primitive; primordial; rudimentary
  and end: **n.** alpha and omega
  existing at or from the: **a. or adv.** *ab inconabulis; ab initio; ab initium;* aboriginal; primordial; **adv.** *ab ovo*

having no: **adv.** *ab aeterno*
in the: **adv.** *in principio*
just: **a.** inchoate; inchoative; potential;
n. inchoation; nascency
to end, from: **adv.** *ab ovo usque ad mala*
to form: **a.** aborning; nascent; parturient; **n.** nascency

BEHAVIOR: (**see** "conduct") **n.** attitude; bearing; comportment; demeanor; deportment; discipline; ergasia; manner; mien
artificial: **n.** affectation; theatricality; (**pl.** dramatics; histrionics; hysterics; pathetics; sentimentalities; theatrics)
asocial or antisocial: **n.** sociopath(y); **a.** sociopathic
authority on rules of: **n.** *arbiter-elegantiae; arbiter elegantiarum*
bad: (**see** "misconduct") **n.** beastliness; bestiality
bold or licentious: **n.** *grivoiserie;* **a.** *grivois*
childish or infantile: **n.** immaturity; infantility; puerilism; puerility; **a.** infantile; infantilistic
coarse: (**see** "coarseness") **n.** buffoonery
conforming to proper: **see** "standards"
courteous: **n.** benignity; civility; congeniality; cordiality; graciosity
during good: **adv.** *ad vitam aut culpam; quamdiu se bene gesserit*
extravagant or conspicuous: (**see** "*artificial*" *above*) **n.** baboonery; buffoonery; exhibitionism; theatricality; theatrics; **a.** exhibitionistic(al); theatrical
false: **see** "*artificial*" *above*
good: **see** "*courteous*" *above*
influencing by suggesting desirable life goals: **n.** psychagogy; **a.** psychagogic
lofty: **n.** dramatism; theatricality; (**pl.** theatrics)
not conforming to proper: **see** "improper"
one w/ disordered toward other people: **n.** (constitutional) psychopath
science or study of: **n.** behaviorism; ethics; ethology; psychology; **a.** ethological
violent: **a.** manic(al); rampageous; riotous

BEHEAD: **v.** decapitate; guillotine; obtruncate

BEHIND: **n.** *derrière;* gluteus; podex; posterior; **a. or adv.** *en arrière*
force acting from: **n.** *vis a tergo*
from: **adv.** *a tergo;* **a.** posterior

BEING(S): (**see** "existence" **and** "human") **n.** actuality; bios; ens; entity; esse; existent; **a.or adv.** *in esse*
description of nature of: **n.** ontography
for the time (being): **a. or adv.** *ad hoc; pro tem(pore)*
of Beings (supreme): **n.** *Ens Entium*
physical: **see under** "existence"
rel. to: **a.** *ontic; ontological*
science dealing w/ nature of: **n.** metaphysics; ontology; **a.** ontological
small: **n.** animalcule; inchling

BELCH: **v.** eruct(ate); **n.** eructation

BELIEF(S): **n.** acceptation; conviction; credence; creed; doctrine; *idée fixe;* persuasion; philosophy; principle; profession; sentiment; tenet
abandon: **v.** apostatize; **n.** apostasy; apostate
erroneous: **n.** pseudodoxy
in facts only: **n.** materialism; positivism
in one's self: **n.** egoism; solipsism
one holding no particular: **see under** "creed"
reconciliation or union of conflicting: **n.** syncretism; **a.** syncretic; syncretistic; **v.** syncretize
semi-mystical surrounding person or object: **n.** mystique
worthiness of: **see** "believable"

BELIEVABLE: **a.** credible; creditable; plausible; trustworthy; **n.** BELIEVABILITY: credibility; plausibility; trustworthiness

BELIEVER *in all religions:* **n.** omnist

BELITTLE: **v.** debase; decry; defame; denigrate; depreciate; disparage; minimize; stigmatize; vilify; villipend; **a.** BELITTLING: denigratory; depreciatory; derogative; derogatory; minimizing; villipending; **n.** BELITTLEMENT: denigration; derogation; disparagement; minimization; stigmatization

BELL(S), *art of ringing:* **n.** campanology
shaped like: **a.** campaniform; campanular; campanulate
small tinkling: **n.** tintinnabulum; (**pl.** tintinnabula)
sound of: **n.** tintinnabulation; **a.** tintinnabular
study of, or making: **n.** campanology

BELLIGERENT: (see "hostile") **a.** bellicose; umbrageous; **n.** bashi-bazouk

BELLOWING: a. mugient; vociferating; vociferous

BELLY: see "abdomen"
 dance: **n.** *danse du ventre*

BELONG: v. appertain; inhere; **a.** appurtenant; **n.** appurtenance; appurtenant

BELOW: adv. inferior; nether; subalternate; subjacent; suboptimal; subordinate; substrative; underlying
 as: **adv.** *ut infra*

BEND: v. arcuate; circumflex; deflect; incurve; replicate; **n.** arcuation; circumflexion; flexure; flexuosity; incurvation; (in)curvature; sinuosity; tortuosity; **a. see** "bent"

BENEATH, *to place:* **v.** infrapose; **n.** infraposition

BENEFACTOR: n. donor; grantor; patron; philanthropist; Prometheus; Samaritan
 generous: **n.** Maecenas; **n.** Maecenasship: Maecenatism

BENEFICIAL: (see "advantageous") **a.** benefic; opportune; rewarding; salubrious; salutary; sanative

BENEFICIARY: n. cestui; donee; legatee

BENEFICIENT: (see "charitable") **a.** benevolent; munificient; salubrious; salutary

BENEFIT: n. advantage; benefaction; benefice; beneficience; benevolence; blessing
 for whose?: **adv.** *cui bono?*
 of clergy; **n.** *beneficium clericale*

BENEVOLENT: see "charitable"

BENT: a. arcuate; circumflex; determined; flexuous; geniculate; incurvate; pronate; resolved; **n.** (see "inclination") affectation; disposition; penchant; tendency
 backwards, as the body: **n.** opisthotonos; retroflexion; **a.** opisthotonic

BERATE: (see "scold") **v.** castigate; chide; execrate; objurgate; reprove; vituperate; **a.** castigatory; execratory; objurgatory; **n.** execration; objurgation; vituperation

BESEECH: (see "pray") **v.** entreat; impetrate; implore; importune; obsecrate; obtest; solicit; supplicate; **a.** BESEECHING: imploratory; importunate; precative; precatory; solicitous; **n.** imploration; obtestation; solicitation

BESIDE: see "alongside"

BESIEGE: (see "surround") **v:** beleaguer

BEST, *all is for the:* **a.** Panglossian
 cond. or fact of being: **n.** optimity; optimum; preeminent; preeminence; superiority; **a.** optimum; *par excellence;* superordinary; superordinate
 make (best) of: **v.** optimize
 -man: **n.** *garçon d'honneur;* paranymph
 the, or the very: (see "choice") **n.** *crème de la crème; nec plus supra; nec plus ultra;* **adv. or a.** *par excellence;* **adv.** preeminent; supereminent

BETRAYAL: n. apostasy; duplicity; perfidy; prodition; treachery; treason; triplicity
 of trust: **n.** perfidy; prodition; seduction; **a.** perfidious; treacherous

BETRAYER: n. apostate; recreant; traitor

BETROTHAL: n. affiance; engagement; espousal; troth; **pl.** sponsalia

BETS, *series of:* **n.** parlay

BETTER, *for want of anything:* **n.** *faute de mieux;* Hobson's choice
 quality or cond. of being: **n.** meliority; optimity; **a.** optimum; superordinary; superordinate
 so much the: **adv.** *tant mieux*
 to make or become: **v.** (a)meliorate; **a.** meliorative; **n.** melioration

BETTERMENT *of society by improving health conds., etc.:* **n.** meliorism

BETWEEN: a. interjacent; intermediate; intervening; **n.** interjacency
 ourselves: **adv.** *entre nous; inter nous*
 three: **adv.** *à trois*
 two: **adv.** *à deux*
 two fires: **adv.** *entre deux feux*

two points or events: **a.** intermediary; intermediate; intervenient; intervening; parenthetical

BEVERAGE: **n.** draught; libation; potable; potation

BEWAIL: **v.** bemoan; deplore; lament; **a.** deprecable; lamentable; plangorous; **n.** BEWAILMENT: deploration; deprecation; lamentation

BEWARE: **adv.** *prenez garde*

BEWILDER: **v.** astonish; astound; bemuse; electrify; flabbergast; metagrobolize; obfuscate; perplex; **a.** BEWILDERED: (see "confused") bemused; *désorienté;* disconnected; distraught; electrified; *éperdu;* thunderstruck; **n.** BEWILDERMENT: (see "confusion") disorientation; embranglement; obfuscation; perplexity

BEWITCH: (**see** "enchant") **v.** captivate; ensorcel(1); exorcise; fascinate

BIAS: **n.** inclination; partiality; *parti pris;* predilection; prejudice; prepossession; tendency; **a.** BIASED: diagonal; oblique; opinionated; prejudiced; prejudicial; slanting; tendentious

BIBLE, *adherence to letter of:* **n.** Biblicism; Biblicist; fundamentalism
   books not recognized: **n.pl.** apocrypha; anagignoskomena
   books recognized as authoritative (N. Test.): **n.pl.** homolog(o)umena; **a.** protocanonical
   pert. to: **a.** biblical; scriptural; **n.** biblicality; scripturality
   student of: **n.** Biblicist; Biblist
   worship of: **n.** Bibliolatry

BIG: (**see** "huge") **a.** preeminent; pregnant; pretentious
   -bellied: **a.** abdominous; ventripotent
   -bug: (**see** "person, important") **n.** bigwig; celebrity; cynosure; grandee; luminary; magnate; magnifico; notability; panjandrum; personage
   -headed: (**see** "conceited") **a.** megacephalic; megacephalous

BIGOT: see "person, narrow-minded"; **a.** BIGOTED: (see "narrow-minded") inegalitarian; **n.** BIGOTRY: fanaticism; intolerance; (pen)insularity; provincialism; sectarianism; sectionalism

BILATERAL: **a.** bipartisan; reciprocal; synal(l)agamatic; **n.** BILATERALITY: bipartisanship; duality

BILK: (**see** "cheat") **v.** disappoint; frustrate; swindle

BILL *having multiple purposes:* **n.** omnibus (bill)

BIND: **v.** colligate; constrain; contract; ligate; restrain; restrict; shackle
   something which (binds): **n.** ligation; ligature; linchpin

BINDING: **a.** astrictive; (a)stringent; indissoluble; obligatory; **n.** astriction; astrictive; colligation; contraction; ligation; ligature; stringency
   by, or as if by, oath or covenant: **n.** objurgation; **a.** sacramental

BIOGRAPHICAL *novel, developing character fr. child to adulthood:* **n.** entwicklungsroman
   sketches, collection or production of: **n.** prosopography

BIOGRAPHY: **n.** anamensis; *curriculum vitae;* memoir(s); personalia; prosopography; reminiscence(s)
   short: **n.** profile

BIOLOGICAL *development:* **n.** ontology; **a.** ontological

BIOLOGICALLY *defective or deficient:* **a.** dysgenic

BIRD(S), *collector of eggs:* **n.** oologist; oology
   loving or fond of: **a.** ornithophilous
   of a region or area: **n.** avifauna; ornithofauna
   pert. to: **a.** avian; ornithic; ornithoid
   rearing and care of: **n.** aviculture
   study of: **n.** ornithology
   -watching: **n.** ornithoscopy

BIRTH: **n.** accouchement; ancestry; confinement; debut; embarcation; extraction; genesis; geniture; inauguration; inchoation; insipience; lineage; nativity; procreation
   about to give, or giving: **a.** aborning; *in statu nascendi;* parturient
   after (subsequent to): **a.** postnatal; postpartum

asst. at: **n.** accoucher; midwife; obstetrician; (**fem.** accoucheuse; midwife)
at moment of: **a. or adv.** aborning; **a.** parturient; **n.** parturition
before: **a.** antemundane; antenatal; antepartum; prenatal; **adv.** *in utero*
bringing forth young by: **a.** parturient; proligerous; viviparous; **n.** viviparity
bringing forth young by eggs: **a.** oviparous; ovoviparous; **n.** oviparity; ovoviparity
existing from or before: **a.** congenital; connatal; connate; familial; genetous; hereditary; inherent; innate; primeval
giving to live beings: **see** "bringing forth young by" *above*
illegitimate: **n.** bar sinister
land of one's: **n.** *natale solum*
occurring at or about time of: **a.** aborning; parturient; perinatal
of gentle: **a.** gentilitial; gentilitious; **n.** gentility; gentry
pert. to: **a.** aborning; natal; parturient
rate of: **n.** natality
resident of place or region of: **n.** sedens
room set apart for, as in hosp.: **n.** natuary

BIRTHDAY, *pert. to:* **a.** genethliac(al)
poem: **n.** genethliacon

BISEXUAL: **a.** androgynous; hermaphroditic(al); **n.** androgyne; hermaphrodite; **n.** BISEXUALITY: androgyneity; androgyny; hermaphroditism

BIT: **n.** driblet; granule; minimum; minum; modicum; morceau; morsel; smack; tincture; tinge

BITING: (**see** "sarcastic") **a.** acidulous; acrid; acrimonious; caustic; censorious; corrosive; incisive; mordacious; mordant; piquant; poignant; vinegary
of nails: **n.** onychophagia; onychophagy; phaneromania
remarks: **n.** causticity; mordacity; spinosity

BITTER: (**see** "sarcastic") **a.** acrimonious; caustic; determined; distasteful; grievous; poignant; relentless; unpalatable; unsavory; vehement; **n.** BITTERNESS: acerbity; acridity; acrimony; poignancy
in temperament: (**see** "biting") **a.** acerb(ic); **n.** acerbity
something which is: **n.** wormwood (**or** gall and wormwood)

BIZARRE: (**see** "odd") **a.** atypical; baroque; chimerical; daedal(ic); daedalian; fantastic; grotesque; **n. see** "oddity"
quality: **n.** bizarrerie

BLACK: **a.** atramental; atramentous; discreditable; dishonorable; nigrescent; swart; **n.** BLACKNESS: nigrescence; nigritude
beast (*figurative*): **n.** *bête noir*
magic: **n.** necromancy; sorcery
sheep (*figurative*): (**see** "scamp") **n.** *mauvais sujet*

BLACKEN: **v.** nigrify; **a.** BLACKISH: nigrescent; nigricant
name of: **v.** defame; denigrate; depreciate; disparage; revile; sully; vilify; vilipend; **n.** denigration; vilification; **a.** denigratory

BLACKHEAD: **n.** comedo

BLACKMAIL: **n.** chantage

BLAME: **v.** accuse; animadvert; censure; condemn; criticize; impute; incriminate; inculpate; reprehend; reprimand; reproach; reprove; upbraid; **n.** animadversion; culpa(bility); obloquy; onus; reprehension; **a.** BLAMABLE (or BLAMEWORTHY): (**see** "guilty") censurable; condemnatory; culpable; demeritorious; peccable; reprehensible; reprovable
free from: **v.** absolve; exculpate; exonerate; vindicate; **n.** exculpation; exoneration; vindication; **a.** exculpable; exculpatory

BLAMELESS: (**see** "innocent") **a.** impeccable; impeccant; inculpable; irreproachable; unimpeachable; **n.** BLAMELESSNESS: impeccability

BLAND: (**see** "soothing") **a.** affable; anodyne; anodynic; anodynous; benign; complaisant; favonian; halcyon; ingratiating; lenient; suave; tasteless; unconcerned; unperturbed; urbane

BLARE: **see** "fanfare"

BLAZING: **see** "fiery"

BLEACH: **v.** achromatize; decolorize; etiolate
from lack of sun or light: **v:** etiolate; **n.** etiolation

32

BLEEDING, *hereditary disease of:* **n.** hemophilia; hemophiliac

BLEMISH: **n.** cloud; imperfection; macula-(tion); stigma

BLEND: **v.** amalgamate; coalesce; harmonize; inosculate; **n.** amalgamation; coalescence; tincture

BLESS: **v.** consecrate; macarize; sanctify; **a.** BLESSING: benedictory; invocatory; macarian; **n.** (**see** "approval") beatitude; benediction; benison; felicitation; invocation

BLESSED *are the peacemakers:* **adv.** *beati pacifici*

BLIND: **a.** amaurotic; **adv.** BLINDLY: *à tâtons*
-alley: **n.** cul-de-sac; deadlock; impasse
drive or impulse: **n.** ate
envy is: invidia est caeca
partially: **a.** purblind; **n.** hemianopsia

BLINDNESS: **n.** ablepsia; amaurosis; anopsia; cecity
night-: **n.** nyctalopia
one-sided: **n.** homonymous hemianopsia
study of: **n.** typhlology

BLINK: **v.** nict(it)ate; twinkle; **n.** nictitation

BLISS: (**see** "happiness") **n.** beatitude; ecstasy; elysium; felicity; paradise; transport; **a.** BLISSFUL: beatific; beatified; ecstatic; Edenic; elysian; enchanted; felicific; felicitous; halcyon; paradisiacal; rapturous; transported
consummate: **n.** beatitude; **a.** beatific

BLOCK: **v.** impede; obstruct; occlude; oppilate; **n.** hindrance; impediment; occlusion; oppilation; **a.** impedimental; occlusive

BLOOD: **n.** consanguinity; gore; lineage; **a.** BLOODY: gory, merciless; murderous; sanguinary
bad: **n.** *mauvais sang*
color of: **a.** sanguine(ous)
feeding on: **a.** hematophagous; sanguinivorous; sanguivorous
having excess of: **a.** plethoric; **n.** plethora
impurity of: **n.** acatharsia; septicemia

not of pure: (**see** "half-breed") **a.** unpedigreed
of, containing, or tinged w/: **a.** sanguinolent
-pressure instrument; **n.** sphygmomanometer
supply, local, temp. lack of: **n.** ischemia; **a.** ischemic
-thirsty: **a.** murderous; sanguinary; sanguineous; **n.** acharnement

BLOODSHED, *place of:* **n.** Aceldama; Armageddon

BLOOM: **v.** burgeon; effloresce; flourish; **n.** burgeoning; (ef)florescence; heyday; maturescence
full: **n.** anthesis; maturescence

BLOOMING: **a.** burgeoning; (ef)florescent; (ef)floriferous; prosperous
again: **a.** recrudescent; remontant

BLOTCH: **a.** imperfection; macula(tion); **a.** macular; maculate

BLOW: **v.** bluster; fulminate; squander; **n.** assault; calamity; concussion; coup; impact; trauma(tism)
knockdown: **n.** recumbentibus
physical or mental: **n.** trauma(tism); **a.** traumatic; **v.** traumatize
taking effect elsewhere: **n.** contrecoup
without a: **adv.** *sine ictu*

BLUE: **a.** depressed; melancholy; puritanical; unpromising; **n.** "BLUES": despondency; doldrum(s); megrim(s); melancholy
deep clear: **a.** cerulean
ribbon (highest distinction): **n.** *cordon bleu; grand prix*

BLUENESS *of skin:* **n.** cyanosis; **a.** cyanotic

BLUESTOCKING: **n.** *bas bleu;* (**fem.** *femme savante*)

BLUNDER: **v.** botch; bungle; mismanage; **n.** (**see** "stupidity") *faux pas; gaffe;* parapraxia; parapraxis
in speech: **n.** parapraxia; solecism; **a.** solecistic(al)
social: **n.** *faux pas; gaffe;* solecism

BLUNT: (**see** "frank") **v.** anesthesize; hebetate; narcotize; **a.** brusque; hebetate;

insensible; insensitive; obtund; obtuse; unceremonious; untactful; **n.** BLUNTNESS: brusquerie; hebetude; insensibility; obtusity

BLUSH: **n.** erubescence; rubedo; **a.** erubescent

BLUSTER: **see** "boast" **and** "swagger;" **n.** BLUSTERER: (**see** "boaster") swashbuckler

BOARDER: **n.** *pensionnaire*

BOAST: (**see** "swagger") **v.** bluster; flaunt; flourish; gasconade; preen; rodomontade; swashbuckle; **n.** BOASTER: braggadocio; braggart; bravado; cockalorum; fanfaron; gasconade; hector; jackanapes; megalomaniac; rodomont; Scaramouche; swashbuckler; **n.** BOASTING: (**see** "bombast") fanfaronade; jactitation; pomposity; rodomontade; vainglory; vaporing

BOASTFUL: **a.** bombastic; braggadocian; grandiose; grandiloquent; magniloquent; ostentatious; pompous; rodomontade; sonorous; swashbuckling; thrasonic(al); vainglorious; vaporing; vaunting
person: see "boaster"
talk, speech or action: **n.** bravado; cockalorum; fanfaronade; gasconade; rodomontade

BOAT-SHAPED: **a.** navicular

BODY: **n.** cadaver; corpus; quantum; (**pl.** quanta); substance; substantiality; torso; **a.** BODILY: constitutional; corpor(e)al; incarnate; physical; somantic
abnormal cond. of: **n.** dyscrasia; pathology
and mind, rel. to: **a.** psychosomatic
and soul: **n.** *corpus et âme*
build: (**see** "type" below) **n.** habitus; physique
cavity, opening of: **n.** introitus; os
dead: **n.** cadaver; corpse
discharge(s): see "excrement(s)"
form into: **v.** corporify; embody; incarnate
freed from the: **a.** disincarnate
having a: **a.** corporality; corporeity; incarnate; materiality
having abnormally large: **a.** macrosomatic; macrosomatous; **n.** macrosomia

having small: **a.** microsomatic; microsomatous
human: **n.** tenement
movement, pert. to: **a.** gestic
originating within: **a.** autogenic; autogenous; endogenous; psychogenic; psychosomatic; physiogenic; somatogenic
originating w/o: **a.** exogenous; heterogeneous
pert. to: **a.** constitutional; corpor(e)al; musculo-skeletal; physical; somatic; **n.** somatization
preoccupied with the: **n.** physicality
sensations, recognition of location of: **n.** stereognosis; topognosis; **a.** stereognostic
sensations, rel. to: **a.** somesthetic
type, human:
    light or asthenic: **a.** ectomorphic; leptosome; **n.** ectomorph; hyperontomorph; leptosome
    muscular or athletic: **a.** eumorphic; mesomorphic; **n.** mesomorph
    short, broad, round: **a.** endomorphic, pyknic; **n.** endomorph; pyknic
    thick, robust, powerful: **n.** meso-ontomorph

BOG: **n.** morass; quagmire; **a.** quaggy

BOGUS: (**see** "sham") **a.** artificial; Brummagem; counterfeit; factitious; fraudulent; spurious

BOIL (*sore*): **n.** furuncule; **a.** furuncular; (**n.pl.** furunculosis)

BOILING: **a.** ebullient; effervescent; seething; torrid; **n.** ebullition; effervescence

BOISTEROUS: (**see** "noisy") **a.** brawling; disorderly; raucus; robustious; robustuous; roisterous; termagant; truculent; tumultuous; **n.** BOISTEROUSNESS: raucity; raucousness

BOLD: (**see** "brave") **a.** adventurous; (ad)venturesome; arrogant; audacious; chivalrous; courageous; doughty; enterprising; harageous; impertinent; impudent; intrepid; malapert; presumptuous; prominent; resolute; valiant; **adv.** *con bravura;* **n.** BOLDNESS: assumption; audacity; doughtiness; effrontery; impudence; intrepidity; pertness; presumption; temerity
attempt: **n.** bravura
or courageous when drunk: **a.** potvaliant

showy type of (boldness): **n.** bravado; **a.** doughty; vainglorious

BOMBAST: **n.** balderdash; braggadocio; fustian; gasconade; grandiloquence; magniloquence; pomposity; rhapsody; rodomontade; tumidity; turgescence; turgidity; tympany; **a.** BOMBASTIC: (**see** "boastful") fustian; grandiloquent; grandiose; *guindé;* inflated; magniloquent; pompous; tumescent; tumid; turgescent; turgid; vainglorious
in speech or writing: **n.** fustian; gasconade; grandiloquence; grandiosity; magniloquence; rodomontade; **a.** (**see** "rhetorical") declamatory; fustian; grandiloquent; grandiose; stilted

BOND(S): **n.** collateral; covenant; debenture; liaison; ligation; ligature; obligation; nexus; recognizance; shackle
of matrimony: **n.** vinculum matrimonii
strong or inextricable: **n.** Gordian knot; **a.** Gordian

BONE(S), *growth on:* **n.** exostosis
pert. to or resembling: **a.** osseous
place for: **n.** charnel house; ossuary
union of two: **n.** ankylosis; synostosis; **a.** ankylotic

BONFIRE: **n.** *feu de joie*

BONUS: **n.** cumshaw; dividend; lagniappe

BOOBS, *class of persons considered:* **n.** booboisie

BOOK(S), *binder of:* **n.** bibliopegist; **a.** bibliopegistic(al)
catalogue of: **n.** bibliotheca
censorship of: **see** "list of banned or proscribed" **below**
collecting, esp. rare: **n.** bibliomania
collection: **n.** bibliotheca
collector: **n.** bibliophile; **a.** bibliophilic
dealer: **n.** bibliopole; bibliopolist
destroyer or mutilator of: **n.** biblioclast
edition containing variant readings of the text: **n.** variorum (edition)
extreme preoccupation w/: **n.** bibliomania
first edition: **n.** princeps
guide or travel: **n.** Baedeker
hater or hatred of: **n.** biliophobe; bibliophobia
history and science of: **n.** bibliology

hoarder: **n.** bibliotaph(e); **a.** bibliotaphic
license to print: **n.** imprimatur
list of banned or proscribed: **n.** *index expurgatorius;* (**pl.** *index expurgatorii*); *index librorum prohibitorum*
love or lover of: **n.** bibliolater; bibliomania; bibliomaniac; bibliophage; bibliophile; bibliophilism; bibliophilist; bibliophily; philobiblist
mania for acquiring: **n.** bibliomania
of no interest of worth: **n.pl.** *biblia abiblia*
one having great knowledge of: **n.** bibliognost; **a.** bibliognostic
printed before 1501: **n.** incunabulum
production of: **n.** bibliogony
reference: (**see** "handbook") **n.** manual; promptuary; *vade mecum*
second-hand dealer in: **n.** *bouquiniste*
seller, esp. rare: **n.** bibliopole; bibliopoly; **a.** bibliopolic
series of five: **n.** pentalogy
of four: **n.** tetrad; tetralogy
of three: **n.** triad; trilogy
stealer of: **n.** biblioklept
strange or unusual: **n.pl.** curiosa; erotica; facetiae
unknown writer of: **n.** anonym(e)
-worm: **n.** bibliophage; *helluo librorum;* **a.** bibliophagous
worship or worshipper: **n.** bibliolatry; Bibliolatry (Bible); bibliolater; Bibliolater (Bible); **a.** bibliolatrous

BOOKCASE: **n.** bibliotheca

BOOKISH: **a.** bibliognostic; erudite; pedantic; scholastic; **n.** bibliognost

BOOKLET: **n.** brochure; monograph; pamphlet

BOON: **a.** convivial; intimate; jovial; merry
companion: **n.** alter ego; *bon camarade*

BOOR: **n.** bromide; bumpkin; churl; clodhopper; dullard; grobian; yokel; **a.** BOORISH: (**see** "rude") churlish; clownish; gauche; loutish; **n.** BOORISHNESS: gaucherie; grobianism; rudeness; rusticity

BORDER: (**see** "boundary") **n.** confine; extremity; margin; periphery; verge
have a distinct: **a.** discrete; limbate
situated on (border) or frontier: **a.** limitrophe

BORDERLINE: **a.** dubious; intermediate; liminal; limitrophe; marginal; peripheral; questionable; **n. see** "boundary"

BOREDOM: **n.** ennui; tedium; wearisomeness; **a.** BORED: *ennuyé;* (**fem.** *ennuyée*); **adv.** *ad nauseam*

BORING: **see** "dull" **and** "tiresome"

BORN *after father's death:* **a.** posthumous
   being (*born*) *or produced:* **a.** aborning; *in statu nascendi;* nascent; parturient; **n.** nascency; parturition

BORROWING *makes sorrowing: borgen macht sorgen*

BOTHER: **see** "annoy"

BOUNCE: **v.** rebound; resile; ricochet; **a.** resilient; *n.* resilience; resiliency; ricochet

BOUND(S): (**see** "leap," "restrain" **and** "scope") **n.** ambit; circumscription; environs; precinct; **v.** circumscribe; confine; delineate; embosom; encompass
   by a single: **a. or adv.** *per saltum*
   keep within: **adv.** *sevare modum*

BOUNDARY: **n.** circumference; confines; perimeter; periphery; terminal; termination; terminus; **a.** circumferential
   having common: **a.** conterminal; conterminous; contiguous; **n.** contiguity
   line: **n.** perimeter; periphery

BOUNDED: **a.** circumscribed; finite; limited; **n.** finitude

BOUNDLESS: (**see** "eternal") **a.** illimitable; immeasurable; impenetrable; inexhaustible; infinite; limitless; measureless; unbounded; uncircumscribed; unfathomable; **n.** BOUNDLESSNESS: illimitability; infinitude; infinity

BOW, *with humiliation or penance:* **v.** go to Canossa

BOWELS, *act of relieving:* **n.** cacation; defecation; excretion
   excretion from: **see** "feces"
   remove: **v.** disembowel; eviscerate; exenterate
   rumbling of: **n.** borborygmus; crepitation; flatus; **a.** borborygmic

BOXER: **n.** pugilist
   clumsy: **n.** stumblebum

BOXING: **n.** pugilism; **a.** pugilant; pugilistic
   rules of: **n.** Marquis of Queensberry
   world of: **n.** fistiana; pugilism

BOY *kept for sexual purposes:* **n.** catamite; pathic

BOYISH: **a.** ephebic; immature; juvenile; puerile; youthful; **n.** BOYISHNESS: juvenility; puerilism; puerility

BRACELET, *of or like:* **a.** armillary

BRACING: **a.** invigorating; roborant; salubrious; tonic, vigorous; zestful

BRAG: (**see** "boast") **v.** gasconade; **n.** (**see** "boaster") braggadoccio; fanfaron; rodomontade; **n.** Scaramouche; BRAGGING: **see** "boasting"

BRAIN: **n.** cerebrum; encephalon; intellect; intelligence; psyche; sensorium
   action: (**see** "thought") **n.** cerebration
   having very small: **a.** micrencephalous; **n.** micrencephaly

BRAINY: **see** "intellectual"

BRAN, *of or like:* **a.** furfuraceous

BRANCH(ES): **n.** arborization; bifurcation; divarication; divergence; ramification; ramus; **v.** arborize; (bi)furcate; divaricate; diverge; ramify; subdivide
   comprised of more than two: **a.** polychotomous
   having many small: **a.** ramulose
   having two: **a.** biramose; biramous
   producing: **a.** sarmentose; sarmentous

BRANCHING: **a.** bifurcate(d); biramose; biramous; cladose; divergent; radial; radiating; ramose; ramous
   in all directions: **a.** radial; radiating; ramifying; tentacular

BRANDY: **n.** *eau de vie*

BRASH: **see** "reckless"

BRASS: **n.** audacity; effrontery; hubris; impertinence; impudence; insolence; presumption; temerity; **a. see** "brazen"

BRAVADO: (see "swagger") n. panache

BRAVE: (see "bold") a. audacious; cavalier; chivalresque; chivalric; chivalrous; courageous; dauntless; doughty; fortitudinous; heroic; intrepid; martial; resolute; Spartan(ic); undaunted; valiant; valorous; v. beard; challenge; defy
and gallant man, as one who liberates victims of tyranny: n. pimpernel
fortune favors the: adv. *fortes fortuna (ad) juvat*

BRAVERY: n. audacity; bravado; chivalry; dauntlessness; derring-do; doughtiness; fortitude; gallantry; hardihood; intrepidity; intrepidness; prowess; temerity; valiancy; valor
show of: n. bravado; bravura; panache; swagger; verve

BRAWL: n. altercation; brannigan; brouhaha; contention; controversy; disputation; dissention; donny-brook; fracas; tumult; wrangle

BRAZEN: (see "shameless") a. arrogant; audacious; brassy; clangorous; gaudy; hubristic; presumptuous; unscrupulous

BREACH: n. abruption; (ab)scission; crevasse; desuetude; dissension; hiatus; infraction; infringement; nonfulfillment; non-observance; rupture; schism; transgression; violation; a. dissentious; schismatic(al)
of etiquette: n. barbarism; *faux pas;* impropriety; solecism; a. indecorous; solecistic(al)
of trust: n. *trahison des clercs*

BREAD, *quality or state of being:* n. paneity

BREAK: (see "breach") v. bankrupt; fracture; fragment(al)ize; fragmentate; rupture; transgress; violate; n. abruption; abscission; armistice; c(a)esura; cessation; discontinuity; disruption; hiatus; interim; interruption; lacuna; recess; respite; schism; scission; a. hiatal
as in continued series: n. discontinuity; interregnum; lacuna
not possible to: see "unbreakable"
up: v. comminute; decompose; disjoin; divaricate; fractionalize; fractionate; liquidate; pulverize; schismatize; triturate; n. comminution; disintegration; dissolution; fragmentation; liquidation; trituration

BREAKABLE: a. fracturable; fragile; frangible; friable; n. fragility; frangibility; friability

BREAKING *down* (or BREAK-DOWN): n. catabolism; cataclasm; decomposition; disintegration; disruption; dissolution; prostration
process of (biological): n. catabolism
of faith: n. apostasy; perfidy; a. perfidious; traitorous
of status or situation, sudden: n. abscission
off: n. abruption; cessation; disruption
up: see under "break"

BREAST(S): n.pl. mammae; a. mammary; pectoral
excessive development: n. macromastia; a. bathycolpian; pneumatic
from the inmost: adv. *imo pectore*
having: a. mammiferous
having small: n. micromastia
having two: a. bimastic; n. bimasticism; bimasty
male, excessive development: n. gynecomastia
muscles: n.pl. pectorals
pin or ornament: n. pectoral

BREATH: n. anima(tion); emanation; exhalation; flatus; halitus; inhalation; inspiration; suggestion; utterance; vitality
of life: n. *élan vital;* pneuma; prana
shortness of: n. anhelation; brachypnea; dyspn(o)ea

BREATHING: n. inhalation; inspiration
difficult or painful: n. dyspn(o)ea; a. dyspneic
heavy: a. suspirious; n. suspiration
rapid: n. hyperpnea; hyperventilation; polypnea

BREECH: see "blunder" and "break"

BREED: (see "beget") v. multiply; pullulate
-half or mixed: n. hybrid; mestizo; *métis;* mongrel; mulatto
quickly or *abundantly:* v. pullulate; n. pullulation

BREVITY: (see "brief") n. conciseness; laconism; monosyllabicity; succinctness; terseness
in speech or expression: n. brachylogy; breviloquence; laconism; monosyllabicity;

a. breviloquent; cryptic(al); laconic(al); monosyllabic; succinct; **adv.** *paucis verbis*

BREW: **v.** concoct; contrive; decoct; **n.** concoction; decoction

BRIBE: **v.** suborn; **n.** douceur; gratuity; pourboire; sop to Cerberus; subornation *capable of taking:* **a.** mercenary; venal *one taking fr. both sides:* **n.** ambidexter *willingness to take:* **n.** venality

BRIDEGROOM: **n.** *garçon d'honneur;* paranymph

BRIEF: (see "concise") **a.** compendiary; compendious; cryptic(al); ephemeral; epigrammatic; evanescent; fugacious; fugitive; laconic(al); monosyllabic; pithy; succinct; summary; telegramm(at)ic; terse; transient; transitory; vanishing; volatile; **n.** (see "brevity") abstract; compendium; epitome; inventory; summarization; summary; syllabus; **adv.** BRIEFLY: *en abrégé; paucis verbis* *in:* **adv.** *paucis verbis* *in answering or talking:* (see "brevity") **a.** monosyllabic; **n.** *monosyllabicity* *visit or stay:* **n. or v.** sojourn

BRIGHT: **a.** auroral; aurorean; effulgent; illustrious; incandescent; irradiant; luminous; lustrous; nitid; opalescent; (re)fulgent; resplendent; scintillating; undimmed; **v.** BRIGHTEN: effulge; illuminate; refurbish; **n.** BRIGHTNESS: brilliance; effulgence; fulgor; fluorescence; incandescence; luminance; luminescence; luminosity; luster; nitidity; refulgence; refulgency; resplendence; resplendency; scintillation; vivacity *(promising):* **a.** auspicious *witty and (bright), characterized by being:* **a.** spirituel(le)

BRILLIANT: (see "bright") **a.** effulgent; glittering; illustrious; luminescent; luminous; meteoric; opalescent; scintillant; scintillating; splendent; splendrous; virtuosic; **n.** BRILLIANCE (or BRILLIANCY) *éclat;* effulgence; incandescence; luminance; luminescence; luminosity; luster; nitidity; refulgence; refulgency; resplendence; resplendency; scintillation; virtuosity; vivacity *and witty, to be:* **a.** lambent; scintillating; scintillescent; spirituel(le); **n.** lambency; scintillation; **v.** scintillate *array or assemblage:* **n.** galaxy

execution, as of mus.: **n.** bravura; *tour de force;* virtuosity; **a.** virtuosic *in color:* **a.** iridescent; opalescent; **n.** iridescence; opalescence *momentarily:* **a.** meteoric

BRING(ING) *forth, or about to:* **n.** parturition; **a.** aborning; parturient *together:* (see "assemble") **v. or a.** correlate; **n.** correlation

BRINK: **n.** precipice

BRISK: **a.** alacritous; ebullient; effervescent; energetic; galvanic; spirited; stimulating; **a. or adv.** allegro; *con brio;* **n.** BRISKNESS: alacrity; ebullience; effervescence; spiritedness; vivacity; vividity

BRISTLES, *bearing:* **a.** chaetigerous; chaetophorous *having:* (see "spiny") **a.** aristate; barbellate; exhinate; hispid; setaceous; setarious; setiferous; setigerose; setose

BRITTLE: **a.** evanescent; fragile; frangible; friable; perishable; tenuous; transitory; **n.** BRITTLENESS: fragility; frangibility; friability

BROKEN: **a.** bankrupt; contrite; disconnected; discrete; disunited; fractional; fractured; fragmental; fragmentary; humbled; interrupted; ruptured; spasmodic; subdued *-down:* **a.** dilapidated; disreputable; tatterdemalion *that which cannot be:* (see "unbreakable") **n.** irrefrangability; **a.** immarcescible; imperishable; indestructible; irrefrangable

BROTHEL: **n.** bagnio; bordel(lo); lupanar; seraglio *under police supervision:* **n.** *maison de tolérance*

BROTHER *or sister:* **n. or a.** sibling

BROTHERHOOD: **n.** alliance; companionship; confraternity; confraternization; confrerie; fellowship; fraternity; sodality

BROTHERLY: **a.** affectionate; amicable; fraternal

BROWBEAT: **v.** bully; dictate; domineer; dragoon; hector; intimidate; overawe;

subdue; swashbuckle; **a.** dictatorial; domineering; swashbuckling; tyrannical; tyrannous

BROWN, *dark:* **a.** bruneous; brunescent; cordovan
  beige: **a.** *café au lait;* fulvous

BRUISE: **v.** contuse; disable; traumatize; **n.** contusion; ecchymosis; laceration; lividity; petechia; trauma(tism)

BRUSQUE: **a.** see "abrupt"; **n.** BRUSQUENESS: abruptness; brusquerie

BRUTAL: **a.** barbarous; bestial; brutish; Caliban; feral; inhuman; Procrustean; troglodytic; vindictive

BRUTALITY: **n.** barbarity; brutishness; ferity; inhumanity
  one practicing or advocating: **n.** brutalitarian; sadist

BUBBLING: **a.** ebullient; effervescent; effusive; exuberant; yeasty; **n.** ebulliency; effervescence; effusiveness; exuberance; yeastiness

BUD: **v.** burgeon; germinate; pullulate; **a.** BUDDING: burgeoning; emanating; emergent; pullulant; **n.** burgeoning; efflorescence; pullulation

BUFFOON: **n.** grobian; harlequin; merry-andrew; **n.** BUFFOONERY: harlequinade

BUGBEAR: **n.** *bête noire;* hobgoblin; *loup-garou*

BUILD: **v.** chisel; compose; contrive; fabricate; fashion; manufacture; **n.** composition; makeup; physique; stature
  as to body type: **see under** "body"

BUILDING: **n.** edifice; fabrication; structure
  pert. to: **a.** (archi)tectonic; architectural; constructional

BULGE: **v.** beetle; protrude; protuberate; **n.** convexity; gibbosity; protuberance; protrusion; **a.** (see "swollen") gibbous; obtrusive; protuberant; protrudent; protrusive

BULK: (**see** "largeness") **n.** aggregate; dimension; magnitude; majority; quantum; (**pl.** quanta); **a.** BULKY: corpulent; magnitudinous; massive; ponderous; unwield(l)y; voluminous; **n.** BULKINESS: corpulency; massivity; ponderosity; voluminosity

BULLY: (**see** "browbeat") **v.** bluster; hector; **n.** blusterer; hector

BUNGLING: **a.** amateurish; awkward; gauche; inept; inexpert; maladroit; unskillful; **n.** BUNGLER: *blanc-bec*

BURDEN: **v.** (en)cumber; freight; **n.** albatross; encumbrance; hindrance; impediment; imposition; incubus; infliction; millstone; obligation; onus; *onus probandi;* perplexity; responsibility; **a.** BURDENED: (en)cumbered; freighted; impedimental; impeditive; impregnated; obstructive; oppressed; **a.** BURDENSOME: cumbersome; cumbrous; formidable; grievous; onerous; oppressive; overpowering; ponderous; superincumbent
  equal to the: **adv.** *par oneri*
  of proof: **n.** onus; *onus probandi*

BUREAUCRAT: **n.** mandarin

BURIAL: **n.** deposition; inhumation; interment
  ceremony: **n.** exequy; obsequy
  clothes: **n.** cerecloth; cerement; shroud
  pert. to: **a.** cemeterial; cinerary; funebrial; funereal; mortuary; sepulchral

BURLESKING *cynic:* **n.** pantagruelist; **a.** pantagruelian; **n.** pantagruelism

BURN: **v.** cauterize; deflagrate; incinerate; oxidize; scorify; torrify

BURNABLE: **a.** combustible; conflagrant; conflagratory; ignescent; (in)flammable; inflammatory

BURNING: **a.** ardent; conflagrant; consuming; urgent; vehement; **n.** cineration; conflagration; cremation; ustulation
  to ashes: **n.** cineration
  words: **n.pl.** *ardentia verba*

BURST *forth:* (**see** "blossom") **v.** burgeon; effloresce; **n.** efflorescence; proruption *or split open:* **v.** dehisce; **a.** dehiscent; dissilient; **n.** dehiscence; dissilience

BURSTING: **a.** burgeoning; dehiscent; efflorescent; **n.** dehiscence; efflorescence
open: **a.** dehiscent; dissilient; **n.** dehiscence; dissilience

BUSH, *beat about the:* **v.** *battre la campagne*

BUSINESS: **n.** clientele; commerce; commercialism; *commercium;* industrialism; industry; *jus commercii; métier;* merchantilism; patronage; pursuit

BUSINESSMAN: **n.** *homme d'affaires;* (**pl.** *gens d'affaires*)
uncultivated and conventional: **n.** Babbitt; **a.** Babbitical

BUSY: (**see** "diligent") **a.** assiduous; engaged; engrossed; industrious; occupied; operose; sedulous; **n.** assiduity; engagement; operosity; sedulity

BUSYBODY: **n.** gadfly; intermeddler; polypragmatist; pragmatic; quidnunc; zealot

BUTCHER, *rel. to:* **a.** carnificial

BUTTER, *resembling, yielding or containing:* **a.** butyraceous

BUTTERFLY, *pert. to or characteristic of:* **a.** lepidopterological; lepidopterous

BUTTOCKS: **n.** *derrière;* fundament; gluteus (maximus); (**pl.** glutei maximi); podex; posterior; **a.** pygal
enlarged or fatty: **n.** steatopygia; steatopygy; **a.** steatopygic; steatopygous
having beautiful or shapely: **a.** callipygian; callipygous

BUXOM: **a.** Junoesque

BUY *at own risk:* **n.** or **a.** *caveat emptor*
insane desire to: **n.** oniomania

BUYER: **n.** consumer; emptor; purchaser; vendee
beware, let the: **n.** or **a.** *caveat emptor*
of products or services of several sellers: **n.** monopsonist; monopsony; **a.** monopsonistic

BUYING *or selling of church office or preferment:* **n.** simony

BUZZ: **v.** bombinate; **n.** bombilation; bombination

BY *courage and faith:* **adv.** *animo et fide*
force of arms: **adv.** *vi et armis*
grace of God: **adv.** *Dei gratia*
hook or crook: **adv.** *à bis ou à blanc*
my fault: **adv.** *meâ culpâ*
the month: **adv.** *per mensem*
the way: **adv.** *en passant*
this sign thou wilt conquer: **adv.** *in hoc signo vinces*
virtue of being: **adv.** *qua*
way of example: **adv.** *exempli gratia* (*abb.* e.g.)
words of present tense: **adv.** *per verba de praesenti*

BYEGONE: **a.** extinct; outmoded; *passé;* quondam; **adv.** whilom; **n.** ancien regime; antiquity

BYPASS: (**see** "evade") **v.** circumnavigate; circumvent; detour; **n.** circumnavigation; circumvention; detour

BYWORD: **see** "proverb"

C

CABBAGE *warmed over* (*old story*): **n.** *crambe repetita*

CAESAR'S *river:* **n.** Rubicon

CALAMITY: **n.** cataclysm; catastrophe; holocaust; **a.** CALAMITOUS: cataclysmic; cataclysmal; catastrophic(al); holocaustic

CALCULATE: **see** "infer" **and** "predict"

CALCULATING, *art of:* **n.** algorism; **a.** algorismic

CALENDAR, *add to* (*as in leap year*): **v.** intercalate; **a.** intercalary; **n.** intercalation
present in use: **n.** Gregorian

CALF *of leg, muscle of:* **n.** gastrocnemius; (**pl.** gastrocnemii)
of leg, pert. to: **a.** gastrocnemial; sural
worship the golden: adorer le veau d'or

CALL: (**see** "name") **v.** denominate; entitle
forth: **v.** evocate; **a.** evocative; evocatory; **n.** evocation
together: **v.** convocate; muster; **a.** convocational; **n.** convocation; muster

CALLOUS: (**see** "cruel") **a.** adamant; anesthetic; dedolent; impertinent; impiteous; indifferent; indurative; inexorable; insensible; obdurate; unfeeling; **n.** CALLOUSNESS: impenitence; impenitency; induration
(*hardening of skin*): **n.** callosity

CALM: (**see** "appease") **v.** assuage; placate; temper; tranquilize; **a.** (**see** "peaceful") apathetic; assuasive; composed; dispassive; dispassionate; equanimous; grave; halcyon; hermetic(al); impartial; impassive; imperturable; imperturbed; impervious; insensate; judicial; lenitive; nepenthean; nonchalant; oasitic; pacific; philo-

sophic(al); phlegmatic(al); phlegmatous; phlegmonic; placid; (re)quiescent; sedate; self-possessed; serene; sober; staid; stoic(al); stolid; tempean; temperate; tranquil; unagitated; unalarmed; unblinking; undisturbed; unexcited; unimpassioned; unperturbed; unruffled; untroubled; **n. see** "calmness"
act of making: **n.** sedation; tranquilization; **a.** sedative; tranquilizing
become: **v.** quiesce; tranquilize
medicine or agent for making: **n.** nepenthe; sedative; tranquilizer
(*sober*): **adv.** *mens aequa in arduis*
(*unconcerned*): **a.** indifferent; insouciant; lackadaisical; phlegmatic; pococurante; **n.** equanimity; insouciance; lackadaisy; phlegm

CALMING: **a.** anodynic; calmant; calmative; hesychastic; nepenthean; placative; placatory; sedative; tranquilizing; **adv.** *placidamente;* **n.** placation; propitiation

CALMNESS: **n.** apathy; assuagement; ataraxia; ataraxy; composure; *détente;* dispassion; equability; equanimity; forbearance; gravity; impassivity; imperturbability; imperturbation; indifference; lackadaisy; lassitude; nepenthe; nonchalance; passivity; phlegm; placidity; pococurantism; quietude; repose; (re)quiescence; *sang-froid;* sedation; serenity; sobriety; solemnity; tranquility; tranquilization; unexcitedness
of mind: **n.** *aequo animo;* equanimity

CAMP, *laying out or establishment of:* **n.** castrametation
rel. to: **a.** castrensian
temporary, or for the night: **n.** or **v.** bivouac; **n.** *pied-à-terre*

CANCEL: **v.** abolish; abrogate; countermand; delete; efface; expunge; invalidate; neutralize; nullify; obliterate; repudiate; rescind; revoke; vacate; **a.** CAN-

41

CELLABLE: abrogative; recissory; revocable; revocatory; revokable; **n.** CANCELLATION: abrogation; cessation; deletion; disaffirmance; disaffirmation; expunction; invalidation; nullification; recision
   not capable of being (canceled): (**see** "unbreakable") **a.** inalienable; indefeasible

CANCER: **n.** carcinoma; malignancy; malignant neoplasm; sarcoma; **a.** CANCEROUS: cancroid; carcinomatous; malignant; sarcomatous
   -producing: **a.** carcinogenic; **n.** carcinogen

CANDID: **a.** artless; disinterested; guileless; impartial; implicit; ingenuous; naive; straightforward; unfeigned; unflattering; unprejudiced; unreserved; unsophisticated; unsubtle; unvarnished; wholehearted

CANDIDATE *for admission:* **n.** postulance; postulancy; postulant

CANDLE, *burn both ends: brûler la chandelle par les deux bouts*

CANE *or reed, like or pert. to:* **a.** arundinaceous

CANNIBAL: **n.** anthropophaginian; anthropophagite; anthropophagus; (**pl.** anthropophagi); **n.** CANNIBALISM: anthropophagism; anthropophagy; cannibality; exophagy; **a.** CANNIBALISTIC: anthropophagous

CAPABLE: (**see** "able") **a.** accomplished; adequate; competent; consummate; qualified; sciential; virtuosic

CAPACITY: **n.** amplitude; attainment; capability; endowment; genius; intellect; intelligence; latitude; magnitude; potentiality; puissance; qualification; talent; virtuosity
   increase: **v.** augment; enhance; potentiate; **n.** augmentation; enhancement; potentiation

CAPER: (**see** "frolic") **n.** capriccio; capriole; caracole; curvet; gambade; gambado; gambol; marlock; saltation

CAPITAL *letter(s):* **n.** factotum; majuscule
   letter(s), written in: **a.** majuscule

CAPITALIST: **n.** bourgeois; Philistine (**usu.** disparaging)
   class: **n.** proprietariat; **a.** bourgeois; proprietarian

CAPRICE: see "whim"

CAPTIVATE: (**see** "allure" **and** "charm") **v.** enamor; enrapture; ensorcel(1); enthral(1); fascinate; transport; **n. see** "alluring"

CAPTURE, *open to:* **a.** expugnable; pregnable; vulnerable

CARAVAN: **n.** cavalcade; convoy; expedition; peregrination; safari

CARD(S), *by the:* **adv.** *à la carte*
   fortune-telling by: **n.** cartomancy
   lay one's on table: **n. or v.** *abattre son jeu*

CARE: **n.** attention; attentiveness; circumspection; consideration; custody; guardianship; management; paternalism; precaution; prudence; solicitude; supervision; tutelage; vigilance; **a.** custodial; supervisory; tutelary; tutorial
   marked by great: **a.** solicitous; solicitudinous
   take good: gardez bien
   without: (**see** "carefree") **adv.** *sans souci; sine cura*

CAREFREE: **a.** debonair(e); *dégagé;* incautious; insouciant; irresponsible; jaunty; *sans souci;* undemanding; **n.** insouciance

CAREFUL: (**see** "cautious") **a.** analytical; attentive; calculating; circumspect(ive); conscientious; discreet; discriminating; discriminatory; heedful; judicious; meticulous; observant; provident; prudent(ial); punctilious; punctual; regardful; scrupulous; solicitous; vigilant; **n.** CAREFULNESS: (**see** "caution") circumspection; meticulosity; prudence; scrupulosity; solicitude
   excessively: **a.** fastidious; finical; hypercritical; meticulous; particularistic; pedantic; punctilious; rabbinic(al); scrupulous; **n.** circumspection; fastidiousness; meticulosity; punctiliousness; scrupulosity; scrupulousness
   of details: **a.** conscientious; meticulous; scrupulous; **n.** meticulosity; particularity; scrupulosity; scrupulousness

CARELESS: (see "indifferent") a. apathetic; casual; cursory; heedless; improvident; imprudent; inattentive; incautious; incurious; indiscreet; neglectful; negligent; oblivious; perfunctory; pococurante; promiscuous; random; slovenly; superficial; unconcerned; unfastidious; unmindful; unsolicitous

CARELESSNESS: n. improvidence; imprudence; inattention; incaution; incuriosity; indifference; indiscretion; neglect; negligence; nonchalance; perfunctoriness; pococurantism; promiscuity; remission; superficiality
through: adv. *per incuriam*
toward duty: n. laches

CARESS: v. embrace; fondle; a. CARESSIVE: affectionate; amative; endearing

CARETAKER: n. concierge; superintendent

CARNIVAL: n. *Mardi Gras*
like a: a. carnivalesque; festive

CAROUSE: v. roister; royster; n. CAROUSER: bacchanal; bacchant; (fem. bacchante); reveler; roysterer; a. CAROUSING: bacchanal(ian); bacchanalic; roystering; roysterous

CARP: v. cavil; censure; criticize; disparage; pettifog; n. cavil; pettifoggery; stricture; a. captious; hypercritical

CARRIAGE: (see "bearing") n. posture
porch for: n. *porte cochère*

CARRY-*all:* n. omnibus
away: v. ablate; disembogue; meander; a. ablative; deferent; efferent; n. ablation
out: see "accomplish" and "fulfill"

CARTHAGE *must be destroyed:* n. *delenda est Carthago*

CASE, *famous or celebrated:* n. *cause célèbre*
hard protective: n. carapace

CASH, *convert into:* v. liquidate; n. liquidation

CAST: n. matrix
off, as skin or shell: v. desquamate; exfoliate; exuviate; a. desquamative; des-

quamatory; exuvial; n. desquamation; exuviation

CASTE, *person of high:* n. Brahmin; kshatriya
person of low: n. pariah; sudra

CASTLE *in Spain (or in the air):* n. *château en Espagne*

CASTOR AND POLLUX, *of or like:* a. dioscuric

CASTRATE: v. asexualize; desexualize; emasculate; eunuchize; geld; spay; n. CASTRATION: asexualization; demasculinization; emasculation; eunuchism; gonadectomy; mutilation; orchidectomy

CASUAL: a. accidental; adventitious; dishabille; fortuitous; haphazard; impromptu; incidental; informal; precarious; random; uncertain; unexpected; unimportant; unstudied

CAT(S), *abnormal fear of:* n. aelurophobia; ailurophobia
characteristic of: a. feline; n. felinity
fondness for: n. ailurophilia; galeophilia
hater or hatred of: n. aelurophobe; ailurophobe; ailurophobia; galeophobia; gatophobia
having claws like: a. aeluropodous; ailuropodous; cheliferous
killing of: n. felicide
-lover: n. aelurophile; ailurophile
make sound like: v. or n. caterwaul
old (usu. fem.) n. grimalkin
resembling: a. feliform; feline; n. felinity

CATALOG(UE): n. *catalogue raisonné;* compendium; *repertorium;* repertory; a. catalogical

CATASTROPHE: n. Armageddon; holocaust
heightened action leading to: n. catastasis
violent and disordered: n. gotterdammerung

CATEGORY: (see "class") n. classification; concept; genre; lexicon; rubric

CATER *to passions and prejudices:* v. pander

43

CAUGHT *in the act:* **adv.** *in actu;* (*in*) *flagrante delicto;* **a.** redhanded

CAUSE: (**see** origin") **n.** determinant; etiology; genesis; provenance; **a.** etiological
and effect, rel. bet.: **n.** causality
final: **n.** *causa finalis*
final, containing or realizing: **n.** entelechy
final, study of: **n.** entelechy; teleology; **a.** teleological
for war: **n.** *casus belli*
nothing is w/o a (theory) : **n.** causality
of unknown: **a.** agnogenic; idiopathic; ignogenic
to effect: **n.** *a priori;* apriority; **a.** aprioristic

CAUSTIC: (**see** "biting" and "keen") **a.** acidulous; acrimonious; corrosive; incisive; malevolent; mordant; pyrotic; sarcastic; satirical; scathing; trenchant; virulent; vitriolic; **n.** CAUSTICITY: malevolence; mordacity; spinosity; virulence

CAUTION (or CAUTIOUSNESS): **n.** admonishment; (ad)monition; calculation; caveat; chariness; circumspection; cunctation; discretion; exhortation; heedfulness; meticulosity; prudence; vigilance; wariness; **v.** admonish; sermonize
from abundant: ex abundanti cautela

CAUTIOUS: (**see** "careful") **a.** admonitory; Argus-eyed; attentive; calculating; circumspect(ive) ; discreet; expectant; judicious; meticulous; monitorial; Nestorian; provident; prudent(ial) ; scrupulous
to be: (**see** "careful") **adv.** *festina lente* (make haste slowly)

CAVE-*dweller:* **n.** troglodyte; **a.** troglodytic(al)
explorer: **n.** speleologist; spelunker
science of exploring: **n.** speleology; **a.** speleological

CAVERN(S), *inhabiting:* **a.** cavernicolous

CAVIL: **v. see** "carp"; **n.** CAVILER: *advocatus diaboli* (devil's advocate)

CELEBRATE: **v.** commemorate; solemnize; **a.** commemoratory; **n.** CELEBRATION: commemoration; jubilation; jubilee; ovation; potlatch; solemnization

CELEBRATED *case:* **n.** *cause célèbre*

CELEBRITY: (**see** "big-wig") **n.** luminary
treat as: **v.** lionize

CELESTIAL: **see** "spiritual"
mysteries: **n. pl.** *arcana caelestia*

CELL *division, direct:* **n.** mitosis

CEMETERY: **n.** *campo santo;* Golgotha; necropolis

CENSOR *of morals or manners:* **n.** *censor morum*

CENSORIOUS: (**see** "faultfinding") **a.** calumnious; castigative; censorial; condemnatory; defamatory; excoriative; slanderous; stigmatic(al) ; vituperative

CENSORSHIP: **see** "censureship" and "exclusion"
of books, etc: **see under** "book(s)"
sign or mark of approval: **n.** imprimatur

CENSURE: (**see** "abuse") **v.** animadvert; berate; calumniate; castigate; chastise; excoriate; lambaste; opprobriate; reprobate; revile; scarify; stigmatize; vilify; vituperate; **n.** CENSURESHIP: animadversion; calumniation; excoriation; reprehension; reprobation; reproof; stricture; **a.** CENSURABLE: blameworthy; condemnatory; reprehensible

CENTER(S): **n.** axis; focus; ganglion; nidus; nucleus; omphalos; pivot; umbilicus; **v.** concentrate; converge; focus
as of development: **n.** nucleus
away from the: **a.** decentralizing; efferent; excentric
being in, or tending to stay at or near: **a.** centrality; centricity
force to the, or tending toward: **n.** centripetence
having common: **a.** concentric; **n.** concentricity
having many: **a.** decentralized; polycentric
having single: **a.** unicentric
moving from: **a.** centrifugal; efferent; **n.** centrifugalization; decentralization
moving to: **a.** afferent; centripetal; **n.** centripetalism
of attraction, interest or activity: **n.** cynosure; epicenter; Mecca; polestar

off, or w/o a: **a.** acentric; excentric(al)
originating in: **a.** centrogenic

CENTRAL: (**see** "basic") **a.** concentric; dominant; equidistant; essential; middlemost; pivotal; principal; umbilical; **a.** CENTRALIZING: amalgamative; centripetal; integrative; **n.** centrality

CENTURY: **n.** centenary; centennial; *siècle;* **a.** centenary; centennial
pert. to beg. of: **a.** centurial
pert. to close of: **a.** *fin-de-siècle*

CEREMONIAL: (**see** "formal") **a.** ceremonious; conventional; punctilious; ritualistic; solemn
attire: **n.** *grande toilette;* panoply
fuss: **n.** panjandrum

CEREMONIES, *master of:* **n.** ceremoniarius; compere; officiator

CEREMONY: (**see** "pomp") **n.** accolade; formality; ostentation; protocol; ritual(ity)
without: **adv.** *sans cérémonie; sans façon*

CERTAIN: **a.** absolute; apodictic(al); conclusive; explicit; incontestable; incontrovertible; indisputable; indubitable; ineluctable; inevitable; irrefrangible; irrefutable; undeniable; unequivocal; unerring; unmistakable; unquestionable; **adv.** CERTAINLY: *bien entendu;* ineluctably; inevitably; *sans doute;* unquestionably
absolutely: **a.** apodictic(al); indisputable; inevitable; irrefutable; unequivocal

CERTAINTY: **n.** accuracy; assurance; certitude; incontrovertibility; indisputability; indubitability; ineluctability; infallibility; positivism; reality; securement
believer in impossibility of: **n.** acataleptic; probabilism; probabilorism; probabilorist; **a.** acataleptic; probabilistic

CHAFE: see "annoy"

CHAIN: **v.** catenate; fetter; **n.** catena-(tion); concatenation; vinculum

CHAIR, *from the:* **a.** or **n.** *ex cathedra*
protector for: **n.** antimacassar

CHAMBER(S): **n.** camera; concameration; cubiculum
divided into: **n.** cameration

CHANCE: **v.** hazard; venture; **n.** accidentality; *casus fortuitus;* contingency; fortuitiveness; fortuity; haphazardry; opportunity; peradventure; random; speculation; tychism; **a.** accidental; casual; contingent; fortuitous; haphazard; random
by: **a.** fortuitous; *par hasard; per accidens*
goodess of: **n.** Tyche
rule by: **n.** casualism; tychism

CHANGE(S): **v.** alchemize; alternate; commute; diversify; metamorphose; permutate; reciprocate; renegotiate; substitute; transfigure; transform; transmogrify; transmute; transplant; **n.** alternance; alternation; heterization; metamorphosis; materialization; modification; modulation; (per)mutation; reciprocation; (r)evolution; substitution; transfiguration; transformation; transition; transmogrification; transmutation; transplantation; variation
alternating: **n.** alternation; reciprocation; vicissitude
capable of: (**see** "correctable") **a.** alterable; labile; mutable; tractable
characterized by: **a.** chameleonic; inconstant; labile; variational; **n.** lability
completely, as in grotesque or strange manner: **v.** transmogrify; **n.** transmogrification
figure, form or outward appearance; **v.** transfigure; **n.** transfiguration
from one stage, cond., etc. to another: **n.** evolution; metastasis; transition; **a.** metastatic
hater or hatred of: **n.** misoneism; misoneist; **a.** misoneistic
in process of: **a.** transitional
in shape, form, substance, etc.: **v.** metamorphose; **n.** heterization; metamorphism; metamorphosis; **a.** metamorphic; metamorphous
liable to: (**see** "changeable") **a.** labile; mutable; **n.** lability; mutability
magic power to: **n.** alchemy; **a.** alchemic; alchemistic
necessary (changes) having been made: **adv.** *mutatis mutandis*
not capable of: see "unbreakable" **and** "unchangeable"
"of life": **n.** climacteric; climacterium; involution; menopause; **a.** climacteric; involutional; menopausal
of mind or heart (to better): **n.** penitence; reformation; repentance; resipiscence; **a.** penitent; penitential; repentent
of one thing into another, position, state

or form: **v.** metamorphose; metastasize; **a.** metamorphic; metamorphous; metastatic; **n.** heterization; metamorphosis; metastasis
  one capable of indefinite: **n.** Proteus
  one substance into another: **v.** transubstantiate; **n.** transubstantiation
  subject to: (**see** "changeable") **a.** chameleonic; labile; mutable; protean
  sudden: **n.** saltation
  tendency against: **n.** inertia; **a.** immutable; inertial
  tending to: **see** "liable to" **above**
  times and customs: **adv.** *autre temps, autre moeurs*
  wine and bread to blood and body of Christ (doctrine): **n.** transubstantiation

CHANGEABLE: **a.** adaptable; alterable; ambivalent; amenable; amphibolic; amphibolous; capricious; chameleonic; fickle; fluctuating; inconstant; iridescent; itinerant; labile; mercurial; mutable; nomadic; protean; Proteus-like; quicksilver; temperamental; unstable; vagrant; variational; versatile; whimsical; **n.** CHANGEABLENESS: adaptability; ambivalence; fickleness; iridescence; lability; mutability; versatility; volatility; volubility; whimsicality

CHANGING: **a.** evolutionary; transitional
  constantly: **a.** kaleidoscopic
  frequently or foolishly: **a.** capricious; chameleonic; protean; vertiginous
  one form to another: **n.** heterization; metamorphosis; transmogrification; transubstantiation
  patterns: **a.** kaleidoscopic

CHANNELED: (**see** "grooved") **a.** canalicular; canaliculate; cannel(l)ated; chamfered

CHAOS: **see** "confusion"

CHAPERON(E): **n.** *gouvernante;* governess; surveillant

CHAPTER, *as of an organization, member of:* **n.** capitulary
  rel. to: **a.** capitulary

CHARACTER(S): **n.** constitution; disposition; reputation; temperament; texture
  concealment of real: **n.** hypocrisy; hypocrite; **a.** hypocritical
  in drama, etc.: **n.** persona; (**pl.** *corps dramatique; dramatis personae; personae*)
  main, in story, drama, etc.: **n.** protagonist
  pursuits influence: **n.** *abeunt studia in mores*
  rel. to: **a.** characterological
  standards, etc., of race or group: **n.** ethos; mores
  study of development of: **n.** characterology; ethology; **a.** characterological; ethological

CHARACTERISTIC(S): **n.** accoutrement; attribute; haecceity; individuality; singularity; symptom; **a.** diacritical; distinguishing; individual; pathognomonic(al); peculiar; quintessential; symbolic(al); symptomatic(al); typical
  odd or peculiar: (**see** "peculiarity") **n.** eccentricity; idiosyncrasy; oddity; singularity; vagary
  quality: **n.** savor
  study of acquired: **n.** ctetology; psychology
  though untrue: **a.** *ben trovato*

CHARGE: **v.** enjoin; indict; **n.** accusation; ascription; behest; imposition; imputation; indictment; injunction; mandate; management; supervision
  (accusation): **n.** gravamen

CHARGING: **a.** accusable; ascribable; attributive; imputable; imputative; mandatory
  by, or as if by, oath: **n.** objuration

CHARITABLE: (**see** "generous") **a.** benefic(ent); benevolent; eleemosynary; gracious; humanitarian; lenient; philanthropic
  person: **n.** charitarian; eleemosynar; humanitarian; philanthropist; Samaritan

CHARITY: (**see** "mercy") **n.** benefaction; beneficence; benevolence; generosity; largess(e); lenity; liberality; philanthropy

CHARLATAN: **see** "pretender"

CHARM: (**see** "entice") **v.** bewitch; captivate; enchant; enrapture; ensorcel(l); enthral(l); fascinate; transport; **n.** abracadabra; abraxis; amiability; amulet; enchantment; fetish; geegree; incantation; madstone; obeah; periapt; phylactery; seduction; talisman; witchery; **a.** CHARMING: (**see** "pleasing") arresting; bewitching; captivating; enchanting; fascinating; felicitous; irresistible; magnetic; mesmeric; personable; phylacteric; winsome

CHARTER: **n.** canon; constitution
of civil or political liberties: **n.** constitution; decalogue; *Magna C(h)arta*

CHARWOMAN: **n.** *femme de chambre; femme de ménage*

CHASE: **see** "hunting"
goddess of the: **n.** Artemis; Diana

CHASTITY: **n.** continence; pucelage; pudicity
vow of: **n.** *votum castitatis*

CHAT: (**see** "talk") **v.** confabulate; **n.** causerie; confabulation; conversation; **a.** CHATTY: discursive; garrulous; loquacious; **n.** CHATTER (*small talk*): bavardage

CHATTERBOX: **n.** *moulin à paroles*

CHEAP: (**see** "bargain") **a.** bedizened; Brummagem; chintzy; inexpensive; meretricious; picayune; picayunish; pinchback; tawdry; **n.** CHEAPNESS: bedizenment; flummery; trumpery
  (*bargain*): **a.** *à bon marché*
  (*flashy*): **a.** raffish; tawdry; trumpery

CHEAT: **v.** bamboozle; beguile; chicane; circumvent; cozen; defraud; delude; foist; victimize; **n.** CHEATER: **see** "pretender"; **n.** CHEATING: circumvention; cozenage; defraudation; imposture

CHECK: **v.** abort; checkmate; counteract; counterbalance; counterpoise; inhibit; obstruct; acclude; rebuff; repress; restrain; slacken; stymie; **a.** CHECKING: abortive; inhibitory; **n.** abortifacient; inhibition

CHEEK(S), *pert. to:* **a.** buccal

CHEER: **v.** inspirit; invigorate; solace; **n.** acclamation; applause; *éclat*

CHEERFUL: **a.** blithe; buoyant; ebullient; eudaemonic; euphoric; eupeptic; exhilarative; genial; jocular; jocund; optimistic; sanguinary; sanguine; sprightly; viva-

cious; volatile; **a. or adv.** allegro; *gemütlich; adv. de bonne grâce*
overly and irritatingly: **a.** Pollyannish; **n.** Pollyanna; Pollyannism

CHEERFULNESS: (**see** "merriment") **n.** ebullience; euphoria; exhilaration; geniality; jocularity; jocundity; joviality; sanguinity; sprightliness; vivacity
excessive: **n.** Pollyannism

CHEF: **n.** *chef de cuisine; cuisinier;* (**fem.** *cuisinière*); culinarian

CHERISH: **v.** embosom; enshrine; foster; idolize; spiritualize

CHEST: **n.** thorax; **a.** thoracic
pert. to (or lungs): **a.** pectoral; thoracic

CHEW: **v.** manducate; masticate; **a.** manducatory; masticatory; **n.** manducation; mastication; rumination

CHIEF: **a.** capital; cardinal; foremost; paramount; predominant; (pre)eminent; principal; sovereign; superior; supreme; **n.** (**see** "leader") director; hierarch; *imperator;* pendragon; sachem; sovereign; superior
item of a group: **n.** *pièce de résistance*
work: **n.** *chef d'oeuvre; magnum opus; meisterwerk*

CHILD: (**see** "children" **and** "offspring")
n. changeling; infant; issue; juvenile; (s)cion; **a.** filial
  attracted to parent of opp. sex:
    daughter to father: **n.** Electra complex
    son to mother: **n.** Oedipus complex
  befitting a: **a.** dutiful; filial
  gifted: **n.** prodigy; *wunderkind*
  illegitimate; **n.** *filius nullius; filius populi;* mongrel; **a.** bar sinister
  not befitting a: **a.** unduteous; undutiful; unfilial
  of or rel. to study of: **a.** pedologic(al); **n.** pedologist; pedology
  relationship or attitude of parent to: **n.** filiality
  spoiled: **n.** *enfant gâté; enfant terrible*
  state or period of development when becomes interested in opp. sex: **n.** altrigenderism
  unmanageable; **n.** *enfant terrible*

CHILDBIRTH: **n.** accouchement; delivery; labor; parturition; travail; **a.** parturient

after: **a.** post-natal; post-partum
before: **a.** antenatal; antepartum; prenatal; prepartum
convalescent period following: **n.** puerperium
father takes bed during: **n.** couvade

CHILDHOOD: **n.** *jeune âge;* juniority
from: **adv.** *ab incunabilis*
lit. works designed for: **n.pl.** juvenilia
rel. to: **a.** juvenile; puerile
second: **n.** dotage
writings, drawings, etc. of: **n. pl.** juvenilia

CHILDISH: (**see** "petty") **a.** immature; infantile; infantine; infantive; juvenile; pantywaist; puerile; **n.** CHILDISHNESS: dotage; immaturity; infantility; juvenility; puerilism; puerility
behavior: **see under** "behavior"

CHILDREN: (**see** "offspring") **n.pl.** descendants; progeny; posterity; (s)cions
diseases of, study: **n.** pediatrics; **a.** pediatric; **n.** pediatrician
hatred or hater of: **n.** misopaedia; misopaedist
science or study of life and development of: **n.** pedology; pedologist
sexual inclination toward: **n.** pedophilia; pedophiliac

CHILL: **v.** infrigidate; **n.** frisson

CHIN: **n.** mental prominence (**or** protuberance)
pert. to: **a.** mental
point of: **n.** pogonion

CHINESE, *one fond of:* **n.** sinophil(e)

CHINK(S): **n.** aperture; cranny; interstice; lacuna
full of: **a.** rimose; rimous; rimulose

CHITCHAT: **n.** bavardage; small talk

CHIVALROUS *fighter:* **n.** *preux chevalier*

CHIVALRY, *having spirit or manners of:* **a.** chivalresque

CHOICE: (**see** "best") **n.** alternant; alternate; alternative; candidate; election; option; **a.** (**see** "choosing") discriminative; elegant; exquisite; fastidious; optimum;

recherché; sumptuous; supernacular; supernal
power of: **n.** alternativity; option
where no real, or for want of better; **n.** *faute de mieux;* Hobson's choice

CHOIRMASTER: **n.** *chorypheus; maestro di cappella*

CHOOSE: **see** "determine"; **a.** CHOOSING: discretional; eclectic; optional; preferential; **a.** CHOOSY: **see** "careful"
or reject, ability to: **n.** alternativity; discretion; option

CHORUS *leader:* **see** "choirmaster"
of or pert. to: **a.** choreutic; choric

CHRONIC: (**see** "habitual") **a.** confirmed; deep-seated; ingrained; intractable; inveterate; irradicable; lingering; obstinate; persistent; prolonged; routine

CHRONOLOGICAL *error:* **n.** anachronism; prochronism; prolepsis; **a.** anachronistic; anachronous; proleptic

CHRIST, *doctrine that human being only:* **n.** psilanthropy; psilanthropism; psilanthropist
marks resembling wounds of: **n.pl.** stigmata

CHURCH *body:* **n.** diocese; episcopate; hierarchy
buying or selling of office or preferment: **n.** simony
excessive devotion to: **n.** ecclesiasticism; ecclesiolatry
leader: (**see** "priest") **n.** archimandrite; hegumen; hierophant; **a.** hierophantic
one estranged from: **n.** publican
pert. to: **a.** apostolic; ecclesiastic(al); ecclesiologic(al); ecumenical; encyclic(al); episcopal; hierarchial; sacerdotal; **n.** apostolicity
policy, also study of doctrines of: **n.** ecclesiology
sphere of authority: **n.** diocese; episcopate; hierarchy

CIRCLE: **see** "group"
reasoning in a: **n.** *circulus in probando*

CIRCUIT: **n.** ambit; circumference; circumnavigation; gyre; periplus; revolution; **a.** circumferential; peripheral
(journey): **n.** itineration

CIRCULAR: **a.** annular; cyclic(al); cycloid(al); cylindrical; elliptic(al); nummiform; nummular; orbicular; rotund; spherical; spheroid(al)
> *in definition:* **n.** *circulus in definiendo*
> *movement:* **n.** circumduction; circumgyration; **v.** circumduct; circumgyrate
> *state of being:* **n.** circularity; rotundity; spheroidicity

CIRCUMFERENCE: **n.** ambit; perimeter; periphery; **a.** circumferential; peripheral

CIRCUMSTANCE(S): (**see** "condition") **n.** concomitant; contingency; episode; eventuality; inadvertency; incident; occurrence; particularity; posture; **a.** CIRCUMSTANTIAL: adventitious; contingent; inadvertent; incidental
> *bow to:* **v.** temporize; **adv.** *tempori parendum* (one must yield to the times)
> *by force of:* **adv.** perforce
> *dependent upon:* (**see** "chance") **a.** precarious
> *suited to the:* **a.** expedient; opportune; opportunistic; politic
> *taking advantage of:* **a.** opportunistic; **n.** expediency; opportunism; opportunist

CITIZEN(S): **n.** burgher; citoyen; constituency; constituent; denizen; *habitué;* national; oppidan
> *leading:* **n.pl.** *lumina civitatis*
> *of town:* **n.** burgher; oppidan
> *of world:* **n.** cosmopolitan; cosmopolite; **a.** cosmopolitan
> *of yesterday:* **n.** *hesterni quirites*

CITIZENSHIP *of child determined by parent's:* **n.** *jus sanguinis*

CITY: **n.** metropolis; municipality; **a.** metropolitan; municipal; urban
> *very large:* **n.** megalopolis
> *world-important, or of many nationalities:* **n.** cosmopolis; **a.** cosmopolitan

CIVIL: (**see** "courteous") **a.** cultured; educated; genteel; nonclerical; parliamentary; secular; sophistical; **n.** laity
> *affairs, pert. to:* **a.** communal; metropolitan; municipal; urban
> *liberties, advocate of:* **n.** libertarian; **a.** libertarian
> *or civic pride, lack of:* **n.** incivilism
> *order:* **n.** polity
> *power or authority:* **n.** temporality

CIVILITIES: **n.pl.** amenities; (the) proprieties; urbanities

CIVILIZED: (**see** "refined") **a.** debarbarized; **v.** debarbarize; **n.** debarbarization

CLAIM: **v.** maintain; postulate; **a.** CLAIMED: alleged; assertive
> *to possession:* **n.** arrogation; **v.** appropriate; arrogate

CLAMOR: (**see** "uproar") **n.** alarum; alarums and excursions; brouhaha; hubbub; tumult; **a.** CLAMOROUS: blatant; boisterous; clangorous; demonstrative; importunate; pressing; strepitant; strepitous; vociferant; vociferous
> *of the forum:* **n.** *forensic strepitus*

CLARIFICATION: **n.** *éclaircissement;* elucidation; enlightenment; exegesis; interpretation; **v.** CLARIFY: defecate; depurate; elucidate; elutriate; enlighten; explicate; illume; interpret; resolve; subtilize; unscramble; **a.** CLARIFYING: elucidative; elucidatory; exegetic(al); explanatory
> *further:* **n.** epexegesis; **a.** epexegetic(al)

CLASH: **v.** encroach; impinge; **n.** see "conflict"

CLASS: (**see** "classification") **n.** category; clique; coterie; denomination; genre; (**pl.** genera); genus; phylum; (**pl.** phyla); rubric; **a.** categorical; generic; phyletic
> *by itself:* **a.** *sui generis*
> *divided into many* (*classes*): **a.** multipartite; polychotomous; polytomous; **n.** polychotomy
> *lesser nobility:* **n.** *petite noblesse*
> *low:* **n.** canaille; rabble; riffraff
> *lower middle* (*also members of*): **n.** petite bourgeoisie
> *middle:* **n.** Babbit(t)ry (**usu.** disparaging); bourgeois(ie); proletariat; **a.** Philistine (**usu.** disparaging); proletarian
> *of no definite:* **a.** mongrel
> *propertied or capitalist* (*also members of*): **n.** proprietariat; **a.** proprietarian
> *upper:* (**see** "aristocrat") **n.** aristocracy; (**pl.** aristoi); gentry; nobility; patrician

CLASSICAL, *state or quality of being:* **n.** classicality

CLASSIFICATION: (**see** "class") **n.** categorization; category; compartmentaliza-

tion; departmentalization; departmenta- tion; hierarchization; individualization; stratification; subordination; taxonomy; **a.** classificatory
> *science of:* **n.** taxonomy; **a.** taxonomic(al)
> *something that escapes:* **n.** *tertium quid*

CLASSIFY: **v.** alphabetize; categorize; collimate; compartmentalize; departmentalize; hierarchize; individualize; synthesize
> *difficult to:* **a.** nondescript; **n.** *tertium quid*
> *not possible to:* **a.** acategorical; amorphous; heterogeneous; unclassifiable

CLAWS, *bearing:* **a.** cheliferous
> *having (or nails):* **a.** unguiferate

CLAY, *pert. to:* **a.** argillaceous

CLEAN: **v.** absterge; depurate; deterge; elutriate; expiate; expurgate; mundify; **a.** abstrusive; hygienic; immaculate; kosher; sportsmanlike; sterile; thoroughgoing; undefiled; unspoiled; unstained; unsullied; **n.** CLEANLINESS: immaculacy; sterility
> *slate:* **n.** *tabula rasa*

CLEANSING: **a.** abstersive; cathartic; expiatory; purgatorial; **n.** ablution; abstersion; balneation; depuration; elutriation; expiation; lavage; lavation; lustration; purgation; purification
> *ceremonial:* **n.** purgation
> *religious (washing):* **n.** ablution; maundy

CLEAR: **v.** see "clarify"; **a.** (see "transparent") accessible; crystal(line); definitive; demonstrable; diaphanous; evident; exoteric; explicit; limpid; luculent; luminous; manifest; palpable; patent; pellucid; perspicacious; perspicuous; (trans)lucent; transpicuous; unambiguous; unencrypted; unequivocal; unhampered; unimpeded; unmistakable; unquestionable; unquestioned; **n.** CLEARNESS: clarity; diaphaneity; distinctness; explication; limpidity; luminosity; (pel)lucidity; perspicacity; perspicuity; sonority; translucence; translucency; transparency
> *and simple in style:* **a.** limpid; unambiguous; unencrypted; unequivocal; **n.** limpidity
> *as a bell:* **a.** orotund; resonant; sono-

rous; **n.** orotundity; sonority; sonorousness
> *as glass:* **a.** crystal(line); hyaline
> *-cut:* (see "decided") **a.** crystalline; inconfused
> *in lit. style:* **a.** Addisonian
> *to make:* (see "clarify") **v.** explicate; manifest; subtilize
> *to understanding:* **a.** explicit; lucid; perspicacious; perspicuous; unequivocal; **n.** comprehensibility; lucidity; perspicuity

CLEARLY *presented or spoken:* **a.** articulate; explicatory; lucid

CLEFT *in two:* **a.** bipartient; bipartite; bisulcate; cloven; dichotomous; schismatic(al)

CLERGY(MAN): (see "church") **n.** cleric; ecclesiastic; hierophant; man of the cloth; prelate; pulpitarian; (**pl.** *gens d'église*)
> *function(s) of:* **n.** clericature; (**pl.** spiritualities)
> *pert. to:* **a.** clerical; ecclesiastical; ministerial; parsonic(al); prelatical; pulpitarian; sacerdotal; sacerdotical; **n.** clericality; ecclesiasticism
> *position of:* **n.** clericature

CLERK, *pert. to:* **a.** clerical; **n.** clericality
> *position or function of:* **n.** clericature

CLEVER **a.** adroit; astute; dexterous; discerning; habile; heady; ingenious; penetrating; perspicacious; resourceful; sagacious; sapient; **n.** CLEVERNESS: acumen; adroitness; astucity; dexterity; discernment; esprit; hability; ingeniosity; ingenuity; inventiveness; resourcefulness
> *feat:* see "feat"
> *(skillful):* **a.** adept; adroit; dexterous; habile; **n.** adroitness; dexterity; hability
> *turn of phrase* (see "witticism") **n.** *jeu d'esprit*

CLEW (*or* CLUE): **n.** characteristic; criterion; (**pl.** criteria); indication; landmark; symptom

CLIMATE: (see "environment") **n.** clime; milieu
> *lit. or artistic, pert. to:* **a.** *fin de siècle*

CLIMAX: (see "acme") **n.** climacterium; consummation; culmination; denouement;

flood tide; meridian; orgasm; pinnacle; summit; zenith

CLIMBER, *social:* **n.** arriviste; *nouveau riche;* opportunist; parvenu

CLINGING: **a.** adherent; adherescent; agglutinant; tenacious; viscous
by feet, as certain birds; **a.** adhamant

CLIPPINGS (*writings, etc.*): **n.pl.** excerpta; scrapiana

CLIQUE: **n.** cabal; camarilla; charmed circle; conclave; *corps d'élite;* coterie; junto; sodality
for dishonest or dishonorable ends: **n.** camorra

CLOAKED: **a.** cabalistic; clandestine; disguised; larvate(d); screened

CLOG: **v.** impede; obstruct; occlude; oppilate; **n.** impediment; occlusion; oppilation

CLOISTER, *confined in, or as if in:* **n.** claustration

CLOSE: (**see** "discontinue" **and** "near") **v.** obturate; occlude; **a.** CLOSED: imperforate; **a.** CLOSING. operculated; **n.** occlusion; obturation; **n.** CLOSENESS: (**see** "nearness") propinquity; proximity
at hand: **a.** adjacent; contiguous; imminent; **n.** adjacency; contiguity; imminence
together, to place: **v.** juxtapose; **a.** (**see** "adjacent") juxtapositional

CLOSURE *of passage or opening:* **n.** atresia; obturation; occlusion; stenosis
or limitation of debate: **n.** cloture

CLOT: **v.** coagulate; thrombose; **n.** coagulation; thrombosis

CLOTHE: **v.** accouter; array; caparison; habilitate; invest; portray; represent; swathe

CLOTHING (or CLOTHES): (**see** "dress") **n.pl.** accouterments; apparel; array(ment); attire; habiliments; regalia; toggery; vestments; vesture
act of: **n.** investiture
addicted to those of opp. sex: **a.** transvestic; **n.** transvestism; transvestite

pert. to (*esp. men's*): **a.** sartorial
splendid: **n. pl.** regalia

CLOUD(S): **v.** obfuscate; tarnish; **n.** nebula; nimbus; stigma; **a.** CLOUDY (or CLOUDED): fuliginous; murky; nebular; nebulated; nebulose; nebulous; nimbose; nubilous; obscure; overcast; roily; turbid; **n.** CLOUDINESS: fuliginosity; nebulosity; obnubilation; tenuosity; turbidity
in the: **adv.** *in nubibus*
rain: **n.** nimbus
scientific observation of: **n.** nepholognosy

CLOVEN: (**see** "cleft") **a.** bisulcate

CLOWN: **n.** buffoon; grobian; harlequin; jester; lubber; merry-andrew; Pierrot; **n.** CLOWNING: baboonery; buffoonery; clownery; clownishness; **a.** baboonish; buffoonish
boastful: **n.** scaramouche

CLUB: **n.** association; consortium; coterie; fraternity; sodality; sorority
lit. or scientific: **n.** athen(a)eum
of both sexes: **n.** fratority

CLUE: see "clew"

CLUMPS, *growing in:* (**see** "clustered") *a.* caespitose

CLUMSY: (**see** "awkward") **a.** cumbersome; cumbrous; elephantine; gauche; loutish; lumbering; maladroit; ponderous; ungainly; unwield(l)y; **n.** CLUMSINESS: cumbrousness; gaucherie; maladroitness; ponderosity; ungainliness

CLUSTER: **v.** agglomerate; aggregate; nucleate; **n.** agglomeration; aggregation; fascicle; nucleation; **a.** CLUSTERED: acervate; acervuline; aciniform; agglomerated; aggregatory; caespitose; fascicular

COARSE: **a.** artless; barbarous; brutish; earthy; Falstaffian; gauche; immature; incondite; indelicate; inelegant; inurbane; plebeian; ribald; scurrilous; squalid; tramontane; troglodytic; uncouth; unpolished; unrefined; vulgarian; **v.** COARSEN: vulgarize; **n.** COARSENESS: barbarism; barbarity; buffoonery; gaucherie; *grossiereté;* indelicacy; inurbanity; rascality; scurrility; vulgarity

and witty writings or books: **n. pl.** facetiae
person: **see under** "person"

COASTAL *region:* **n.** littoral

COATING, *hard:* **n.** carapace; incrustation
resulting fr. age or wear: **n.** patina

COAX: **v.** cajole; wheedle; **n.** cajolery; cajolement

COCKTAIL: **n.** apertif

CODE *message:* **n.** cryptogram
of conduct, accepted: **see under** "standards

COERCE: **v.** compel; discipline; dragoon;
necessitate; **a.** COERCIVE: compelling;
compulsatory; compulsory; obligatory; **n.**
see "duress"
ability to: **n.** puissance

COEXIST(ING): **see** "living"
ability to: **a.** compossible; symbiotic;
n. compossibility; symbiosis

COFFEE, *black:* **n.** *café noir*
small serving: **n.** *café noir;* demitasse
with cream: **n.** *café-crème*
with milk: **n.** *café au lait*

COFFIN: **n.** bier; catafalque; sarcophagus

COHERE: (**see** "stick") **v. or a.** conglutinate; **n.** conglutination

COIL: (**see** "spiral") **n.** convolution; entanglement; perplexity; whorl; **a.**
COILED: convolute(d); gyrate; mean-
drine; tortile; volute

COIN *collector:* **n.** numismatist; **a.** numis-
matic(al)
of small value; **n.** picayune
-shaped: **a.** nummiform; nummular

COINCIDE: **v. see** "agree"; **a.** congruent;
congruous

COLD: (**see** "unfeeling") **a.** arctic; boreal;
frigid; glacial; hyperborean; marmoreal;
n. frigidity; glaciation; gelidity
-blooded: (**see** "cruel") **a.** indurate;
marblehearted; poikilothermal; poikilo-
thermic; poikilothermous; premeditated;
n. *sang-froid*

hands, warm heart: *froides manis,
chaudes amours*
make: **v.** infrigidate
pert. to or producing: **a.** frigorific

COLLAPSE: (**see** "failure") **n.** dissolution;
prostration; **v.** founder
catastrophic: **n.** cataclysm; *götterdämmerung;* holocaust

COLLECT: (**see** "accumulate") **v.** agglutinate; conflate; conglomerate; congregate;
convoke; muster

COLLECTION: **n.** agglomeration; agglutination; aggregation; collectivity; colluvies; compendium; conflation; conglomeration; congregation; fascicle; ingather-
ing; miscellaneity; nucleation; repertory;
sylloge; (**pl.** congeries)
literary: **n.** anthology; crestomathy;
(**pl.** adversaria; analecta; collectanea; *disjecta membra*)
*of biographical sketches (or production
of):* **n.** prosopography
*of stories by same author or on one sub-
ject:* **n.** omnibus
of things in general: **n.** collectanea; heterogeneity; hodgepodge; miscellanea; miscellaneity; miscellany

COLLECTOR, *bird-egg:* **n.** oologist
coins: **n.** numismatist; **n.** numismatics
curios or objets d'art: **n.** curioso
postcards: **n.** deltiologist
shells: **n.** conchologist; conchology
stamps: **n.** philatelist; philately

COLLEGE, *life within walls of:* **a.** intramural; parietal; **n.** academe; academia
teaching or teachers: **n.** professordom;
professoriat(e)

COLLISION: **n.** encroachment; impingement; infringement; renitency; retroac-
tion; **a.** COLLIDING: encroaching; im-
pingent

COLONIZER: **n.** oecist

COLONY: **n.** habituation; installation; pro-
tectorate; settlement

COLOR(S), *deprive of:* **v.** achromatize; decolorize; etiolate; **a. see** "colorless"
having many: **a.** heterochromous; multi-
colored; polychrom(at)ic; polychromat-
ous; variegated

having one: **a.** homochromatic; monochrom(at)ic; unicolorous

having two: **a.** bichromatic; bichrome; bicolored; bicolorous; dichrom(at)ic

having various, or changeable in: **a.** allochromatic; chatoyant; iridescent; kaleidoscopic; varicolored; versicolor(ed)

neutral in: **a.** achromatic

of flesh: **a.** incarnadine

of same (uniform in): **a.** concolorate; concolorous

pert. to different, or having complex pattern of: **a.** heterochrom(at)ic; heterochromous; kaleidoscopic

COLORLESS: (**see** "dull") **a.** achlorophyllaceous; achlorophyllous; achromatic; achromatous; achromic; achromous; diatonic; **n.** achromatism

COLOSSAL: **see** "huge"

COLUMNIST: **n.** feuilletonist

COMA: **n.** carus; stupor; torpidity; torpor; **a.** comatose; stuporous; torpid; torporific

COMBAT: **v. see** "contend"; **n.** rencontre; **a.** COMBATIVE: (**see** "hostile") agonistic; armigerous; bellicose; belligerent; disputatious; martial; militant; oppugnant; pugnacious; taurine; unpacific

mock or futile: **n.** sciamachy

COMBINATION: (**see** "collection") **n.** agglutination; amalgamation; coalescence; coalition; conjoinment; conjugation; conjunction; conjuncture; consolidation; lamination; merger; (poly)synthesis; syncretism; synergism; **v.** COMBINE: (**see** "join") amalgamate; coalesce; conjoin; consolidate; laminate; syncretize; synthesize

of diff. ideas, persons or things: **n.** amalgam(ation); heterogeneity

of many elements into one: **n.** polysynthesis(m)

COMBINED *action of drug or agent:* **n.** synergism; **v.** synergize; **a.** synergetic; synergic(al); synergistic(al)

COMBINING: **a.** amalgamative; coalescent; synergetic; synergic(al)

more than one use or quality: **a.** portmanteau

of various ideas, forces, etc. into workable result: **v.** synthesize; **n.** synthesis

two into one: **a.** biune; biunial

COME *between:* **v.** intermediate; interpose; intervene; **n.** intermediation; interposition; intervention

together: (**see** "meet") **v.** converge; rencounter; **n.** convergence; convergency

COMEDOWN: **n.** anticlimax; bathos; comeuppance; denigration; disappointment; setback; **a.** anticlimactic; bathetic; denigratory

COMEDY, *broad and low:* **n.** burlesk; burlesque; **a.** Aristophanic; Falstaffian; Rabelaisian

muse of: **n.** Thalia

plotless: **n.** harlequinade

COMFORT: **see** "ease"; **n.** COMFORTER: intercessor; paraclete; **a.** COMFORTING: consolatory; nepenthean; tranquilizing

drug or agent for: **n.** nepenthe; tranquilizer; **a.** nepenthean

COMIC: **n.** comedian; *farceur;* (**fem.** *farceuse*); harlequin; **a.** COMICAL: Aristophanic; burlesk; burlesque; farcical; harlequin; ludicrous; opera buffe; risible

talent: **n.** *vis comica*

COMMAND: (**see** "order" **and** "rule") **v.** imperate **n.** adjuration; caveat; fiat; imperative; mandament; mandate; mastery; precept

authoritative: **n.** caveat; fiat; mandate

COMMANDER: **n.** imperator

COMMANDING: **a.** august; authoritative; autocratic; exalted; grandiose; imperative; imperial; imperious; imposing; mandatory; peremptory; predominant

air: **n.** bravura

COMMEMORATE: **v.** celebrate; elegize; signalize; solemnize

COMMENCE: **see** "begin"

COMMENDABLE: **a.** admirable; approbatory; commendatory; complimentary; creditable; encomiastic(al); estimable; eulogistic; exemplary; honorific; laudable; laudative; laudatory; meritorious; panegyric(al); praiseworthy

COMMEND: **see** "extol"; **n.** COMMENDATION: (**see** "praise") approbation;

compliment; encomium; laudation; panegyric

COMMENTATOR: **n.** annotator; exegete; exegetist; expositor; glossator; scholiast

COMMERCIAL: **a.** mercantile; mercenary

COMMODIOUS: (**see** "roomy") **a.** baronial; capacious; cavernous; spacious

COMMON: **a.** communal; customary; demotic; epidemic; generic; habitual; hackneyed; heathenish; pagan; plebeian; prevalent; scurrile; scurrilous; undistinguished; universal; unrefined; vulgar; **n.** COMMONNESS: commonality; peasantry; prevalence; unrefinement; vulgarity
   consent, by; **adv.** *communi consensu*
   danger produces concord: **adv.** *commune periculum concordiam parit*
   good: **n.** *commune bonum*
   origin, having: **a.** monogen(et)ic; monogenistic
   people: (**see under** "people") **n.** commonalty; proletariat(e); **a.** lumpen; plebeian; proletarian; proletariat(e)
   sense: **n.** *bon sens;* prudence; sophrosyne
   to both male and female: **a.** (am)bisexual; ambosexual; epicene; hermaphrodite; hermaphroditic(al)
   to make: (**see** "debase" *and* "lower") **v.** heathenize; paganize; vulgarize

COMMONER: **n.** bourgeois; plebeian; roturier

COMMONPLACE: (**see** "dull") **a.** banal; bourgeois; *cliché;* hackneyed; pedestrian; platitudinal; platitudinous; plebeian; prosaic(al); stereotyped; stereotypical; trite; twice-told; uneventful; unglamorous; unglorified; **n.** COMMONPLACENESS: banality; bathos; peasantry; pedestrianism; platitudinism; triteness
   expression or remark: **n.** bromide; *cliché;* platitude; shibboleth; stereotype; truism; **a.** bromidic; hackneyed; platitudinal; platitudinous; stereotyped; **v.** platitudinize
   person addicted to use of the: **n.** platitudinarian

COMMOTION: **n.** agitation; Babelism; bouleversement; brouhaha; convulsion; flurriment; hurly-burly; perturbation; tempest in a teapot; tumult; turbulence; turmoil; **a.** perturbational; turbulent

COMMUNICATION: (**see** "speech") **n.** impartment; transmission
   without means of: **a.** incommunicado

COMMUNITY: **n.** environment; environs; fellowship, microcosm; milieu; **a.** environmental; microcosmic(al)
   affairs, active in: **a.** pragmatic
   affairs, disinterested in: **n.** incivilism
   of interest: **n.** affinity

COMPACT: **a.** compendious; consolidated; succinct; **n.** alliance; compendium; covenant

COMPANION: **n.** accessory; chaperone; cohort; compeer; consort; counterpart; escort
   at table: **n.** commensal; **a.** commensal; **n.** commensality
   boon: **n.** *alter ego; bon camarade*
   close: **n** *alter ego*
   gay and often irresponsible: **n.** Trojan
   ghostly: **n.** doppelganger; doubleganger
   he is known by his (companions): nosci-tur ex sociis
   traveling: **n.** *compagnon de voyage*

COMPARABLE: (**see** "similar") **a.** commensurate; corresponding; equipollent; equiponderant; equivalent; homogeneous; homologous; proportionate; **n.** COMPARABILITY: commensurability; commensuration; equiponderance; equivalence; homogeneity

COMPARE: **v.** collate; contrast; equate; **a.** COMPARATIVE: analogical; analogous; approximate; metaphorical

COMPARISON: **n.** analogy; collation; metaphor; parable; simile; similitude
   beyond: (**see** "superior") **a.** *ne plus supra; ne plus ultra; par excellence;* preeminent; supereminent
   not capable of: **a.** incommensurable; incomparable; **n.** incommensurability

COMPASS: **see** "scope"

COMPASSION: (**see** "sympathy") **n.** commiseration
   appeal(ing) to: **adv. or n.** *(argumentum) ad miserecordiam*

COMPASSIONATE: **see** "kind" **and** "sympathetic"
   person: **n.** almoner; charitarian; elee-

mosynar; humanitarian; philanthropist; Samaritan

COMPATIBLE: (see "harmonious") a. congenial; congruent; consentaneous; consonant; homogenous; n. COMPATIBILITY: congeniality; congruity; consentaneousness; homogeneity

COMPEL: v. commandeer; discipline; dragoon; necessitate; a. COMPELLING: cogent; convincing; impelling; n. cogency

COMPENDIUM: (see "abstract") n. lexicon; sylloge

COMPENSATE: (see "offset") v. atone; counterbalance; counterpoise; countervail; recompense; remunerate; requite; n. COMPENSATION: honorarium; perquisite; recompense; remuneration; requital; restitution; solatium

COMPETENT: (see "able") a. adequate; capax; ingenious; panurgic; proficient; puissant; n. COMPETENCE: (see "ability") versatility
in many things: a. ambidextrous; ingenious; panurgic; versatile; n. ambidexterity; ingeniosity; panurgy; versatility
mentally: n. *compos mentis*

COMPETITION: n. concours; rivalry; a. COMPETITIVE: rivalrous
out of, or excluded from: a. or adv. *hors concours;* adv. *hors de combat*

COMPLAIN: (see "protest") v. bewail; expostulate; inveigh; lament; remonstrate; repine; a. COMPLAINING: clamorous; complaintive; querimonious; querulent; querulous
person who (complains): n. complainant; plaintiff; querulist

COMPLAINT: (see "objection") n. allegation; expostulation; jeremiad; lamentation; protest(ation); querulity; remonstration; remonstrance
essential part of: n. gravamen
sad: n. jeremiad; lamentation

COMPLETE: v. accomplish; complement; consummate; finalize; realize; a. accomplished; consummate; consummative; integral; plenary; replete; saturative; unabridged; unexpurgated; a. COMPLETED: (see "done") accomplished; concluded; consummated; established; finalized; realized; adv. COMPLETELY: *a capite ad calcem; à fond; cap-a-pie;* diametrically; *in toto;* utterly; a. COMPLETING: (see "ending") concluding; consummatory; n. COMPLETION: (see "accomplishment") actuality; actualization; complement; consummation; *coup de grâce; fait accompli;* finality; realization
it is (completed): adv. *consummatum est; fait accompli*

COMPLETENESS: n. consummation; finality; integrality; integrity; wholeness
in general: n. entelechy

COMPLEX: (see "abstract" and "intricate") a. complicated; daedal(ic); heterogeneous; labyrinthian; labyrinthine; sinuous; sophisticated; n. COMPLEXITY: complexus; complicacy; compositeness; entanglement; intricacy; involvement; labyrinth; maelstrom; sinuosity

COMPLIANCE: n. assiduity; concord; condescendence; conformance; facilitation; facility; harmony; obsequence; obsequency; obsequity; sequacity; a. COMPLIANT: accommodating; amenable; assentatious; assiduous; complaisant; docile; ductile; facile; malleable; obsequious; pliable; sequacious; servile; submissive; subservient; tractable; yielding

COMPLICATED: (see "complex") a. abstruse; Gordian; involuted; prolix; recondite; n. COMPLICATION: (see "complexity") complexus; complicacy; entanglement; intricacy; involution; involvement; sinuosity
aggregation or situation: n. complexus

COMPOSED: see "calm"; n. COMPOSURE: (see "serenity") countenance; equability; equanimity; phlegm; placidity; poise; posture; repose; *sang-froid;* self-possession; stability; temperament

COMPOUND: see "mixture"

COMPREHENSION: (see "knowledge") n. connotation; inclusion; intuition; understanding; v. COMPREHEND: see "understand"
beyond: (see "obscure") a. transcendent
by intellect alone: n. cognition; noesis; a. cognitive; noetic

COMPREHENSIVE: (see "universal") **a.** catholic; connotative; consolidated; ecumenical; encyclic; encyclopedic(al); intensive; synoptic; transcendental
  all: **see under** "all"
  view or range: **n.** panorama

COMPROMISE: **v.** adjust; arbitrate; embarrass; endanger; expose; humiliate; jeopardize; **n.** abatement; arbitration; concession; conciliation; embarrassment; humiliation; jeopardy; understanding
  arrangement pending final settlement: **n.** *modus vivendi*

COMPULSORY: **see** "imperative"

COMPUNCTION: **n.** contrition; penitence; qualm; scruple; **a.** COMPUNCTIOUS: contrite; penitent(ial); qualmish; remorseful

COMRADE: **n.** associate; colleague; compeer; confrere; **n.** COMRADESHIP: *camaraderie; esprit de corps;* geniality
  close or boon: **n.** *alter ego; bon camarade*

CONCEALMENT: **n.** clandestinity; delitescence; dissimulation; eclipse; obscuration; occultation; **v.** CONCEAL: camouflage; cache; dissemble; ensconce; obscure; secrete; sequester; **a.** CONCEALED: (see "hidden") abeyant; clandestine; covert; delitescent; dormant; larvate(d); latent; potential; quiescent; surreptitious; veiled
  from law: **n.** abscondence
  of crime: **n.** misprision
  of facts: (see "fraud") **n.** subreption; *suppressio veri*

CONCEDE: **v.** acknowledge; acquiesce; capitulate; surrender

CONCEIT: **n.** *amour-propre;* caprice; egocentricity; egomania; ego(t)ism; flatulence; hauteur; *mauvaise honte; outrecuidance;* pomposity; presumption; self-esteem; **a.** CONCEITED: arrogant; bumptious; egomaniac(al); ego(t)istical; haughty; hubristic; opinionated; overweening; pragmatic; priggish; presumptuous
  abnormal: **n.** egomania; hubris; **a.** egomaniac(al); hubristic
  disagreeable: **n.** bumptiousness; presumptiousness
  person with: **n.** cockalorum; egomaniac

CONCEIVE: **v.** apprehend; comprehend; concoct; contrive; fabricate; formulate; ideate; **a.** ideational; **n.** (see "concept") ideation

CONCENTRATE: (see "condense") **v.** agglutinate; assemble; centralize; conglomerate; consolidate; epitomize; nucleate; **a.** CONCENTRATED: inspissated; **n. see** "concentration"

CONCENTRATION: **n.** agglutination; concentrate; essence; inspissation; nucleation; polarization; quintessence
  of power or authority: **n.** centralization
  point: **n.** nidus; nucleus

CONCEPT(ION): (see "category") **n.** envisagement; hypothesis; ideation; postulate; presupposition; prochronism; prolepsis; rubric

CONCERN: **n.** altruism; anxiety; apprehension; concernment; solicitude; **a.** CONCERNED: apprehensive; distressed; disturbed; interested; solicitous; solicitudinous; versant; **adv.** CONCERNING: anent; *in re;* regarding; respecting
  it's my own: **n.** *c'est mon affaire*

CONCESSION: **n.** acknowledgement; capitulation; condescendence; indulgence

CONCILIATE: **v.** appease; mollify; pacify; placate; propitiate; reconcile; tranquilize; **n.** CONCILIATION: appeasement; mollification; pacification; propitiation; tranquilization; **a.** CONCILIATORY: mollifying; pacific; placatory; propitiatory; propitious
  offer or gesture of (conciliation): **n.** olive branch

CONCISE: (see "terse") **a.** aphoristic; compendious; comprehensive; cryptic(al); epigrammatic; laconic(al); pregnant; sententious; succinct; Tacitean; telegraphic; trenchant
  in speech or expression: (see **under** "brevity") **n.** brachylogy; **a.** aphoristic

CONCLUSION: **n.** cessation; coda; consequence; consummation; (d)eduction; envoi; epilogue; finality; finalization; gradation; illation; inference; liquidation; settlement; termination
  terminus ad quem: **a. see** "ending"

exclamatory sentence or striking comment at (conclusion) of discourse: **n.** epiphonema
expressing a: **a.** desitive

CONCLUSIVE: (**see** "final") **a.** consummative; consummatory; decisive; definitive; determinative; illative; irrefutable; terminal; unanswerable; unequivocal

CONCORD: (**see** "agreement") **n.** congeniality; harmony; rapprochement; simultaneity; synchroneity; unanimity
in: see "harmonious"
restoring of: **n.** rapprochement

CONCRETE, *dealing with the:* **a.** idiographic; materialistic; pragmatic
entity: **n.** concretum; (**pl.** concreta)

CONCURRENCE: **n.** simultaneity; synchroneity; unanimity; **v.** CONCUR: **see** "agree"
not in: **a.** anachronous; asynchronistic; asynchronous; **n.** asynchronism

CONDEMN: **see** "censure"; **a.** CONDEMNING: condemnatory; damnatory
what is not understood: damnat quod non intelligunt

CONDENSE: **v.** abbreviate; abridge; compress; concentrate; consolidate; epitomize; inspissate
in rhetoric to emphasize: **n.** paraleipsis

CONDENSED *expression:* **n.** (**see** "maxim") aphorism; brachylogy

CONDESCENDING: (**see** "yielding") **a.** hoity-toity; patronizing
air or manner, with a: **a. or adv.** *de haut en bas*

CONDITION: **n.** circumstance; contingency; eventuality; facet; obstacle; plight; predicament; (pre)requisite; provision; proviso; reservation; status; stipulation
at any previous time: **n.** *status quo ante*
at any specified time: **n.** *status quo*
in same or existing: **n. or adv.** *in statu quo; status quo*
indispensable: see "indispensable"

CONDITIONAL: **a.** circumstantial; contingent; limitative; provisional; provisory; tentative; **n.** CONDITIONALITY: tentativeness

CONDOLE: **v.** commiserate; lament; **n.** CONDOLENCE: commiseration; compassion; **a.** CONDOLENT: compassionate

CONDUCT: (**see** "manage") **v.** escort; negotiate; **n.** (**see** "behavior") comport(ment); demeanor; deportment; management; mien; praxis
bad: see "misbehavior"
brutish or grotesque: **n.** baboonery; grossness; vulgarity
correctness of: **n.** correctitude; rectitude; scrupulosity
extravagant, shamelessly flamboyant or vainglorious: **n.pl.** heroics; theatrics
gracious acts of: **n.pl.** amenities; proprieties; urbanities
nice point of: **n.** meticulosity; punctilio
reasoning about, or false application of principles to: **n.** casuistry; **a.** casuistic
right or wrong, judge of: **n.** casuist; censor morum;* moral sophist
study of human: **n.** praxeology; praxiology
usual or conventional: **n.** praxis

CONFEDERATE: **see** "associate"

CONFEDERATION: **see** "alliance"

CONFERENCE: **n.** caucus; colloquium; colloquy; confabulation; consultation; deliberation; dialogue; discussion; palaver; parley; seminar; symposium; **v.** CONFER: bestow; confabulate; consult; deliberate; endow
preliminary or informal: **n.** pourparler

CONFESSON(S), *receiver of:* **n.** confessarius
sacrament of: **n.** penance

CONFIDENCE: **n.** assurance; certainty; certitude; credence; positivism; presumption; **a.** CONFIDENT: assured; peremptory; presumptious; sanguine
bold show of: **n.** bravura; doughtiness; *tour de force*
lack of: **n.** diffidence; inferiority complex
over-: **n.** presumptiousness
tending to inspire: **a.** prepossessing

CONFIDENTIAL: (**see** "secret") **a.** classified; covert; esoteric; trustworthy; **adv.** CONFENTIALLY: covertly; *entre nous; inter nos; sub rosa*

CONFINE: **v.** circumscribe; demarcate; encompass; immure, impale; impound; imprison; incarcerate; **n.** CONFINEMENT: accouchement; circumscription; immurement; incarceration
place of: **n.** limbo

CONFIRM: (**see** "verify") **v.** authenticate; corroborate; establish; substantiate; validate; **n.** CONFIRMATION: affirmation; authentication; corroboration; investiture; substantiation; validation; **a.** CONFIRMATIVE: confirmatory; corroborative; corroboratory

CONFISCATE: **see** "take"

CONFLICT: (**see** "fight") **n.** antagonism; collision; encroachment; friction; impingement; **a.** CONFLICTING: antagonistic; antithetical; contending; contradictory; incompatible; incongruous; inconsistent; inharmonious; irreconcilable; **n.** CONFLICTION: antagonism; contrariety; disharmony; incompatibility; irreconcilability
vast, final, or conclusive: **n.** Armageddon

CONFORM: **see** "adapt"; **a.** CONFORMABLE: **see** "accepted"
one who (conforms): **n.** conventionalist; ritualist

CONFORMING *to standards:* (**see** "according to rule" **and** "standards") **a.** canonical; conventional; ethical; **adv.** *en règle;* **n.** canonicity; conventionality; propriety; rituality

CONFORMITY *at any cost, or by force:* **a.** procrustean
lack of: **n.** difformity; impropriety; recusancy; unconventionality

CONFUSE: (**see** "bewilder") **v.** bemuse; confound; disconcert; disorient; embrangle; obfuscate; perplex; perturb
by sounds, or by mingling of diff. language or cultures: **n.** Babelism; **v.** Babelize

CONFUSED (**or** CONFUSING): (**see** "baffling" **and** "bewildered") bemused; chaotic; disconcerted; *désorienté;* disordered; distraught; frantic; higgledy-piggledy (**or** higglety-pigglety); hugger-mugger; incoherent; indiscriminate; muddled; obfuscated; obfuscatory; perplexed

state of mind: **n.** disorientation; incoherence; obnubilation

CONFUSION: (**see** "disorder") **n.** anarchy; ataxia; Babelism; bewilderment; brouhaha; chaos; delirium; disarrangement; disarray; discomfiture; disorientation; embranglement; hugger-mugger; incoherence; katzenjammer; obfuscation; perplexity; turbidity; turmoil; welter; witches' brew
in: **adv.** *à l'abandon;* higgledy-piggledy; topsy-turvy
of sound or sense: **n.** Babelism
place or scene of: **n.** Bedlam

CONGRATULATE: **v.** commend; felicitate; macarize; **a.** CONGRATULATORY: gratulant; **n.** CONGRATULATION: commendation; felicitation

CONJECTURE: **n.** hypothesis; postulation; presumption; (pre)supposition; speculation; surmise; theorem; **a.** CONJECTURAL: hypothetical; stochastic; suppositional; supposi(ti)ous; theoretical

CONJUNCTION(S): (**see** "union") **n.** association
connecting by (words or sentences): **a.** syndetic
omission of in sentence: **n.** asyndeton; **a.** asyndetic
repetition of many in succession: **n.** polysyndeton; **a.** polysyndetic

CONJURER: **see** "magician"

CONNECTION: (**see** "association") **n.** affinity; alliance; colligation; conjunction; consanguinity; contiguity; continuity; liaison; ligature; nexus; relationship; symphysis; **a.** CONNECTED (**or** CONNECTING): affined; anastomotic; articulate(d); coadunate; coadunative; conjunctive; contiguous; osculant; syndetic
as by descent or derivation: **n.** apparentation; **v.** apparent
blood vessels or channels: **n.** anastomosis; **a.** anastomotic
necessary: **n.** causality
nerve(s): **n.** synapse; **a.** synaptic

CONQUER: **v.** overthrow; subdue; subjugate; surmount; vanquish; **n. see** "conquest"
or die: aut vincere aut mori

CONQUERABLE: **a.** domitable; expugnable; surmountable; vincible; vulnerable; **n.** CONQUERABILITY: domitability; expugnability; surmountability; vincibility
not: see **under** "conquered"

CONQUERED, *capable of being:* see "conquerable"
incapable of being: **a.** impregnable; inconquerable; inexpugnable; insurmountable; invulnerable; **n.** impregnability; inexpugnability; insurmountability; invincibility
woe to the: **adv.** *vae victis*

CONQUEROR: **n.** conquistador

CONQUEST: **n.** acquisition; debellation; reduction; subjection; subjugation; triumph

CONSCIOUS *of:* (see "aware") **a.** cognizable; cognizant; sensible; sentient; **n.** cognizance

CONSCIOUSNESS: (see "awareness") **n.** cognizance; percipience; percipiency; sentience; sentiency
below threshold or outside area of: **a.** subliminal; **n.** sublimination
twinge of: **n.** compunction; qualm; scruple; **a.** qualmish; scrupulous; **n.** scrupulosity

CONSECUTIVE: **a.** alphabetical; categorical; chronologic(al); sequel; sequent(ial); successional; successive

CONSENT: (see "accord" **and** "assent") **n.** approbation; concurrence; corroboration; permission; ratification; sufferance; unanimity
against, or against will: **adv.** *in invitum*
by common: **adv.** *communi consensu; d'un commun accord*
silence gives: chi tace assonsenti; qui tacet consentit
with general: **a.** consentaneous; consentient; consensual; unanimous; **n.** consension; consensus; unanimity

CONSEQUENCE(S): (see "weight") **n.** consecution; contrecoup; corollary; emanation; importance; ramification; residual; residue; residuum; sequala(e); **a.** CONSEQUENTIAL: corollary; residual; rational; self-important; sequent(ial)

CONSERVATION: **n.** economy; husbandry; perpetuation; planned management; preservation; sustentation; sustention; **a.** sustentative; **v.** CONSERVE: see "manage"

CONSERVATIVE: (see "old-fashioned") **a.** conventional; lethargic; reactionary; traditionalistic; unenterprising; **n.** mossback; Old-Guard(ist); pr(a)etorian; reactionary; standpatter; traditionalist; **n.** CONSERVATISM: conventionality; fundamentalism; traditionalism; traditionality
politically: **a.** Old-Guard; Metternichian

CONSIDERATION: **n.** advisement; attention; contemplation; deliberation; estimation; (ex)cogitation; honorarium; perpension; *quid pro quo;* reward; **v.** CONSIDER: (see "reflect") contemplate; deliberate; (ex)cogitate; perpend; ponder; take under advisement
for further: **adv.** *ad referendum*

CONSISTENT: (see "constant") **a.** commensurate; compatible; comportable; concordant; congenial; congruous; consentaneous; consonant; harmonious; invariable; isogenous; **n.** CONSISTENCY: compatibility; correspondence; harmony; homogeneity; isogeny; persistency
not: see "inconsistent"

CONSOLE: see "condole"

CONSOLIDATE: see "combine"

CONSPICUOUS: (see "outstanding") **a.** eminent; manifest; striking
by his absence: **adv.** *briller par son absence*
extremely: **a.** supereminent; **n.** supereminence

CONSPIRE: **v.** collude; connive; contrive; machinate; **a.** CONSPIRATIVE (**or** CONSPIRATORIAL) cabalistic; Catilinarian; collusive; collusory; conniving; **n.** CONSPIRACY: (see "plot") *association illégale;* cabal; collusion; confederacy; conjuration; connivance; intrigue; junto; machination

CONSTANT: (see "steady") **a.** continent; continual; continuous; immutable; incessant; invariable; perennial; persevering; resolute; steadfast; unceasing; undeviating; unfading; unfailing; uniform; unswerving

CONSTITUTION: **n.** character; decalogue; disposition; lustihood; Magna C(h)arta; ordinance; physique; stamina; temperament; virility
individual: **n.** crasis

CONSTRAINT: **see** "duress"

CONSTRICTION: (**see** "obstruction") **n.** coarctation; stenosis; strangulation

CONSTRUCT: (**see** "build") **v.** compose; confect; fabricate; improvisate; improvise; manufacture

CONSTRUCTION, *art of:* **n.pl.** (archi)-tectonics
pert. to: **a.** (archi)tectonic; constructional

CONSTRUCTIVE: **a.** affirmative; architectonic; definitive; inferred

CONSUMING: **a.** devouring; edacious; voracious; **n.** edacity; voracity

CONTACTING: **a.** contiguous; juxtapositional; tangential; **n.** (**see** "touching") apposition; contiguity; contingence; juxtaposition; tangency

CONTAGIOUS: **a.** communicable; epidemic; noxious; pestilential; **n.** contagium
state of being: **n.** contagiosity

CONTAMINATED: **a.** defiled; insanitary; polluted; septic; **v.** CONTAMINATE: **see** "defile"
morally: **a.** scrofulous; **n.** scrofulosis
not possible to (*contaminate*): **a.** incontaminable; incontaminate

CONTEMPLATION: **n.** anticipation; (ex)cogitation; expectation; meditation; **v.** CONTEMPLATE: anticipate; envisage; (ex)cogitate; meditate; ponder; postulate
mystical: **n.** orison

CONTEMPORARY: **a.** coetaneous; coeternal; coeval; coincident; concomitant; concurrent; contemporaneous; isochronous; simultaneous; synchronous; **n.** CONTEMPORARINESS: coetaneity; coeval-

(ity); contemporaneity; simultaneity; synchroneity

CONTEMPT: **n.** contumacy; contumely; denigration; depreciation; derision; despiciency; disdain; disparagement; hauteur; hubris; misprision; scurviness; **a.** CONTEMPTIBLE: contemptuous; contumelious; denigrating; derisible; derisive; despicable; despiteous; disdainful; haughty; hubristic; pitiable; scurrile; scurrilous; scurvy; toplofty
as a token of: **adv.** *par signe de mépris*
hold in: **v.** denigrate; deride; disdain; disparage; misprize
person regarded with: **n.** pilgarlic

CONTEND: **v.** antagonize; grapple; oppugn; **n.** CONTENTION: (**see** "controversy") altercation; competition; contestation; dissidence; donny-brook; litigiosity; rivalry; **a.** CONTENTIOUS: (**see** "hostile") belligerent; contradictious; disputable; disputatious; dissentious; factious; litigious; mutinous; seditious; tauraine; turbulent

CONTENT(ED): (**see** "calm") **a.** *sans souci;* unperturbed; **n.** CONTENTMENT: complacency; eudaemonia; eudaemony; euphoria; felicity; repose; satisfaction; tranquility

CONTEST: (**see** "oppose" **and** *"fight"*) **n.** agon; tournament; **n.** CONTESTING: agonistic(al); **n.** CONTESTANT: agonist
slight: **n.** skirmish; vellitation

CONTINGENCY: **n.** accidentality; casualty; eventuality; fortuitousness; fortuity; juncture

CONTINUE: **v.** perdure; perpetuate; perseverate; persevere; persist; **n.** CONTINUATION: (**see** "continuousness") perduration; perpetuation; perpetuality; perpetuity; perseveration; persistence; persistency; prolongation

CONTINUOUS (**or** CONTINUAL): **a.** consecutive; incessant; inveterate; perdurant; perennial; perpetual; persistent; progressive; recurrent; sempiternal; successive; unceasing; uninterrupted; **n.** CONTINUOUSNESS: (**see** "continuation") continuity; continuum; incessancy;

incessantness; inveterateness; perpetuality; perpetuity; perseveration; sempiternity
something which is: **n.** continuum

CONTOUR: (**see** "outline") **n.** configuration; conformation; silhouette

CONTRACT, *power to:* **n.** contractility

CONTRACTING: **a.** astrictive; binding; **n.** astriction; astrictive

CONTRADICTING *no one:* **adv.** *nemine contradicente* (**abb.** *nem con*); *nemine dissentiente*

CONTRADICTION: **n.** anomaly; antilogy; antinomy; antithesis; contrariety; incompatibility; paradox
in terms or ideas: **n.** antilogy; *contradictio in adjecto*

CONTRADICTORY: **a.** ambivalent; antonymous; contradictious; incompatible; inconsistent; paradoxical; repugnant; schizoid
attitude: **n.** ambivalence; paradoxicality

CONTRARY: (**see** "opposite" **and** "stubborn") **a.** absonant; adverse; ambivalent; antagonistic; antipodal; antithetic(al); cantankerous; contradictious; contrariant; contrarious; diametrical; discrepant; fractious; froward; incompatible; inverse; perverse; petulant; refractory
on the: **adv.** *per contra*
quite the: **adv.** *à rebours; tout au contraire; tout bien ou rien*
state of being: **n.** antithesis; contrariety; (**n.pl.** antipodes)
to the: **adv.** *a contrario; au contraire*

CONTRIBUTION, *small but all one can afford:* **n.** widow's mite

CONTRIBUTORY: (**see** "supplemental") **a.** accessorial; accessory; adjuvant; auxiliary; complemental; complementary; **n.** complementarity

CONTRIVE: **see** "invent"

CONTROL: (**see** "manage") **v.** dominate; govern; hierarchize; influence; manipulate; regulate; restrain; subdue; subjugate; superintend; **n.** (**see** "power") hierarchization; jurisdiction; manipula-

tion; restraint; subjugation; **n.** CONTROLLER: comptroller; governor; manipulator; regulator; superintendent; supervisor
easy to: (**see** "pliant") **a.** controllable; educable; educatable; manipulatory; tractable; vulnerable; **n.** dirigibility; educa(ta)bility; tractability; vulnerability
impossible to: **a.** incoercible; incorrigible; irrepressible
of another, one who is under: **n.** *homo alieni juris*
self-: **see under** "self"

CONTROVERSY: **n.** argumentation; altercation; brannigan; contestation; disputation; dissention; polemics; **a.** CONTROVERSIAL: argumentative; contentious; dialectic; discursory; disputatious; eristic; polemic(al)
famous or celebrated: **n.** *cause célèbre*

CONVENIENCE: **n.** advantage; expedience; expediency; opportunity; **a.** CONVENIENT: advantageous; expedient; expeditional; opportune; seasonable

CONVENT, *occupant of:* **n.** cenobite; solitudinarian; **a.** cenobitic; solitudinarian

CONVENTION: **n.** academicism; decorum; (**pl.** decora); orthodoxy; proprieties; propriety
one who defies: **n.** beatnik; Bohemian; iconoclast; solecist; transgressor
outside: **a.** extracurricular

CONVENTIONAL: (**see** "accepted") **a.** academic; artificial; *au fait;* Babbit(t)ical; bourgeois; ceremonial; ceremonious; conventionalized; decorous; formal; nomic; orthodox(ical); pedantic; Philistine; stilted; traditional; tralatitious; **n.** CONVENTIONALITY: **n.** academicism; commonplaceness; conformity; conventionalism; formalism; (**pl. see** "proprieties")
person: **n.** academician; Babbitt; bourgeois; orthodoxian; Philistine; proprietarian
social usage, form or propriety: **n.** convenance; (the) amenities; (the) proprieties
to make: **v.** conventionalize; stylize

CONVERGENCE: **n.** concurrency; confluence; conflux; convergency; **a.** CONVERGENT: confluent

CONVERSANT: see "informed"

CONVERSATION: (see "discussion") n. causerie; colloquy; confabulation; conversazione; interlocution; parlance
clever or witty: n. repartee
of three: n. trialog(ue)
preliminary: n. pourparler
room set aside for: n. ex(h)edra; locutory

CONVERSATIONAL: a. colloquial; interlocutory; n. CONVERSATIONALIST: n. causeur; (fem. causeuse); raconteur
style, writing in: n. causerie; journalese

CONVERT: v. persuade; transform; transmute; n. disciple; neophyte; novice; proselyte
from another sect, belief, etc.: v. or n. proselyte

CONVINCING: (see "authoritative" and "evident") a. cogent; compelling; luculent; (per)suasive; plausible; telling

CONVULSION: n. grand mal; jactitation; orgasm; paroxysm; petit mal; seizure; a. CONVULSIVE: convulsionary; eclamptic; orgasmic; paroxysmal; spasmic; spasmodic(al)
state of: n. eclampsia

COOK, *chief:* n. *chef de cuisine; cuisinier;* (fem. *cuisinière*); culinarian
under- or assistant: n. *aide de cuisine*

COOKED *plainly:* a. *au naturel (also uncooked)*
well: adv. *bien cuit*

COOKING, *art of:* n. cuisine; epicurism; gastronomy; magirics
fine or high-class: n. *haute cuisine*
pert. to: a. culinary
plain: n. *cuisine bourgeoise*
prepared as at home: a. *bonne femme*
style of: n. cuisine; gastronomy

COOL: (see "calm" and "indifferent") a. composed; dispassionate; imperturbable; judicial; nonchalant; unperturbed; unruffled; a. COOLING: frigorific; n. COOLNESS: equanimity; indifference; nonchalance; phlegm; *sang-froid;* self-possession

COOPERATION: n. coadjuvancy; collaboration; commensalism; mutuality; reciprocality; reciprocity; symbiosis; synergism; synergy; v. COOPERATE: (see "unite") collaborate; n. COOPERATOR: collaborateur; collaborator; colleague; co-worker; phalansterian
bet. persons, animals or groups which may be otherwise incompatible: n. commensalism; mutualism; nutricism; parasitism; symbiosis; a. symbiotic(al)

COOPERATIVE: a. associative; collaborative; synergetic(al); synergic; synergistic
group living together; also building so used: n. phalansterianism; phalanstery

COORDINATION, *lack of:* n. astasia abasia; asynergia

COPPER, *bearing or containing:* a. cupriferous
pert. to, or to color of: a. cupr(e)ous

COPY: (see "imitate") v. duplicate; reproduce; transcribe; n. apograph; counterpart; duplicate; duplication; ectype; facsimile; replica; reproduction; transcription; a. apographal; ectypal
act or process of making: n. transumption

CORDIALITY: see "warmth"; adv. CORDIALLY: *à bras ouverts*

CORE: see "heart"

CORN (*on toe*): n. callosity; clavus; ecphyma

CORPSE, *like a:* a. cachectic; cadaverous

CORRECT: v. castigate; chasten; discipline; expiate; rectify; a. accurate; *au fait;* conventional; decorous; legitimate; orthodox; precise; rectitudinous; scrupulous
deviating from what is: see "deviating" and "deviation"
overly: a. meticulous; scrupulous; n. meticulosity; precisian; scrupulosity

CORRECTABLE: a. amenable; corrigible; perfectible; tractable; n. amenability; corrigibility; tractability

CORRECTION: (see "rebuke") n. amendment; chastening; chastenment; emendation; rectification; reformation

beyond: **a.** incorrigible; irreclaimable; irredeemable; irreformable; irremediable; irreparable
order for, of error: **n.** corrigendum; erratum; (**pl.** corrigenda; errata)

CORRECTIVE: **a.** amenable; amendatory; castigatory; correctional; emendatory; penal

CORRECTNESS: (**see** "accuracy") **n.** orthodoxy; scrupulosity
of judgment: **n.** rectitude

CORRESPONDING: **a.** accompanying; commensurable; commensurate; equivalent; homologous; isonomous; proportionate; **n.** CORRESPONDENCE: commensurability; commensuration; correlation; equiponderance; equivalence; homogeneity; reciprocation; **v.** CORRESPOND: (**see** "agree") coincide; correlate; equate; reciprocate
in value, structure, or position: **a.** homologous
person or thing: **n.** counterpart; homolog(ue)

CORROBORATIVE: **a.** adminicular; confirmatory; corroboratory; justificatory; vindicatory

CORRUPT: **v.** adulterate; debase; debauch; defile; demoralize; deprave; inquinate; pervert; pollute; putrefy; vitiate; **a.** CORRUPT (**or** CORRUPTIVE): Augean; cankerous; contaminated; contaminating; degenerate; demoralizing; immoral; infectious; mercenary; peccant; putrescent; putrid; tainted; venal
morally: **a.** degenerate; scrofulous; **n.** scrofulosis

CORRUPTION: **n.** contamination; debasement; debauchment; debauchery; degeneracy; defilement; demoralization; depravation; depravity; flagitiousness; putrefaction; putrescence; putridity; scrofulosis; squalor; venality
moral: **n.** degeneracy; scrofulosis; **a.** degenerate; scrofulous

COSMOS: **see** "universe"
worship of: **n.** cosmotheism

COST, *regardless of* (*or what it may*): **adv.** *à tout prix; coûte que coûte*

COSTLY: **a.** dispendious; exorbitant; extortionate; extravagant; inestimable; invaluable; lavish; prodgial
victory: **n.** Cadmean victory; Pyrrhic victory

COSTUME: **see** "attire"

COUNCIL: **n.** assembly; quorum
of state (*privy council*): **n.** *conseil d'état*

COUNSEL: **see** "advice" **and** "advocate"

COUNTENANCE: **n.** appearance; comportment; lineament; mien; physiognomy; sanction; visage; **v.** (**see** "support") encourage; sanction
is index of the soul: vultus est index animi

COUNTERACT: **v.** antagonize; contrapose; neutralize; nullify; **n. see** "opposition"

COUNTERATTACK: **n.** counteroffensive; repartee; ripost(e)

COUNTERCHARGE: **v.** recriminate; retaliate; **n.** recrimination; retaliation; **a.** recriminative; recriminatory; retaliative; retaliatory

COUNTERFEIT: (**see** "false") **v.** feign; imitate; pretend; simulate; **a.** (**see** "imitative") affected; apocryphal; artificial; Brummagem; colorable; delusive; ersatz; factitious; fraudulent; inauthentic; pretended; pseudo; simulated; spurious; supposititious; synthetic(al); uncanonical; **n. see** "imitation"

COUNTERFEITER: **n.** adulterator; imitant; impostor; imposture; mountebank; pretender

COUNTERMOVE: **n.** counteraction; *démarche*

COUNTLESS: **a.** incalculable; infinite; innumerable; legion; multitudinous; myriad; **n.** infinitude

COUNTRIFIED (**or** COUNTRYFIED): (**see** "rural") **a.** agrestic; bucolic; provincial; rustic; unsophisticated; **n.** peninsularity; provincialism; provinciality; rusticity

COUNTRY, *back* (*away fr. coast or cities*):
n. hinterland
   born or living in the: **a.** rurigenous
   girl or sweetheart: **n.** amaryllis
   go to, live, or stay in: **v.** rusticate; **n.**
rustication
   holiday or retreat: **n.** villeggiatura
   house or farm: **n.** villa; **a.** villatic
   in the: **adv.** *en pays*
   of or like: **a.** agrestic; countrified; idyllic; pastoral; provincial; rustic; Theocritean; unsophisticated
   one's own: **n.** fatherland; **a.** patrial
   person: **n.** agrestian; bucolic; provincial; rustic
   person who came up in the world: **n.**
paysan parvenu
   pert. to a particular: **a.** autochthonous;
enchorial; indigenous

COUNTRYMAN, *fellow:* **n.** compatriot

COUPLE: (**see** "unite") **v.** conjugate; **a.**
COUPLED: coadunate; coadunative; conjugate
   (*as hus. and wife*): **n.** dyad; **a.** dyadic

COUPLING: (**see** "union") **n.** accouplement; articulation; conjugation; copulation; junction; juncture; symphysis

COURAGE: **n.** audacity; dauntlessness;
fortitude; gallantry; intrepidity; mettle;
prowess; resolution; tenacity; **a.** COU-
RAGEOUS: (**see** "bold") audacious;
chivalrous; fortitudinous; Herculean; intrepid; resolute; Spartan
   and faith, by: **adv.** *animo et fide*
   incitement to: **n.** *sursum corda*
   pretended: **n.** bravado; doughtiness
   reckless: **n.** bravado; derring-do;
doughtiness

COURSE: **v.** pulsate; surge; transverse; **n.**
(**see** "journey" **and** "schedule") *démarche;*
maneuver; procedure
   of: **adv.** *bien entendu;* **int.** *parbleu!*

COURT(S), *authority or power of:* **n.** judicature; judiciary; jurisdiction
   before, or under consideration by: **adv.**
sub judice
   capable or suitable for cons. by: **a.** justiciable
   of law: **n.** judicature
   pert. to: **a.** aulic; forensic; judicial;
judiciary; juridical; juristic

COURTEOUS: (**see** "affable") **a.** attentive; chivalric; chivalrous; debonair(e);
deferential; hospitable; ingratiating; parliamentary; suave; urbane
   acts: **n. pl.** (the) amenities; (the) proprieties; urbanities
   overly: **a.** deferential; obeisant; obsequious; servile; **n.** deferentiality; obeisance;
obsequence; obsequiousness; obsequity;
servility

COURTESY: **n.** address; *agréments;* amenity; civility; courtliness; deference; deferentiality; gentility; graciousness; gratuity; homage; indulgence; obeisance; politeness; politesse; protocol; suavity; urbanity; (**pl.** COURTESIES: *agréments;*
amenities; proprieties; urbanities)
   act of: **n.** devoir
   given as a: **a.** complimentary; gratis

COURTLY: (**see** "courteous" **and** "polite")
a. aulic; obsequious; stately; suave; unctuous

COVER: **v.** superimpose
   under: **adv.** *à couvert*

COVERING: **n.** canopy; envelope; integument; marquee; operculum; superimposi-
tion

COVETOUS: **a.** acquisitive; *alieni appetens;* avaracious; extortionate; miserly;
parsimonious; penurious; prehensile; rapacious; **n.** COVETOUSNESS: avarice;
cupidity; pleonexia; venality

COW: **v.** browbeat; bulldoze; dishearten;
intimidate; overawe; **n.** bovine; (**pl.** bovidae) ruminant

COWARD: **n.** caitiff; craven; dastard; poltroon; recreant; **a.** COWARDLY: caitiff;
craven; dastardly; irresolute; lily-livered;
poltroon(ish); pusillanimous; recreant;
timorous; tremulous; **n.** COWARDICE:
cowardliness; dastardliness; poltroonery;
pusillanimity; recreancy; timidity

COWLED: **a.** cucullate(d)

COXCOMB: **n.** jackanapes; macaroni; popinjay

COY: **a:** coquettish; **n.** COYNESS: coquetry; dalliance; minauderie

COZY: **a:** gemultlich; intimate
place: **n.** snuggery

CRABBY: (**see** "cranky") **a.** *acariâtre;*
acerb(ic); acidulent; acidulous; choleric;
churlish; rebarbative; splenetic; vinegary;
n. CRABBINESS: acerbity; asperity
person: **n.** crotcheteer; curmudgeon

CRACKLING: **a.** crepitant; **n.** crepitation

CRACKS, *full of:* **a.** rimose; rimulose

CRADLE: **n.** *crèche;* incunabula; infancy;
matrix
from the: **adv.** *ab incunabulis*
song: **n.** berceuse

CRAFTSMAN: **n.** artificer; artisan

CRAFTY: (**see** "cunning") **a.** artful; astucious; astute; ingenious; insidious; in-
sinuating; Machiavellian; politic; sophisticated; subtle; vulpine; **n.** CRAFTINESS:
astuteness; astucity; callidity; diablerie;
ingeniosity
esp. political: **a.** Machiavellian; **n.**
Machiavellianism

CRAMPED: **a.** incapacious; incommodious

CRANKY: (**see** "crabby" **and** "peevish") **a.**
cantankerous; choleric; crochety; irascible; petulant; querulous; splenetic; vinegary; **n.** CRANKINESS: (**see** "peevishness") acerbity; angularity; asperity;
crotchiness; distemper; irascibility; querulousness

CRAVING: **a.** appetant; appetitious; desiderative; **n.** appetence; appetency; appetition; desideration; desideratum; yearning

CRAWLING, *adapted to:* (**see** "creeping")
a. subreptary

CRAZED: **a.** berserk; distraught; frantic;
frenetic; harassed; maniac(al); **n.**
CRAZE: **see** "fad"
for one thing: **a.** monomaniac(al); **n.**
monomania; monomaniac

CRAZY: **see** "insane"

CREATING, *all:* **see under** "all"

CREATION: **n.** cosmos; genesis; masterpiece; poiesis; universe; **v.** CREATE:

(**see** "build") fabricate; generate; invent;
reproduce
before: **a.** antemundane; premundane

CREATIVE: (**see** "original") **a.** constructive; demiurgic; formative; genetic; imaginative; ingenious; poietic; Promethean;
(re)productive; **n.** poiesis
person: **n.** Prometheus
principle: **n.** *élan vital*

CREATIVELY *striving:* **a.** Dionysian

CREDIT: **n.** acknowledg(e)ment; ascription; recognition
for authorship, etc.: **n.** attribution; **a.**
attributive
giving: **n.** ascription
letter of: **n.** *lettre de créance*
worthy of: **a.** commendable; creditable;
n. creditability

CREDULOUS: **a.** gullible; naïve (**also**
"naive"); naïvety; **n.** CREDULITY: gullibility; *naïveté* (**also** "naiveté")
person: **n.** gobemouche

CREED: (**see** "belief") **n.** confession; denomination; doctrine; dogma; philosophy;
tenet
abandon: **v.** apostatize; **n.** apostate;
apostasy; **a.** apostate; apostatic
one with no particular: **n.** anythingarian;
aporetic; latitudinarian; nullifidian

CREEPING: **a.** procumbent; prostrate; reptant; reptatorial; reptilian; serpentine;
serpiginous; subreptary

CREMATION: **n.** cineration

CRESCENT-*shaped:* **a.** lunate; lunular;
lunulate; meniscoid

CRESTED: **a.** cristate; **n.** CREST: **see**
"crown"

CRIME: **n.** defalcation; delict; embezzlement; felony; infraction; iniquity; malefaction; malfeasance; misdemeanor; offense; transgression
against state or king: **n.** *lèse majesté;*
treason
associate in: **n.** accessory; *particeps
criminis; socius criminis;* sorcerer's apprentice
capable of committing: **a.** *capax doli*
charge w/: **v.** (in)criminate; indict; **a.**

criminatory; (in)criminative; **n.** (in)crimination

   concealment of: **n.** misprision; subreption

   concernment w/: **a.** criminous

   fact(s) necessary to establish: **n.** *corpus delicti*

   minor: **n.** misdemeanor; transgression

   on acct. of conviction for: **adv.** *propter delictum*

   tending to involve in: **v.** incriminate; **a.** criminogenic; incriminatory; **n.** incrimination

CRIMINAL: **a.** blameworthy; culpable; disgraceful; extortionate; felonious; flagitious; illicit; iniquitous; malefic; malevolent; malignant; nefarious; nocent; reprehensive; unlawful; **n.** convict; culprit; delinquent; felon; infractor; malefactor; malfeasant; miscreant

   intent: **n.** *mens rea*

CRINKLED: **a.** convoluted; crispate

CRIPPLED: see "lame"

CRISIS: **n.** climacteric; climacterium; (con)juncture; criticality; cruciality; crux; dilemma; exigency; predicament; **a.** CRISIC: (see "critical") dilemmatic; predicamental

CRITERION: see "standard"

CRITIC: (see "faultfinder") **n.** aristarch; carper; caviler; exegete; feuilletonist; pundit

   bitter and envious; **n.** Zoilus; **a.** Zoilean

   carping: **n.** momus

   learned and severe: **n.** Aristarch(us)

   of art(s) and fashion(s): **n.** cognoscente; connoisseur

CRITICAL: (see "crucial" **and** "dangerous") **a.** captious; censorial; censorious; climacteric(al); climactic(al); condemnatory; cynical; definitive; derisive; dilemmatic; exigent; imminent; resolute; scrupulous; squeamish

   (*dangerous*): **a.** parlous

   essay, exam. or analysis: **n.** critique; exegesis

   moment: see "crisis"

CRITICISM: (see "censure") **n.** animadversion; critique; derision; diatribe; evaluation; impugnation; scarification; stricture

   above or beyond: **a.** impregnable; invulnerable; unassailable

   insensitive to: **a.** pachydermatous

CRITICIZE: (see "censure") **v.** animadvert; castigate; evaluate; execrate; fustigate; impugn; reprehend; upbraid

   sharply: **v.** scarify

CRITICIZING *another for what he criticizes in others:* **n.** *tu quoque*

CROOKED: **a.** circuitous; devious; fraudulent; insidious; perfidious; sinuous; stealthy; surreptitious; tortuous; unconscionable; unprincipled; unscrupulous; vermiculate; villainous; **n.** CROOKEDNESS: circuity; deviousness; indirection; insidiousness; perfidy; surreption; tortuosity; unscrupulosity; villainy

CROP(S), *goddess of:* **n.** Annona; Ops

   production, study of: **n.** agronomics; agronomy; agronomist

CROSS: **a.** acidulous; bilious; choleric; contentious; decussate; fractious; irascible; perverse

   -breeding, animal or plant produced by: (see "half-breed") **n.** hybrid; mongrel

   -fertilization; **n.** allogamy; xenogamy; **a.** allogamous; xenogamous

   making sign of the: **n.** signation

   pert. to: **a.** crucial; cruciate

   shaped like: **a.** cruciate; cruciform

   swastica type: **n.** flyfot; gammadion; hakenkreuz

   type of: **n.** avellan; *botonée; clechée; fleuretée;* Maltese; moline; patonce; quadrate

   worship of (or crucifix): **n.** staurolatry

CROSSNG: **n.** chiasma; decussation; intersection

   like an "x": **n.** decussation; **v.** decussate

CROSS-ROADS: **n.** carrefour; quadrivium; **a.** quadrivial

   goddess of: **n.** Hecate; Trivia

CROUCHING: **a.** crouchant; couchant

CROW, *like or pert. to:* **a.** corvine

CROWD(S): see "multitude"

   abnormal fear of: **n.** ochlophobia

   in. a: **adv.** *en foule*

to please the: **adv.** ad captandum (vulgus)

CROWN: **n.** coronet; culmination; diadem; scepter; sovereignty; tiara
-prince; **n.** atheling; dauphin; (**fem.** dauphine; dauphiness)
with laurel: **n. or v.** laureate

CRUCIAL: (see "critical") **a.** climacteric(al); climactic(al); decisive; searching; **n.** CRUCIALITY: (see "crisis") criticality
experiment: **n.** experimentum crucis

CRUCIFIX: worship of (or cross): **n.** staurolatory

CRUDE: (see "undeveloped") **a.** artless; gauche; immature; inapt; incondite; inept; primitive; primordial; rustic; unpolished; unskil(l)ful
person: **n.** buffoon; grobian; rustic

CRUDENESS (or CRUDITY): **n.** gaucherie; grobianism; impoliteness; immaturity; ineptness; ineptitude; pleb(e)ianism; primitivity; rusticity
social or lit.: **n.** gaucherie

CRUEL: (see "wicked") **a.** barbarous; despiteful; diabolical; dispiteous; Draconian; ferocious; impiteous; inexorable; inhuman; malicious; marblehearted; merciless; Neronian; procrustean; remorseless; ruthless; sadistic; satanic; Tarquinian; truculent; tyrannical; tyrannous; **n.** CRUELTY: barbarism; barbarity; callousness; ferity; induration; inhumanity; sadism

CRUMBLY: **a.** frangbile; friable; pulverous; pulverulent

CRUSADER: **n.** Messiah; messiahship; **a.** CRUSADING: evangelical; evangelistic; messianic; zealous

CRUSH: see "annihilate" **and** "pulverize"

CRUTCH: **n.** prosthesis

CRY(ING): **n.** deploration; lachrymation; lacrimation; lamentation; ululation; **a.** lachrymal; lacrimal; lachrymose; lachrymatory; lacrimatory; larmoyant

CULMINATION: (see "acme") **n.** apogee; climacteric; climacterium; climax; con-

summation; meridian; zenith; **a.** CULMINANT: climacteric

CULTURE(S), assimilation of: **n.** enculturation; socialization
human, study of: **n.** ethnology; **a.** ethnologic(al)
imparting of or conditioning to: **v.** acculturize; **n.** acculturation
lacking in: (see "uncouth") **a.** bourgeoise; Philistinic; Philistinish; **n.** Babbitt; grobian; Philistine
mingling or confusion of: **n.** Babelism; **v.** Babelize
trend of (gen. moral state, etc.): **n.** zeitgeist

CULTURED **a.** (a)esthetic; cultivated; literate; polished; refined; urbane
not: see "culture, lacking in"

CUNNING: **a.** artful; artistic; astucious; astute; callid; crafty; daedal(ian); daedalic; dexterous; diplomatic; duplicitous; expedient; ingenious; insidious; parlous; sagacious; unscrupulous; **n.** artifice; astucity; callidity; craftiness; dexterity; ingeniosity; ingenuity; insidiousness

CURABLE: (see "remedial") **a.** curative; medicable; remediable; sanable; sanative; sanatory; therapeutic(al); tractable; vulnerary; **a.** CURATIVE: see "healing"

CURE: (see "remedy") **n.** remediation
-all: **n.** catholicon; elixir; nostrum; panacea; theriac

CURIO: **n.** bibelot; bric-a-brac; curiosity; knickknack; virtu; (**pl.** objet d'art)

CURIOSITY: **n.** inquisitiveness; piquancy; prurience; pruriency; rarity; (**pl.** curiosa)
arousing: **a.** provocative; provocatory

CURIOUS: **a.** inquisitive; inquisitorial; piquant; provocative; prurient
person: **n.** Pandora; quidnunc

CURLY: **a.** convolute(d); crispate; oundy; **n.** convolution; crispation

CURRENT (see "modern") **a.** coetaneous; coeval; contemporaneous; contemporary; existing; extant; popular; prevailing; prevalent; topical; **n.** contemporaneity; modernity; prevalence; topicality

CURSED (or CURSING): (see "detestable) **a.** accursed; anathematic(al); comminatory; execrable; imprecatory; maledictory; odious; **v.** CURSE: anathematize; blaspheme; comminate; execrate; imprecate; maledict; objurgate; **n.** anathema(tization); blasphemy; contamination; denunciation; execration; imprecation; malediction; malison; scourge
   person or thing which is (cursed): **n.** anathema

CURT: (see "terse") **a.** brusque; condensed; laconic(al); unceremonious

CURTAIL: **v.** abbreviate; abridge; truncate

CURVE: **v.** arcuate; circumflex; **n.** arcuation; circumflexion; convolution; flexure; parabola; sinuosity; **a.** CURVED (or CURVING): archiform; arcuate; circumflex; convolute(d); crescentic; curvaceous; falciform; flexuous; undulating
   inward: **a.** involute(d); **n.** concavity; incurvation; involution
   outward: **n.** convexity

CUSTODIAN: **n.** Cerberus; chaperone; claviger; concierge; guardian; shepherd; superintendent

CUSTOM(S): (see "habit") **n.** consuetude; habitude; habituation; mores; observance; patronage; praxis; precedent; prescription; protocol; rubric
   according to: (see "customary") **adv.** *ad usum* (**abb.** *ad us.*) *ex more; comme il faut*
   depicting local or regional in lit. or art: **n.** costumbrista

group: **n. pl.** conventionalities; ethos; mores

CUSTOMARY: **a.** censuetudinary; conventional; *de rigueur; de règle;* nomic; prescriptive; prevalent; traditional; **adv.** *ad amussim; ad us(um); ex more*

CUT *off:* **v.** abscind; abscise; amputate; **n.** ablation; (ab)scission; amputation
   out: **v.** ablate; bowdlerize; emasculate; enucleate; excise; expurgate; extirpate; resect
   short: **v.** abbreviate; decapitate; syncopate

CUTE: see "coy"

CUTTING: (see "keen") **a.** acrimonious; caustic; incisive; mordant; penetrating; piquant; poignant; sarcastic; trenchant; **n.** excision; extirpation; rescission; scission
   down: **n.** retrenchment
   in parts: **a.** disjunction; dismemberment; dissolution; disunion; excision; mutilation; sundering

CYCLE(S), *life, or of organism:* **n.** ontogeny; ontogenesis; **a.** ontogenetic
   moving or arranged in: **a.** cyclic(al); periodical; rhythmic(al)

CYNIC: **n.** Antisthenes; Diogenes; misanthrope; skeptic; Timon; **a.** CYNICAL: derisive; ironical; misanthropic(al); pessimistic; sarcastic; sardonic; satirical; **n.** CYNICISM: Dadism; derision; irony; pessimism; sarcasm; sardonicism; satire
   burlesquing: **a.** pangruelian; **n.** pangruelism; pangruelist

D

DABBLER: (see "collector") n. amateur; dilettante; novice; sciolist

DAILY: a. diurnal; quotidian
anything that occurs: n. quotidian
occurring twice: a. semidiurnal

DAINTY: (see "airy") a. decorous; etherial; exquisite; fastidious; gossamery; *recherché;* DAINTINESS: (see "delicacy") ethereality; *friandise*

DALLY: v. dawdle; loiter; philander; procrastinate; shilly-shally; vacillate

DALLYING, *relaxed:* n. desipience; desipiency; a. *dégagé;* desipient

DAMAGES, *payment for:* n. remuneration; reparation(s)

DAMAGING: (see "injurious") a. destructive; detrimental; hurtful; inimical; malignant; nocent; nocuous; noxious; prejudicial; venomous

DAMN: see "curse"

DAMNATION, *also place of:* n. perdition

DANCE, *belly:* n. *danse du ventre*
for two persons; n. *pas de deux*
of death: n. *danse macabre*
tea: n. *thé dansant*

DANCER(S), *ballet, esp. star:* n. *coryphée* (fem.)
responsive movement bet. two, or groups of: n. antiphony; a. antiphonal; antiphonic

DANCING: n. choreography; terpsichore
muse of: n. Terpsichore
pert. to: a. saltatorial; saltatory; terpsichorean

DANDRUFF, *covered w/:* a. furfuraceous; scurfy

DANDY: n. Beau Brummel; coxcomb; dandiprat; *incroyable;* jackanapes; macaroni; *petit-maître;* popinjay; n. DANDYISM: foppishness

DANGER: (see "peril") n. Charybdis; crisis; imperilment; insecurity; instability; jeopardy; v. see "endanger"
common, produces concord: commune periculum concordiam parit
hidden: n. *anguis in herba* (snake in the grass); Trojan horse
impending: n. powder keg; sword of Damocles; a. Damoclean
pushing to limit of: n. brinksmanship
serving as warning of: a. sematic; n. *memento mori;* skull and crossbones

DANGEROUS: (see "menacing") a. critical; formidible; hazardous; ignitable; imminent; jeopardous; parlous; periculous; perilous; precarious; venturesome; venturous; vulnerable; n. DANGEROUSNESS: criticality; ignitability; jeopardy; venturousness; vulnerability
situation: n. hazard; jeopardy; precipice
to morals or social welfare: a. pernicious; pestiferous; pestilent(ial)

DARE *to know:* adv. *aude sapere*

DARING: (see "bold" and "dangerous") a. (ad)venturous; audacious; courageous; fortitudinous; Icarian; intrepid; perilous; picaresque; unconventional
action: n. bravura; derring-do
or reckless experience: n. escapade
romantic story of: n. bravura; derring-do; *tour de force;* a. picaresque
show of: n. bravura; derring-do; *tour de force*

DARK: (see "gloomy") a. adiaphanous; adumbral; atramental; atramentous; caliginous; Cimmerian; fuliginous; ignorant; inexplicable; iniquitous (see "wicked"); murky; mysterious; opaque; sinister; somber; stygian; tenebrous

69

in color, complexion or cast: **a.** nigrescent; swart(hy)

DARLING: **see** "favorite"

DARKEN: **v.** adumbrate; denigrate; obfuscate; obscure
as if by shadowing: **v.** obtenebrate

DARKNESS: (**see** "night") **n.** fuliginosity; nigrescence; nigritude; obscurity; tenebrosity
after, comes light: **adv.** *post tenebras lux*
causing: **a.** tenebrific
comparative: **n.** umbra(ge)
of complexion: **n.** nigrescence; **a.** nigrescent; swart(hy)
Prince of: **n.** Ahriman
surrounded by: **a.** benighted; unenlightened

DASH: (**see** "spirit") **n.** dollop
headlong: **n.** tantivy

DATA, *factual or speculative:* **n.** armentarium; (**pl.** armamentaria)

DATE, *out of:* **see under** "out"

DAUGHTER *or son, pert. to:* **a.** filial; sibling; **n.** sibling

DAWDLE: (**see** "dally" **and** "delay") **a. n. or v.** shilly-shally

DAWN: **n.** aurora; **a.** auroral; aurorean; eoan
before: **a.** antelucan
goddess of: **n.** Aurora; Eos

DAY, *live for or enjoy the:* **n.** *carpe diem; in diem vivere; in horam vivere*
lucky: **n.** *dies fa(u)stus*
occurring three times per: **a.** terdiurnal
of this: **a.** hodiernal
of wrath or judgment: **n.** *dies irae*
pert. to: (**see** "daily") **a.** diurnal
pert. to half a: **a.** semidiurnal
to day, from: **adv.** *de die in diem* (**abb.** d.d. in d.)
unlucky: **n.** *dies infa(u)stus;* (**pl.** *nefasti dies*)
w/o a (day) being set: **a.** *sine die*

DAYDREAM(ING): **n.** autism; introspection; introspectiveness; phantasm; phantasy; reverie; stargazing; woolgathering; **a.** autistic; introspective; phantasmal

DAYLIGHT, *in broad:* **adv.** *en plein jour*

DAZE: **see** "bewilder"

DAZZLING: **a.** foudroyant; fulgent; fulgurant; fulgurating; fulgurous; iridescent; meteoric; prismatic; pyrotechnic; radiant; resplendent; splendorous; **n.** DAZZLEMENT: radiance; resplendence; resplendency

DEAD: (**see** "death") **a.** *ad patres;* amort; barren; deceased; defunct; demised; deserted; exanimate; extinct; inanimate; inert; inorganic; insensible; insentient; irrevocable; lifeless; monotonous; moribund; unresponsive
abnormal attachment to (corpses, etc.): **n.** necrophilia(c); necrophilism
abnormal fear of: **n.** necrophobia
civilly (dead): **a.** *civiliter mortuus*
communication with (claimed): **n.** necromancy; **n.** necromancer; **a.** necromantic
fear of the: **n.** necrophobia
hymn to: **n.** requiem
place for: (**see** "cemetery") **n.** charnel house; ossuary
place for burial of honored: **n.** pantheon
prayer for: **n.** *requiescat; requiescat in pace* (**abb.** r.i.p.)
say nothing but good of: **adv.** *de mortuis nil nisi bonum*
world of the: **n.** netherworld
worship of or excessive reverence for: **n.** manism; necrolatry; **a.** manistic; necrolatrous

DEADEN: **v.** anesthesize; benumb; hebetate; obscure; obtund; paralyze; stupefy; **n.** anesthesia; hebetation; hebetude; stupefaction; **a.** anesthetic; obtund(ent); stupefacient

DEAD-END (**or** DEADLOCK): (**see** "impasse") **n.** cul-de-sac

DEADLY: **a.** baneful; cadaverous; devastating; fatal; feral; implacable; internecine; lethal; lethiferous; malignant; malicious; mortal; mortiferous; noxious; pernicious; pestilent(ial); stygian; terminal; venomous; viperish; **n.** DEADLINESS: fatality; lethality; mortality
less than: **a.** subcritical; sublethal

DEAF, *sign lang. of:* **n.** dactylology

DEAFNESS: **n.** surdity

DEAL: see "apportion"

DEAR: see "expensive"

DEATH: (see "dead") **n.** annihilation; consummation; *debitum naturae;* defunction; demise; evanishment; exitus; extinction; fatality; mortality; quietus; **a.** DEATHLESS: see "eternal"; **n.** DEATHLESS: eternality; imperishableness; perpetuity; **a.** DEATHLY: (*see* "deadly") cachectic; cadaverous; morbid; moribund; stygian; terminal
  abnormal fear of: **n.** necrophobia; necrophobiac
  abode after of unbaptised: **n.** limbo
  after: **a.** *post-mortem; post obitum;* posthumous
  appearance of face when near: **n.** Hippocratic facies; **a.** cadaverous
  arising, continuing, born or published after: **a.** posthumous
  be mindful of: memento mori
  before: **a.** antemortem
  characteristic of: (see "deadly") **a.** stygian
  easy and painless: **n.** euthanasia
  evidence of (sometimes figurative) : **n.** rigor mortis
  exam. after: **n.** autopsy; necropsy; post mortem; **a.** post-mortem
  exempt from: **n.** immortability; immortality; **a.** immortal
  fated or foredoomed to: **a.** fey; moribund
  fear of: **n.** thanatophobia
  -like: see "deathly"
  likely to cause: see "deadly"
  made by reason or in expectation of: **a.** *mortis causa*
  made or done after: **a.** post-mortem; posthumous
  mercy: **n.** euthanasia
  notice of: **n.** obituary; necrology; **a.** obitual; obituary; **v.** obituarize
  occurring after: **a.** post-mortem; posthumous
  occurring before: **a.** premortal; premortem; preterminal
  of a part (local) : **n.** necrosis
  pert. to: **a.** mortuary
  poem, song or oration of mourning: **n.** elegy; monody; threnody; **a.** elegaic; monodic
  rate: **n** mortality

  resembling: **a.** thanatoid
  stiffening of body after: **n.** rigor mortis
  to the: **a.** *à outrance;* lethal; mortal; mortiferous
  to the point of: **adv.** *à l'extrémité; in extremis*
  warning or reminder of: **n.** *memento mori;* skull and crossbones

DEBASE: **v.** adulterate; bastardize; contaminate; corrupt; defame; deglamorize; degrade; demean; denigrate; deteriorate; discredit; dishonor; heathenize; humble; minimize; paganzie; pejorate; pervert; stigmatize; sully; vilify; vitiate; vulgarize; **n.** DEBASEMENT: adulteration; degeneracy; deglamorization; depravation; depravity; dishonor; humiliation; squalidity; squalor; **a.** see "degrading"

DEBATE: **v.** argue; deliberate; discuss; **n.** argumentation; controversy; dialectic; disputation; dissension; **a.** DEBATABLE: contentious; controversial; controvertible; dialectical; disputatious; dubious; dubitable; equivocal; forensic; polemical; questionable; quodlibetic(al)
  pert. to or suitable for: **a.** forensic; quodlibetic(al)
  practice of: **n.pl.** forensics; polemics

DEBILITY: (see "weakness") **n.** adynamia; asthenia; cachexia; cachexy; debilitation; decrepitude; enervation; impotence; impotency; languor; **a.** DEBILITATED: (see "weak") adynamic; asthenic; cachectic; impotent
  general, or fatigue: **n.** adynamia; myasthenia; myasthenia gravis

DEBRIS: (see "rubbish") **n.pl.** detritus; fragments; oddments; orts; trivia

DEBTS, *able to pay:* **a.** solvent; **n.** solvency
  unable to pay: **a.** insolvent; **n.** insolvency

DEBUTANTE: **n.** ingenue

DECADENT: (see "out-of-date") **a.** antediluvian; archaic; archaistic; *démodé; fin-de-siècle;* moribund; obsolescent; *passé;* **n.** DECADENCE: see "deterioration"

DECAMP: see "elope"

DECAY: (see "rot") **v.** disintegrate; putrefy; putresce; **n.** decadence; decadency; decomposition; decrepitude; *délabrement;*

deterioration; dilapidation; disintegration; dissolution; labefaction; necrosis; putrefaction; putrescence; putridity
from old age: **n.** consenescence; **a.** consenescent
not subject to: **a.** indefectible; **n.** indefectibility

DECAYING *matter, feeding on:* **a.** saprophagous; saprophytic
matter, thriving on: **a.** saprophytic; **n.** saprophyte

DECEIT: (**see** "deception") **n.** artifice; chicanery; circumvention; cozenage; defraudation; desipience; dissimulation; duplicity; fabrication; hypocrisy; imposture; indirection; inveiglement; legerdemain; mendacity; obliquity; perfidy; sinuosity; stratagem; tortuosity; **a.** DECEITFUL: (**see** "deceptive" **and** "tricky") dissimulative; duplicitous; gnathonic; mendacious; obliquitous; perfidious; **n.** DECEITFULNESS: (**see** "deception") disingenuity; dissimulation; duplicity; fraudulence; indirection; obliquity

DECEIVE: **v.** bamboozle; beguile; cajole; camouflage; circumvent; cozen; defraud; dissemble; dissimulate; double-cross; ensnare; inveigle; mislead; outwit; victimize; **n.** DECEIVER: charlatan; dissembler; dissimulator; imposter; mountebank; rogue

DECENT: **a.** adequate; appropriate; chaste; decorous; demure; **n.** DECENCY: decorum; modesty; propriety; pudency; (**pl.** conventionalities; conventions; decencies; decora; proprieties)

DECEPTION: (**see** "deceit" **and** "trickery") **n.** artifice; bamboozlement; camouflage; chicanery; cozenage; defraudation; dissimulation; duplicity; fourberie; gambit; hanky-panky; hocus-pocus; ignis fatuus; legerdemain; mirage; obliquity; phonus-bolonus; prestidigitation; ·simulation; sinuosity; speciosity; stratagem; subterfuge; will-of-the-wisp
act of: **n.** beguilement; defraudation; duplicity; ludification; speciosity; triplicity
of the eye, as by painting: **n.** *trompe l'oeil*

DECEPTIVE: (**see** "misleading") **a.** alluring; barmecidal; cabalistic; clandestine; deceptious; dissembling; duplicitous; fallacious; illusional; illusory; mendacious; sirenic(al); specious; surreptitious

DECIDE: **see** "determine"
inability to: (**see** "waver") **n.** indecision; irresolution; vacillation
power to: **n.** discretion; **a.** discretionary
question or case: **v.** adjudicate; **n.** adjudication; **a.** adjudicative

DECIDED: (**see** "decisive") **n.** *fait accompli; res judicata*
that which can be: **a.** justiciable; resoluble; **n.** justiciability; resolubility

DECIDING, *act of:* **n.** adjudication; arbitrament; determination; umpirage; volition

DECISION: **n.** adjudication; arbitrament; conclusion; definitude; determination; judgment; mandate; resolution; settlement
irrevocable: **n.** (crossing the) Rubicon; point of no return

DECISIVE: (**see** "conclusive" **and** "final") **a.** absolute; authoritative; categorical; clear-cut; conclusive; crucial; definitive; determinative; implacable; indomitable; inexorable; unalterable; unmistakable; unequivocal
blow or answer: **n.** sockdolager
or authoritative group or tribunal: **n.** Aerophagus; **a.** Aerophagitic; **n.** Aerophagite
period or stage: **see** "crisis"
ultimately: **a.** apocalyptic(al)

DECLAMATORY: **a.** bombastic; Ciceronian; elocutionary; grandiloquent; oratorical; rhetorical

DECLARE: **v.** annunciate; asseverate; nuncupate; predicate; proclaim; promulgate; **n.** DECLARATION: manifesto; white paper; **a.** DECLARATORY: affirmative; assertorial; assertive; enunciative; expository; proclamatory
positively: **v.** asseverate; **n.** asseveration; **a.** asseverative

DECLINE: (**see** "decrease") **v.** degenerate; renege; retrocede; retrogress; retrograde; **n.** DECLINATION: decadence; degeneration; degenerescence; degradation; *dégringolade;* demotion; retrocession; retrogression
gradual, as fever or disease: **n.** lysis
in function, as organ or body; **n.** involution

period of: **n.** decadence; decadency; involution; **a.** decadent; involutional
rapid: **n.** *de gringolade*

DECORATE: **v.** adorn; embellish; emblazon; enrich; furbish; ornament; **n.** DECORATION: adornment; atmosphere; caparison; citation; decor; embellishment; emblazonment; embroidery; garnish(ment); garniture; medallion; **a.** DECORATIVE: see "attractive"

DECORUM: see "propriety"

DECREASE: (see "lessen") **v.** abate; diminish; dwindle; **n.** abatement; attenuation; declination; decrement; decrescence; decrescendo; degregation; degression; depreciation; diminuendo; diminution; retrenchment; retrogression; **a.** DECREASING: declinatory; decrescendo; decrescent; degressive; diminishing; reductionistic; reductive
gradual: **a. or n.** decrescendo; diminuendo; **n.** lysis

DECREE: **n.** decretum; fiat; judgment; mandate; ordinance; proclamation; pronouncement; pronunciamento

DECRY: see "belittle"

DEDICATE: **v.** consecrate; enshrine; hallow; sanctify; **a.** DEDICATORY: consecratory; dedicatorial; **n.** DEDICATION: consecration; devotion; devotement; enthusiasm; faithfulness; sanctification

DEDUCE: **v.** conclude; estimate; hariolate; **a.** see "deductive"; **n.** DEDUCTION: abatement; corollary; deductibility; hariolation; inference; inferentiality

DEDUCTIVE: **a.** deducible; illative; inferential
logic or reasoning: **n.** *a priori;* apriority; syllogism; synthesis; **a.** *a priori;* aprioristic; syllogistic(al)

DEED(S): **n.** achievement; exploit; gest(e); performance; *res geste;* transaction; **n.pl.** acta
justified by result: exitus acta probat
not words: facta non verba
not words are needed: non verbis sed factis opus est

DEEP: (see "mysterious") **a.** abstruse; abysmal; cavernous; hermetic(al); penetrating; profound; recondite; subterranean; unfathomed; **n.** (see "depth") bottomless
-bosomed: **a.** bathycolpian; pneumatic
-seated: **a.** adamant; chronic; confirmed; habitual; ingrained; inveterate; irradicable; obstinate; subterranean

DEEPEST *distress, from:* **n.** *de profundis*

DEEPNESS: (see "depth") **n.** abstrusity; profundity

DEFACE: see "disfigure"

DEFAME: (see "libel") **v.** asperse; calumniate; denigrate; disparage; malign; revile; slander; sully; traduce; vilify; **n.** DEFAMATION: aspersion; denigration; **a.** DEFAMATORY: calumnious; denigratory; slanderous; libelous

DEFEAT: (see "baffle") **v.** checkmate; conquer; frustrate; nullify; overcome; overthrow; subjugate; surmount; **n.** bouleversement; debacle; defeasance; discomfiture; downfall; frustration; labefaction; overthrow; repulse; subjugation; Waterloo
fear of: **n.** defeatism; **a. or n.** defeatist

DEFECT: (see "blemish" and "weakness") **n.** deficiency; foible; handicap; impediment; lacuna; shortcoming
because of a: **adv.** *propter defectum*
free of: (see "flawless") **a.** immaculate

DEFECTIVE: (see "imperfect") **a.** deficient; impedimental; incomplete; infelicitous; insufficient; lacunal; lacunar; *manqué;* mediocre; unsound; **n.** DEFECTIVENESS: defectibility
biologically: **a.** dysgenic

DEFENSE: **n.** aegis; apologia; argument; bulwark; extenuation; justification; (**pl.** apologetics; apologiae) **a.** DEFENSELESS: exposed; impotent; vulnerable; **n.** DEFENSELESSNESS· impotence; impotency; vulnerability; **a.** DEFENSIBLE: see "reasonable"
incapable of: (see "defenseless") **a.** indefensible; inexcusable; unjustifiable; untenable
means of: **n.** armament; (**pl.** armamen-

taria) ; *matériel;* muniment ; munitions ;
weaponry
  position for: **n.** *en garde*
  systematic, as of a doctrine or particular
  action(s) : **n.pl.** apologetics

DEFER : **v.** capitulate ; continue ; intermit ;
postpone ; prorogue ; surrender ; temporize ;
n. continuance ; prorogation

DEFERENCE : **n.** capitulation ; deferentiality ; devoir ; fealty ; homage ; humility ;
obeisance ; veneration ; **a.** DEFEREN-
TIAL : reverential ; venerative

DEFIANT : (**see** "bold") **a.** antagonistic ;
audacious ; challenging ; insolent ; recalcitrant ; refractory ; **n.** DEFIANCE : audacity ; challenge ; confrontation ; effrontery ; impudence ; opposition ; refractoriness ; temerity

DEFICIENT : (**see** "defective") **a.** mediocre ; **n.** DEFICIENCY : dearth ; *faiblesse;* foible ; handicap ; impediment ; imperfection ; inadequacy ; lacuna ; *manqué;*
ullage ; weakness
  biologically or racially: **a.** dysgenic

DEFILE : **v.** befoul ; contaminate ; pollute ;
ravish ; tarnish ; violate ; vitiate ; **a.** DE-
FILED : contaminated ; maculate ; polluted ; vitiated ; **n.** DEFILEMENT : contamination ; corruption ; pollution

DEFINE : **v.** circumscribe ; delineate ; diagnose ; diagnosticate ; distinguish ; identify ;
interpret
  what is to be (defined) : **n.** definiendum
  what serves to: **n.** defimens

DEFINING *technical terms, science of:* **n.**
orismology ; **a.** orismological

DEFINITE : **a.** absolute ; circumscribed ;
cogent ; definitive ; determinate ; determinative ; dogmatic(al) ; explicit ; material ;
mathematical ; objective ; particular ; positive ; tangible ; unqualified ; **n.** DEFI-
NITENESS : (de)finitude ; finality ; inevitability ; precision ; tangibility

DEFLATED : **a.** kaput

DEFRAUD : (**see** "cheat") **v.** cozen ; victimize ; **n.** DEFRAUDATION : cozenage ; defraudment

DEFY : **see** "oppose"

DEGENERATE : (**see** "decay") **a.** cor-
rupt(ed) ; devitalized ; effete ; retrograde ;
n. DEGENERACY : *abâtardissement;*
declination ; degeneration ; profligacy ; retrogression

DEGRADE : (**see** "debase") **v.** demean ; demote ; denigrate ; humble ; humiliate ; im-
brute ; pejorate ; relegate ; **n.** DEGRADA-
TION : debasement ; declination ; humiliation ; pejoration ; squalidity ; squalor ; **a.**
DEGRADING : (**see** "dishonorable") humiliating ; humiliative ; ignoble ; ignominious ; menial ; mortifying ; sordid ; squalid

DEGREE : **see** "measure"
  bachelor's: **a. or n.** baccalaureate

DEHUMANIZE : **v.** automate ; automatize ;
barbarize ; brutalize ; mechanize ; robotize

DEIFY : (**see** "exalt") **v.** apotheosize ;
canonize ; enshrine ; hallow ; sanctify ; spiritualize ; transcend ; transfigure ; **n.** DE-
IFICATION : apotheosis ; canonization ;
sanctification ; transfiguration

DEITY : **see** "god"
  evil: **n.** (**see** "devil") Ahriman ; caco-
d(a)emon
  good: **n.** agathod(a)emon ; ormuzd
  local: **n.** numen

DEJECT : **v.** discourage ; dishearten ; dispirit ; **a.** DEJECTED : abased : *à la mort;*
disconsolate ; disheartened ; dispirited ; funereal ; humbled ; inconsolable ; inconso-
late ; melancholic ; melancholy ; prostrate ;
n. DEJECTION : **see** "depression" **and**
"gloominess"

DELAY : **v.** continue ; defer ; impede ; postpone ; procrastinate ; protract ; retard ;
temporize ; **n.** armistice ; continuance ;
cunctation ; deferment ; detention ; impediment ; moratorium ; obstructionism ; postponement ; procrastination ; protraction ;
respite ; retardation ; suspension ; temporization ; **a.** DELAYING : impedimental ;
obstructive ; procrastinating ; procrastinatory ; protractive
  inexcusable: **n.** laches
  there's danger in: periculum in morâ
  without: **adv.** instanter ; *sine morâ*

DELEGATE : **v.** commission ; commit ; de-
pute ; **n.** commissioner ; deputy ; representative ; surrogate ; **a.** DELEGATED : dep-
uted ; substitutionary ; vicarial ; vicarious

DELIBERATE: **v.** excogitate; meditate; ponder; **a.** (see "intentional") calculated; considered; premeditated; studied; **n.** DELIBERATION: attention; deliberateness; excogitation; ponderation; premeditation; reflection

DELICACY: **n.** *bonne bouche;* confection; *délicatesse;* ethereality; fragility; *friandise;* kickshaw; tidbit
extreme: **n.** fastidiousness; meticulosity; overniceness; overnicety; preciosity; squeamishness

DELICATE: (**see** "dainty") **a.** epicene; ethereal; fastidious; fragile; overnice; precarious; refined; sensitive; squeamish; superfine; uncertain

DELICIOUS: (**see** "appetizing") **a.** ambrosiac; ambrosial; delectable; delightful; enchanting; esculent; nectarean; nectareous; palatable; savory

DELIGHT: (**see** "charm") **n.** delectation; ecstasy; exuberance; exultation; festivity; gratification; jubilation; merriment; oblectation; rapture; ravishment; transport; **a.** DELIGHTFUL: delectable; delicious; Edenic; entrancing; felicitous; gratifying; luscious; paradisiacal

DELIRIOUS: **a.** frantic; frenetic(al); maniac(al); phrenetic(al); rabid; **n.** DELIRIUM: **see** "frenzy"

DELIVERANCE: **n.** atonement; emancipation; exoneration; extrication; liberation; manumission; reclamation; redemption; salvation; **a.** emancipative; extricable; redemptive; redemptory; salvatory; salvific

DELUDE: (**see** "deceive") **v.** bamboozle; circumvent; cozen; mislead; victimize; **n.** DELUSION: (**see** "deception") artifice; chimera; circumvention; cozenage; hallucination; *ignis fatuus;* illusion; phantasm(agoria); phantasma; (**pl.** phantasmata); wile; will-of-the-wisp; **a.** DELUSIVE: beguiling; deceptive; delusional; delusory; fallacious; phantasmagoric(al); unrealistic

DEMAGOGUE: **n.** ochlocrat; rabblerouser; **a.** DEMAGOGIC(AL) rabblerousing; **n.** DEMAGOGISM: demagogery; demagogy

DEMAND: (**see** "pray") **v.** expostulate; importune; necessitate; **a.** DEMANDING: (**see** "persistent") arduous; clamorous; exacting; importunate; onerous; taxing; vociferous

DEMOCRATIC: **a.** egalitarian; equalitarian; **n.** democratization; egalitarianism; *égalité;* popularization

DEMON(S): **see** "devil"
abode of all: **n.** pandemonium; **a.** pandemoniac(al)
like or pert. to: **a.** demoniac(al); demonic(al); fiendish; frantic; frenzied
lore of: **n.** diablerie; diabology
worship of: **n.** demonolatry

DEMONSTRATION: **n.** apod(e)ixis; effusion; effusiveness; exhibition; manifestation; **v.** DEMONSTRATE: exhibit; manifest; promulgate; reflect; **a.** DEMONSTRATIVE: (**see** "theatrical") apod(e)ictic(al); deictic; effusive; epideictic; exhibitive; gushing; overflowing; probative; unreserved; unrestrained
capable of: **a.** apodictic(al)

DEMORALIZING: **see** "corrupt"

DEMOTE: (**see** "depreciate") **v.** denigrate; minify; minimize; pejorate; **n.** DEMOTION: denigration; pejoration; relegation

DENIAL: **n.** (ab)negation; denegation; disaffirmance; disaffirmation; disavowal; disclaimer; renunciation; repudiation; **a.** disclamatory; elenc(h)tic; renunciative; renunciatory
self-: **see under** "self"
that admits or involves affirmative implication: **n.** negative pregnant

DENOUNCE: (**see** "censure") **v.** abrade; comminate; delate; denunciate; excoriate; inveigh; lambaste; stigmatize

DENSE: **see** "stupid"

DENUNCIATION(S): (**see** "accusation") **n.** anathema; commination; diatribe; fulmination; invective; vituperation; **a.** DENUNCIATORY: anathematic(al); comminatory; denunciative; fulminous; vituperative
shout or thunder forth: **v.** fulminate; **a.** fulminous; **n.** fulmination

75

DENY: (see "denial") v. abjure; (ab)negate; disclaim; disown; gainsay; renege; repudiate
   not possible to: a. incontrovertible; irrefrangable; irrefutable

DEPENDABLE: a. authentic; authoritative; calculable; inerrable; inerrant; inerratic; infallible; predictable; trustworthy; yeomanly; n. see "reliability"

DEPENDANCE: n. reliance; relativity; succorance

DEPENDENT: a. adjective; adjectival; auxiliary; circumstantial; collateral; contingent; derivative; subsidiary; succursal
   mutually: a. complementary; symbiotic(al)
   servile: n. minion

DEPLORABLE: (see "wretched") a. calamitous; contemptible; despicable; disreputable; execrable; grievous; lamentable; odious; shocking; unfortunate; n. DEPLORATION: bewailment; lamentation

DEPORTMENT: (see "bearing") n. address; behavior; comportment; demeanor; mien

DEPOSIT: (see "sediment") n. deposition

DEPRAVE: v. corrupt; demoralize; depreciate; malign; pervert; pollute; a. DEPRAVED: (see "lewd") degenerate; dissolute; Neronian; putrid; vitiated; n. DEPRAVITY: degeneracy; demoralization; iniquity; putridity; turpitude

DEPRECIATE: (see "demote") v. denigrate; deprecate; disparage; minify; minimize; pejorate; revile; traduce; undervalue; vilify; vilipend; n. DEPRECIATION: denigration; disparagement; pejoration

DEPRESS: v. degrade; deject; dishearten; dispirit; humble; a. DEPRESSED: (see "sad") *à la mort;* dejected; dispirited; downcast; melancholic; vaporish; a. DEPRESSING: dispiriting; melancholy; *triste*

DEPRESSION: n. dejection; dispiritedness; doldrums; downswing; humiliation; mortification; nadir; *taedium vitae; tristesse*

greatest depth of: n. nadir
of spirit(s) n. melancholia; melancholy; (pl. doldrums; megrims)

DEPRIVATION *of authority:* n. deposition; dispossession; divestation; divestiture

DEPRIVING, *or tending to:* a. divestive; privative

DEPTH(S): n. abstrusity; acumen; acuteness; penetration; perspicacity; profundity
   great: (see "deep") n. profundity
   out of the: adv. *de profundis*

DEPUTY: (see "delegate") n. surrogate; representative

DERANGED: (see "disordered") a. *détraqué;* maniac(al); psychopathic

DERISION: n. asteism; burlesk; burlesque; caricature; contumely; denigration; irrision; ridicule; a. DERISIVE: ironical; irrisory; sarcastic; sardonic; satiric(al); scurrilous

DERIVATION: (see "descent" and "lineage") n. epiphenomenon; etiology; etymology; genesis; lineage; pedigree; provenance; stemma; a. DERIVATIVE: derivational; epiphenomenal; etiological; secondary; supplemental

DESCARTE'S *philosophy:* n. *cogito ergo sum*

DESCENDANT(S): n. issue; progeny; posterity; (s)cion; (pl. *les arrière-neveux*)

DESCENT: (see "derivation") n. ancestry; declension; declination; declivity; degradation; extraction; lineage; origination; pedigree; phylum; stemma; a. declinatory; declivitous
   connect by: v. apparent; n. apparentation; derivation
   fr. promising to disappointing: n. anticlimax; bathos; a. anticlimactic(al); bathetic
   line of: n. ancestry; lineage; pedigree; a. phyletic
   sudden: n. anticlimax; a. anticlimactic(al); bathetic
   thru father: a. patrilineal; patrilinear
   thru mother: a. matrilineal; matrilinear

DESCRIPTION : **n.** delineation; depiction; portraiture; portrayal; portrayment; **v.** DESCRIBE : delineate; depict; portray *vivid picturesque:* **n.** hypotyposis

DESCRIPTIVE : **a.** delineative; descriptory; illuminating; illuminative; picturesque
list: **n.** *catalogue raisonné*

DESECRATION : (**see** "debasement") **n.** defilement; profanation; violation; vulgarization; **a.** profanatory

DESERT : **v.** abandon; abdicate; abscond; absquatulate; decamp; elope; forsake; renege; **n.** DESERTER : apostate; renegade; turncoat; **n.** DESERTION : abandonment; abdication; abrogation; abscondence; absentation; absquatulation; apostasy; defection; renunciation; tergiversation
a cause, party, etc.: **v.** apostasize; tergiversate

DESERVED : **a.** condign; merited; warranted

DESIGN : (**see** "purpose") **n.** arrangement; decoration; delineation; intendment; motif; scheme; DESIGNING : **see** "crafty"
evidence of in nature: **n.** teleology; **a.** teleological

DESIGNATE : **v.** circumscribe; identify; nominate; signify; specify; stigmatize; stipulate; **n.** DESIGNATION : (**see** "name") assignment; circumscription; connotation; nomination; specification; stipulation

DESIRABLE : (**see** "attractive") **a.** advantageous; advisable; appetible; appetitious; desiderative; expedient; optative; optimal; orective
less than: **a.** suboptimal; **a. or n.** suboptimum

DESIRE : **v.** covet; crave; desiderate; **n.** appetency; appetibility; appetite; appetition; aspiration; desideration; (**pl.** desiderata) ; Eros; inclination; orexis; passion; proclivity; propensity
appealing to: **a.** appetible; appetitive; **n.** appetibility
ardent: **n.** aspiration; desiderium; **a.** aspirational; desiderative
expressing: **a.** optative

habitual or uncontrollable: **n.** cacoethes
having great: **a.** gluttonous; insatiable; omnivorous; voracious; **n. see** "gluttony"
innate: **n.** conatus
lack of: **n.** inappetence
pert. to: **a.** appetitive; desiderative; epithumetic; orectic
sexual: **n.** concupiscence; Eros; libido
strong: **n.** appetency; appetition; desiderium; (**pl.** desiderata; desideria) ; **a.** appetitious
unsatisfied: **n.** insatiability; insatiety; **a.** insatiable
very weak: **n.** velleity

DESIRED, *something to be:* **n.** desideratum; desiderium; (**pl.** desiderata; desideria) ; optative

DESOLATE : (**see** "barren") **a.** dejected; *désolé;* melancholy; *triste*

DESPAIR : **n.** (**see** "depression") desperation; futility; hopelessness
expression of: **n.** *de profundis*
fashionable: **n.** *fin-de-siècle*
in: **adv.** *au désespoir;* **n.pl.** doldrums; megrims
never: **adv.** *nil desperandum*

DESPERATELY : **adv.** *à corps perdu;* appallingly; compelling; impetuously; indispensably; intensely; **a.** DESPERATE : (**see** "helpless") crucial; despondent; outrageous; overmastering; overpowering; **n.** DESPERATION : (**see** "despair") cruciality

DESPISABLE : **a.** contemptible; contemptuous; contumelious; despicable; execrable; leprous

DESPITE : **prep.** *malgré;* notwithstanding

DESPONDENT : **a.** disconsolate; discouraged; disheartened; dispirited; forlorn; hypochondriacal; melancholy; **n.** DESPONDENCY : apathetic inertia; dejection; dispiritment; hypochondriasis; melancholia; melancholy; (**pl.** doldrums; megrims)

DESPOT : **n.** anarch; autarch; authoritarian; autocrat; disciplinarian; martinet; rigorist; satrap; totalitarian; tyrant; **n.** DESPOTISM : absolutism; autocracy; totalitarianism; tyranny

DESPOTIC: **a.** absolute; absolutistic; anarchistic; arbitrary; autarchic(al); authoritarian; autocratic; dictatorial; dogmatic; domineering; hierarchic(al); imperative; imperious; Neronian; peremptory; rigorist(ic); totalitarian; tyrannical
official: **n.** satrap; totalitarian; **n.** satrapy

DESTINATION: (**see** "goal") **n.** terminus; *terminus ad quem*

DESTINY: (**see** "fate") **n.** doom; fortune
Hindu: **n.** karma
individual: **n.** *moira;* (**pl.** moirae)
of man, study or science of: **n.** eschatology; **a.** eschatological

DESTITUTE: (**see** "poor") **a.** impecunious; impoverished; indigent; **n.** DESTITUTION: (**see** "poverty") impecuniosity; impecuniousness; indigence; insolvency; mendicancy; pauperism; penury; squalor

DESTROY: **v.** annihilate; decapitate; deracinate; devastate; eradicate; exterminate; extirpate; immolate; **a.** DESTROYED: decimated; devastated; eradicated; kaput; **n.** DESTROYER: predator
large number: **v.** decimate; **n.** decimation

DESTRUCTION: **n.** annihilation; cataclysm; corrosion; demolition; deracination; devastation; dissolution; extinction; extirpation; immolation; invalidation; perdition
capacity for: **n.** destructivity
great or widespread: **n.** catastrophe; cataclysm; *götterdämmerung;* holocaust
malicious, of materials, machinery, etc.: **v. or n.** sabotage
place of: **see** "hell"

DESTRUCTIVE: (**see** "deadly") **a.** annihilative; annihilatory; baneful; corrosive; deleterious; devastating; devastative; inimical; malignant; noxious; pernicious; ruinous; subversive
metabolism: **n.** catabolism
mutually: **a.** internecine
of life: (**see** "deadly") **a.** lethal; malignant; pernicious; pestilent; pestiferous

DETACHED: (**see** "separate") **a.** aloof; discrete; dissociated; disunited; enisled; fragmented; hermetic(al); insular; insulated; isolated; segregated; unaffiliated;

unbiased; **n.** DETACHMENT: abruption; dissociation; disunion; fragmentation; indifference; insularity; isolation; segregaton; unworldliness

DETAIL(S): **n.** circumstance; circumstantiality; meticulosity; minutia(e); particular(ity); specificality; **v.** particularize
excessively careful about: **a.** chromatic; finical; meticulous; minutiose; minutious; picayune; rabbinic(al); scrupulous
small: **n.** minutia; (**pl.** inconsequentia; minutiae; particularities; trivia[lities])

DETECT: **v.** apprehend; ascertain; descry; discern; elicit; unmask; **n.** DETECTION: ascertainment; discernment; discovery; elicitation; revelation; **a.** DETECTIVE: discerning; revelative; revelatory

DETERIORATION: (**see** "declination") **n.** decadence; declension; degeneration; degenerescence; *dégringolade; délabrement;* labefaction; retrocession; retrogression; **a.** DETERIORATING: decadent; declensional; declinatory; degenerative; deteriorative; retrograde; retrogressive

DETERMINE: **v.** adjudicate; ascertain; dijudicate; foreordain; regulate; resolve; **n.** DETERMINATION: (**see** "decision") conclusion; impulsion; resoluteness; resolution
nature or cause: **v.** diagnosticate; **a.** diagnostic; pathognomonic(al)

DETERMINED (**or** DETERMINING): **a.** decisive; definitive; dominative; foreordained; immovable; indomitable; predestined; preemptory; resolute; resolved; tenacious; unalterable; unwavering
person: **n.** Trojan

DETEST: (**see** "hate" **and** "loathe"); **a.** DETESTABLE: (**see** "bad") abhorrent; abominable; anathematic(al); contemptible; despicable; execrable; grievous; imprecatory; loathsome; odious; **n.** DETESTATION: abhorrence; abomination; anathema; contempt; despicability; loathsomeness; odium
person or thing (*detested*): **n.** abomination; anathema

DETRACT: (**see** "debase") **v.** calumniate; defame; denigrate; derogate; disparage; minify; minimize; **a.** DETRACTING:

denigratory; derogative; derogatory; disparaging; **n.** DETRACTION: (**see** "censure") calumny; denigration; derogation; disparagement; subtraction

DETRIMENTAL: (**see** "adverse") **a.** baneful; deleterious; hurtful; inimical; injurious; malefic; malignant; nocuous; noisome; pernicious; prejudicial

DEVELOP: **v.** burgeon; differentiate; evolve; effloresce; expound; flourish; incubate; maturate; mature
 fail to: **v.** abort

DEVELOPED: **a.** calminant; differentiated; matured
 in course of being: **adv.** *in statu nascendi;* **a.** aborning; burgeoning; florescent; maturescent; nascent; parturient
 prematurely: **a.** precocious; **n.** precocity

DEVELOPMENT: (**see** "advancement") **n.** consummation; differentiation; evolution; florescence; incubation; maturation; maturescence; maturity; morphosis; ontogeny
 capable of: **a.** viable; **n.** viability
 in course of: **see under** "developed"
 mode of, as organism or part: **n.** morphosis; **a.** morphotic
 path or line of: **n.** trajectory
 period of in young: **n.** puberty; pubescence; **a.** maturescent; pubertal; pubescent

DEVIATING: (**see** "devious" **and** "straying") **a.** aberrant; circuitous; divaricative; divergent; excursional; excursionary; excursive; parenthetic(al); serpentine; tortuous; **n.** DEVIATION: aberrance; aberration; circuity; detour; divergence; divagation; eccentricity; intransigence; sinuosity; tangency; tortuosity
 fr. previous course: **a.** aberrant; tangent; **n.** aberration; tangency
 fr. principles or rules: **a.** (ab)errant; aberrative; heteroclite; obliquitous; **n.** deviate; deviationist; heteroclite

DEVICE: **n.** accouterment; artifice; contrivance; insigne; (**pl.** insignia); invention; machination; stratagem

DEVIL(S): **n.** Apollyon; Beelzebub; Belial; cacod(a)emon; Diabolus; incubus (**pl.** incubi); Lucifer; Mephistopheles; succubus (**pl.** succubi)

advocate: **n.** *advocatus diaboli*
crafty and malevolent: **n.** Mephistopheles; **a.** Mephistophelian
follower of: **n.** diabolonian
govt. by: **n.** diabolarchy; diabolocracy
one possessed of: **n.** energumen
study of: **n.** demonology; demonologist; diabology
 to pay, the: **n.** *diable à quatre; faire le diable à quatre*
 work of: **n.** diablerie
 worshipper of: **n.** diabolist; **n.** demonolatry

DEVILISH: (**see** "fiendish") **a.** demoniac(al); demonic(al); diabolic(al); diabolonian; ghoulish; hellish; infernal; Luciferian; malicious; Mephistophelian; Satanic(al); saturnine; **n.** DEVILTRY (**or** DEVILRY) diablerie; diabolism

DEVIOUS: (**see** "roundabout") **a.** ambagious; anfractuous; circuitous; labyrinthian; labyrinthine; louche; oblique; perverse; serpentine; sinister; sinuate; sinuous; tortuous; unscrupulous; **n.** DEVIOUSNESS: (**see** "deviation") anfractuosity; circuity; circumbendibus; indirection; sinuosity; tortuosity

DEVISE: **v.** bequeath; contrive; fabricate; machinate; premeditate
 with evil intent: **v.** machinate; **n.** machination

DEVITALIZE: **v.** debilitate; desiccate; disembowel; emasculate; enervate; eviscerate; exenterate; **n.** DEVITALIZATION: see "weakness"

DEVOTEE: (**see** "follower") **n.** adherent; aficionado; (**fem.** aficionada); amateur; apostle; enthusiast; fanatic; liege man; minion; votary; zealot
 fanatical or hired: **n.** energumen; mercenary; minion

DEVOTION: (**see** "worship") **n.** allegiance; enthusiasm; fealty; fidelity; loyalty; piety; reverence
 fervent: **n.** fanaticism; fetishism; zealotry; **a.** fetishistic; zealous
 to church, excessive: **n.** ecclesiolatry; religiosity; **a.** religiose

DEVOURING: **a.** annihilatory; consuming; corrosive; edacious; gluttonous; voracious

DEVOUT: **a.** devotional; pietistic(al); religiose; sacrosanct; sanctimonious
hypocritically: **a.** pietistic(al); religiose; sanctimonious; **n.** piosity; religiosity

DEW, *generating:* **a.** roriferous
rel. to: **a.** roric

DEXTERITY: **see** "agility"

DIAGNOSE: **v.** diagnosticate; identify; **a.** DIAGNOSTIC: distinctive; pathognomonic(al); prodromal; symptomatic

DIAGRAM: **n.** schema; (**pl.** schemata); **a.** diagrammatic(al); schematic

DIALECT(S), *local or provincial:* **n.** cant; colloquialism; jargon; vernacular(ism); vernacularity
student or study of: **n.** dialectologist; dialoctology; **a.** dialectological

DIALOGUE: **n.** causerie; collocution; colloquy; confabulation; interlocution
art of discussion and reason by: **n.** dialectics; **a.** dialectic(al)
pert. to: **a.** dialectic(al); dialogic; dialogistic; interlocutory

DIAMETRICALLY *opposite:* **a.** antipodal; antipodic; antithetic(al); **n.** antipode; antithesis

DIAMOND(S), *like in luster:* **a.** adamantine
to set with: **v.** diamondize
yielding: **a.** diamondiferous

DIARY, *private:* **n.** *journal intime*

DICE, *lowest number in:* **n.** ambsace

DICTATOR: **n.** anarch; authoritarian; autocrat; caudillo; commissar; despot; man on horseback; oligarch; tyrant; **a.** DICTATORIAL: arbitrary; authoritarian; autocratic; cavalier; despotic; doctrinaire; dogmatic(al); domineering; hierarchic(al); imperative; imperious; magisterial; oracular; overbearing; peremptory; totalitarian; **n.** DICTATORSHIP: absolutism; autocracy; Caesarism; monopolization; totalitarianism

DICTION: **n.** enunciation; phraseology; verbiage; vocabulary
bad: **n.** cacology

DICTIONARY, *author or compiler of:* **n.** lexicographer; lexicography
of names and terms: **n.** nomenclature; onomasticon
pert. to: **a.** lexicographic(al); Websterian

DIE *has been cast: jacta alea est*
we who are about to, salute: morituri te salutamus

DIET: **see** "menu"

DIFFER: **see** "disagree"

DIFFERENCE(S): (**see** "controversy")
n. cleavage; differentia; discrepancy; discrimination; disparity; dissention; dissimilarity; dissimilitude; dissonance; distinction; divergence; diversity; heterogeneity; heterology; nuance; incongruity; inequality; (**pl.** differentiae)
in nature or kind: **n.** allogeneity; heterogeneity; **a.** allogeneous; heterogeneous
process of perceiving or expressing: **n.** differentiation
slight degree of: **n.** nuance
w/ the respective differences having been considered: mutatis mutandis

DIFFERENT: **a.** antipodal; antithetic(al); disparate; dissimilar; divergent; diverse; heterogeneous; heterologous; incongruent; incongruous; sundry
in operation or effect: **a.** heteropathic
quality or state of being: **n.** alterity; antipodes; antithesis; heterogeneity; incongruity

DIFFERING: **a.** antagonistic; differential; discordant; discrepant; discriminative; dissenting; dissonant; diverse; heterogeneous; incongruous; inharmonious; unharmonious
fr. standard(s) or norm: (**see** "impropriety") **a.** heteromorphic; **n.** heteromorphism; heteromorphosis; mutation; sport

DIFFICULT: (**see** "hard") **a.** arduous; devastating; exacting; formidable; frenetic; hectic; Herculean; incorrigible; intractable; intricate; involved; laborious; murderous; onerous; operose; overwhelming; perplexing; perverse; scabrous; strenuous; toilsome; unaccommodating; unmanageable; unyielding; vicissitudinous

position: **n.** dilemma; quagmire; quandary

problem: **n.** dilemma; entanglement; Gordian knot

route, passage, or series of experiences: **n.** *via dolorosa*

DIFFICULTY: (**see** "problem") **n.** dilemma; embarrassment; embroilment; entanglement; Gordian knot; imbroglio; impediment; maelstrom; obstacle; predicament; riptide; quagmire; quandary; strenuosity; vicissitude; vortex
in great: **adv.** *in extremis*
without: **adv.** *sans peine*

DIFFUSE: (**see** "wordy") **a.** osmotic; prolix; verbose; **n.** DIFFUSION: dispersion; dissemination; osmosis; prolixity; promulgation

DIG *up:* **v.** disentomb; disinter; exhume; **n.** exhumation

DIGESTION: **n.** assimilation; metabolism; **v.** DIGEST: assimilate; codify; comprehend; metabolize; **n.** (**see** "summary") abridgement; breviary; compilation; conspectus; pandect; prospectus; summation
having good: **a.** eupeptic; **n.** eupepsia
pert. to: **a.** peptic

DIGIT, *having but one* (*toe, finger, claw*): **a.** monodactylous
having six: **n.** hexadactylism

DIGNITY: **n.** courtliness; decorum; eminence; ennoblement; gentility; grandeur; lordliness; majesty; nobility; solemnity; stateliness; (**pl.** amenities; civilities; convenances; conventions; decora; [the] proprieties); **v.** DIGNIFY: (**see** "exalt") aggrandize; ennoble; nobilitate; pedestal; **a.** DIGNIFIED: (**see** "stately") august; eminent; grandiose; imperial; magisterial; togated
affront to: **n.** *lèse majesté*
beneath one's: **a.** *infra dignitatem* (**abb.** infra dig.)
extreme or exaggerated: **n.** imperialism; magistrality; pomposity; pompousness; pontificality; pontification
high: **n.** sublimity
to maintain: *se faire valoir*

DIGRESS: **v.** detour; deviate; divaricate, divagate; diverge; meander; parenthesize; **n.** DIGRESSION: aberration; apostro-

phe; detour; discursion; divagation; divarication; ecbole; excursus; excursion; irrelevancy; parenthesis; tangency; tangent; **a.** DIGRESSIVE: aberrant; apostrophic; circuitous; devious; discursive; divaricative; divergent; excursional; excursionary; excursive; parenthetic(al); sinuous; tangent(i)al; Thackerayan; tortuous; vagrant
in rhetoric: **n.** ecbole; excursus
in speech or writing(*s*)*:* **n.** apostrophe; excursus; **a.** apostrophic; excursive

DILAPIDATED: **a.** beggarly; disreputable; retrogressive; tatterdemalian; **n.** DILAPIDATION: see "decay"

DILEMMA: (**see** "predicament") **n.** nonplus; quagmire; quandary; **a.** DILEMMATIC: nonplussed

DILIGENT: **a.** assiduous; indefatigable; industrious; operose; painstaking; persevering; sedulous; solicitous; steadfast; **n.** DILIGENCE: (**see** "attention") assiduity; operosity; perseverance; sedulity; steadfastness

DILUTED: **a.** attenuated; homeopathic

DIM: (**see** "obscure") **v.** becloud; befog; eclipse; obfuscate; obnubilate; obscurify; **a.** caliginous; crepuscular; fuliginous; lackluster; opaque; **n.** DIMNESS: crepuscle; *demi-jour;* fuliginosity; nebulosity; obscuration

DIMINISHMENT: **n.** attenuation; declination; depreciation; diminuendo; diminution; extenuation; regression; retrenchment; **v.** DIMINISH: abate; attenuate; depreciate; dwindle; extenuate; palliate; recede, regress; retrench; **a.** DIMINISHING: ablatitious; decrescendo; diminuendo; extenuatory; regressive
in volume or force: **n. or a.** diminuendo

DIN: see "uproar"

DINING *hall:* **n.** refectory; *salle à manger*
science or art of: **n.** aristology

DINNER, *after:* **a.** postcibal; postprandial
before: **a.** precibal; preprandial

DIPLOMATIC *corps:* **n.** *corps diplomatique*

DIRE: (see "deadly") **a.** awesome; calamitous; catastrophic(al); cheerless; deplorable; desolate; desperate; disastrous; dispiriting; extreme; grievous; horrendous; horrific; implacable; mortal; overpowering

DIRECT: **v.** administer; focus; superintend; superscribe; supervise; **a.** absolute; categorical; explicit; immediate; pertinent; positive; unconditional; undeviating; unequivocal; **n.** DIRECTNESS: immediacy

DIRECTION: (see "control") **n.** command; inclination; objective; presidence; superintendence; superscription; supervision
    maintenance of: **n.** directionality
    reverse or change: **v.** commutate; **n.** commutation
    to find right: **v.** orientate; **n.** orientation

DIRECTLY *opposite:* (see "diametrically opposite") **a.** antipodal; diametrical

DIRECTOR: **n.** administrant; comptroller; conductor; regisseur; superintendent
    as opera: **n.** impresario

DIRGE: see "funeral ode or hymn"

DIRTY: **a.** Augean; bawdy; despicable; dishonorable; disreputable; excrementitious; feculent; filthy; immund; insanitary; ordurous; putrid; saprogenic; sordid; squalid; stercoraceous; unsportsmanlike; **n.** DIRTINESS: (see "filthiness") immundity; putridity; sordidness; squalidity; squalor

DISABLE: (see "weaken") **v.** disqualify; handicap; incapacitate; **a.** DISABLED: incapacitated; kaput; **adv.** *hors de combat;* **n.** DISABILITY: disadvantage; handicap; incapacity; incapacitation; invalidity
    become (disabled): **v.** founder

DISAGREE: (see "dispute") **v.** contradict; contravene; **a.** DISAGREEING (or DISAGREEABLE): (see "discordant") antagonistic; disputatious; dissentient; dissenting; dissentious; dissentive; dissident; dissonant; distasteful; incompatible; incongruous; inconsistent; inconsonant; inharmonious; unharmonious; unpalatable;

unpleasant; unsavory; **n.** DISAGREEMENT: (see "breach") contravention; *désagrément;* disharmony; disparity; disputation; dissentience; dissidence; dissonance; embroilment; entanglement; imbroglio; incompatibility; incongruity; inconsonance

DISAPPEARANCE: **n.** abscondence; depletion; diminution; evanishment; evanition

DISAPPOINTMENT: (see "defeat") **n.** anticlimax; bathos; contretemps; frustration; **a.** DISAPPOINTING: anticlimactic(al); bathetic; suboptimal

DISAPPROVAL: **n.** admonition; censure; condemnation; deprecation; disapprobation; reprobation; **v.** DISAPPROVE: (see "reject") censure; condemn; deprecate; discommend; discountenance; disparage; reprobate; **a.** DISAPPROVING: admonitory; censorious; deprecatory; deprecative; disapprobative; disapprobatory; **adv.** *en mauvaise odeur*
    expression of: **adv.** or **n.** *à bas*

DISARRAY: (see "confusion") **n.** derangement; disarrangement; discomfiture; hodge-podge; mish-mash

DISASTER: **n.** adversity; calamity; cataclysm; catastrophe; debacle; holocaust; misadventure; mischance; **a.** DISASTROUS: calamitous; cataclysmal; cataclysmic; catastrophal; catastrophic(al); unpropitious
    heightened point of action leading to: **n.** catastasis; epitasis
    impending: **n.** imminence; sword of Damocles
    sudden great: **n.** catastrophe; debacle; holocaust (*esp. fire*)

DISAVOWAL: **n.** disclamation; renunciation; repudiation

DISBELIEVER: (see "skeptic") **n.** agnostic; aporetic; dissenter; dissident; doubting Thomas; giaour; heretic; infidel; nullifidian; pyrrhonist; recusant; skeptic; theophobist; **n.** DISBELIEF: (see "doubt") incredibility; incredulity; misbelief; miscreance; skepticism; **a.** DISBELIEVING: see "skeptical"
    (*freethinker:*) **n.** latitudinarian

DISCARD(ING): (see "abandon") **n.** abandonment; banishment; defenestration; repudiation

DISCERNMENT: **n.** acumen; astucity; clairvoyance; clear-sightedness; detection; discrimination; judgment; penetration; perception; perspicacity; profundity; sagacity; sapiency; telegnosis; **a.** DISCERNING: analytical; astucious; astute; clairvoyant; discriminatory; discriminating; judicious; knowledgeable; penetrating; penetrative; perspicacious; sagacious; trenchant
   impaired: **n.** astigmatism; impalpability; myopia; **a.** astigmatic(al); myopic

DISCHARGE: (see "dismissal") **n.** acquittance; elimination; profluvium

DISCIPLE: (see "follower" **and** "learner") **n.** adherent; apostle; proselyte; satellite; sectary; sectator; votary; **a.** DISCIPULAR: apostolic(al)

DISCIPLINARIAN, *strict:* **n.** martinet; precisian; rigorist; sabbatarian; tyrant

DISCIPLINARY: **a.** ascetic; austere; castigatory; disciplinatory; penitentiary; punitive
   course or conduct: **n.** ascesis; asceticism; self-mortification

DISCIPLINE: **v.** castigate; chasten; chastise; **n.** (see "punishment") approach; castigation; chastenment; chastisement; method; self-restraint
   subject to rigid: **v.** hierarchize; regiment

DISCIPLINED, *hardy:* **a.** *aguerri;* Spartan(ic)
   self-: **a.** ascetic; **n.** ascesis; ascetic(ism); self-mortification

DISCLOSURE: **n.** apocalypse; divulgation; divulgence; exposition; exposure; manifestation; publication; revelation; **a.** DISCLOSING: expository; revelative; revelatory; **v.** DISCLOSE: (see "demonstrate") unbosom
   prophetic: **n.** apocalypse; revelation; **a.** apocalyptic(al); apostolic(al); revelatory

DISCOLORATION *from bruise:* **n.** ecchymosis; petechia(e)
   on skin: **n.** ecchymosis; macula; petechia(e); **a.** ecchymotic; petechial

DISCOMFORT: **n.** annoyance; chagrin; discomfiture; discomposure; disquietude; dysphoria; embarrassment; inquietude; malaise

DISCONNECTED: **a.** desultory; discrete; dissociated; disunited; fractional; rambling; staccato; **n.** DISCONNECTION: see "separation"

DISCONTENT(MENT): **n.** discomfiture; dissatisfaction; dysphoria; frustration; insubordination; malaise; sedition; **a.** DISCONTENTED: dissatisfied; insubordinate; malcontent; seditious; unsatisfied
   stirring up: **a.** insubordinate; rebellious; seditious; turbulent

DISCONTINUE: (see "pause") **v.** abandon; intermit; interrupt; sever; surcease; suspend; terminate; **n.** DISCONTINUANCE: (see "removal") cessation; desistance; intermission; interruption; surcease; termination
   from use: **v.** obsolesce; **n.** desuetude; obsolescence; **a.** archaic; obsolescent; obsolete
   or end a session: **v.** prorogue; **n.** prorogation; *sine die*

DISCORD: **n.** antagonism; *brouillerie;* cacophony; disharmony; disruption; dissension; dissonance; incongruity; inharmony; scission; variance; **a** DISCORDANT: (see "stubborn") absonant; cacophonous; contradictory; disputatious; dissociable; dissonant; gladiatorial; heterogeneous; incongruous; inconsonant; irreconcilable; quarrelsome
   goddess of: **n.** Eris
   harmony of (discordant harmony): **n.** *concordia discors*

DISCOURAGE: **v.** daunt; dishearten; dismay; dispirit; dissuade; intimidate; obstruct; **n.** DISCOURAGEMENT: (see "despondency") dissuasion

DISCOURSE: (see "lecture") **n.** conversation; descant; disquisition; dissertation; expiation; narration; treatise
   formal: **n.** disquisition

DISCOURTESY: **n.** brusqueness; *brusquerie;* contumely; disrespect; impoliteness; incivility; insuavity; inurbanity; profanation; **a.** DISCOURTEOUS: see "disrespectful"

DISCOVER: **v.** ascertain; descry; determine; disinter; exhume; unearth; **n.** DISCOVERER: Columbus; pathfinder; trailblazer
by careful exam.: **v.** expiscate; **n.** expiscation; **a.** expiscatory

DISCOVERY: **n.** ascertainment; detection; disclosure; revelation
accidental: **n.** serendipity; **a.** serendipitous
helping, guiding or serving to: **a.** heuristic

DISCRETION: **n.** circumspection; diplomacy; finesse; moderation; prudence; restraint; **a.** DISCREET: (**see** "cautious" **and** "prudent") circumspect(ive); judicious; politic; reticent; silentious; taciturn
age of: **n.** âge de raison
marked by notable: **a.** Solomonic

DISCUSSION(S): (**see** "conversation") **n.** argumentation; colloquium; colloquy; confabulation; disputation; disquisition; exposition; expostulation; seminar; symposium; (**pl.** symposia); **v.** DISCUSS: confabulate; deliberate; expostulate
formal: **n.** disquisition; (**pl.** dialectics; forensics)
incidental: **n.** excursus
informal: **n.** causerie
on subtle or debatable point: **n.** quodlibet
pert. to: **a.** dialectic; forensic; quodlibetic
preliminary: **n.** pourparler
Socratic type: **n.** dialectics; **a.** dialectic(al)

DISEASE(S): **n.** affection; affliction; ailment; distemper; indisposition; infirmity; malady; malignancy; morbus; pathology; pathosis; visitation; **a.** DISEASED: contaminated; malignant; morbid; morbific(al); morbose; leprous; pathological; peccant; unwholesome
after-effects of: **n.** residual(s) residuum; sequala(e); **a.** residual; sequential
bringing, carrying or infected w/: **a.** pestiferous; pestilent(ial)
carrier: **n.** vector
causing or capable of causing: **a.** morbific(al); pathogenetic; pathogenic; **n.** pathogenicity
characteristic of a particular: **a.** pathognomonic(al); symptomatic

classification of: **n.** nosography; nosology; pathology
description of: **n.** nosography; nosology; pathology
imaginary: **n.** malade imaginaire
increase in: **n.** anabasis; exacerbation; **a.** anabatic; **v.** exacerbate
infectious or contagious: **a.** zymogenic; zymogenous; zymotic
made up of various symptoms: **n.** syndrome
not capable of causing: **a.** apathogenic; nonpathogenic; physiological; sterile
origination and development of: **n.** pathogenesis; pathogenicity; pathogeny; **a.** pathogen(et)ic; pathological
place of origin or orig. location: **n.** nidus; situs
produced by physician or treatment: **a.** iatrogenic
shifting in body location: **n.** metastasis; **v.** metastasize; **a.** metastatic
sign(s) of: **n.** stigma; (**pl.** stigmata); symptomatology
simulation of: **n.** malingering; pathomimesis
stage when outcome doubtful: **n.** amphibolia
study of: **n.** pathology
study of symptoms of: **n.** diagnostics; semeiotics; symptomatology
symptoms of: **n.** symptomatology; syndrome; **a.** diagnostic; pathognomonic(al); semeiotic; symptomatic; symptomatologic(al); syndromic
w/o recognized cause: **a.** essential; idiopathic

DISFAVOR: **n.** detriment; disadvantage; disesteem; disrepute; odium; **a.** detrimental; disadvantageous; disreputable; odious

DISFIGURE: **v.** maim; mutilate; scarify; uglify; **n.** DISFIGUREMENT: defacement; disfiguration; mayhem; scarification; uglification

DISGRACE: **v.** stigmatize; **n.** (**see** "contempt") dishonor; disrepute; ignominy; infamy; obloquy; odium; opprobrium; stigma; turpitude; **a.** DISGRACEFUL: (**see** "disreputable") criminal; dishonorable; ignominious; indign; infamous; inglorious; notorious; obloquious; opprobrious; shameful; stigmatical; unbecoming
mark of: **n.** odium; opprobrium; stigma; (**pl.** stigmata)

DISGUISE: **v.** or **n.** camouflage; counterfeit; masquerade; **a.** DISGUISED: clandestine; covert; incognito; obscure; surreptitious; *travesti(e)*
  woman in: **n.** incognita

DISGUST: **v.** abominate; nauseate; **n.** abhorrence; abomination; antipathy; nausea; odium; repugnance; **a.** DISGUSTING: abhorrent; fulsome; loathsome; nauseating; *nauséeux;* odious; offensive; repugnant; repulsive; sickening; unpalatable; **adv.** *ad nauseam*
  to the point of: **adv.** *ad nauseam*

DISH, *main or principal:* **n.** *pièce de résistance; plat du jour*
  next to main: **n.** *entrée*
  side: **n.** entremet(s)

DISHARMONIOUS: (see "divisive") **a.** allometric; cacophonic; cacophonous; discordant; disharmonic(al); disputatious; dissident; dissociable; dissonant; incongruous; **n.** DISHARMONY: (see "disagreement") antagonism; cacophony; discord(ance); dissention; dissidence; dissonance; incongruity; variance

DISHONEST: (see "dishonorable" **and** "tricky") **a.** deceitful; disingenuous; duplicitous; fraudulent; ignominious; knavish; Machiavellian; mendacious; perfidious; roguish; sinister; sinuate; sinuous; surreptitious; treacherous; unscrupulous; **n.** DISHONESTY: dishonor; disingenuity; duplicity; improbity; indirection; indirectness; infamy; knavishness; perfidy; roguery; roguishness; sinuosity; unscrupulosity; villany

DISHONOR: **n.** disrepute; ignominy; improbity; infamy; obloquy; opprobrium; stigma; **a.** DISHONORABLE: (see "base" **and** "dishonest") despicable; disesteemed; disgraceful; disreputable; ignoble; ignominious; infamous; inglorious; obloquious

DISINCLINATION *to act:* (see "laziness") **n.** inertia; inertness; **a.** inertial

DISINTEGRATION: **n.** decentralization; decomposition; demoralization; dissolution; fragmentation; putrefaction; **a.** DISINTEGRATIVE: disintegrable; putrefactive

of society or personal standards: **n.** anomie

DISINTERESTED: **a.** candid; impassionate; impersonal; **n.** DISINTERESTEDNESS: inertia; objectivity; passivity
  adviser: **n.** *amicus curiae* (friend of the court)

DISJOIN(T): **v.** disarticulate; disarrange; discerp; dismember; luxate; **a.** DISJOINTED: disconnected; disordered; dissociated; inarticulate; incoherent; **n.** DISJOINTING: (see "separation") disarticulation; discerption; disjointure; dissociation

DISLIKE: (see "hate") **n.** abhorrence; alienation; antipathy; aversion; detestation; disaffection; disapprobation; disfavor; disinclination; displeasure; estrangement; hostility; odium; repugnance; **a.** DISLIKABLE: abhorrent; antipathetical; averse; odious; repugnant

DISLOCATION: **n.** disarticulation; displacement; disruption; luxation; **a.** see "displaced"

DISLOYAL: (see "disobedient" **and** "treacherous") **a.** disaffected; faithless; mutinous; perfidious; recreant; seditious; traitorous; unfaithful; **n.** DISLOYALTY: infidelity; perfidy; recreancy; sedition; traitorship; treachery; villainy
  person: **n.** apostate; conspirator; recreant; renegade; traitor; villain
  to country or govt.: **n.** anarchy; incivilism; traitorousness; treachery

DISMAL: (see "gloomy") **a.** Acheronian; Acherontic; calamitous; dispirited; dispiriting; funebrial; funebrous; funerary; funereal; lachrymose; lugubrious; melancholic; melancholy; **n.** DISMALITY: lugubrosity; melancholia

DISMAY: (see "fear") **n.** consternation; disenchantment; disillusionment; perturbation

DISMISSAL: **n.** *congé;* manumission
  from office: **n.** deprivation; divestation; divestiture

DISOBEDIENCE: **n.** insubjection; insubordination; intractableness; mutiny; perfidy; recusance; recusancy; refractoriness;

85

treachery; unruliness; **a.** DISOBEDI-ENT: (**see** "disloyal") insubmissive; insubordinate; intractable; mutinous; recalcitrant; recusant; refractory; unruly

DISORDER: (**see** "confusion") **n.** alarums and excursions; anarchism; anarchy; Babelism; Bedlam; bouleversement; brouhaha; chaos; disarrangement; discomposure; dishevelment; disorganization; distemper; embroilment; irregularity; pandemonium; turbulence; turmoil; **a.** DISORDERED: chaotic; dishevel(l)ed; disorganized; farraginous; immethodic(al); inchoate; inchoative; incoherent; pandemoniac(al); turbulent; unhinged; **a.** DISORDERLY: (**see** "riotous") inordinate
　in: **adv.** *à l'abandon*
　place of great: **n.** Bedlam; capharnaum; mare's nest; pandemonium
　wild: **n.** mania; pandemonium; **a.** maniac(al); pandemoniac(al)

DISORGANIZED: (**see** "disordered") **a.** deranged; disarranged; fragmental; fragmentary; indecisive; inveterate; unhinged; **n.** DISORGANIZATION: **see** "disorder"

DISOWN: **v.** abjure; disclaim; repudiate

DISPARAGING: **a.** denigrating; depreciatory; derogative; minimizing; pejorative; **n.** DISPARAGEMENT: denigration; deprecation; disgrace, indignity; meiosis; minimization; pejoration
　word or phrase: **n.** epithet; **a.** epithetical

DISPARATE: (**see** "different") **a.** unequal

DISPLACED: **a.** *dépaysé;* ectopic; luxated; **n. see** "dislocation"

DISPLACEMENT, *as a bone:* **n.** luxation

DISPLAY: **v.** disclose; manifest; ostentate; **n.** blazonry; *étalage;* exhibition; fanfare; manifestation; ostent(ation); pageant; panoply; pomp; spectacle
　colorful, rich (or empty): **n.** pageantry; panoply; **a. see** "showy" **and** "theatrical"

DISPLEASURE: **n.** annoyance; disapproval; discomposure; indignation; pique; umbrage; **a.** DISPLEASING: **see** "annoying"

DISPOSE *of, by killing or otherwise:* **v.** liquidate; **n.** liquidation

DISPOSED: (**see** "favorable") **a.** amenable; congenial; inclinable; inclinatory; suasive; tractable

DISPOSITION: (**see** "mood") **n.** administration; arrangement; character; diathesis; idiosyncrasy; inclination; liquidation; management; predisposition; proclivity; propensity

DISPOSSESS: **v.** commandeer; confiscate; expropriate; oust; sequester; usurp; **n.** DISPOSSESSION: abstraction; deprivation; divestiture; divestment; expropriation; ouster; sequestration; usurpation; **a.** DISPOSSESSED: (**see** "displaced") lumpen; uprooted

DISPROOF: **n.** confutation; refutation; **a.** DISPROVING: refutative; refutatory; **v.** DISPROVE: confute; controvert; rebut; refute

DISPROVED, *not capable of being:* **a.** incontrovertible; irrecusable; irrefutable

DISPUTE: **v.** contend; contest; contravene; controvert; polemize; **n.** DISPUTE (**or** DISPUTATION): (**see** "controversy") altercation; argument(ation); contravention; controversy; debate; dissension; invective; polemic; velitation; **a.** DISPUTATIOUS: (**see** "argumentative") controversial
　one who (disputes): **n.** controversalist; disputant; polemic
　practice of (disputation): **n.** dialectic(s); polemic(s); **a.** dialectic(al); polemic(al)
　subject to (dispute): **a.** contentious; controvertible; controversial; debatable; disputatious; polemic(al)

DISQUIET(UDE): **n.** agitation; anxiety; chemistry; dyspathy; dysphoria; excitement; ferment; restlessness; uneasiness; unrest; **a. see** "annoying"

DISREGARD: **see** "ignore"

DISREPUTABLE: (**see** "disgraceful") **a.** despicable; ignoble; ignominious; infamous; inglorious; notorious; opprobrious; squalid; unrespectable

DISRESPECTFUL: **a.** contemptuous; contumelious; derisive; despicable; discourteous; impertinent; impolite; infamous; opprobrious; scurrilous; uncivil; **n.** DISRESPECT: contumely; discourtesy; incivility; misesteem; profanation
to things held sacred: **a.** profanatory; profane; sacrilegious

DISRUPTION: **n.** cataclasm; intrigue; **a.** DISRUPTIVE: cataclasmic

DISSATISFACTION: **n.** disapprobation; discontent; displeasure; dissidence; **a.** DISSATISFIED: (**see** "discontented") dissentious; factious; mutinous

DISSENT: (**see** "disagree") **n.** cleavage; disagreement; dissidence; nonconcurrence; recusance; recusancy

DISSENTER: **n.** dissentient; dissident; recusant; **n.** DISSENSION: **see** "dissent"

DISSENTING: **a.** dissentient; dissentious; dissident; factious; heretical; nonconforming
with no one; **adv.** *nemine dissiente*

DISSIMILAR: **a.** anomalistic; anomalous; disparate; incongruous; heterogeneous; **n.** DISSIMILARITY: anomalism; anomaly; divergence; divergency; heterogeneity; unlikeness

DISSOLUTE: **see** "lewd"

DISSOLVE: **v.** abrogate; decompose; deliquesce; disintegrate; liquefy; **a.** DISSOLVING: deliquescent; liquefactive; **n.** (**see** "disintegration") deliquescence; liquefaction

DISTANCE, *seeing at, or knowledge of things at:* **n.** clairvoyance; telegnosis

DISTANT: (**see** "haughty" **and** "remote") **a.** forane; tramontane; ultramontane; **n.** light year; ultima Thule

DISTASTE: **n.** abhorrence; abomination; antipathy; disinclination; disrelish; repugnance; revulsion; **a.** DISTASTEFUL: (**see** "disagreeable") augean; fastuous; fulsome; impalatable; insufferable; loathsome; nauseating; nauseous; noisome; obnoxious; offensive; repellant; repugnant; repulsive; revulsive; unpalatable
mood of scornful: **n.** fastidium

DISTENDED: (**see** "swollen") **a.** dilated; dila(ta)tive; gravid; inflated; patulous; tumescent; tumid; tympanic; **n.** DISTENTION: dila(ta)tion; tumescence; tumidity; turgescence; tympanites; tympany

DISTINCT: (**see** "separate") **a.** articulate; cogent; definitive; determinate; discernible; discrete; manifest; palpable; patent

DISTINCTION(S): (**see** "eminence") **n.** cachet; differentiation; discrimination; disparity; dissimilarity; subtlety
given to subtle or ridiculously fine: **a.** quodlibetic; **n.** subtlety; tenuosity
great: **n.** flamboyance
marked by appearance of: **a.** *distingué* person of, in his field; **n.** *cordon bleu;* laureate; paladin
trifling or subtle: **n.** distinguo; nuance; quiddity; subtlety; tenuosity; **a.** quodlibetic

DISTINCTIVE: **a.** characteristic; diacritic; diagnostic; discriminating; *distingué;* flamboyant; honorific; illustrious; majestic; peculiar; signal; transcendent
character or tone: **n.** cachet; timbre
feature or characteristic: **n.** lineament
mark: **n.** cachet
or subtle quality: **n.** bouquet; cachet
property (of a thing): **n.** savo(u)r

DISTINGUISHED: **a.** celebrated; conspicuous; *distingué;* eminent; honorific; illustrious; majestic; prominent; signal; transcendent; **v.** DISTINGUISH: differentiate; discriminate; perceive; signalize; typify
in profession or field: **n.** *cordon bleu;* laureate; paladin

DISTINGUISHING: **a.** definitive; diagnostic; differential; signal
mark(s) on property (brand, etc.): **n.** differentia; differentiation; stigma; (**pl.** differentiae; stigmata)

DISTORTED: **a.** circuitous; tortuous; **n.** tortuosity; tortuousness

DISTORTION, *exaggerated or ludicrous:* **n.** caricature; Munchausenism

DISTRACTED: **a.** absent-minded; aloof; bemused; detached; disconcerted; distraught; perplexed; preoccupied; **n.** DISTRACTION: (**see** "confusion") perplexity; perturbation

DISTRESS: **n.** adversity; affliction; *angoisse;* bereavement; calamity; consternation; cruciation; mortification; penance; tribulation; **a.** DISTRESSED: harrowed; lacerated; tortured; **a.** DISTRESSING: agonizing; atrocious; calamitous; deplorable; flagrant; grievous; harrowing; heinous; hurtful; macaber; macabre; necessitous; vexatious
mental: **n.** dysphoria; psychalgia

DISTRIBUTION *center:* **n.** entrepôt

DISTRUST: **v.** misdoubt; **n.** apprehension; misdoubt; misgiving; suspicion

DISTURB: **v.** agitate; discompose; disconcert; disquiet; perturb; **n.** DISTURBANCE: (**see** "disorder") commotion; discomposure; interruption; perturbation; rabblement; tumult(ation); **a.** DISTURBING: (**see** "distressing") vexatious; **a.** DISTURBED: **see** "agitated"

DISUNITE: (**see** "disjoint") **v.** alienate; dissociate; **n.** DISUNITY: (**see** "separation") alienation; dissension; dissociation

DISUSE: **n.** desuetude; obsolescence

DIVERGE: **v.** bifurcate; detour; digress; divagate; divaricate; parenthesize; **n.** DIVERGENCE: bifurcation; detour; deviation; digression; dissimilarity; divagation; divarication; obliquity; parenthesis; tangency; **a.** DIVERGENT: deviant; deviating; parenthetical; tangent(ial)

DIVERSE: (**see** "distinct") **a.** heterogeneous; manifold; motley; multifarious; multiform; multiplex; multiplicious; multivarious; protean; variegated; **n.** DIVERSITY: (**see** "variety") diversification; heterogeneity; rotation; variegation; **v.** DIVERSIFY: intersperse; rotate; variegate

DIVIDE: (**see** "separate") **v.** alienate; bifurcate; dis(as)sociate; disjoint; dismember; disunite; divaricate; diverge; fractionalize; fractionate; **n.** see "division"
and rule: **adv.** *divide et impera*

into equal parts: **n., v. or a.** aliquot
into three parts: **see under** "divided"
unable to: **a.** indivisible; inextricable; inseparable

DIVIDED (**or** DIVIDING): **a.** bisulcate; cleft; cloven; discrete; disunited; divaricate; divergent; partite
into many parts or branches: **a.** multipartite; polychotomous; polytomous
into three parts: **a.** trichotomous; tripartite; **n.** trichotomy; tripartition; **v.** trisect
into two parts: **a.** bisected; bipartient; bipartite; dichotomous; **n.** bifurcation; dichotomy; **v.** bifurcate; bisect; dichotomize; halve
wall: **n.** septum

DIVINATION: (**see** "fortune-telling") **n.** metagnomy
false: **n.** pseudomancy; **a.** pseudomantic
forms of: **n.** astragalomancy; astromancy; catoptromancy; cleromancy; haruspication; numerology; omoplastoscopy; oneiromancy; ornithomancy; rhabdomancy; scapulimancy; sortilege

DIVINE: (*see* "sacred") **a.** ambrosiac; ambrosial; celestial; deific; olympian; superhuman; supernal
and human combined or working jointly: **n.** theanthropism; theanthrophy; **a.** theandric; theanthrophic
guidance or care: **n.** Providence
influence or inspiration: **n.** afflation; afflatus; theopneusty; **a.** theopneust(ic)
law: **n.** *jus divinum; jus ecclesiasticum*
law, by: **adv.** *jure divino*
making (divine): **v.** apotheosize; canonize; celestialize; deify; etherealize; spiritualize; **n.** apotheosis; deification; spiritualization
power, alleged: **n.** charism(a); **a.** charismatic
wisdom: **n.** Sophia; **a.** Sophian

DIVINELY *inspired:* **a.** charismatic; theopneust(ic)

DIVINITY, *good:* **n.** agathod(a)emon
individual opn. on: **n.** theologoumenon

DIVISIBLE: **a.** discerptible

DIVISION(S): **n.** alienation; apportionment; category; cleavage; decentralization; detachment; disagreement; discerp-

tion; disjunction; dismemberment; dissolution; distribution; disunity; divarication; divergence; fission; partition; phylum; polychotomy; schism; scission; separation; sundering
comprising more than two: **a.** polychotomous
cut into small: **a.** sectile; **n.** sectility
having many lateral: **a.** ramose; ramous
into independent or semi-independent units: **n.** compartmentalization; compartmentation; deparmentalization; departmentation; **v.** compartmentalize; departmentalize
into two opposites, or bet. two enemies: **n.** polarization; **v.** polarize
pert. to: **a.** divisional; fractional; phyletic; schismatic(al)
plant and animal kingdoms: **n.** phylum; regnum; (**pl.** genera; regna); **a.** phyletic

DIVISIVE: **a.** centrifugal; disharmonious; disintegrative; disjunctive; dissentious; dissociable; dissociative; factional; fissiparous; schismatic(al); schizoid; separatist; **n.** (**see** "division") fissiparousness

DIZZY: **a.** vertiginous; **n.** DIZZINESS: vertigo

DO: **see** "complete"
what you are doing (concentrate on business at hand): age quod agis

DOCTOR(S), *medical, pert. to:* **a.** Aesculapian; iatric(al)
pert. to disease or disorder caused by: **a.** iatrogenic; medicamentous

DOCTRINE(S): **n.** creed; (**pl.** credenda); dogma; philosophy; precept; tenet; theory
body of: **n.** organon
pert. to: **a.** doctrinaire; dogmatic(al)
secret or occult: **n.** cabala; cabalism; occultism; **a.** cabalistic

DOER: **n.** executant; facient

DOG(S), *abnormal fear of:* **n.** cynophobia
beware the: **adv.** cave canem
expert in training and care of: **n.** cynologist
genus: **n.** canis
in manger: canis in praesepi
let sleeping lie: quieta non movere
love me, love my (dog): qui m'aime, aime mon chien
lover of: **n.** canophilist; cynolatrist

pert. to or resembling: **a.** canine; cynoid
resembling or like: **a.** cyanoid
study of: **n.** cynology
the race, or qualities of: **n.** caninity; dogginess
trainer of: **n.** cynologist
worship of: **n.** cynolatry; **n.** cynolatrist

DOGMATIC: **a.** authoritative; dictatorial; doctrinaire; doctrinal; magisterial; opinionated; pronunciative; sophomoric; **n.** DOGMA: **see** "creed" **and** "doctrine"
assertion: **n.** dixit
statement(s): **n.** dictum; (**pl.** dicta); dogmatism; *ipse dixit;* ipsedixitism

DOLLAR, *love of:* **n.** amor nummi; plutolatry

DOMAIN (**or** DOMINION): (**see** "estate") **n.** arrondissement; demesne; jurisdiction; principality; sovereignty

DOMESTIC: **a.** enchorial; indigenous; internal; **n.** domesticity; domesticality
animals and plants, science of propagation: **n.** thremmatology
establishment: **n.** menage

DOMESTICATED: (**see** "tame") **a.** domitae naturae

DOMICILE: **see** "abode"

DOMINANT: (**see** "powerful") **a.** (pre)-eminent; prepotent; prevalent; transcendent; **n.** DOMINATION: (**see** authority") ascendency; dominance; sovereignty; **a.** DOMINATING: (**see** "commanding") autocratic; dominative; hegemonic; **n.** DOMINANCE: ascendency; preeminence; superordination; transcendency

DOMINION: **n.** dominance; domination; jurisdiction; seign(i)ority; sovereignty; supremacy; suzerainty; transcendency

DONATION: **see** "gratuity"

DONE: **a.** consummate(d); **n.** consummation; *factum est; fait accompli;* kaput
it is: actum est
that which was to be: quod erat faciendum (**abb.** q.e.f.)

DOOM, *foreshadowed:* (**see** "fate") **n.** handwriting on the wall; sword of Damocles; **a.** apocalyptic(al); Damoclean *prophet of:* **n.** Jeremiah; (**fem.** Cassandra)

DOOMED: **a.** destined; fey

DOOR(S), *behind or w/ closed:* **adv.** *à huis clos; januis clausis*
  -keeper: **n.** concierge; ostiary; tiler; tyler

DOPEY: **see** "sluggish"

DORMANT: **a.** abeyant; comatose; cryptic; hibernant; latent; lethargic; potential; quiescent; stationary; torpid; **n.** DORMANCY: hibernation; latency; latescence; quiescence

DOT: **n.** punctation; punctum; **a.** DOTTED: motley; piebald; punctate(d); punctiform; variegated

DOTARD: **see** "fool"

DOUBLE: **a.** bigeminal; binary; duplex; **n.** *alter ego;* counterpart; duplicate; image; semblance; similitude; substitute; understudy; **n.** DOUBLENESS: dichotomy; duality; **a.** dualistic
  -dealing: **n.** ambidexterity; duplicity; **a.** ambidextrous; duplicitous; Janus-faced; Janus-like; Machiavellian
  -dealing, extreme: **n.** triplicity
  meaning: **n.** double entendre; double entente; equivoque; (*also* equivoke); **a.** equivocal
  vision: **n.** diplopia; **a.** diplopic

DOUBT: (**see** "skepticism" **and** "uncertainty") **n.** ambiguity; ambivalence; distrust; dubiety; dubiosity; dubitation; incertitude; incredulity; indecision; irresolution; miscreance; skepsis; skepticism; suspicion; **a.** DOUBTING: aporetic; dubitant; dubitative; incredulous; irresolute; skeptical; **n.** DOUBTER: (**see** "disbeliever") aporetic; doubting Thomas; nullifidian; pyrrhonist; skeptic
  covert expression of: **n.** addubitation
  expression of as where truth lies: **n.** *non liquet*
  in: **adv.** *in ambiguo; in dubio*
  lack of: **n.** credulity; gullibility; **a.** credulous; gullible
  not open to: **see under** "question"
  philosophical: **n.** skepsis
  problem presenting, or passgae in speech or writing presenting a: **n.** aporia; (**pl.** aporiae)

room for: **n.** *ambigendi locus;* **a.** dubious
  when in, do nothing: **adv.** *dans le doute, abstiens-toi*
  without: (**see** "incontrovertible") **adv.** *sans doute; sine dubio*

DOUBTFUL: (**see** "vague") **a.** ambivalent; dubious; dubitable; equivocal; fabular; factious; improbable; incredible; incredulous; legendary; perilous; problematic(al); questionable; unlikely; unpredictable; unpromising
  group (morally or legally): **n.** demimonde
  outlook: **n.** skepsis

DOUGHY: **a.** magmatic; **n.** magma

DOWDY: **see** "untidy"

DOWN: **n.** floccus; lanugo; pubescence; **a.** DOWNY: (**see** "woolly") floccose; flocculent; lanuginous; puberulent; pubescent; villous
  with: **adv.** *à bas*

DOWNCAST: (**see** "sad") **a.** cheerless; dejected; disheartened; dispirited; melancholic; melancholy; **n.pl.** doldrums; lachrymals, megrims

DOWNFALL: (**see** "ruin") **n.** debasement; degradation; *dégringolade;* labefaction; Waterloo

DOWNRIGHT: (**see** "out-and-out") **a.** arrant; forthright; unmitigated; utter

DOWNWARD: **a.** netherward
  moving or bending: **a.** declensional; declinatory; **n.** declension; declination

DRAB: (**see** "dull") **a.** insipid; somber; subfusc(ous)

DRAFT, *rough:* **n.** *brouillon; ébauche*

DRAMA, *culminating event of:* **n.** catastrophe; climax; dénouement
  featuring gruesome or horrible: **n.** guignol
  heightened action, or complication leading to climax: **n.** catastasis
  juvenile lead in: **n.** *jeune premier*
  pert. to: **a.** dramatic; histrionic; theatric(al); thespian
  problem (drama or play): **n.** *pièce à thèse*

DRAMATIC: (see "showy") **a.** artificial; compelling; declamatory; elocutionary; histrionic; operatic; stagy; theatric(al); thespian; **n.** DRAMATIST: dramaturge; playwright; **a.** dramaturgic(al)

DRASTIC: see "rigorous"
as to methods: **a.** procrustean

DRAW *away;* **v.** abduct; abstract; **n.** abduction; abstraction; **a.** ablatitious
back (or in): **v.** adduct; retract; **n.** adduction; retraction; retrenchment; **a.** retractile
forth (or out): **v.** attenuate; elicit; extract; protract; **n.** attenuation; elicitation; evocation

DRAWBACK: (see "hindrance") **n.** stultification

DRAWING(S), *pert. to:* **a.** delineative; graphic
scratched on walls, etc.: **n.** graffito; (**pl.** graffiti)
young person's (children): **n.pl.** juvenilia

DREAD: **a.** doughty; formidable; perilous; portentious; redoubtable; **n.** (see "anxiety") angst; apprehension; trepidation; trepidity; **a.** DREADFUL: (see "dire") awesome; fearful; horrendous; horrific; revolting

DREAM(S): **n.** chimera; fantasia; fantasy; *insomnium;* phantasm; (**pl.** phantasmata); **v.** fantasize; **n.** DREAMER: (see "visionary") fantasist; fantast; ideologist; ideologue; phantast; romancer; romanticist; utopian; **a.** DREAMY: (see "impractical") chimerical; fantastic; fantasque; languid; langorous; utopian
art of interpretation, or foretelling by: **n.** oneiromancy
day-: see "daydream"
god of: **n.** Oneiros
pert. to: **a.** chimerical; fantastic: oneiric; utopian
sick man's: **n.** *aegri somnis*
sick man's empty: **n.** *aegri somnia vana*
unrealistic or unrealizable: **n.** *chateau en Espagne;* chimera; **a.** chimerical; fantastic; utopian

DREARY: see "dismal"
quality or state of being: **n.** dreariment

DREGS: (see "rubbish") **n.** debris; exuviate; feculence; orts, residue; residuum; sediment; sordor

DRENCH: see "imbrue"

DRESS: (see "attire") **v.** accouter; accoutre; **n.** accoutrement(s); apparel; array(ment); drapery; habiliments; (in)-vestments; regalia; toggery; toilette; trappings; vesture
ceremonial: **n.** *grande toilette;* panoply; regalia
in full: **adv.** *en grande tenue; en grande toilette; endimanché*
-maker: **n.** *couturier;* (**fem.** *couturière*)
pert. to (esp. men's): **a.** sartorial; **n.** haberdashery
richly: **v.** caparison
up: **v.** caparison; tit(t)ivate; **n.** caparison; panoply; ragalia; tit(t)ivation

DRESSED *carelessly or partly:* **n.** deshabille; dishabille; **adv.** *en déshabillé*

DRESSING *gown:* **n.** *robe de chambre*

DRIFTER(S): **n.** flotsam and jetsam; gaberlunzie; itinerant; vagrant

DRINK: **v.** imbibe; **n.** beverage; potable; potation; libation
alcoholic: **n.** libation
ceremonial or as sacrifice: **n.** libation
craving for (as alcoholic): **n.** dipsomania; oenomania; potomania; **a.** dipsomaniac(al)
fit to (drinkable): **a.** potable; **n.** potability
greedily: **v.** ingurgitate
not fit to: **a.** impotable; undrinkable
of the gods (or any delicious): **n.** nectar; **a.** nectarean; nectareous

DRINKING: (see "alcoholism") **n.** bibation; inhibition; ingurgitation; libation; potation
addicted to: see "drunken"
bold or courageous when: **a.** pot-valiant
bout, or together: (see "spree" **below**) **n.** carouse; compotation
companion: **n.** compotator
fond of: **a.** convivial; crapulous; intemperate
mania for: **n.** dipsomania; *mania a potu*
rel. to: **a.** bibacious; bibitory; bibulous
song or light lyric: **n.** *air à boire;* Anacreontic

91

sparing in: **a.** abstemious; abstentinent; abstentious; **n.** abstentation; moderation
spree: **n.** bacchanal(ia); bender; brannigan; carouse; compotation

DRIVE: **v.** coerce; flagellate; impel; **n.** (**see** "incentive") conation; conatus; dynamism; impetus; momentum; vector; **a.** DRIVING: conational; conative; dynamic
away: **v.** aroint; dispel

DROLLERY: **n.** *drôlerie;* raillery; whims(e)y; whimsicality; whimsicalness

DROOPING: **a.** enervated; flaccid; lackadaisical; languid; languorous; lethargic; nutant; **n.** flaccidity; lackadaisy; languor; lethargy

DROP *by drop:* **adv.** *goutte à goutte*
falling in (drops): **a.** stillatitious
to the last **adv.** supernaculum

DROSS: (**see** "remains" **and** "sediment") **n.** *caput mortuum;* (**pl.** *caput mortua*)

DROWNING, *execution by:* **n.** noyade; Republican marriage

DROWSY: **a.** comatose; hypnogenic; hypnogenous; hypnogogic; lethargic; oscitant; somnolent; torpid; **n.** DROWSINESS: oscitancy; oscitation; somnolence

DRUG(S), (**see** "medicine") *combined action of* **n.** synergism; **a.** synergic(al); synergistic(al)
habit: **n.** narcoticism; opiumism
science of **n.** materia medica; pharmaceutics; pharmacology; **a.** pharmaceutic(al); pharmacological

DRUMMER: **n.** tympanist

DRUNK: **see** "alcoholic" **and** "drunken
bold or courageous when: **a.** pot-valiant; **n.** Dutch courage; pot-valor
to make: **v.** inebriate; intoxicate
weepingly: **a.** maudlin

DRUNKARD: (**see** "alcoholic") **n.** bacchanal; bacchant; (**fem.** bacchante); debauchee; dipsomaniac; inebriate; libertine; oenophilist; winebibber; **n.** DRUNKENNESS: (**see** "alcoholism") dipsomania;

ebrosity; inebriation; (in)ebriety; intoxication; potomania

DRUNKEN: **a.** bacchanal(ian); bacchantic; bibacious; bibulous; crapulent; crapulous; dipsomaniacal; inebriate(d); inebrious
feast or party: **n.** bacchanal(ia); bender; brannigan; carouse; compotation orgy

DRY: (**see** "dull") **a.** anhydrous; arenaceous; dehydrated; desiccated; desiccative; jejune; monotonous; uninteresting; xerotic; **n.** DRYNESS: aridity; dehydration; desiccation; xerosis

DUCT, *body:* **n.** meatus

DUAL: **see** "two-fold"

DUEL: **n.** *affaire d'honneur;* rencounter; rencontre

DUET: **n.** *pas de deux*

DULL: (**see** "bland" **and** "commonplace") **a.** adenoid(al); anserine; apathetic; asinine; bromidic; brutish; comatose; conventional(ized); gleamless; hebetate; hebetudinous; insipid; jejune; lackadaisical; lackluster; languid; languorous; lethargic; lumbering; monotonous; moronic; obtuse; opaque; oscitant; pedestrian; phlegmatic(al); pointless; ponderous; prosaic; routinized; stolid; stereotyped; stylized; triste; unadventurous; uninspired; unresponsive; unsensational; vapid
(lifeless): **a.** comatose; inanimate; lethargic
or blunt, to make: **v.** hebetate; obtund
passage (as of book, play or music): **n.** longueur
statement: **n.** platitude
(uninteresting): **a.** insipid; jejune; prosaic(al); **n.** insipidity; jejunity

DULLARD: (**see** "person, dull," etc.) **n.** Boeotian; bromide

DULLNESS: **n.** apathy; hebetude; inanity; infestivity; insensitivity; insipidity; jejunity; lethargy; mirthlessness; monotony; obtuseness; opacity; oscitancy; platitude; ponderosity; prosaism; stereotypy; stoginess; stolidity; stupidity; tepidity; tristesse *mental:* **n.** crassitude; hebetude; mental retardation; moronity; obtuseness; obtusity; stupidity

DUMMY: **n.** *homme de paille* (man of straw)

DUNG: (**see** "feces") **n.** ordure; (**pl.** rejectamenta)
containing or like: **a.** fecal; ordurous; stercoraceous
living in: **a.** fimicolous; merdivorous; stercoricolous

DUPE: **see** "deceive"

DUPLICATE: (**see** "double") **n.** counterfeit; counterpart; facsimile

DURATION: (**see** "endurance") **n.** longanimity; perseverance; protension
unlimited: **n.** infinitude; infinity; perpetuality; perpetuity; saeculum

DURESS: **n.** coercion; constraint; durance; imprisonment; incarceration; restraint

DUSKY: **a.** somber; obfusc(ous)

DUST, *abnormal fear of:* **n.** amathophobia
covered with: **a.** pulverulent

DUSTY: **a.** pulverous; pulverulent

DUTIFUL: **a.** deferent(ial); duteous; filial; **n.** deference; deferentiality

DUTY: **n.** devoir; dharma; liability; obligation; onus; responsibility
abandonment of: **n.** abdication; apostasy; defection
ethics of: **n.** deontology; **a.** deontological
misconduct or neglect of: **n.** irresponsibility; maladministration; misfeasance; misprision
of nobility or rich to less fortunate: **n.** *noblesse oblige*
outside regular: **a.** extracurricular; supererogative; supererogatory
rel. to: **a.** deontic; duteous; obligatory
required by: **a.** *de règle; de rigueur;* imperative; obligatory; preemptory
to do my: faire mon devoir

DWARF: **n.** diminutive; homunculus; (**pl.** homunculi); lilliputian; Rumpelstiltskin; sesquipedal; **a.** DWARFISH: diminutive; homuncular; lilliputian; microscopic; nanitic; nanous; sesquipedalian; **n.** DWARFISHNESS: dwarfism; nanism

DWELLING: **n.** domicile; habitation; **a.** domiciliated; imminent; inherent; residentiary

DYE: **v.** imbue; tinge

DYING: **a.** agonal; expiring; fey; moribund; **adv.** *in articulo mortis; in extremis*
person: **n.** moribund

DYNAMIC: (**see** "powerful") **a.** kinetic

E

EACH *his own, to: suum cuique*

EAGER: (**see** "ardent") **a.** agog; desirous; ecstatic; enthusiastic; fanatical; fervent; impetuous; importunate; insatiable; intent; rapturous; ravenous; solicitous; voracious; zealous; **n.** EAGERNESS: (**see** "enthusiasm") ardor; demonstrativeness; empressement; lust; solicitude
  for gratification: **a.** gluttonous; rapacious; ravenous; voracious
  for praise: **a.** esurient; **n.** captation; esurience

EAGLE *does not catch flies: aquilla non capit muscas*
  of or like an: **a.** aquiline

EARLIEST: **a.** primeval; primitive; primordial
  in time: **a.** primordial; ultimate
  part or stage: **n.** primordium; (**pl.** primordia)

EARLY: **a.** embryonic; incipient; matinal; matutinal; nascent; precipitate; premundane; primeval; primitive; primordial; punctual; seasonable; timely
  development: **n.** precocity; **a.** precocious
  stage, in: **a.** embryonic; incipient; incunabulum; infancy; nascent; rudimentary
  work of art, book, record, etc.: **n.** incunabulum; (**pl.** incunabula)

EARNEST: (**see** "eager") **a.** fervent

EARS, *excessive largeness of:* **n.** macrotia; **a.** macrotous
  having: **a.** auriculate
  pricked up: **n.** *arrectis aribus*

EARTH: (**see** "universe") **n.** *terra firma*
  and heavens, rel. to or affecting both: **a.** cosmotellurian
  as a center: **n.** geocentricism; **a.** geocentric(al)
  deep within the: **a.** chthonian; chthonic; plutonic; subterranean
  goddess of: **n.** Ceres; Tellus Mater
  inhabited portion: **n.** ecumene
  inhabitant of: (**see** "man") **n.** earthling; tellurian; **a.** terrigenous
  lying beneath: **a.** nether; subterranean
  lying, dwelling or active on or above: **a.** superterranean; superterraneous; **n.** superterranean; superterrene
  of or arising from: **a.** telluric; terrestrial
  of this: see "worldly"
  power of people of: **n.** cosmocracy
  rel. to: **a.** planetary; telluric; terranean; terraneous; terrestrial
  theory of origin, etc.: **n.** cosmogony

EARTHBORN: **a.** human; terrigenous

EARTHEN: **a.** terraceous

EARTHLY: (**see** "earthly") **a.** cosmopolitan; factual; global; mundane; planetary; realistic; sublunary; telluric; temporal; terrene; terrestrial

EARTHQUAKES, *pert. to:* **a.** seismic(al)
  study of: **n.** seismology

EARTHY: (**see** "vulgar") **a.** carnal; chthonian; chthonic; Falstaffian; heathenish; Hogarthian; mortal; mundane; pagan; Rabelaisian; *risqué;* terrestrial; worldly

EASE: **v.** alleviate; assuage; compromise; extenuate; mitigate; moderate; placate; relax; tranquilize; **n.** alleviation; assuagement; detachment; disengagement; leisure; naturalness; palliation; quietude; relaxation; repose; tranquility; **a. see** "easy"
  at: **adv.** *à l'aise*
  difficult to, or incapable of (easing): **a.** implacable; inexorable; intractable; unappeasable
  something which (eases): **n.** alleviant; lenitive; nepenthe; palliative; tranquilizer
  tending to: **a.** alleviative; alleviatory; conciliatory; extenuating; extenuative;

lenitive; mitigating; nepenthean; palliative; placative; placatory; tranquilizing
with dignity: **n.** *otium cum dignitate*
without dignity: **n.** *otium sine dignitate*

EASILY: **adv.** *sans gêne*
managed, taught or controlled: **a.** docile; educable; educatable; governable; malleable; maniable; manipulable; manipulative; manipulatory; pliable; tractable; **n.** docility; malleability; tractability

EASING: **a.** alleviative; alleviatory; anesthetic; consolatory; lenitive; nepenthean; mitigative; palliative; palliatory; **n.** alleviation; *détente;* mitigation; palliation; tranquilization

EAST: **n.** Levant; Orient; **a.** see "oriental"
face or turn to: **v.** orientate

EASTER *or Lent, pert. to:* **a.** lenten; paschal; quadragesimal

EASTERN: **a.** oriental; ortative
hemisphere, rel. to: **a.** gerontogeous

EASY: **a.** accessible; complaisant; effortless; facile; indulgent; lenient; tractable
and casual in manner: **a.** cavalier; *dégagé;* jaunty; unconcerned; unconstrained; **adv.** *sans gêne;* **n.** *un air aisé*
come (easy) go (easy): **n.** *cito parit; quod cito acquiritur*
going: **a.** apathetic; *dégagé;* indifferent; jaunty; unconstrained
job: **n.** sinecure

EAT: **v.** consume; corrode; devour; ingest; ingurgitate; manducate

EATABLE: (**see** "food") **n.** comestible; edible; **a.** alimentary; cibarious; comestible; edible; esculent
not: **a.** inedible; inesculent
state of being: **n.** edibility

EATER: **n.** gastronome(r)
gluttonous: **n.** bon-vivant; cormorant; glutton; gourmand; **a.** crapulent; edacious; omnivorous
heavy: **n.** cormorant; gourmand; trencherman

EATING: **n.** ingestion; ingurgitation; manducation; **a.** consuming; corrosive; devouring; edacious; ingestible; ingestive; voracious

after: **a.** post-cibal; post-prandial
any sort of food: **a.** omnivorous; pantophagous
before: **a.** ante cibum
both animal and vegetable food: **a.** amphivorous
earth, dirt, clay, etc.: **n.** geophagy; pica
fast: **n.** tachyphagia
fond of: **a.** convivial; gluttonous; gourmand; **n.** *bon-vivant;* epicure; gastronome(r); gourmand; gourmet; sybarite; trencherman; **a.** epicurean
huge capacity for: **n.** edacity; gluttony; voracity
injurious, unusual or nonedible things: **n.** allotriophagy; geophagy; paroexia; pica
science of good: **n.** cuisine; epicureanism; gastronomy
sparing: **a.** abstemious
together: **a.** commensal; **n.** commensal(ity)

ECCENTRIC: (**see** "peculiar") **a.** aberrant; anomalous; atypical; bizarre; cantankerous; capricious; crotchety; fantastic; idiosyncratic; off-center; **n.** aberrant; Bohemian; deviant; **n.** ECCENTRICITY: (**see** "peculiarity") aberrance; aberrancy; aberration; *bizarrerie;* idiosyncrasy; quiddity; quirk

ECHO: **n.** polyphony; repercussion; reverberation; **a.** echoic; polyphonic; polyphonous; reverborative; reverboratory

ECONOMICS: **n.** plutology; plutonomy; **a.** ECONOMIC(AL): frugal; profitable; prudent
(economic) satisfaction: **n.** ophelimity

ECONOMY: **n.** frugality; husbandry; prudence; retrenchment; **v.** ECONOMIZE: curtail; husband; retrench
extreme: **n.** austerity
unreasonable: **n.** parsimony; **a.** cheeseparing; parsimonious

EDDY: **n.** Charybdis; vortex; whirlpool; **a.** vortiginous

EDIBLE: **see** "eatable"

EDICT: **n.** fiat; mandate; mandatum; manifesto; ordinance; proclamation; pronouncement; pronunciamento; ukase; **a.** edictal

EDIT: **v.** compile; emend; redact; **n.** redaction; **n.** EDITOR: diaskeuast; *redacteur;* redactor

EDITION, *first:* **n.** *editio princeps;* princeps

EDUCATED: **a.** enlightened; erudite; learned; lettered; literate; philomathic(al); scholarly; tutored; **v.** EDUCATE: see "teach"
or enlightened class: **n.pl.** cognoscenti; illuminati; intelligensia; literati; **n.** cognoscente; clerisy; litterateur; literatus; savant
self-: **a.** autodidactic; **n.** autodidact

EDUCATION: (see "background" and "learning") **n.** breeding; curriculum; discipline; erudition; instruction; learning; pedagogics; pedagogy; refinement; scholarship; scholasticism; tuition; **a.** EDUCATIONAL: academic; didactic; doctrinal; educative; instructive; pedagogic(al); propaedeutic(al); scholastic(al); tutorial
general (education) and breeding: **n.** curriculum

EDUCATOR(S): (see "teacher(s)") **n.** pedagog(ue)
pretentious speech or writing(s) of: **n.** pedag(u)ese; pedantry

EERIE: **a.** fantastic; grotesque; mysterious; phantasmal; phantasmic; uncanny; weird; **n.** grotesquerie

EFFECT: **v.** accomplish; execute; **n.** (see "outcome" and "result") appearance; causatum; consequence; encroachment; impingement; infringement; manifestation; residuum; sequel; sequela; (**pl.** sequelae)
done for: see "stagy"
to cause: **n.** *a posteriori;* **a.** aposterioristic

EFFECTIVE (or EFFECTUAL): **a.** consequential; efficacious; efficient; executive; substantious; telling; **n.** EFFECTIVENESS: effectivity; efficacity; efficacy
make more: **v.** augment; enhance; potentiate; **n.** augmentation; enhancement; potentiation

EFFEMINATE: **a.** gynecoid; muliebral; womanlike; **n.** EFFEMINACY: androgyny; femineity; femininity; muliebrity
boy or man: **n.** androgyne; androgynus; milksop

EFFICIENCY: **n.** accomplishment; competency; consummation; effectiveness; effectuality; efficacity; efficacy; expedition; ingenuity; **a.** EFFICIENT: accomplished; adept; competent; consummate; dexterous; effective; efficacious; expeditious; ingenious; professional; proficient; virtuosic

EFFIGY, *to form or represent as:* (see "model") **v.** effigiate; **n.** effigiation; **a.** effigial
used in primitive magic: **n.** envoûtement

EFFORT: **n.** application; conatus; endeavor; exertion; nisus
act of making: **n.** conation; **a.** conative
close or continuous: (see "diligence") **n.** assiduousness; assiduity; **a.** assiduous
requiring constant and often ineffective: **a.** Sisyphean; Sisyphian

EFFUSIVE: **a.** demonstrative; ebullient; exuberant; gushing; scaturient; unreserved; unrestrained; **n.** EFFUSIVENESS: ebullience; ebulliency; ebullition; exuberance; unreserve; unrestraint

EGG(S), *collector or student of bird:* **n.** oologist; oology; **a.** oologic(al)
having young by: **a.** oviparous; ovoviviparous; **n.** oviparity; ovoviviparity
living or feeding on: **a.** oophagous
membrane: **n.** oolemma; vitilline (membrane)
-shaped or like: **a.** ooid(al); ovate; ovicular; oviform; ovoid(al)

EGGHEAD: see "intellectual"

EGOTISM: see "selfishness" and "self-importance"

EGYPTIAN *writing, ancient:* **n.** cuneiform; hieroglyphic(s)

EIGHT, *pert. to or group or series of:* **a.** octadic; **n.** octad
-sided or angled figure: **n.** octagon; **a.** octagonal
years, happening every or lasting for: **a.** octennial

EIGHTY *to 90 years, person of, or rel. to this period:* **a.** or **no.** octogenarian

EINSTEIN'S *theory:* $e = mc^2$

EITHER *to conquer or to die: aut vincere aut mori*

EJECT: (**see** "banish") **v.** disbar; dispossess; oust; regurgitate

ELABORATE: **v.** (**see** "develop") expaciate: **a.** (**see** "large") complicated; diligent; intricate; painstaking; stupendous; **n.** ELABORATION: exegesis; expaciation
   in ornamentation: **a.** garish; rococo
   production: **n.** extravaganza; spectacular

ELATED: **a.** buoyant; ecstatic; enraptured; eudamonic(al); euphoric; exhilarated; exultant; heady; intoxicated; rapturous; **n.** ELATION: (**see** "rapture") ecstasy; euphoria; exultation; rapture; transport

ELDER: **n.** patriarch; **a.** ELDERLY: (**see** "aged") anile; antiquated; *d'un certain âge;* senile; venerated; **n.** anility; antiquity; senescence; senility

ELECTIONS, *scientific study of:* **n.** psephology; **a.** psephological; **n.** psephologist

ELEGANCE: **n.** comeliness; concinnity; courtliness; gentility; luxe; refinement; *savoir faire;* sumptuosity; urbanity; **a.** ELEGANT: concinnous; exquisite; luxurious; polished; *recherché;* sumptuous; supernacular; supernal
   of simple: **adv.** *simplex munditiis*

ELEGANTLY *dressed or maintained:* **a.** *soigné;* (**fem.** *soignée*); modish; well-groomed

ELEGY: **see** "funeral ode or hymn"

ELEMENT: **n.** component; constituent; factor; ingredient; integral; integrant; **a.** ELEMENTAL: (**see** "fundamental") hypostatic(al); integral; introductory; ultimate
   out of one's: **a.** *dépaysé*

ELEMENTARY: (**see** "fundamental") **a.** abecedarian; abecedary; inchoate; incomplex; initiatory; primitive; primordial; rudimental; rudimentary
   instruction: **n.** propaedeutics; **a.** propaedeutic(al)

ELEPHANT(S): **n.** pachyderm
   do not catch mice: elephantus non capit murem

ELEVATE: (**see** "raise") **v.** edify; enhance; enlighten; ennoble; escalate; exhilarate; pedestal; refine; spiritualize; sublimate; transcend; **n.** ELEVATION: edification; enhancement; enlightenment; **a.** edificatory
   character of: **v.** ennoble; spiritualize; sublimate; **n.** ennoblement; spiritualization; sublimation

ELIMINATE: (**see** "abolish") **v.** decimate; dele(te); exclude; expunge; exscind; extirpate; oust; resect; **n.** ELIMINATION: decimation; deletion; deracination; divestation; extirpation; ouster
   not capable of (elimination): **a.** ineliminable; ineradicable; inexterminable; inextinguishable; inextirpable; irradicable; irrepressible; unquenchable

ELITE: (**see** "aristocrat" **and** "superior") **n.** aristocracy; (**pl.** aristoi); *bas bleu;* bluestocking; *crème de la crème;* magnifico; *ne plus supra; ne plus ultra;* supernaculum; (**pl.** *gens de condition*)
   principles and practices of the: **n.** aristocratism

ELOPE: **v.** abscond; absquatulate; **n.** ELOPEMENT: abscondence; absquatulation

ELOQUENCE: (**see** "speech") **n.** facundity; **a.** ELOQUENT: Ciceronian; Demosthenic; Demosthenian; facund; impassioned; oratorial; oratoric(al)

ELUSIVE: (**see** "baffling") **a.** impalpable; insidious; intangible; lubric(i)ous; saponaceous; subtle; **n.** ELUSIVENESS: insidiousness; intangibility; lubricity; subtility

EMACIATED: **a.** attenuated; cadaverous; enfeebled; macilent; marasmic; tabescent; **n.** EMACIATION: atrophy; attenuation; macies; marasmus; tabefaction; tabescence

EMANATION: (**see** "outcome") **n.** aura; cachet; effluence; effluvium; efflux

EMBARRASSMENT: **n.** abashment; chagrin; discomfiture; discomposure; disconcertion; discountenance; encumbrance; frustration; humiliation; impediment; mortification; perturbation; **v.** EMBARRASS: daunt; discomfit; discompose; disconcert; humble; humiliate; mortify
without: **adv.** *sans gêne*

EMBEDDED: **a.** encapsulated; impacted; nidulant

EMBELLISH: see "adorn"

EMBEZZLE: **v.** appropriate; defalcate; misappropriate; peculate; purloin; **n.** EMBEZZLER: defalcator; peculator

EMBEZZLEMENT: **n.** abstraction; defalcation; malversation; (mis)appropriation; peculation; substraction

EMBITTER: (**see** "anger") **v.** exacerbate; **n.** exacerbation; exacerbescence; rancor; **a.** EMBITTERED: rancorous

EMBLEM(S): **n.** insigne; (**pl.** insignia); symbol; **a.** EMBLEMATIC: representative; symbolic(al)
for a book: **n.** colophon

EMBODIMENT: (**see** "personify") **n.** avatar; epiphany; incarnation; incorporation; (im)personification; quintessence

EMBRACE: **v.** adopt; circumscribe; comprehend; comprise; embosom; encompass; enfold; incorporate; undertake; **n.** EMBRACEMENT: accolade; comprehension; incorporation; **a.** EMBRACING: circumscriptive; comprehensive; encircling; enclosing; inclusive; incorporated; osculant

EMERGE: **v.** burgeon; debouch; disembogue; effloresce; egress; emanate; evolve; materialize; **n.** EMERGENCE: burgeoning; debouchment; debut; efflorescence; egression; emanation; evolution
as a river: **v.** disembogue
as from outlet: **v.** debouch

EMERGENCY: **n.** crisis; dilemma; exigency; **a. see** "critical"

EMIGRATION: (**see** "flight") **n.** egression; exodus; hegira

EMINENCE: **n.** conspicuity; conspicuousness; esteem; magnificence; majesty; paramouncy; prestige; prominence; resplendency; salience; saliency; superiority; transcendence; transcendency
great: **n.** preeminence; principality

EMINENT: (**see** "famous" **and** "illustrious") **a.** august; celebrated; conspicuous; *distingué;* distinguished; estimable; honorific; immortal; inimitable; leonine; magnific(al); magnificent; majestic; paramount; prestigious; prominent; (re)splendent; sovereign; superlative; transcendent
in rank or authority: **n.** *cordon bleu*
person: (**see** "person of high rank, etc.") **n.** eminentissimo

EMOTION(S): (**see** "feeling") **n.** affectivity; ecstasy; emotionality; emotivism; emotivity; rapture; rhapsody; vehemence
appeal(ing) to: **adv.** *ad captandum (vulgus)*
display of: **n.pl.** histrionics; hysterics; melodramatics
frenzy of: **n.** nympholepsy; orgasm; Saturnalia
lacking or incapable of: **see under** "feeling"
relieved by talking, etc.: **n.** abreaction; catharsis; **a.** abreactive; cathartic

EMOTIONAL: **a.** affective; ecstatic; effusive; emotive; histrionic; hysteric(al); (melo)dramatic; passionate; rhapsodic; theatric(al); vehement; **n.** emotionality
interest or involvement: **n.** ecstasy; empressement; fervor
wildly: **a.** dithyrambic; rapturous; rhapsodic(al)

EMPHASIZE: **v.** accelerate; accent(uate); enhance; exacerbate

EMPHATIC: **a.** coercive; cogent; compelling; dogmatic; forceful; imperative; pronounced; vehement; vigorous
in speaking: **a.** lexical
statement: **n.** adjuration; asseveration

EMPIRE *within an empire:* **n.** *imperium in imperio*

EMPTY: **a.** barren; frivolous; fustian; inane; meaningless; pretentious; uninhabited; unoccupied; vacuous; **n.** EMPTINESS: barrenness; inanition; inanity;

nihility; nullibicity; nullibiety; senseless-
ness; shallowness; vacuity; vacuum
  as by pouring, or as a river: **v.** disembogue
  (*pretentious*): **n.** flummery; pageantry
  space: **n.** vacuity; vacuum
  spaces, aversion to: **n.** *horror vacui*

ENABLING: (**see** "permissive") **a.** empowering; facultative

ENCAMPMENT: **n.** castrametation; etape

ENCHANT: (**see** "allure") **v.** bewitch;
captivate; ensorcel(1); enthral(1); mesmerize; **a.** ENCHANTING: captivating;
Circean; fascinating; sirenic(al); **n.** EN-
CHANTMENT: bewitchment; captiva-
tion; conjuration; ensorcel(1)ment; fascination; gramary(e); incantation; necromancy; sorcery; sortilege

ENCHANTRESS: **n.** *charmeuse;* Circe;
femme fatale; lamia; vampire

ENCIRCLE: (**see** "surround") **v.** circumnavigate; circumscribe; circumvallate;
embosom; embrace; encompass; impale;
immure; **a.** ENCIRCLING: circumambient; circumferential; encompassing; peripheral

ENCLOSE: (**see** "encircle") **v.** circumscribe; embosom; environ; incarcerate;
invaginate; sheathe; **n.** ENCLOSURE:
empalement

ENCLOSED *tract, territory, etc.:* **n.** en-
clave

ENCOMPASSING: (**see** "encircling") **a.**
ambient; circumferential; enveloping

ENCOURAGE: **v.** animate; embolden; expostulate; exhort; foment; hearten; inspire; inspirit; instigate; promote; sanction; stimulate; **n.** ENCOURAGE-
MENT: approbation; excitation; exhortation; expostulation; fomentation; incentive; instigation; patronage; protreptic;
sanction; sponsorship; **a.** ENCOURAG-
ING: auspicious; (ex)hortative; (ex)-
hortatory; inspirational; inspiriting; persuasive; propitious; protreptic(al); psychagogic; sanctionative

ENCUMBRANCE: **n.** embarrassment; impediment; incubus; perplexity; **a.** impedimental

END: (**see** "conclusion," "discontinue,"
"ending" **and** "objective") **v.** abolish; abrogate; consummate; culminate; dis(as)so-
ciate; terminate; **n.** abrogation; accomplishment; achievement; annihilation;
coda; consequence; consummation; culmination; denouement; destination; dis-
(as)sociation; dissolution; eventuality;
exitus; expiration; finality; finis; goal;
omega; *sine die;* termination; terminus;
a. ENDED: **see** "completed"
  act or stroke that (ends): **n.** *coup de
  grâce*
  beginning of the: **n.** *commencement de la
  fin*
  coming to an: **a.** moribund
  crowns the work: finis coronat opus
  directed or tending toward an: **a.** teleological; telic
  impossible to: **a.** inconclusible
  in itself, having: **a.** autotelic
  in or at the: **adv.** *in fine*
  look to the: respicere finem
  near the: **a.** subterminal
  to the bitter: **adv.** *à outrance*
  to the, or at the: **adv.** *ad fin(em)*
  weigh well the: **adv.** *aviser la fin*

ENDANGER: **v.** imperil; jeopardize

ENDEARMENT, *short term of* (*pet
name*): **n.** hypocorism; hypocoristic; **a.**
hypocoristic

ENDEAVOR: **v.** essay; strive; **n.** conatus;
essay; experiment; nisus; speculation; undertaking; venture; **a.** conative; experimental; speculative; venturous

ENDING: (**see** "conclusion" **and** "end")
n. desinence; disintegration; dissolution;
epilogue; finis; liquidation; **a.** consummative; desinent(ial); desitive; finitive; terminal; terminative; terminatory; **a.**
ENDED: **see** "finished"

ENDLESS (**see** "enduring" **and** "everlasting") **a.** boundless; illimitable; incessant;
infinite; interminable; interminate; measureless; perpetual; protracted; sempiternal; unceasing; **adv.** *ad infinitum*
  in time: (**see** "eternity") **n.** infinity;
  perpetuity

ENDOWMENT: **n.** accomplishment; ap-
(p)anage; largess(e); perquisite; talent

ENDURANCE: **n.** continuance; continuity;
diuturnity; fortitude; longanimity; longev-

ity; monumentality; perdurability; perdurance; permanence; perseverance; perseveration; propensity; sempiternity; stamina; sufferance; tolerance; toleration; **v.** ENDURE: abide; brook; countenance; perdure; survive; tolerate; undergo; withstand; **a.** ENDURING: (**see** "chronic") abiding; classic; diuturnal; established; immarcescible; long-suffering; monotonous; monumental; patient; (per)durable; permanent; perseverant; persistent; protensive; sempiternal
  contest: **n.** marathon

ENDURES, *he conquers who: vincit qui patitur*

ENEMY: **n.** adversary; antagonist; competitor; opponent

ENERGY: **n.** dynamism; gusto; impetus; motivity; potency; puissance; verve; vivacity; **a.** ENERGETIC: (**see** "brisk") dynamic(al); forceful; resolute; strenuous; vigorous; **adv.** *con brio*
  generating: **a.** calorigenic
  intense: **n.** athleticism; strenuosity
  lacking in: (**see** "weak") **a.** lymphatic(al)
  science of: **n.** dynamics; energetics

ENFORCED: **a.** coercive; compulsory; disciplinary; mandatory; obligatory; peremptory; tyrannical; **n.** ENFORCEMENT: coercion; compulsoriness; duress; oppression

ENFORCER *of discipline:* (**see** "disciplinarian") **n.** martinet; rigorist; tyrant

ENGAGE: **v.** betroth; participate; plight; **n.** ENGAGEMENT: assignation; betrothal; betrothment; espousal; involvement; plight; prepossession; rendezvous; tryst

ENGLAND (**or** ENGLISH), *hate(r) of:* **n.** anglophobe; anglophobia; **a.** anglophobic
  love(r) of: **n.** anglomania; anglomaniac; anglophile; anglophilia; **a.** anglomaniacal; anglophilic
  study of lang. or lit. of: **n.** anglistics

ENGLISHMAN: **n.** Sassenach

ENJOY *the present:* **n.** *carpe diem; in diem vivere; in horam vivere*

ENJOYMENT: (**see** "pleasure") **n.** delectation; ecstasy; exultation; gusto; zest; **a.** ENJOYABLE: (**see** "pleasurable") delectable; entertaining; zestful
  devoted to: **a.** apolaustic; hedonic; hedonistic; sensuous; sybaritic; voluptuous
  of foolish trifles: **n.** desipience; desipiency

ENLARGE: **v.** aggrandize; amplify; dilate; elaborate; enhance; exacerbate; expatiate; hypertrophy; intumesce; magnify; omnify; protuberate; tumefy; **a.** ENLARGED: augmented; enhanced; hypertrophic; (in)tumescent; tumefactive; turgescent; turgid; **n.** ENLARGEMENT: accession; aggrandizement; augmentation; expansion; expaciation; (in)tumescence; majoration; tumefaction; tumidity; turgescence

ENLARGING *upon:* **a.** amplificatory; augmentative; **n.** augmentation; enhancement; expatiation

ENLIGHTENMENT: (**see** "revelation") **n.** *éclaircissement;* edification; illumination; **v.** ENLIGHTEN: (**see** "teach") edify; educate; elucidate; illuminate; irradiate; **a.** ENLIGHTENING: edificatory; illuminant; illuminating; illuminative
  person of high: **n.** illuminato; (**pl.** cognoscenti; illuminati; intelligensia)

ENLIVEN: **v.** animate; exhilarate; inspirit; invigorate; quicken; vivify

ENMITY: (**see** "hate") **n.** animosity; animus; antagonism; antipathy; malevolence; pique; rancor; **a.** antagonistic(al); antipathetic(al); malevolent; provocative; rancorous

ENORMOUS: (**see** "huge") **a.** colossal; cyclopean; cyclopic; gargantuan; inordinate; magnitudinous; titanic; **n.** ENORMITY: amplitude; colossality; magnitude

ENOUGH: (**see** "ample") **a.** adequate; copious; **adv.** *quantum sufficit* (**abb.** q.s.)
  and more: satis superque
  is as good as a feast: satis quod sufficit (what suffices satisfies)

ENRICH: (**see** "adorn") **v.** diamondize; fertilize; garnish; lard

ENROLL: **v.** impanel; matriculate; **n.** matriculation

ENSNARE: (**see** "deceive" **and** "entice") **v.** circumvent; entrap; **n.** circumvention; entrapment

ENSUING: **see** "following"

ENTANGLE: **v.** confuse; embrangle; embroil; ensnare; entrap; **n.** ENTANGLEMENT: complexity; complication; embranglement; embroilment; imbroglio; intricacy; involution; labyrinth; maelstrom; morass

ENTER: **v.** infiltrate; ingress; penetrate; permeate; **n.** ENTERING (**or** ENTRY): incursion; ingression; invasion; penetration
   freedom or right to: **n.** access; *entrée;* ingress
   not permitting to: **a.** impenetrable; imperforate; impermeable; imperviable; impervious

ENTERTAINMENT: (**see** "amusement") **n.** diversion; divertissement; recreation; **a.** ENTERTAINING: (**see** "amusing") divertive; festive; recreative
   of strangers: **n.** xenodochy

ENTHUSIASM: **n.** ardor; dash; ebullience; ebulliency; ecstasy; *élan;* euphoria; exhilaration; exuberance; fanaticism; fervency; impetuosity; transport; vehemence; vigor; zest; **a.** ENTHUSIASTIC: ardent; dithyrambic; ebullient; ecstatic; euphoric; exuberant; fervent; flamboyant; glowing; impassioned; intense; lyrical; (per) fervid; profuse; rapturous; rhapsodic(al); unrestrained; vehement; zealous; zestful; **n.** ENTHUSIAST: buff; devotee; energumen; *exalté;* fanatic; zealot
   unrestrained: **n.** lyricism; **a.** dithyrambic; lyrical; rhapsodic(al)

ENTICE: (**see** "charm") **v.** allure; attract; cajole; captivate; entrap; inveigle; **a.** ENTICING: alluring; beguiling; bewitching; captivating; Circean; engaging; exotic; glamorous; orphic; picturesque; prepossessing; seducible; seductive; sirenic(al); **n.** ENTICEMENT: allure(ment); entrapment; inveiglement; seducement; seduction; temptation

ENTIRE: **a.** comprehensive; integral; *pur et simple;* undiminished; undivided; unexpurgated; unimpaired; **adv.** ENTIRELY: (**see** "completely") *in toto; tout à fait;* **n.** ENTIRETY: aggregate; integrality; integrity; totality
   something which is: **n.** integral; totality

ENTITY: **n.** existent; monad
   abstract: **see under** "abstract"

ENTRAILS, *pert. to:* **a.** enteral; enteric; intestinal; splanchnic; visceral
   remove: **v.** disembowel; eviscerate; exenterate
   soothsayer who examined: **n.** haruspex; **a.** haruspical

ENTRANCE: **n.** access; adit(us); atrium; *entrée;* ingress(ion); introitus; os
   rel. to: **a.** liminal

ENTRANCING: (**see** "enticing") **a.** delightful; rapturous
   as of music: **a.** orphic(al)

ENTREAT: (**see** "beseech" **and** "pray") **v.** adjure; implore; supplicate; **a.** ENTREATING: adjuratory; precative; precatory; supplicative; supplicatory; **n.** ENTREATY: (**see** "prayer") adjuration; imprecation; obsecration; petition; solicitation; supplication

ENTRY: **see** "entering"
   violent or forceful: **n.** intrusion; irruption

ENVELOP(E): (**see** "surround") **n.** container; integument; wrapper; **a.** ENVELOPING: ambient; circumferential; encompassing; pervading; pervasive

ENVIRONMENT: (**see** "background") **n.** ambiance; ambience; ambiente; entourage; environs; habitat; milieu; *mise en scène;* surroundings; vicinage; vicinity
   adaptation to: **n.** acclimatization; bionomics; ecology; habitation; inurement; orientation
   in artificial: **a. or adv.** *in vitro*
   local: **n.** habitat; milieu; vicinage; vicinity; (**pl.** environs)
   molded by: **a.** alloplastic; **n.** alloplasticity
   native or natural: **n.** habitat(ion)
   pert. to: **a.** ecological; environmental; vicinal

responsive to and in harmony w/: **a.** syntonic; syntonous; **n.** syntony

serving to bring in rel. w/: **a.** projicient; **n.** projicience

study of w/ rel. to living organisms: **n.** behavioristics; bionomics; ecology; **a.** behavioristic; bionomic; ecological

ENVY: **n.** jaundice; prejudice; resentment

is blind: invidia est caeca

without: adv. *sine invidia*

EQUAL: (**see** "equalize") **v.** equate; **a.** adequative; commensurable; commensurate; coordinate; corresponding; equable; equipollent; equiponderant; equivalent; isometric; proportionate; tantamount; uniform; **n.** (**see** "equality") coeval; compeer; equivalent; peer

age or period: **n.** coetaneity; contemporaneity; **a.** coetaneous; coeval; contemporaneous; contemporary

first among (equals): **n.** *primus inter pares*

in (equal) fault: adv. *in pari delicto*

in force, weight or rank: **a.** equipollent; equiponderant; equivalent; isonomic

in status or rank: a. coeval; coordinate; isonomous; **n.** coeval; compeer; contemporary; isonomy

make: **v.** adequate; equate; **a.** adequative; **n.** adequation

obligations w/ mutual rights and duties: **a.** reciprocal; syna(1)lagamatic

other things being: adv. *c(a)etera desunt; ceteris paribus*

pace or proportion: **a.** or adv. *pari passu*

to each person: **a.** or adv. *per capita*

to the burden: adv. *par oneri*

without: adv. *hors concours; sans pareil*

EQUALITY: **n.** adequation; commensurability; equiponderance; equivalence; isonomy; parity; uniformity

before law: **a.** isonomous; **n.** isonomy

conducive to: **a.** democratic; egalitarian

favoring: **a.** democratic; equalitarian; Rouseauesque; Rouseauistic

one who advocates: **n.** egalitarian; equalitarian; libertarian; Rouseauist

EQUALIZATION: n. adequation, balance; equilibrium; equipoise; equiponderance; equiponderation; isonomy; osmosis; proportionality; stabilization; **v.** EQUALIZE: equate; equiponderate; librate; neutralize; stabilize; unify; **a.** EQUALIZ-

ING: egalitarian; isonomous; osmotic; unifying

EQUILIBRIUM, *internal:* **n.** homeostasis; **a.** homeostatic

EQUIP: **v.** accouter; accoutre; capacitate; caparison; habilitate; **n.** EQUIPMENT: accouterment(s); accoutrement(s); apparatus; appointments; appurtenance(s); armamentaria; caparison; equipage; habiliment(s); impedimenta; instrumentaria; *matériel;* panoply; paraphernalia; trappings

EQUIVALENT: (**see** "equal") **a.** adequative; commensurate; congruent; counterpart; equipollent; equiponderant; homogeneous; isonomous; synonymous; tantamount

an: (**see under** "equal") **n.** *quid pro quo*

in meaning or result: **a.** equipollent; equiponderant; synonymous; **n.** equiponderance; **v.** equiponderate

treat or regard as: **v.** equate

word or phrase: **n.** equivoque (**also** equivoke)

EQUIVOCAL: (**see** "evasive") **a.** ambiguous; ambivalent; amphibologic(al); cryptic; dubious; enigmatic; indeterminate; multivocal; problematic(al); questionable

ERA, *pert. to end of:* **a.** *fin de siècle*

ERADICATE: **v.** annihilate; decimate; deracinate; exterminate

ERASE: (**see** "eliminate") **v.** dele(te); expunge; obliterate; **n.** ERASURE: deletion; excision; expunction; extirpation; obliteration

incapable of being (erased): **a.** immarcescible; imperishable; indelible; ineradicable; inexpungeable; inexpungible; inextirpable; irradicable; **n.** indelibility; ineradicableness; inextirpableness; inexpungibility

ERECT: (**see** "vertical") **v.** construct

posture, pert. to: **a.** orthograde; orthostatic

state or quality of being: **n.** perpendicularity; verticality

walking: **a.** orthograde; orthostatic

EROSION: **n.** ablation; cavitation; cor-
rasion; corrosion; denudation; depletion;
deterioration; detrition; ulceration
　carry away by: **v.** ablate; **a.** ablative
　formed by: **a.** terrigenous
　products of: **n.pl.** detritus

EROTIC: **see** "lewd"
　books, pictures, etc.: **n.pl.** erotica; esoterica; facetiae; pornography

ERR (*to*), *is human: errare humanum est;
humanum est errare*

ERRATIC (or ERRING): **a.** (ab)errant;
capricious; circuitous; desultory; devious; eccentric; fallible; fluctuating; nomadic; tangent(ial); unpredictable; vagarious; vagrant; **n.** aberrancy; caprice;
deviation; eccentricity; erraticism; fallibility; vagary

ERRONEOUS: (**see** "incorrect") **a.** apocryphal; fallacious; inaccurate
　doctrine or belief: **n.** pseudodox(y); **a.**
pseudodox

ERROR: (**see** "blunder") **n.** corrigendum;
deviation; discrepancy; erratum; fallacy;
faux pas; inaccuracy; indiscretion; *lapsus
linguae;* miscalculation; misconception;
misinformation; transgression
　acknowledgment w/ apology: **n.** *amende
honorable;* apologia
　capable of: **v.** fallible; **n.** fallibility
　correction of, order for: **n.** corrigendum;
erratum; (**pl.** corrigenda; errata)
　fond of finding in others: **a.** captious
　grammatical: **n.** catachresis; parapraxia; solecism; **a.** catachrestic(al);
solecistic(al)
　incapable of: **a.** inerrable; inerrant; infallible; **n.** inerrability; inerrancy; infallibility
　social, or in etiquette: **n.** barbarism;
faux pas; gaffe; grivoiserie; impropriety;
lapsus linguae; solecism
　word pointing out: **adv.** sic

ESCAPADE: (**see** "adventure") **n.** gambit; gest(e); harlequinade; peccadillo;
ploy

ESCAPE: **see** "elope"
　to have a narrow: **v.** *échapper belle*

ESCORT: **v. or n.** chaperone; shepherd; **n.**
cicerone; entourage; retinue; *vis-à-vis*

ESSAY: **v. or n.** endeavor; **n.** (*see* "treatise") discourse; disquisition; dissertation; exegesis; **n.** ESSAYIST: feuilletonist; polemist; polemicist

ESSENCE: (**see** "embodiment") **n.** attribute; aura; cachet; concoction; decoction;
epitome; principle; virtuality
　having (essence) or substance: **a.** coessential; consubstantial; **n.** consubstantiality
　in: **adv.** basically; essentially; fundamentally
　of the: **a.** essential; indispensable
　purest or ultimate: **n.** quintessence; **a.**
quintessential

ESSENTIAL: (**see** "basic") **a.** cardinal;
characteristic; componental; constitutional; fundamental; hypostatic(al); idiopathic; indispensable; inherent; integral;
intrinsic; quintessential; substantial; substantive; vital; **adv.** ESSENTIALLY:
au fond; basically; fundamentally; inherently; **n.** (**see** "requirement") component;
constituent; essentiality; indispensability;
prerequisite; *sine qua non;* **n.** desideratum; desiderium; integrality; (**pl.** desiderate; desideria)
　cond. or qualification: **n.** prerequisite;
sine qua non
　in form or nature: **adv.** *sub specie
aeternitatis;* **n.** quiddity; quintessence
　nature or meaning: (**see** "embodiment")
n. epiphany
　not quite: **a.** subessential; suboptimal
　part: **n.** component; constituent; quintessence
　part(s), deprive of: **v.** devitalize; disembowel; emasculate; eviscerate; exenterate
　quality, fact or thing: **n.** essentiality;
fundamentality; indispensability; quiddity;
quintessence

ESTABLISHED: **a.** conclusive; determinate; determinative; documented; en-
sconced; enshrined; ingrained; institutive;
inveterate; ordained; substantiated; **v.**
ESTABLISH: endow, ensconce; inaugurate; institute; ordain
　long and firmly: **a.** chronic; inveterate
　something conclusively: **n.** probatum;
(**pl.** probata)

ESTABLISHMENT: **n.** installation; institution
　doctrine of opposition to: **n.** antiestab-

lishmentarianism; disestablishmentarianism

    opposing disestablishmentarianism: **n.** antidisestablishmentarianism

ESTATE: **n.** ap(p)anage; demesne; freehold; hereditament(s); patrimony; principality; tenure

ESTEEM: (**see** "honor") **v.** appreciate; venerate; **n.** deference; distinction; eminence; estimableness; estimation; illustriousness; majesty; popularity; prestige; prominence; reverence; veneration; **a.** ESTEEMED: (**see** "eminent") celebrated; commendatory; estimable; illustrious; majestic; meritorious; praiseworthy; prestigious; venerated
    place of highest: **n.** hall of fame; pantheon
    state of being in high: **n.** perihelion
    worthy of: **see** "esteemed" **above**

ETERNAL: (**see** "everlasting") **a.** ceaseless; diuturnal; immarcescible; immortal; immutable; indefectible; infinite; perpetual; sempiternal; supertemporal
    make: **v.** eternalize; perpetuate
    state of being: **n.** diuturnity; eternality; perpetuity
    truths or realities: **n.pl.** (the) eternities

ETERNITY: **n.** diuturnity; eon; eternality; eviternity; Ewigkeit; immortability; immortality; infinitude; infinity; perpetuality; perpetuity; sempiternity
    from: **adv.** *ab aeterno*
    to: **adv.** *in aeternum*

ETHEREAL: **a.** celestial; diaphanous; empyreal; empyrean; exquisite; heavenly; insubstantial; tenuous; **n.** ETHEREALITY: diaphaneity; insubstantiality; tenuity

ETHICAL: **see** "accepted" **and** "moral"
    quality or character: **n.** ethicality

ETIQUETTE: **n.** ceremony; conventiality; decorum; formality; protocol
    breach of: **n.** barbarism; *faux pas; gaffe;* impropriety; solecism

EULOGY: (**see** "praise") **n.** commendation; encomium; eulogium; laudation; panegyric; **a.** EULOGISTIC(AL): (**see** "praiseworthy") commendatory; elegaic; encomiastic; laudatory; panegyrical

EVASION: **n.** artifice; circumvention; equivocation; stratagem; subterfuge; tergiversation; **v.** EVADE: circumvent; equivocate; finesse; maneuver; tergiversate; **a.** EVASIVE: disingenuous; duplicitous; equivocal; evanescent; nebulous; oblique
    in speech: **n.** circumbendibus; circumlocution; periphrasis; sophistry; **a.** circumlocutious; circumlocutory; periphrastic

EVEN: (**see** "equal") **a.** equable; impartial; serene; uniform; unruffled
    mind in circumstances of difficulty: mens aequa in arduis

EVENING, *of the, occurring or appearing at:* **a.** crepuscular; vespertinal; vespertine
    party or gathering: **n.** *soirée*

EVENT(S): **n.** circumstance; circumstantiality; contingency; episode; experience; occurrence; phenomenon
    important: **n.** breakthrough; landmark
    in all: **adv.** *en tout cas*
    prepared for either: **adv.** *in utrumque paratus*
    series of: **n.** chain reaction; continuity; continuum

EVENTUAL: **see** "final" **and** "inescapable"

EVER: **see** "everlasting"
    for: **adv.** *in aeternum;* in perpetuity; *in perpetuum*
    for (ever) and (ever): **adv.** *in saecula saeculorum*

EVERGREEN: **a.** perennial; perpetual; sempervirent; unceasing

EVERLASTING: (**see** "forever") **a.** (a)eonian; amaranthine; diuturnal; continual; eternal; immarcescible; imperishable; incessant; indefectible; indelible; indestructible; *in saecula saeculorum;* interminable; perpetual; sempiternal; unceasing; unfadable; unfading; **n.** EVERLASTINGNESS: (**see** "eternity") diuturnity; eviternity; immortability; immortality; perpetuity; sempiternity

EVERYONE: **pron.** *tout le monde*

EVERYWHERE: **a.** boundless; infinite; omnipresent; peregrine; prevalent; ubiquitous; universal; **n.** omnipresence; ubiquity; universality

EVIDENCE: **n.** criterion; (**pl.** criteria); demonstration; indication; manifestation; symptom; testimony; token; **a.** EVIDENT: (**see** "apparent") cognizable; conspicuous; demonstrable; discernible; luculent; manifest; palpable; patent; perceivable; perceptible; ponderable; rampant; recognizable; sensible; symptomatic; tangible

EVIL: (**see** "wicked") **a.** baleful; depraved; demoniacal; diabolic(al); guileful; iniquitous; malefic(ent); malevolent; malicious; malign(ant); miscreant; noxious; pernicious; pestiferous; pestilent; serpentine; sinister; sinistrous; vicious; **n.** (**see** "wickedness") abomination; calamity; depravity; diabolism; disaster; malefaction; maleficence; malum; misfortune; sinisterity
and good, theory that world divided into: **n.** Manichaeism; **a.** Manichaeistic
because prohibited by law: **adv.** *malum prohibitum*
designed to avert or turn aside: **a.** apotropaic
-doer: **n.** criminal; culprit; delinquent; felon; malefactor; miscreant
in itself, or inherently: **adv.** *malum in se*
intent: **n.** malice aforethought; *malus animus;* **adv.** maliciously; *malo animo*
magic ritual, etc. to avert or overcome: **n.** apotropaism; **a.** apotropaic
mark of: **n.** mark of the beast; stigma; (**pl.** stigmata)
spirit(s): **n.** cacod(a)emon
person possessed by: **n.** demonaic; energumen
to him who (evil) thinks: honi soit qui mal y pense
to invoke: **v.** anathematize; imprecate; **a.** anathematic(al); imprecatory; **n.** anathema; imprecation
world is (doctrine): **n.** malism

EVOLUTION: (**see** "advancement" **and** "change") **n.** development; metamorphosis; ontogeny; phylogeny; transformation; unfoldment; **n.** EVOLUTIONIST: developmentarian
regressive: **n.** categenesis; **a.** catagenetic

EX (*former*): **a. or n.** ci-devant; emeritus

EXACT: (**see** "precise") **v.** extort; **a.** ceremonious; conscientious; definitive; determinate; literal; literatim; mathematical; meticulous; punctilious; scrupulous; slavish; undeviating; verbatim; word-for-word; **n.** EXACTNESS: (**see** "accuracy") definitude; determinacy; exactitude; fidelity; meticulosity; precision; scrupulosity
information: **n.** chapter and verse
minutely: **adv.** *à la lettre; ad literam;* meticulous; punctilious; scrupulous
not: (**see** "inexact") **a.** imponderable

EXACTING: (**see** "demanding") **a.** arduous; exigent; fastidious; meticulous; onerous; precise; scrupulous

EXACTLY: (**see** "exact" **and** "literally") **adv.** accurately; *ad amussim*
as written: (**see** "word-for-word") **adv.** *ad lit(t)eram;* verbatim

EXAGGERATE: **v.** amplify; enhance; magnify
tendency to: **n.** meglomania; mythomania; **a.** megalomaniac(al); Munchausen

EXAGGERATED (or EXAGGERATIVE): **a.** amplificatory; bizarre; eccentric; extravagant; fustian; hyperbolic(al); mythomaniac(al); *outré;* overweening

EXAGGERATION: **n.** megalomania; Munchausenism; mythomania; phantasm(ata)
extravagant or for effect: **n.** hyperbole; **a.** hyperbolic(al)

EXALTATION: **n.** aggrandizement; apotheosis; canonization; deification; enhancement; ennoblement; enshrinement; nobilitation; spiritualization; stellification; transcendence; transfiguration; **v.** EXALT: aggrandize; apotheosize; canonize; deify; enhance; ennoble; enshrine; nobilitate; pedestal; spiritualize; stellify; subtilize; transcend; transfigure; **a.** EXALTED: aggrandized; apotheosized; canonized; deified; enhanced; ennobled; enshrined; magnific(al); nobilated; pedestalized; stellified; transfigured
of mood or spirits: **n.** euphoria; *sursum corda;* **a.** euphoric

EXAMINATION: (**see** "analysis") **n.** anatomy; critique; exploration; inquest; inquiry; inquisition; investigation; perlustration; perscrutation; probe; **a.** analytic(al); exploratory; inquisitive; inquisitorial
critical: **n.** critique

EXAMINE: **v.** analyze; anatomize; collate; explore; interrogate; investigate; perlustrate; scrutinize
minutely: **v.** analyze; anatomize

EXAMPLE: **n.** archetype; exemplar; exemplification; exemplum; paradigm; paragon; precedent; prototype; specimen; typification; **a. see** "exemplary"
chief: **n.** *nec plus supra*
for, or by way of: **n. or adv.** *exempli gratia* (**abb.** e.g.)
most typical: **n.** quintessence; **a.** quintessential
to others, an: **n.** *instar omnium*
to serve as: **v.** exemplify; typify; **n.** exemplification; typification

EXCEED: **v.** excel; surpass; transcend; **a.** EXCEEDING: inordinate; transcendent; **adv.** parlous; **n.** transcendency

EXCELLENCE: **n.** arete; preeminence; superiority; transcendence; **a.** EXCELLENT: (**see** "best" **and** "finest") admirable; *euge;* marvelous; meritorious; mirific; *ne plus ultra; nulli secundus;* paramount; preeminent; prominent; signal; significant; supernal; superordinary; surpassing; stellar; transcendent; unparalleled; unprecedented; valiant; **adv.** *à la bonne heure; catexochen; par excellence*
model of: (**see** "example") **n.** paragon; phoenix

EXCELLING: **a.** preeminent; supereminent; transcending; **v.** EXCEL: see "exceed"

EXEMPTION, *not subject to:* **a.** irrecusable
taking: **a.** excipient
to a rule: **n.** nonobstant

EXCEPTIONAL: (**see** "choice") **a.** extraordinary; inexplicable; nonpareil; novel; preternatural; supernal; supernatural; superordinary; unexampled; unprecedented

EXCERPTS, *literary:* **n.pl.** analecta; analects; collectanea; chrestomathy; *disjecta membra;* miscellanea; *morceaux choisis;* scrapiana

EXCESS: **n.** copiosity; exorbitance; exorbitancy; extravagance; inordinateness; intemperance; luxus; nimiety; plethora; prodigality; redundancy; satiety; *satis superque;* superabundance; superabundancy; supererogation; superfluity; superflux; surfeit; surplusage; **a.** EXCESSIVE: (**see** "extravagant") copious; exorbitant; extreme; immoderate; inconsolable; inordinant; intemperant; lavish; nimious; pleonastic; plethoric; profuse; redundant; replete; superabundant; superfluous; superlative; unconscionable
avoid: **adv.** *nec quid nimis*
in number: **a.** superfluous; supernumerary; **n.** superfluity; superflux; supernumerary
of words: **n.** prolixity; redundancy; verbiage; verbosity

EXCHANGE: **v.** barter; commute; reciprocate; substitute; **n.** commutation; *quid pro quo;* reciprocity; **a.** commutable
science of, esp. international: **n.** cambistry

EXCITED: (**see** "delirious") **a.** agitato; febrile; frenetic; hectic; **v.** EXCITE: (**see** "stir") fillip; inflame; stimulate; suscitate; **a.** EXCITATORY: excitable; hysteric(al); ignitable; incitatory; incitative; provocative; riotous; stimulatory
capable of being: (**see** "excitatory" **above**) **n.** ignitability
extremely: **a. or adv.** berserk; rapturous(ly)

EXCITEMENT: **n.** agitation; fomentation; furore; incitation; incitement; instigation; rapture; transport
great: **n.** alarum; alarums and excursions; orgasm; **a.** orgasmic; orgiastic
intense emotional: **n.** ecstasy; raptus; **a.** ecstatic; **v.** ecstasiate; ecstasize
state of: **n.** agitation; fanteeg; fantigue; raptus

EXCLAMATION: **n.** ecphonesis; ejaculation; expletive; vociferation; **a.** EXCLAMATORY: ejaculatory; expletive; expletory; vociferant; vociferous

EXCLUDE: **v.** debar; disbar; eliminate; excommunicate; ghettoize; ostrasize; preclude; prohibit; reject; segregate; **n.** EXCLUSION: (**see** "separation") censorship; debarring; excommunication; ostracism; rejection; segregation; sequestration

107

EXCLUSIVE: **a.** exclusivistic; fashionable; stylish; undividéd; **n.** exclusivism; exclusivity
 group: (**see** "clique") **n.** cabal; charmed circle; *corps d'elite;* coterie

EXCOMMUNICATE: **v.** anathematize; interdict; ostracize; **n.** EXCOMMUNICATION: anathema(tism); anathematization; ostracism; **a.** anathematic(al)

EXCREMENT(S): **n.** defecation; elimination; feculence; ordure; (**pl.** dejecta; egesta; excreta; feces); **v.** EXCRETE: defecate; egest; eliminate; **a.** EXCRETORY: depurant; egestive; excretious
 abnormal interest in: **n.** coprophilia; **a.** coprophilous
 rel. to or to study of: **a.** excremental; scatologic(al)
 study of or interest in: **n.** coprology; scatology; skatology

EXCUSE: **v.** absolve; conciliate; condone; extenuate; intellectualize; overlook; palliate; pardon; rationalize; **n.** absolution; amnesty; condonation; dispensation; extenuation; indulgence; intellectualization; justification; palliation; pardon; provocation; rationalization; remission; **a.** EXCUSABLE: apologetic; conciliatory; condonable; *ein mal, kein mal;* excusatory; justificatory; pardonable; placable; venial; vindicatory
 he who (excuses) himself, accuses himself: qui s'excuse, s'accuse

EXECUTION, *means of:* **n.** decapitation; electrocution; garrote; guillotine; lapidation; noyade; Republican marriage; strangulation

EXECUTIONER, *rel. to:* **a.** carnificial

EXEMPLARY: (**see** "commendable") **a.** exemplificative; exemplificatory; monitory; paradigmatic(al); prototypal; prototypic(al)

EXEMPTION: (**see** "freedom") **n.** dispensation; immunity; impunity

EXHALATION: **n.** effluvium; emanation; expiration; flatus; **a.** effluvial

EXHAUST: **v.** deplete; discharge; evacuate; **n.** effluvium; (**pl.** effluvia); **a.** EX-HAUSTED: depleted; effete; impoverished; **n.** EXHAUSTION: depletion; inanition
 riches or supplies: **v.** depauperate; improverish; pauperize

EXHIBITION, *boastful:* **n.** ostentation; **a.** ostentatious

EXHILARATED: (**see** "cheerful") **a.** ebullient; euphoric; exhilarative; heady; intoxicated; rapturous; zestful

EXILE: **v.** banish; expatriate; ostracize; relegate; **n.** banishment; Diaspora; expatriation; fugitivity; ostracism; relegation

EXISTENCE: (**see** "being") **n.** actuality; entity; reality
 as a person or individual: **n.** individuation
 beginning to have: **a.** aborning; nascent; parturient; **adv.** *in fieri*
 capacity to compete for: **n.** vagility
 cause or ground of: **n.** *ratio essendi*
 physical: **n.** corporality; corporeity; materiality; substantiality; substantivity; **a.** corporeal; substantive
 rel. to: **a.** noumenal; ontic; ontological
 science or study of: **n.** ontology; **a.** ontological
 something w/o: **n.** ethereality; nonentity; nullity

EXISTING: **a.** existential; extant; **adv.** *in esse*
 at same time: **see** "contemporary"
 something which is: **n.** actuality; corporality; corporeity; entity; existent; materiality; reality; substantiality

EXIT: **n.** egress(ion); exeunt

EXONERATE: **v.** absolve; exculpate; vindicate; **n.** EXONERATION: exculpation; **a.** EXONERATED: exculpable; exculpatory

EXORBITANT: (**see** "excessive") **adv.** *hors de prix*

EXPAND: **v.** amplify; augment; delate; dilate; enhance; inflate; intumesce; tumefy; **a.** EXPANDING: proliferous; tumefactive; tumescent; **n.** EXPANSION: amplification; development; exacerbation; proliferation; tumescence; tympany

EXPANDED *or spread out:* (**see** "expand-ing") **a.** patulous

EXPECTED: **a.** anticipated; contemplated; contingent; inchoate; inchoative; incipient; potential; prospective; **n.** EXPECTATION: anticipation; assumption; contemplation; expectancy; prospect; supposition
act or conduct: **n.** devoir
doing more than: **a.** supererogative; supererogatory; **n.** supererogation; **v.** supererogate

EXPECTING: **a.** anticipant; anticipatory; **n.** anticipant

EXPEDIENT: (**see** "fit") **a.** advisable; astucious; astute; expediential; opportune; opportunistic; politic; **n.** EXPEDIENCY (**or** EXPEDIENCE): makeshift; temporization
last: **n.** *à outrance; dernier ressort; pis aller*

EXPEDITION: (**see** "quest") **n.** acceleration; entrada; promptness; reconnaissance; safari

EXPEL (**or** EXPULSION): see "exile"

EXPENDITURE: **n.** disbursement; dispensation

EXPENSE(S), *at great:* **adv.** *à grands frais*
regulating: **a.** sumptuary

EXPENSIVE: (**see** "costly") **a.** confiscatory; dispenditious; extravagant; lavish; sumptuous
very: **a.** exorbitant; **adv.** *hors de prix*

EXPERIENCE: (**see** "background" **and** "knowledge") **n.** versatility; **a.** EXPERIENCED: adept; capable; competent; consummate; knowledgeable; practiced; seasoned; versant; versatile
based on: **a.** empirical; existential; experiential; materialistic; pragmatic; utilitarian
beyond or outside of: **a.** intuitive; met-empirical; **n.** fourth dimension
brief but unpleasant: **n.** *mauvais quart d'heure*
is mistress of fools: experientia stultorum magistra

reliance on rather than science: **a.** empiric(al); **n.** empiric(ism)
teaches: **n.** *experientia docet*
thru imaginary participation: **n.** identification; vicariousness; **a.** vicarious

EXPERIMENT, *crucial:* **n.** *experimentum crucis*

EXPERIMENTAL: **a.** contingent; empirical; tentative

EXPERT: (**see** "skillful") **a.** adept; (ambi)dexterous; *au fait;* proficient; versatile; virtuosic; **n.** adept; ambidexterity; artiste; connoisseur; expertise; past master (**or** mistress); virtuoso
in realms of fine arts or fashion: **n.** artiste; cognoscente; connoisseur; doyen; (**fem.** doyenne); esthete; illuminato; **a.** esthetic
opinion: **n.** expertise

EXPERTNESS: (**see** "skill") **n.** (ambi)-dexterity; deftness; expertise; hability; virtuosity
degree of: **n.** habilitation; technique; virtuosity

EXPLAIN: **v.** elucidate; expatiate; explicate; exposit; expound; interpret; justify; rationalize; resolve; translate; **n.** EXPLAINER: elucidator; exegete; exegetist; explanator; exponent; interpreter; translator
not able to: (**see** "mysterious") **a.** inexplicable; insoluble

EXPLANATION: (**see** "justification") **n.** clarification; *éclaircissement;* elucidation; exegesis; expatiation; explication; exposition; interpretation; rationale; rationality; translation
additional: **n.** excursus; epexegesis
art of: **n.** exegetics; hermeneutics
avoid by giving reasonable, but not too plausible (explanation): **v.** intellectualize; rationalize; **n.** intellectualization; rationalization
making more obscure by: obscurum per obscurius

EXPLANATORY: **a.** analytical; discursive; epexegetic(al); essayistic; exegetic(al); explicative; explicatory; expository; expositive; hermeneutic; interpretative; paraphrastic(al); resolutive; resolutory *article:* **n.** disquisition; exegesis; interpretation

EXPLODE: **v.** detonate; fulminate; **a.** EXPLOSIVE: detonative; fulminous; pyrotechnic(al); **n.** EXPLOSION: detonation; fiasco; fulmination

EXPLOIT: **v.** cultivate; manipulate; utilize; **n.** (see "deed") achievement; gest(e); **a.** EXPLOITING: predaceous; predacious; predatory; **n.** EXPLOITATION; predacity; utilization

EXPLORE: **v.** examine; investigate; probe; reconnoiter; **n.** EXPLORATION: (see "survey") examination; inquest; investigation; probe; prospection; reconnaissance; reconnoiter; safari

EXPOSE: **v.** denudate; denude; unmask; **n.** denudation; *exposé;* **a.** EXPOSING: denudative; **a.** EXPOSED: see "attack, open to"

EXPOUND: **see** "explain"; **n.** EXPOUNDER: advocate; exegete; exponent

EXPRESSION: (**see** "remark") **n.** diction; locution; manifestation; mien; phraseology; physiognomy; utterance
  concise or condensed: **n.** aphorism; brachylogy
  extravagant or high-flown: **n.** vaporing; **a.** vaporing; vaporizing; **v.** vaporize
  facial, denoting disorder, etc.: **n.** facies
  lacking in: **a.** inexpressible; impassive; **n.** impassivity
  nice facility of: **n.** *curiosa felicitas*
  pedantic or academic: **n.** scholasm
  polite: **n.** euphemism; **a.** euphemistic
  studied facility of: **n.** curiosa felicitas

EXPRESSIVE: **a.** articulate; eloquent; emphatic; indicative; meaningful; sententious; significant; **n.** EXPRESSIVENESS: eloquence; expressivity; plangency

EXPURGATE: **v.** bowdlerize; emasculate; expunge; purge

EXTEMPORARY: (see "off-hand") **a.** autoschediastic; extemporaneous; extempore; impromptu; improvised; improviso; spontaneous; unpremeditated; **n.** EXTEMPORIZATION: autoschediasm; extemporaneity; improvisation; improviso;

spontaneity; **v.** EXTEMPORIZE: *ad lib;* improvise

EXTENT: (see "scope") **n.** ambit; amplitude; caliber; compass; comprehensiveness; latitude; **a.** EXTENSIVE: comprehensive; (en)cyclopedic(al); far-reaching; illimitable; latitudinal; latitudinous; magnitudinous; measureless; panoramic
  to a certain: **adv.** *pro tanto*
  to indicate the: **v.** quantify

EXTENUATE: see "ease"

EXTERMINATE: (see "destroy") **v.** abolish; annihilate; decimate; demolish; deracinate; eradicate; execute; extirpate; **n.** EXTERMINATION: abolishment; annihilation; decimation; eradication; extirpation

EXTERNAL (or EXTERIOR): **a.** adventitious; ectal; exogenous; exoteric; extraneous; extrinsic(al); foreign; peripheral; superficial; ulterior; **n.** EXTERNALITY: exteriority; extraneity; periphery
  appearance: **see under** "aspect"
  control, subject to: **a.** heteronomous

EXTOL: (see "exalt") **v.** applaud; approbate; commend; deify; glorify; enhance; enshrine; eulogize; laud; panegyrize; spiritualize; **a.** EXTOLLING: (see "commendable") eulogistic; panegyric(al)

EXTRA: **a.** accessory; additional; adjunctive; *de trop;* redundant; superfluous; superior; supernumerary; **n.** redundance; redundancy; superabundance; supererogation; superfluity; supernumerary

WORK: **n.** supererogation; **a.** supererogant; supererogatory

EXTRACT: (see "abstract") **n.** concentrate; decoction; decoctum; elicitation; extraction; genealogy; (quint)essence

EXTRANEOUS: (see "foreign") **a.** accidental; extrinsic; irrelevant; ulterior; unrelated; **n.** accidentality; extraneity

EXTRAORDINARY: (see "rare") **a.** bizarre; *extraordinaire;* inordinate; melodramatic; phenomenal; prodigious; sensational *person or thing:* **n.** anomaly; extravaganza; mutation; phenomenality; phenomenon; prodigality; prodigy; *rara avis;* spectacular; sport

EXTRASENSORY *perception:* **n.** telesthesia

EXTRAVAGANCE: **n.** enthusiasm; exorbitance; extravagancy; extravaganza; luxuriance; nimiety; opulence; prodigality; profligacy; profusion; rampancy; redundance; superabundance; superfluity; superflux; wantonness; **a.** EXTRAVAGANT: (see "superfluous") dispendious; exorbitant; gothic; immoderate; inordinate; intemperate; lavish; luxuriant; luxurious; nimious; prodigal; profligate; rampant; redundant; unrestrained; wanton
controlling or regulating: **a.** sumptuary

EXTREME(S): (see "odd") **a.** arrant; bizarre; consummate; eccentric; egregious; extravagant; fanatical; fantastic(al); immoderate; inordinate; maximum; notorious; *outré;* overweening; ultimate; uncompromising; **adv.** unco
act(s): **n.** ultraism
at the: **adv.** *ad extremum*
circumstances, in: **adv.** *in articulo mortis; in extremis*
course bet. two: **a.** or **n.** *via media*
limit: (see "extremity") **n.** outrance

EXTREMIST(S): (see "radical") **n.** *avant-garde;* ultraist
opinions, principles, etc. of: **n.** ultraism
pert. to: **a.** *avant-garde;* fanatical; ultraistic(al)

EXTREMITY, *last or utmost:* **n.** *à outrance; dernier ressort;* outrance; *pis aller*

EXTRICATE: see "free"

EXUBERANT: see "rank" and "unbridled"

EXUDE: **v.** emanate; osmose; percolate; transude; **n.** EXUDATION: extravasation; osmosis; transudate; transudation; **a.** EXUDATIVE: osmotic; transudative

EYE(S), *almond-shaped:* **n.** *yeux en amande*
bulging: **a.** exophthalmic; **n.** exophthalmos (**also** exophthalmus)
cross: **n.** exotropia; exotropism
glance of the: **n.** oeillade
having or involving one: **a.** monocular; monophthalmic
having or pert. to two: **a.** binocular
inequality in size of pupils: **n.** anisocoria
quick movement of, fr. one point to another: **n.** saccadic (movement)
study or student of: **n.** ophthalmology; ophthalmologist
twinkling of: **n.** *clin d'oeil*
watering of: **n.** epiphora
with naked: **adv.** nudis oculis; **a.** macroscopic

EYEBROW(S): **n.** supercilium; (**pl.** supercilia)
loss of: **n.** anaphalantiasis

EYELASH: **n.** cilium; (**pl.** cilia); **a.** ciliary

EYELID(S): **n.** blepharon; palpebrum; (**pl.** palpebra); **a.** palpebral

F

FABLE: **n.** allegory; apologue; fabrication; fabulosity; legend; myth; untruth; **a.** FABULAR (**or** FABULOUS): allegorical; apocryphal; fictitious; mythical; parabolical; Scheheradazian; **n.** FABLER: allegorist; fabulist; improvisatore; (**fem.** improvisatrice); improvisor; mythmaker; mythologist; parabolist
  express in: **v.** allegorize; fabulize; mythasize; mythologize; parabolize
  pert. to: **a.** Aesopian; Aesopic; allegoric(al); fabular; mythologic(al); parabolical

FABRICATE: (**see** "construct") **v.** fabulize; improvisate; improvise; **a.** improvisatorial; improvisatory

FACE: **v.** beard; brave; challenge; **n.** assurance; audacity; countenance; effrontery; facade; facet; impudence; obverse; physiognomy; visage
  having large: **a.** megaprosopous
  makeup: **n.** maquillage
  rel. to: **a.** prosopic
  -to-face: **adv.** *affronté; front à front; tête-à-tête; vis-à-vis;* **n.** confrontation
  trust not the: fronti nulla fides; ne fronti crede

FACIAL *feature or expression:* (**see** "countenance") **n.** lineament; mien; physiognomy; (**pl.** facies); **a.** physiognom(on)-ic(al)
  feature(s) where sign of disease: **n.pl.** facies (**or** Hippocratic facies)
  makeup (cosmetic, as paint, etc.) **n.** maquillage

FACING: **see** "face-to-face"

FACT(S). **n.** actuality; circumstance; datum; (**pl.** data); *fait accompli;* occurrence; **a.** FACTUAL: (**see** "earthly") empirical; **n.** FACTUALITY: facticity
  after the: **a.** *ex post facto; post-factum;* retrospective

by the: **a. or n.** *ipso facto;* **a.** *de facto consider (something unreal) as (fact):* **v.** materialize; pragmatize; rationalize
  fraudulent concealment of: **n.** subreption
  ignorance of the (excuses): ignoranti facti (excusat); **pl.** *ignoranti factorum (excusat)*
  inescapable and unalterable: **n.** facticity
  speak for themselves: res ipso loquitur
  state of being a: **n.** facticity; factuality
  surrounding a crime, etc.: **n.pl.** *res geste w/o ref. to pertinent (facts) or materials:* **adv.** *in vacuo*

FACTIONAL: **see** "divisive"

FAD: (**see** "fancy") **n.** caprice; foible; megrim; monomania; vagary; whim
  latest: **n.** *dernier cri*

FADE: **v.** etiolate; evanesce; languish; **a.** FADELESS: amaranthine; immarcescible; indelible

FAIL, *as in health:* **v.** decline; flag; languish; retrogress
  to develop: **v.** abort; **a. or adv.** abortive

FAILURE: **n.** abstention; bankruptcy; *brutum fulmen;* catastrophe; *culbute;* defalcation; defection; delinquency; dereliction; deterioration; fiasco; insolvency; miscarriage; neglect; omission; pretermission
  to act: **n.** inexecution; laches; misfeasance; nonfeasance; nonperformance
  to appear: **n.** absentation; abstention
  utter: **n.** catastrophe; **a.** catastrophic(al)

FAINT: **n.** swoon; syncope; **a.** (**see** "dim") caliginous; indistinct; obscure
  -hearted: **a.** irresolute; pusillanimous; **n.** pusillaniminity

FAIR: (**see** "honest") **a.** comely; dispassionate; equitable; honorable; impartial;

impersonal; judicial; moderate; unbiased; unprejudiced; **n.** FAIRNESS: detachment; disinterestedness; equity; impartiality; judiciality

FAITH: (**see** "belief" **and** "religion") **n.** assurance; confidence; conviction; doctrine
　abandon: **v.** apostasize; **n.** apostate; apostasy
　acceptance of dogmatic statements on: **n.** fideism
　alone assures salvation: **n.** solifidianism
　articles of: **n.** credenda
　bad, with or in: **adv.** or **a.** mala fide(s)
　branch of theology dealing w/: **n.** pistology
　defender of the: **n.** fidei defensor
　good: **n.** uberrima fides
　implicit: **n.** uberrima fides
　pert. to or explaining: **a.** pistic
　reliance on alone: **n.** fideism

FAITHFUL: **a.** accurate; incorruptible; reliable; resolute; staunch; steadfast; **n.** unswerving; unwavering; **n.** FAITHFULNESS: allegiance; devotion; fealty; fidelity; loyalty; obedience; steadfastness

FAITHLESS: **see** "false" **and** "treacherous"

FAKE: **see** "counterfeit"

FALL, *sudden:* **n.** anticlimax; **a.** anticlimactic(al)

FALLACY: (**see** "deception") **n.** casuistry; idolum; illogicality; illusion; paradox(icality); phantasy; pseudology; pseudoxy; sophism; sophistry; **a.** FALLACIOUS: (**see** "deceptive" **and** "false") apocryphal; illogical; paralogistic; pseudological; pseudox; sophistical
　formal: **n.** paralogism; **a.** paralogistic
　in thinking: **see under** "thinking"
　logical: **n.** petitio principii

FALLING *of organ or part:* **n.** prolapse; prolapsus; ptosis
　steeply: **a.** precipitant; precipitate; precipitous

FALSE: (**see** "artificial" **and** "hypocritical") **a.** apocryphal; arrant; apostate; apostatic; barmecidal; counterfeit (**q.v.**); dishonorable; duplicitous; faithless; fictitious; fictive; ignominious; illusional; il-

lusive; illusory; inauthentic; infamous; Machiavellian; mendacious; meretricious; mythical; paradoxical; perfidious; pseudological; pseudo(x); renegade; specious; spectral; spurious; traitorous; treacherous; treasonable; unauthentic; untrustworthy; **n.** FALSENESS: (**see** "hypocrisy") duplicity; inaccuracy; inveracity; mendacity; misrepresentation; paradoxicality; perfidy; speciosity; treachery; unfaithfulness
　and scandalous story, esp. in politics: **n.** canard; roorback
　belief or conception: **n.** delusion; hallucination; misconception; pseudodox: **a.** delusional; delusionary; delusive; pseudodox
　fantastically or romantically: **a.** Munchausen; pseudological; **n.** Munchausenism
　front: **n.** Potemkin village; Trojan horse
　modesty or shame: **n.** malus pudor; **a.** puritanical
　notably or splendidly: **adv.** splendide mendax
　opinion or doctrine: **n.** or **a.** pseudodox; **n.** pseudodoxy
　pathos: **n.** bathos; maudlinism; sentimentalism
　pretense: (**see** "sham") **n.** dissemblance; dissimulation; Trojan horse
　reasoning: (**see** "illogical") **v.** paralogize
　suggestion: **n.** suggestio falsi
　swearing: **n.** perjury; **a.** perjur(i)ous
　thinking, form of: (**see under** "thinking") **n.** idolum
　writing(s) **see** "falsely or wrongly attributed writing(s)"

FALSEHOOD: (**see** "lie") **n.** canard; cretinism; fabrication; fabulation; falsity; invention; inveracity; mendacity; misrepresentation; pretense; pseudology; roorback; unveracity
　hint of: **n.** suggestio falsi
　minor: **n.** fib; tarradiddle
　suggestion of: **n.** suggestio falsi

FALSELY *or wrongly attributed writing(s):* **n.** apocryph; pseudepigraph; pseudograph; (**pl.** anagignoskomena; apocrypha; pseudepigraphia) **a.** apocryphal; pseudepigraphic(al); pseudepigraphous

FALSIFIED, *fantastically:* **a.** Munchausen; pseudological; **n.** Munchausenism

FAME: (see "eminence") n. distinction; *éclat;* notability; notoriety; prestige; renown; reputation; repute

FAMILIARITY: n. confidentiality; informality; intimacy; a. FAMILIAR: *au fait;* confidential; conversant; customary; intimate; intrusive; proverbial; unceremonious; versed; v. FAMILIARIZE: (see "accustom") acclimatize; acquaint; habituate; orientate; popularize
    acting with: a. avuncular
    too much breeds contempt: nimia familiaritas parit contemptum

FAMILY, *centered around husband's:* a. patrilocal
    centered around mother's: a. matrilocal
    head of (fem.): n. materfamilias; matriarch; a. matriarchal
    head of (m.): n. paterfamilias; patriarch; *père de famille;* a. patriarchal
    life: n. domesticity; ménage
    relating or peculiar to a: a. gentilitial; gentilitious
    pert. to: a. familial; familistic
    tree: n. ancestry; genealogy; lineage; paternity; pedigree

FAMINE: n. dearth; exigency; starvation

FAMOUS: (see "eminent") a. celebrious; celebrated; classic; *distingué;* distinguished; illustratory; illustrious; leonine; notable; notorious; renowned; reputable; venerable
    incident or case: n. *cause célèbre*

FAN: (see "follower") n. *aficionado;* (fem. *aficionada*); apostle; buff; devotee; enthusiast; votary
    shaped like: a. rhipidate

FANATIC: (see "radical") n. bigot; energumen; enthusiast

FANCY: (see "fad" and "daydream") n. capriccio; caprice; chimera; *fata morgana;* megrim; phantasm(ata); phantasy; vaporosity; a. extravagant; premium; whimsical; a. FANCIFUL: (see "fantastic") capricious; chimerical; ethereal; grotesque; imaginary; quixotic; romantic; vaporous; whimsical; n. ethereality; fantasticality; grotesquerie; whimsicality
    food or dish: n. kickshaw; tidbit
    impossible or foolish: n. chimera; fantasy; a. chimerical; fantastic; utopian

FANFARE: n. blazonry; fanfaron; fanfaronade; flourish; tantara; tantatara

FANTASTIC(AL): (see "fanciful" and "odd") a. baroque; bizarre; capricious; eccentric; extravagant; fantasque; gothic; grotesque; irrational; preposterous, preternatural; supernatural; unearthly; unrealistic; n. FANTASTICALITY: ethereality; grotesquerie; whimsicality
    render (fantastic): v. fantasticate; n. fantastication; fantasticism

FANTASY: n. apparition; autism; ethereality; fantasticality; hallucination; phantasm(ata); reverie; vagary
    lit. or mus.: n. extravaganza; fantasia

FAR: (see "remote") a. forane; tramontane; ultramontane; ultramundane
    away place: n. ultima Thule

FARCE: n. buffoonery; burlesque; extravaganza; forcemeat; harlequinade; opera bouffe; ridiculosity

FARCICAL *character:* n. harlequin; opera bouffe

FAREWELL: (see "goodbye") n. adieu; *chant du cygne* (swan song); *congé;* envoi; valediction
    a last: n. *ultimum vale*
    bidding or saying, or farewell utterance: n. valediction; a. apopemptic; valedictory
    hymn or ode: n. or a. apopemptic

FAR-FETCHED: (see "ridiculous") a. catachrestic(al); laborious; preposterous; *recherché*

FARMING: n. agrarianism; agriculture; agronomics; agronomy; geoponics; husbandry; n. FARMER: agriculturist; agronomist; granger; husbandman; ruralist
    pert. to: a. agrarian; agricultural; agronomical; geoponic

FAR-OFF *or unknown region:* n. ultima Thule; a. tramontane; ultramontane; ultramundane

FARSIGHTED: (see "prophetic[al]") a. hyperopic; presbyopic; presbytic; n. presbyopia

FARTHEST: **a.** farthermost; remotest; ultimate
>*possible point or limit:* **n.** ultima Thule

FASCINATING: **a.** captivating; Circean; enchanting; enthralling; irresistible; mesmeric; sirenic(al); **v.** FASCINATE: (**see** "allure") bewitch; captivate; enamor; enchant; ensorcel(1); enthral(1); mesmerize
>*woman:* **n.** Circe; *femme fatale;* intrig(u)ante

FASHION: (**see** "make" **and** "fad") **n.** *dernier cri*
>*after a:* ad instar
>*high:* **n.** *beau monde; haute couture; haut ton*
>*in a cavilier:* **adv.** *à la hussarde*
>*latest:* **n.** *dernier cri*
>*man of:* **n.** *homme du monde*
>*people of:* **n.pl.** *gens du monde*
>*woman of:* **n.** *femme du monde;* mondaine; sophisticate

FASHIONABLE: **a.** *à la mode;* jaunty; *le bon ton;* modish; mondain(e); *recherché; soigné(e)* ; sophisticated; ton(n)ish
>*despair:* **a.** *fin-de-siècle*
>*society:* **n.** *beau monde;* (**pl.** *beaux mondes*) ; *grand monde; haut monde*
>*world:* **n.** *le beau monde; le monde*

FAST: (**see** "prompt") **a.** accelerated; *à corps perdu;* celeritous; expeditious; expeditive; Gaderine; intemperate; meteoric; precipitate; precipitous; velocious; **adv. or a.** allegro
>*day:* **n.** *jour maigre*

FAT: (**see** "stout") **a.** adipose; corpulent; pinguid; **n.** (**see** "fattiness" **and** "obesity") adiposity; corpulence; pinguidity
>*excess on hips or buttocks:* **n.** steatopygia; steatopygy; **a.** steatopygic; steatopygous
>*formation of:* **n.** adipogenesis; **a.** adipogenous; adipogenetic
>*inclined to be:* **a.** liparous
>*pert. to:* **a.** adipose; corpulent; pinguid
>*producing or causing:* see "fattening"

FATAL: (**see** "deadly") **a.** calamitous; disastrous; feral; lethal; lethiferous; malicious; malignant; mortal; mortiferous; pernicious; pestilent(ial)

FATALISM: **n.** determinism; necessarianism; predestination; predetermination

FATE(S): (**see** "doom") **n.** destiny; disaster; Moira; (**pl.** Moirai) ; portion; predestination; predetermination; Providence; will of the gods
>*Hindu:* **n.** karma
>*omen of* (*esp. one's own*): **n.** handwriting on the wall
>*oppose:* **n.** *Fata obstant*
>*The Three:* (or "Destinies") : Greece (Moerae **or** Moirai) ; Clotho (spins thread of life) ; Lachesis (assigns each to his destiny) ; **and** Atropos (cuts thread at death) ; Roman counterparts (Parcae): Nona; Decuma; Morta

FATHER: **n.** ancestor; author; genitor; patriarch; precursor; predecessor; procreator; prototype
>*centered upon:* **a.** patricentric
>*derived fr. name of:* **a.** patronymic(al)
>*descended thru:* **a.** patrilineal; patronymic(al) ; **n.** patrilineage
>*inherited from:* **a.** patriclinous; patroclinous; **n.** patrimony
>*killing of, also killer:* **n.** patricide
>*like a:* **a.** paternal(istic) ; **n.** paternalism
>*like (father), like son:* tel père, tel fils
>*marked by authority of:* **a.** patripotestal
>*of the family:* **n.** paterfamilias; patriarch; père de famille; **a.** patriarchal
>*pert. to duty to:* **a.** filial
>*power of:* **n.** *patria potestas;* **a.** patripotestal
>*relationship thru:* **n.** agnate; agnation; patrilineage; **a.** agnatic; patrilineal; patronymic(al)
>*side of family:* **a.** paternal

FATHERHOOD: **n.** paternality; paternity; **a.** paternal

FATHERLY *care or conduct:* **n. or a.** paternality; **n.** paternalism; **a.** paternalistic

FATIGUE: **n.** dyspn(o)ea; enervation; exhaustion; hypokinesia; hypokinesis; impuissance; lackadaisy; languor; lassitude; lethargy; listlessness; weariness; **a.** FATIGUED: adynamic; dyspn(o)eic; enervated; languescent; languorous; lassitudinous; lethargic
>*becoming (fatigued):* **a.** languescent

FATTENING: **a.** lipogenous; pinguescent; steatogenous; **a.** FATTY: adipose; oleaginous; unctious; unctuous; **n.** FATTINESS: (**see** "obesity") adiposis; lipomatosis

FAULT(S): **n.** culpa(bility); delinquency; dereliction; foible; imperfection; misdemeanor; neglect; negligence; peccadillo
by my: **a.** *mea culpa*
every man has his: nemo sine vitiis nascitur
in equal: **adv.** (*in*) *pari delicto*
slight: **n.** foible; peccadillo; veniality

FAULTFINDING: (**see** "critical") **a.** captious; carping; censorial; censorious; condemnatory; cynical; hypercritical; querulous; scrupulous; **n.** FAULTFINDER: carper; caviler; censor; critic; cynic; *frondeur;* malcontent; momus
given to: **n.** captiousness; cynicism; scrupulosity

FAULTLESS: (**see** "innocent") **a.** immaculate; impeccable; impeccant; indefectible; infallible; irreproachable; undeviating; unerring; **n.** FAULTLESSNESS: immaculacy; impeccability; indefectibility

FAULTY: (**see** "imperfect") **a.** amiss; dilapidated; suboptimal; substandard; unsound
in reasoning or logic: **a.** paralogistic; **n.** paralogism
or mixed use of metaphors: **n.** catachresis; **a.** catachrestic(al)

FAVOR: **v.** abet; countenance; encourage; **n.** approbation; condescension; indulgence; patronage; sponsorship
as a: **adv. or a.** ex gratia; **a.** complimentary; gratis; gratuitous
popular: **n.** *aura popularis*
to find, or bring into good: **v.** ingratiate; **a.** ingratiating; ingratiatory

FAVORABLE: (**see** "advantageous") **a.** approbative; approbatory; auspicious; beneficial; benign(ant); commendatory; condescending; disposed; gracious; inclinable; ingratiating; preferential; propitious; salutary; strategetic; strategic(al); tendentious; wholesome
most: **a. or n.** optimal; optimum
omen: **n.** *omen faustum*

FAVORED, *person highly:* **n.** *persona grata;* (**pl.** *personae gratissimae*)

FAVORITE: **n.** cosset; *mignon;* partisan; *persona grata*
servile: **n.** minion; toady

FAVORITISM: **n.** bias; cordiality; encouragement; partiality; patronage; predilection; sanction
in placing in desirable jobs: **n.** nepotism; **a.** nepotal; nepotic; **n.** nepotist

FAWN: **v. or n.** grovel; kow-tow; **a.** FAWNING: deferential; gnathonic; obsequious; oleaginous; parasitical; servile; sycophantic; toadying; unctuous; **n.** deference; obsequiousness; obsequity; servility; sycophancy; toadying; unctuosity; unctuousness

FEAR: **n.** apprehension; consternation; disquietude; misgiving; timidity; trepidation; **v.** apprehend; cower; eschew; suspect
abnormal, of animals: **n.** zoophobia
of being alone: **n.** autophobia; monophobia
of being buried alive: **n.** taphephobia
of being chastized: **n.** rhabdophobia
of being touched: **n.** aichmophobia
of cat(s): **n.** aileurophobia; ailurophobia; galeophobia; gatophobia
of close(d) places or being shut in: **n.** claustrophobia
of crowds: **n.** ochlophobia
of darkness: **n.** nyctophobia
of death or dead: **n.** necrophobia; thantophobia
of disease: **n.** hypochondria; pathophobia
of dog(s): **n.** cynophobia
of drafts or wind: **n.** aerophobia; anemophobia
of dust: **n.** amathophobia
of fire: **n.** pyrophobia
of foreigners or what is foreign: **n.** xenophobia
of God's wrath: **n.** theophobia
of heights or high places: **n.** acrophobia
of human society: **n.** apanthropophobia; apanthropia; apanthropy
of ideas: **n.** ideophobia
of insanity or going insane: **n.** lyssophobia
of lightning or storms: **n.** astrophobia
of male sex: **n.** androphobia; apandria
of meeting people: **see** "of human society" **above**
of night or darkness: **n.** nyctophobia
of number 13: **n.** triadaidekaphobia
of open or public places: **n.** agoraphobia
of pain: **n.** algophobia

117

of particular place(s) : **n.** topophobia
of poisoning: **n.** toxiphobia
of pollution by contact w/ objects, or of being unclean: **n.** mysophobia
of punishment: **n.** rhabdophobia
of Satan: **n.** Satanophobia
of sharp-pointed objects: **n.** aichmophobia
of sleep: **n.** hypnophobia
of society: **see** "of human society" **above**
of solitude: **n.** autophobia; monophobia
of sound(s) : **n.** phonophobia
of storms or lightning: **n.** astrophobia
of thunder: **n.** astrophobia; brontophobia; tontitrophobia; tonitruphobia
of uncleanliness: **n.** mysophobia
of winds or drafts: **n.** aerophobia; anemophobia
of woman or women: **n.** gynephobia
of work: **n.** ergasiophobia; ergophobia
of wrath of God: **n.** theophobia

FEARFUL: **a.** appalling; apprehensive; horrendous; horrific; pavid; timorous; **a.** FEARLESS: (**see** "brave") audacious; chivalrous; courageous; dauntless; impavid; indomitable; intrepid; *sans peur;* temerarious; undauntable; undaunted; **n.** FEARLESSNESS: audacity; chivalry; fortitude; intrepidity; **a.** FEARSOME: awe-inspiring; doughty; formidable; horrendous; redoubtable

FEASIBLE: **see** "possible"

FEAST: **n.** convivium; **n.** FEASTING: conviviality; epulation; **a.** convivial; epulary; festive

FEAT *of arms:* **n.** *action d'éclat*
of strength, skill or ingenuity: **n.** gymnastic(s) ; gyration; *passe-passe; tour de force*

FEATHER(S), *birds of a:* **n.pl.** *gens de même famille*
loss of: **n.** deplumation; molting; **a.** callow; deplumate

FEATURE(S): **n.** characteristic; facies; landmark; lineament; peculiarity; physiognomy
facial or distinguishing: **n.** countenance; facies; habitus; lineament; physiognomy; physique; visage; **a.** lineamental; physiognomic(al) ; physiognomonic(al)

odd, peculiar or remarkable: **n.** eccentricity; oddity; peculiarity; singularity
outward: **n.** physiognomy
surface or natural: **n.** topography

FEBRUARY *29th:* **n.** bissextile (day) ; intercalary (day)

FECES: (**see** "dung") **n.** excrement; feculence; ordure; (**pl.** (d)ejecta; egesta; excreta; (r)ejectamenta) ; **a.** FECAL: excremental; excrementi(ti)ous; scatologic(al) ; steracoraceous; stercoral
abnormal interest in: **n.** coprophilia

FEE: (**see** "wage") **n.** emolument; honorarium
one taking fr. both sides: **n.** ambidexter

FEEBLE: **a.** adynamic; asthenic; debilitated; decrepit; flaccid; impotent; impuissant; insipid; insubstantial; languid; languorous; pointless; unsubstantial; **n.** FEEBLENESS: (**see** "fatigue" **and** "weakness") adynamia; decrepitude; impotence; impotency; impuissance; tenuity
-mindedness: **n.** amentia; cretinism; idiocy; imbecility; moronity; oligophrenia

FEEL: (**see** "felt") **v.** palpate; **n.** experience; palpation; sensation
ability to: **n.** esthesia; sentience; sentiency
one's way: **v.** *aller à tâtons*

FEELING: (**see** "enthusiasm") **n.** affectation; affection; atmosphere; consciousness; conviction; emotion; fondness; impression; opinion; perception; responsiveness; sensation; sensibility; sentience; sentiency; senitment
arouse: **v.** impassion; **a.** (**see** "ardent") impassionate; impassioned
capable of: **a.** conscious; esthetic; sensible; sentient
drug or agent to destroy: **n.** analgesic; anesthesia; anesthetic; anodyne
examine by: **v.** palpate; **n.** palpation
for others: **n.** altropathy; altruism; **a.** altruistic
for those in same situation as oneself: **n.** alter-egoism; identification
incapable of: (**see** "unfeeling") **a.** impassible; impassive; impiteous; **n.** impassibility
lacking in: **a.** anesthetic; apathetic; expressionless; impassive; impiteous; inanimate; incompassionate; indurate; indura-

tive; insensate; insensitive; insentient; phlegmatic; stoical; unimpressionable; unfeeling; **n.** analgesia; anesthesia; anesthetic; impassivity; insensitivity; insentiency
 loss of: **n.** analgesia; anesthesia; **a.** analgesic; anesthetic; anodynic
 loss of power to recognize by: **n.** asterognosis
 of having been at place before: **n.** *déjà vu(e)* ; parmnesia
 power to recognize by: **n.** stereognosis
 sudden or violent change in: **n.** revulsion
 tender or sorrowful: **n.** pathos; **a.** pathetic
 with: **adv.** *con expressione;* **n.** pathos; **a.** pathetic
 without: **see** "unfeeling"

FEET, *hanging by, as certain birds:* **a.** adhamant
 having: **a.** pedigerous
 having four: **a.** quadrupedal; tetrapod; tetrapodous; **n.** quadruped; tetrapod
 having large: **a.** *or* **n.** macropod; **n.** macropodia; **a.** sciapodopous
 having many: **a.** *or* **n.** multiped; polyped
 having small: **a.** micropodal; micropodous; **n.** micropod
 having two: **a.** biped(al); **n.** biped
 pert. to or accomplished by the: **a.** pedal; podal(ic)

FEIGN: (**see** "pretend") **v.** allege; fabricate; **a.** FEIGNED: (**see** "artificial") fictitious
 illness: **v.** malinger; **n.** malingerer; malingering; pathomimesis

FELLOW, *good:* **n.** bon ami; bon enfant
 member or worker: (**see** "associate") **n.** coadjutor; coeval; confrere; cohort; colleague

FELLOWSHIP: **n.** alliance; association; brotherhood; camaraderie; comity; communion; foundation; fraternity; sociality; sodality
 good: **a.** *bon camaraderie;* bonhom(m)ie; conviviality; *esprit de corps;* geniality
 united in: **a.** consociate; consociative

FELT, *capable of being:* **a.** palpable; tactual; tangible; **n.** tactility; tangibility
 incapable of being: **a.** impalpable; insentient; intangible

FEMALE: (**see** "woman") **a.** (**see** "feminine") distaff; effeminate; womanish; womanlike
 centering or centered on: **a.** gynecocentric
 diseases of (incl. study): **n.** gynecology; **a.** gynecological
 external genitals of: **n.pl.** muliebria; pudenda; **n.** vulva
 govt. by: **n.** gynecocracy
 having form or structure like: **a.** gynecomorphic; gynecomorphous
 homosexual: **n.** lesbian; sapphist; tribadist; uranist; urning; **a.** homoerotic; lesbian
 leader, leading figure, etc.: **n.** doyenne
 seductive: **see** "enchantress"
 small: **n.** microgyne; *petite dame*

FEMININE: **a.** distaff; effeminate; feminal; gynecian; gynecic; maidenly; muliebral; womanish; womanly; **n.** FEMININITY: effeminacy; feminality; femineity; muliebriety
 domination by or emphasizing interests of: **n.** gynecocentrism; **a.** gynecocentric
 loss of qualities: **n.** defeminization; masculinization
 the eternal: **n.** Ewig-Weibliche

FENCE: **v.** circumscribe; equivocate; impale; **n.** bulwark; circumscription; impalement; palisade; septum; stockade

FENCER: **n.** foilsman; sabreur; swordsman

FERMENTATION, *rel. to or caused by:* **a.** fermentative; zymotic
 science dealing with: **n.** zymology

FEROCITY: **n.** acharnement; barbarity; ferity; impetuosity; savagery; truculency; **a.** FEROCIOUS: (**see** "barbaric") feral; sanguinary; tartarly; vandalic

FERTILE: (**see** "fruitful") **a.** abounding; abundant; exuberant; fecund; fructuous; productive; profuse; prolific; proligerous; uberous; **n.** FERTILITY: (**see** "fruitfulness") fecundity; prolificity; **v.** FERTILIZE: enrich; fecundate; fecundify; fructify; generate; impregnate; pollinate; prolificate; spermatize; **n.** FERTILIZATION: enrichment; fecundation; impregnation; pollination; prolification

FERVOR: **see** "zeal"

FESTER: **v.** corrupt; maturate; putrefy; suppurate; **a.** putrefactive; suppurative; **n.** maturation; putrefaction; suppuration

FESTIVE: **a.** carnivalesque; celebrious; convivial; festivous; *Mardi Gras;* sportive; **n.** FESTIVAL: conviviality; epulation; jamboree; *Mardi Gras;* symposium; **n.** FESTIVITY: (**see** "gaiety") jollification; jollity; merrymaking

FEUD: *as bet. families:* **n.** vendetta

FEVER: **n.** agitation; calenture; delirium; febricity; (hyper)pyrexia; impetuosity; **a.** FEVERISH: (**see** "fiery") febrile; inflammatory; pyretic; pyrexial; pyrexic; **n.** FEVERISHNESS: febrility
  abnormally high: **n.** hyperpyrexia; **a.** hyperpyrectic
  something to reduce: **n.** antipyretic; febrifuge; **a.** antipyretic
  subsidence of: **n.** defervescence; lysis; **a.** defervescent; lytic

FEW: **n.** minority; sparcity; sparsity
  govt. by or state so governed: **n.** oligarchy; **a.** oligarchic(al)
  words, in a: (**see** "brevity") **adv.** *paucis verbis*

FEWNESS: (**see** "scarcity") **n.** dearth; exigency; exiguity; paucity; scantiness; sparcity; sparsity

FIB, *minor:* **n.** prevarication; taradiddle; white lie

FICKLE: **a.** capricious; chameleonic; crotchety; erratic; flighty; inconstant; mercurial; quicksilver; unpredictable; whimsical; **n.** FICKLENESS: *légèreté;* mercurality; quicksilver

FICTIONAL: **see** "imaginary"

FICTITIOUS: **see** "illusory"

FIDDLE, *resembling in outline:* **a.** pandurate; panduriform

FIDGETY: (**see** "nervous") **a.** restive; restless

FIELD(S): **see** "domain"
  growing in or pert. to: **a.** agrarian; agrest(i)al; agrestic; campestral
  of interest or authority: **n.** baliwick; domain; jurisdiction; *métier;* milieu; province; sphere

FIEND: **n.** demon; energumen; fanatic; **a.** FIENDISH: avernal; demoniac(al); demonic(al); diabolical; frantic; frenzied; infernal; malevolent; Mephistophel(i)an; sardonic; satanic; saturnine
  crafty and malevolent: **n.** Mephistopheles

FIERCE: (**see** "cruel") **a.** feral; ferine; ferocious; inhuman; leonine; lupine; merciless; pugnacious; taurine; truculent; **n.** see "ferocity"

FIERY: (**see** "rash") **a.** animated; ardent; blazing; choleric; combustible; evangelistic; fervent; fervid; feverish; flammable; igneous; impassioned; impetuous; inflamed; irascible; mettlesome; passionate; spirited; vehement; vivacious

FIFTEEN *year existence or celebration:* **n.** or **a.** quindecennial

FIFTEENTH *century:* **n.** or **a.** quattrocento

FIFTH *day, occurring every:* **a.** quintan

FIGHT: **v.** impugn; **n.** belligerency; contention; contest; controversy; engagement
  against: **v.** contest; militate

FIGHTER: (**see** "boxer") **n.** pugilist
  chivalrous: **n.** *preux chevalier*

FIGHTING, *given to:* **a.** agnostic; antagonistic; bellicose; belligerent; disputations; militant; oppugnant; pugnacious; taurine; truculent; **n.** bellicosity; pugnacity

FIGMENT *of the mind:* (**see** "ghost") **n.** apparition; phantasm(agoria); phantom; specter

FIGURATIVE: **a.** allegorical; anagogical; metaphoric(al); parabolic(al); synecdochic(al); tralatitious; tropological
  language: **n.** tropology

FIGURE: **v.** calculate; compute; **n.** digit; numeral
  fine: **n.** *belle tournure*
  having shapely or well-developed: **a.** curvaceous; pneumatic
  of speech: **n.** litotes; metaphor; simile;

synecdoche; tralatition; trope; **a.** meta-
phoric(al); synecdochic(al); tralatitious;
v. metaphorize
  use of: **n.** tropology; **a.** tropological

FILE: **n.** dossier

FILLED: (**see** "full") **a.** gravid; replete

FILMY: **a.** diaphanous; ethereal; insubstantial; membranous; pellucid; pellicular;
pelliculate; tenuous

FILTH (**or** FILTHINESS): **n.** contamination; corruption; defilement; excrement; excreta; fecula; feculence; immundity; offal; ordure; pollution; putrefaction; putrescence; putridity; recrement;
sordidness;   squalidity;   squalor;   **a.**
FILTHY: (**see** "obscene") augean; excremental; excrementitious; feculent; immund; impetiginous; noxious; ordurous;
putrid; scatologic(al); sordid; squalid;
stercoraceous; verminous
  abnormal attraction to: **n.** coprophilia;
mysophilia; scatology
  covered with or abounding in: **a.** feculent; **n.** feculence
  interest in: **n.** scatology; **a.** scatological
  *produced by, or originating fr. decompo-
sition of:* **a.** pythogenic
  worship of: **n.** aischrolatreia

FINAL: (**see** "conclusive" **and** "decisive")
a. consummative; consummatory; (de)-
finitive; dernier; last-ditch; telic; terminal; terminative; ultimate; **adv.** FI-
NALLY: *ad extremum; en fin;* eventu-
ally; ultimately; **n.** FINALITY: (de)fini-
tude; inevitability; perfection; teleology;
ultimateness
  act or appearance: **n.** *chant du cygne*
(swan song)
  argument: **n.** *ultimo ratio*
  cause: **n.** *causa finalis*
  destiny or purpose of man. study of: **n.**
eschatology
  part: **n.** epilogue
  proposition or condition: **n.** ultimatum

FINANCES: **n.** exchequer
  rel. to: (**see** "money, pert. to") **a.** financial; fiscal; sumptuary
  rel. to public: **a.** cameralistic
  science of public: **n.** cameralistics

FINANCIALLY *responsible:* **a.** solvent; **n.**
solvency

FIND: (**see** "discover") **n.** *découverte*
  impossible to: **a.** introuvable
  lucky: **n.** *ben trovato;* serendipity; **a.**
serendipitous
  rich: **n.** bonanza; El Dorado
  when looking for something else: **n.**
serendipity; **a.** serendipitous; **n.** seren-
dipitist

FINE: **a.** attenuated; comminuted; excellent; exquisite; homeopathic; tenuous; **n.**
FINEST: *crème de crème; élite; nec plus
supra; nec plus ultra;* nonpareil; nonesuch; *rara avis*
  arts: **n.pl.** *beaux-arts*
  extremely: **a.** homeopathic; impalpable
  or penalty: **n.** amercement; **v.** amerce
  writing(s): **n.pl.** *belles-lettres;* **a.** belletristic

FINERY: **n.** adornment; caparison; frip-
pery; ornamentation; regalia

FINGER(S) (**or** toe): **n.** dactyl(u)s; digit
  abnormal size: **n.** dactylomegaly
  having five: **a.** pentadactyl(ate); **n.**
pentadactylism
  having six: **n.** hexadactylism
  holding up two: **n.** bidigitation; **v.** bi-
digitate
  interlock as in folded hands: **v.** interdigitate
  little: **n.** minimus; pinkie; pinky
  middle: **n.** medius
  resembling or shaped like: **a.** dactyloid;
digitate; digitiform
  ring: **n.** annulary
  thumb: **n.** pollux
  use in sign language: **n.** dactylology

FINGERPRINT(S): **n.** dactylogram
  study of: **n.** dactylography; **n.** dactylog-
rapher

FINICAL: **see** "overnice"

FINISH: **see** "complete"; **a.** FINISHED:
accomplished; *au fait;* consummated; cul-
minated; kaput; perfected; proficient;
soigné; (**fem.** *soignée*); terminated

FINISHING: (**see** "ending") **a.** consummatory
  stroke or blow: **n.** *coup de grâce*

FIRE(S): **n.** combustion; conflagration;
holocaust; **a.** conflagratory; igneous
  add oil to: oleum addere camino

bet. two: **adv.** *entre deux feux*
catch: **v.** conflagrate; ignite; **a.** ignescent
   divination by use of: **n.** pyromancy
   fear of: **n.** pyrophobia
   formed by: **a.** igneous; pyrogenic
   great destructive, or great destruction by: **n.** holocaust
   hypothetical principle of: **n.** phlogiston
   one w/ compulsion to start or watch: **n.** firebug; pyromaniac
   wilfully causing: (**see** "firebug") **n.** arson; **n.** or **a.** incendiary
   -yielding: **a.** pyrophoric

FIREBUG: **n.** arsonist; incendiary; pyromaniac; pyrophile

FIREWORKS (*incl. verbal*) : **n.** girandole; petard; pyrotechnic(s); (**pl.** *feux d'artifice*) ; **a.** pyrotechnic(al)

FIRM: (**see** "steady") **a.** adamantine; determined; established; impregnable; indissoluble; ineradicable; inexpugnable; inflexible; preemptory; resolute; sustained; unassailable; unconquerable; unfaltering; unflinching; unshaken; unwavering; unyielding; **n.** FIRMNESS: adhesiveness; determination; indissolubility; persistency; resolution; solidarity; solidity; tenacity; vertebration
   of purpose: **adv.** *tenax propositi*

FIRST: **a.** (ab)original; elementary; embryonic; inaugural; inceptive; inchoate; indigenous; initial; initiatory; introductory; maiden; nascent; preeminent; primeval; primitive; primo(rdial); primogenital; pristine; rudimental; rudimentary; **adv.** *ab ovo;* **n.** aboriginal; aborigine; alpha; preeminence; princeps
   among equals: **n.** *primus inter pares*
   at: **adv.** *d'abord; au premier abord;* **a.** *prima facie*
   attempt: **n.** *coup d'essai*
   born, rights of: **n.** primogeniture
   edition: **n.** *editio princeps; princeps*
   in rank, etc.: **n.** precedence; preeminence; primacy; priority; supremacy
   in time: **a.** primordial
   one, or that which is: **n.** premier; princeps
   or among the: **adv.** imprimis
   place, in the: **adv.** imprimis
   principles, science of: **n.** archelogy
   prize or award: **n.** *cordon bleu; grand prix*

-rate: **a.** *soigné;* (**fem.** *soignée*) ; stellar
step: **n.** *premier pas*
to last, from: **adv.** *ad primo ad ultimum*

FISH *chowder:* **n.** bouillabaisse
   -eating: **a.** ichthyophagous; piscivorous; **n.** ichthyophagist
   expert on science of: **n.** ichthyologist
   feeding on: **see** "eating" *above*
   of a region: **n.** piscifauna
   pert. to or resembling: **a.** ichthyic; ichthyoid; ichthyological; piscatorial; piscatory; piscine
   shaped like, or having some features of: **a.** ichthyomorphic
   state of being: **n.** piscinity
   study of or treatise on: **n.** halieutics; ichthyology; piscatology

FISHERMAN: **n.** angler; piscator; Waltonian

FISHING: **n.** piscation
   art of or treatise on: **n.** halieutics; ichthyology; piscatology
   pert. to: **a.** halieutic(al); ichthyological; piscatorial; piscatory

FISSURE: **n.** sulcus; **a.** sulcate

FIT(S) : (**see** "fitting") **a.** condign; expedient; felicitous; ideal; idoneous; kosher; legitimate; pertinent; prudent; **n.** paroxysm; seizure; tantrum; **n.** FITNESS: (**see** "suitability") adaptability; adaptitude; appropriateness; aptitude; competency; decorum; (**pl.** decora) ; eligibility; expediency; idoneity; propriety; seemliness; soundness; suitability
   and starts, by: **adv.** *par accès*
   out: see "equip"

FITTING: (**see** "appropriate") **a.** apropros; *comme il faut;* congruent; congruous; consonant; decorous; idoneous; legitimate; pertinent; relevant; seemly; **n.** accessory; adjunct; aproposity; attachment; idoneity
   to be: **v.** behoove
   together, as ends of bone: **n.** coaptation

FIVE: **n.** cinque; pentad
   arranged in sets of, or divided into 5 parts: **a.** pentamerous; quinary; quinate
   articles or points, rel. to: **a.** quinquarticular
   athletic events: **n.** penthalon

consisting of, or 5th in rank: **a.** quinary ; quinate
consisting of or including, or 5 times as great: **a. or v.** qunituple ; **n.** quintuplet
figure w/ 5 sides and angles: **n.** pentagon ; **a.** pentagonal
objects in square, one each corner and one in middle: **n.** quincunx ; **a.** quincuncial
-sided: **a.** pentagonal
the number, group of, or period of 5 years: **n.** pentad
-year event or celebration: **n.** quniquennial ; quinquennium
years, period of: **n.** lustrum ; pentad ; quinquennium
years, taking place every or lasting: **a.** quinquennial

FIX : **v.** arrange ; attach ; concentrate ; determine ; implant ; install ; radicate ; stabilize ; **n.** cruciality ; dilemma ; implantation ; plight ; predicament ; **a.** dilemmatical ; predicamental

FIXED : (see "firm" and "stubborn") **a.** immobile ; immovable ; immotile ; immutable ; inadaptable ; inalterable ; incommutable ; inerratic ; inflexible ; irrevocable ; irreversible ; sedentary ; sessile ; stab(i)le ; stabilized ; unswerving ; unyielding ; **n. see** "inflexibility"
idea: **n.** delusion ; *idée fixe;* obsession

FLABBY : **a.** ductile ; flaccid ; languid ; plastic ; supple

FLAG : **n.** colors, ensign ; pennant ; pennon ; standard ; vexillum
for boat: **n.** bougee ; burgee
of devotion or courage: **n.** oriflamme
-waver: **n.** chauvinist ; jingoist ; patrioteer ; (**pl.** patriotics)

FLAGRANT : (see "wicked") **a.** egregious ; execrable ; flagitious ; glaring ; heinous ; malicious ; nefarious ; rampant ; vicious

FLAKE : **v.** desquamate ; exfoliate ; **n.** desquamation ; exfoliation ; lamina ; **a.** FLAKING : desquamative ; desquamatory ; exfoliative ; lamellar ; lamelliform ; laminar

FLAME : **n.** luminescence
bursting into: **a.** fulgurating ; ignescent ; inflammatory ; volatile

producing, or bright with: **a.** flammiferous ; ignescent

FLARING : (see "showy") **a.** bouffant(e) ; dazzling

FLASH, *as lightning or spiritual:* **n.** fulguration

FLASHING : **a.** fulgurating ; meteoric ; pyrotechnic(al)
as colors: **a.** iridescent ; **n.** iridescence
as pain: **a.** fulgurant ; fulgurating ; fulgurous ; lancinating

FLASHY : (see "gaudy") **a.** garish ; meretricious ; ostentatious ; tawdry

FLAT : (see "bland") **a.** horizontal ; immature ; insipid ; jejune ; juvenile ; monotonous ; planar ; palnate ; prostrate ; uninteresting ; **n.** horizontality ; insipidity ; jejunity ; monotony ; prostration

FLATTER : **v.** beguile ; blandish ; cajole ; ingratiate ; panegyrize ; sycophantize ; wheedle ; **n.** FLATTERY : adulation ; allurement ; banishment(s) ; cajolement ; cajolery ; obsequiousness ; sycophancy ; unction ; unctuosity ; **n.** FLATTERER : adulateur ; (**fem.** adulatrice) ; eulogist ; proneur ; sycophant

FLATTERING : **a.** adulatory ; ingratiating ; ingratiatory ; panegyric(al) ; sycophantic(al) ; unctuous
falsely: **a.** gnathonic ; sycophantic(al) ; toadying

FLAVOR, *high:* (see "taste") **n.** *haut goût*

FLAWLESS : (see "perfect") **a.** immaculate ; impeccable ; impeccant ; indefectible ; irreproachable ; **n.** FLAWLESSNESS : (see "perfection") immaculacy ; impeccability ; indefectibility

FLEE : **v.** absquatulate ; elope ; evade ; fugitate ; **n. see** "flight"

FLEECY : (see "woolly") **a.** lanate ; laniferous

FLEETING : (see "vanishing") **a.** deciduous ; diaphanous ; ephemeral ; ephemerous ; ethereal ; evanescent ; fugacious ; gossamer ; impermanent ; instantaneous ; momentary ; perishable ; preterient ; semelfactive; shadowy; temporal; transient; transitory; unenduring; vaporous; volatile; unsubstantial; **n.** caudicity; diaphaneity; ephemerality; ethereality; fugacity; impermanence; volatility

FLESH-*colored:* **a.** incarnadine
   -eating: **a.** carnivorous; creophagous; sarcophagic; sarcophagous; sarcophilous; **n.** carnivority; creophagy; sarcophagy
   embody in: **v.** humanize; incarnate; **a.** incarnate
   of or composed of: **a.** sarcous
   used as food: **n.** carnivosity; creophagy; sarcophagy

FLESHINESS: (**see** "obesity") **n.** corpulence

FLEXIBLE: **a.** complaint; lissom(e); lithe(some); manageable; pliable; resilient; supple; tractable; willowy; **n.** FLEXIBILITY: amenability; elasticity; lissomeness; maneuverability; mobility; plasticity; tractability

FLICKERING: **a.** fulgurating; lancinating; lambent; meteoric; uncertain

FLIGHT: **n.** elopement; fugitation; hegira; migration; volitation
   capable of: **a.** volitant
   engaged in headlong: **a.** Gaderine

FLIGHTY: **a.** anile; capricious; helter-skelter; hoity-toity; frivolous; imaginative; mercurial; pompous; quicksilver; quixotic; scatterbrained; utopian; volatile

FLIMSY: **a.** diaphanous; enfeebled; ethereal; ineffective; insubstantial; superficial; tenuous; trifling; unsubstantial; **n.** FLIMSINESS: diaphaneity; ethereality; tenuity; tenuousness; unsubstantiality

FLIPPANCY *in writing or speech:* **n.** persiflage; **v.** persiflate; **n.** persifleur

FLIRT: **v.** philander; **n.** coquet(te); philanderer; **a.** FLIRTATIOUS: amorous; vampirish; **n.** FLIRTATION: coquetry; dalliance; passade; philander; toying
   amorous (flirtation): **n.** *oeillade*
   female (flirt): **n.** amourette; amoureuse; coquette; intrigante; nymph(et)
   male (flirt): **n.** coquet; philander(er)

FLOAT(ING) *in air:* **n.** levitation; **v.** levitate
   on surface: **a.** supernatant

FLOCKS, *living in:* **a.** gregarious

FLOG: **v.** chastise; flagellate; lambaste

FLOOD: **v.** deluge; inundate; overflow; **n.** cataclysm; cataract; deluge; freshet; inundation; spate; **a.** FLOODED (or FLOODING): cataclysmic(al): deluginous; diluvial; inundatory
   after the (Biblical): **a.** postdiluvian
   before the: **a.** antediluvian
   fresh, or sudden heavy rain: **n.** freshet; spate
   violent: **n.** avalanche; cataclysm; debacle; deluge

FLORID: (**see** "ornate" **and** "showy") **a.** erubescent; melismatic; rubescent; rubicund; rufous; **n.** FLORIDITY: erubescence; rubescence; rubicundity

FLOUR *or meal, of or like or made from:* **a.** farinaceous

FLOURISH: **v.** blossom; brandish; burgeon; effloresce; flaunt; prosper; **a.** FLOURISHING: affluent; efflorescent; palmy; prosperous; rampant; **n.** affluence; efflorescence; fanfare; tan(a)tara
   rhetorical: **n.** circumgyration

FLOWERING *again:* **a.** reefflorescent; remontant

FLOWERLESS: **a.** agamous; cryptogamous

FLOWERS, *bearing:* **a.** anthophorous; floriferous
   description of: **n.** anthography
   feeding on: **a.** anthophagous; anthophilous
   living among: **a.** anthophilous

FLOWERY: (**see** "showy") **a.** bombastic; (ef)florescent; embellished; euphuistic; floriferous; florulent; grandiloquent; inflated; rhapsodic; rubescent

FLOWING: **a.** canorous: cantable; (con)-fluent; cursive; derivative; deriving; effluent; emanant; mellifluent; mellifluous; mellisonant; perfluent; **n.** liquidity
   back: **a.** refluent; reflux; regurgitate; **n.** refluence

musically: **a.** canorous; cantable; sonorous
out or forth: **a.** effluent; profluent; **n.** effluence; emanation; profluvium
sweetly or smoothly: **a.** mellifluent; mellifluous; mellisonant; profluent; sonorous
together: **a.** confluent; coursing; cursive

FLUCTUATE: (see "waver") **v.** oscillate; undulate; vacillate; **n.** FLUCTUATION: ambivalence; oscillation; vacillation; **a.** ambivalent; mercurial

FLUENCY *of speech:* **n.** *copia verborum;* eloquence; facundity; grandiloquence; liquidity; loquaciousness; loquacity; mellifluence; verbosity; **a.** FLUENT: euphonious; facile; liquid; loquacious; mellifluous; unembarrassed; verbose

FLUFFY: (see "woolly") **a.** flocculent

FLUORESCENCE: **n.** luminescence; phosphorescence

FLUSHED, *to become (or red):* **v.** empurple; **n.** rubescent

FLUTED: **a.** cannel(l)ated; channeled

FLUTTER: **v.** fluctuate; palpitate; quiver; vibrate; volitate; **a.** FLUTTERING: (see "confusion") palpitant; volitant; **n.** palpitation; vibration; volitation

FLY, *able to (or flying):* **a.** volitant; volitorial
as hither and thither: **v.** volitate

FOCAL *point (focus):* **n.** centrum; cynosure; epicenter; nidus; nucleus; omphalos; umbilicus

FOE: **n.** adversary; antagonist; combatant; competitor; opponent

FOG: **n.** bewilderment; brume; perplexity; uncertainty; vapor; **a.** FOGGY: brumous; caliginous; confused; nubilous; tenuous; vague; vaporous

FOIL, *person serving as:* **n.** deuteragonist

FOLD: **v.** embosom; envelop(e); intertwine; plicate; **n.** congregation; (con)-volution
or bend back: **v.** replicate

FOLIAGE, *shade-giving;* **n.** boscage; umbrage; **a.** foliaceous; umbrageous

FOLKWAYS: **n.pl.** mores
study of: **n.** ethnology; **a.** ethnological

FOLLOW(S), *disposition to:* **n.** sequacity; tractability
it does not: **n.** *non sequitur* (**abb.** non seq.)
that (or those) which: **n.** *et sequens* (**abb.** et seq.); (**pl.** *et sequentes; et sequentia;* (**abb.** et seq., et seqq. **or** et sqq.))
that which does not: **n.** *lucus a non lucendo; non sequitur* (**abb.** non seq.)
that which logically: **n.** *sequitur*

FOLLOWER(S): **n.** abettor; acolyte; adherent; aficionado; (**fem.** aficionada); apostle; attendant; audience; claque; clique; cohort; devotee; disciple; enthusiast; entourage; escort; fanatic; henchman; liege man; partisan; retainer; retinue; sectary; sectator; votary; zealot; **a.** FOLLOWING: consecutive; (con)sequential; ensuant; ensuing; sequent
loyal or hired: (see "mercenary") **n.** Hessian; janissary; janizary; liege man; minion
small group of: **n.** claque; corporal's guard
zealous: **n.** militant; minion; sectary

FOLLY: **n.** absurdity; *bêtise;* desipience; fatuity; imprudence; inanity; indiscretion; indulgence; infatuation; lunacy
utter: **n.** idio(t)cy

FOND: (see "loving") **a.** affectionate; amatory; amorous; ardent; devoted; enamored; **n.** FONDNESS: (see "appetite") affection; attachment; diathesis; partiality; penchant; predilection; propensity

FOOD(S): (see "cooking") **n.** aliment; comestible(s); cuisine; edible(s); grist; ingesta; nourishment; nutrient; nutriment; nutrition; nutritive; pabulum; provender; subsistence; sustenance; sustentation
American Indian: **n.** pem(m)ican
and drink: **n.** refection
art of preparation: **n.** cuisine; gastronomy
assimilation of: **n.** anabolism; **a.** anabolic
conversion into energy: **n.** metabolism; **a.** metabolic

craving for unnatural articles of: **n.** allotriophagy; geophagy; parorexia; pica
dry, for livestock: **n.** provender
eating any sort of: **a.** omnivorous; pantophagic; pantophagous; polyphagous
eating both animal and veg.: **a.** amphivorous
eating living organisms: **a.** biophagous
eating only a few kinds of: **a.** oligophagous
eating single kind of: **a.** monophagous
high class: **n.** haute cuisine
judge or lover of fine: **n.** bon-vivant; epicure; gastronome(r); gourmet; sybarite; trencherman
living on many or various kinds of: **a.** pantophagous; polyphagous; **n.** polyphagia
lover of good: see "judge or lover of fine" **above**
manner of preparing: **n.** cuisine; gastronomy
pert. to: **a.** alimental; alimentary; alimentative; cibarian; cibarous; culinary; gastronomic(al); nutrimental; nutritious; nutritive; trophic; **n.** gastronomy
reheated (left over): **n. or a.** réchauffé
science of: **n.** cuisine; dietetics; gastronomy; nutrition; sitology; trophology
uncooked: **adv.** au naturel
warmed over: **n. or a.** réchauffé

FOOL(S): (see "fop") **n.** Abderite; idiot; imbecile; nincompoop; *radoteur;* simpleton
fortune favors: fortuna favet fatuis
learned: **n.** morosoph
not such a: pas si bête

FOOLED, *people wish to be: populus vult decipi*
world wishes to be: mundus vult decipi

FOOLHARDY: (see "reckless") **a.** adventurous; Icarian; incautious; temerarious

FOOLISH: (see "silly") **a.** fatuous; inane; inept; infatuated; preposterous; puerile; **n.** FOOLISHNESS: (see "irrationality") fatuity; ineptitude; insipidity; *niaiserie*
act or remark: (see "absurdity") **n.** *bêtise; gaffe;* ridiculosity; solecism
cause to appear: **v.** infatuate; stultify
laughing: **a.** Abderian

FOOT: (see "feet") **n.** pedal extremity
done or going on: **a.** *à pied;* pedestrian
having but one: **n. or a.** monopod

FOOTPRINT: **n.** spoor; vestige; (**pl.** vestigia)

FOP: (see "dandy") **n.** Beau Brummel; coxcomb; incroyable; jack-a-dandy; jack-anapes; *petit maître;* popinjay; **a.** FOPPISH: dandiacal; dandified

FOR *and against:* **adv.** *pro et contra*
ever and ever: (see "everlasting") **adv.** *in saecula saeculorum*
now: **adv.** *pro tunc*
public good: **adv.** *pro bono publico*
so much: **adv.** *pro tanto*
the present: **adv.** *pro nunc*
this occasion only: **adv.** *pro hoc vice*
this purpose: **adv.** *ad hoc*
virgins and for boys: virginibus puerlesque
want of better: **adv.** *faute de mieux*
whose benefit (or what purpose)?: **adv.** *cui bono?*

FORBEARANCE: (see "mercy") **n.** clemency; compassion; fortitude; leniency; lenity; longanimity; long-suffering; patience; resignation; toleration; **a.** FORBEARING: (see "patient") compassionate; indulgent; lenient; longanimous; tolerant

FORBIDDEN: **a.** inhibitory; prohibited; taboo; tabu; verboten; **v.** FORBID: (see "ban") enjoin; inhibit; interdict; prohibit; **a.** FORBIDDING: (see "dangerous") disagreeable; formidable; hazardous; inhibitory; menacing; repellant
list of books, etc.: **n.** *index expurgatorious; index liborum prohibitorum*

FORCE: **v.** coerce; constrain; dragoon; oblige; **n.** coercion; cogency; compulsion; constraint; duress; dynamism; impetus; import; impulsion; potency; restraint; validity; vis
acting from behind: **n.** *vis a tergo*
appealing to: **a. or adv.** *a baculo*
by main: **adv.** *manu forti*
by its own: **adv.** *proprio vigore*
creative or decisive (as institution, idea or person): **n.** demiurge
dynamic or creative: **n.** numen
equal, having: **a.** equiponderant; equivalent; tantamount
equal, use against: **v.** countervail
from behind: **n.** *vis a tergo*
from the front: **n.** *vis a fronte*
life: see *"vital"* **below**

marked by great: **a.** dynamic; Herculean; Samsonian; titanic; titanian
moving or impelling: **n.** animus; impetus
of or by own: **adv.** *(ex) proprio vigore; proprio motu*
overwhelming, as of nature: **n.** *force majeure; vis major*
powerful or angry, effect or expression of: **n.** *terribilita*
rel. to: **a.** dynamic(al); **n.** dynamism
terrible or irresistible: **n.** juggernaut
vital: **n.** *anima mundi; élan vital;* mana
w/ the whole: viribus totis

FORCED: see "coercive"; **a.** FORCEFUL: (see "emphatic" **and** "vigorous") dynamic; impactful; intrusive; resounding
acceptance: **n.** Hobson's choice

FOREARM: **n.** antebrachium

FOREBODING: (see "foretelling") **a.** apprehensive; portentous; premonitory; **n.** apprehension; augury; portent; premonition; presage; presentiment; prognostication
disaster or doom: **a.** apocalyptic(al); handwriting on the wall

FORECAST: (see "foretell") **v.** prognosticate; prophesy; **n.** prognosis; prognostication; **a.** divinatory; oracular; orphic; prognostic; prophetic

FOREFATHER(S): **n.** ancestor; antecedent; ascendant; forebear; forerunner; precursor; primogenitor; procreator; progenitor; (**fem.** progenitress; progenetrix); prototype
pert. to: **a.** ancestorial; ancestral; primogenitorial; primogenitive

FOREFRONT: **n.** *avant-garde;* van-(guard)

FOREGO: (see "renounce") **v.** precede; **a.** FOREGOING: antecedent; preceding

FOREGROUND: **n.** proscenium

FOREHEAD: **n.** frons; metopion; sinciput; **a.** metopic; sinciputal

FOREIGN: **a.** adventitious; exotic; extraneous; extrinsic; forane; irrelevant; heterochthnous; heterogeneous; peregrinate; tramontane; **n.** FOREIGNNESS: extraneity; heterogeneity

(far-off): **a.** ultramontane; untramundane; **n.** ultima Thule
one attracted to (foreign) things, people or places: **n.** xenophile; **a.** xenophilous
to: **prep.** dehors
to the subject: **adv.** *à propos de bottes; à propos de rien;* irrelevant

FOREIGNER: **n.** alien; auslander; exoteric; outlander; peregrine; Philistine; tramontane
abnormal fear of, or what is foreign: **n.** xenophobia; **a.** xenophobic; **n.** xenophobe

FOREKNOWLEDGE: (see "intuition") **n.** precognition; precognitum; prescience; **a.** precognitive; prescient

FORERUNNER: **n.** ancestor; antecedent; antecessor; *avant coureur; avant-garde;* forebear; harbinger; herald; pioneer; precursor; predecessor; premonitor; trailblazer; vanguard

FORESEE: (see "foretell") **v.** adumbrate; anticipate; divine; envisage

FORESHADOW: see "foretell"

FORESIGHT: (see "institution") **n.** foreknowledge; precognition; prescience; *prospicience;* prospection; prudence; **a.** precognitive; prescient
deficiency of: **n.** amblyopia; astigmatism; myopia; **a.** astigmatic; myopic
having, or characterized by: **a.** precognitive; prescient

FOREST(S), *pert. to or inhabiting:* **a.** nemoral; sylvan; sylvatic; sylvestrian

FORETASTE: **n.** prelibation

FORETELLING: (see "foreboding") **a.** adumbrated; apocalyptic(al); Delphian; Delphic; divinatory; fatidic; oracular; presageful; prophetic(al); pythonic; **n.** adumbration; divination; foreshadowing; prognostication; **v.** FORETELL: adumbrate; augur; auspicate; forecast; predict; prefigure; presage; presignify; prognosticate; prophesy; portend; vaticinate
imminent disaster or doom: **a.** apocalyptic(al); **n.** apocalypse

FOREVER: (see "everlasting") **adv.** *ab aeterno; ad infinitum; in adfinitum; in aeternum;* incessantly; in perpetuity; *in perpetuum; in saecula saeculorum*

127

FOREWARNED *is forearmed: praemonitus praemunitus*

FOREWORD: see "preface"

FORFEIT, *take over on:* **v.** amerce; confiscate; **a.** confiscatory; **n.** FORFEITURE: amercement; confiscation

FORGED: **a.** counterfeit; spurious; supposititious; **n.** FORGERY: counterfeit; fabrication; invention; pseudograph; supposition

FORGET: **v.** obliviate; **a.** FORGETFUL: (see "careless") abstracted; oblivious; unmindful
do not: **adv.** *ne obliviscaris*

FORGETFULNESS: **n.** lethe; oblivescence; oblivion; obliviscence
rel. to or causing: **a.** Lethean
something causing (as drug, potion, etc.): **n.** nepenthe; **a.** nepenthean

FORGIVABLE: see "excusable"; **n.** FORGIVENESS: absolution; amnesty; conciliation; condonation; indulgence; remission; **a.** FORGIVING: absolutory; clement; compassionate; conciliatory; indulgent; placable; magnanimous; merciful

FORGOTTEN, *cond. or fact of being:* **n.** oblivescence; oblivion; obliviscence

FORK: **v.** bifurcate; dichotomize; divaricate; **n.** FORK (or FORKING): bifurcation; dichotomization; dichotomy; divarication; **a.** FORKED: bidigitate(d); bifid; bifurcate(d); dichotomous; forcipate; forficulate; furcate; furciform

FORM(S): (see "outline") **n.** ceremony; configuration; conformation; contour; conventionality; liturgy; perspective; ritual; silhouette; **v.** see "make"
according to: (see "rule") **a.** conventional; *de règle; de rigueur;* formal; ritualistic
as a matter of (form) only: **a.** perfunctory; *pro forma (tantum)*
assuming various: **a.** polymorphic; polymorphous; **n.** polymorphism; polymorphy; **n.** polymorph
beautiful: **n.** *belle tournure*
beginning to: **a.** aborning; nascent; parturient; **adv.** *in fieri*

combining human and animal: **a.** therianthropic; **n.** therianthropism
existing in different: **a.** allotrophic; **n.** allotrophy
for sake of: see "as matter of" **above**
give individual (form) to: **v.** individualize; individuate; **n.** individualization; individuation
having a single: **a.** monomorphic; monomorphous
having more than one: **a.** pleomorphic; pleomorphous; polymorphic; polymorphous
having, occurring or passing through several or various: **a.** polymorphic; polymorphous; **n.** polymorphism
having identical or similar: **a.** isomorphic; **n.** isomorphism
in its essential: **adv.** *sub specie aeternitatis*
varied in: **a.** allotropic; **n.** allotropy
word (form) or formation, study of: **n.** morphology

FORMAL: **a.** academic; ceremonial; ceremonious; conventional; dogmatic; formalistic; liturgical; mechanical; pedantic; pharisaic(al); punctilious; ritualistic; scholastic(al); stylized; syntactical

FORMALITIES, *observance of trivial or petty:* **n.** punctilio; **a.** punctilious

FORMALITY: **n.** academicism; ceremonial(ism); ceremony; conventionality; liturgy; pedantry; regularity; ritual(ism); rituality; solemnity

FORMATION, *in course of:* **a.** aborning; in production; *in statu nascendi;* nascent; parturient; **n.** nascency
in layers: **n.** hierarchization; stratification; **a.** stratified; stratose
in line or series: **n.** echelon; linearity

FORMATIVE: (see "creative") **a.** constructive; demiurgic; developmental; fictile; impressionable; nascent; plastic

FORMER: **n.** antecedent; cidevant; emeritus; (**pl.** emeriti); **a.** ancient; antecedent; anterior; bygone; cidevant; elapsed; onetime; quondam; **adv.** erewhile; whilom
life, supposed remembering of: **n.** anamnesis; **a.** anamnestic
system, govt., etc.: **n.** *ancien régime*

FORMLESS: **a.** amorphous; chaotic; heterogeneous; immaterial; inchoate; incor-

poreal; nebulous; spiritual; **n.** FORM-
LESSNESS: heterogeneity; immateriality; incorporeality; incorporeity; nebulosity

FORMULA: **n.** doctrine; philosophy; prescription; recipe; **a.** doctrinaire; doctrinal; formulaic
   magic: alkahest
   secret: **n.** nostrum

FORMULATE: **v.** confect; concretize; fabricate; forge; materialize; synthesize

FORTIFY: **v.** lace; munify; **a.** castellated

FORTUNATE: **a.** auspicious; beneficial;
benign(ant); dexter; opportune; propitious; prosperous; reasonable; timely
   man: **n.** *homme de fortune*

FORTUNE: (**see** "fate") **n.** destiny; fortuity; prosperity; success
   accident of: **n.** serendipity; vicissitude;
a. serendipitous; vicissitudinous
   favors bold: audaces fortuna juvat
   favors brave: fortes fortuna adjuvat
   favors daring: audentes fortuna juvat
   favors fools: fortuna favet fatuis
   goddess of: **n.** Tyche
   *helps those who help themselves: faber
est quisque fortunae suae*
   if (fortune) favors: si fortuna fuvat

FORTUNE-TELLER: **n.** necromancer;
Nostradamus; prognosticator; physiogno-
mist; soothsayer

FORTUNE-TELLING: (**see** "propheti-
c(al)") **n.** prognostication
   by cards: **n.** cartomancy
   by crystal-gazing or mirrors: **n.** catoptromancy
   by dreams: **n.** oneiromancy

FORTY, *lasting 40 days or consisting of:*
a. quadragesimal
   persons 40 to 50 years of age: **n. or a.**
quadragenarian; **a.** quadragenarious

FORUM, *clamor of the:* **n.** *forensis strepitus*

FORWARD: **a.** *en avant*

FOUL: **a.** carious; disagreeable; entangled;
feculent; fetid; leprous; loathsome; mephitic; noisome; noxious; pestilent(ial);

polluted; putrescent; putrid; treacherous
   -smelling: **see** "stink" **and** "stinking"

FOULNESS: **n.** feculence; fetidness;
loathsomeness; mephitis; noisomeness;
pestilence; pollution; putrefaction; putrescence; putrescency; putridity; stench
   accumulation of: **n.** colluvies

FOUNDATION: (**see** "base") **n.** endowment; fundament; *point d'appui;* princi-
pum; substratum
   from the: de fond en comble

FOUR, *consisting of, including or multiplied
by:* **n. or a.** quadruple; **a.** quaternary
   *directions, leading in or meeting at a
point:* **a.** quadrivial; **n.** quadrivium
   -fold: **a. or n.** quadrigeminal; tetrad;
a. quadruple; quadruplicate
   group or set of, or composed of 4 parts:
n. or a. quaternary; quaternity; tetrad; **a.**
quarternate
     member of such group: **n.** quaternary
   in sets or groups of: **a. or n.** quaternary;
a. quaternate
   -letter word: **n.** tetragram
   liberal arts: **n.** quadrivium; **a.** quadrivial
   lines, stanza or poem of: **n.** quatrain
   parts, divide into: **v.** quadrisect; **n.**
quadripartition; **a.** quadripartite
   persons, group of: **n.** *partie carée;* quad-
rumvirate; quartet; quaternary; tetrad
   series of, as books, operas, etc.: **n.**
tetralogy
   -sided or angled figure: **n.** quadrangle;
n. or a. quadrilateral
   threatening forces: **n.** Four Horsemen
(of the Apocalypse)
   union of: **n.** quaternity
   years, lasting or occurring every: **n.
or a.** quadrennial
   years, period of: **n.** Olympiad; quadrennium

FOURTH *anniversary:* **n.** quadrennium; **a.**
quadrennial
   in order: **a.** quaternary

FOWLS, *domestic, science of:* **n.** alectryo-
nology

FOX-*like:* **a.** alopecoid; vulpine

FRACTION: **n.** fragment; modicum; moiety; quantum; (**pl.** quanta); segment; **a.**
FRACTIONAL: aliquot; fragmental;

fragmentary; inconsiderable; insignificant; segmental

FRAGILE: (**see** "fleeting") **a.** diaphanous; ephemeral; ethereal; evanescent; frangible; nebulous; tenuous; unsubstantial; **n.** FRAGILITY: diaphaneity; ephemerality; ethereality; evanescence; nebulosity; tenuity

FRAGMENT(S): (**see** "fraction") **n.** detritus; morceau; morsel; residue; segment; **a. see** "fractional"
assembled to make picture, etc.: **n.** collage; montage
of erosion, etc.: **n.** detritus
scattered or lit.: **n.pl.** analecta; collectanea; disjecta membra; scrapiana; **n.** chrestomathy

FRAGRANT: (**see** "savory") **a.** ambrosiac; ambrosial; aromatic; balmy; redolent; refreshing; **n.** FRAGRANCE: aroma(ticity); bouquet; effluvium; emanation; redolence
to make: **v.** aromatize

FRAILTY: **n.** infirmity; insubstantiality; susceptibility; tenuousness; tenuity; **a.** FRAIL: (**see** "brittle" **and** "sickly") fragile; frangible; infirm; valetudinarian
in character: **n.** foible

FRAMEWORK: **n.** anatomy; cadre; parenchyma; skeleton

FRANCE: **see** "French"

FRANK: (**see** "candid") **a.** artless; demonstrative; guileless; *ingénu;* (*fem. ingénue*); ingenuous; manifest; straightforward; unreserved; unvarnished

FRANTIC: **a.** berserk; delirious; demoniac(al); demonic(al); frenzied; maniac(al); phrenetic; rabid; **n. see** "frenzy"

FRAUD: **n.** adventurer; artifice; charlatan; circumvention; conjurer; deception; delusion; dissimulation; duplicity; empiric; fraudulence; humbug; hypocrite; imposition; imposter; imposture; mountebank; prestidigitator; pretender; stratagem; subreption; trickster; **a.** FRAUDULENT: (**see** "counterfeit") duplicitous; perfidious; sinister
marked or done by: **a.** clandestine; duplicitous; fraudulent; surreptitious
pious: **n.** *fraus pia*

FREAK: **n.** capriccio; caprice; crochet; lusus; monstrosity; mutation; sport; vagary; whimsey; whimsicality; **a.** FREAKISH: bizarre; capricious; crochety; eccentric; fanciful; notional; uncertain; vagarious; whimsical
of nature: **n.** *lusus naturae;* monstrosity; mutation; sport

FRECKLE(S): **n.** ephelis; (**pl.** ephelides); lentigo; **a.** lentiginous

FREE: **v.** absolve; detach; disburden; disencumber; disentangle; emancipate; enfranchise; manumit; unfetter; unshackle; unyoke; **a.** (**see** "unrestrained") autonomic; autonomous; complimentary; emancipated; exempt; frank; generous; gratis; gratuitous; independent; ingenuous; prodigal; self-determining; sovereign; spontaneous; unburdened; unbuttoned; unconfined; unencumbered; unenslaved; unenthralled; unfettered; unhampered; unlimited; unobstructed; unrestricted; untrammeled; voluntary; **adv.** FREELY: *avec abandon*
and easy: **a.** apathetic; cavalier; *dégagé;* indifferent; jaunty; lenient; unconcerned; unconstrained; **adv.** capriccioso; *sans gêne; sans souci*
choice or will: **n.** *liberum arbitrium*
-for-all: **n.** donny-brook
from blame: **v.** absolve; exculpate; exonerate; vindicate; **n.** exculpation; vindication; **a.** exculpable; exculpatory
gift: **n.** gratuity; lagniappe; largess(e); **a.** complimentary; gratis
not: **see** "restrained"
set (free): **v.** disencumber; disentangle; emancipate; extricate
to move about: **a.** vagile
will or choice: **n.** *liberum arbitrium*

FREEDOM: **n.** authority; autonomy; *carte blanche;* dispensation; emancipation; immunity; impunity; independence; liberation; license; manumission; self-determination; unrestraint; unrestrictedness
from obligation: **n.** disengagement; disentanglement; immunity; impunity
having: **a.** latitudinal; latitudinous
of conduct or action: **n.** impunity; latitude
prevent: **v.** immobilize

FREETHINKER: **n.** agnostic; aporetic; *esprit fort;* latitudinarian; nullifidian; **n.** FREETHINKING: agnosticism; latitudinarianism; nescience

FREEZING *to solid or semi-solid:* n. congealation; a. congealative

FRENCH, *hater of anything:* n. Francophobe; gallophobe; n. Francophobia; gallophobia
  lover of anything: n. Francophile; gallophile
  prejudice in favor of: n. gallomania; gallophobia

FRENZY: n. deliration; delirium; fanaticism; mania; orgasm; rabidity; raptus; a. FRENZIED: (see "frantic") berserk; corybantic; furibund; hectic; orgasmic; orgiastic
  of emotion: n. nympholepsy; a. nympholeptic

FREQUENCY: n. commonality; perpetuality; prevalence

FREQUENTER: n. *habitué*

FRESH: (see "sassy") a. additional; blooming; inexperienced; invigorating; neoteric; original; succulent; unspoiled; untainted; unwilted; vernal; youthful; v. FRESHEN: refurbish; renovate; modernize; vernalize; n. FRESHENING (or FRESHNESS): crispness; innovation; invigoration; refurbishment; renovation; spontaneity; succulency; vernalization; vividity; youthfulness

FRETFUL: (see "irritable") a. fractious; ill-humored; impatient; irascible; peevish; pettish; petulant; querulous; restive; restless; waspish; n. see "irritability"

FRICTION, *wearing by:* n. attrition; erosion

FRIEND(S): (see "follower") n. adherent; benefactor; colleague; compeer; companion; confrere; confidant; Damon and Pythias; devotee; partisan; patron; *protégé*
  are proved by adversity: amici probantur rebus adversis
  close or bosom: n. *alter ego; ami de coeur*
  close and trusted (intimate): n. *alter ego;* catercousin; confidant; (fem. confidante); *fidus Achates*
  dear: n. *bon ami; cher ami;* (fem. *chère amie*); *mon vieux*
  next (one who acts for incompetent, as

minor or person non compos): n. *prochein ami*
  of the court: n. *amicus curiae*
  of the human race: n. *amicus humani generis*
  old: n. *mon vieux*
  true and faithful: n. confidant(e); *fidus Achates;* partisan; sectary

FRIENDLESS: adv. *sans amis*

FRIENDLY: a. accessible; affable; affectionate; ami(c)able; amical; bonhomous; companionable; compatible; (con)genial; convivial; courteous; favorable; fraternal; gregarious; neighborly; propitious; sociable; sympathetic; n. FRIENDLINESS: affinity; amicability; bonhom(m)ie; camaraderie; (con)geniality; conviviality; cordiality; *esprit de corps;* geniality; graciosity; graciousness; gregariousness; hospitality; intimacy; joviality; sociability
  warmly: a. bonhomous

FRIENDSHIP: (see "friendliness") a. affinity; amicability; intimacy
  act of gaining or contracting: n. contesseration
  making or restoration of: n. *rapprochement*

FRIGHTEN: v. intimidate; petrify; terrorize; a. FRIGHTFUL (or FRIGHTENING): (see "ghastly") appalling; formidable; grotesque; hideous; horrendous; horrific; perilous; portentous; prodigious; redoubtable

FRIGID: (see "cold") a. gelid; glacial; hyperborean; passionless; n. frigidity; gelidity

FRILL: n. affectation; bauble; extravagance; flummadiddle; superfluity

FRINGED: a. circumferential; lacinate; laciniose

FRIVOLOUS: (see "gay" and "playful") a. frolicsome; hoity-toity; inconsequential; irrelevant; light-minded; superficial; yeasty; n. FRIVOLITY: absurdity; irrationality; *légèreté;* levity; nugacity; superficiality; yeastiness
  person: n. or a. futilitarian
  young woman: n. soubrette

FROGS *and mice, parody on (Homer?):* n. Batrachomyomachy

feeding on: **a.** batrachophagous
of, like, or pert. to: **a.** batrachian; batrachoid

FROLIC: (**see** "caper") **n.** boutade; caprice; carousal; *espièglerie;* festivity; *fredaine;* gambol; marlock; vagary; **a.** FROLICSOME: (**see** "playful") antic; *espiègle; folâtre;* larkish; mirthful; prankish; **n.** FROLICSOMENESS: *gaminerie;* roguery

FROM *a part one may infer the whole:* **n.** *ex pede Herculem; ex ungue leonem*
a single instance one may infer the whole: ab uno disce omnes
day to day: **adv.** *de die in diem*
deepest distress: **n.** *de profundis*
elsewhere, or other source: **a. or adv.** *aliunde*
olden time: **adv.** *ab antiquo*
one, learn all: ab uno disce omnes
the beginning: **see** "beginning"
the chair: **a. or adv.** *ex cathedra*
the greatest to the least: a maximus ad minima
the part may recognize the whole: **n.** *ex pede Herculem; ex ungue leonem*
within: **adv.** *ab intra;* **a.** endogenous
without: (**see** "foreign") **a.** exogenous

FRONT: **n.** anterior; anticus; *avant coureur; avant-garde;* countenance; façade; obverse; physiognomy; vanguard
as of coin or medal: **n.** obverse
being in: **a.** anterior; *avant-garde;* **n.** anteriority

FRONTIER: **see** "border"

FROSTY: **a.** boreal; gelid; pruinose; pruinous; unfriendly; **n.** FROSTNESS: gelidity

FROTH: **n.** despumation; effervescence; spume; **a.** FROTHY: effervescent; spumescent

FROWZY (or FROWSY): **a.** scabrous; slatternly; squalid; unkempt

FROZEN: (**see** "cold") **a.** gelid; hyperborean; immobile; petrified; refrigerated; solidified; **n.** gelidity

FRUGALITY: (**see** "thrift") **n.** exiguity; parcity; parsimony; paucity

FRUIT, *bear:* **v.** fructify; **a.** fructiferous; fructuous; **n.** fruition
bearing none: **a.** acarpous; barren; infertile; infructuous; sterile
business of growing, marketing, etc.: **n.** pomology; **n.** pomologist
-eating: **a.** carpophagous; frugivorous
residuum after expressing juice: **n.** magma

FRUITFUL: (**see** "fertile") **a.** abounding; exuberant; fecund; feracious; fructiferous; fructificative; fructuous; fruitive; gravid; procreant; prolific; proligerous; uberous; **n.** FRUITFULNESS: fecundity; frutescence; gravidity; productiveness; prolificacy
to make: **v.** fructify

FRUITLESS: **see** "futile"

FRUSTRATE: (**see** "baffle") **v.** circumvent; impede; outwit; stultify; **n.** FRUSTRATION: circumvention; disappointment; impediment; stultification; **a.** FRUSTRATING: self-defeating; stultifying

FULFILL: **v.** accomplish; consummate; execute; fructify; implement; **n.** FULFILLMENT: (**see** "end") accomplishment; consummation; execution; fruition; implementation; **a.** consummative; implementary

FULL: **a.** abounding; abundant; comprehensive; copious; orotund; plenary; plentitudinous; plethoric; replete; sated; surfeited; torrential; unexpurgated; **n.** FUL(L)NESS: abundance; amplitude; copiosity; copiousness; plen(t)itude; plethora; repletion; satiation; satiety; surfeit
in: **adv.** *in extenso; in pleno*
-toned: **a.** resonant; rotund; sonorous

FUNCTION(S): **see** "purpose" **and** "occupation"
having various: **a.** polymorphic; polymorphous; **n.** polymorphism; polymorphy
impaired or abnormal: **n.** dysfunction; malfunction; **a.** afunctional; malfunctional
lack of, not due to apparent injury or disease: **n.** abiotrophy; hysteria; **a.** abiotrophic; hysterical
of office, etc.: **n.** attribute; attribution; perquisite; **a.** attributive

FUNCTIONAL: **a.** occupational; psychogen(et)ic; psychological; psychosomatic;

physiological; utilitarian; **n.** psychogenesis; psychosomatics

FUNCTIONING, *normal, of organism, pert. to:* **a.** functional; operational; psysiological

FUNDAMENTAL: (**see** "basic") **a.** constitutional; essential; indispensable; inherent; primal; primary; primitive; substratal; substrate; substrative; underlying; ultimate; **adv.** *au fond;* **n.** FUNDAMENTALITY: essentiality; intrinsicality; primality; primitivity; quintessence; ultimacy; (**pl.** ultimacies)

FUNERAL: **n.** exequy; (**or pl.** exequies); inhumation; interment; obsequy; (**pl.** obsequies); sepulcher; sepulchre; sepulture; solemnities
ode, hymn or commendation: **n.** coronach; dirge; elegy; epicede; epicedium; epitaph; monody; obituary; requiem; threnody; **a.** elegiac; epicedial; epicedian; monodic; threnodial; threnodic
oration: **n.** eloge; elogy; encomium
service(s): **n.pl.** exequies; obsequies; solemnities
song: **see** "ode, hymn, etc." **above**
suitable for or pert. to: **a.** exequial; funebrial; funebrous; funereal; funerary; mortuary; sepulchral

FUN-*loving:* **a.** gelogenic; jocular; roguish

FUNNY: (**see** "laughable") **a.** facetious; farcical; gelastic; harlequin; humorous; jocose; ludicrous; risible
action or remark: **n.** facetiosity; farcicality; ridiculosity
yet serious: **a.** ludicropathetic; ludicroserious

FURIOUSLY: **see** "mercilessly"

FURNITURE, *household, of or rel. to:* **a.** mobiliary

FUROR(E): **see** "hubbub"

FURROW: **n.** chamfer; sulcus; **a.** sulcate

FURTHER: **a.** additional; ulterior

FURY: (**see** "anger" **and** "madness") **n.** acharnement; agitation; frenzy; impetuosity; rabidity; truculence; truculency; vehemence; **a.** FURIOUS: energetic; frenzied; furibund; impetuous; maniac(al); turbulent

FUSE: **v.** amalgamate; ankylose; anneal; coalesce; conflate; connate; syncretize; synchronize; **n.** amalgamation; ankylosis; conflation; connation; syncretism; synchronism

FUSS: **see** "hubbub;" **a.** FUSSY: (**see** "overnice") grandmotherly

FUTILE: **a.** abortive; frivolous; fruitless; futilitarian; inadequate; ineffective; ineffectual; otiose; sterile; unrewarding; **n.** FUTILITY: frivolity; fruitlessness; inadequacy; ineffectuality; otiosity; uselessness
one engaged in (futile) pursuits, or believing in futility of human striving: **n. or a.** futilitarian

FUTURE: **a.** prospective; subsequent; **n.** futurity
in the: **adv.** *in futuro*

G

GAIETY: **n.** animation; buoyancy; ebullience; euphrosyne; exhilaration; exuberance; festivity; *gaieté de coeur;* geniality; jocularity; jocundity; jollification; jollity; joviality; jubilation; lightheartedness; merrymaking; nepenthe; nonchalance; revelry; sprightliness; vivacity; yeastiness; **a. see** "gay"

GAIN: **n.** acquirement; acquisition; aggrandizement; augmentation; compensation; enhancement; emolument; increment; **a.** GAINFUL: (**see** "profitable") compensatory; remunerative; remuneratory
   for sake of: **adv.** *lucri causâ*
   interested in or undertaken for: **a.** commercial; mercenary; mercantile; quaestuary; venal
   spirit of: **n.** fiscality

GALL: (**see** "anger") **n.** acerbity; assurance; audacity; effrontery; impudence; presumption; rancor; temerity; **a. see** "annoying"; **v. see** "annoy"

GALLANT: (**see** "brave") **a.** cavalier; chivalresque; chivalric; chivalrous; magnanimous; stately; urbane; **n.** (**see** "lover") cavalier; *cavalier servant;* chevalier; cicisbeo; **n.** GALLANTRY: **see** "bravery"
   and dashing man, as in liberating victims of tyranny: **n.** pimpernel

GALLOP, *rapid, or at a:* **n. or a.** tantivy

GAMBLING, *pert to:* **a.** aleatory

GANG: (**see** "mob") **n.** camorra; canaille; carbonari
   member of: **n.** camorrista

GAP: **n.** aperture; caesura; chasm; discontinuity; hiatus; interim; intermission; interregnum; interruption; interspace; interstice; interval; lacuna; parenthesis; va-

cuity; **a.** hiatal; lacunal; lacunar; parenthetical

GAPE: **v.** dehisce; oscitate; **n.** dehiscence; oscitance; oscitation; **a.** GAPING: cavernous; oscitant; patulous

GARBAGE: (**see** "waste") **n.** offal; recrement; refuse; sordes

GARDEN *party:* **n.** *fête champêtre*
   pert. to or suitable for: **a.** hortensial
   vegetables, herbs, etc.: **n.** potagerie(s)

GARMENT: **n.** habiliment; vestment
   ecclesiastical: **n.** cassock; chasuble; soutane
   worn as sign of mourning, penitence or project: **n.** sackcloth

GARNISH: **v.** adorn; diamondize; embellish; furbish; lard; **n.** GARNISH (**or** GARNISHMENT): adornment; embellishment; ostentation; panoply

GARTER, *Order of, motto: honi soit qui mal y pense*

GAS, *intestinal:* **n.** borborygmus; crepitation; crepitus; flatulence; flatus

GATHER: **v.** agglutinate; assemble; coagulate; collate; concentrate; conclude; conglomerate; infer; marshal(l); muster; **n.** GATHERING: (**see** "collection") agglutination; assemblage; assembly; colluvies; concourse; congregation; coterie; parliament

GAUDY: (**see** "ornate" **and** "showy") **a.** baronial; baroque; bedizened; blatant; brummagem; chintzy; extravagant; flamboyant; garish; grotesque; meretricious; ornate; rococco; **n.** GAUDINESS: bedizenment; blatancy; flamboyance; ostentation; panoply; showiness

135

GAUZY: see "filmy"

GAY: **a.** Anacreontic; affable; amiable; blithe(ful); buoyant; carnivalesque; cavalier; convivial; debonair(e); ebullient; ecstatic; effervescent; euphoric; exuberant; frivolous; frolicsome; genial; hoitytoity; jaunty; jocular; jocund; jovial; joyous; jubilant; nonchalant; phrenetic; Pythian; revelrous; rhapsodic(al); riant; roguish; *sans-souci;* spirited; vivacious; volatile; yeasty; **n. see** "gaiety"

GEAR: (see "equipment") **n.pl.** accoutrements; apparatus; appointments; paraphernalia; toggery; trappings

GEM, *surface of:* **n.** bezel; facet
uncut but somewhat polished: **n.** cabochon

GENERAL: **a.** cosmic; cosmopolitan; customary; ecumenical; encyclic(al); encyclopedic(al); generic; pandemic; prevalent; universal; unrestricted; **n.** GENERALITY: catholicity; ecumenicity; universality
effect: **n.** tout ensemble
in: **adv.** en masse

GENERATION: **n.** development; procreation; production
spontaneous: **n.** abiogenesis; autogenesis

GENERATIVE *principle in nature, worship of:* **n.** phallicism

GENEROUS: (see "charitable") **a.** altruistic; beneficent; benevolent; bountiful; charitable; chivalrous; copious; indulgent; lavish; munificent; philanthropic(al); profuse; **n.** GENEROSITY: beneficence; benevolence; largess(e); liberality; magnanimity; munificence; openhandedness; philanthropy; prodigality
extremely: **a.** lavish; prodigal; **n.** prodigality
person: (see "person, charitable") **n.** philanthropist; Samaritan

GENIAL: (see "friendly") **a.** affable; amiable; benignant; bonhomous; debonair(e); genteel; nonchalant; **n.** GENIALITY: (bon)camaraderie; bonhom(m)ie; conviviality; *esprit de corps;* gentility; joviality

GENITALS, *external, either sex:* **n.pl.** genitalia; pudenda

female: **n.pl.** genitalia; muliebria; pudenda; vulva

GENIUS. **n.** aptitude; disposition; intellect; propensity; talent
local, or of a place: **n.** genius loci

GENTLE: **a.** chivalresque; chivalric; chivalrous; conciliatory; considerate; courteous; courtly; docile; favonian; genteel; lenient; pacific; placid; tractable; tranquil; **n.** GENTLENESS: chivalry; docility; gentility; leniency; lenity; mansuetude; refinement

GENTLEMAN: **n.** galantuomo; gentilhomme; mynheer; seignior; seigneur; **a.** GENTLEMANLY: seigneurial; seign(i)orial
young: **n.** yo(u)nker

GENUINE: (see "sincere") **a.** apostolic(al); authentic; authoritative; *bona fide;* canonical; documented; ingenuous; kosher; legitimate; official; orthodox; simon-pure; straightforward; unadulterated; unaffected; unalloyed; unfeigned; **n.** GENUINENESS: apostolicity; canonicity; ingenuousness; legitimacy; sincerity
not: **see** "counterfeit"

GESTURE(S): **v.** gesticulate; **n.** deportment; gesticulation; **a.** gesticulatory
fine, graceful or pleasing, but sometimes meaningless and overcourteous: **n.** beau geste
study of, as means of communication: **n.** pasimology

GET: **v.** acquire; comprehend; obtain; secure; **n.** acquisition; acquirement; comprehension; obtainment; obtention; procurement; securement

GHASTLY: (see "frightful") **a.** awesome; cadaverous; corpselike; grisly; gruesome; hideous; livid; macabre; morbid; repellent; repulsive; spectral; terrifying; **n.** GHASTLINESS: grisliness; lividity; morbidity; repulsiveness

GHOST: **n.** animus; apparition; chimera; *deceptio visus;* delusion; eidelon; manes; phantasm(ata); phantom; poltergeist; revenant; shadow; specter; wraith; **a.** GHOSTLY: chthonian; delusive; illusory; shadowy; spectral; spiritual; supermundane; supernatural

(ghostly) counterpart or companion: **n.** alter ego; doppelganger
noisy: **n.** poltergeist

GIANT: **n.** behemoth; brobdingnagian; colossus; Gargantua; goliath; Paul Bunyan; Polypheme; **a.** GIGANTIC: (**see** "huge") behemothian; brobdingnagian; Bunyanesque; cyclopean; cyclopic; elephantine; Gargantuan; giantesque; Herculean; polyphemian; polyphemic; polyphemous; prodigious; **n.** GIANTISM: gigantism; macrosomia
with a (giant) stride: **adv.** *à pas de géant*

GIDDY: **a.** capricious; flighty; frivolous; gyratory; heady; vertiginous; volatile; **n.** vertigo

GIFT: (**see** "gratuity") **n.** aptitude; benefaction; benefice; beneficence; bequest; devise; faculty; largesse(e)
free: **n.** gratuity; lagniappe; largess(e); **a.** complimentary; gratis
giver adds to the: autcor pretiosa facit of kindness: **n.** benefaction; benefice; beneficence; benevolence; **a.** beneficent; benevolent

GIFTED *person or thing:* **n.** *bel esprit;* prodigality; prodigy

GILDED: **a.** aureate; festooned; luxurious; meretricious; ornate; prosperous; tassellated; tawdry; **v.** GILD: **see** "adorn"
"youth": **n.** *jeunesse doré;* (**fem.** *dorée*)

GIN: **n.** *spiritus juniperi*

GIRL: **n.** belle; colleen; damsel; demoiselle; mademoiselle; maid(en); minx; nymph
adolescent or immature: **n.** backfisch(e)
country: **n.** amaryllis
mischievous, bold or boisterous: **n.** gamine; hoyden; minx; tomboy; **a.** gamine; hoydenish
promiscuous but technically virgin: **n.** *demi-vierge*
slender: **n.** sylph; **a.** sylphic; sylphlike
young: **n.** ingénue; *jeune fille;* junior miss; soubrette

GIST: **n.** essence; quintessence; sum and substance

GIVE-*and-take:* **v.** reciprocate; **n.** compromise; *quid pro quo;* reciprocation; reci-

procity; **a.** reciprocative
in: **see** "yielding"
out: **v.** administer; dispense; distribute; **n.** administration; disbursement; dispensation; distribution
up: **v.** abjure; capitulate; disclaim; divest; relinquish; submit; surrender; **n.** abjuration; capitulation; relinquishment; resignation; submission
with expectation of receiving: **n. or v.** potlatch

GIVER: **n.** benefactor; donor; eleemosyner; grantor; philanthropist; testator
adds value to gift: auctor pretiosa facit

GLANCE: (**see** "glimpse" **and** "rebound")
v. effleurer; ricochet
amorous: **n.** *oeillade*
brief: **n.** *aperçu; clin d'oeil*
rapid, or covering wide field: **n.** *coup d'oeil*

GLARING: (**see** "gaudy") **a.** audacious; flagrant; garish; glowering; impudent

GLASS, *of or like:* **a.** crystal(line); hyaline; sanidinic; vitreous; vitric

GLEAM: **v.** coruscate; fulgurate; phosphoresce; radiate; rutilate; scintillate; **n.** coruscation; fluorescence; fulguration; phosphorescence; **a.** GLEAMING: clinquant; corsucant; coruscating; fulgent; fulgurant; lambent; luminous; lustrous; phosphorescent; rutilant; **n.** clinquant; coruscation; fulguration; lambency; luminosity; phosphorescence

GLIMPSE: (**see** "glance") **n.** adumbration; *aperçu; clin d'oeil; coup d'oeil;* inking

GLOOM (or GLOOMINESS): **n.** dejection; depression; despondency; disconsolation; hypochondria(sis); melancholia; melancholy; morbidity; morosity; murkishness; pessimism; sableness; saturninity unsociability; (**pl.** doldrums; lachrymals; megrims)
causing: **a.** luctiferous; tenebrific

GLOOMY: (**see** "peevish") **a.** Acheronian; Acheronic(al); Cimmerian; dejected; disconsolate; disheartened; disheartening; dolorous; dyspeptic; funebrial; funebr(i)ous; funereal; hypochondriacal; inconsolable; melancholic; melancholy; morose; pessimistic; plutonian; plutonic; satur-

nine; sepulchral; splenetic; stygian; tene-brific; tenebrous; unsociable
    person: **n.** atrabilarian; hypochondriac; melancholiac; pessimist

GLORY: **n.** effulgence; eminence; grandilo-quence; grandiosity; illustriousness; lu-minosity; luster; magnificence; repute; re-splendence; resplendency; splendor; sub-limity; **v.** GLORIFY: (**see** "exalt") apotheosize; deify; glamorize; idealize; romanticize; stellify; **n.** GLORIFICA-TION: apotheosis; canonization; deifica-tion; exaltation; glamorization; sanctifi-cation; stellification
    born to: **adv.** *natus ad gloriam*
    cloud of: **n.** nimbus
    to the Father (God): **n.** ascription; Gloria in Excelsis; Gloria Patri

GLOSS: **see** "veneer"; **a.** GLOSSY: lus-trous; nitid; **n.** GLOSSINESS: (**see** "sheen") luster; nitidity

GLOW, *sunrise or sunset:* **n.** alpenglow

GLOWING: **a.** ardent; candent; enthusias-tic; fervent; impassioned; (in)candescent; intense; (per)fervid; phosphorescent; refulgent; **n.** (in)candescence; phospho-rescence; refulgence; refulgency

GLUEY: **a.** glutinous; tenacious; viscous; **n.** glutinosity; tenacity; viscosity

GLUM: **see** "gloomy"

GLUTTON: **n.** apician; cormorant; epi-cure; gormand(izer); gourmand; gour-met; **v.** gormandize; **a.** GLUTTONOUS: bulimic; cormorant; crapulent; crapulous; edacious; epicurean; polyphagous; rapa-cious; ventripotent; voracious; **n.** GLUT-TONY: (**see** "appetite, excessive") bu-limia; crapulence; edacity; gulosity; in-satiability; rapacity; voracity

GO: (**see** going") **v.** depart; diminish; elapse; proceed; wane
    before: (see "going before" **and** "pre-liminary") **v.** precede; transcend; **n.** prece-dent
    -between: **n.** diplomat(ist); emissary; *entrepreneur;* (fem. *entrepreneuse*); inter-cessor; intermediary; internuncio; media-tor; moderator; propitiator
    in peace: **adv.** *vade in pace*
    permission to: **n.** *congé*

GOAL: (**see** "aim" **and** "intent") **n.** ambi-tion; destination; ideal; intention; Mecca; terminus; *terminus ad quem*
    distant: **n.** Thule; *ultima Thule*
    extreme or highest: **n.** consummation

GOAT, *of or like:* **a.** capric; caprid; cap-rine; hircine

GOD(S): **n.** Almighty; divinity; Jehovah; Pantocrator; Providence
    appearance or revelatory manifestation of: **n.** epiphany; **a.** epiphanic
    as center, central interest or ultimate concern: **n.** theocentrism; **a.** theocentric
    bad: **n.** Ahriman; cacod(a)emon; (**see** "devil")
    being willing, or w/ sanction of: **adv.** *Deo volente*
    belief in or worship of several or many: **n.** polytheism; **a.** polytheistic(al)
    blood of the (gods): **n.** ichor
    by grace of: **adv.** *Dei gratia*
    doctrine that but one: **n.** monotheism; **a.** monotheistic(al)
    drink of the (gods): **n.** nectar
    favored our undertakings: annuit coeptus
    fear of wrath of: **n.** theophobia
    festival honoring the (gods): **n.** pane-gyris
    fit for, or food for (gods): **n.** ambrosia; **a.** ambrosial
    forbid: **adv.** *absit omen*
    formed an image of: **a.** theomorphic; **n.** theomorphism
    from machine; deux ex machinâ
    glory to: **see** "praise to" **below**
    good or beneficial: **n.** agathod(a)emon
    government or rule by: **n.** theocracy; theonomy; **a.** theocratic; theonomous
    hatred or hater of: **n.** theophobia; theo-phobist
    having ruled otherwise: diis (or dis) aliter visum
    having appearance or nature of a: **a.** Adonic; deiform
    helps those who help themselves: otiosis nullus adsistit Deus
    humbles the proud: Dieu abaisse les superbes
    hymn to: **n.** doxology; *te deum;* theody
    incarnation of: **n.** epiphany
    inferior or subordinate: **n.** demiurge; subdeity
    narrative of miraculous deeds of (god) or hero: **n.** aretalogy
    of the people (popular or state-recog-nized): **n.** pantheon

praise be to: **adv.** *laus Deo*
praise to: **n.** ascription; doxology; *Gloria in Excelsis; Gloria Patria; laus Deo;* **a.** doxological; **v.** doxologize
revelation or manifestation of: **n.** epiphany
thanks to: **n.** *Deo gratias*
will of the: **n.** *moira*
will provide: Deus providebit; Dominus providebit
wills it: Deus vult
with us: **adv.** *Dieu avec nous*
worship of a: **n.** theolatry
worship of all: **n.** pantheism; **a.** pantheistic(al); **n.** omnist; pantheist
worship of foreign or unsanctioned: **n.** allotheism
worship of many: **n.** polytheism; **a.** polytheistic(al)
worship of one: **n.** henotheism; monolatry; monotheism; **a.** monolatrous; monotheistic

GODLINESS: **n.** *pietas*

GOD-MAN: **n.** theanthropos

GODSEND: **n.** *trouvaille*

GOING *before:* (**see** "preliminary") **a.** antecedent; anticipating; anticipatory; expectant; introductory; precedent; preceding; precursory; prefatorial; premonitory; prevenient; **n.** precedent
out: **v.** egress; **n.** egression

GOLD, *accursed greed of: auri sacra fames*
bearing or containing: **a.** auric; auriferous; aurous
cloth of: **n.** *drap d'or*
distinctive properties of: **n.** aureity
pert. to or like: **a.** auric; aurous
supposed element to produce: **n.** elixir; philosopher's stone

GOLDEN: **a.** aureate; aurelian; aureous; auric; auriferous; aurulent; halcyon
age: **n.** millennium; (**pl.** millennia); *siècle d'or*
calf, worship of: **n.** *adorer le veau d'or*
mean: **n.** *ariston metron; aurea mediocritas; le juste milieu*

GOOD: **a.** adequate; admirable; advantageous; beatific; blissful; cardinal; decorous; delicious; nutritious; prime; propitious; profitable; saintly; salubrious; salutary; seraphic; superlative; worthy

all things tend to ultimate (theory): **n.** agathism; agathist
and evil, composed of both: **a.** agathocacological; agathokakological; Jekyll-and-Hyde
and evil, theory that world divided into: **n.** Manichaeism; **a.** Manichaeistic
appearing to be: **a.** hypocritical; religiose; sanctimonious; **n.** hypocrisy; odor of sanctity; religiosity; sanctimoniousness; sanctimony
auspices: **n.** *bonis avibus*
breeding or manners: **n.** *bon ton;* gentility; *savoir faire;* suavity; urbanity
common: **n.** *commune bonum*
deed or act: **n.** benefaction; benefice; beneficence; benevolence; mitzvah; **a.** benefic(ent); benevolent
doctrine of: **n.** agathology
-evening: **n.** *bonsoir*
faith: **n.** *aberrima fides; bona fide(s); bonne foi*
-fellowship: **n.** (*bon*) *camaraderie; bonhom(m)ie;* conviviality; *esprit de corps;* geniality; joviality; **a.** bonhomous; convivial; genial; jovial
-for-nothing: **a.** fustian
for whose?: **n.** *cui bono?*
genius: **n.** agathod(a)emon
great: **n.** *magnum bonum*
help: **n.** *bon secours*
highest or greatest: **n.** *summum bonum*
-humored: **see** "gay"
incapable of either harm or good: **a.** adiaphoristic; adiaphorous
-looking: **a.** comely; personable; pulchritudinous
-morning: **n.** *bonjour; buenas dias*
-natured: **a.** affable; amiable; benign; (con)genial; gracious
-night: **n.** *buenas noches*
order or management: **n.** eutaxy; husbandry
position for observation or action: **n.** coign (of vantage)
pretending to be: **see** "appearing to be" **above**
science or doctrine of: **n.** agathology
supreme or highest: **n.** *summum bonum*
taste: **n.** *decorum;* **a.** *decorous*
to the (good) all things are (good): omnia bona bonis
-will: **n.** benevolence; *bienveillance; bonne volonté; bonté*

GOODBYE: **n.** *à bientôt;* adeus; adieu; *à tout à l'heure; au revoir; auf wiedersehen; bene vale; bon voyage; congé; riverderchi* *biding or pert. to:* **a.** apopemtic; valedictory

GOODNESS, *appearance or reputation of:* **n.** hypocrisy; odor of sanctity; religiosity; sanctimoniousness

GOOSE, *like a:* **a.** anserine
-pimples: **n.** *arrectores pilorum; cutis anserina;* horripilation

GORGE: **v.** gormandize; satiate; surfeit; **n.** gluttony; satiation; satiety

GORGEOUS: (**see** "grand") **a.** dazzling; flamboyant; magnificent; resplendent; splendaceous; splendacious

GOSSIP: **n.** blatherskite; *caqueterie;* magpie; quidnunc; rumormonger; scuttlebutt
piece of: **n.** *on-dit*
unsavory: **n.** *chronique scandaleuse*

GOURMET: (**see** "glutton") **n.** *bonvivant;* epicure; gastronome(r); gourmand; trencherman

GOVERN: **see** "command"

GOVERNMENT(S): **n.** administration; bureaucracy; dominion; polity; regime(n); sovereignty
by all the people: **n.** pantarchy; pantisocracy; **a.** pantocratic
by best men: **n.** aristarchy
by fools: **n.** foolocracy
by devil(s): **n.** diabolarchy; diabolocracy
by few, also state so governed: **n.** oligarchy: **a.** oligarchic(al)
by harlots: **n.** pornocracy
by many persons: **n.** polyarchy; **a.** polyarchic
by middle class: **n.** mesocracy
by old men: **n.** gerontocracy
by one person: **n.** autocracy; dictatorship; monarchy; monocracy
by rich: **n.** plutocracy
by small ruling class: **n.** aristocracy
by two persons: **n.** diarchy; duumvirate; dyarchy
by woman or women: **n.** gynarchy; gynecocracy; matriarchy
by worst men: **n.** kakistocracy
ceremonial forms of dealing bet.: **n.** protocol
former or old: **n.** *ancien regime*

founded on system or code of laws: **n.** nomocracy
military: **n.** stratocracy
rel. to: **a.** governmental; gubernatorial; statal; **n.** statecraft
subject to that of another (govt.) **n.** heteronomy; **a.** heteronomous
suspension of, or interval bet. leaders: **n.** interregnum
within a govt.: **n.** *imperium in imperio*
without a head: **a.** acephalous

GRAB: **v.** appropriate; arrogate; capture; confiscate; sequester; **n.** appropriation; arrogation; capture; confiscation; sequestration

GRACE: **n.** attractiveness; benefaction; clemency; considerateness; dispensation; elegance; felicity; lenity; polish; thoughtfulness
characterized by exquisite (grace) and refinement: **a.** spirituel(le)
(prayer): **n.** benediction; invocation; **a.** benedictory; invocatory
with good: **adv.** *de bonne grâce*

GRACEFUL: **a.** gracile; lissome; lithe(some); nymphean; nymphlike; soigné(e); svelt(e); sylphic; sylphlike; symmetrical; **n.** GRACEFULNESS: **see** "slenderness"

GRACIOUS: (**see** "courteous") **a.** affable; auspicious; benign(ant); merciful; **adv.** GRACIOUSLY: *de bonne grâce;* **n.** GRACIOUSNESS: (**see** "grace") benignity; condescension; graciosity; lenity; mercifulness

GRADE: (**see** "rank") **n.** echelon; gradation; standing; station

GRADUAL: **a.** fractional; fragmentary; imperceptible; incremental; piecemeal; progressive; subtle; **adv.** GRADUALLY: *di grado in grado;* inchmeal; *poco a poco*
state or quality of being: **n.** graduality; imperceptibility

GRAIN, *against the:* **adv.** *à contre coeur; à rebours*
of or like: **a.** farinaceous; frumentaceous

GRAMMATICAL *arrangement:* **n.** syntax
inflection: **n.** conjugation

GRAND: (see "great") **a.** august; baronial; cosmic; exalted; flamboyant; grandiloquent; grandiose; Homeric; illustrious; imposing; impressive; magnificent; magniloquent; majestic; ostentatious; preeminent; princely; prominent; rococo; stately; sublime; sumptuous; transcendent
state of being or feeling: **see** "grandeur"

GRANDEUR: **n.** flamboyancy; grandiloquence; grandiosity; grandity; impressiveness; magnificence; majesty; regality; sublimity; sumptuousness
delusions of: **n.** megalomania; **a.** megalomaniacal; **n.** megalomaniac

GRANDIOSE: (see "grand") **a.** apocalyptic(al); bombastic; cosmic; Homeric; imposing; majestic; turgid
in speech or expression: (see "flowery") **a.** grandiloquent; magniloquent; rubescent

GRANT: **v.** award; concede; vouchsafe; **n.** see "gratuity

GRANTED, *taken for:* (see "self-evident") **adv.** sub silento

GRANTING, *act of:* **n.** accordance; concession

GRAPES, *clustered or shaped like:* **a.** aciniform; botryoid(al); botryose; racemose

GRASPING: (see "greedy") **a.** acquisitive; *alieni appetens;* avaricious; covetous; miserly; prehensile; prehensive; tenacious
adapted for: **n.** prehensile; prehensive; **n.** prehension; prehensility
person: **n.** curmudgeon

GRASS(ES), *feeding on:* **a.** graminivorous
rel. to or resembling: **a.** gramineal; gramineous; graminoid
study of: **n.** agrostology; **n.** agrostologist

GRATIFICATION: **n.** delectation; satiation; satiety
showing: **a.** congratulatory; gratulant

GRATIFY: (see "please") **v.** delectate; indulge; satiate
that which (gratifies): **n.** emollient; placebo; tranquilizer; unction

GRATING: **a.** strident; stridulous; **n.** crepitus; stridor; stridulation

GRATUITY: **n.** benefaction; benefice; beneficence; benevolence; douceur; honorarium; lagniappe; largess(e); perquisite; pourboire
given w/ a purchase: **n.** lagniappe

GRAVE: (see "important") **a.** authoritative; funereal; melancholy; mortuary; saturnine; sepulchral; sombrous; tumular(y); **n.** columbarium; mausoleum; ossuary; repository; sepulcher; terminus
cloth: see **under** "burial"

GRAVESTONE *inscription:* **n.** epitaph; *hic jacet*

GREASY: **a.** adipose; butyraceous; oleaginous; lardaceous; pinguid; saponaceous; sebaceous; unctuous; **n.** GREASINESS: lubricity; pinguidity; unctuosity; unctuousness

GREAT: (see "grand") **a.** distinguished; estimable; incalculable; incomputable; magnanimous; monumental; predominant; (pre)eminent; prominent; renowned
events or deeds: **n.** magnalia; magnality
in amount: **n.** abundance; magnitude; plethora; preponderance
in magnitude and extent: **a.** cosmic; encyclopedic(al); magnitudinous; panoramic
very: **a.** incalculable; inestimable; supereminent; transcendent
work: **n.** *chef-d'oeuvre; magnum opus; meisterwerk; piece de résistance*
year: **n.** *annus magnus*

GREATER, *in amount, weight, power, etc.:* **a.** preponderant; **n.** plurality; preponderance

GREATEST: **a.** maximal; maximum; *nec plus supra; nec plus ultra;* paramount; preeminent; sovereign; utmost
degree: **n.** optimum
from the (greatest) to the least: a *maximus ad minima*

GREATNESS: **n.** grandeur; grandiosity; magnanimity; magnitude; monumentality; nobleness; predominance; (pre)eminence; prominence; renown; sublimity; transcendence
delusions of: see **under** "grandeur"
personal: **n.** grandeur

GREECE, *worship or veneration of:* **n.** Hellenism; philhellenism; **a.** philhellene; philhellenic; **n.** philhellene; philhellenist

GREEDY: (**see** "grasping") **a.** acquisitive; avaricious; bourgeois; covetous; extortionate; gluttonous; insatiable; mercenary; parasitic(al); prehensile; prehensive; rapacious; ravenous; venal; voracious; **n.** GREED(INESS): (**see** "avarice") covetousness; cupidity; eagerness; miserliness; rapacity; voracity
    person: (**see** "glutton") **n. or a.** cormorant

GREEN: (**see** "immature") **a.** ultramarine; verdant; verdurous; virescent; virid; **n.** GREENNESS: verdancy; verdure; virescence; viridity; **a.** GREENISH: aeruginous; verdigrisy; virescent; viridescent

GREENHORN: (**see** "amateur") **n.** *blanc-bec*

GREENSICKNESS: **n.** chlorosis

GREET: **v.** accost; address; salute; welcome

GREETING, *act of:* **n.** devoir; salaam; salutation; salute; **a.** salutatory
    or opening, as in a letter: **n.** salutation; **a.** salutational; salutatory

GRIEF: **n.** affliction; desolation; dolor; heartache; lamentation; melancholy; misadventure; misfortune; mortification; tribulation; tristesse; **a.** GRIEVED: disconsolate; inconsolable; lamented
    banishing or mitigating: **a.** nepenthean; **n.** dolorfuge; nepenthe
    causing: **a.** dolorific
    characterized by: **a.** dolorous; funereal; grievous; lamentable; melancholy
    come to: **v.** founder
    road or course of: **n.** *via doloroso*
    scene or occasion of great: **n.** Gethsemane

GRIEVANCE: **n.** annoyance; displeasure; gravamen; lament(ation); oppression

GRIM: (**see** "ghastly") **a.** ferocious; forbidding; gruesome; grisly; inexorable; macabre; morbid; moribund; obdurate; plutonian; plutonic; relentless; ruthless; uncompromising

GRIMACE: **n.** moue; *simagrée*

GRIMY: (**see** "dirty") **a.** scabrous; squalid; sullied; **n.** squalidity; squalor

GRIND: **v.** abrade; comminute; harass; masticate; pulverize; triturate

GRITTY: **a.** arenaceous; plucky; resolute; sabulous

GROOVED: **a.** caniculate; cannellated; chamfered; channeled; scorbiculate; sulcate; **n.** GROOVE: **n.** chamfer; sulcus
    two-: **a.** bisulcate

GROPE: **v.** *aller à tâtons;* **n.** GROPING: *tatonnement*

GROSSNESS: **n.** barbarity; crassitude; crassness; indecency; scurrility; vulgarity

GROTESQUE: **see** "odd"
    manifestation(s): **n.** bizarrerie; fantasia; *fata morgana;* grotesquerie; grotesquery; *ignis fatuus;* phantasmagoria; will-of-the-wisp

GROUCHY: **see** "irritable"

GROUND(S): (**see** "justification") **n.** foundation; rationale; terrain
    contour of: **n.** terrain; topography
    growing in the: **a.** terrestrial
    growing on the: **a.** terricolous
    living under: **a. or n.** subterranean; subterrestrial; **n.** subterrene
    solid: **n.** *terra firma*
    under the: **a.** submundane; subterranean; subterrestrial

GROUNDLESS: **a.** baseless; unfounded

GROUP(S): (**see** "classify") **v.** agglutinate; assemble; categorize; coagulate; colligate; conglomerate; congregate; muster; **n.** (**see** "class" **and** "collection") assemblage; battery
    authoritative: **n.** Areophagus; **a.** Areophagitic; **n.** Areophagite
    centered in one's social: **a.** egocentric; ethnocentric; sociocentric; **n.** sociocentrism
    comprising more than two: **a.** polychotomous
    controlling: **n.** hierarchy; **a.** hierarchic(al)

degraded or contemptible: **n.** lumpen proletarial; **a.** lumpen

elder and often reactionary member of: **n.** mandarin

entire membership of: **n.** plenum; **a.** plenary

exclusive: **n.** cabal; charmed circle; claque; clique; *corps d'élite;* coterie

gathering in a: (**see** "sociable") **a.** gregarious; **n.** gregariousness

general, as a corporation: **n.** commonal(i)ty

habits, manners and customs of: **n.** mores

in a: **adv.** *en masse*

large: **n.** hecatomb; legion; multitude

list of members of: **n.** matricula; roster; rota

literary, philosophical or artistic: **n.** athen(a)eum; cenacle

living together cooperatively: **n.** phalanstery; **a.** or **n.** phalansterian

member of: **n.** congregant

miscellaneous: **n.** omnium-gatherum

of best in any category; **n.** *corps d'élite;* crème de la crème

of many tribes, kingdoms, etc: **n.** polyarchy; **n.** polyarchic

of miscellaneous persons: **n.** menagerie

of three: **n.** *ménage à trois;* ternion; triad; trio; triumvirate

one who secedes and forms new: **n.** Adullamite

opinions, doctrines, etc. of a: **n.** ideology

powerful, effective, well-organized, etc.: **n.** powerhouse

scientific or literary: **n.** athen(a)eum; cenacle

secret: **n.** cabel; junta; **a.** cabalistic

select: **n.** charmed circle; *corps d'élite;* quorum

GROUPING: **a.** agglutinative; aggregatory; cumulative; **n.** alignment; pattern

GROVE: **n.** boscage
rel. to or inhabiting: **a.** nemoral

GROVELING: (**see** "servile") **a.** reptilian

GROW: **v.** augment; enhance; maturate; mature; **n. see** "growth"
together: **v.** ankylose; coalesce; **n.** accretion; ankylosis; coadunation; coalescence; concrescence; concretion; conglomeration; **a.** ankylosed; coadunate; coadunative

GROWING *at high elevations:* **a.** alpestrine
luxuriantly: **a.** rampant; **n.** rampancy
on living tissues: **a.** biogenous
wild, in fields, etc.: **a.** agrest(i)al

GROWTH: **n.** accretion; augmentation; concrescence; development; differentiation; enhancement; evolution; excrescence; maturation; maturescence; neoplasm; proliferation; ramification
gradual: **n.** accrescence; accretion; evolution
or enlargement: **n.** excrescence; neoplasm
original (of anything, as new industry, etc.) : **n.** naissance
over-: **n.** hypertrophy; **a.** hypertrophic
source of natural: **n.** physis
under-: **n.** atrophy; degeneration; hypotrophy

GRUDGE: (**see** "hatred") **n.** animosity; animus; malice; pique; resentment

GRUESOME: (**see** "ghastly") **a.** cadaverous; grisly; macabre; morbid; morbific; morbose; sinister

GUARANTOR: **n.** adpromissor; protector; warrantor

GUARDIAN *of manners or morals:* **n.** custos morum
spirit: **n.** *alter ego*
watchful: **n.** Argus; Cerberus; chaperone

GUARDIANSHIP: (**see** "care") **n.** paternalism

GUARDS, *who guards the?: quis custodiet ipsos custodes?*

GUESS: **v.** anticipate; conjecture; deduce; divine; estimate; hariolate; hypothesize; infer; postulate; presage; prognosticate; surmise; **n.** augury; conjecture; deduction; divination; estimation; hariolation; hypothesis; postulation; prognosis; prognostication; prophesy; supposition; surmise; **a.** GUESSING: academic; conjectural; divinatory; hypothetical; postulatory, presumptive; prophetic(al); suppositional; supposititious; suppositive; theoretical

GUESSWORK: **n.** conjecture; hariolation; haruspication; postulation; supposition

GUEST: **n.** invitee

GUIDE: (**see** "measure") **n.** cicerone; cynosure; dragoman; mentor; polestar; precedent; supervisor; **n.** GUIDANCE: (**see** "supervision") chaperonage; ciceronage; guardianship; paternalism
   serving to: **a.** didactic; heuristic; normative; prescriptive
   sightseeing: **n.** cicerone

GUIDEBOOK: (**see** "handbook") **n.** Baedeker; itinerary; *vade mecum*

GUIDING, *as by hand:* **n.** manuducation; **a.** manuducative; manuducatory

GUILE: **n.** artifice; deceit; dissimulation; duplicity; rascality; stratagem; subtlety; treachery; **a.** GUILELESS: artless; credulous; gullible; ingenuous; naive; **n.** GUILELESSNESS: artlessness; credulity; cullibility; gullibility; ingenuousness; *naïveté*

GUILT: **n.** criminality; culpa(bility); delinquency; dereliction; reprehensibility; reprehension
   acknowledgment of personal: **n.** *mea culpa*
   confession of: **n.** peccavi
   feeling of: **n.** compunction; contrition; penitence; remorse; repentance
   freeing or forgiveness from: **n.** absolution; amnesty; atonement; expiation; purgation; redemption; **a.** absolutory; expiatory; redemptive
   impute: **v.** incriminate; inculpate
   sense of: **n.** compunction; contrition; penitence; remorse; **a.** compunctious; contrite; intropunitive; penitent; remorseful; self-accusatory

GUILTY: **a.** blameworthy; contrite; culpable; demeritorious; indictable; nocent; penitent; reprehensible; reprehensive
   person: **n.** criminal; culprit; felon; misdemeanant; misfeasor

GULLIBLE: **a.** credulous; naïve; **n.** GULLIBILITY: credulity; cullibility; *naïveté*

GUMMY: **a.** glutinous; viscous

GUSH: **v.** regurgitate; **n.** regurgitation; **a.** GUSHING: **see** "demonstrative"
   forth: (**see** "effusive") **a.** scaturient

GYPSIES, *of or rel. to:* **a.** tzigane

H

HABIT(S) : **n.** addiction; assuetude; constitution; consuetude; demeanor; disposition; habitude; pattern; physique; praxis; rota; rote; routine
  bad or uncontrollable: **n.** cacoethes
  become accustomed to: **v.** habituate; **n.** habituation
  great is the power of: magna est vis consuetudinis
  group: **n.pl.** mores
  law(s) regulating on religious or moral grounds: **n.** sumptuary (law)
  person addicted to: **n.** *habitué;* routineer
  state of being controlled by: **n.** habituality; habituation

HABITUAL: (see "chronic") **a.** adamant; confirmed; consuetudinal; customary; inveterate; persistent; routine; HABITUATE: **see** "accustom"
  pursuits pass over into character: abeunt studia in mores

HAIR: **n.** capillus; chevelure; pilus; thatch
  covered w/ fine or wool: **a.** lanate; lanuginose; lanuginous; laniferous; pubescent; velutinous; villoid
  crew-cut: **n.** *(cheveux) en brosse*
  erection due to cold, fear, etc.: **n.** *cutis anserina;* horripilation; piloerection
  falling out of: **n.** depilation; psilosis; **a.** psilotic
  false: **n.** postiche; toupee
  golden: **a.** aurocephalous
  grayness or whiteness of: **n.** canities
  having dark or black: **a.** melanocomous; melanous
  having red: **a.** hirsutorufous; rufous; xanthous; phrrhotism
  having straight smooth: **a.** leiotrichous; lissotrichous
  having wooly or curly: **a.** ulotrichous; **n.** ulotrichy
  having yellowish, red, auburn or brown: **a.** xanthous
  kinky or crinkled, pert. to: **a.** encomic
  like a: **a.** capilliform

loss of coloring in: **n.** canites; poliosis
of the head: **n.** chevelure
pubic: **n.** byssus; escutcheon
  site of: **n.** *mons veneris* (**fem.**) pubic triangle
rel. or pert. to: **see** "hairy"
remove: **v.** depilate; **n.** depilant; depilatory; depilation
study of: **n.** trichology
wavy, having: **a.** cymotrichous

HAIR-RAISING: **a.** horripilant; **a.** HAIR-SPLITTING: casuistic; sophistical; specious; **n.** casuistry; dialectics; pilpul; sophistry; speciosity

HAIRY: **a.** ciliate; comose; comous; crinate; criniferous; crinitory; hirsutal; hirsute; piliferous; pilose; pilous; polytrichous; villous; **n.** HAIRNESS: crinosity; hirsutism; pilosis; pilosism; pilosity; trichosis; **a.** HAIRLESS: atrichic; atrichous; depilous; glabrate; glabrescent; glabrous
  covering, as animal's: **n.** pelage
  growth, covered w/: **a.** crinate; criniferous; **n.** crinosity; pelage
  or threadlike: **a.** capillaceous; **n.** capilliform

HALF: (see "halved") **a.** imperfect; partial; **n.** mediety; moiety
  -"baked :" **a.** immature; malentendu
  -*breed:* (**see under** "breed") **n.** hybrid; mestizo; *métis;* mongrel

HALL, *of or pert. to:* **a.** aularian

HALLOWED *place:* **n.** bethel; bethesda; halidom(e) ; sanctuary; *sanctum sanctorum*

HALLUCINATION(S), *that which produces:* **n.** hallucinogen

HALO: **n.** aura; aureola; aurora; anthelion; corona; nimbus

HALT: see "discontinue"

HALTING *place:* (see "hostelry") **n.** anchorage; haven; étape; terminus

HALVED: **a.** bifid; bipartite; bisected; cloven; dichotomous; dimidiate; **n.** bifurcation; dichotomy; dimidiation

HAND(S), *enlargement of:* **n.** chiromegaly
  having four: **a.** quadrumanous
  having no: **a.** amanous
  having or pert. to two: **a.** ambidextrous; bimanous; bimanual
  largeness of: **n.** chiromegaly
  leading by the: **n.** manuducation; **a.** manuductive; manuductory
  left: **n.** *mano sinistra;* **a.** sinistral
  on the other: **adv.** *per contra*
  *opened so as to show palm; **a.** ap-(p)aumé*
  pert. to, made or worked by: **a.** manual
  right: **n.** dextrality; *mano destra;* **a.** dextral; **a. or adv.** *main droite*
  seizure by: **n.** manucaption; **n. or v.** manucapture
  sign lang. by use of: **n.** dactylology
  use of in talking: **v.** gesticulate; **n.** gesticulation; **a.** gesticulatory
  use of both equally: **n.** ambidexterity; **a.** ambidextrous; bimanual
  use of one: **a.** unidextral
  with a strong: **adv.** *manu forti*

HANDBOOK: **n.** Baedeker; enchiridion; manual; promptuary; *vade mecum*

HANDED *down:* (see "traditional") **a.** tralatitious

HANDICAP: (see "disability") **n.** encumbrance; impediment; incubus

HANDSOME: **a.** adonic; comely; *fait à peindre;* personable
  young man: **n.** Adonis; *un beau garçon*

HANDWRITING: **n.** chirography; (manu)script(ion); **a.** chirographic
  bad or careless: **n.** cacography; griffonage; scrawl
  fine or beautiful: **n.** calligraphy; **a.** calligraphic; **n.** calligrapher
  illegible: **n.** hieroglyphic(s)
  large: **n.** macrography; **a.** macrographic
  of author, written in: **a.** holographic(al); onomastic; **n.** holograph
  on the wall: mene, mene; tekel, upharsin

  one's own: **n.** autograph; autography; **a.** autographic(al)
  pert. to: **a.** scriptorial; scriptory
  study of: **n.** bibliotics; graphology
  written in one's own: **a.** autographic(al); holographic; onomastic

HANDY: (see "convenient") **a.** adroit; dext(e)rous; facile; habile; ingenious; resourceful; **n.** HANDINESS: adeptness; dexterity; expertise; virtuosity
  -man: **n.** factotum; *genius loci*

HANG: **v.** (im)pend; pendulate; suspend; **a.** HANGING: (see "impending") abeyant; appendicular; pendent; pendulant; pendular; pendulous; pensile; suspended; **n.** pendency; pendulation; pendulosity; pendulousness

HAPHAZARD: see "random"

HAPPENING: see "contingency" **and** "incident"; **v.** HAPPEN: befall; betide; supervene; transpire
  at same time: see **under** "time"

HAPPINESS: **n.** beatitude; bliss; ecstasy; eud(a)emonia; euda(e)monism; felicity; seventh heaven; transport
  bringing, or designed to promote: **a.** beatific; felicific; **v.** beatify
  incapacity for: **n.** anhedonia; **a.** anhedonic
  place of blissful: **n.** Eden; Elysium; paradise
  "science of:" **n.** eudaemonics
  transcendent: **n.** beatitude; ecstasy; **a.** beatific; ecstatic

HAPPY: (see "blissful") **a.** appropriate; auspicious; blithesome; buoyant; ecstatic; edenic; elysian; eud(e)emonic(al); felicific; felicitous; gelastic; gelogenic; halcyon; harmonious; opportune; rapturous; revelrous; *sans-souci*
  always: **adv.** *semper felix*
  extremely: **a.** dithyrambic; ecstatic; euda(e)monic(al); rapturous; rhapsodic(al)
  make extremely: **v.** enrapture; imparadise; transport

HARASS: **v.** bedevil; dragoon; exhaust; importune

HARD: (see "difficult" **and** "stern") **a.** adamant(ine); arduous; exacting; griev-

ous; impenetrable; incorrigible; inflexible; intractable; laborious; ruthless; strenuous; unrelenting; unsparing; **v.** HARDEN: concretize; fortify; habituate; indurate; inure; ossify; petrify; **a.** HARDENED: adamantine; concretive; confirmed; congelative; impenitent; indurated; insensate; insusceptible; inured; inveterate; marmoreal; obdurate; ossified; petrous; unrepentant; **n.** HARDNESS: impenitence: induration; petrification; sclerosis; strenuosity
-hearted: (**see** "unfeeling") **a.** impenitent; impervious; obdurate; unemotional
like marble: **a.** adamantine; marmoreal; petrous

HARDENING: **n.** concretization; congealment; congelation; induration; ossification; petrification
of the arteries: **n.** arteriosclerosis; **a.** arteriosclerotic

HARE: **n.** coney; lagomorph; **a.** leporid
-brained: **a.** *écervelé*
-lip: **n.** cheilognathus; cheiloschisis

HARM: (**see** "injury") molestation
immune to: **a.** impassible; invulnerable; **n.** impassibility; invulnerability
incapable of (harm) or good: **a.** adiaphoristic; adiaphorous

HARMFUL: (**see** "bad") **a.** baleful; baneful; deleterious; detrimental; inimical; malefic; malevolent; malicious; malign(ant); nocent; nocuous; noxious; prejudicial; scatheful; sinister; unbenevolent; venomous; virulent; **n.** HARMFULNESS: maleficence; malevolence; malignancy; sinisterity; toxicity
to health or morals: **a.** malign(ant); noxious; pernicious; venomous; virulent

HARMLESS: (**see** "innocent") **a.** beneficent; benign(ant); impotent; inoffensive; innocuous; innoxious; insipid; salutary
something which is: **n.** innocuity

HARMONIOUS: **a.** affable; Apollonian; Apollonic; Apollonistic; assonant; canorous; companionable; compatible; concinnous; concordant; congruent; congruous; consonant; *en rapport;* euphonic(al); euphonious; eurhythmic; mellifluent; mellifluous; mellisonant; melodic; melodious; **reconciliatory**; rhythmic(al); sociable;

sonorous; symphonic; symphonious; synchronic(al); synchronous; syncretic; syncretistic; unisonant
not: (**see** "harsh") **a.** cacophonous; discordant; dissident; dissonant; incompatible; incongruous; inharmonious; **n.** atonality; cacophony; discordance; dissonance

HARMONIZE: (**see** "agree") **v.** coordinate; correlate; mediate; orchestrate; reconcile symphonize; synchronize; syncretize; tranquilize
having power or tendency to: **a.** conciliatory, henotic; irenic; pacific(atory); tranquilizing

HARMONY: **n.** affability; amity; assonance; compatibility; concinnity; concordance; congruence; congruency; congruity; consonance; coordination; cosmos; euphony; mutuality; orchestration; rapport; reconciliation; reconcilement; symmetry; symphony; synchroneity; syncretism; tranquility; unanimity
discordant; **n.** *concordia discors*
in: (**see** "harmonious) **a.** *en rapport*
in art, etc.: **n.** synaesthesis

HARSH: (**see** "rigorous" and "severe") **a.** acerb(ic); acidulous; antagonistic; asperous; astringent; cacophonous; discordant; disharmonious; dissonant; Draconian; ferocious; inclement; relentless; ruthless; strident; truculent; uncharitable; unharmonious; **n.** HARSHNESS: acerbity; asperity; discordance; discordancy; inclemency; mordacity; rigor
in temperament: **a.** acidulent; acidulous; vinegary
sound(s): **n.** cacophony; **a.** cacophonic; cacophonous; discordant; dissonant; immelodious; ineuphonious; strident; unharmonious

HAS-BEEN: **n. or a.** ci-devant; emeritus; **a.** quondam

HASH: **n.** gallimaufry; goulash; haricot; heterogeneity; hodgepodge; medley; olla podrida; potpourri; ragout; *réchauffé;* salmagundi; slumgullion

HASTE: (**see** "abruptness") **n.** acceleration; alacrity; celerity; dispatch; *empressement;* expediency; expedition; facility; impetuosity; impulsivity; precipitateness; precipitancy; precipitation; rapidity; su-

perficiality; n. HASTINESS: alacrity; celerity; festination; rapidity; superficiality; a. HASTY: (see "rash") accelerated; celeritous; cursory; desultory; festinate; impatient; impulsive; incautious; indiscreet; precipitant; precipitate; precipitous; subitaneous; superficial
make (haste) slowly: adv. *eile mit weile; festina lente; speude bradeos*

HASTENER: n. accelerant; catalyst; gadfly; precipitator; stimulator

HATE: (see "hatred" and "loathe") v. abhor; abominate; anathematize; a. HATEFUL: abhorrent; abominable; anathematic(al); defamatory; despicable; detestable; excreable; fastuous; heinous; invidious; loathsome; nauseous; objectionable; obnoxious; odious; opprobrious; outrageous; repellent; repugnant; repulsive; n. HATER: antipathist
object of: n. *bête noir(e)*

HATRED: (see "aversion") n. abhorrence; abomination; anathema; animosity; animus; antagonism; antipathy; detestation; enmity; malevolence; malice; malignity; odium; rancor; repugnance; repugnancy
arousing: a. antipathetic(al); antipathic
without: adv. *sine odio*

HAUGHTY: (see "proud") a. arrogant; cavalier; contemptuous; contumelious; despiteful; disdainful; egotistical; fastuous; grandiose; hoity-toity; hubristic; patronizing; petulant; pompous; pontifical; portentous; preemptory; prideful; supercilious; toploftical; toplofty; n. HAUGHTINESS: arrogance; contempt; contumacy; despicableness; despicability; disdain; fastuosity; hauteur; hubris; lordliness; morgue; vainglory

HAUNT: n. environ(s); habitat; milieu; purlieu; rendezvous

HAWK, *resembling*: a. accipitral; accipitrine

HAZARD: see "danger"

HAZY: a. ethereal; indefinite; indistinct; nebular; nebulose; nebulous; obscure; tenuous; vague; n. HAZINESS: (see "cloudiness") ethereality; nebulosity; tenuosity; vaporosity

HEAD(S): n. caput; (pl. capita); cranium
affecting both sides of: a. amphicranial; bicranial
affecting one side of: a. hemicranial
back of: n. occiput; a. occipital
bald: n. pilgarlic
black-: n. comedo
golden-colored: a. aurecephalous
having a: a. cephalous
having abnormally small: a. microcephalic; microcephalous; n. microcephaly
having large: a. megacephalic; megacephalous; n. megacephaly
having many: a. hydra-headed
of the house, fem.: n. *mater familias*; matriarch
of the house, male: n. *chef de famille; pater familias*; patriarch
out of the (fr. memory): adv. *ex capite*
pain in: (see "headache") n. *cephalalgia*
pert. to: a. capital; cephalic; cranial
pointed: a. acrocephalic; n. acrocephaly
tax: n. capitation; a. capitation; per capita
thickness of (or skull): n. pachycephalia; pachycephaly
to foot, from: adv. *cap à pied*
to heel, from (completely): adv. *capite ad calcem*
to remove: v. decapitate; guillotine; obtruncate; n. decapitation
toward the: adv. cephalad
two better than one: *due teste valgano più d'una sola; nemo solus satis sapit*
without a: a. acephalic; acephalous; n. acephalia

HEADACHE: n. cephalalgia; cephalodynia; *mal de tête*; megrim; migraine
both sides: n. amphicrania; bicrania; a. amphicranial; bicranial
one side: n. hemicrania; a. hemicranial

HEADLONG: (see "rash") a. Gaderine; impetuous; precipitant; precipitate; precipitous; adv. *à corps perdu; tête baissée*

HEADSTRONG: see "stubborn"

HEALING: a. assuasive; balsamic; curative; lenitive; medicamental; medicamentous; medicative; medicinable; medicinal; remedial; resoluble; restorative; sanative; therapeutic(al); vulnerary
agent (as medicine or plant): n. therapeutant
by first intention: a. *per primam*

power of nature: **n.** *vis medicatrix naturae*
  promoting of: (**see** "healthful") **a.** curative; lenitive; remedial; restorative; sanative; therapeutic(al); vulnerary
  science of: **n.** iatrics; iatrology; therapeusis; therapeutics
  slow in: **a.** indolent

HEALTH: **n.** prosperity; robusticity; tonicity; vigor; vitality
  abnormal anxiety over: **n.** hypochondria(sis); **a.** hypochondriacal; valetudinarian; **n.** hypochondriac; valetudinarian
  conducive to: **see** "healthful" **and** "healing"
  goddess of: **n.** Hygeia; Salus
  in normal or good: **n.** eucrasia; eudaemonia; euphoria; normality
  in poor: **n.** dyscrasia; **a.** valetudinarian
  recovery or restoration of: **v.** convalesce; recuperate; **n.** convalescence; recuperation; **a.** convalescent; recuperative; recuperatory

HEALTHFUL: **a.** curative; hygienic; invigorating; restorative; salubrious; salutary; salutiferous; wholesome; **n.** HEALTHFULNESS: salubrity; salutariness; wholesomeness
  not: **see** "unhealthy"

HEAP: **n.** accumulation; acervation; agglomeration; aggregation; congeries; **a.** acervuline; cumulative; pyramidal

HEAR *the other side:* **adv.** *audi alteram partem*
  willing to: **a.** acousmatic

HEARSAY: **n.** *on dit; oui-dire;* scuttlebutt

HEART: (**see** "gist") **n.** affection; cardia; cor(e); disposition; interior
  coming fr. the (as subjective or emotional): **a.** pectoral; **adv.** *imo pectore*
  fast beating of: **n.** tachycardia
  fear of disease of: **n.** cardiophobia
  from bottom of one's: **adv.** *imo pectore;* **a.** pectoral
  from the: **see** "sincere"
  of the matter, in: **adv.** *in medias res*
  pert. to, or to disease of: **a.** cardiac; cardiological
  shaped like: **a.** cordate; cordiform
  slow beating of: **n.** bradycardia
  study of disease of: **n.** cardiology; **n.** cardiologist

HEARTH, *goddess of:* **n.** Hestia; Vestia

HEAT: (**see** "hot") **n.** calefaction; calescence; candescence; temperature
  formed by, as rock: **a.** igneous
  generating: **a.** calorigenic; igneous
  great: **n.** candescence
  pert. to: **a.** calefacient; calefactory; calescent; calorific; ignescent; igneous; pyrogenic; pyrogenous; thermal; thermic
  producing or produced by: **a.** calefacient; igneous; pyrogenic; pyrogenous; thermal; thermic
  treatment by use of: **n.** thermotherapy
  unusual sensitiveness to: **n.** hyperthermalgesia

HEATHEN: **n.** idolater; pagan; **n.** HEATHENISM: heathendom; heathenry; idolatry; paganism; **a.** HEATHENISH: foreign; irreligious; pagan; uncircumcised; unenlightened; unfamiliar

HEAVEN(S): (**see** "sky") **n.** celestial sphere; Eden; Elysium; empyrean; firmament; paradise; Utopia; Valhalla; **a.** HEAVENLY: (arch) angelic; beatific; blissful; (super) celestial; edenic; elysian; empyreal; ethereal; firmamental; Olympian; paradisiac(al); paradisial; paradisian; rapturous; sublime; supernal
  above the: **a.** supercelestial
  and earth, rel. to or affecting both: **a.** cosmotellurian
  of or from the: **a.** ethereal; supernal
  study of: **n.** astronomy; uranology
  there is rest in: in coelo quies
  up to the (ref. to theory that land ownership includes air above): **adv.** *usque ad coelum*

HEAVY: **a.** burdensome; consequential; elephantine; grievous; massive; oppressive; ponderous; saturnine; substantious; weighty

HEDGE: **n.** septum; **v.** encircle; equivocate; obstruct

HEED: (**see** "attention") **n.** apprehension; attentiveness; circumspection; cognizance; perception; **a.** HEEDFUL: advertent; calculating; cautious; circumspect; mindful; vigilant; wary; **a.** HEEDLESS: (**see** "reckless") inattentive; incautious; incogitable; incogitant; neglectful; oblivious; precipitate; remiss; unobservant; unmindful; **n.** HEEDLESSNESS: *étourderie;* inattention; inobservance

HEIGHT(S): (**see** "acme") **n.** altitude; elevation; eminence; pinnacle
  fear of: **n.** acrophobia; **a.** acrophobic
  natural: **n.** stature
  pert. to: **a.** altitudinous; culminant

HEIGHTEN: **v.** accent; aggravate; augment; enhance; exacerbate; exaggerate; exalt; intensify

HEIR *apparent:* **n.** atheling; crown prince; dauphin; **n.** primogeniture(ship)

HELL: **n.** Abaddon; Acheron; Avernus; barathrum; gehenna; Hades; inferno; limbo; Pandemonium; perdition; Sheol; Tartarus; **a.** HELLISH: Acheronian; Acherontic(al); chthonian; chthonic; demoniac(al); devilish; infernal; pandemoniac(al); sheolic; sulfurous; sulphurous; stygian
  descent to is easy: facilis descensus Averno

HELP: **v.** abet; alleviate; collaborate; facilitate; participate; succor; **n.** (**see** "assistance") adminicle; administeration; (co)adjuvancy; cooperation; encouragement; **int.** *au secours!;* **a.** HELPFUL: (**see** "beneficial") accessory; advantageous; alleviatory; auspicious; constructive; convenient; cooperative; obliging; opportune; propitious; remedial; salutary; subsidiary; therapeutic (**see** "curative"); **a.** HELPING: adminicular; auxiliary; cooperative; corroborative; participative; **a.** HELPLESS: (**see** "defenseless") bewildered; *brutum fulmen;* feckless; impotent; impuissant; incapacitated; incompetent; ineffective; inefficient; nugatory; powerless; **n.** HELPLESSNESS: impotency; impuissance; inability; incapacity; incapability
  designed to: **a.** alleviatory; cooperative; remedial
  good: **n.** *bon secours*
  with God's: **adv.** *Dieu aidant*
  yourself and heaven will help you: aide-toi, le ceil t'aidera

HELPER: (**see** "aide") **n.** accessory; adjutant; adjuvant; adminicle; aide-decamp; ancillary; auxiliary; benefactor; coadjutor; (**fem.** coadjutress; coadjutrix); collaborator; collaborateur; col-

league; confederate; confrere; participant; participator

HENCHMAN: **n.** mercenary; minion; *particeps criminis;* participant; satrap; *socius criminis*

HERALD: (**see** "forerunner") **n.** *avant-courrier; avant-garde;* harbinger; precursor

HERBS, *living on:* **a.** herbivorous
  study of: **n.** phytology; **n.** botanist; phytologist

HERD(S), *leader of:* **n.** patriarch
  living in: **a.** gregarious

HERE *and everywhere:* **adv.** *hic et ubique*
  and there: **adv.** *par ci par là; passim*
  lies: **adv.** *hic jacet*
  there, and everywhere: **adv.** *hic et ubique*
  today, gone tomorrow: **adv.** *aujourd'hui roi, demain rien*

HEREDITARY: (**see** "inborn") **a.** ancestral; congenital; familial; hereditable; innate; lineal; linear; paternal; patriarchal; patrimonial
  disposition (to disease, etc.): **n.** diathesis

HERETIC: (**see** "unbeliever") **n.** apostate; heresiarch; nonconformist; schismatic; **a.** HERETICAL: see "unorthodox"
  labeling as a: **n.** mark of the beast

HERETOFORE: **a.** cidivant; hitherto; quondam; **n.** ci-devant; has-been; *status quo ante*

HERITABLE *property:* **n.** hereditament(s); patrimony

HERITAGE: **n.** hereditament; inheritance; legacy; patrimony; **a.** patrimonial

HERMIT: **n.** anchorite; cenobite; eremite; isolate; recluse; solitudinarian; troglodyte
  like a, or pert. to: **a.** anchoritic; cenobitic; eremitic(al); hermitic; troglodytic

HERO: **n.** Argonaut; demigod(dess)
  in a play: **n.** protagonist

HEROIC: **a.** chivalrous; courageous; dauntless; extreme; Homerian; Homeric; il-

lustrious; intrepid; powerful; radical; resolute; Samsonian; undaunted
mockingly or satirical: **a.** Hudibrastic

HESITATE: **v.** demur; fluctuate; linger; shilly-shally; vacillate; **a.** HESITANT: (**see** "indisposed") dubitant; dubitative; shilly-shally; vacillatory; **n.** HESITATION: demur; dubitation; indisposition; pausation; vacillation

HICCUP (or HICCOUGH): **n.** singultus

HICK: **see** "boor"

HIDDEN: (**see** "secret") **a.** abeyant; abstruse; arcane; cabalistic; clandestine; covert; cryptic(al); cryptogenic; delitescent; dormant; enigmatic(al); esoteric; inapparent; inherent; larvate(d); latent; occult; potential; quiescent; recondite; surreptitious; ulterior; undercurrent; undisclosed; unexplained; veiled
danger: **see under** "danger"
significance, having a: **a.** cryptogrammic
state of being, or something that is: **n.** abstrusity; arcanum; clandestinity; obscuration; occultation; sequestration

HIDE: **v.** abscond; cache; camouflage; conceal; ensconce; obscure; secrete; sequester; **n.** (**see** "skin") abscondence; obscuration; sequestration
away: **v.** abscond; cache; **n.** HIDEAWAY: hermitage; nidus; redoubt; refuge; retreat
from law: **v.** abscond; fugitate; **n.** abscondence; fugitation
one's self: **v.** abscond; ensconce

HIGH: (**see** "lofty") **a.** altitudinous; eminent; extravagant; sublime; supernal; top-echelon; towering
extremely: **a.** stratospheric(al); supernal
fashion or social standing: **n.** bon ton; haut ton; **a.** à la hussarde
-flown: **see** "pretentious"
in class or field: **a.** aristocrat; Brahmin; *cordon bleu;* eminentissimo; luminary; magnifico; mahatma; minion; nonesuch; paladin; panjandrum; paradigm; paragon; patrician; **a.** (super)eminent; supernal
point: **see** "apex"
society: **n.** grand monde; haut monde

-sounding: **a.** grandiloquent; magnific(al)
spirits: **n.** ebullience; ebulliency; ebullition; ecstasy; euphoria; exuberance; **a.** (**see** "spirited") ebullient; ecstatic; euphoric; exuberant
status or prestige: **n.** cachet

HIGHEST: **a.** classic; meridional; paramount; preeminent; supereminent; supernal; supreme
distinction: **n.** cordon bleu; grand prix
in the: **adv.** in excelsis
point: **see** "apex"
region(s): **n.** *1.* stratosphere; *2.* inosphere; *3.* mesosphere; *4.* exosphere
type: **n.** nec plus supra; nec plus ultra

HIGHWAY, *main:* **n.** camino real

HILL, *small or low:* **n.** hillock; hummock; namelon; monticule; monticulus; **a.** HILLY: tumular; tumulose; tumulous

HINDER: (**see** "block") **v.** impede; **n.** HINDRANCE: barnacle(s); barrier; encumbrance; impediment; obstruction; perplexity; stultification; **a.** impedimental; obstructive

HINT: **v.** allude; imply; insinuate; suggest; **n.** forewarning; illusion; innuendo; insinuation; insinuendo; suggestion; **a.** insinuative; insinuatory
that something is worse than said: **n.** parale(i)psis; paralipsis

HIRED: **a.** commercial; mercenary; mercantile; venal; **n.** HIRELING: (**see** "mercenary") myrmidon; pensionary

HISS: **v.** (as)sibilate; **n.** sibilance; sibilant; sibilation; **a.** sibilant

HISTORIAN: **n.** analyst; annalist; chronicler; Herodotus; historiographer

HISTORIC, *state of being:* **n.** historicity
to render or make: **v.** historify; historicize

HISTORICAL *records:* **n.pl.** annals; **a.** annalistic

HISTORY: (**see** "ancestry") **n.** annals; biography; chronicle; historiography
as of word or custom: **n.** phylogenesis;

phylogeny; **a.** phylogenic; **n.** phylogenist
  *give appearance of (historical) verity
  or significance:* **v.** historicize
  goddess of: **n.** Saga
  muse of: **n.** Clio
  of immaterial thing, as word or custom:
  n. phylogenics; phylogeny; **a.** phylogenic
  period just before recorded: **n.** protohistory; **a.** protohistoric(al)
  personal: **see** "autobiography"
  record in, or as: **v.** historicize; historify
  study or knowledge of: **n.** historiology
  writing of: (**see** "historian") **n.** historiography; **a.** historiographic(al); **v.** historicize; historify

HIT *or miss:* **adv.** *à tort et à travers;* (at)
random; **a.** aimless; desultory; haphazard; random

HITCH: **n.** contretemps; misadventure;
mishap

HOARSE: **a.** raucous; strident; stridulent;
stridulous; **n.** HOARSENESS: phonasthenia; raucity; stridency; stridor; stridulation; strid(ul)ence

HOAX: (**see** "fraud") **n.** imposture; mare's
nest

HOCUS-POCUS: (**see** "nonsense") **n.** abracadabra; legerdemain; prestidigitation;
thaumaturgy

HODGE-PODGE: (**see** "hash" **and** "mixture") **n.** colluvies; gallimaufry; *macédoine; omnium-gatherum;* pasticcio; pastiche; potpourri; ragout; smorgasbord

HOG(S), *like or rel. to:* **a.** porcine; suoid;
swinish

HOLE: **n.** aperture; (con)cavity; excavation; lacuna; orifice; perforation; punctulum; puncture
  in body: **n.** aperture; fistula; foramen;
  (**pl.** foramina); meatus; orifice; os

HOLLOW: **n.** concavity; sinus; **a.** concave;
insincere; lacunal; lacunar; treacherous
  -sounding: **a.** tympanic; tympanitic

HOLY: (**see** "sacred") **a.** hallowed; immaculate; sacrosanct; saintly; sanctified;
a. HOLIER-THAN-THOU: Pecksniffian; religiose; sacrosanct; sanctimonious;
n. Pecksniffianism; religiosity; sanctimo

niousness; sanctity; **n.** HOLINESS:
godliness; sacramentality; sacredness;
saintliness; sanctification; sanctitude;
sanctity
  of holies: **n.** adytum; sanctum; *sanctum
  sanctorum*
  place: **n.** bethesda; halidom(e); sanctuary
  pretending to be: **see** "holier-than-thou"
  above
  Roman Empire: **n.** *Sacrum Romanum
  Imperium* (**abb.** S.R.I.)
  thing considered: **n.** halidom(e)

HOMAGE: **a.** adoration; allegiance; deference; deferentiality; fealty; fidelity; obeisance; reverence; sacredness; veneration
  supreme: **n.** latria

HOME: **n.** abode; domicile; habitation;
headquarters; hearthstone; ingleside; *lares
et penates*
  love of: **n.** inhabitiveness
  sweet: **n.** *dulce domum*

HOMELAND, *extreme or exaggerated love
of:* **n.** chauvinism
  pert. to: **a.** compatristic; patrial

HOMELESS: **adv.** *sans abri*

HOMESICKNESS: **n.** *mal du pays;* nostalgia; **a.** nostalgic

HONEST: **a.** *bona fide;* candid; conscientious; equitable; honorable; impartial;
incorrupted; incorruptible; ingenuous;
judicial; legitimate; meticulous; rectitudinous; reputable; scrupulous; uncorrupt(ed); upright; **n.** HONESTY: *bona
fide(s); bonne foi;* candor; fidelity; integrity; judiciality; probity; propriety;
rectitude; scrupulosity; sincerity; truthfulness; uprightness; veracity

HONEY-*colored:* **a.** melichrous; nectarous
  containing or resembling: **a.** melleous;
  nectarous
  producing: **a.** melliferous; nectariferous

HONEYCOMB, *like a:* **a.** alveolate; faveolate; faviform

HONEYED, *as words or speech:* **a.** melodic; melleous; melliferous; mellifluent;
mellifluous; mellisonant
  words: **n.** *paroles mielleuses*

HONOR(S) : (see "esteem") **v.** canonize; commemorate; deify; dignify; elevate; enhalo; ennoble; laureate; revere; worship; **n.** approbation; deference; deferentiality; eminence; ennoblement; homage; integrity; izzat; obeisance; prestige; reverence; veneration
> *as a token of:* **a.** or **adv.** *causa honoris; honoris causa*
> *conferring, conveying or implying:* **a.** commendatory; eulogistic; honorific; laudatory
> *with:* **adv.** or **a.** *cum laude*
> *with high:* **adv.** or **a.** *magna cum laude*
> *with highest:* **adv.** or **a.** *summa cum laude*
> *word of:* **n.** *parole d'honneur*
> *worthy of:* (see "praiseworthy") **a.** laureate

HONORABLE (or HONORED): **a.** belaurel(1)ed; chivalric; chivalrous; estimable; illustrious; laureated; laurel(1)ed; prestigious; reputable; respectable; revered; venerable; venerated; **n.** HONORABLENESS: honorificabilitudinitatibus; honorificabilitudininity; prestige; prestigiousness; reputability; respectability

HOODED (or HOODSHAPED): **a.** cowled; cucullate

HOOFS, *animal having:* **n.** ungulate
> *shaped like or having:* **a.** ungular; ungulate

HOOK *or by crook:* **adv.** *à bis ou à blanc*
> *shaped like:* **a.** aduncous; ancistroid; ankyroid; aquilline; falciform; **n.** aduncity

HOOT, *as an owl:* **v.** ululate; **n.** ululation; **a.** ululant

HOPE: **n.** anticipation; confidence; enthusiasm; expectancy; optimism; reliance; **a.** HOPEFUL: auspicious; confident; enthusiastic; euphoric; expectant; optimistic; promising; sanguine; utopian; **n.** HOPEFULNESS: buoyancy; confidence; enthusiasm; euphoria; expectancy; sanguinity; optimism; **a.** HOPELESS: immitigable; incorrigible; irreclaimable; irredeemable; irretrievable
> *anchor of:* **n.** *ancora spei*
> *faint:* **n.** velleity

good: **n.** *spes bona*
while I breathe I (hope): *spero dum spiro*

HORIZONTAL: **a.** decumbent; prone; prostrate; recumbent; supine; **n.** HORIZONTALITY: decumbency; reclination; recumbency

HORN(S), *having:* **a.** corniculate
> *having two:* **a.** bicorn(ed); bicornous; bicornuate
> *of plenty:* **n.** *corne d'abondance;* cornucopia; **a.** cornucopian
> *without:* **a.** aceratophorous; polled

HORNY (or HORNLIKE) **a.** corneous

HORRIBLE: (see "ghastly") **a.** abhorrent; abominable; appalling; excruciating; execrable; formidable; grisly; gruesome; horrendous; horrific; macabre
> *to relate:* **adv.** *horribile dictu*

HORROR, *something that provokes:* **n.** *danse macabre*

HORSE(S), *art of riding or training:* **n.** equitation; manège
> *broken-down:* **n.** rosinante
> *caper or circle:* **n.** or **v.** caracole
> *-drawn vehicle:* **n.** hippomobile
> *family or species:* **n.** equidae; **a.** equine
> *flesh, eating of:* **n.** hippophagous; hippophagism; **n.** hippophagist
> *-loving:* **a.** philhippic
> *pert. to:* **a.** equestrian; equinal; equine; hippoid
> *rearing on hind legs:* **n.** pesade
> *study or student of:* **n.** hippologist; hippology
> *turn on one spot:* **n.** caracole; passade
> *violent check by pull on reins:* **n.** saccade

HORSEBACK: **adv.** *à cheval*

HORSEMAN: **n.** cavalier; chevalier; dragoon; equestrian; (**fem.** equestrienne); **n.** HORSEMANSHIP: equestrianism; equitation; *haute école;* manège

HORSESHOE-*shaped:* **a.** hippocrepiform

HOSPITAL: **n.** *maison-dieu; maison de santé*
> *for contagious diseases:* **n.** lazaretto

HOSPITALITY: **n.** amicability; bonhom-(m)ie; camaraderie; (con)geniality; convivality; cordiality; graciosity; graciousness; xenodochy; **a.** HOSPITABLE: amicable; bonhomous; companionable; (con)genial; convivial; cordial; gracious; gregarious; neighborly; receptive; sociable
to strangers: **n.** xenodochy

HOST *at dinner:* **n.** amphitryon

HOSTEL(RY): (**see** "hotel") caravansary; xenodochium

HOSTILE: (**see** "aggressive") **a.** a(d)verse; antagonistic; antipathetic; bellicose; belligerent; contentious; discordant; disaffected; feral; gladiatorial; inimicable; inimical; irreconcilable; malevolent; martial; mutinous; provocative; pugilistic; pugnacious; rancorous; rebellious; repugnant; truculent; umbrageous; unassuageable; unfavorable; unfriendly; vehement; warlike; **n.** HOSTILITY: animosity; animus; antagonism, antipathy; bellicosity; cleavage; combativeness; combativity; disaffection; discordance; ferity; friction; inimicalness; irreconcilability; pugnacity; rancor; truculence; umbrage; vehemence
bitterly: **a.** venomous; virulent
in (hostile) or unfavorable surroundings: **adv.** in partibus (infidelium)
meeting: **n.** rencontre

HOT: **a.** ardent; candent; choleric; fervent; impetuous; incalescent; incandescent; pungent; thermal; thermic; vehement
and moist: **a.** sulfurous; sulphurous; sultry; sweltering; torrid; **n.** torridity

HOTEL(S): **n.** caravansary; hostel(ry); imaret; xenodochium
and inns, lore of: **n.** xenodocheinology

HOUR, *live for the:* **adv.** carpe diem; in horam vivere

HOUSE: **v.** contain; shelter; **n.** (**see** "abode") chateau; domicile; habitation; mansion; tenement
head of: **see under** "head"
mistress of: **n.** chatelaine; materfamilias

HOUSEHOLD, *also persons who share:* **n.** menage
deities or tutelaries: **n.pl.** lares; penates
effects, most valued: **n.pl.** lares and penates

mistress of: **n.** chatelaine; materfamilias; matron
of misc. persons: **n.** menagerie
of three, one the lover of one of spouses: **n.** ménage à trois

HOUSEKEEPING: **n.** ménage

HOVER: **v.** cower; librate; linger

HOW: **adv.** *quo modo?*

HOWLING *joyously:* **a.** roborant; **v.** HOWL: ululate; **n.** ululation

HUBBUB: (**see** "ado") **n.** agitation; Babelism; brouhaha; coil; hullabaloo; turmoil

HUE: **n.** aspect; complexion; tincture

HUG: **v.** embosom

HUGE: (**see** "giant") **a.** amplitudinous; astronomical; behemoth(ian); brobdi(n)gnagian; Bunyanesque; colossal; cyclopean; dinosauric; elephantine; gargantuan; gigantesque; gigantic; Herculean; heroic; Homeric; immeasurable; imposing; leviathan; macroscopic; magnitudinous; mammoth; mastadonic; monstrous; monumental; oceanic; Olympian; polyphemian; polyphemic; polyphemous; prodigious; pyramidal; pythonic; stratospheric(al); titanic; tremendous; **n.** HUGENESS: (**see** "immensity") amplitude; colossality; enormity; indefinitude; magnitude; prodigality
grotesquely: **a.** gigantesque
something that is: **n.** behemoth; colossus; leviathan; titan

HULLABALOO: **see** "hubbub" **and** "ado"

HUM: **v.** bombinate; murmur; susurrate; **n.** bombination; murmur; susurration

HUMAN(S): (**see** "man" **and** "mankind") **n.** Adamite; anthropoid; earthling; hominid(ae); *homo sapiens;* individual; mortal; **a.** anthropoid(al); anthropomorphic; anthropopathic; compassionate; earthborn; finite; humane; mortal; sympathetic
action, produced or induced by: **a.** (arti)factitious; **n.** artifact; (**pl.** *fructus industriales*)
affairs, pert. to: **a.** mundane

154

and animal forms combined (as centaur): **n.** therianthropism; **a.** therianthropic

below: **a.** infrahuman; subhuman

characteristics, ascription to animal(s): **n.** anthropomorphism; anthropopathism; **a.** anthropomorphic; anthropopathic

characteristics, ascription to god(s): **n.** anthropopathy; anthropophuism; embodiment; incarnation; **n.** anthropopathite

characteristics, ascription to inanimate objects: **n.** humanization; pathetic fallacy; personification

feelings, ascribed to something not human: **a.** anthropopathic; **n.** anthropopathism

figure, as architectural support: **n.** antic; caryatid (**fem.**); telamon (**male**)

figure, representation of: **n.** anthropomorph; humunculus; manikin

figure, use in primitive magic: **n.** *envoûtement*

flesh, eating of: see "cannibalism"

form, changing into: **n.** anthropomorphosis; (**pl.** anthropomorphoses); **a.** anthropomorphic; anthropomorphous

form, in: **a.** incarnate; personified; **n.** embodiment; incarnation

form or shape, having: **a.** anthropomorphic; anthropomorphous

law, by: **adv.** *jure humano*

less than: **a.** infrahuman; subhuman

pert. to: **a.** anthropoid; anthropogenic; anthropic(al); mortal

qualities, attributed to nature or objects: **n.** embodiment; humanization; incarnation; pathetic fallacy

qualities, deprive of: **v.** barbarize; brutalize; dehumanize; robotize

resembling: **a.** anthropomorphic; anthropomorphous; anthropoid(al); humanoid

study of in rel. to environment and to other organisms: **n.** anthropomony; ecology

study of origin and development: **n.** anthropogenesis; **a.** anthropogenetic

study or student of: **n.** anthropologist; anthropology; **a.** anthropological

unsuitable for: **a.** subhuman

wisdom about: **n.** anthroposophy

HUMANE: see "human"

HUMANITARIAN: see "person, charitable"

HUMANITY: (**see** "man" **and** "mankind") **n.** anthropopathy

HUMANIZE: **v.** civilize; incarnate; personify; refine; **n.** HUMANIZATION: civilization; embodiment; incarnation; personification; refinement

animals or things: **v.** anthropomorphize; personify; **n.** anthropomorphism; embodiment; incarnation; pathetic fallacy; personification; **a.** anthropomorphic; anthropomorphous

HUMBLE: **v.** debase; degrade; demean; denigrate; humiliate; minify: **a.** (**see** "meek") genuflectory; modest; self-effacing; submissive; unpretentious; **n.** HUMBLENESS: see "humility"

people: **n.pl.** *gens de peu*

HUMBUG: **n.** blague; flummery; hypocrisy; hypocrite; imposter; pretension

HUMILIATING: **a.** degrading; humiliative; ignominious; mortifying; **n.** HUMILIATION: abasement; abashment; chagrin; chastenment; debasement; mortification; **n.** HUMILITY: (**see** "self-denial") abjection; abnegation; humbleness; self-effacement

place of (humiliation): **n.** Canossa

HUMOR: **n.** badinage; caprice; comicality; disposition; farcicality; inclination; jocosity; jocularity; joviality; temperament; **n.** HUMORIST: *farceur;* (**fem.** *farceuse*)

bad: (**see** "ill-humored") **n.** distemper; dudgeon

coarse: **a.** Falstaffian; Rabelaisian

cynical: **n.** Pantagruelism; **a.** Pantagruelic; Pantagruelian; **n.** Pantagruelist

sense of: **n.pl.** risibles

HUMORLESS: **a.** serious; unmirthful

HUMOROUS: (**see** "laughable") **a.** facetious; farcical; jocose; jocular; jovial; ludicrous; Rabelaisian; risible; waggish; whimsical; **n.** HUMOROUSNESS: *espièglerie;* ludicrousness; waggishness; whimsicality

action or remark: **n.** farcicality; jocosity

grotesquely: **a.** baboonish; **n.** baboonery

HUMPBACK: **n.** gibbosity; kyphosis; **a.** gibbous; kyphotic

HUNDRED *fold:* **a.** or **v.** centuplicate;
a. HUNDREDTH: centisimal
years: **see** "one hundred"

HUNGER: (**see** "appetite") **n.** edacity;
gulosity; voracity; **a.** HUNGRY: gluttonous; insatiable; rapacious; ravenous;
voracious
abnormal or continuous: **n.** bulimia; hyperorexia; **a.** bulimic; hyperorectic
*acknowledges no law: la fame non vuol
leggi*
for praise, honor, etc.: **n.** captation; esurience; **a.** esurient

HUNTING: **n.** (the) chase; venation; **n.**
HUNTER: chasseur; huntsman; ja(e)-
ger; Nimrod
as art or sport: **n.** cynegetics; shikar;
venery
expedition: **n.** safari
goddess of: **n.** Artemis; Diana
of, used for, fond of or living by: **a.**
venatic
rel. to: **a.** cynegetic; venatic

HURRAH!: **int.** *evviva!;* ole!

HURRIEDLY: **adv.** *à corps perdu; à la
volée;* impetuously

HURTFUL: (**see** "injurious") **a.** atrocious; baneful; deleterious; flagrant;
grievous; heinous; inimical; malignant;
nocent; nocuous; noxious; pernicious;
traumatic; venomous

HUSBAND(S): **n.** consort; spouse
and wife: **n.** *vir et uxor*
dear: **n.** *caro sposo*
having one at a time: **n.** monandry;
monogamy; **n.** monandrist; monogamist;
a. monandrous; monogamic; monogamous
having two or more at a time: **n.** bigamy; polyandry; polygamy; **n.** bigamist;
polyandrist; polygamist; **a.** bigamous;
polyandrous; polygamous
located or centered around family of: **a.**
patrilocal
*or wives, having more than one at a
time:* **n.** bigamy; polygyny; **n.** bigamist;
polygamist; polygynist; **a.** bigamous;
polygamous; polygynous
right of the: **n.** *jus mariti*

HUZZY: **n.** doxy; slattern; trollop; wench

HYMN *of praise or thinksgiving:* (**see under** "praise") **n.** doxology; magnificat;
te deum; theody

HYPOCRISY: (**see** "pretense") **n.** (dis)-
simulation; duplicity; Pharisaism; piosity;
religiosity; sanctimoniousness; self-right-
eousness; speciosity; Tartuffery; **n.**
HYPOCRITE: (**see** "pretender") dissembler; dissimulator; Pecksniffian; Tar-
tuf(f)e; **a.** HYPOCRITICAL: dissimulative; Pecksniffian; pretentious; religiose;
sanctimonious; specious; Tartuffian; **adv.**
à la Tartuffe

HYPOTHETICAL: **see** "theoretical"
principle of fire: **n.** phlogiston

156

I

I, *excessive use of letter:* **n.** iotacism
  think, therefore I am: cogito ergo sum

IDEA(S) : (**see** "notion") **n.** abstraction;
  concept(ion) ; conceptus; (**pl.** concepti) ;
  impression; percept(ion) ; supposition
    advanced in: **a.** *avant-garde; fin-de-*
    siècle; **n.** *avant-garde; avant-gardist(e)* ;
    visionary
    contradiction in: **n.** antilogy
    express variously by means of syno-
    nyms: **v.** synonymize
    fear or distrust of: **n.** ideophobia
    fixed: **n.** *idée fixe*
    formulate: **v.** conceptualize; ideate; **n.**
    conceptualization; ideation; **a.** concep-
    tualistic; ideational; ideative
    full of or pregnant w/: **a.** tumefacient
    happy: **n.** *curiosa felicitas*
    one accepting new: **n.** neoteric
    one hating new: **n.** misoneist
    originating: **a.** ideogenetic
    suggestive of, rel. to or concerned w/:
    a. ideologic(al)
    with no exact word for: **n.** anonym(e)

IDEAL(ISTIC) : **a.** aerial; altitudinarian;
  chimerical; doctrinaire; messianic; para-
  disaic(al) ; paradisical; paradisial; para-
  disic; platonic; platonistic; poetic(al) ;
  romantic; sentimental; quixotic(al) ; utopian; visionary; **n.** IDEALIST: altitudinarian; *avant-gardist(e)* ; Don Quixote;
  utopian; visionary; **n.** IDEALIZATION:
  apotheosis; canonization; deification;
  spiritualization; stellification; **v.** IDEAL-
  IZE: apotheosize; canonize; deify; spiritualize; stellify

IDEALOGY: **see** "ideology"

IDENTICAL: (**see** "equal") **a.** congruent;
  equivalent; indistinguishable; isonomous;
  synonymous; tantamount; **n.** IDENTI-
  CALITY : equivalence; selfsameness; synonymity

IDENTIFICATION, *sympathetic:* **n.** empathy; **a.** empath(et)ic; heteropathic; **v.**
  IDENTIFY: diagnosticate; recognize; **n.**
  IDENTIFIABILITY: identification; **a.**
  identificatory

IDENTITY, *individual:* **n.** individuality;
  ipseity
    in essence or substance:
    of nature, meaning or significance: **n.**
    synonymity
    self w/ another: **n.** empathy; identifica-
    tion; **a.** empath(et)ic; heteropathic

IDEOLOGY: **n.** philosophy; speculation;
  weltanschauung

IDIOM: **n.** colloquialism; parlance; patois;
  vernacular

IDIOTIC: **see** "stupid"

IDLE: **a.** *désoeuvré;* faineant; groundless;
  indolent; lackadaisical; *le bras croisés;*
  otiose; slothful; superfluous; trivial;
  vacuous
    remark: **n.** vaporing
    talk: **n.** caquet
    the (unemployed persons) : **n.pl.** flotsam
    and jetsam; *les sans-travail*

IDLENESS (or IDLING): (**see** "inaction") **n.** aimlessness; disoccupation;
  flânerie; idlesse; inactivity; indolence;
  leisure; otiosity; sedentation; triviality
    pleasant: **n.** *dolce far niente*

IDLER: **n.** badaud; dawdler; *fainéant;*
  flaneur; (**fem.** *flaneuse*); loiterer; slug-
  gard, vagrant

IDOL: (**see** "image") **n.** effigy; demigod-
  (dess)
    worship: **n.** am harrez (Jewish); icon-
    olatry; idolatry

157

IGNORANCE: **n.** agnosticism; benightedness; *bêtise;* crassitude; ignoration; illiteracy; inscience; nescience; rusticity; sciolism
appealing to: **adv.** *ad ignorantum*
of the fact(s) excuses: ignoranti facti excusat; (**pl.**) *ignoranti factorum excusat*
of the law excuses no one: ignorantia legis nemnem excusat
gross: **n.** *ignorance crasse*
state of: ignoration; incognoscibility

IGNORANT: **a.** agnostic; analphabetic; artless; benighted; illiterate; incognoscible; inerudite; inscient; nescient; unbookish; uncultured; unenlightened; uninstructed; unlearned; unlettered; unschooled; unsophisticated; untaught; untutored
person: **n.** am haarez; analphabet; ignoramus; illiterate; Philistine; sciolist

IGNORE: (**see** "neglect") **v.** disregard; elide; **n.** IGNORATION: disregard; elision

ILL: (**see** "sick") **a.** *à la mort;* aeger; hurtful; inauspicious; indisposed; infirm; maladive; morbid; morbific; morbose; pernicious; unpropitious; untoward; valetudinarian
-advised: **adv.** *mal avisé*
breeding: **n.** *mauvais ton*
health: **n.** cachexia; malaise; **a.** cachectic
-humored: **a.** cantankerous; captious; churlish; contentious; disputatious; irascible; pettish; petulant; pugnacious; querulous; waspish; **n.** distemper; dudgeon
-mannered or ill-bred: **a.** *mal elevé(e)*
-ma⁺ched: **a.** disparate; dissociable; heterogen(e)ous; incompatible; incongruous
-natured or tempered: (**see under** "bad") **a.** bilious; cantankerous; irascible; perverse; surly
-will: (**see** "hostility") **n.** animosity; animus; antagonism; enmity; malevolence; malice; malignity; rancor
-will, full of or moved by: **a.** antagonistic; contemptuous; despiteful; despiteous; malevolent; malicious; rancorous
will, let there be no: **adv.** *absit invidia*

ILLEGAL: (**see** "unlawful") **a.** adulterine; contraband; criminal; illegitimate; illicit; misbegotten; nugatory; unauthorized; unsound

performance of legal act: **n.** malfeasance; misfeasance

ILLEGITIMATE: **a.** counterfeit; debased; erratic; illogical; irregular; misbegotten; spurious; supposititious; unwarranted
birth: **n.** *bar sinister*
child: **n.** *filius nullius; filius populi;* mongrel

ILLICIT *love affair:* **n.** amour; intrigue; liaison; rendezvous

ILLITERATE: (**see** "ignorant") **a.** analphabetic; **n.** analphabet(ic)

ILLNESS, *recovery period:* **n.** convalescent; recuperation; **a.** convalescent; recuperative

ILLOGICAL: (**see** "unreasonable") **a.** acategorical; equivocal; fallacious; incoherent; incongruous; inconsequent; inconsistent; parabolical; paralogical; paralogistic; rambling; **n.** ILLOGICALITY: incoherence; incoherency; paralogism; unreasonableness; unsoundness
explanation: **n.** *lucus a non lucendo; non sequitur* (**abb.** non sec.)

ILLUMINATING: **a.** enlightening; fluorescent; incandescent; luminescent; luminiferous

ILLUSION: **n.** anamorphosis; apparition; chimera; *fata morgana;* hallucination; hallucinosis; *ignis fatuuis;* mirage; misapprehension; misconception; phantasm(ata); revenant; spectrum
of being somewhere before: **n.** *déjà vu(e)* (phenomenon); paramnesia

ILLUSIVE: (**see** "ghostly") **a.** barmecidal; chimerical; deceptive; fatuitous; fictitious; illusionistic; illusory; imaginary; phantasmagoric(al); phantasmal; phantasmic; phantom, prestidigitatorial; prestidigitatory; spectral

ILLUSTRATIVE (or ILLUSTRATIONAL): **a.** delineative; demonstrative; descriptive; descriptory; pictorial; picturesque; representative; **n.** ILLUSTRATION: see "picture"

ILLUSTRIOUS: (**see** "eminent") **a.** august; celebrated; distinguished; formidable; honorific; immortal; luscent; magnific(al); magnificent; majestic; prestigious; redoubtable; regal; (re)splendent; signal; transcendent

IMAGE(S): (see "likeness") **n.** *alter ego;* conception; counterpart; effigy; portrait; replica; (re)semblance; sculpture; similitude; simulacrum
    breaker of: **n.** iconoclast; a. iconoclastic
    pert. to: **a.** conceptual; concipient
    use in primitive magic: **n.** *envoûtement*
    veneration of: **n.** fetishism; iconoduly
    worship of: **n.** fetishism; iconolatry; idolatry

IMAGINARY: (see "illusive") **a.** apocryphal; apparitional; chimerical; fanciful; fictitious; fictive; idealistic; ideational; imaginational; *in nubibus;* insubstantial; legendary; mythical; quixotic; simulated; supposititious; unreal(istic); utopian; veritable; visionary; **v.** IMAGINE: conceive; fabricate; fictionalize; ideate; meditate; mythologize; surmise
    animal or thing: **n.** centaur; chimera; cyclops; *ens rationis;* griffon; gyascutus; kraken; mermaid; minotaur; phoenix; sphinx
    creature, regarded as embodiment of absolute absurdity: **n.** coquecigrue
    disease: **n.** *malade imaginaire*
    invalid: **n.** hypochondriac; valetudinarian
    perception, auditory or visual: **n.** delusion; hallucination; hallucinosis; **a.** hallucinatory
    place: **n.** never-never country; *weissnichtwo*
    place of high romance: **n.** Graustark; **a.** Graustarkian

IMAGINATION: **n.** genius; phantasy; resourcefulness; unreality
    capacity for: **n.** ideaphoria
    fantastic: **n.** *fata morgana*
    lacking in: **a.** frigid; insipid; monotonous; pedantic; pedestrian; pointless; prosaic; unimaginative; unleavened

IMBECILE: **n.** *impos animi*

IMITATION: **n.** burlesque; caricature; counterfeit; emulation; imitant; mimesis; mimicry; mockery; parody; postiche; pretense; sequacity; simulacrum; simulation; **v.** IMITATE: counterfeit; emulate; feign; pretend; reproduce; simulate; **a.** IMITATIVE: (see "counterfeit") deriv-

ative; echoic; emulatory; emulous; epigonic; epigonous; mimetic; onomatopoe(t)ic; sequacoius; slavish; **n.** IMITATIVENESS: imitancy; **n.** IMITATOR: (see "impostor") epigone
    as of speech or behavior: **n.** mimesis; mimicry; **a.** mimetic; mimical
    lit. or mus. work: **n.** epigonism; postiche
    satirical or grotesque: **n. or v.** burlesque; caricature

IMMATERIAL: **a.** apparitional; asomatous; diaphanous; ethereal; gossamery; illusionary; incorporeal; insubstantial; irrelevant; spiritual; transcendent; unimportant; **n.** IMMATERIALITY: diaphaneity; ethereality; incorporeality; incorporeity; insubstantiality; irrelevancy

IMMATURE: **a.** fledgling; impubic; infantile; infantilistic; juvenile; nouveau; puerile; unfinished; unripe; **n.** IMMATURITY: incunabulum; infancy; infantility; juniority; juvenility; nonage; puerilism; puerility; verdancy

IMMEASURABLE: (see "vast") **a.** imponderable; incommensurable; infinite; unfathomable

IMMEASURABLY *great or low:* **a.** abysmal

IMMEDIATE: (see "direct") **a.** presto; proximate; **adv.** IMMEDIATELY: forthwith; instanter; straightway; *tout de suite;* **n.** IMMEDIACY: directness; instantaneity

IMMENSE: see "huge"; **n.** IMMENSITY: colossality; immeasurability; indefinitude; magnitude; vastitude; vastity

IMMODERATE: **a.** bizarre; eccentric; exaggerated; exorbitant; extravagant; inordinate; intemperate: *outré;* overweening; unreasonable; **n.** IMMODERATION: extravagance; gulosity; inordinancy; insobriety; intemperance

IMMODEST: **a.** brazen; *grivois;* indecorous; indelicate; uninhibited; unrestrained; unseemly; **n.** IMMODESTY: boldness; forwardness; impropriety; impudicity; indecency; indecorum; indelicacy

IMMORAL: (see "lewd") **a.** dissolute; licentious; pornographic; profligate; unedi-

fying; unprincipled; unsavory; wanton;
n. IMMORALITY: (**see** "lewdness")
obliquity
  excess of (*immorality*): **n.** orgy; Saturnalia; **a.** orgiastic; Saturnalian

IMMORTAL: **see** "eternal"

IMMOVABLE: (**see** "fixed") **a.** implanted;
obdurate; sessile

IMPARTIAL: **a.** candid; dispassionate;
equitable; impersonal; judicial; judicious;
unbiased; unprejudiced; **n.** IMPARTI-
ALITY: detachment; disinterestedness;
fairness

IMPASSABLE: (**see** "unconquerable") **a.**
impenetrable; imperforate; impermeable;
impervious; insurmountable; **n.** impenetrability; impermeability

IMPASSE: **n.** cul-de-sac; deadlock; (horns
of a) dilemma; obstruction; predicament;
stalemate

IMPASSIONED: **a.** delirious; dithyrambic; evangelistic; fanatical; hysterical;
impetuous; maniac(al); (per)fervid; vehement; zealous

IMPASSIVE: (**see** "calm") **a.** apathetic;
comatose; expressionless; hermetic(al);
imperturbable; inanimate; insensate; invertebrate; motionless; nonchalant; phlegmatic; spineless; stolid; torpid; torporific;
unimpressible; unperturbed

IMPATIENT: **a.** anxious; apprehensive;
choleric; fidgety; impetuous; intolerant;
pettish; petulant; precipitate; premature;
previous; restive; waspish

IMPEDIMENT: (**see** "hindrance") **n.** cul-
de-sac; embarrassment; encumbrance; obstruction

IMPENDING: (**see** "pressing") **a.** ap-
proaching; emergent; imminent; incumbent; inevitable; threatening
  disaster or doom: **n.** handwriting on the
wall; sword of Damocles; **a.** apocalyp-
tic(al); Damoclean

IMPERATIVE: (**see** "required") **a.** compulsory; *de rigueur; de règle;* obligatory;
preemptory; prerequisite; **n.** command;
injunction; mandate; mandatum; prerequisite

IMPERCEPTIBLE: **a.** gradual; subliminal; subtle; **n.** IMPERCEPTIBILITY:
graduality
  to touch or mind: **a.** impalpable; subliminal

IMPERFECT: (**see** "defective") **a.** atelic;
contingent; dilapidated; imperfective; inadequate; inchoate; inchoative; incipient;
potential; rudimentary; suboptimal; substandard; **n.** IMPERFECTION: **see**
"blemish"

IMPERIOUS: **see** "lordly"

IMPERISHABLE: (**see** "eternal") **a.** immarcescible; immarcescible; immortal; indestructable; perpetual; **n.** IMPERISH-
ABLENESS: eternality; perpetuality;
perpetuity; subtility

IMPERSONAL: (**see** "impartial") **a.** infrahuman; inhuman; mechanical; **n.** personality
  to make: **v.** dehumanize; depersonalize;
robotize; **n.** dehumanization; depersonalization

IMPERSONATION: **see** "personation"

IMPETUOUS: (**see** "abrupt" **and** "hasty")
a. *à corps perdu;* impassioned; impulsive;
intractable; (per)fervid; precipitate; restive; vehement; **n.** impetuosity; impulsivity

IMPISH: (**see** "whimsical") **a.** puckish; **n.**
IMPISHNESS: puckishness; whimsical-
ity

IMPLEMENT(S): **see** "equipment"

IMPLICATION: **n.** connotation; deduction; entanglement; inference; insinuation;
insinuendo; significance; signification; **a.**
IMPLIED: connotative; implicit; inferred; insinuated; tacit; **v.** IMPLY: allude; connote; infer; insinuate; intimate;
purport
  affirmative: **n.** negative pregnant

IMPLYING *something beyond what is obvious:* **a.** subintelligential

IMPOLITE: (**see** "rude") **a.** dedecorous;
discourteous; indecorous; inurbane; uncivil; uncourtly; uncouth; unmannerly;
unpolished; unrefined; **n.** IMPOLITE-
NESS: (**see** "discourteousy") incivility;
inurbanity

IMPORTANCE: **n.** concernment; consequence; cruciality; eminence; moment; prestige; signality; significance
of great: **a.** basilic(al); crucial; monumental
person of little: **n.** nonentity
thing of: **n.** *pièce de résistance*
thing of little: (**see** "trifle") **n.** bagatelle; bauble; geegaw; gewgaw; gimcrack; inconsequence; inconsequentiality; infinitesimality; minutia; nihility; nullity; (**pl.** inconsequentia; minutiae; trivia)

IMPORTANT: **a.** acute; basic; basilic(al); consequential; crucial; determinative; fundamental; impactful; impactive; influential; momentous; monumental; paramount; pivotal; prominent; signal; significant; strategic; stratagetic
feeling or acting: **a.** consequential; pompous; **n.** flatulence; pomposity; pontificality; pursiness
matters or events: **n.** memorabilia
person or thing: **n.** bashaw; colossus; mogul; panjandrum; potentate; sachem; sagamore; tycoon

IMPOSING: (**see** "commanding") **a.** august; exalted; grandiose; imperial; magnific(al); magnificent; majestic; regal; **n.** grandiosity; majesty; regality
in style: (**see** "pretentious") **a.** grandiloquent; sonorous
upon: **n.** imposture

IMPOSSIBLE: **a.** chimerical; fantastic; impracticable; insuperable; insurmountable; invincible; unacceptable; unrealistic; unsurpassable; **n.** IMPOSSIBILITY: impracticability; insuperability; invincibility
advocacy of something that is: **n.** impossibilism; **n. or a.** impossibilist

IMPOSTOR (or IMPOSTER): **n.** Cagliostro; charlatan; epigone; humbug; mountebank; Pharisee; pretender; quacksalver; **n.** IMPOSTURE: charlatanry; hocus-pocus; mountebankery

IMPOTENCE: **n.** fecklessness; feebleness; helplessness; sterility; weakness
sexual: **n.** anaphrodisia; impotency

IMPRACTICABLE: **a.** imprudent; infeasible; insuperable; unrealistic

IMPRACTICAL: (**see** "visionary") **a.** academic; doctrinaire; dogmatic(al); escap-

ist; feckless; idealistic; implausible; inexcutable; irresponsible; ivory-tower(ed); pedantic; poetic(al); quixotic(al); romantic; speculative; theoretic(al); unfeasible; visionary

IMPREGNATION: **n.** fecundation; fertilization; indoctrination; spermatization
by external contact only: **n.** adosculation

IMPRESSION: **n.** impact; imprint; indentation; influence
brief: **n.** *aperçu*
total or over-all: **n.** *tout ensemble*

IMPRESSIVE: (**see** "grand" and "imposing") **a.** impactful; penetrative; **n.** IMPRESSIVENESS: grandeur; grandiloquence; grandiosity; magnificence; opulency; penetrativity

IMPRISON: **v.** confine; immure; incarcerate; restrain; **n.** IMPRISONMENT: confinement; durance (vile); immuration; immurement; incarceration; limbo; restraint

IMPROBABLE: **see** "uncertain"

IMPROMPTU: (**see** "off-hand") **a.** *ad lib-(itum)*; autoschediastic; extemporaneous; extemporary; extempore; improvisatorial; improvisatory; improviso; impulsive; spontaneous; unpremeditated; unstudied; **v. see** "improvise"; **n.** ad lib; autoschediasm; improvisation

IMPROPER: (**see** "unwise") **a.** *à propos de rien*; errant; illicit; immodest; impertinent; inaccurate; inappropriate; incongruous; indecent; indecorous; indelicate; inexpedient; insubordinate; insurgent; irrelevant; rebellious; scabrous; solecistic; unacceptable; unbecoming; uncomely; unethical; unseasonable; unseemly; untoward; **n.** IMPROPRIETY: barbarism; *faux pas; gaffe; grivoiserie;* solecism
action or behavior: (**see** "impropriety") **n.** insubordination; insurgence; insurgency; insurrection
highly: **a.** malodorous

IMPROVE: **v.** (a)meliorate; augment; enhance; rectify; refine; **a.** ameliorative; **n.** IMPROVEMENT: (a)melioration; enhancement; perfectionment; refinement; reformation

capable of (*improvement*) : (see "correctable") **a.** perfectible
designed to (*improve*) : see "remedial"
not subject to (*improvement*) : see **under** "correction" **and** "incurable"

IMPROVISE: **v.** *ad lib;* extemporize; improvisate; **n.** IMPROVISATION: *ad lib*(*itum*) ; autoschediasm; **a.** IMPROVISED: see "impromptu"

IMPRUDENT: (see "rash" **and** "unwise") **a.** audacious; impolitic; impracticable; improvident; injudicious; procacious

IMPUDENT: (see "sassy") **a.** audacious; contemptuous; contumelious; disrespectful; forward; insolent; malapert; shameless; supercilious; toplofty; unmannerly; **n.** IMPUDENCE: (see "sassiness") cheekiness; impudency; incivility; procacity

IMPULSE: (see "incentive") **n.** impetus; incitement; instigation; nisus; spontaneity; **a.** IMPULSIVE: (see "rash" ballistic; capricious; impetuous; spontaneous; unpremeditated; **n.** IMPULSIVENESS: impetuosity; impetuousness; impulsivity; spontaneity

IMPURE: (see "lewd") **a.** adulterated; defiled; macular; unchaste; unrectified; unwholesome; **n.** IMPURITY: adulteration; contamination; corruption; defilement; pollution; putrescence
make: **v.** adulterate; debauch; defile; impurify

IN *a few words:* **adv.** *paucis verbis*
all events: **adv.** *en tout cas*
all seriousness: **adv.** *au grand sérieux*
bad faith: **adv.** *mala fide*(*s*)
being: **a.** or **adv.** *in esse;* **n.** existent
equal fault: **adv.** (*in*) *pari delicto*
few words: **adv.** *paucis verbis*
one way or another: **adv.** *à bis ou à blanc*
passing: **adv.** *en passant*
short, or in a word: **adv.** *ad summam*
so many words: **adv.** *totidem verbis*
spite of: **prep.** mauger; maugre; notwithstanding; *quand même*
spite of oneself: **adv.** *malgré lui*
the first place: **adv.** *imprimis*
the first place cited: **adv.** *loco primo citato* (**abb.** *loc. primo cit.*)

the function, capacity or character of: **adv.** qua
the place cited or quoted: **adv.** *loco citato* (**abb.** *loc. cit.*)
the same place: **adv.** *ibidem* (**abb.** *ibid.*)
the work cited or quoted: **adv.** *opere citato* (**abb.** *op. cit.*)
this place: **adv.** *hoc loco*
what manner or way?: **adv.** *quo modo?*

INABILITY: see "helplessness" **and** "weakness"
statement expressing: **n.** *non possumus*

INACCURATE: (see "incorrect") **a.** apocryphal; discrepant; erroneous; fallacious; inexact; **n.** INACCURACY: discrepancy; erratum; fallacy; imprecision; inexactitude; inexactness; misconception

INACTION: (see "sloth") **n.** acedia; deliquescence; dormancy; ennui; fecklessness; idleness; indolence; inertia; inertness; lassitude; lethargy; otiosity; passivity; quiescence; quietude; slothfulness; supinity; torpidity; torpor; **a.** INACTIVE: anergic; comatose; deliquescent; dormant; faineant; feckless; inanimate; indolent; inoperative; latent; lethargic; otiose; quiescent; sedentary; slothful; supine; torpid; withdrawn; **n.** INACTIVITY: (see "idleness") faineance; faineancy; *fainéantise;* idleness; inertia; otiosity; paralysis; passivity; quiescence; sedentation; stasis; *status quo*
pleasant: **n.** *dolce far niente*

INADEQUATE: (see "ineffective") **a.** deficient; disabled; disproportionate; futile; impotent; inefficacious; insufficient; perfunctory; **n.** INADEQUACY: (see "deficiency") dearth; incapacitation; inefficacy; insufficiency

INADVISABLE: **a.** contraindicative; disadvantageous; impolitic; impracticable; inappropriate; inexpedient; inopportune; **n.** INADVISABILITY: contraindication

INANE: (see "empty") **a.** fatu(it)ous; feckless; insubstantial; jejune; pointless; puerile; shallow; stratospheric(al); vacant; vacuous; **n.** INANITY: (see "emptiness") hollowness; inanition; lethargy; marasmus; shallowness; vacuity

INAPPROPRIATE: (see "unsuitable") **a.** impertinent; inapposite; inapt; incongruous; inexpedient; infelicitous; inopportune; malapropos; unbecoming

INATTENTIVE: **a.** absent-minded; abstracted; astigmatic; bemused; distant; distraught; harum-scarum; heedless; incogitable; incogitant; incurious; negligent; oscitant; preoccupied; remiss; **n.** INATTENTION: (**see** "neglect") abstraction; heedlessness; ignoration; inadvertency; incogitancy; incuriosity; misfeasance; oscitancy; oscitation; preoccupation; remission

INAUGURATE: **v.** auspicate; induct; initiate; install; institute; introduce; invest; **n.** INAUGURATION: accession; induction; installation; institution; investiture; **a.** INAUGURATIVE: auspicatory; initiatory; introductory

INBORN: (**see** "innate") **a.** ancestral; cognate; congenital; connate; constitutional; endogamous; endogenous; familial; hereditary; idiopathic; inbred; indigenous; ingrained; inherent; inherited; intrinsic; institutional; intuitive
tendency: **n.** diathesis; predisposition

INCAPABLE: **a.** feckless; helpless; impotent; powerless; sterile, **n. see** "helplessness"
of being weighed or measured: **a.** immeasurable; imponderable

INCENTIVE: (**see** "incitement") **n.** catalyst; fillip; incitation; inducement; instigation; motivation; provocation; stimulant; stimulation; stimulus

INCEPTION: (**see** "beginning" **and** "origin") **n.** inauguration; initiation; principium

INCIDENTAL: **a.** accessory; adventitious; casual; collateral; concomitant; concurrent; circumstantial; digressive; episodic(al); extraneous; fortuitous; intervenient; parenthetic(al); subordinate; tangential; **adv.** INCIDENTALLY: apropos; casually; en passant; obiter; parenthetically; secondarily; **n.** INCIDENT: (**see** "event") circumstance; circumstantiality; concomitant; contingency; episode; phenomenon
remark or comment: (**see under** "parenthetical") **n.** digression; interlocution; *obiter* (*dictum*); **a.** interlocutory; parenthetical

INCITE: (**see** "stimulate") **v.** actuate; animate; flagellate; foment; instigate; suscitate; **n.** INCITEMENT: concitation; fomentation; incitation; instigation; provocation; **a.** INCITING: animative; catalytic; hortative; hortatory; incitory; provocative; stimulatory
to courage or fervor: **n.** *sursum corda*

INCLINATION(S): **n.** acclivity; affectation; diathesis; gradient; partiality; penchant; predilection; (pre)disposition; prejudice; proclivity; propensity; tendency; versant; **a.** INCLINABLE: (pre)-disposed; suasible; tendentious; **a.** INCLINING: accliv(it)ous; inclinatory
natural born: **n.** diathesis; predisposition; tropism
slight: **n.** velleity
to act in response to stimulus: **n.** tropism
worldly: **n.pl.** mundanities

INCLUSIVE: **a.** capacious; comprehensive; cyclopedic(al); encompassing; **n.** INCLUSIVENESS: comprehensibility; **v.** INCLUDE: see "embrace"
all-: **see under** "all"

INCOMPATIBLE: (**see** "disagreeing") **a.** discordant; immiscible; incongruous; inconsistent; irreconcilable; repugnant; uncongenial

INCOMPETENT: **a.** impertinent; inapt; incapacitated; inept; unqualified; **n.** INCOMPETENCE: inaptitude; incapacitation; incapacity
as evidence: **a.** impertinent; inadmissible
mentally: **a.** *non compos* (*mentis*)
totally: **a. or n.** *asinus ad lyram* (ass at the lyre)

INCOMPLETE: (**see** "partial" **and** "rudimentary") **a.** contingent; defective; deficient; elementary; fractional; fractionary; fragmental; fragmentary; imperfect(ed); inchoate; inchoative; incipient; potential; truncated; unperfected

INCOMPREHENSIBLE: **a.** ambiguous; enigmatic(al); impenetrable; indefinite; nebulous; numinous; undecipherable; unintelligible; **n.** INCOMPREHENSIBILITY; ambiguity; enigma; indefinitude; nebulosity

INCONSISTENT: **a.** antagonistic; contradictuous; discordant; discrepant; immiscible; incompatible; incongruous; inharmonious; irreconcilable; paradoxical; repugnant; **n.** INCONSISTENCY: contrariety; incompatibility; incongruity; misalliance; *non sequitur* (**abb.** *non seq*); paradox(icality); (**pl.** contrarieties)

INCONSTANT: (**see** "fickle") **a.** alternating; ambivalent; capricious; chameleonic; fluctuating; mercurial; mutable; quicksilver; spasmodic; unstable; vacillating; vagrant; variable; vertiginous

INCONTROVERTIBLE: (**see** "certain") **a.** immutable; incontestable; indisputable; irrecusable; irrefrangible; irrefutable; **adv.** *sans doute; sine dubio*

INCONVENIENT: **a.** disadvantageous; discommodious; embarrassing; inappropriate; incommodious; inexpedient; inopportune; unseasonable; **n.** INCONVENIENCE: disadvantage; handicap; impediment; **v.** (**see** "annoy") discommode; embarrass; incommode

INCORPORATION: **n.** amalgamation; embodiment; incarnation; inclusion

INCORRECT: (**see** "erroneous" **and** "unseemly") **a.** fallacious; imprecise; improper; inaccurate; solecistic; unbecoming; **n.** fallacy; imprecision; impropriety; inaccuracy
spelling, writing or printing of words: **n.** cacography; pseudography

INCREASE: (**see** "multiply") **v.** aggrandize; augment; enhance; exacerbate; propagate; **n.** accruement; accumulation; additament; advancement; agglutination; aggrandizement; augmentation; concrescence; enhancement; exacerbation; increment; intensification; majoration; multiplication; progress(ion)
gradual: **n.** accrescence; accretion; agglutination; **a.** incremental
in severity, as disease: **v.** exacerbate; **n.** exacerbation; exacerbescence
in size, as organ or part: **v.** hypertrophy; tumesce; **n.** hypertrophy; tumescence
rel. to: **a.** accessorial
size, power, riches, etc.: **v.** aggrandize; augment; **n.** aggrandizement; augmentation
to utmost: **v.** maximalize

INCREASING: **a.** (ac)cumulative; augmentative; escalating; exacerbative; multiplicative; pyramiding
capable of: **a.** accumulable

INCURABLE: **a.** immedicable; incorrigible; insanable; intractable; irremediable; irreparable
wound: **n.** *immedicable vulnus*

INDECENCY: (**see** "immodesty" **and** "obscenity") **n.** grossness; impudicity; indelicacy; ribaldry; scurrility; **a.** INDECENT: (**see** "improper" **and** "lewd") *grivois;* immodest; ribald; scurrilous; unseemly
concerned with or replete with: **a.** cloacal; coprophilous; scatologic(al)

INDECISION: (**see** "doubt") **n.** ambivalence; fluctuation; incertitude; indecisiveness; irresolution; **a.** INDECISIVE: (**see** "vague") ambivalent; capricious; inconclusive; indefinite; indistinct; invertebrate; irresolute; vacillating; wavering

INDECISIVENESS, *pathological:* **n.** *folie du doute*

INDEFINITE: (**see** "ambiguous," "uncertain" **and** "vague") **a.** aoristic; equivocal; heterogeneous; imprecise; inconclusive; indeterminable; indeterminate; indefinitive; *sine die;* unformalized; unmathematical; **n.** INDEFINITENESS: (**see** "uncertainty") ambiguity; indefinitude; nebulosity
in form: **a.** amorphous; ethereal; nebular; nebulous; vaporous
period, for an: **a. or adv.** *sine die*

INDELICATE: (**see** "coarse" **and** "lewd") **a.** immodest; salacious; scabrous; tactless; unrefined; **n.** INDELICACY: immodesty; salaciousness; salacity; scabrousness

INDEPENDENT: (**see** "free") **a.** autonomic; autonomous; individualistic; objective; self-governing; sovereign; unconstrained; undoctrinaire; unregimented; **n.** INDEPENDENCE: autarchy; autonomy; emancipation; objectification; sovereignty; unconstraint

INDESCRIBABLE: (**see** "awful") **a.** ineffable; inenarrable

INDESTRUCTIBLE: (**see** "everlasting") **a.** adamantine; immarcescible; irrefragable; inviolable; **n.** see "everlastingness"

INDETERMINATE: (see "indefinite") **a.** aoristic; capricious; dubious; indefinitive; irresolute

INDEX: (see "indication") **n.** concordance; repertory; token; (**n.pl.** indexes; indices) *of forbidden books:* **n.** *index expurgatorius; index liborum prohibitorum of topics:* **n.** *index rerum of words or terms:* **n.** *index verborum*

INDIA, *of or rel. to:* **a.** Bharati; Indic *study of, or its people:* **n.** Indology; **a.** Indological

INDIAN *food:* **n.** pem(m)ican

INDICATION: (see "clew") **n.** criterion; gesticulation; hallmark; insigne; (**pl.** insignia); symbol; symptom; **a.** INDICATIVE: emblematic(al); pathognomonic(al); prodromal; significant; significative; significatory; suggestive; symbolic(al); symptomatic

INDICATOR: see "measure"

INDIFFERENCE: (see "apathy") **n.** acedia; detachment; inappetency; inertia; insouciance; lackadaisicalness; lackadaisy; languor; listlessness; minauderie; nonchalance; phlegm; pococurantism; *sangfroid;* stoicism; stolidity; supineness; supinity *religious or moral:* **n.** adiaphoria; adiaphorism; agnosticism; **a.** adiaphorous; agnostic; laodicean

INDIFFERENT: (see "aloof" **and** "careless") **a.** anapodictic; apathetic; cursory; detached; disinterested; imperturbable; incurious; insipid; insouciant; insusceptible; invertebrate; lackadaisical; languid; languorous; laodicean; lethargic; mechanical; nonchalant; phlegmatic; pococurante; stolid; unconcerned; unenthusiastic *person:* **n.** adiaphorist; laodicean; pococurante

INDIGNATION: see "anger"; **n.** INDIGNITY: affront; infamy; *lèse majesté;* unpleasantry

INDIRECT: **a.** ambagious; circumlocutious; circumlocutory; circuitous; circumstantial; collateral; consequential; deceitful; devious; mediate; oblique; roundabout; serpentine; **n.** INDIRECTION:

ambiguity; circuity; circumbendibus; circumlocution; circumstantiality; deceitfulness; deviousness; duplicity; sinuosity; tortuosity *in expression:* **a.** circumlocutious; circumlocutory *in speaking or writing:* **a.** circumlocutory; **n.** circumbendibus; circumlocution; *oratio obliqua ways or proceedings:* **n.** ambage(s)

INDISCREET: (see "rash") **a.** heedless; imprudent; incautious; inconsiderate; injudicious; untactful; **n.** INDISCRETION: heedlessness; imprudence; incaution; injudiciousness; untactfulness

INDISCRIMINATE: **a.** desultory; haphazard; heterogeneous; hit-or-miss; indistinguishable; promiscuous; random; **n.** INDISCRIMINATION: heterogeneity; promiscuity

INDISPENSABLE: **a.** *de rigueur;* essential; fundamental; obligatory; (pre)requisite; *sine qua non condition or thing:* **n.** condition precedent; *conditio sine qua non;* essentiality; indispensability; (pre)requisite

INDISPOSED: **a.** aeger; a(d)verse; disinclined; hesitant; loath; reluctant; unfriendly; unwilling

INDISPUTABLE: (see "incontrovertible") **a.** apodictic(al); incontestable; indubitable; irrefrangible; undeniable; unquestionable

INDISTINCT: (see "hazy" **and** "vague") **a.** amorphous; ethereal; nebulous; nebular; vaporous *area:* **n.** penumbra; twilight zone

INDIVIDUAL: **a.** idiomatic(al); ontogenetic; personal; **n.** see "person" *characteristic:* **n.** haecceity; individuality *entity or being, as dist. from a group:* **n.** individuum *identity:* **n.** individuality; ipseity *mark or signature:* **n.** idiograph

INDOLENCE: see "inactivity"

INDUCTIVE *reasoning:* **n.** empiricism; epagoge; **a.** *a posteriori;* aposterioristic; empirical; inductive

INDUSTRIAL *workers:* **n.** proletariat; **n. or a.** proletarian

INDUSTRIOUS: (**see** "busy") **a.** assiduous; attentive; diligent; indefatigable; operóse; persevering; zealous

INDUSTRY: (**see** "diligence") **n.** assiduity; diligence; industriousness; laboriousness; operosity; perseverance; sedulity; steadfastness
   leisurely: **n.** *otiosa sedulitas*

INEFFECTIVE: **a.** abortive; feckless; flaccid; impotent; incapable; ineffectual; inefficacious; **n.** INEFFECTIVENESS: flaccidity; impotency; ineffectuality

INEFFICIENT: **a.** inept; **n.** INEFFICIENCY: maladministration; **v.** maladminister

INEQUALITY: **n.** anomalism; anomaly; disparity; disproportion; dissimilarity; divergence; diversity; imparity; inequity; injustice; **a. see** "unequal"
   of rank, quality, form, etc.: **n.** imparity

INERTIA: **n.** indisposition; inertness; *vis inertiae*

INESCAPABLE: (**see** "certain") **a.** *che sarà sarà;* ineluctable; ineludible; inevitable; unavoidable; unescapable; **n.** INESCAPABILITY: ineluctability; inevitability; inevitableness

INEXACT: (**see** "incorrect") **a.** desultory; equivocal; erroneous; imponderable; imprecise; **n.** INEXACTITUDE: equivocality; imponderability; imprecision; inevitability
   things which are: **n.pl.** *imponderabilia*

INEXCUSEABLE: **a.** inexpiable; irremissible; unforgivable; unjustifiable; unpardonable; unprovoked

INEXISTENCE: **n.** nonentity; nonexistence; nullibicity; nullity

INEXPERIENCED: (**see** "immature") **a.** amateurish; callow; fledgling; incompetent; inconversant; inexpert; maladroit; unfledged; uninitiated; unseasoned; unskilled; untrained; verdant
   person or thing: **n.** fledgling

INEXPLICABLE: **a.** preternatural; supermundane; supernatural

INFALLIBILITY: **see** "perfection"

INFAMOUS: **a.** abhorrent; arrant; atrocious; dedecorous; despicable; execrable; heinous; ignominious; inglorious; nefarious; obloquial; opprobrious; **n.** INFAMY: abasement; ignominy; obloquy; odium; opprobrium

INFANCY: **n.** *bas âge;* incunabulum; (**pl.** incunabula); minority; nonage
   in: **adv.** *in statu pupillari*

INFATUATION: (**see** "passion") **n.** *béguin*

INFECTION: **n.** contagion; corruption; pathology; septicity; **a.** INFECTIOUS (**or** INFECTIVE): communicable; contagious; contaminating; corruptive; demoralizing; pathological; septic; **n.** INFECTIVENESS: contagiosity; infectivity
   source or center of: **n.** nidus

INFER: **v.** conclude; (d)educe; surmise; **n.** INFERENCE: conclusion; corollary; (d)eduction; illation; **a.** INFERENTIAL: denotative; illative; putative
   from a trend: **v.** extrapolate; **n.** extrapolation

INFERIOR: **a.** *déclassé;* mediocre; nether; subaltern(ate); subnormal; suboptimal; subordinate; substandard; **n.** INFERIORITY: mediocrity; subnormality; subordination
   as a judge: **n.** puisne
   in status or quality: **a.** subaltern(ate); suboptimal; **n.** subaltern(ant); subalternation

INFERNAL: (**see** "hellish") **a.** avernal; chthonian; chthonic; diabolical; fiendish; flagitous; horrific; malevolent; Mephistophelian; (pan)demoniac(al); stygian; tartarean

INFERTILE: (**see** "barren") **a.** infecund; sterile; unfruitful; unproductive; **n.** INFERTILITY: barrenness; infecundity; sterility

INFINITE: (**see** "eternal") **a.** boundless; cosmic; illimitable; immeasurable; inex-

haustible; limitless; unlimited; **n. see** "eternity"
  amount: **n.** inconsequentiality; infinitesimality; iota; negligibility; scintilla; **a.** infinitesimal

INFIRM: **see** "weak"

INFLAMMATION: **n.** congestion; phlegmasia; phlogosis; suppuration; **a.** INFLAMMATORY: ignescent; incendiary; phlogenic; phlogenetic; phlogistic; provocative; seditious; suppurative
  allaying: **n. or a.** antiphlogistic; calmative
  producing: **a.** phlogenetic

INFLATED: (**see** "swollen") **a.** bombastic; exaggerated; flatulent; incrassate; magniloquent; pompous; portentous; tumescent; turgescent; turgid; tympanic; tympanitic; **n.** INFLATION: distention; flatulence; (in)tumescence; pomposity; tumidity; turgidity; turgidness; tympany

INFLEXIBLE: (**see** "stubborn") **a.** immutable; implacable; implastic; impliable; indocile; inductile; indurate; indurative; inexorable; intransigeant; intransigent; irreconcilable; obstinant; refractory; relentless; retractable; unalterable; uncompromising; unmodifiable; unrelenting; unyielding; **n.** INFLEXIBILITY: immutability; immutableness; implacability; implacableness; implasticity; indocility; induration; inexorability; intransigence; intransigentism; obstinacy; refractoriness; relentlessness; rigidification; rigidity; unalterability; unmodifiability; unyieldingness

INFLICT: **v.** impose; perpetrate

INFLUENCE: **v.** actuate; affect; impel; impregnate; infuse; modify; predominate; **n.** (**see** "authority") impulsion; patronage; predomination; prestige; puissance; **a.** INFLUENTIAL: (**see** "powerful") effective; hierarchic(al); potent; prominent
  divine: (**see** "halo") **n.** afflation; afflatus; charism(a)
  impervious to: (**see** "impassive") **a.** hermetic(al); unperturbed
  pervasive or noxious: **n.** miasma; **a.** miasmal; miasm(at)ic

INFORM: **v.** acquaint; delate; enlighten; instruct; **a.** INFORMED: (**see** "up-to-date") *au courant; au fait;* cognizant; conversant

INFORMAL: **a.** colloquial; *en famille;* irregular; unceremonious; unconventional; unofficial; unorthodox; **adv.** *en famille; sans façon;* unceremoniously

INFORMER: **n.** delator; quidnunc

INFRINGE: **v.** contravene; encroach; intrude; transgress; trespass; violate; **n.** INFRINGEMENT: breach; contravention; encroachment; infraction; intrusion; nonfulfillment; piracy; plagiarism; transgression; trespass

INFURIATED: **see** "mad"

INGREDIENT: (**see** "part") **n.** component; constituent; element; **a.** componental

INHERENT: (**see** "inborn") **a.** connatal; connate; essential; immanent; inalienable; indwelling; inseparable; intrinsic; latent; native; potential; subjective; **n.** essentiality; intrinsicality
  not: (**see** "foreign") **a.** adventitious; extraneous; peripheral

INHERITABLE: **a.** descendible; hereditable; hereditary; transmissible
  characteristic: **n.** mutation
  tendency **n.** diathesis; tropism; **a.** diathetic

INHERITANCE: **n.** benefaction; heritage; hereditament(s); legacy; patrimony
  esp. from father: **n.** patrimony

INHERITED: (**see** "inborn") **a.** congenital; hereditary; innate
  fr. father or paternal line: **a.** patroclinical; patroclinic; **n.** patrimony
  fr. mother or maternal line: **a.** matroclinical; matroclinic; matroclinous

INHUMAN: (**see** "cruel") **a.** barbarous; diabolical; dispiteous; Draconian; impersonal; infrahuman; inhumane; mechanical (q.v.); Neronian; ruthless; satanic; subhuman; superhuman; truculent; **n. see** "cruelty"
  to make: **v.** dehumanize; mechanize; robotize

INITIAL: (**see** "beginning") **a.** incipient; inchoative; initiatory; rudimental; **adv.** INITIALLY: *ab initio;* aborigine; *ab ovo*

INITIATED, *known only to the:* **a.** epoptic; esoteric
one who has been: **n.** epopt; initiate

INITIATIVE, *by one's own:* **adv.** *proprio motu*

INITIATOR: **n.** actuator; bellwether; catalyst; inceptor; originator

INJURIOUS: (**see** "harmful") **a.** deleterious; inimical; invidious; malignant; pernicious
to health: **a.** contagious; inimical; malignant; nocuous; nocent; noisome; noxious; pernicious; venomous

INJURY: **n.** detriment; impairment; lesion; mayhem; mutilation; trauma(tism)
by violence or force: **a.** traumatic; **v.** traumatize; **n.** mayhem; trauma(tism)
following, or result of: **a.** post-traumatic; residual
patient endurance of: **n.** forbearance; longanimity; long-suffering; **a.** longanimous
residual(s) or result(s) of: **n.** disablement; disability; handicap; impairment; incapacitation; residuum; sequala; (**pl.** sequalae)
unmerited: **n.** crown of thorns; martyrdom

INKY: **a.** atramental; atramentous

INN (or LODGE): **n.** auberge; caravansary; hospice; hostel(ry); poseda; xenodochium

INNATE: (**see** "inborn") **a.** congenital; hereditary; idiopathic; inherited; intrinsic
desire: **n.** conatus
intelligence: **n.** *élan vital;* entelechy
quality: **n.** largesse

INNER *nature or character:* **n.** interiority

INNERMOST *part(s):* **n.** penetrale; (**pl.** penetralia); sanctuary; *sanctum sanctorum*

INNOCENT: **a.** Arcadian; artless; blameless; candid; cherubic; faultless; guileless; immaculate; impeccable; impeccant; inculpable; ingenuous; innocuous; inoffensive; irreproachable; lily-white; *naïve* (also naive); pastoral; seraphic; unaware; undefiled; undisguised; undissembled; unsullied; unsuspecting; untainted; virtuous; **n.** INNOCENCE: artlessness; blamelessness; immaculacy; impeccability; inculpability; ingenuousness; innocuousness; *naïveté;* simplicity; verdancy
something which is: **n.** innocuity

INNUENDO: (**see** "hint") **n.** aspersion; connotation; insinuation

INOFFENSIVE: (**see** "peaceful") inobnoxious

INOPPORTUNE: (**see** "untimely") **a.** impracticable; inappropriate; inconvenient; inexpedient; intempestive; malapropos; unseasonable; unsuitable

INQUIRY: (**see** "investigation") **n.** disquisition; inquest; inquisition; **a.** INQUISITIVE: disquisitive; inquisitorial

INSANE: **a.** chaotic; compulsive; delirious; frantic; frenzied; incompetent; irrational; lunatic; maniacal; *non compos (mentis);* psychotic; *tête exaltée;* (tête exaltée)
fear of becoming: **n.** lyssophobia
wildly: **a.** berserk; dithyrambic; maniac(al)

INSANITY: **n.** aberration; alienation; *amentia folie;* dementia; incompetency; lunacy; psychosis
of two (hus. and wife): **n.** *folie à deux*
religious: **n.** theomania

INSCRIPTION(S), *on plaque, monument, etc.:* (**see** "gravestone") **n.** epigraph
scratched on walls, etc.: **n.** graffito; (**pl.** graffiti)

INSECURITY: **n.** apprehensiveness; apprehension; incertitude; instability; jeopardy; peril

INSENSITIVE: **a.** analgesic; anesthetic; apathetic; inanimate; insensate; insentient; lethargic; obtuse; pachydermatous; philistine; philistinic; unimpressionable; **n.** INSENSIBILITY (or INSENSITIV-

ITY) : analgesia ; apathy ; carus ; coma ; insentience ; lethargy ; obtuseness ; obtusity ; stupor ; torpor ; trance
person: **n.** pachyderm ; **a.** pachydermatous

INSERT : **v.** intercalate ; interlard ; interpolate ; interpose ; intromit ; **n.** entredeux ; intercalation ; interpolation ; **a.** INSERTING (or INSERTED) : intercalary ; interlarded ; interpolated
at intervals: **v.** intersperse
bet. two: **n.** entredeux

INSIGHT : **n.** acumen ; clairvoyance ; discernment ; discrimination ; empathy ; intuition ; penetration ; perception ; perspicacity ; perspicuity ; understanding
gifted w/ mental or moral: **a.** prehensile ; prescient ; spirituel (le)
intuitive: **n.** aperçu ; intuition ; prescience
natural: **n.** *lumen naturale*

INSIGNIFICANT : (**see** "small") **a.** commonplace ; contemptible ; immaterial ; infinitesimal ; irrelevant ; minuscule ; trivial ; **n.** INSIGNIFICANCE : infinitesimality ; minitude ; triviality
thing(s): **see** "importance, things of little or slight"

INSINCERE : **a.** artificial ; counterfeit ; deceitful ; disingenuous ; duplicitous ; fulsome ; hypocritical ; meretricious ; specious ; theatrical ; **a. or adv.** tongue in cheek ; **n.** INSINCERITY : artificiality ; bathos ; dissimulation ; duplicity ; hypocrisy ; sentimentalism ; sentimentality ; theatricality
person: **n.** charlatan ; mountebank ; *poseur;* (**fem.** *poseuse*) ; pretender

INSIPID : (**see** "bland") **a.** cloying ; commonplace ; jejune ; mawkish ; savorless ; trite ; uninteresting ; unsavory ; vapid ; **n.** INSIPIDITY : jejunity ; vapidity

INSISTENT : (**see** "urgent") **a.** conspicuous ; exigent ; importunate ; persevering ; persistent ; pressing ; prominent

INSOLENT : (**see** "sassy") **a.** arrogant ; audacious ; contemptuous ; contumelious ; hubristic ; impudent ; overbearing ; **adv.** INSOLENTLY : *avec audace;* **n.** INSOLENCE : arrogance ; audacity ; cheekiness ; contempt (uousness) ; contumacy ;

contumely ; effrontery ; flippery ; haughtiness ; hubris ; impertinence ; impudence ; protervity ; sauciness
person: **n.** jackanapes

INSPECTION : (**see** "examination") **n.** probe ; reconnaissance ; scrutiny ; surveillance ; **a.** inspectorial
person(s) making: **n.** inspectorate ; surveillant

INSPIRATION : **n.** afflation ; afflatus ; enthusiasm ; inhalation ; stimulant ; stimulation ; **v.** INSPIRE : animate ; encourage ; exhilarate ; imbue ; infuse ; inhale ; motivate ; prompt ; **a.** INSPIRING : (**see** "stimulating") afflated ; infusive

INSTABILITY : (**see** "unbalance") **n.** apprehensiveness ; incertitude ; inconstancy ; insecurity

INSTALLMENT (S), *printed in:* **n.** feuilleton

INSTANCE : **n.** circumstance ; exception ; illustration ; suggestion
for: **adv.** *exempli gratia* (**abb.** e.g.)

INSTANT : **n.** *clin d'oeil;* instantaneity ; **a.** INSTANTANEOUS : momentary ; semelfactive ; simultaneous ; **n.** simultaneity

INSTIL(L) : **v.** implant ; indoctrinate ; infiltrate ; innoculate ; insinuate ; introduce

INSTINCT : **n.** appetency ; intuition ; propensity

INSTRUCTION : (**see** "teaching") **n.** disciple ; education ; indoctrination ; information ; precept ; **v.** INSTRUCT : discipline ; edify ; educate ; indoctrinate ; **a.** INSTRUCTIVE : didactic (al) ; edificatory ; educational ; expository ; moralistic ; preceptive
elementary or preparatory: **n.** propaedeutics ; **a.** propaedeutic (al)
oral: **n.** catechesis ; **a.** catechetic (al) ; catechistic ; **v.** catechize
theory of art of: **n.** didactics ; propaedeutics ; pedagogy

INSTRUMENT (S) : (**see** "equipment")
n.pl. armamentaria ; instrumentaria

INSUFFICIENCY: **n.** dearth; deficiency; inability; inadequacy; incompetency; paucity

INSULT: **see** "indignity"

INTACT: **see** "whole"

INTANGIBLE: **a.** aeriform; amorphous; diaphanous; ephemeral; impalpable; imperceptible; incorporeal; insubstantial; nebular; nebulous; vague; vaporous; **n.** INTANGIBILITY: aeriality; ephemerality; (**pl.** ephemera; ephemeralities) incorporeality; insubstantiality; nebulosity
   process or function: **n.** chemistry; mystique

INTEGRATIVE: (**see** "unifying") **a.** centralizing; centripetal; integrable

INTEGRITY: **n.** candor; completeness; entireness; sincerity; soundness

INTELLECT: **see** "reason"
   comprehension by: **n.** cognition; noesis; **a.** cognitive; noetic

INTELLECTUAL(S): **n.** academe; *bel esprit;* cognoscente; illuminato; literato; literatus; luminary; pedant; savant; sophist; (**pl.** cognoscenti; illuminati; intelligentsia; literati) ; **a.** cerebral; cognitive; dianoetic; epistemic; epistemological; gnostic; sagacious; sophic(al)
   depth: **n.** intellectuality; profundity; rationality
   food (figurative): **n.** pabulum
   hostility toward: **n.** anti-intellectualism
   state of being, or intellectual power: **n.** intellectuality; luminosity; sagacity
   treat or analyze (intellectually): **v.** intellectualize; rationalize; **n.** intellectualization; rationalization
   wandering or quest: **n.** odyssey; **a.** odyssean

INTELLIGENCE: **n.** acquaintance; acumen; comprehension; information; intellectuality; luminosity; mentality; perspicacity; perspicuity; sagacity; sapience; **a.** INTELLIGENT: **see** "intellectual" and "rational"
   innate: **n.** élan vital; entelechy
   lack of: **n.** amentia; insipience; moronity; nescience
   pert. to or having: **a.** intelligential

INTEMPERATE: **a.** immoderate; inclement; incontinent; inordinate; **n.** INTEMPERANCE: acrasia; acrasy; immoderation; inclemency; incontinence; insobriety
   in eating or drinking: (**see** "alcoholic" **and** "glutton") **a.** crapulent; crapulous; **n.** crapulence; gulosity

INTENSE (or INTENSIVE): (**see** "burning") **a.** comprehensive; consuming; consummatory; inspissate(d); vehement; zealous; **n.** INTENSIFICATION (or INTENSITY): concentration; enhancement; enthusiasm; exacerbation; potency; profundity; saturation; strenuosity; temperature; vehemency; **v.** INTENSIFY: accentuate; augment; deepen; emphasize; enhance; exacerbate; exaggerate; sharpen; strengthen

INTENT (or INTENTION): (**see** "design" **and** "motive") **n.** ambition; animus; contemplation; determination; import; intendment; purport; resolve; significance
   criminal: **n.** malice aforethought; malice prepense; *mens rea;* premeditation
   with evil: (**see under** "evil") **adv.** maliciously; *malo animo*
   without: (**see** "accidental") **a.** unpremeditated; unmotivated

INTENTIONAL: **a.** calculated; deliberate; designed; permissive; premeditated; purposeful; voluntary
   quality or state of being: **n.** designedness; intentionality

INTENTIONALLY *so written:* **adv.** *sic*

INTERCHANGE: **v.** alternate; reciprocate; **n.** alternation; mutuality; *quid pro quo;* reciprocation; reciprocity; **a.** INTERCHANGEABLE: alternating; commutable; mutual; reciprocal; reciprocative

INTERCONNECTING: **a.** anastomotic; syndetic

INTEREST(S): (**see** "concern") **n.** attraction; consciousness; curiosity; inquisitiveness
   center of: **n.** cynosure; Mecca; polestar
   community of: **n.** affinity
   in others: **a.** allocentric
   in self: **a.** egocentric; **n.** egocentricity
   lack of: **n.** acedia; ennui; lackadaisy;

melancholia; otiosity; slothfulness; tepidity; torpor; unconcern
level of: **n.** intensity; temperature
of local or current: **a.** topical; **n.** topicality
one having great diversity of: **n.** Proteus
rate higher than legal: **n.** usury; **a.** usurious

INTERESTING: **a.** absorbing; attractive; divertive; engrossing; intriguing; piquant; provocative; succulent; **a.** INTERESTED: (**see** "concerned") versant

INTERFERE: **v.** intercede; interlope; intermeddle; interpose; interrupt; intervene; intrude; obtrude; supervene; **n.** INTERFERENCE: ingerence; intercession; interposition; intervention; intrusion; **a.** INTERFERING: adventitious; supervenient
do not: **adv.** *noli me tangere*

INTERIOR: (**see** "internal") **a.** domestic; **n.** INTERIORITY: domesticality; internality; internalization
country: **n.** hinterland; **a. or n.** up-country

INTERLOCK: **v.** interdigitate; interlace; **n.** interdigitation

INTERLUDE: **n.** armistice; hiatus; intermezzio; intermission; interregnum; interruption; parenthesis; respite; stasimon

INTERMEDIATE: **a.** equidistant; medial; mesothetic

INTERMISSION: (**see** "pause") **n.** armistice; *entr'acte;* interlude; interruption

INTERNAL: **a.** domestic; endogenous; inherent; internecine; intestinal; intramural; intraneous; intrinsic; municipal
state of being: **n.** domesticality; interiority; internality; internalization
to make: **v.** interiorize; internalize; **n.** interiorization; internalization

INTERNATIONAL *law:* **n.** *jus gentium; jus inter gentes*
state or cond. of being: **n.** internationality

INTERPOSE: (**see** "interfere") **v.** arbitrate; interpolate; intervene; mediate; mediatize; **n.** INTERPOSITION: arbitration; interpolation; mediation

INTERPRETATION: **n.** elucidation; exegesis; explanation; explication; exposition; **a.** INTERPRE(TA)TIVE: divinatory; exegetic(al); explanatory; expository; hermeneutic; prophetic(al); revelatory; significative; **v.** INTERPRET: (**see** "clarify") construe; decipher; elucidate; explicate; illustrate; translate
additional: **n.** epexegesis
by reading into it one's own: **n.** eisegesis; **a.** eisegetical
science of: **n.** exegetics; hermeneutics

INTERPRETER: **n.** annotator; dragoman; exegete; exponent; expounder; expositor; hierophant; scholiast
of dreams: **n.** oneirocritic

INTERRUPT: (**see** "interfere") **v.** arrest; intercept: intermit; pretermit; **n.** INTERRUPTION: (**see** "pause") armistice; arrest; disruption; hiatus; interlocution; intermission; interpolation; pretermission; suspension

INTERRUPTIVE *utterance:* **n.** interlocution

INTERSECT: **v.** anastomose; bisect; collide; decussate; transect; **n.** INTERSECTION: anastomosis; chiasma; collision; decussation

INTERVAL: (**see** "gap," "interlude"; **and** "pause") **n.** armistice; c(a)esura; hiatus; intermission; interstice; parenthesis; rupture
bet. two reigns: **n.** interregnum

INTERVENE: (**see** "interfere") **v.** arbitrate; interject; interpose; mediate; **a.** INTERVENING: interjacent; interjaculatory; interjectional; interpolated; intervenient; mediatorial; mediatory; parenthetical
one who does: **n.** intercessor; intermediary; intervenient; mediator

INTERVENTION: **n.** arbitration; intercession; interposition; intervenience; (inter)mediation
supernatural, into human affairs: **n.** theurgy

INTESTINES: **n.pl.** viscera
pert to: **a.** alvine; splanchnic; visceral
rumbling sound(s) in: borborygmus; crepitation; flatus; **a.** borborygmic

171

INTIMATE: (see "familiar") **a. or adv.** *à deux;* **a.** contubernal; *tête-à-tête*

INTIMIDATE: **v.** browbeat; bulldoze; bully; cow; daunt; dishearten; dragoon; hector; terrorize

INTOXICATED: (see "drunken") **a.** heady; inebriated
person: see "alcoholic"
that which (intoxicates): **n.** inebriant; intoxicant

INTRICATE: **a.** abstruse; convoluted; daedalian; daedal(ic); entangled; Gordian; inexplicable; inextricable; involuted; labyrinthian; labyrinthine; **n.** INTRICACY: abstrusity; complexity; labyrinth

INTRIGUE: (see "plot") **n.** artifice; cabal; chicanery; collusion; coup; machination; subtlety; **a.** INTRIGUING: see "attractive"

INTRIGUER, *female:* **n.** Circe; *femme fatale;* intrig(u)ante; siren

INTRINSIC: see "inborn" **and** 'inherent"

INTRODUCTION: (see "preface") **n.** debut; exordium; innovation; manduction; preamble; prelude; prelusion; preparation; proem; prolegomenon; prologue; prolusion; propaedeutic; unveiling; **v.** INTRODUCE: see "open"
brief: **n.** proem
literary: **n.** isagoge

INTRODUCTORY: **a.** antecedent; elementary; inductive; initiatory; innovatory; isagogic(al); liminary; manductive; manductory; precursory; prefatorial; prefatory; preliminary; preludial; preludious; prelusive; premonitory; presaging; prolegomenous; prolusory; propaedeutic(al); rudimentary
study, as of Bible history, etc.: **n.pl.** isagogics
work (lit.) **n.** prodromus

INTROSPECTIVE: **a.** autistic; **n.** INTROSPECTION: autism; introspectiveness; introspectivity; reverie; self-examination

INTRUDE: see "interfere"

INTUITION: **n.** anschauung; apprehension; clairvoyance; conception; eidos; foreknowledge; percipience; precognition; prescience; **a.** INTUITIVE: (see "inborn") clairvoyant; percipient; prescient
learn by: **v.** intuit
reasoning by: **n.** *a priori;* apriority; **a.** aprioristic

INVADER: **n.** incursionist

INVALID: **a.** nugatory; null and void; unlawful; unsound; **n. or a.** valetudinarian

INVALIDATE: (see "weaken") **v.** nullify; repeal; stultify; vitiate

INVALUABLE: **a.** incalculable; inestimable; priceless

INVASION: **n.** aggression; assault; encroachment; incursion; inroad; transgression; **a.** incursionary; invasive

INVENT: **v.** contrive; create; devise; excogitate; fabricate; machinate; originate; **a.** INVENTIVE: creative; ingenious; innovational; **n.** INVENTIVENESS: creativity; ingeniosity; ingenuity

INVENTORY: **n.** catalog(ue); compendium; schedule; summary; survey; syllabus; tariff

INVESTIGATION: **n.** catechesis; catechism; disquisition; inquest; inquisition; interrogation; perscrutation; reconnaissance; scrutiny; survey; **a.** INVESTIGATIVE: disquisitive; exploratory; investigational; probative; zetetic; **v.** INVESTIGATE: inquisit; probe; **n.** INVESTIGATOR: see "searcher"

INVIGORATING: **a.** animating; bracing; exhilarative; roborant; stimulating; tonic

INVINCIBLE: (see "unconquerable") **a.** Achillean; unswerving

INVITATION, *pert. to or containing:* **a.** invitatory

INVOCATION: (see "prayer") **n.** *absit omen;* bismillah; enforcement; incantation; supplication

INVOLUNTARY: **a.** accidental; automatic; autonomic; inexorable; instinctive; irreparable; mechanical; uncontrollable; unmotivated; unwilling; **n.** automaticity; mechanicality

INVOLVE: **v.** complicate; embarrass; embroil; entangle; implicate; interpenetrate; permeate; **a.** INVOLVED: abstruse; complicated; confused; inextricable; intricate; involute(d); labyrinthian; labyrinthine; **n.** INVOLVEMENT: (**see** "confusion") complexity; embroilment; entanglement; involution

INWARD: **a.** centripetal; domestic; endogenous; immanent; intrinsic; **n.** INWARDNESS: immanence; intrinsicality; intrinsicalness

IRE: see "anger"

IRIDESCENT: **a.** kaleidoscopic; lustrous; margaritaceous; nacereous; opalescent; pavonine

IRK: see "annoy"; **n.** IRKSOMENESS: (**see** "depression") *taedium vitae*

IRON, *containing or bearing:* **a.** ferric; ferriferous; ferruginous
pert. to: **a.** ferric; ferruginous

IRONIC(AL): (**see** "biting") **a.** Hudibrastic; sarcastic; satirical; **a. or adv.** tongue in cheek; **n.** IRONY: asteism; contempt; disapprobation; dissimultation; satire; sarcasm
buffoonery: **n.** Pantagruelism; **a.** Pantagruelian; **n.** Pantagruelist

IRRATIONAL: (**see** "absurd") **a.** addlepated (**or** brained); alogical; asinine; Dionysian; fatuous; grotesque; imbecilic; illogical; psychotic; rattle-brained; unbounded; **n.** IRRATIONALITY: absurdity; fatuity; foolishness; imbecility; psychosis; unreasonableness
action or speech: **n.** deliration; delirium
statement or reasoning: **n.** alogism

IRREGULAR: (**see** "abnormal") **a.** anomalous; arrhythmic; atypical; baroque; clandestine; distorted; diverse; eccentric; heteroclite; heteromorphic; inordinate; intermittent; promiscuous; sporadic; tumultuary; **n.** IRREGULARITY: aberration; anomaly; arrythmia; asymmetry; caprice; delinquency; deviation; eccentricity; promiscuity; sporadicity; unevenness

IRRELEVANT: (**see** "unrelated") **a.** *à propos de bottes; à propos de rien;* ex-traneous; extrinsic; heterogeneous; impertinent; inapplicable; inapposite; inconsequential; *nihil ad rem;* tangential; **n.** IRRELEVANCE: extraneity; impertinence; inappositeness; inconsequentiality; irrelevancy

IRREPARABLE: **a.** intractable; irremediable; irretrievable; irreversible
injury: **n.** *immedicable vulnus*

IRRESISTIBLE: (**see** "alluring" **and** "charming") **a.** mesmeric

IRRESOLUTE: **see** "undecided"

IRRESPONSIBLE: (**see** "irrational") **a.** arbitrary; feckless; harum-scarum; impractical; scatterbrained; visionary

IRREVERENCE: **n.** blasphemy; impiety; irreligiosity; *lèse majesté;* profanation; sacrilege; undutifulness; ungodliness; **a.** IRREVERENT: atheistic; blasphemous; impious; irreligious; irreverential; sacrilegious; undutiful; worldly

IRRITABILITY: **n.** animosity; fretfulness; iracundity; irascibility; petulance; querulousness; waspishness; **a.** IRRITABLE: (**see** "peevish") acrimonious; bilious; cankered; cantankerous; caustic; choleric; churlish; crochety; fretful; fractious; iracund; irascible; perverse; pettish; petulent; splenetic(al); testy; touchy; waspish
being in state of: **n.** fantod(s)

IRRITATE: (**see** "aggravate") **v.** abrade; annoy; chafe; exacerbate; exasperate; gall; incense; intensify; nettle; provoke; stimulate; **a.** IRRITATING: see "annoying"; **n. or a.** IRRITANT: abradant; provocative; **n.** provocation

ISLAND(S), *group or cluster of:* **n.** archipelago
inhabiting an: **a.** enisled; insular; nesiote
pert. to: **a.** insular; **n.** insularity

ISOLATE: **v.** detach; enisle; ghettoize; immure; maroon; quarantine; seclude; segregate; **a.** ISOLATED: discrete; ivory-towered; quarantined; segmental; segmentary; segregated; sporadic; **n.** ISOLATION: ascesis; decentralization; immurement; incarceration; insularity; insulation; quarantine; segregation; sequestration

ISSUE: **v.** circulate; debouch; disembogue; egress; emanate; evacuate; extravasate; **n.** (**see** "child") debouchment; eggress-(ion); emanation; emergence; extravasation; issuance; outflow
without: **adv.** *sine prole*
IT *is done:* **n.** *factum est; fait accompli;* **a.** *is said:* **n.** *on-dit*
consummated

ITEM, *lavishly decorated or utilitarian:* **n.** botique

ITCH: **n.** agitation; ferment; prurience; pruritus; restlessness
to do something: **n.** cacoethes

ITSELF, *by or in:* **adv.** inherently; intrinsically; *per se;* simpliciter; **n.** perseity

J

JACK-*of-all-trades:* **n.** factotem; *homme à tout faire;* pantologist; Proteus

JAGGED: (**see** "uneven") **a.** lancinate; lancinose; serrate(d)

JARGON: (**see** "slang") **n.** abracadabra; argot; balderdash; baragouin; cant; Chinook; Choctaw; dialect; gibberish; lingo; patois

JAUNTY: **a.** affable; affected; debonair(e); fashionable; genial; nonchalant; raffish; rakish; *soigné(e)*; sprightly; stylish; **n.** geniality; nonchalance; sprightliness

JAW(S), *having large:* **a.** pachygnathous
having long: **a.** longirostrine
having projecting: **a.** prognathous
having receding lower: **a.** opistognathous
pert. to: **a.** gnathic
pert. to lower: **a.** genial; mandibular; mental

JEALOUSY, *professional:* **n.** *jalousie de métier;* **a.** JEALOUS: invidious

JERKY: **a.** saccadic

JEST: **n.** banter; *drôlerie;* drollery; *mot pour rire; plaisanterie;* **n.** JESTER: (**see** "fool") *farceur;* (**fem.** *farceuse*); merry-andrew; railleur
in: **adv.** *pour rire*

JEW(S), *of or rel. to:* **a.** Hebraic; Judaic(al); **n.** Hebraism; Judaism
things or lit. pert. to: **n.** Hebraica; Judaica

JEWEL(S): **n.** bijou(terie)
imitation: **n. or a.** Brummagem

JEWISH *boy at age 13, also rite;* **n.** bar mitzvah (*also* bar mitzvot(h))
girl at age 13, also rite: **n.** bath (**or** bas **or** bat) mitzvah

JOB, *soft or easy:* **see** "snap"

JOINED: (**see** "coupled") **a.** affined; associated; concatenate; contiguous; intercatenated; **a.** JOINING: convergent; **n.** colligation; communication; concatenation; conjugation; copulation; juncture; **v.** JOIN: agglutinate; amalgamate; articulate; associate; coagment; coalesce; colligate; communicate; concatenate; conjugate; consolidate; copulate; harness; interconnect; interlock; matriculate

JOINT: **n.** articulation; commisure; juncture; synchondrosis; **a.** JOINTED (**or** JOINED): (**see** "connected") articulate

JOKE: (**see** "jest") **n.** facetiosity; farcicality; jocosity; jocularity; jocundity; **a.** JOKING: (**see** "jolly") facetious; jocose; jocular; jocund; jovial
for sake of the: **adv.** *joci causâ*

JOKER: **n.** *farceur;* (**fem.** *farceuse*); humorist; railleur

JOLLY: **a.** convivial; genial; jocular; jocund; jovial; sportive; **n. see** "joviality"

JOURNEY: **v.** itinerate; peregrinate; safari; **n.** entrada; expedition; itinerary; itineration; odyssey; peregrination; pilgrimage; safari
extended: **n.** odyssey
for safety (flight): **n.** hegira
have a pleasant: **adv.** *bon voyage*
pert. to: **a.** itinerant; Odyssean; peripatetic; viatic(al)

JOVIALITY: **n.** conviviality; jocosity; jocundity; jocularity

JOY: (**see** "delight") **n.** allégresse; beatitude; ecstasy; exuberance; exaltation; felicity; festivity; gaiety; gratification; jubilation; merriment; transport; **a.** JOY-

FUL (or JOYOUS) : (**see** "gay") blithe; buoyant; carnivalesque; ecstatic; elated; exuberant; exultant; gratulant; jovial; jubilant; jubilean; rapturous; triumphant; zestful; **n.** JOYFULNESS: exuberance; exultation; joviality; jubilance; jubilation; jubilee
foretaste of: **n.** *joie anticipée*
of living: **n.** *joie de vivre;* zest
shout for: **v.** jubilate; **n.** jubilation; **n.** jubilarian

JUDGE(S) : **v.** adjudicate; analyze; arbitrate; discriminate; **n.** (ad)judicator; arbitrator; arbiter; connoisseur; critic; judicature; judiciary
junior: **n.** puisne
of arts or fashion: **n.** cognoscente; connoisseur
rigorous: **n.** Rhadamanthus; **a.** rhadamanthine
wise: **n.** Solomon

JUDGED, *capable of or liable to be:* **a.** judicable; justiciable

JUDGING : **a.** analytical; discretionary; discriminatory; judicative; judicial; judicious

JUDGMENT : **n.** acumen; circumspection; criticism; discernment; discretion; discrimination; insight; intuition; judicality; judicium; penetration; perception; prudence; rationality; sagacity; wisdom; **a.** judgmental
lacking: **a.** immature; malentendu
sound or soundness of: **n.** sagacity; **a.** **see** "judicious"

JUDICIOUS : (**see** "wise") **a.** circumspect; discerning; judgmatic(al) ; rational; sagacious

JUGGLING, *skillful feat of:* **n.** legerdemain; *passe-passe;* prestidigitation; *tour de force*

JUICY : **a.** piquant; racy; succulent; **n.** piquancy; succulence; succulency

JUMBLE : (**see** "confusion") **n.** colluvies; disarrangement; farrago; *fatras;* gallimaufry; heterogeneity; hodge-podge; medley; olla podrida; potpourri; salmagundi; **a.** JUMBLED: disarranged; farraginous; hugger-mugger; indiscriminate; macaronic
confused: **n.** capharnaum; mare's nest

JUNCTION : **see** "union"

JUMP : **v.** saltate; **n.** saltation; **a.** capering; salient; saltant

JUNIOR : **a.** or **n.** puisne; subaltern(ate) ; subordinate; **a.** juvenile; youthful
state of being: **n.** juniority

JURISDICTION : **n.** authority; bailiwick; cognizance; control; domain; province; sovereignty; territory
being within: **n.** *intra vires;* **a.** justiciable
having full: **a.** plentary; plenipotent(ial) ; plenipotentiary; **n.** plenipotentiary
state of exceeding: **n.** *ultra vires*

JURY, *act of influencing illegally:* **n.** embracery

JUST : **a.** accurate; conscientious; deserved; equitable; impartial; incorruptible; merited; rectitudinous; righteous; unbiased
cause: **n.** *justa causa*
inflexibly: **a.** Rhadamanthine
once, nothing counts: ein mal, kein mal

JUSTICE : **n.** dharma; equity; impartiality; integrity; rectitude; righteousness; rightfulness
pert. to: **a.** forensic; judicatory; juridical; juristic; justiciary
rel. to administration of: **a.** justiciary
with. **adv.** *à bon droit*

JUSTIFIABLE : (**see** "legal") **a.** legitimate; justificatory; vindicatory; warrantable

JUSTIFICATION : **n.** apologia, exoneration; extenuation; rationale; vindication

JUSTIFIED, *something that is to be:* **n.** justificandum

JUSTIFY, *something that serves to:* **n.** justificans; justification; **a.** justificative; justificatory

JUSTIFYING : **a.** extenuative; justificative; justificatory; vindicatory

JUTTING : **a.** bulbous; protuberant; salient; **n.** protuberance; protuberancy; salience; saliency

JUVENILE: (**see** "young" **and** "youthful") **a.** ephebic; immature; puerile; **n.** juniority; juvenility
lead in a play: **n.** *jeune premier*

K

KEEN: (see "caustic") **a.** acrimonious; appercipient; astucious; astute; discerning; incisive; moradacious; mordant; penetrating; perspicacious; piquant; poignant; pungent; sagacious; trenchant; **n.** KEENNESS: acumen; asperity; astucity; perspicacity; piquancy; poignancy; pungency; sagacity
    mindedness: **n.** acumen; astucity; astuteness; perspicacity; **a.** acuminous; analytical; appercipient; astute; perspicacious

KEEP *silent and be counted a philosopher:* **n.** *sile, et philosophus esto*

KEEPSAKE. **n.** bibelot; knickknack; memento; *objet d'art;* virtu

KERNEL: **n.** chromosome; nidus; nucleus; quintessence

KEY, *pass or master:* **n.** *passe partout*
    to riddle or puzzle: **n.** *le mot de l'eigme*

KICK: **n.** *coup de pied*

KILL: (see "annihilate") **v.** assassinate; decapitate; dispatch; execute; immolate; suppress
    by cutting throat: **v.** jugulate
    by stoning: **v.** lapidate; **n.** lapidation

KILLING *of brother, also the killer:* **n.** fratricide; **a.** fratricidal
    same for father: **n.** patricide; **a.** patricidal
    same for husband by wife: **n.** matricide; **a.** matricidal
    same for inafnt: **n.** infanticide; **a.** infanticidal
    same for king: **n.** regicide; **a.** regicidal
    same for mother: **n.** matricide; **a.** matricidal
    same for parent: **n.** parenticide; parricide; **a.** parricidal; parricidious
    same for sister: **n.** sorocide; **a.** sorocidal
    same for wife by hus.: **n.** matricide;

uxoricide; **a.** uxoricidal
    same for woman or women: **n.** femicide; **a.** femicidal

KIND(S): **a.** amiable; auspicious; beneficent; benevolent; benign(ant); charitable; clement; compassionate; cordial; gracious; grandfatherly; humane; indulgent; philanthropic; propitious; Samaritan; sympathetic; **n. see** "class"
    all, pert. to or producing: **a.** omnifarious
    having same (kind) or nature: **a.** consubstantial; **n.** consubstantiality
    of another: alieni generis
    of its own: **a.** *sui generis*
    only one of his or its: **a.** *sui generis;* unique; **n.** uniquity

KINDNESS: **n.** amiability; benevolence; benignancy; benignity; clemency; complaisance; congeniality; cordiality; lenity; philanthropy; *prévenance*

KINDRED: **a.** cognate; congeneric; congenerous; congenital; consanguineous; sympathetic; **n. see** "kinship"

KING(S): **n.** dynast; emperor; imperator; monarch; regulus; rex; sovereign
    last of the: **n.** *ultimus regnum*
    petty or vassal: **n.** (sub)regulus
    right and privileges of: **n.** regalia; regality
    today, tomorrow nothing; aujourd'hui roi, demain rien
    who has lost power (do-nothing king): **n.** *roi fainéant*

KINGDOM: **n.** demesne; domain; dominion; dukedom; jurisdiction; principality; realm; sultonate; vizierate

KINGLY: **a.** august; basilic(al); imperial; leonine; majestic; monarchial; palatine; regal; royal; sovereign

KINSHIP: **n.** affinity; agnation; consanguinity; congener; propinquity; relationship

KISS: **v.** caress; osculate; **n.** osculation
parting: **n.** baiser d'adieu

KISSING: **a.** osculant; oscular; osculatory; **n.** osculation
"science of:" **n.** philematology

KITCHEN: **n.** cuisine
pert. to: **a.** culinary
utensils: **n.** batterie de cuisine

KNAVISH: (**see** "dishonest") **a.** deceitful; fraudulent; frolicsome; unscrupulous; **n.** KNAVISHNESS: (**see** "dishonesty") unscrupulosity; **n.** KNAVE: (**see** "scamp") scapin

KNEE-*cap:* **n.** patella; **a.** patellar
-*like:* **a.** geniculate
space behind: **n.** popliteal (space)
to bend, as in reverence: **v.** or **a.** geniculate; kow-tow; **v.** genuflex; **n.** genuflection; genuflexion

KNEEL(ING): **n.** genuflection; genuflexion; **adv.** à genoux; **a.** genuflectory
in respect: **see under** "knee"

KNIGHT: **n.** chevalier; Galahad; paladin; protagonist; templar
gallant: **n.** preux chevalier
like a: **a.** chivalresque; chivalric; chivalrous; equestrian

KNOCKDOWN *blow:* **n.** recumbentibus

KNOLL: **n.** hillock; hummock; tumulus

KNOT: **n.** excrescence; exostosis; gibbosity; knurl; protuberance; **a.** KNOTTY: **see** "difficult"

KNOW, *dare to:* **adv.** aude sapere
-*how:* **n.** expertise; *savoir-faire;* technique; virtuosity
in the: **adv.** (be) à la page
thyself: **adv.** gnothi seauton; nosce te ipsum; te nosce

KNOWABLE: **a.** cognoscible; cognoscitative; cognizable; knowledg(e)able; perceivable; percipient; ratiocinative

KNOWING: **a.** apprehensive; astute; cognitative; cognitional; cognitive; cognoscible; cognoscitive; discerning; epistemonic(al); gnostic; intelligenced; knowledg(e)able; penetrating; perceptive; percipient; sagacious; scient(ial); sophisticated
all things: **a.** omniscient; pansophic(al); **n.** omniscience; pansophism
before hand: **a.** precognitive; **n.** precognition; **v.** precognize
having power of: **a.** cognoscitive

KNOWLEDGE: (**see** "learning") **n.** acquaintance; apperception; cognition; cognizance; comprehension; episteme; erudition; information; perception; sagacity; scholarship; science; scientia; sophistication
denial of any basis for: **n.** nihilism; **a.** nihilistic; **n.** nihilist
depreciation of or opposition to: **n.** anti-intellectualism; obscurantism; **a.** obscurant(ic)
ground of: **n.** ratio cognoscendi
having great or infinite: **a.** bibliognostic; encyclopedic(al); omniscent; pansophic(al); **n.** encyclopedism; omniscence; pansophism; **n.** bibliognost; pansophist; virtuoso
great or penetrating: **n.** profundity; **a.** encyclopedic(al)
half-: **n.** demi-savoir
imparting: (**see** "teaching") **a.** informative; instructive; tutorial
impossibility of arriving at certain: **n.** acatelepsy; **a.** acataleptic
instinctive: (**see** "intuition") **n.** Anschauung; cognition; *savoir-faire;* **a.** cognitive; intuitive
intellectually certain: **n.** episteme; **a.** epistemic; epistemological
investigation or study of nature of: **n.** epistemology; gnosology
lack of: **n.** ignoration; inscience; nescience
love of: **n.** epistemophilia; philomathy
method, means or agency of communicating: **n.** organon
one interested in pursuit of: **n.** co(g)-noscente; illuminato; savant; virtuoso
possessing great or extensive: **a.** (en)cyclopedic(al); omniscient; pansophic(al)
preliminary: **n.** foreknowledge; praecognitum; precognition
private or secret bet. two persons: **n.** privity; **a.** à deux

process of: **n.** cognition; **a.** cognitional; cognitive

rel. or pert. to: **a.** cognitional; cognitive; epistemonic(al); gnostic; sciental

sacred, body of: **n.** hierology; **a.** hierologic(al); **n.** hierologist

secret or mysterious: **n.** arcanum; (**pl.** arcana); **a.** arcane

show of: **n.** didacticism; pedantry; sciolism; **a.** pedantic; sciolistic; sciolous

study or theory of: **n.** epistemology; gnosology; **a.** epistemonic(al)

superficial: **n.** sciolism; **a.** sciolistic; sciolous; **n.** sciolist

theory of: **n.** epistemology; gnosology; **a.** epistemonic(al)

universal, or system embracing all: **n.** pansophism; pansophy; **a.** pansophic(al)

useful, pert. to: **a.** chrestomathic(al)

L

L, *excessive use of letter, as in stuttering:* **n.** lallation; lambdacism

LABOR, *characterized by great:* (**see** "laborious") **a.** Herculean; yeoman
conquers all: labor omnia vincit convict, system of: **n.** peonage
the palm is not gained w/o (labor): palma non sine pulvere

LABORIOUS: **a.** arduous; Herculean; industrious; onerous; operose; slavish; toilsome; yeoman; **n.** LABORIOUSNESS: operosity
very (unending toil): **a.** Sisyphean

LABORIOUSLY *study, etc.:* **v.** lucubrate; **n.** lucubration

LACKING: **a.** desiderative; deficient; devoid; exiguous; insufficient; **n.** LACK: (**see** "deficiency") dearth; deficiency; desideratum; desiderium; (**pl.** desideria); exigency; exiguity; famine; inadequacy; insufficiency; requirement
in factual or historical basis; **a.** fictional; mythologic(al)

LADY: **n.** domina; donna
beautiful: **n.** belle dame
beautiful w/o mercy: **n.** la belle dame sans merci
great or aristocratic: **n.** grande dame
young: **n.** damsel; demoiselle; ingenue; jeune fille

LAKES, *pert. to or found in:* **a.** lacustral; lacustrine
situated bet.: **a.** interlacustrine

LAMB, *as gentle as a:* **n.** doux comme un agneau
of God: **n.** agnus Dei

LAME: **a.** claudicant; halting; maimed; spavined; **n.** claudication

LAMENT: (**see** "bewail") **v.** deplore; elegize; **n.** elegy; epicede; epicedium; threnody; **a.** LAMENTABLE: deplorable; despicable; doleful; grievous; lachrymose; mournful; plaintive; plangorous; sorrowful; **n.** LAMENTATION: (**see** "complaint") epicedium; lachrymation; languishment

LAND: (**see** "earth") **n.** domain; dominion; terrain
and water, consisting of both: **a.** amphibian; terraqueous; **n.** amphibian
area: **n.** terrain; terrene; topography
doctrine of equitable distribution: **n.** agrarianism
living or growing on or in: **a.** terrestrial; terricolous
native, pert. to: **a.** compatriotic; patrial
of one's birth: **n.** natale solum
promised: **n.** (land of) Canaan
rel. to: **a.** agrarian; terrene
take for public use: **v.** expropriate; sequester; **n.** eminent domain; expropriation; sequestration

LANDHOLDING, *vast or extensive:* **n.** barony

LANDMARK: **n.** cairn

LANDSCAPE: **n.** panorama; paysage; scenery; terrain; topography

LANGUAGE(S): **n.** idiom; parlance; tongue; vernacular
abusive: **n.** billingsgate; invective; scurrility; vituperation; **a.** scurrilous; vituperative
affectation in: **n.** preciosity
ambiguity in: **n.** amphibology; circumlocution; **a.** amphibological; amphibolous; circumlocutious
artificial, affected, or excessive elegance of: **n.** ephuism; preciosity; **a.** euphuistic(al); phraseological

181

careful in lit. style: **a.** Addisonian; stylistic
characteristic of a particular: **a.** idiomatic; provincial
characterized by mixture of: **a.** macaronic; **n.** Babelism
clear and polished: **a.** Addisonian
clear in: **a.** explicit; limpid; unambiguous; uncryptic; unequivocal
common, or functioning as (signs, etc.): **n.** *lingua franca*
common, ordinary, local or native: **n.** patois; vernacular(ism); vernacularity; vulgate
confused: (see "jargon") **n.** Babelization; Babelism
confusion of: **n.** Babelism; polyglot
containing several: **a.** polyglot; polylingual
deceptive: **n.** flummery
expert in: see "linguist"
familiar w/ or using but one: **a.** monoglot; monolingual
familiar w/ or using two or more: **a.** bilingual (*two*); polyglot; polylingual
figurative: **n.** tropology
foolish: **n.** balderdash; flatulence; flummery; gasconade; gibberish; jaberwock(y); kompology; lallation; **a.** jargonistic; **v.** jargonize
having same: **a.** colingual
high-sounding and usu. unimportant: **a.** bombastic; euphuistic; grandiloquent; rhapsodic; rubescent; **n.** bombast; grandiloquent; rubescence
in plain: **adv. or a.** *en clair;* **adv.** *nudis verbis*
incorrect use of: **n.** abusage
informal or conversational: **n.** colloquialism; vernacular; **a.** colloquial; vernacular
knowledge of: **n.** linguistry; philology
international: see "universal" **below**
living: **n.** vernacular
native: (see "regional or local" **below**) **a. or n.** vernacular; **n.** patois
nonsense: see "foolish" **above**
obscene, uncontrollable or excessive use of: **n.** coprolalia
of criminals: **n.** argot
preciseness or over-preciseness of: **n.** preciosity; purism; **n.** precieuse; purist
regional or local: **a. or n.** vernacular; **n.** colloquialism; dialect; dialectalism; koine; patois; villagism; **a.** dialectal
rel. to: **a.** glottological; lingual; linguistic; phonetic
rel. to origin of: **a.** dialectic; glottogonic; lingual(istic); vernacular

science of: **n.** glottology; linguistics; philology
sign: **n.** dactylology; *lingua franca*
smallest unit of: **n.** glosseme
speaking in unknown or imaginary: **n.** glossolalia
speaking one: **a.** monoglot; monolingual
speaking or pert. to two: **a.** bilingual; **n.** bilingualism; bilinguality
speaking or pert. to several: **a.** multilingual; polyglot; polylingual
specialist in: see "linguist"
specialist in English: **n.** anglicist
study of: **n.** glottology; linguistics; linguistry
study of English: **n.pl.** anglistics
universal: **n.** esperanto; pasigraphy
use of substandard: **n.** barbarism; vernacularism; vernacularity; vulgarism

LAPEL *flower(s):* **n.** boutonniere

LAPSE: (see "pause") **n.** apostasy; backslide; caudicity; declination; decline
as of memory: **n.** parapraxia; parapraxis

LARD, *of or like:* **a.** amyloid; lardaceous; oleaginous

LARGE: (see "huge") **a.** abundant; capacious; comprehensive; copious; formidable; generous; grandiose; immeasurable; lavish; magnitudinous; monstrous; portentous; prodigal; spacious; **n.** LARGENESS: colossality; comprehensiveness; grandiosity; immensity; magnitude; massivity; monumentality; vastity; voluminosity
and ornate: **a.** baronial; magnificent; palatial
fantastically: **a.** Bunyanesque
in body: **a.** macrosomatic; macrosomatous; **n.** macrosomatic
number: **n.** hecatomb; legion; multitude; spate

LASSITUDE: (see "laziness") **n.** adynamia; enervation; ennui; hypokinesia; lackadaisy; languor; lethargy; listlessness; weariness; **a.** LASSITUDINOUS: adynamic; comatose; hypokinesic; lackadaisic(al); languorous; lethargic

LAST: (see "final" and "endure") **v.** abide; perdure; **a.** conclusive; concluding; definitive; dernier; eventual; extreme; terminal; ultimate

at: **adv.** *ad extremum*
but one (next to last): **n.** penult; **a.** penultimate
but two: **n.** antepenult; **a.** antepenultimate
degree: **adv.** *ad extremum*
resort: **n.** *dernier ressort; pis aller; ultima ratio*
word (most modern): **n.** *dernier cri;* ultimate

LASTING: (see "eternal") **a.** abiding; boundless; diuturnal; indelible; indissoluble; inefaceable; interminable; perseverant; pertinacious; protracted; unceasing; **n.** diuturnity; indissolubility; perpetuality; perpetuity; pertinacity
indefinitely: **a.** aeonian; in perpetuity

LASTLY: **adv.** *en fin*

LATE: (see "recent") **a.** advanced; dilatory; procrastinative; procrastinatory; neoteric; **n.** LATENESS: eleventh hour; **a.** LATER: (see "after") posterior; subsequent; succedent

LATENT: **a.** abeyant; delitescent; dormant; inactive; potential; quiescent; sessile; **n.** LATENCY: (see "possibility") deliquescence; dormancy; incubation; potentiality; quiescence; quietude

LATEST *fashion, or most authoritative thing:* **n.** *dernier cri*

LATIN, *of or pert. to:* **a.** Latinian; Latinic; **n.** Latinism; Latinity; latinization

LAUD: **v.** acclaim; applaud; approbate; commend; deify; extol; felicitate; macarize; panegyrize; **a.** LAUDABLE (or LAUDATORY): commendatory; encomiastic; eulogistic; panegyrical; praiseworthy; **n.** LAUDATION: approbation; commendation; deification; encomium; eulogy; extolment; panegyric

LAUGH: **v.** cachinnate; ridicule; **n.** cachinnation
able to or inclined to: **a.** risible; **n.** risibility

LAUGHABLE: (see "funny") **a.** cachinnatory; farcical; ludicrous; mirthful; *pour rire;* riant; ridiculous; risible
yet serious: **a.** ludicropathetic; ludicroserious

LAUGHTER: **n.** cachinnation; **risibility**
causing or pert. to: **a.** gelastic; gelogenic; risible; **n.** risibility
given to: **a.** Abderian
inextinguishable: **n.** *asbestos gelos*
loud or unrestrained: **n.** cachinnation; **a.** cachinnatory
sarcastic: **n.** irrision
to excite: **v.** *pour faire rire*

LAVISH: **v.** squander; **a.** affluent; Babylonian; Babylonic; exorbitant; extravagant; exuberant; improvident; inordinate; Lucullan; luxurious; magnificent; opulent; prodigal; profuse; (super)abundant; sumptuous; unstinted; **n.** LAVISHNESS: (see "abundance") affluence; affluency; extravagance; exuberance; magnificence; opulence; opulency; prodigality; sumptuosity

LAW(S): **n.** canon; code; command(ment); covenant; enactment; formula; jurisprudence; legislation; mandate; ordinance; precept; procedure; regulation; statute
according to: **adv.** *secundum legem;* **a.** nomological
based on: **a.** *de jure;* nomothetic
basic: **n.** constitution; decalogue; *Magna C(h)arta*
by reason or by operation of: **a.** *ipso jure*
by right of: **a.** *de jure*
civil order under good: **n.** eunomy
common: see "unwritten" **below**
conformity to: **n.** dharma; legitimation
digest of: **n.** *corpus juris;* pandect
divine: **n.** *jus divinum; jus ecclesiasticum*
divine, by: **adv.** *jure divino*
exact: **n.** *strictum jus; summum jus*
-giver: **n.** Solon; thesmothete
govt. founded on system of: **n.** nomocracy
having no standing in (w/o legal effect or validity): **a.** invalid; *nullius juris*
human, by: **adv.** *jure humano*
international: **n.** *jus gentium; jus inter gentes*
letter of (strict): **n.** *strictum jus (or ius);* **adv.** *stricti(ssimi) juris*
-maker: see "-giver" **above**
moral: **n.** dharma
natural: **n.** *jus naturae; jus naturale*
of marriage: **n.** *jus con(n)ubii*
of nations: see "international" **above**
of organic life: **n.** organonomy
of place or locality: **n.** *lex loci*

of retaliation: n. *lex talions*
of the land: n. *lex terrae*
pert. to or in accordance w/: a. judicatory; juridical; juristic; nomological
public: n. *jus publicum*
regulating habits (moral or religious grounds): n. sumptuary (law); a. sumptuary
science or system of: n. jurisprudence
spirit of the: n. *mens legis*
strict: see under "letter of" above
under color of: adv. *sub colore juris*
unwritten or common: n. *jus commune; lex non scripta*
written or statute: n. *jus scriptum*

LAWFUL: (see "legal") a. authorized; canonical; constitutional; legitimate; permitted; rightful; adv. *de jure;* n. LAWFULNESS: see "legality"

LAWLESS: (see "unrestrained") a. anarchic; anomalous; contumacious; Dionysian; disobedient; insubordinate; insurgent; mutinous; piratical; recalcitrant; recusant; refractory; riotous; seditious; transgressive; unbounded; ungoverned; unlicensed

LAWMAKING *or drafting:* n. nomography; nomology

LAWSUIT(S), *given to carrying on:* a. litigious
in action or pending: adv. *pendente lite*

LAWYER: (see "advocate") n. attorney; barrister; counselor
pert. to: a. advocatory; barristerial
woman: n. Portia

LAX: (see "remiss") a. immoral; undutiful; unobservant; unprincipled

LAYER: n. hierarchization; lamina; stratification; stratum; a. LAYERED: laminal; laminar; laminated; stratal; stratified; superimposed

LAYMAN: n. esoteric; (pl. laity)

LAZY: a. comatose; dilatory; faineant; hebetudinous; hypnotic; indolent; inertial; lackadaisical; languid; lethargic; oscitant; otiose; remiss; slothful; sluggish; somniferous; spiritless; torpescent; torpid; unenterprising; n. LAZINESS: (see "sloth") faineancy; *fainéantise;* inanition;

inertia; indolence; lackadaisy; lassitude; lethargy; oscitancy; otiosity; remission; sluggishness; supinity; torpidity
an idle person: n. faineant

LEACH: v. lixiviate; n. lixiviation; a. lixivious

LEAD, *containing or producing:* a. plumbiferous
having color of: a. plumbeous

LEADER(S): (see "guide") n. archimandrite; bellwether; chairman; conductor; executive; governor; hierophant; maestro; pacemaker; premier; president; primate; protagonist; speaker; spokesman; wheelhorse; n. LEADERSHIP: aegis; authority; chieftainry; command
masterful and potent: n. mogul; tycoon
military, or w/ mil. following: n. caudillo
of a chorus: n. choragus; choregus; coryphaeus
of a school, as painting, music, writing, etc.: n. *chef d'école*
of a group or body: n. dean; doyen; (fem. doyenne)
of thought, taste, or opn.: n. *avant-garde;* connoisseur; vanguard
politics: n. sachem
sect: n. coryph(a)eus; hierarch; a. hierarchic(al)
tending to follow any: a. sequacious; n. sequacity
without a: a. acephalic; acephalous

LEADING: (see "chief") a. enlightened; foremost; principal; salient; signal; stellar
act of: n. manuduction; a. manuductive; manuductory
"-light": n. luminary
position in a movement, etc., also those leading: n. *avant-garde;* vanguard

LEAGUE: (see "association") n. alliance; amalgamation; coalition; confederation; entente

LEAN: a. angular; attenuated; deficient; emaciated; infertile; macilent; tabescent; unproductive; unremunerative; n. LEANNESS: angularity; emaciation; macilency; tabescence

LEANING: (see "tendency") n. conatus; flair; partiality; penchant; predilection; (pre)disposition; prejudice; propensity; susceptibility; a. inclinatory; tendentious

LEAP(S): **n.** catapault; gambade; gambado; gambol; saltation
   proceeding by: **a.** saltatory
   -year: **n.** bisextile (year)

LEAPING: **a.** capering; saltant; saltatorial; saltatorian; saltatory; subsultory; subsultive
   adapted for or rel. to: **a.** saltatorial

LEARN: **v.** acquire; ascertain; memorize
   all from one: **adv.** *ab uno disce omnes*
   by intuition: **v.** *intuit*

LEARNED: (**see** "educated") **a.** academic; Aristotelian; enlightened; erudite; lettered; literate; omniscient; pansophic; philomatic(al); polymathic(al); profound; scholarly
   affectedly: **a.** bookish; pedantic; pansophist
   exhaustedly: **a.** omniscient; pansophic(al); **n.** omniscience; pansophism; pansophy
   person: **see under** "person"
   world, the: **n.** *le monde savant*

LEARNER: (**see** "beginner") **n.** abecedarian; alphabetarian; apprentice; catechumen; inceptor; novice; novitiate; probationer; trainee; understudy
   who begins late in life: **n.** *opsimath*

LEARNING: (**see** "knowledge") **n.** culture; enlightenment; erudition; omniscience; philology; sapience; scholarship; schoolcraft
   encyclopedic: **n.** polymath(y): **a.** polyhistoric; polymathic(al); **n.** polyhistor(ian)
   given to excess: **a.** intellectualistic; **n.** intellectualism; intellectualist; rationalism
   helping, serving or guiding in: **a.** heuristic
   hostility to: **n.** anti-intellectualism; anti-intellectualist
   lover or love of: **n.** intellectualist; intellectualism; philologist; philomath(y); **a.** philomathic(al)
   man of great: **see** "person, learned"
   one of encyclopedic: **n.** polyhistor(ian); polymath
   one who parades: **n.** pedant; sciolist; **a.** pedantic; sciolistic; sciolous; **n.** pedanticism; pedantry; sciolism
   period of: **n.** apprenticeship; catecumnenate; novitiate
   person of great: **see** "person, learned"

pert. to: **a.** erudite; palladian
   pretender to: **n.** pedant; sciolist; **a.** pedantic; sciolistic; sciolous
   show of: **n.** didacticism: intellectuality; pedanticism; pedantry; sciolism
   useful, pert. to: **a.** chrestomathic(al)

LEATHER, *pert. to* (*leathery*): **a.** coriaceous

LEAVE, *by your:* **adv.** *pace tua*
   for travel, education, etc.: **n.** sabbatical; shemittah; **a.** sabbatical
   -taking: (**see** "goodbye") **n.** adieu; *congé;* devoir; valediction; **a.** valedictory

LEAVES, *feeding on:* **a.** phyllophagic; phyllophagous
   shedding: **a.** deciduous
   to strip off: **v.** defoliate; **n.** defoliation

LECHEROUS: **see** "lustful"

LECTURE: (**see** "discussion") **n.** castigation; colloquium; colloquy; discourse; disquisition; dissertation; dressing-down; excursus; homily; reprimand; reproof; riotact; symposium; treatise; **v.** castigate; reprimand; reprove; sermonize; **n.** LECTURER: (**see** "speaker") *conférencier*
   pert. to: **a.** admonitory; castigatory; disquisitional; dissertative; homiletic

LEFT: **a.** larboard; port; sinistral
   hand: **n.** *mano sinistra;* minor hand
   handed but trained to use right hand in writing: **a.** dextrosinistral
   -handedness: **n.** maneinism; sinistrality; **a.** sinistral; sinistromanual
   toward or on the: **a.** gauche; sinister; sinistrad; sinistral
   turning to: **a.** levogyrate; levogyre; levorota(to)ry; **n.** levogyration; levorotation

LEG(S), *front of the:* **n.** antecnemion
   having long: **a. or n.** macropod; **a.** macropodal
   having short: **a.** brachyskelic; brachyskelous
   lower portion of: **n.** cnemis; tibia
   rel. to: **a.** crural; femoral
   upper portion of: **n.** femur

LEGAL: **a.** authorized; constitutional; *de jure;* juridical; juristic; justifiable; lawful; legitimate; licit; official; permissive;

permitted; statutory; warrantable; **n.**
LEGALITY: legitimacy, lawfulness
　capacity, power or jurisdiction: **n.** competence
　effect, w/o: **a.** nugatory; null and void; **n.** *nullius juris*
　ineligibility or incompetency: **n.** incapacity; incompetency; *non compos (mentis)* **a.** *doli incapax;* incompetent; *non compos (mentis)*
　it is: **n.** licit
　person: **n.** *homo legalis*

LEGALLY *competent:* **a.** *capax negotii; compos mentis; doli capax; sui juris*
　incompetent: **see under** "legal"

LEGENDARY: **a.** aprocryphal; fabulous; fictitious; mythical; mythological; traditional; tralatitious; unwritten

LEGIBLE: **a.** comprehensible; decipherable; scrutable; understandable

LEGITIMATE: **see** "legal"

LEISURE, *at:* **a.** otiose; **adv.** *en retraite;* **n.** otiosity
　breeds vice: otia dant vitia

LENGTH, *at:* **a. or adv.** *in extenso*
　pert. to: **a.** longitudinal
　speak or write at: **v.** expatiate; **n.** expatiation

LENGTHEN: **v.** elongate; expand; extend; prolong; protract; **a.** LENGTHENING: protractive; **n.** protraction; **a.** LENGTHWISE: longitudinal

LEOPARD, *pert. to or resembling:* **a.** pardine

LESS: *so much the: quoad minus*
　than required: **a.** submarginal; subminimal; subnormal; suboptional; substandard

LESSEN: (**see** "decrease") **v.** abbreviate; adulterate; alleviate; attenuate; demote; depreciate; disparage; extenuate; minify; mitigate; mollify; palliate; temper
　repute or esteem of: **v.** decry; degrade; denigrate; derogate; disparage; minify; pejorate; **n.** degradation; denigration; derogation; disparagement; pejoration; **a.** degradative; denigratory; derogative; derogatory
　seriousness of: **v.** dulcify; extenuate; minify; mitigate; mollify; palliate

LESSENING: (**see** "reduction") **n.** abatement; attenuation; decrescendo; demotion; diminution; diminuendo; extenuation; mitigation; mollification; palliation; **a.** ablatitious; alleviatory; decrescent; extenuative; palliative; palliatory; subtractive
　of virulence: **n.** attenuation

LETHARGY: (**see** "lassitude" **and** "laziness") **n.** apathy; lassitude; **a.** LETHARGIC: **see** "slow"

LETTER(S), *devotion to or worship of:* **n.** grammatolatry
　-for-letter: **a.** literally; literatim; verbatim; **n.** literality
　-for-letter and word-for-word: **adv.** *literatim et verbatim*
　men of: **n.pl.** *gens de lettres; hommes de lettres*
　observing the, rather than spirit: **a.** formal; hypocritical; pharisaic(al); ritualistic
　of credit: **n.** *lettre de créance*
　opening of: **n.** salutation; superscription
　person of: **n.** *homme de lettres; littérateur; litterato; litteratus;* (**pl.** *gens de lettres; hommes de lettres; intelligentsia; literati*)
　pert. to: **a.** epistolary
　representing diff. sounds in diff. words: **n.** heterography
　transposition of, as in reading or writing: **n.** metathesis; strephosymbolia
　-writer: **n.** epistolarian; **a.** epistolary
　-writing, practice or art of: **n.** epistolography; **a.** epistolary

LEVEL: **n.** echelon; plateau; **a.** balanced; equipotential; horizontal; planate; unexcited; uniform; **n.** horizontality

LEWD: **a.** Anacreontic; aphrodisiac; carnal; concupiscent; concupiscible; cyprian; debauched; depraved; dissolute; ithyphallic; lascivious; lecherous; libidinous; licentious; lubricious; lustful; obliquitous; obscene; pornographic; profligate; prurient; salacious; satyric; scrofulous; sensual; venereal; venereous; wanton; **n.**
LEWDNESS: amorosity; carnality; concupiscence; debauchery; depravity; impudicity; lasciviency; lasciviousness; lechery; libidinousness; lubricity; obliquity; obscenity; profligacy; pruriency; salacity; sensuality; wantonness
　person: **see** "libertine"

LIABILITY: **n.** drawback; likelihood; obligation; obnoxiety; responsibility

LIAR: **n.** Ananias; fabricator; fabulist; prevaricator; pseudologist; pseudologue
consummate: **n.** *menteur à triple étage*
pathological: **n.** pseudologue
should have good memory: mendacem memorem esse oportet

LIBEL (**see** "defame") **n.** aspersion; calumny; defamation; lampoon; satire; slander; **a.** LIBELOUS: calumnious; defamatory; slanderous

LIBERAL: **a.** abundant; bounteous; bountiful; copious; generous; hospitable; knowledg(e)able; latitudinarian; lavish; magnanimous; munificent; philanthropic; prodigal; **n.** latitudinarian; philanthropist; Young Turk; **n.** LIBERALITY: copiosity; generosity; hospitality; munificence; openhandedness; philanthropy

LIBERATE: **see** "free"; **n.** LIBERATOR: emancipator; manumitter; Messiah; redeemer; redemptor; (**fem.** redemptrix); **a.** messianic

LIBERTINE: **n.** cyprian; debauchee; lecher; paillard; profligate; sensualist; satyr; thelemite; voluptuary
state of being: **n.** debauchery; lechery; libertinage; profligacy; sensuality

LIBERTY, *destruction or destroyer of:* **a.** or **n.** liberticide

LIBRARY: **n.** athenaeum; atheneum; bibliotheca; *bibliothèque;* **n.** LIBRARIAN: *bibliothécaire; bibliothecarian*

LICE, *pert. to or infected w/:* **a.** pedicular; pediculous; verminous; **n.** pediculosis

LICENSE: (**see** "unrestraint") **n.** franchise; privilege; licentiousness
poetic: **n.** *licientia vatum*
to publish or print (under censorship): **n.** imprimatur

LIE: (**see** "falsehood") **v.** equivocate; fabricate; fabulate; prevaricate; tergiversate; **n.** (**see** "liar") canard; equivocation; exaggeration; fabrication; fabulation; hyperbole; inveracity; mendacity; prevarication; pseudology; roorback; tergiversation; **a.** prevaricative; tergiversatory

abnormal tendency to: **n.** mythomania; pseudology
pathological or exaggerated: **n.** Munchausenism; pseudology

LIEN: **n.** encumbrance; hypothecation; mortgage

LIFE: (**see** "biography") **n.** animation; spirit; vitality; vivaciousness; vivacity
absence of: (**see** "death") **n.** abiosis; defunction; **a.** abiotic
centering in or on: **a.** bio-centric; **n.** bio-centrist
cycle, single organism: **n.** ontogeny; **a.** ontological
development fr. preexisting: **n.** biogenesis; biogeny; **a.** biogenic; biogenous
during: **adv.** *durante vita; intra vitam*
force: **n.** *anima mundi; élan vital;* mana
full of: **see** "lively"
generating of: **n.** (bio)genesis; **a.** biogenetic(al); biogenous
history: **see** "biography"
long or great span of: **n.** longevity; macrobiosis; **a.** macrobian; macrobiotic
necessity of: (**see** "food") **n.** aliment; **a.** alimental; alimentary
organic, law of: **n.** organonomy
philosophy of: **n.** ideology; weltanschauung
prime of: **n.** *fleur de l'âge*
prolonging, art of: **n.** macrobiotics
process: **n.** anabolism; **a.** anabolic
producing: **n.** (bio)genesis; **a.** biogenetic(al); biogenous
return to: **n.** anabiosis; resurrection; resuscitation; reviviscence
science and development: **n.** biology; **a.** biologic(al)
scientific investigation of: **n.** biognosis; (**pl.** biognoses)
such is: c'est la vie; sic eunt fata hominum
vigor of: **n.** *élan vital; vis vitae*
way of: **n.** *modus vivendi*
weariness of: **n.** *taedium vitae*

LIFELESS: (**see** "spiritless") **a.** adenoid-(al); amort; apathetic; colorless; comatose; defunct; exanimate; inanimate; inert; insensible; insentient; insipid; lethargic; quiescent; torpid; unconscious; unresponsive; vapid; **n.** LIFELESSNESS: defunction; immobility; insentience; insipidity; quiescence; quietude; torpidity; vapidity

LIGHT: (**see** "easy") **a.** diaphanous; ethereal; imponderous; inconsiderable; luminary; luminiferous; luminous; weightless; **n.** fluorescence; illumination; incandescence; luminary; luminescence; luminosity; phosphorescence; scintillation
   abnormal fear of or sensitivity to: **n.** photophobia; **a.** photophobic
   (*airy*), *as in mus. dir.:* **a.** sfogato
   and brilliant: **a.** lambent; scintillating; scintillescent; **n.** lambency; scintillescence; **v.** scintillate
   and shade (*as in painting*), *interplay of:* **n.** chiaroscuro
   avoiding: **a.** lucifugal; lucifugous; photophobic
   impervious to: **a.** opaque; **n.** opacity
   let there be: **adv.** fiat lux
   movement in response to: **n.** photokinesis; tropism; **a.** photokinetic
   of the world: **n.** lux mundi
   producing or giving off: **n.** illuminant; incandescence; luminosity; **a.** incandescent; lucific; luminescent; luminiferous; luminous; phosphorescent; photogenic
   reflected, pert. to: **a.** catoptric(al)
   requiring abundant: **a.** photophilic; photophilous
   science of: **n.** actinology; catoptrics; optics; photics
   sensitivity to: **n.** photophobia; **a.** photophobic
   spirit of: **n.** Ormuzd
   thriving in or loving: **a.** photophilic; photophilous
   treatment by use of: **n.** actinotherapy; heliotherapy

LIGHTHEARTEDNESS: **n.** blitheness; buoyancy; ebullience; euphoria; jauntiness; nonchalance; sprightliness

LIGHTNING, *abnormal fear of:* **n.** astrophobia
   of or like: **a.** fulgurant; fulgurous; fulmin(e)ous
   strikes highest peaks: feriuntque summos fulgura montes

LIKABLE: **a.** appealing; attractive; comely; contential; personable; simpatico; sympathetic; **n.** LIKABLENESS: likability

LIKE: (**see** "akin" **and** "similar") **v.** esteem; relish
   delights in like: similis simili gaudet

LIKELY: (**see** "possible") **a.** apparent; conjectural; credible; ostensible; plausible; presumable; presumptive; probable; *prima facie;* promising; specious; verisimilar; *vraisemblable;* **n.** LIKELIHOOD: liability; probability; speciosity; verisimilitude; verisimility; *vraisemblance*

LIKENESS: (**see** "image") **n.** analogy; counterpart; equivalence; facsimile; parity; (re)semblance; similarity; similitude
   bad or ludicrous: **n.** caricature
   or affinity of nature: **n.** assonance
   rough: **n.** assonance, caricature

LIKING: **n.** diathesis; gusto; inclination; penchant; predilection; preference; propensity; relish
   preconceived: **n.** inclination; predilection; predisposition; prejudice; propensity
   strong: **n.** penchant

LIMBER: (**see** "pliant") **a.** flaccid; gracile; lissom(e); lithe(some); **n.** flaccidity; lissomeness; lithesomeness

LIMBS, *having those adapted to grasping:* **a.** prehensile
   having those adapted to running: **a.** cursorial

LIMIT(S): (**see** "confine") **v.** circumscribe; demarcate; discriminate; regulate; **n.** boundary; circumscription; demarcation; restriction; solstice; terminus; (**pl.** confines; purlieus); **a.** LIMITED (**or** LIMITING): adjectival; adjective; circumscribed; cloistral; confined; confining; demarcative; denominational; finite; parochial; prescribed; provincial; qualificatory; restrictive; sectarian
   established: **n.pl.** metes and bounds
   without: **adv.** ad infinitum; **a.** inexhaustible; infinite; limitless; **n.** infinitude; infinity

LIMITATION: (**see** "limit") **n.** circumscription; delimitation; finitude; restriction
   of debate: **n.** clôture

LIMITLESS: (**see** "unrestrained") **a.** boundless; uncircumscribed; unmeasured

LIMP: **a.** flaccid, spiritless; **n.** claudication; flaccidity; **a.** LIMPING: claudicant; **n.** claudication

LINE(S), *formation in, or series:* **n.** collineation; echelon; regimentation
in straight: **a.** (col)linear; **n.** .collineation; linearity
marked with: **a.** linear(istic); lineate; **n.** lineation
of action: **n.** demarche; maneuver
of or rel. to a: **a.** lineal; linear
situated bet.: **a.** interlineal; interlinear; **v.** interlineate; **n.** interlineation

LINEAGE: (**see** "derivation" **and** "descent") **n.** ancestry; background; genealogy; heredity; pedigree; stemma

LINGUIST: **n.** glottologist; linguistician; philologist; **a.** glottological; linguistic(al); philologic(al)

LINIMENT: **n.** embrocation; linimentum

LINK: (**see** "join") **v.** (con)catenate; interlock; **n.** catena; concatenation; juncture; liaison; nexus; suture; vinculum; **a.** LINKED: (**see** "joined") concatenate; intercatenated

LION, *characteristic of or resembling:* **a.** leonine
fr. the claw one may recognize the: ex ungue leonem

LIP(S): **n.** labium; (**pl.** labia); **a.** labial
biting of: **n.** cheilophagia
having large: **a.** macrocheilous; **n.** macrocheilia
moving as in speech or singing but w/o sound: **n.** mussitation
produce sound by: **v.** labialize; phonate

LIQUID, *becoming:* **a.** liquescent
reduce to: **v.** liquefy; **n.** liquefaction

LIST(S): **n.** agendum; (**pl.** agenda); catalog(ue); enumeration; inventory; repertory; tariff; **a.** catalogical
of banned books, etc.: **see under** "books"

LISTENING: **a.** acousmatic; audient

LISTLESS: (**see** "lazy") **a.** comatose; dilatory; dispirited; enervated; inattentive; lackadaisical; lackluster; languid; languorous; lethargic; spiritless; supine; vacuous; **n.** LISTLESSNESS: abiotrophy; apathy; lackadaisy; languor; lassitude; lethargy; otiosity

LITANY: **n.** rogation; supplication

LITERAL: (**see** "word-for-word") **a.** categorical; exact; obvious; prosaic; textual; unimaginative; **adv.** LITERALLY: *à la lettre; au pied de la lettre;* explicitly; virtually; **n.** LITERALITY: exactitude; grammatolatry; prosaism

LITERARY: (**see** "bookish") **a.** erudite; scholarly
adaptation: **n.** rifacimento
attack: **n.** *coup de plume*
collection: **n.** anthology; chrestomathy; collectanea; *disjecta membra;* (**pl.** adversaria; analecta; collectanea; miscellanea); **a.** anthologized; **v.** anthologize
composition, short and reminiscent: **n.** feuilleton
crudity: **n.** gaucherie
excerpts or fragments: **see** "excerpts" **and** "collection" **above**
group or coterie: **n.** *cénacle*
ornamentation: **n.** asiaticism; floridity; grandiloquence; mandarinism; rubescence; **a.** mandarin
patron(age): **n.** Maecenas; Maecenasship; Maecenatism
person: **n.** belletrist; bellelettrist; *homme de lettres; litterateur; literato(r); literatus;* (**pl.** *gens de lettres; hommes de lettres; intelligentsia; literati*)
scraps, misc.: (**see** "collection" **above**) **n.pl.** ana; scrapiana
selected passages: **n.pl.** analecta; analects; collectanea; *morceaux choisis*
sketch: **n.** feuilleton
style, clear and polished: **a.** Addisonian
lofty: **n.** *la morgue littéraire*
ornate and complex: **see** "ornamentation" **above**
ornate, exaggerated or artificial: **n.** gongorism; lyricism; rubescence
popular: **n.** journalese
sublimity of: **a.** Miltonic
theft: **n.** piracy; plagiarism; **a.** piratical; plagiaristic; **v.** plagiarize
work, catering to popular taste: **n.** feuilleton; **n. or a.** journalese
chief: **see under** "chief"
closely imitating previous work: **n.** pastiche
containing two parts contrasting or matching each other: **n.** diptych
developing character fr. child to adulthood: **n.** entwicklungsroman
early development or spiritual education of main character: **n.** Bildungsroman

ornamental embellishment or accessory to: **n.** paregon; **(pl.** parega)
prelim, or introductory: **n.** prodromus; prologue
w/ notes by diff. persons, or w/ variant readings of the text: **n. or a.** variorum
w/ real persons, events, etc. disguised: **n.** *roman à clef*

LITERATURE, *high-class:* **n.** *belles-lettres;* **a.** belletristic; **n.** belletrist; bellelettrist
lover of: **n.** belletrist; bellelettrist; literarian; philologist
morbid or scandalous creation in: **n.** *chronique scandaleuse; fleur du mal*
specialist in: **see** "literary person"
specialist in English: **n.** anglicist
study of: **n.** philology
substandard or sensational: **n.** kitsch
undue interest in: **n.** belletrism; belles-lettrism

LITHE: **see** "graceful"

LITIGATION, *rel. to:* **a.** litigious; *n.* litigiosity

LITTLE: **(see** "petty" **and** "small") **a.** contemptible; diminutive; exiguous; inconsiderable; lilliputian; microscopic; miniature; paltry; trifling; trivial
bit: **see** "in quantity" **below**
-by-little: **adv.** inchmeal; piecemeal; *petit à petit; peu à peu; poco a poco*
ever so (little): **adv.** *tant soit peu*
in quantity: **(see** "touch") **n.** modicum; moiety; *soupçon;* triviality; *un peu*
man: **n.** homunculus
minds are caught w/ trifles: parva leves capiunt animas
things befit little man: parvum parva decent

LIVE: **v.** dwell; reside; subsist; **a. see** "lively"; **n.** **(see** "life") viability
ability to (live) elegantly: **n.** *savoir vivre*
beings, bringing forth: **a.** parturient; proligerous; viviparous; **n.** parturition; viviparity
for the day: **n.** *carpe diem; in diem vivre; in horam vivere*
while we (live), let us (live): *dum vivimus, vivamus*

LIVELY: **(see** "sprightly") **a.** alacritous; animated; blithe; ebullient; effervescent;

exhilarative; exuberant; fervent; fervid; frolicksome; impassioned; intense; light-hearted; piquant; spirited; spiritous; vehement; vigorous; vital; vivacious; volatile; **n.** LIVELINESS: **(see** "animation") ebullience; effervescence; exhilaration; intoxication; invigoration; sprightliness; vivacity
in music: **a.** *animo; capricio; con brio*

LIVING *again:* **a.** redivivus; reincarnated; resurgent; resurrected; **n.** resurgence; resurrection
high and well, one who does: **n.** bonvivant; boulevardier; epicurean; flâneur; gastronome(r); gourmet; **a.** epicurean; sybaritic
manner of: **n.** *modus vivendi*
pledge: **n.** *vivum vadium*
things, produced from or inhabiting: **a.** biogenous
together: **a.** cohabiting; contubernal; **n.** cohabitation
dissimilar organisms where advantageous to both: **n.** symbionticism; symbiosis; **a.** symbiotic(al)

LOAD: **(see** "burden") **n.** encumbrance; impediment; incubus; ponderosity

LOAFER: **n.** chairwarmer; flaneur; loiterer; vagrant; **(pl.** flotsam and jetsam)

LOATH: **see** "indisposed"

LOATHE: **v.** abhor; abominate; anathematize; detest; execrate; **a.** LOATHING **(or** LOATHSOME): **(see** "hateful") abhorrent; abominable; anathematic(al); cloying; detestable; disgusting; odious; offensive; repugnant; unprincipled; **n.** abhorrence; abomination; antipathy; aversion; detestation; execration; *nausée;* odium; qualmishness; repugnance; repugnancy

LOCAL: **(see** "native") **a.** autochthonous; edaphic; parochial; peninsular; provincial; regional; sectional; topical; vicinal
as to country: **a.** enchorial
in viewpoint, customs, etc.: **n.** parochialism; peninsularity; provincialism

LOCALITY: **n.** locus; **(pl.** loci); milieu; purlieu; vicinage; vicinity

LODGING, *esp. temporary:* **n.** *pied-à-terre*

LOFTY: **(see** "high") **a.** altitudinous; celestial; divine; eminent; ethereal; **gran-**

diloquent; heavenly; magniloquent; Olympian; stately; supreme; supernal; towering
    thoughts, ideas, etc., or given to: **a. or n.** altitudinarian; **a.** spirituel(le)

LOGIC: **n.** *ars artium;* syntactics
    bad: **n.** sophism; sophistry; **a.** alogical; sophistical
    beyond scope of: **a.** metaphysical
    contrary to: (**see** "illogical") **n.** affirmation (**or** assertion) of the consequent; alogism; denial of the antecedent; dereism; formal fallacy; *ignoratio elenchi;* illicit process; paralogism; *petitio principii;* material fallacy; verbal fallacy; **a.** alogical; dereistic; paralogistic; sophistical
    specialist in: **n.** dialectician; logician

LOGICAL: (**see** "rational" **and** "reasonable") **a.** Aristotelian; Cartesian; cogent; coherent; consistent; dialectical; dianoetic
    argumentation: **n.** dialectic(s); **a.** dialectical
    result: **n.** consequence; logicality; **a.** consequential

LOITERER: (**see** "loafer") **n.** flaneur; vagrant

LONG: **v.** desiderate; hanker; languish; pine; yearn; **a.** (**see** "eternal") diuturnal; elongated; sempiternal; seven-league; **n.** diuturnity; sempiternity
    life: **n.** longanimity; longevity; macrobiosis; **a.** longanimous
    lived, also one who has lived long: **n. or a.** centenarian; macrobian; **a.** longevous
    story or account: **n.** iliad
    -winded: **a.** garrulous; loquacious; prolix; repetitious; verbose; **n.** garrulity; loquaciousness; loquacity; verbosity
    word(s): **see under** "word"

LONGING: (**see** "craving") **a.** appetent; appetitious; desiderative; **n.** appetency; appetite; appetition; desiderata; desideration
    ardent: **n.** desiderium; (**pl.** desideria)

LOOK(S): **n.** appearance; aspect; countenance; expression; mien; physiognomy; semblance; visage
    acquired fr. long custom or settled use: **n.** patina
    good: **n.** *beaux yeux*

LOOP, *shaped like:* **a.** ansiform

LOOSE: **a.** desultory; detached; disengaged; dissolute; licentious; rampant; unconnected; wanton

LOOSENING, *gradual, as in disease:* **n.** lysis
    of restraint: **n.** (re)laxation

LOPSIDED: (**see** "uneven") **a.** asymmetric(al); unsymmetric(al)

LORD: **n.** kyrios; (**also** kurios)
    be with you: Dominus vobiscum
    direct us: Domine dirige nos

LORDLY: (**see** "overbearing") **a.** archidiaconal; arrogant; dignified; honorable; honored; imperial; imperious; majestic; stately
    personage: **n.** magnifico
    style, in: **a.** baronial; *en grand seigneur*

LORDSHIP: **n.** domain; dominion; seigneury; seign(i)ory; sovereignty

LORE: **see** "learning"

LOSS: **n.** casualty; depreciation; (de)privation; destruction; detriment; diminution; disintegration; divestation; elimination; eradication; forfeiture; misfortune; perdition
    complete or irreparable: **n.** perdition; **a.** irretrievable

LOST, *likelihood or capability of being:* **n.** amissibility; **a.** amissible
    not capable of being: **a.** inamissible; **n.** inamissibility

LOT: **see** "fate"

LOTION: **n.** embrocation; emollient; liniment

LOTS, *act of casting:* **n.** sortition
    divination or prophecy by: **n.** cleromancy; sortilege

LOUD: **a.** blatant; clamorous; clangorous; forte; multivocal; ostentatious; stentorian; stentorious; tumultous; vociferous
    and abusive: **a.** scurrilous; thersitical
    and piercing: **a.** calliopean; stentorian; stentorious; stertorous
    moderately: **adv.** *mezzo-forte*

very: **a.** stentorian; stentorious; stentorophonic; (**mus.** forte; fortissimo)

LOUDNESS: **n.** amplitude; blatancy; magnitude; volume
   increasing in: **a. or n.** crescendo

LOUSY: **a.** pedicular; pediculous; verminous; **n.** pediculosis

LOUT: **n.** grobian; oaf; yokel

LOVE: **n.** affection; amorosity; amorousness; amour; benevolence; devotion; *la belle passion; la grande passion;* passion; tenderness
   affair: **n.** *affaire d'amour; affaire de coeur*
     esp. if secret or illicit: **n.** amour; intrigue; liaison; rendezvous; tryst
     passing: **n.** amourette; passade
     trifling or ephemeral, also woman involved: **n.** amourette
   conquers all: amor vincit omnia
   devotee of: **n.** amo(u)rist; gallant
   goddess of: **n.** Aphrodite; Venus
   great (also object of great): **n.** *grand(e) passion*
   illicit: **n.** amour; intrigue; liaison; rendezvous; **a.** Paphian; wanton
   in: **a.** amorous; enamored; infatuated
   -letter or note: **n.** *billet d'amour; billet doux*
   -making: **n.** amour(s); courtship
   natural: **n.** affection; storge
   non-sensual: **a.** Platonic; **a.** Platonism
   of country: **n.** *amor patriae*
   of friends or one's fellows: **n.** philia
   of offspring: see **under** "offspring"
   of possession: **n.** *amor habendi*
   of the dollar (money): **n.** *amor nummi;* plutolatry
   overcomes all things: omnia vincit amor; amor vincit omnia
   overwhelming (love) at first sight: **n.** *coup de foudre*
   passionately, to: **v.** *aimer éperdument*
   pledge of: **n.** *gage d'amour*
   renewal of: **n.** *redintegratio amoris*
   self-: **n.** *amour de soi; amour-propre;* autophilia; autotheism; egocentricity; ego-(t)ism; iotacism; narcissism; **a.** autotheistic(al); egocentric; narcissan; narcissistic; narcistic; **n.** autophiliac; egocentrist; narcissist
   to distraction, to: *aimer éperdument*
   writings about: **n.** amoristics

LOVER(S): **n.** amour; amo(u)rist; Casanova; cavalier; devotee; gallant; inamorato; Lothario; paramour; Romeo; servente; (**fem.** inamorata; paramour)
   are fools: amantes amentes
   daring or romantic: **n.** cavalier; Lochinvar
   of married man or woman: **n.** paramour
   of married woman: **n.** cicisbeo
   promiscuous and unscrupulous: **n.** Casanova

LOVING: (**see** "amative") **a.** affectionate; amatory; amorous; enamored; painstaking
   state of: **n.** amorosity; amorousness

LOW: (**see** "despondent" **and** "vulgar") **a.** contemptible; despicable; dishonorable; groveling; Hogarthian; ignoble; ignominious; leprous; plebeian; reptilian; vulgarian
   fellow: **n.** *polisson;* vulgarian
   state of being: **n.** contemptibility; despicability; ignobility; ignominy; vulgarity

LOWER: (**see** "debase") **a.** inferior; nether
   in status, esteem, character, quality, etc.: **v.** animalize; bastardize; deglamorize; degrade; dehumanize; demean; denigrate; derogate; devalorize; devaluate; disparage; humble; minify; minimize; pejorate; traduce; **n.** debasement; declension; deglamorization; degradation; demotion; denigration; minimization; pejoration; plebification; traduction
   morale of: **v.** debauch; demoralize; **n.** debauchment; demoralization
   to middle or intermediate position: **v.** mediatize
   world, of or rel. to: **a.** chthonian; plutonian; plutonic; subterranean

LOWERING *in social status or class:* (**see under** "lower") **a.** *déclassé;* declensional; declinatory

LOWEST: **a.** bathetic; nethermost
   point: **n.** bathos; nadir; perigee

LOWING (*as do cows*): **n. or a.** mugient

LOWLY: see "humble"

LOYAL: **a.** abiding; adhering; allegiant; faithful; obedient; tenacious; unswerving; yeomanly

follower: **n.** aficionado; devotee; janissary; mercenary; minion
in everything: loyal en tout

LOYALTY: **n.** allegiance; constancy; devotion; faithfulness; fealty; fidelity
among friends: **n.** *bonhom(m)ie; camaraderie; esprit de corps;* philia
in name or form only: **n.** lip service

LUCK, *bad:* **n.** ambsace; misfortune; **a. see** "unlucky"
good, charm for: **see** "charm"
pert. to: **a.** aleatory

LUCKY: (**see** "fortunate") **a.** auspicious; favorable; miraculous; providential; **adv.** *benigno numine*
day: **n.** *dies fa(u)stus*
find: **n.** *ben trovato;* serendipity; **a.** serendipitous

LUKEWARM, *esp. in religion:* **n. or a.** Laodicean
quality or state of being: **n.** tepidity

LULLABY: **n.** berceuse

LUMP: **n.** protuberance
in one: **a.** *en masse; en toto;* holusbolus
in throat: **n.** *globus hystericus*

LUNCH(EON): **n.** *déjeûner;* tiffin

LUNGE (*incl. verbal*): **n.** repartee; ripost(e)

LUNGS, *or chest, pert. to:* **a.** pectoral; pneumonic; pulmonic; respiratory; thoracic

LURE: (**see** "entice") **v.** inveigle; **n.** inveiglement

LUSH: see "luxuriant"

LUST: (**see** "lewdness") **n.** carnality; concupiscence; eagerness; enthusiasm; **a.** LUSTFUL: (**see** "lewd") lecherous; paphian; randy

LUXURIANT: (**see** "fertile") **a.** affluent; exuberant; florid; flourishing; inventive; opulent; plenteous; prodigal; profuse; proliferous; sumptuous; superabundant; uberous

LUXURIOUS: (**see** "lavish") **a.** Babylonian; baronial; Lucull(i)an; opulent; palatial; sumptuous; sybaritic; *voluptuaire;* voluptuous; voluptuary

LUXURY: **n.** affluence; extravagance; luxe; luxuriousness; princeliness; sensuality; *volupté;* voluptuosity; voluptuousness
one fond of: **see under** "pleasure"
take delight in: **v.** luxuriate; revel; voluptuate

LYING: **a.** equivocative; mendacious; prevaricative; tergiversatory
down: **a.** couchant; decubital; decumbent; incumbent; recumbent; supine; **n.** accumbency; deambulation; decubation; decubitus; decumbency; reclination; recumbency
down with head up: **a.** couchant
face down: **a.** procumbent; prone; prostrate
on back: **a.** decubital; supine; **n.** decubation; dorsal decubitus; reclination; recumbency; supinity

LYNX, *like or pert. to:* **a.** lyncean

M

MACHINE: **n.** apparatus; appliance; automaton; engine
God from a: **n.** *deus ex machinâ*
like a: **a.** automatous; mechanical; mechanomorphic; **n.** mechanicality
to make like: **v.** automate; automatize; dehumanize; mechanize; robotize

MAD: (**see** "angry") **a.** bedlamite; berserk; demented; distracted; furious; impetuous; lunatic; maniac(al); senseless; **n.** MADNESS: aberration; acharnement; deliration; delirium; derangement; ecstasy; fanaticism; hallucination; insanity; lunacy; mania; rashness
(*out of one's mind*): **a.** *acharné; aliéné;* berserk; demented; fey; maniac(al); psychotic
whom Jupiter wishes to destroy he first makes (mad): quem Juppiter vult perdere, dementat prius

MADMAN: **n.** bedlamite; maniac; noncompos; psychopath

MAGAZINE *or newspaper style of writing:* **n. or a.** journalese

MAGIC: abracadabra; alchemy; conjuration; conjury; diablerie; enchantment; gramary(e); incantation; legerdemain; necromancy; prestidigitation; sorcery; thaumaturgy; theurgy; witchcraft; witchery; wizardy; **a.** MAGICAL: alchemic(al); alchemistic(al); cabalistic; hermetic(al); incantatory; mystic; necromantic; numinous; phylacteric; recondite; sorcerous; talismanic(al)
black: **n.** necromancy
formula: **n.** alkahest
power (magical): **n.** alchemy
primitive, using image or likeness: **n.** *envoûtement*
spell or sorcery: **n.** alchemy; conjuration; incantation
symbol of: (**see** "charm") **n.** pentacle; pentagram; talisman
word: **n.** abracadabra; abraxis; presto

MAGICIAN: **n.** conjurer; enchanter; magus; (**pl.** magi); necromancer; prestidigitator; shaman; sorcerer; soothsayer; thaumaturge; thaumaturgist; theurgist; wizard; warlock
great: **n.** archimage

MAGNANIMITY: **n.** chivalry; generosity; philanthropy; **a.** MAGNANIMOUS: (**see** "liberal") chivalric; chivalrous; philanthropic

MAGNATE: **n.** nobleman; peer; tycoon
local (big-bug): **n.** panjandrum

MAGNIFICENT: (**see** "grand") **a.** imperial; leonine; majestic; palatial; regal; spectacular; sumptuous; **n. see** "grandeur"

MAID, *lady's:* **n.** Abigail; soubrette
of honor: **n.** *dame d'honneur; fille d'honneur*

MAIDENLY: **a.** daphnean; maidenish; modest; virginal

MAIMED: **a.** mangled; mutilated; truncated; **n.** mayhem

MAIN *item or event, or main dish at meal:* **n.** *pièce de résistance*

MAINTENANCE: **n.** alimentation; sustenance; sustentation; **a.** sustentative

MAJESTIC: (**see** "kingly") **a.** grandiose; imperial; regal; statuesque; **n. see** "grandeur"

MAJORITY: **n.** adulthood; maturity; predominance; predominancy
rule of the: **n.** arithmocracy

MAKE: **v.** concoct; confect; contrive; fabricate; fashion; invent; manufacture; synthesize
  haste slowly: **adv.** *festina lente; speude bradeos*
  up: **v.** compose; fabricate; improvisate; improvise; recoup; **n.** improvisation; morphology; recoupment; **a.** improvisatorial; improvisatory
    facial (paint, cosmetics, etc.): **n.** maquillage
  up for: **v.** requite; **n.** requital

MAKER: **n.** artificier; author; craftsman; fabricator; manufacturer; producer

MAKESHIFT: **n.** expediency; expedient; improvisation; *pis aller;* **a.** emergency; extemporaneous; (ex)temporary; improvisatorial; impromptu

MAKEUP: **n.** aggregate; arrangement; chemistry; composition; disposition; morphology
  of face: **n.** maquillage

MALE(S), *abnormal fear of or aversion to:* **n.** androphobia; apandria
  and female, common to both: **a.** ambisexual; ambosexual; bisexual; epicene
  attracted to the (human) **a.** androphilic; anthropophilic; anthropophilous
  centering or centered on: **a.** androcentric
  diseases of (study): **n.** andrology
  dominated by: **a.** androcentric; androcratic; **n.** androcracy
  generative organ: **n.** membrum virile; penis; phallus; priapium; **a.** phallic; priapic
  homosexual: **n.** uranist; urning; **n.** uranism
  political and social supremacy of: **n.** androcracy
  producing or tending to produce: **a.** androgenous
  shape and appearance of: **a.** andromorphous; masculine; **n.** masculinity
  worship of generative organ (as principle of nature): **n.** phallicism

MALIGN: (**see** "censure") **v.** calumniate; **a.** baneful; malevolent; malignant; pernicious; sinister

MALIGNANT: (**see** "poisonous") **a.** baleful; baneful; cancerous; injurious; lethal

MALNUTRITION: **n.** cachexia; cacotrophy; malnourishment; tabescence

MAN: (**see** "mankind" **and** "person") **n.** anthropoid; earthling; hominian; hominid; hominoid; *homo (sapiens);* mortal; terrene; (**pl.** *hominidae*)
  -about-town: **n.** *bon vivant;* boulevardier; flâneur; (**fem.** flâneuse)
  attracted to: **a.** androphilic; anthropophilic; anthropophilous
  centering on, or as center of all things: **a.** anthropocentric; **n.** anthropocentrism
  chivalrous: **n.** cavalier; chevalier; **a.** cavalier
  differs fr. everything else (theory): **n.** anthropocentrism; anthropopism
  distribution of, study: **n.** anthropogeography; ethnogeography
  effeminate: **n.** androgyn(e); hermaphrodite; **a.** androgynous; hermaphroditic(al)
  state of being (effeminate): **n.** androgyneity; androgynism; androgyny; hermaphroditism
  fall of, before the: **a.** prelapsarian
  family of: **n.pl.** *anthropoidea; hominidae; homo sapiens*
  fit: **n.** *idoneus homo*
  hatred of: **n.** misandry; misanthropy; timonism
  knowledge of nature of: **n.** anthroposophism; anthroposophy; **a.** anthroposophic(al)
  learned: **see** "scholar"
  little (dwarf): **n.** homunculus; (**pl.** homunculi)
  mean or wicked: **n.** caitiff; Procrustean; Sadist
  mechanical: **n.** android; automaton; golem; robot
  melancholy or pensive: **n.** *il pensieroso*
  newly-married: **n.** benedict
  -of-all-work: **see** "jack-of-all-trades"
  of dignity and aristocratic mien: **n.** grand seigneur
  of fashion (or of the world): **n.** *homme du monde*
  of intellect or wit: **n.** *homme d'esprit*
  of iron: **n.** *un homme d'airain*
  of letters: **see under** "person"
  of straw: **n.** *homme de paille*
  of the world: **see under** "world"
  of worth: **n.** *homme de bien;* (**pl.** *gens de condition*)
  pert. to: **a.** android; anthropic; anthropogenic; anthropoidal; anthropomorphic; masculine
  prominent in his field: **n.** Brahmin; doyen; mogul; nabob; tycoon
  resembling: **a.** anthropoid(al)
  rich: **n.** *homme de fortune*

196

sociological study of: n. anthroposociology
study of distribution of: n. anthropogeography; ethnogeography
   of origin and development of: n. anthropogenesis; anthropogeny; a. anthropogenetic
talented or gifted: n. man of parts
wise; n. Nestor; Solomon
worship or deification of: n. anthropolatry
wretched or unfortunate: n. caitiff
young: n. ephebe; yo(u)nker; a. ephebic

MANAGE: (see "control") v. administer; cultivate; direct; govern; husband; manipulate; negotiate; superintend; supervise; n. MANAGEABILITY: docility; manipulability; tractability; a. MANAGEABLE: (see "plastic" and "pliant") governable; tractable
   easy to: see "easily managed"
   hard to: (see "stubborn") a. intractable; obstinate; recalcitrant; refractory

MANAGEMENT: n. administration; cultivation; direction; dispensation; disposition; economy; government; husbandry; manipulation; negotiation; superintendence; supervision
   good or thrifty: n. eutaxy; husbandry
   prudent in: a. politic
   skillful in: (see "expert") a. executive; tactical

MANAGER: n. administrant; administrator; comptroller; director; executive; gerent; impresario; manipulator; superintendent; supervisor; a. MANAGERIAL: administrative; supervisory
   clever and skillful: n. tactician
   of apartment or rooming house: n. concierge
   pert. to duties of: a. administrative; managerial; supervisory

MANDATORY: a. coercive; compelling; compulsory; enforced; exigent; impelling; obligatory; prerequisite; n. coertion; compulsoriness; exigency

MANHOOD: n. adulthood; *âge viril;* majority; masculinity; maturity; potency
   garment (toga) to symbolize: n. *toga virilis*
   Jewish, attaining age 13, also rite: n. bar mitzvah

MANIA: (see "fear") n. cacoethes; delirium; frenzy; hysteria; a. delirious; hysterical; maniac(al)

MANIFESTATION(S): see "embodiment"
   grotesque or bizarre: see "grotesque"

MANIFOLD: (see "many") a. abundant; complex; multifarious; multitudinous; numerous; replicate

MANIPULATED, *that which is to be:* n. manipulandum

MANIPULATION, *skillful feat of:* n. *passe-passe; prestidigitation; tour de force*

MANKIND: (see "man") n. *homo sapiens;* mortality; (pl. *anthropoidae; hominidae*)
   hate or distrust of: n. misandry; misanthropism; misanthropy; timonism
   hater of: n. misanthrope; misanthropist
   study of, or pert. to: a. anthropology; a. anthropological

MANLY: (see "brave") a. masculine; puissant; virile; n. MANLINESS: arete; chivalry; gallantry; masculinity; potency; puissance
   deeds, womanly words (motto of Md.): *fatti maschii, parole femine*

MANNER: n. bearing; demeanor; deportment; mien; ostent; posture; procedure; *quo modo*
   easy: (see "easy") n. *un air aisé*
   in a bad: adv. *malo modo;* a. maladroit
   obliging: n. *prévenance*
   of living: n. *modus vivendi*
   of operating or working: n. *modus operandi*

MANNERISM: n. affectation; artificiality; eccentricity; foible; idiosyncrasy; preciosity; singularity; whimsicality

MANNERS: (see "courtesy") n. breeding; decorum; demeanor; etiquette; savoir-faire; suavity; urbanity; n.pl. mores
   artificial or affected: n.pl. artificialities; histrionics; theatrics
   censor of: n. *censor morum*
   contrary to or against good: adv. *contra bonos mores;* a. *mal élevé(e)*
   fine: n. or a. *bon ton; savoir-faire*
   good: n. *savoir vivre*
   group: n.pl. mores

guardian of: **n.** *censor morum; custos morum*
nice point of: **n.** punctilio; punctilious

MANUAL: (see "handbook") **n.** ench(e)iridion; *vade mecum*
of customs or usages: **n.** consuetudinary

MANURE: (see "dung") **n.** excrement; feculence; ordure; (**pl.** (d)ejecta; excreta; excrementa; feces)

MANY: (**see** "manifold" **and** "numerous")
a. divers(e); multifarious; multifold; multiple(x); multiplicious; multitudinous; myriad; sundry; **n.** multeity; multifariousness; multiplicity; multitude; plurality
-colored: **a.** kaleidoscopic; multi-colored; prismatic
-sided: **a.** multifaceted; multilateral; multiphasic; multivarious; versatile; **n.** versatility
things, having power to do: **a.** multipotent
values, having: **a.** multivalent; multivalued; polyvalent

MAR: see "disfigure"

MARBLE, *of, like or pert. to:* **a.** marmoraceous; marmoreal

MARGINAL: **a.** circumferential; limitrophe; peripheral
note(s): **n.** annotation; apostil(le); postil; scholium; (**pl.** adersaria; marginalia; scholia)
to make: **v.** postil

MARK(S): **n.** characteristic; defacement; disfiguration; indication; scarification; stigma; (**pl.** differentia; stigmata); **v.** characterize; deface; disfigure; scarify; signalize; stigmatize; typify
bearing a: **a.** stigmatiferous
distinguishing: **n.** aura; cachet; earmark; hallmark; imprimatur; stigma; (**pl.** stigmata)
off: **v.** circumscribe; delimit; subtend
of shame or discredit: **n.** mark of the beast; stigma; (**pl.** stigmata)
time: **v.** temporize; **n.** temporization

MARRIAGE: **n.** conjugality; connubiality; espousal; matrimony; nuptials; wedlock
absence, nonregulation or nonrecognition of: **n.** agamy

after: **a.** post-nuptial
before: **a.** antenuptial; premarital
bet. persons unsuited: **n.** *mésalliance;* misalliance
bet. royal and commoner, wife and children not royal: **a. or n.** morganatic
hater or hatred of: **n.** misogamist; misogamy; **a.** misogamic
outside tribe, clan, etc.: **n.** exogamy; **a.** exogamous
pert. to: **a.** conjugial; connubial; epithalmic(al); hymeneal; marital; matrimonial; **n.** conjugality; connubality; matrimony
plural: **n.** bigamy; polyandry; polygamy; polygyny; **a.** bigamous; polandrous; polygamous; polygynous
rate: **n.** nuptiality
related by: **n.** affine
rules and conventions (laws) governing: **n.** *jus con(n)ubii*
second: **n.** deuterogamy; digamy; **a.** digamous
song or poem: **n.** epithalamion; epithalamium; hymenal
state: **n.** connubiality; matrimony
tie: **n.** *vinculum matrimonii*
to one hus. at a time: **n.** monandry; **a.** monandrous
to one person at a time: **n.** monogamy; **a.** monogamous
to one wife at a time: **n.** monogyny; **a.** monogynous
w/ one of lower status: **n.** *mésalliance;* misalliance
w/ one of other race: **n.** miscegenation
within tribe or group: **n.** endogamy; inmarriage; **a.** endogamic; endogamous
w/o tribe or group: **n.** exogamy; **a.** exogamic; exogamous

MARRIAGEABLE: **a.** nubile; **n.** nubility

MARRIED *man, esp. recently:* **n.** benedict
person, one newly: **n.** neogamist

MARSH(ES), *living or thriving in:* **a.** palustrine; uliginose
pert. to: **a.** fenny; paludal; paludous; palustral; uliginose

MARVEL: **n.** miracle; phenomenon; prodigy; (**pl.** mirabilia; phenomena); **a.**
MARVELOUS: meritorious; mirific; transcendent; **adv.** *à merveille; magnifique*

MARY, *worship or veneration of:* **n.** hyperdulia; Mariolatry

MASCULINE: (see "male") **a.** android
characteristics, having (as in fem.) : **a.**
amazonian; android; gynandrous
having shape or appearance: **a.** andromorphous
interests, dominating or emphasizing: **a.**
androcentric

MASCULINITY: **see** "manliness"
female: **n.** amazonism; defeminization
lacking vigorous: **a.** effeminate; epicene;
feminine

MASKED: (see "disguised") **a.** cabalistic;
cryptic; incognito; larvate(d); latent

MASS: **v.** agglomerate; agglutinate; aggregate; assemble; concentrate; conglomerate; muster; **n.** aggregate; agglutination;
conglomeration; magnitude; ponderosity;
spissitude
solidified: **n.** concretion; **a.** concretionary; **v.** concretize

MASSIVE: (see "huge") **a.** elephantine;
monumental; substantial

MASTER: **v.** conquer; dominate; overawe;
overcome; overpower; subdue; subjugate;
vanquish; **n.** MASTERY: ascendency;
command; dominion; subjugation; superiority
of ceremonies: **n.** ceremoniarius; compere; officiator
*of one's own art or profession, also title
for such:* **n.** *cher maître;* virtuoso
of self: **n.** *compos sui*
one who is his own: **n.** *paterfamilias;*
(*homo*) *sui juris;* **a.** *sui juris*
stroke: **n.** *coup de maître*

MASTERFUL: (see "arrogant" and "skillful") **a.** commanding; domineering; imperative; imperious; preemptory; sovereign

MASTERPIECE, *as art or lit.:* **n.** *chef
d'oeuvre; magnus opus;* meisterwerk;
pièce de résistance

MASTURBATION: **n.** autoeroti(ci)sm;
onanism

MAT, *picture:* **n.** *passe partout*

MATCH: **v.** correspond; harmonize; **n.**
counterpart

MATCHLESS: **a.** consummate; incommensurable; incomparable; inimitable; *nec
plus supra; nec plus ultra;* peerless; (super)eminent; superlative; transcendent;
unparalleled; **n.** incommensurability; in-
comparability; inimitability

MATE: **see** "companion"; **n.** MATED: **see**
"coupled"

MATERIAL(S): **a.** corporeal; essential;
important; mechanical; palpable; pertinent; physical; ponderable; relevant; sensible; substantial; tangible; **n.** corporeality; corporeity; materiality; physicality; substantiality; tangibility
array or store of: **n.** armamentarium;
(**pl.** armamentaria; instrumentaria)
not: (see "immaterial") **a.** asomatous;
impalpable; incorporeal; intangible; transcendent
thing: **n.** corporeality; materiality; *matériel;* (**pl.** corporeals; *res corporales;
matériel*)

MATERIALISM: **n.** barbarism; Darwin-
ism; evolution(ism); heterodoxy; Philistinism; physicism; pragmatism; utilitarianism; **n.** MATERIALIST: corporealist;
Darwinist; evolutionist; heterodox; physi-
cist; pragmatist; Sadducee; utilitarian

MATERIALISTIC: **a.** banausic; bourgeois; democritean; faustian; moneymak-
ing; philistine; philistinic; physicalistic;
pragmatic; utilitarian
doctrine or theory: **n.** physicism
world of the: **n.** Philistia

MATERIALIZE: **v.** hypostatize; reify; **n.**
MATERIALIZATION; hypostatization;
reification

MATHEMATICS, *love(r) of:* **n.** philomath; philomathy; **a.** philomathic(al)

MATRIMONY: **see** "marriage"
bonds of: **n.** *vinculum matrimonii*

MATTED: **a.** cespitose

MATTER: (see "material") **n.** corporality;
materiality; substance; substantiality
in heart or substance of the: **adv.** *in
medias res*
it's no: **n.** *n'importe*
-of-fact: (see "prosaic") **a.** literal;
terre à terre; utilitarian; **n.** literality;

practicality; prosaism; pragmatism; utilitarianism
   small: **n.** *peu de chose*

MATURE: (**see** "adult" **and** "develop") **v.** maturate; **n.** MATURITY: adultness; maturation

MAXIM: (**see** "witticism") **n.** adage; aphorism; apothegm; axiom; dictum; epigram; gnome; logion; sententia; **a.** aphoristic; apothegmatic(al); gnomic(al); sentential

MAXIMUM: **see** "greatest"

MAZE: **n.** conglomeration; convolution; intricacy; labyrinth; maelstrom; perplexity; sinuosity
   like: **a.** daedalian; daedal(ic); labyrinthine

MEAGER: **a.** exigous; infinitesimal; **n.** MEAGERNESS: dearth; exiguity; famine; parcity; paucity; squalor; stringency

MEAL: **n.** collation; repast; tiffin
   after: **a.** postcibal; postprandial
   before: **a.** precibal; preprandial
   complete w/ fixed price: **a.** or **n.** *table d'hôte*
   each item at separate price: **a.** or **n.** *à la carte*
   light: **n.** collation; tiffin
   main dish of: **n.** *entree; pièce de résistance; plat de résistance*
   rel. to: **a.** cibarian; prandial
   side dish(es) of: **n.** entremet(s)
   -time: **n.** *heure du repas*

MEAN: **v.** connote; denote; import; signify; **a.** (**see** "wicked") contemptible; despicable; intermediary; intermediate; reptilian; **n.** average; intermediary
   golden: **n.** *ariston metron; aurea mediocritas; juste-milieu*
   person: **n.** Beelzebub; caitiff; procrustean; sadist

MEANING(S): **n.** acceptation; connotation; denotation; drift; gist; import; interpretation; purport; significance; signification; tenor; understanding
   expressing complete substantive: **a.** categorematic
     not: **a.** syncategorematic
   having but one: **a.** or **n.** univocal
   having many: **a.** polysemous; **n.** polysemy

generally accepted, as of word: **n.** acceptation
   identity of: **n.** synonymity; **a.** synonymous
   implied but not expressed: **n.** subaudition; subintelligitur; **a.** tacit
   looseness of: **n.** ambiguity; **a.** ambiguous
   of double or doubtful: **a.** ambiguous; amphibolic(al); amphibolous; equivocal; **n.** ambiguity; amphibologism; amphibology; equivoque
   of similar or same; **n.** synonym; **a.** synonymic; synonymous
   symbolic, or underlying theme: **n.** mythos; (**pl.** mythoi)

MEANINGFUL: **a.** definitive; expressive; knowledg(e)able; pregnant; sententious; significant

MEANINGLESS: (**see** "purposeless") **a.** aimless
   talk: **n.** balderdash; Choctaw; flummery; galimatias; gibberish

MEANNESS: (**see** "wickedness") **n.** despicability; duplicity; knavery; parvanimity; rascality; **a.** despicable; duplicitous; parvanimitous

MEANS: **n.** channel; instrument(ality); instrumentation; intermediary; medium; *modus operandi; quo modo;* resources; vehicle; wherewithal

MEANTIME (**or** MEANWHILE): **n.** interim; interval
   for or in the: **adv.** *ad hoc; ad interim*

MEASURE: **n.** amplitude; barometer; capacity; coefficient; criterion; (**pl.** criteria); indication; magnitude; thermometer; touchstone; yardstick
   beyond: **adv.** *abundantly; à outrance;* excessively
   in things, there is: est modus in rebus

MEASURED: **a.** calculated; deliberate; limited; rhythmical
   capable of being: **a.** commensurable; finite; measurable; mensural; mensurative; ponderable; quantitative
   not capable of being: **a.** imponderable; incommensurable; unfathomable; **n.** incommensurability

MEASURELESS: **see** "boundless"

MEASURING, *act of or pert. to:* n. mensuration; a. mensurable; mensural; mensurative

MECHANICAL: a. automatic; automatous; autonomic; inhuman; involuntary; perfunctorious; perfunctory; stereotyped; n. automaticity; mechanicality; n. MECHANIC; artisan; mechanician
man, or one who acts or thinks as: n. android; automaton; golem; robot
to make: v. automatize; dehumanize; mechanize; robotize; n. automation; automatism; dehumanization; mechanization; robotization

MEDDLE: (**see** "interfere") v. interlope; interpose; intervene; intrude; obtrude; tamper; n. MEDDLER: (**see** "busybody") interloper; intervenient; Meddlesome Mattie; quidnunc; a. MEDDLESOME (or MEDDLING): impertinent; intrusive; officious; (poly)pragmatic(al); n. MEDDLESOMENESS: impertinence; impudicity; intrusiveness; polypragmatism

MEDIATE: **see** "interpose"; n. MEDIATOR: arbitrator; conciliator; intercessor; intermediary; intervenient; placator

MEDICAL: a. Aesculapian; iatric(al)
instruments, equipment, etc.: n.pl. armamentaria; instrumentaria
practitioner: n. Aescalapius; physician; therapist
treatment: n. iatrics; medicament; medicant; medication; therapeusis; therapeutant; therapeutics; therapy

MEDICINE(S): n. medicament; medicant; medication; pharmaceutical; simple; specific; therapeusis; therapeutant; therapeutic; (pl. *materia medica*)
disease caused by, or by med. treatment: a. iatrogenic; medicamentous
false, or to please patient: n. placebo
favorite or quack: n. nostrum; panacea
pert. to: a. Aesculapian; iatric(al); medicative; medicinal; pharmaceutic(al); therapeutic(al); theriac(al)
science or art of: n. iatrics; iatrology; pharmaceutics; therapeutics

MEDICINAL: a. medicative; medicinable; pharmaceutic(al); salutary; sanative; salutiferous; therapeutic(al); theriac(al)

MEDIOCRE: **see** "ordinary"

MEDITATE: v. consider; contemplate; deliberate; (ex)cogitate; lucubrate; ponder; reflect; n. MEDITATION: cerebration; cogitation; contemplation; lucubration; reflection; rumination; a. MEDITATIVE: (**see** "reflective") apollonian; apollonic; apollonistic; cogitable; cogitabund; cogitative; contemplative; deliberative; nomothetic; pensive; purposeful

MEDLEY: n. brouhaha; charivari; farrago; fatras; heterogeneity; hodgepodge; *macédoine; mélange;* miscellany; olla podrida; olio; omnium-gatherum; pastiche; potpourri; salmagundi; *tripotage*
of confused sounds: n. Babelism; brouhaha; gallimaufry; pasticcio; pastiche
of familiar tunes: n. fantasia

MEEK: a. forbearing; humble; invertebrate; phlegmatic; placid; submissive; unpretentious; n. MEEKNESS: abnegation; forbearance; humbleness; humility; mansuetude; submission; submissiveness

MEET: v. assemble; confront; congregate; decussate; encounter; intersect; fulfill; satisfy
casually: v. rencounter

MEETING: n. amalgamation; assemblage; assembly; collocation; concourse; concursion; confluence; conflux; confrontation; congregation; congress; convention; convergence; conversazione; convocation; decussation; encounter; intersection; junction; juncture; rendezvous; tryst
for exchange of ideas; n. symposium
hostile: n. rencounter; rencontre
minimum to conduct: n. quorum
place; or secret: n. concourse; *point de réunion;* rendezvous; tryst
private or secret: **see under** "secret"

MELANCHOLY: (**see** "sad") a. atrabilarious; atrabiliar; atrabilious; dispirited; hypochondriacal; n. MELANCHOLY (or MELANCHOLIA) apanthropia; apanthropy; doldrums; hypochonaria(sis); lachrymals; megrims
person: n. atrabilarian; hypochondriac; melancholiac; valetudinarian
to make, depict as or indulge in: v. melancholize

MELLOW(ED): a. classic; matured; orotund; resonant; sonorous; n. orotundity; sonority

MELODIOUS: **a.** ariose; canorous; cantabile; dulcet; euphonious; lyric(al); mellifluous; melodic; orphic; sirenic(al); sonorous; symphonous; symphonizing; unisonant
  "nonsense": **n.** *nugae canorae*

MELODY: **n.** descant; diapason; euphony; harmonization; harmony; lyric; orchestration; sonority; symphony; syncopation
  art of inventing: **n.** melopoeia; **a.** melopoe(t)ic
  consisting of or rel. to two or more: **a.** contrapuntal; polyphonic; polyphonous; polyrhythmic
  having a single: **a.** monophonic; monophonous
  single dominant or prevailing: **n.** leitmotif; leitmotiv

MELT: (**see** *"dissolve"*) **v.** ablate; deliquesce; disintegrate; dissipate; liquefy; **a.** MELTING: deliquescent; liquescent; **n.** deliquescence; liquefaction

MEMBERS, *attended by all:* **n.** plenum; quorum; **a.** plenary

MEMBRANE, *pass thru:* **v.** osmose; transude; **n.** osmosis; transudate; transudation

MEMORANDUM: (**see** *"reminder"*) **n.** *aide-memoire;* (**pl.** *aides-memoire*); memento; memoir
  preliminary: **n.** protocol

MEMORIAL: **n.** cenotaph; commemoration; memento; monument; plaque; trophy

MEMORY: **n.** recollection; reminiscence; retrospection; **a.** reminiscent(ial)
  aid to: (**see** *"memorandum"*): **n.** *aide-memoire;* (**pl.** *aides-memoire*); *memoria technica;* **a.** mnemonic; **n.** mnemonics
  from: **adv.** *ex capite*
  gap in: **n.** amnesia; **a.** amnesic
  goddess of: **n.** Mnemosyne
  helping: **a.** mnemonic
  increased or exceptionally keen: **n.** hypermnesia
  lack or loss of: **n.** amnesia; **a.** amnesic
  lapse or slip of: **n.** *lapsus memoriae;* parapraxia; parapraxis
  of blessed: **adv.** *beatae memoriae*
  pert. to, helping or meant to help: **a.** mnemonic

science of, or art of improving: **n.** mnemonics
  weak: **n.** *mémoire débile*

MEN: **see** *"man"*
  business: **n.pl.** *gens d'affaires; hommes d'affaires*
  group of best: **n.** *corps d'elite*
  hatred of: **n.** misandry; misanthropy; timonism
  military: **n.pl.** *gens de guerre*
  of lesser merit: **n.pl.** *di minores*
  of letters: **n.pl.** *gens de lettres; hommes de lettres; literati*
  of outstanding merit (eminent): **n.pl.** *di majores*

MENACE: **v.** jeopardize; **n.** anathema; commination; charybdis; jeopardy; minacity; sword of Damocles; **a.** MENACING: (**see** *"dangerous"*) imminent; minacious; minatorial; ominous

MENSTRUATION: **n.** catamenia; menorrhea; menses
  absence of, or abnormal stoppage: **n.** amenorrhea
  end of ("change of life") **n.** menopause; **a.** menopausal
  onset or beg. of (at puberty): **n.** menarche; **a.** menarcheal; menarchial
  painful: **n.** dysmenorrhea
  previous to onset: **n.** premenarche; **a.** premenarcheal; premenstrual
  profuse: **n.** menorrhagia

MENTAL: **a.** appercipient; cerebral; ideological; intellectual; metaphysical; noological; phrenic; psychic(al); psychologic(al); subjective
  aberration: **n.** deliration; delirium; delusion; hallucination; hallucinosis; illusion; mania; psychosis
  activity: **see** *"thought"*
    modified by: **a.** ideoplastic
  confusion or impairment: (**see** *"aberration"* **above**) **n.** dementia; obnubilation; psychosis
  deficiency: **n.** amentia; aphronia; cretinism; feeblemindedness; idiocy; imbecility; moronity; oligophrenia; **a.** cretinous; moronic; oligophrenic
  derangement: (**see** *"aberration"* **above**) **n.** *alienation mentale;* (**or.** *d'esprit*)
  deterioration: **n.** dementia
  disorder: **n.** aberration; alienation; dementia; psychosis; **a.** psychotic

impression: **n.** conception; **a.** conceptual; concipient

pain or distress: **n.** dysphoria; psychalgia

perception: **n.** apperception; prehension; **a.** apperceptionistic

    distorted: **n.** astigmatism; myopia; **a.** astigmatic(al); myopic

phenomena, of or rel. to: **a.** mentalistic; psychological

    study of: **n.** noology; psychology; (**pl.** psychostatics); **a.** noological; psychological

    study of abnormal: **n.** psychiatry; **a.** psychiatric

reservation: **n.** *arrière pensée*

MENTALITY, *lack of:* (see "mental deficiency") **n.** amentia; cretinism; dementia; moronity

    loss of: **n.** dementia; psychosis

MENTALLY *competent:* (see "legally competent" and "sane") **a.** capax; *compos mentis*

    defective but brilliant or apt in some special field: **n.** *idiot savant*

    incompetent or deficient: **a.** amental; cretinous; demented; *doli incapax;* incapacious; *non compos (mentis)*; psychotic

    slow: see "slow-witted"

MENTOR: (see "guide") **n.** cicerone; counsellor; preceptor; tutor

MENU: **n.** *carte du jour;* dietary; regimen

MERCENARY: **n.** condottiere; Hessian; hireling; janissary; Myrmidon; pensionary; **a.** avaricious; commercial; mercantile; venal

MERCY: (see "charity") **n.** benignity; clemency; commiseration; compassion; lenity; toleration; **a.** MERCIFUL: (see "tender") clement; compassionate; forbearing; indulgent; lenient; sympathetic; tolerant; warm-hearted; **a.** MERCILESS: austere; barbarous; disputatious; imperative; implacable; inclement; inexorable; inquisitorial; intolerant; Neronian; obdurate; pitiless; relentless; remorseless; unfeeling; unsympathetic; **adv.** *avec archarnement; sans merci*

    killing: **n.** euthanasia

MERGER: (see "union") **n.** absorption; alliance; amalgamation; coadunation; coalescence; coalition; concursion; confluence; fusion; osmosis; **a.** MERGING: amalgamative; coalescent; confluent; osmotic

MERIT: **n.** commendableness; eminence; estimableness; exemplarity; prestige

    having: (see "meritorious") **a.** eminent; estimable; prestigious

    having no (merit) or demerit: **a.** adiaphorous; **n.** adiaphoron

    of lesser, persons of: **n.** *di minores*

    of outstanding, persons of: **n.** *di majores*

MERITED: **a.** condign; warranted; **a.** MERITORIOUS: commendable; commendatory; creditable; eminent; estimable; exemplary; praiseworthy; prestigious

MERRY: **a.** blithe(some); carnivalesque; debonair; exuberant; exultant; festive; frolicsome; genial; hilarious; jaunty; jocund; jovial; joyous; mirthful; sportive; **n.** MERRIMENT: exuberance; exultation; festivity; geniality; hilarity; jocularity; jocundity; joviality; jubilation; sportiveness

MERRYMAKING, *wild and riotous:* **n.** carousal; orgy; **a.** carnivalesque; orgiastic

MESS: (see "mixture") **n.** conglomeration; heterogeneity; hodgepodge

MESSAGE(S), *code:* **n.** cryptogram

    serving as conveyor of: **a.** internuncial; internunciary

MESSENGER: (see "forerunner") **n.** apostle; harbinger; herald; internuncio

MESSMATE: **a. or n.** commensal; **n.** commensality

METAPHOR(S): **n.** allegory; anagoge; metonymy; synecdoche; trope; **v.** allegorize; metaphorize

    faulty or mixed use of: **n.** catachresis; **a.** catachrestic(al)

METAPHYSICAL: (see "supernatural") **a.** extraphysical; preternatural; stratospheric(al)

METHOD(S): (see "procedure") **n.** approach; discipline; *métier; modus operandi;* technique *lacking in:* (**see** "disordered") **a.** immethodical

of doing things: **n.** expertise; methodology; *modus operandi;* technique; virtuosity

temporary: **n.** *modus vivendi*

METHODICAL: **see** "orderly"

METRICAL *accent:* **n.** cadence; ictus

MIDDAY *meal:* **n.** tiffin
rel. to: **a.** meridian

MIDDLE: **see** "center"
aged: **adv.** *entre deux âges;* **a.** *d'âge moyen*
ages: **n.** or **a.** medieval; *moyen-age*
class: **n.** bourgeois(ie)
course: **see** "way" **below**
ground: (**see** "way" **below**) **n.** limbo
-man: **n.** entrepreneur; (**fem.** entrepreneuse); (inter)mediary; intervenient
of action; or in midst of things: **adv.** *in media(s) res*
-of-the-road, person of: **n.** centrist; moderant; moderate
position: (**see** "intermediate") **a.** mesothetic
put in the: **v.** mediatize
way: **n.** *ariston metron; aurea mediocritas;* golden mean; *juste milieu; mezzo termine; tertium quid; via media*

MIDDLING: **see** "so-so"

MID-MORNING: **a.** or **n.** antemeridian

"MIDNIGHT OIL," *burn the:* **v.** lucubrate; **n.** lucubration

MIDST: **see** "middle"

MIGHT: (**see** "power") **n.** capacity; potency; puissance; resources
w/ all one's: **adv.** *à tout force; manibus pedibusque; totis viribus*

MIGHTY: (**see** "powerful") **a.** efficacious; efficient; extraordinary; Herculean; invincible; momentous; (omni)potent; puissant; Samsonian
in battle or arms: **a.** armipotent

MIGRATION: **n.** diaspora; hegira; **a.** MIGRATORY: nomadic

MILD: (**see** "peaceful") **a.** amiable; assuasive; clement; compassionate; com-

plaisant; considerate; favonian; lenient; lenitive; temperate; tepid; tolerant; tranquil; **n.** MILDNESS: benignity; clemency; compassion; consideration; lenity; tranquility
make or become: **v.** mitigate; mollify; palliate; placate; tranquilize; **a.** mitigatory; palliative; palliatory; placative; placatory

MILITARY *expert:* **n.** Clauzewitz; **a.** Clauzewitzian
government: **n.** stratocracy
pert. to the: **a.** martial
supplies or equipment: **n.pl.** armentaria; armaments; impedimenta; *matériel;* **n.** armamentarium

MILK, *excessive secretion of:* **n.** polygalactia
feeding on: **a.** galactophagous; lactivorous
secretion of: **n.** lactation; **n.** lactescent
yielding or conveying: **a.** galactophorous; lactiferous

MILKY: **a.** lacteous; lactescent; opalescent; **n.** MILKINESS: lactescence; opalescence

MIMICRY: **n.** caricature; imitation; impersonation; mimesis; mimetism; **a.** echoic; mimetic; mimical; onomatopoe(t)ic

MIND(S): **n.** cerebrum; consciousness; faculty; intellect; intelligence; mentality; nous; psyche; rationality; reason; sensorium; sentiment; understanding
absence of: (**see** "absent-mindedness") **n.** *absence d'esprit;* amentia
action of: (**see** "thought") **n.** cerebration; lucubration; mentation
confused or impaired state of: **n.** dementia; obnubilation; psychosis
diversion fr. reality: **n.** escapism; identification
existing in the: **a.** endopsychic; psychogen(et)ic; psychosomatic; **n.** *ens rationalis;* psychogenesis
impress on the: **v.** inculcate; indoctrinate
keenness of : **n.** acumen; discernment; discrimination; perspicacity; perspicuity; shrewdness
little, are caught w/ trifles: parva leves capiunt animas
of or rel. to one's own: **a.** autopsychic
peace of: **see** "contentment"
pert. or rel. to: (**see** "mental") **a.** cere-

bral; intellectual; noological; psychologic(al)
pleasing or acceptable to: **a.** palatable
-reading: **n.** clairvoyance; telepathy; **a.** clairvoyant; telepathic
smallness of: **n.** parvanimity; **a.** lilliputian; parvanimitous
sound: **n.** competent; *compos (mentis);* **n.** competency
sound in sound body: mens sana in corpore sano
study of: **n.** noology; psychiatry; psychology
unsound: **n.** *non compos (mentis)*
weak of: **n. or adv.** *impos animi*
with an equal: **adv.** *aequo animo*
with calmness of: **adv.** *aequo animo;* **n.** equanimity; sophrosyne
with one: (**see** "unanimous") **adv.** *uno animo*

MINE, *rich:* **n.** bonanza; El Dorado

MINERALS, *study of:* **n.** mineralogy; oryctology; **n.** mineralogist; oryctologist

MINGLE: **v.** amalgamate; concoct; confuse; conglomerate; infiltrate; integrate; interlard; interpolate; intertwine

MINIATURE: **a. or n.** diminutive; lilliputian; **n.** epitome
in: **adv.** *en petit; in parvo; in petto*
universe or any large unit: **n.** microcosm; **a.** microcosmic

MINOR: **see** "age, under legal" **and** "secondary"

MINUTE: **see** "small"
(be) up to the: **adv.** (be) *à la page*

MIRACLE(S): **n.** anomy; (**pl.** mirabilia); **a.** miraculous
narrative of those of god or hero: **n.** aretalogy
performance of: **n.** thaumaturgy
performer of: **n.** thaumaturgus; (**n.pl.** thaumaturgi)
pert. to: **a.** thaumaturgic(al)
study or lore of: **n.** thaumatology
worker: **n.** thaumaturge; thaumaturgus; **a.** thaumaturgic(al)

MIRAGE: (**see** "deception") **n.** corposant; *deceptio visus; fata morgana;* St. Elmo's fire

MIRROR(S), *pert. to:* **a.** catoptric(al); specular
study or science of: **n.** catoptrics

MIRTH: **see** "joy"

MISAPPLY: **v.** defalcate; embezzle; misappropriate; **n.** MISAPPLICATION: defalcation; embezzlement; malfeasance; misfeasance; subtraction

MISBEHAVIOR: (**see** "misconduct") **n.** delinquency; malbehavior; malconduct

MISBELIEF: **n.** miscreance

MISCELLANEOUS: **a.** assorted; heterogeneous; hodge-podge; indiscriminate; promiscuous; **n.** MISCELLANY: (**see** "medley") bric-a-brac; heterogeneity; hodge-podge; olla podrida; *omnium gatherum;* (**pl.** miscellanea; varia)
collection, as notes, etc.: **n.pl.** adversaria; collectanea; *disjecta membra;* miscellanea
quality or state of being: **n.** miscellaneity

MISCHANCE: **n.** calamity; catastrophe; contretemps; misadventure; misfortune; mishap

MISCHIEF: **n.** diablerie; hanky-panky; hocus-pocus; impishness; mischievousness
source of great: **n.** Pandora's box

MISCHIEVOUS: **a.** impish; injurious; malevolent; roguish; venomous
antic(s): **n.** escapade; harlequinade; ploy
conduct or manner: **n.** diablerie; impishness

MISCONCEPTION: **n.** delusion; hallucination; illusion; misapprehension; misinterpretation

MISCONDUCT: **n.** beastliness; bestiality; delinquency; malbehavior; malconduct; misbehavior; sociopathy
in office: **n.** defalcation; malfeasance; misfeasance; **a.** malfeasant
one guilty of: **n.** delinquent; malfeasor; misdemeanant; misfeasor

MISDEED: (**see** "offense") **n.** defaction; defalcation; delinquency; felony; malfeasance; misdemeanor; misfeasance

MISERABLE: **a.** contemptible; discreditable; shameful; worthless; wretched
act of making or state of becoming: **n.** immiserization

MISERLY: (**see** "stingy") **a.** acquisitive; avaricious; churlish; covetous; extortionate; frugal; penny-pinching; penurious
person: **n.** curmudgeon; Scrooge

MISERY: **see** "agony"
acute: **n.** purgatory
causing: **a.** afflictive
expression of: **n.** de profundis
place of great: **n.** Gethsemane; purgatory

MISFORTUNE: **n.** adversity; bereavement; calamity; catastrophe; holocaust; misadventure; mishap; tribulation; visitation; **a. see** "unfortunate"
great or sudden: **n.** angoisse; calamity; catastrophe; holocaust; **a.** calamitous; catastrophic(al)
never comes alone: nullium infortunium solum
prophetess of: **n.** Cassandra; **a.** Cassandr(i)an

MISHAP: (**see** "accident") **n.** contretemps

MISLEADING: (**see** "deceptive") **a.** ambiguous; ambivalent; delusional; delusionary; delusive; equivocal; factitious; illusive; **v.** MISLEAD: (**see** "deceive") bamboozle; defraud; delude; equivocate; victimize
ideal: **n.** ignis fatuus; will-of-the-wisp

MISREPRESENTATION: **see** "falsehood" **and** "falseness"

MIST: **n.** brume; nebula; obscurity; **a.** MISTY: brumous; caliginous; crepuscular; nubilous; vaporific; vaporish; vaporous; volatile

MISTAKE: (**see** "fault" **and** "error") **n.** erratum; fallacy; inadvertence; inadvertency; misapprehension; misconception; misperception; misprision; misunderstanding; oversight; **a.** MISTAKEN: **see** "erroneous"
grammatical or social: **see under** "error"

MISTRESS: **n.** amour; inamorata; paramour

of house: **n.** chatelaine; materfamilas; matriarch; matron

MISUNDERSTANDING: **n.** *brouillerie;* disagreement; dissention; imbroglio; malentendu; misapprehension; misinterpretation; misperception; misprision; **v.** MISUNDERSTAND: misapprehend; misinterpret; **a.** MISUNDERSTOOD: malentendu; misapprehended; misinterpreted

MISUSE: **v.** defalcate; embezzle; misappropriate; misapply; **n.** defalcation; embezzlement; misapplication; misappropriation

MIXED: **a.** amalgamated; amalgamative; farraginous; hyphenated; macaronic; **v.** MIX: amalgmate; coalesce; commingle; conglomerate; interfuse; interlard; intermingle; levigate; triturate
capable of being: **a.** miscible; **n.** miscibility
not: **a.** immiscible; incommiscible
origin, race, varieties, etc.: **n.** heterogeneity; hybrid(ization); **a.** heterogeneous; hybrid; **v.** hybridize
use of metaphors: **n.** catachresis; **a.** catachrestic(al)

MIXTURE: **n.** amalgam(ation); commingling; concoction; confection; conglomeration; farrago; gallimaufry; heterogeneity; hodgepodge; hyphenation; medley; miscellanea; miscellaneity; miscellany; pastiche; potpourri; salmagundi; smorgasbord; tagraggery
confused: **n.** farrago
of elements, ideas, peoples, etc.: **n.** amalgam(ation); heterogeneity; tagraggery
of race(s): **n.** miscegenation
produced by or constructed from: **n.** or **a.** hybrid; mongrel

MOANING: **a.** plangorous

MOB: (**see** "gang") **n.** canaille; claque; clique; riffraff; varletry
govt. or rule by: **n.** mobocracy; ochlocracy; **a.** mobocratic; ochlocratic

MOCKERY: **n.** asteism; badinage; burlesque; caricature; counterfeit; derision; futility; imitation; mimesis; mimicry; parody; persiflage; raillery; ridicule; sarcasm; satire
a deplorable: **n.** flebile ludibrium

MODE: see "method"

MODEL: **n.** archetype; *beau idéal;* ectype; exemplar; exemplum; mannequin; man(n)ikin; matrix; microcosm; paradigm; paragon; prototype; replica; **a.** (see "exemplary") archetyp(ic)al
  of human, as for anatomy class: **n.** anthropomorph; homunculus; man(n)ikin
  pert. to: **a.** archetypal; ectypal; exemplar; paradigmatic; prototypal
  quality or state of being: **n.** exemplarity
  use in primitive magic: **n.** evoûtement

MODERATE(S): (see "ease") **v.** mitigate; mollify; restrain; temper; tranquilize; **a.** (see "calm") mitigatory; modest; prudent; reasonable; **adv.** *allegretto; non troppo*
  in eating, drinking, etc.: **a.** abstemious; abstentious; continent; temperate
  one who is: **n.** centrist; moderant; moderate
  something that (moderates): **n.** moderant; tranquilizer

MODERATION: (see "prudence") **n.** abstention; abstinence; continence; discretion; golden mean; moderateness; restraint; temperance
  is best: ariston metron
  wise: **n.** prudence; sophrosyne

MODERN: **a.** *au courant;* contemporary; *dernier cri; fin-de-siècle; moderne;* modernistic; neoteric; progressive; topical; **n.** MODERNITY: modernness; topicality
  person or writer: **n.** *moderne;* neoteric
  state of being: **n.** modernity
  tastelessly or pretentiously: **a.** *moderne*

MODESTY: **n.** demurity; diffidence; maidenliness; pudency; pudibundity; pudicity; verecundity; **a.** MODEST: chaste; decorous; demure; diffident; humble; moderate; unassuming; unboastful; unobtrusive; unostentatious; unpresuming; unpretentious; verecund; virginal; virtuous
  appeal(ing) to: **adv.** *ad verecundiam*
  exaggerated or excessive: **n.** decorousness; priggishness; prudery; pudency; pudibundity; pudicity; **a.** priggish; prudish; pudibund
  false: **n.** *malus pudor*

MODIFY: see "alter"

MODULATED, *capable of being:* **a.** modificatory; modulatory; **n.** modulability

MOISTURE (or MOISTNESS) **n.** aquosity; humectation; humidity; **a.** MOIST: aqueous; hydrogenous
  capable of taking up: **a.** bibitory
  induced by or absorbed fr. air: **a.** hygroscopic

MOLD: (see "model") **n.** matrix

MOLDED, *capable of being:* see "pliant"

MOLT (or MOULT): **v.** deplumate; exfoliate; exuviate; **n.** deplumation; ecdysis; **a.** deciduous; deplumate; exfoliative

MOLTEN *rock:* **n.** magma

MOMENT: **n.** consequence; consideration; instant; weight
  at the: **adv.** *in articulo*
  at the opportune: (see "timely") **adv.** *dextro tempore*

MOMENTARY: (see "fleeting") **a.** ephemeral; evanescent; instantaneous; semelfactive; transient; transitory; **n.** MOMENTARINESS: ephemerality; instantaneity

MOMENTOUS: **a.** consequential; crucial; epochal; memorable; paramount; prominent; signal; weighty

MONASTERY, *occupant of:* **n.** cenobite; **a.** cenobitic; **n.** cenobitism

MONETARY: **a.** financial; numismatic(al); nummary; pecuniary; quaestuary; sumptuary

MONEY, *appeal(ing) to:* **n. or adv.** *(argumentum) ad crumenam*
  as evil, or personified: **n.** mammon
  devoted to getting: **a.** mammonish; **n.** mammonism; mammonist; mammonite
  devotion to or worship of: **n.** *amor nummi;* mammonism; plutolatry; plutomania
  excessive regard for: **n.** fiscality
  having none: (see "poor") **a.** impecunious; indigent; **n.** impecuniosity; indigence
  large sum of: **n.** king's ransom
  love of: **n.** *amor nummi;* mammonism; plutolatry; plutomania
  motivated only by: **a.** commercial(istic); mercantile; mercenary; quaestuary; venal; **n.** commerciality; venality

pert. to control of: **a.** financial; fiscal; sumptuary

pert. to or involving: **a.** financial; fiscal; monetary; numismatic(al); nummary; nummulary; pecuniary; quaestuary; sumptuary; **n.** commerciality

ready: **n.** *argent comptant*

worship of: **n.** plutolatry; plutomania

MONK: **n.** cenobite; monastic; **a.** cenobitic; solitudinarian

MONKEY (or APE): **n.** anthropoid; primate; simian; **a.** anthropoidal; simian; simious; **n.** simianity

MONOTONOUS: (**see** "dull") **a.** banal; stereotyped; stereotypical; **n.** MONOTONY: (**see** "dullness") prosaism

MONSTER: **n.** behemoth; fiend; Frankenstein; leviathan; monstrosity

fabulous: **n.** chimera; dragon; gorgon; ogre; phoenix; sphinx

MONSTROUS: (**see** "huge") **a.** atrocious; Caliban; grotesque; heinous; hideous; prodigious

MONTH(S), *by the:* **adv.** *per mensam*

lasting two: **a.** bimestral

pert. to: **a.** mensual

six: **n.** semester; **a.** semestral

MOOD: **n.** disposition; inclination; proclivity; temper(ament)

in bad: see "irritable"

of scornful distaste: **n.** fastidium; squeamishness; **a.** fastigial

MOODINESS: (**see** "sullenness") **n.** hypochondriasis; melancholia; melancholy; (**pl.** doldrums; megrims); **a.** MOODY: ambivalent; hypochondriacal; melancholic; temperamental

MOON, *full or at time of full:* **a.** plenilune

goddess of: **n.** Artemis; Astarte; Diana; Luna

study of: **n.** selenology

supposed inhabitant of: **n.** lunarian

MORAL(S): **n.** allegory; apologue; ethics; mores; (the) moralities; **a.** allegorical; didactic; righteous; tropological; virtuous

against good: **adv.** *contra bonos mores*

censor of: **n.** *censor morum*

false application of reasoning about: **n.** casuistry; **a.** casuistic

guardian of: **n.** *custos morum*

having no (moral) merit or demerit: **a.** adiaphoristic; adiaphorous; **n.** adiaphorism; adiaphoron; **n.** adiaphorist

law: **n.** dharma

obligation or command: **n.** categorical imperative

obligation, study of: **n.** deontology

outside bounds of: **a.** amoral; immoral; **n.** amorality; immorality

persons who profess strict: **n.** (the) *unco guid*

strictness of: **n.** piosity; precisian; rigorism; sabbatarian; **a.** puritanic(al); sabbatarian

to lower: **v.** debauch; **n.** debauchment; **n.** debaucher

trend or spirit of the time: **n.** zeitgeist

w/o (moral) sensibility, as infants: **n.** or **a.** amoral

MORALISTIC: **a.** admonishing; didactic(al); sabbatarian; sermonic; **v.** MORALIZE: admonish; lecture; sermonize

MORALLY *contaminating:* **a.** scrofulous; **n.** scrofulosis

corrupt or unrestrained: (**see** "lewd") **a.** dissolute; lecherous; libertine; licentious; profligate; scrofulous

degrading, that which is: **n.** ordure

strict: **a.** puritanical; rectitudinous; sabbatarian; **n.** piosity; probity; propriety; rectitude; scrupulosity

those who profess to be: **n.** (the) *unco guid*

weak or unwholesome: **a.** maladive; scrofulous; **n.** scrofulosis

MORBID: (**see** "diseased") **a.** cachectic; cadaverous; grisly; gruesome; maladive; morbose; scrofulous; **n.** MORBIDITY: cachexia

MORNING: **n.** *ante meridiem;* matin

pert. to: **a.** antemeridian; matinal; matutinal

MOROSE: see "gloomy"

MORSEL: see "delicacy"

MORTAL: see "man" **and** "perishable"

MORTGAGE: **n.** hypothecation; **v.** hypothecate; impignorate

MOSAIC: see "variegated" and "variegation"

MOTHER: n. ancestress; genetrix; (pl. genetrices); mater; a. maternal(istic); n. MOTHERHOOD: maternity
  centering on: a. matricentric
  derived or inherited fr. side of: a. matroclinal; matroclinic; matroclinous
  killing of, also killer: n. matricide; a. matricidal
  lineage based on or thru: n. matrilineage; a. matrilineal; matrilinear
  marked by authority of: a. matripotestal
  of the family: n. materfamilias; matriarch; a. matriarchal
  rel. to or to side of family: a. maternal-(istic); matrilateral; matrilinean; matrilinear; n. maternity; matrilineage
  ruler of family or clan: n. materfamilias; matriarch(ate); matriarchy; a. matriarchal; matriarchic

MOTION, *by one's own:* adv. *motu proprio; proprio motu; proprio vigore*
  constantly in: a. volitant; n. volitation
  loss of voluntary: n. catalepsy; paralysis; a. cataleptic; paralytic
  perpetual: n. *moto perpetuo; perpetuum mobile*
  pert. to or resulting from: a. kinetic
  science of: n. dynamics; kinetics

MOTIONLESS: (see "still") a. impassive; quiescent

MOTIVE: n. consideration; design; determinant; fillip; impetus; impulse; incentive; inducement; intendment; intention; motif; motivation; provocation; stimulus
  concealment of false: n. hypocrisy; a. hypocritical; n. hypocrite
  ulterior: n. *arrière-pensée*
  without: a. unmotivated; unpremeditated

MOTOR *control, loss or weakness of:* n. akinesia; akinesis; catalepsy; paralysis; a. akinetic; cataleptic; paralytic

MOTTO: (see "maxim") n. epigraph; epigram
  beginning of book or chapter: n. epigram
  reverse of U.S. seal: annuit coeptus
  U.S.A.: e pluribus unum

MOULT: see "molt"

MOUND: n. hummock; tumulus

MOUNTAIN(S): *are in labor: parturiunt montes*
  beyond the: a. tramontane; transmontane; ultramontane
  climbing: n. alpinism; alpinist
  process of formation: n. orogeny; a. orogenetic; orogenic
  situated at foot or near base of: a. subalpine; submontane
  situated between: a. intermontane
  situated beyond: a. ultramontane
  situated on farthest side of: a. transalpine; transmontane
  situated on nearest side of: a. cismontane
  study of: n. orography; orology
  within the: a. intramontane

MOUNTAINEERS *are always freemen:* n. *montani semper liberi* (motto of W. Va.)

MOUNTAINOUS: a. alpestrine

MOURNFUL: (see "sad") a. deplorable; doleful; lamentable; luctiferous; threnodic; n. MOURNFULNESS: (see "sadness") lugubrosity

MOURNING *garment:* n. sackcloth

MOUTH, *away from:* adv. aborad; aboral
  by way of (as medicine): adv. *per os;* peroral
  having large: a. macrostomus; patulous; n. macrostomia
  having small: a. microstomatus; microstomus; n. microstomia
  pert. to: a. buccal; labial; oral; oscular
  surrounding the: a. circumoral
  w/ closed: adv. *à bouche fermée* a. or adv. bouche fermée

MOVE: v. actuate; advance; affect; (e)migrate; impel; influence; proceed; n. (see "movement") *démarche;* (e)migration; maneuver; transplantation; a. MOVING: impressive; pathetic; persuading; poignant; touching
  with suddenness: v. or n. catapult

MOVEABILITY: n. flexibility; maneuverability; mobility; motility; a. MOVABLE: inconstant; maneuverable; mobile; motile

MOVEMENT: n. activity; advancement; automation; *démarche;* dynamism; (e)migration; impetus; locomotion; maneuver; momentum; proceeding; procession; progression; transition; trend; velocity

MUCH *in little:* **n.** *multum in parvo*

MUDDY: **a.** roiled; roily; turbid; **n.** turbidity

MULTIPLY: (**see** "increase") **v.** augment; burgeon; poliferate; propagate; pullulate; reproduce; **a.** MULTIPLYING: burgeoning; proliferous; reproductive

MULTITUDE: **n.** aggregation; concourse; host; legion; manifold; multiety; multiplicity; myriad; ruck

MURDER: **see** "killing"
mania for: **n.** phonomania

MURKY: **a.** fuliginous; obscure; turbid; **n.** MURKINESS: fuliginosity; obscurity; turbidity

MURMUR: **v.** susurate; **n.** susuration; susurus; **a.** mormorando; purling; susurant; susurus
act of (murmuring): **n.** murmuration

MUSCLE(S): **n.** sinew(s); thews
sense: **n.** kinesthesia; proprioception; **a.** kinesthetic; proprioceptive

MUSCULAR *uncoordination:* **n.** astasia-abasia; astasis; ataxia; **a.** ataxic
power: **n.** thews

MUSES, *the nine:* **n.** Calliope; Clio; Erato; Euterpe; Melpomene; Polymnia; Terpsichore; Thalia; Urania

MUSIC: **n.** harmonization; harmony; melody; syncopation
art or science of writing: **n.** composition; melopoeia; musicography; **a.** melopoe(t)ic
closing piece: **n.** coda; epilogue; postlude; postludium
excessive or abnormal liking for: **n.** melomania; melomaniac
god of: **n.** Apollo
muse of: **n.** Euterpe
opening piece: **n.** overture; pr(a)eludium; prelude
pert. to: **a.** Euterpean; harmonious; melodious; melophonic

study of: **n.** musicology; **a.** musicological; **n.** musicologist

MUSICAL: (**see** "harmonious") **a.** aeolian; canorous; dulcet; euphonic; euphonious; melic; melodious; orotund; sonorous; symphonic; symphonious; **n.** phantasia; revue
composition of varied themes: **n.** medley; montage; pastiche
embellishment: **n.** arabesque
humorous or whimsical melody: **n.** fantasia; quolibet
tones, entire compass of: **n.** diapason; **a.** diapasonal

MUTENESS: **n.** inarticulateness; obmutescence

MUTINOUS: **see** "lawless"

MUTUAL: **a.** alternate; alternating; coincident; common; complementary; correlative; homogeneous; interdependent; reciprocal; respective; synal(1)gamatic; synchronous
quality or state of being: **n.** interdependence; mutuality; reciprocality; synchroneity

MUTUALLY *antagonistic things or qualities:* **n.pl.** incompatibilities
dependent: **a.** complementary; interdependent; reciprocal; symbiotic(al)
destructive: **a.** internecine
not (mutually) possible: **a.** incompossible; **n.** incompossibility

MY *goodness!:* **adv.** *ma foi!*

MYSTERIOUS: (**see** "hidden") **a.** arcane; cabalistic; clandestine; cryptic(al); enigmatic(al); esoteric; exotic; extraphysical; glamorous; hermetic(al); incomprehensible; inexplicable; inscrutable; obscure; occult; oracular; orphic; picturesque; preternatural; recondite; sibylline; supernatural; surreptitious; tenebrific; tenebrious; uncanny; unfathomed; **n.** MYSTERIOUSNESS: incomprehensibility; inscrutability; mysticality
beliefs or attitudes surrounding person or thing: **n.** mystique
invested w/ (mysterious) significance: **a.** fetishistic; **n.** mystique
manner, in a: **a. or adv.** mysterioso
person: **n.** enigma; paradox; sphinx
process or function: **n.** arcanum; (**pl.** arcana); chemistry; mystique

MYSTERY: **n.** arcanum; conundrum; enigma; incomprehensibility; oracularity; paradoxicality; perplexity
celestial: **n.pl.** *arcana caelestia*
interpreter of: **n.** mystagogue
of mysteries: **n.** *arcanum arcanorum*

MYSTIC(AL): (**see** "mysterious") **a.** anagogical; cabalistic; cryptic; enigmatic(al); epoptic; esoteric; mysterial; occult; oracular; orphic(al); paradoxic(al); stratospheric(al); symbolic(al); telestic
beliefs, attitudes, etc. surrounding person or thing: **n.** aura; cachet; halo; mystique; nimbus
doctrine(s): cabala; cabalism; mystagogy; **a.** cabalistic; mystagogic
quality: **n.** mysticality; mystique

teacher or interpreter of the: **n.** mystagogue; **a.** mystagogic

MYSTIFY: **see** "bewilder"

MYTH(S): **n.** anecdote; fabulosity; legend; saga
engaged in making: **a.** mythopoe(t)ic(al); **n.** mythopoesis
to build or construct: **v.** mythologize

MYTHICAL: **a.** allegorical; apocryphal; arcane; fabricated; fabular; fabulous; fantastic; fictitious; legendary; parabolical; visionary
divest of the: **v.** deglamorize; demythologize; **n.** deglamorization; demytholization

N

NAIL(S) : **n.** ungual; unguis
  animal(s) having: **n.** unguiculate; (**pl.**
unguiculata)
  -biting: **n.** onychophagia; onychophagy;
phaneromania
  having: **a.** unguiferate; unguiculate

NAÏVE: **a.** artless; candid; credulous; gullible; ingenuous; innocent; unfeigned; unphilosophic; unsophisticated; **n.** NAÏVETE: artlessness; credulity; gullibility; ingenuosity; ingenuousness; simplicity

NAKED: **a.** *au naturel;* denudate; denuded; destitute; dishabille; divested; exposed; *in puris naturalibus;* obvious; *sans vêtements; tout nu;* unattired; unclothed; undraped; **n.** NAKEDNESS: starkness
  eye, exam. or study by: **n.** macrography; macroscopy; *nudis oculus;* **a.** macroscopic; megascopic
  partly: **n.** dishabille
  practice of going: **n.** Adamitism; gymnosophy; nudism; **n.** gymnosophist
  truth: **n.** *nuda veritas*

NAME(S) : **v.** denominate; designate; entitle; identify; nominate; specify; stipulate; style; **n.** agnomen; appellation; appellative; cognomen(ation); (de)nomination; designation; epithet; eponym; matronym(ic); nomenclature; patronym(ic); rubric; sobriquet
  act of calling or addressing by: **n.** compellation
  additional, as honor (as Eric the Red) : **n.** agnomen
  application of wrong: **n.** misnomer
  assumed, or nickname (**see** "nickname") : **n.** agnomen; alias; hypocoristic; *nom d'emprunt;* sobriquet
  author, assumed by: **see** "fictitious" **below**
  author's own, in: **adv.** *proprio nomine;* **a.** onomastic; onomatous; onymous

  bad or objectionable: **n.** caconym; epithet; **n.pl.** *gros mots*
  bearing no: **a.** anonymous; innominate
  Christian: **see** "first" **below**
  courtesy title (as Hon.) : **n.** honorific
  derived fr. father or male line: **n.** patronym; **a.** patronymic
  derived fr. mother or fem. line: **n.** matronym(ic) ; metronym(ic)
  descriptive, disparaging or abusive: **n.** epithet; **a.** epithetical
  different for same thing, use of: **n.** heteronomy; **a.** heteronymous
  different, having: **a.** heteronymous
  existing in (name) only: **a.** nominal; titular; **n.** titular(it)y
  false or unknown: **n.** anonym(e); anonymity; pseudonym; pseudonymity; **a.** anonymous; pseudonymous
  family, or thru father: **n.** patronym; **a.** patronymic
  family or surname: **n.** cognomen; *nom de famille;* patronym; **a.** patronymic; surnominal
  feminine but used as pseudonym by man: **n.** pseudogyny; **a.** pseudogynous
  fictitious: **n.** alias; allonym; *nom de guerre; nom de plume;* pseudonym; pseudonymity; **a.** pseudonymous
  first or personal: **n.** Christian (name); forename; *nom de baptême; petit nom;* praenomen
  for divine being: **n.** theologumenon
  formed fr. a person's: **n.** antonomasia; eponym; **a.** antonomastic; eponymous
  full or complete: **n.** *nom et prénom*
  god or divine being, for: **n.** theologumenon
  good, or well suited: **n.** euonym; **a.** euonymous
  having no: **a.** anonymous; innominate
  idea, use of person's for: **see** "formed fr. a person's" **above**
  in author's own: **adv.** proprio nomine; **a.** onomatous; onymous
  in (name) only: **a.** nominal; titular; **n.** titular(it)y

inapplication or wrong: **n.** misnomer
known by various: **a.** polyonymous; **n.** polyonymy
  last: **see** "family" **above**
  maiden: **n.** *nom de jeune fille*
  male, but used by fem. as pseudonym: **n.** pseudandry
  many for one person or thing: **n.** polyonymy; **a.** polyonymous
  married woman using maiden: **n.** Lucy Stoner
  mother, derived fr.: **see** "derived" **above**
  no (name), having or bearing: **a.** anonymous; innominate
  objectionable or bad: **n.** caconym; epithet; **a.** epithetic(al)
  of one thing for that of another associated w/ or suggested by it: **n.** antonomasia; metonymy; synecdoche; **a.** antonomastic; metonymic(al); synecdochical
  only, in: **a.** nominal; *pro forma;* titular; **n.** titular(it)y
  pen: **see** "fictitious" **above**
  pet, or of endearment: **n.** hypocorism; hypocoristic; *petit nom*
  place, or indicative of origin, natural locale, etc.: **n.** toponym; **a.** toponymic(al)
  plurality of: **n.** polyonymy; **a.** polyonymous
  same, having: **a.** homonymic; homonymous
  science of: **n.** nomenclature; onomatology; semantics; terminology
  secret: **n.** cryptonym; pseudonym; **a.** cryptonymous; pseudonymous
  stage: **n.** *nom de théâtre*
  study of personal: **n.** anthropoponymy; onomastics
  surname: **see** "family" **above**
  system or catalog(ue) of: **n.** nomenclature; onomasticon
  title or word in place of: **n.** antonomasia; **a.** antonomastic
  two, combined use of: **a.** binomial
  two or more, having: **a.** homonymic; homonymous
  two persons of same, either of: **n.** homonym; **a.** homonymous
  under assumed: **a.** incognito; (**fem.** incognita); pseudonymous
  under the (name) of: **adv.** *sub nomine*
  unmarried: **see** "maiden" **above**
  use of diff. for same thing: **n.** heteronymy; **a.** heteronymous
  use of person's for an idea: **see** "formed fr. a person's" **above**
  use of title or word in place of: **see** "title, etc." **above**

various, having or known by: **a.** polyonymous; **n.** polyonymy
  writer, bearing that of: **see** "author's own" **above**
  wrong: **n.** misnomer

NAMED *suitably:* **a.** eunonymous

NAMELESS: **a.** anonymous; incognito; indescribable; inexpressible; innominate; unacknowledged; **n.** NAMELESSNESS: anonymity

NAMELY: **adv.** *c'est-à-dire;* scilicet (**abb.** scil.); videlicet (**abb.** viz.)

NAMESAKE: **n.** homonym

NARCOTIC: **n.** anesthetic; anodyne; nepenthe; opiate; somniferent; soporific; stupefacient; **a.** anesthetic; somniferous; soporiferous; stupefactive

NARRATIVE: **n.** iliad; narration; odyssey; saga

NARROW: (**see** "petty") **a.** bigoted; circumscribed; illiberal; incapacious; incommodious; insular; parochial; prejudiced; provincial; restricted; sectarian; stenotic
  attachment to sect, party, etc.: **n.** sectarianism; **a.** parochial; sectarian
  limits, having: **a.** municipal; parochial; provincial
  -minded: **a.** bigoted; *borné;* denominational; illiberal; insular; insulated; isolated; parochial; pedantic; peninsular; prejudiced; provincial; sectarian; **n.** NARROW-MINDEDNESS: bigotism; bigotry; exiguity; Grundyism; illiberality; insularism; insularity; parochiality; parvanimity; (pen)insularity; provincialism; sectarianism
  -minded person: **see under** *"person"*

NASTY: **see** "dirty"

NATIONS, *comity of:* **n.** *comitas gentium; comitas inter gentes*
  law of: **see** "law, international"
  understanding bet.: **n.** *entente (cordiale)*

NATIVE: **n.** aboriginal; aborigine; authchthon; domestic; indigen(e); inhabitant; (**pl.** *les aborigènes*); **n.** aboriginality; endemicity; endemism; **a.** aboriginal; autochthonal; autochthonic; autochthonous; demotic; domestic; edaphic; enchorial;

endemial; endemic(al); indigenous; in-herent; innate; original; natal; primitive
   animal, people or plant: **n.** aboriginal; aborigine; autochthon; indigin(e); **a.** abo-riginal; autochthonous
   environment: **n.** habitat(ion); milieu
   land, pert. to: **a.** compatriotic; natal; patrial
   not: (**see** "foreign") **a.** heterochthonous
   soil: **n.** *natale solum*

NATURAL: (**see** "physical" **and** "sin-cere") **a.** artless; candid; congenital; en-dogenous; essential; hereditary; inborn; ingrained; inherent; innate; instinctive; spontaneous; unaffected; unpremeditated; unsophisticated; unstudied; **n.** naturality
   differing fr. or beyond the: (**see** "super-natural") **a.** paraphysical; parapsycho-logical; preternatural; supermundane
   endowment or adjunct: **n.** ap(p)anage
   feeling or behavior: **n.** naturality; **a.** naturalesque
   forces, purposeful use of: **n.** telesia; telesis
   insight: **n.** *lumen naturale*
   law: **n.** *jus naturae; jus naturale*
   not: (**see** "foreign") **a.** artefactitious; artificial; illusive; **n.** artefact; artificiality; Brummagem; counterfeit
   products: **n.pl.** *fructus naturales*
   state: **n.** *al fresco; au naturel*
   state of being: **n.** naturality; **a.** natu-ralesque
   tendency: (**see** "inclination") **n.** ap-petence; appetency; conatus; diathesis; id-iosyncrasy

NATURALIZED: **a.** acclimated; adapted; heterochthonous

NATURE(S): (**see** "character") **n.** con-stitution; inclination; proclivity; propen-sity; (quint)essence; texture
   according to, or second-: **adv.** *secundum naturam*
   as one w/ God (doctrine): **n.** panthe-ism; **a.** pantheistic(al)
   ascription of soul to things: **n.** anthro-popsychism; **a.** anthropopsychic
   being of a diff.: **a.** heterogeneous; het-ero(o)usian
   close to: **n.** primitivism; **a.** primitivistic
   conforming closely to or imitating: **a.** naturalesque
   essential: **n.** quiddity; quintessence; vir-tuality; **a.** quidditive; quintessential; **adv.** *sub specie aeternitatis*

   evidence of design in: **n.** teleology; **a.** teleological
   freak of: **n.** *lasus naturae;* monstrosity; sport
   having same (nature) or kind: **a.** con-substantial; **n.** consubstantiality
   having two or mixed: **a.** amphibious; **n.** amphibian
   healing power of: **n.** *vis medicatrix naturae*
   law of: **see under** "natural"
   of beings, description of: **n.** ontography; **a.** ontographic
   of things, in the: **adv.** *de rerum naturâ; in rerum naturâ*
   pert. to or derived fr. laws of: **a. or n.** cosmonomic
   unbiased or undistorted: **a. or adv.** naturâle; **a.** naturalesque
   wisdom about: **n.** physiosophy
   worship of, or of natural forces: **n.** cos-motheism; pantheism; physiolatry; pri-aprism; **a.** pantheistic(al); physiolatrous; **n.** pantheist; physiolater; physiolatrist

NAUSEA, *to point of: usque ad nauseam*

NAUSEOUS (or NAUSEATING): (**see** "revolting") **a.** abominable; bilious; dis-gusting; fulsome; loathsome; *nauséeux;* offensive; qualmish; repugnant; sicken-ing; squeamish

NAVEL: **n.** omphalos; omphalus; umbilicus
   meditation while gazing at: **n.** omphalo-skepsis; **n.** hesychast; omphalopsychite; **a.** hesychastic
   pert. to: **a.** omphalic; umbilical
   resembling, or depressed like: **a.** um-bilicate(d)

NAVIGATION, *pert. to:* **a.** marine; mari-time; nautical; naval; oceanic

NEAR (or NEARBY): **a.** adjacent; ap-proaching; contiguous; imminent; im-pending; neighboring; propinquant; pro-pinquous; proximate; **adv.** NEARLY: *à peu près;* quasi
   East: **n.** Levant; **a.** Byzantine; Levan-tine
   -sighted: **a.** myopic; purblind; **n.** myopia

NEAREST *in time, relation or degree:* **a.** propinquitous; **n.** prochein; propinquity
   to point of attachment or origin: **a.** proximal; proximate; **adv.** proximad

NEARNESS: **n.** adjacency; (appro)propinquity; contiguity; proximity
in time, place, relationship, etc.: **n.** propinquity; proximity

NEAT: **a.** concinnate; concinnous; fastidious; immaculate; modish; natty; proportional; shipshape; *soigné;* (**fem.** *soignée*); spruce; uncluttered; **a.** NEATNESS: concinnity; fastidiousness

NECESSARY: **a.** essential; imperative; incumbent; inevitable; indispensable; indispensible; inexorable; mandatory; needful; obligatory; (pre)requisite; unavoidable; unpreventable
changes having been made: mutatis mutandis

NECESSITY: (**see** "need") **n.** desideratum; essential(ity); exigency; indispensability; obligation; (pre)requisite; requirement; *sine qua non*
by force of: **adv.** perforce
has no law: necessitas non habet legem
mother of invention (or of arts) : *mater artium necessitas*
of life: **n.** aliment; **a.** alimental

NECK: **n.** cervix; collum; **a.** cervical
having a long: **a.** longicollous; macrauchen

NECKLINE, *low:* **n.** décolletage; **a.** décollete

NEED(S): (**see** "necessity" **and** "poverty") **n.** deficiency; desideratum; desiderium; essential(ity); exigency; indispensability; *manque;* obligation; (pre)requisite; requirement; (**pl.** desiderata; desideria)

NEEDLE, *shaped like:* **a.** acerate; acerose; acerous; acicular; aciculate(d); belonoid

NEEDLESS: **a.** gratuitous; unessential; unnecessary

NEEDY: (**see** "poor") **a.** desiderative; destitute; insolvent; necessitous; pressing

NEGATION: **n.** annihilation; contraindication; denial; disclaimer; nonentity; nullification; obliteration; **a.** NEGATIVE: negatory; neutral; privative; **n.** negativity
expressing: **n.** negatory; **n.** negativism; negativity

but implying affirmation: **n.** negative pregnant

NEGLECT: **v.** disregard; ignore; misprize; pigeonhole; pretermit; **n.** (**see** "failure") delinquency; dereliction; disregard; ignoration; inattention; indifference; indolence; nonobservance; omission; pretermission; procrastination
of duty: **n.** abandonment; delinquency; dereliction; laches; malfeasance; misfeasance
place or condition of: **n.** limbo

NEGLIGENCE: **n.** delinquency; ignoration; inadvertence; inattention; indifference; laches; malfeasance; misfeasance; nonobservance; omission; remission; **a.** NEGLIGENT: delinquent; improvident; inadvertent; inattentive; indifferent; neglectful; remiss; unmindful
gross: **n.** *crassa negligentia; culpa lata*

NEGROES, *dislike or fear of:* **n.** negrophobia; negrophobe
one friendly to: **n.** negrophile

NEIGHBORHOOD: **n.** habitat; milieu; propinquity; proximity; purlieu(s); suburb(s); vicinage; vicinity; (**pl.** alentours; confines; environs); **a.** NEIGHBORING: (**see** "adjacent") attingent; contiguous; limitrophe; propinquant; tangent(i)al; vicinal; **a.** NEIGHBORLY: (**see** "friendly") amicable; gregarious

NEPHEW, *pert. to:* **a.** nepotal; nepotic

NERVE: (**see** "gall") **n.** audacity; effrontery; fortitude; intrepidity; sinew; temerity
center: **n.** plexus
junction: **n.** synapse; **a.** synaptic

NERVOUS: **a.** agitated; apprehensive; excitable; fidgety; hysterical; irritable; neurotic; restless; restive; timorous; volatile; **n.** NERVOUSNESS: agitation; excitation; irritability; nervosity; neurosis; neuroticism; psychoneurosis; psychosis; (**pl.** fantods)
and excited: **a.** agitato

NEST: **n.** abode; aerie; nidus; retreat
build a: **v.** nidify; nidificate; **n.** nidification; nidulation; **a.** nidificant
leaving shortly after hatching: **a.** nidifugous
living in, or sharing w/ another: **a.** nidicolous

NETWORK: **n.** complex; labyrinth; plexus; *reseau;* (**pl.** *reseaux*); reticulation; reticulum

NEUTRAL: (**see** "indifferent") **a.** adiaphorous; disinterested; dispassionate; impersonal; nonpartisan; unbiased; **n.** NEUTRALITY: adiaphoria; detachment; indifference

NEVER *despair: nil desperandum*

NEVERTHELESS: **adv.** *tout de même*

NEW: **a.** immature; inexperienced; modern(istic); nascent; neoteric; novel; nouveau; pristine; renovated; unaccustomed; unexampled; unfamiliar; unprecedented; **n.** NEWNESS: **see** "freshness"
 doctrine: **n.** neology
 hater or hatred of something (*new*) *or strange:* **n.** misoneism; misoneist; xenophobia; xenophobe; **a.** misoneistic; xenophobic
 introducing something (*new*): **a.** innovative; innovatory; **n.** debut; inauguration; innovation
 something which is: **n.** innovation; neoteric
 word or new use for old: **n.** neologism; neoterism

NEWCOMER: (**see** "upstart") **n.** Johnny-come-lately; *nouveau riche; parvenu*

NEWLY *arrived or developed:* **a.** nascent; neoteric; nouveau; **n.** innovation; neoteric

NEWSPAPER *or magazine style of writing:* **n.** journalese

NEXT: (**see** "adjacent") **a.** contiguous; prochein; proximal; sequacious
 to the last: **a.** penultimate

NICE: (**see** "agreeable") **a.** decorous; demure; discriminating
 overly: **a.** fastidious; squeamish; **n.** fastidiousness; preciosity; scrupulosity

NICETY, *to a:* **adv.** *ad unguem*

NICKNAME: **n.** agname; agnomen; cognomen; epithet; hypocorism; hypocoristic; moni(c)ker; *petit nom;* sobriquet

NIGHT: **see** "darkness"
 at: **adv.** *à la belle étoile;* **a.** nocturnal; **n.** nocturnality
 attack by: **n.** camisado
 -blindness: **n.** hemeralopia; nyctalopia
 club: **n.** *boîte de nuit;* truncheon
 functioning at: **a.** nocturnal; **n.** nocturnality
 going about at: **n.** noctambulation; noctivigation; **a.** noctivicant; noctivagous
 -gown: **n.** *robe de nuit*
 happening, active or functioning at: **a.** nocturnal; **n.** nocturnality
 pert. to: **a.** nocturnal; **n.** nocturnality
 stay up or out all: **v.** pernoctate; **n.** pernoctation
 -stick: **n.** truncheon

NIGHTMARE: **n.** apprehension; *cauchemar;* incubus; oneirodynia; *pavor nocturnus;* vexation
 something like: **n.** Walpurgis Night; *Walpurgisnacht*

NIMBLE: (**see** "agile") **a.** dexterous; lissom(e); supple; **n.** NIMBLENESS: agility; dexterity; elasticity; flexibility; legerity; lissomeness; suppleness

NINE, *group or set of:* **n.** ennead; **a.** enneadic
 pert. to or based on: **a.** novenary
 -sided: **n. or a.** nonagon

NINETIETH: **a.** nonagesimal

NINETY, *person over but less than 100:* **n.** nonagenarian
 pert. to such person or period: **a.** nonagenarian

NO *one is sufficiently wise by himself: nemo solus satis sapit*
 sooner said than done: aussitôt dit, aussitôt fait; dictum ac factum

NOBILITY: **n.** aristocracy; eminence; gentility; gentry; grandeur; magnanimity; noblesse; patriciate; peerage; sublimity; (**n.pl.** aristoi) **a.** aristocratic; nobiliary
 duty of: **n.** *noblesse oblige*
 lesser: **n.** *petite noblesse*
 pert. to: **a.** aristocratic; nobiliary; patrician

NOBLE: **a.** aristocratic; eminent; exalted; illustrious; lofty; magnanimous; magnificent; majestic; patrician; princely; sub-

lime; **n.** NOBLEMAN : aristocrat; grandee; magnificio; patrician; peer; (**pl.** aristoi)
  birth or status: **n.** aristocracy; noblesse; patriciate; peerage
  in mind: **a.** magnanimous; spirituel(le)

NOBODY : **n.** *homme de rien; pessorbius orti*

NODDING, *act of, esp involuntary:* **n.** nutation; **a.** nutant; nutational

NOISE : (see "uproar") **n.** acoustics; Bedlam; blatancy; brouhaha; cacophony; charivari; clamor; detonation; pandemonium; phonics; tintamar(re) ; tintinnabulation; tumult; **a.** NOISELESS : see "silent"
  great and confused: **n.** charivari; pandemonium; tintamar(re) ; **a.** pandemoniac(al) ; tintinnabulary; tintinnabulous
  loud: **n.** detonation
  place of: **n.** Bedlam; pandemonium

NOISY : **a.** agitated : Bedlam; blatant; boisterous; cacophonous; clamorous; clangorous; demonstrative; effusive; obstreperous; pandemoniac(al) ; raucous; riotous; roisterous; sonorous; strepitant; strepitus; stridulous; termagant; thunderous; tumultuary; tumultuous; turbulent; undisciplined
  ominously: **a.** thunderous
  rumor: **n.** *fama clamosa*

NONCHALANCE : **see** "indifference"

NONCONFORMISM : **n.** *avant-gardism;* dissidence; heresy; recusance; recusancy; **n.** NONCONFORMIST : (**see** "disbeliever") *avant-garde;* beatnik; Bohemian; dissenter; dissident; heresiarch; heretic; mossback; recusant; renegade; schismatic; schismatist; standpatter; ultraconservative; **n.** NONCONFORMITY : **see under** "conformity"

NONESSENTIAL : **a.** dispensable; gratuitous; supererogant; supererogative; supererogatory; unessential
  items: **n.pl.** marginalia

NONINTERFERENCE, *doctrine of:* **n.** or **a.** *laissez-faire;* (**also** laisser-faire) ; **n.** *caveat emptor*

NONPROFESSIONAL, *as in art:* **n.** amateur; dilettante; **a.** dilettantish; **n.** dilettantism

NONSENSE : **n.** abracadabra; absurdity; amphigory; balderdash; blatherskite; fandangle; fiddle-faddle; flamdoodle; flummadiddle; folderol; hocus-pocus; imbecility; malarkey; *niaiserie;* nugacity; *nugae canorae;* stultiloquence; stultiloquy; tarradiddle; tomfoolery; trumpery; (**pl.** trivia) ; **a.** NONSENSICAL : absurd; amphigoric; capricious; fanciful; imbecilic; ludicrous; macaronic; notional; preposterous; whimsical
  as talk: **n.** Choctaw; galimatias; gibberish; jabberwock(y)
  melodious: **n.** *nugae canorae*
  pretentious: **n.** amphigory; **a.** amphigoric
  verse or prose: **n.** amphigory; **a.** amphigoric

NOON, *before:* **n.** *ante merediem;* **a.** antemeridian
  rel. to: **a.** meridian

NORM(AL), *as to physical function:* **a.** physiological
  conformity to: (**see** "according to rule") **n.** normality
  sub-: **a.** subaverage; suboptimal; substandard

NORTH *star:* **n.** cynosure; lodestar; polestar

NORTHERN : **a.** arctic; boreal; hyperborean; septentrional
  region(s), pert. to: **a.** arctic; hyperborean
  region(s), resident of: **n.** hyperborean

NOSE : **n.** nasus; olfactus; organon; proboscis
  -bleed: **n.** epistaxis; rhinorrhagia
  hair in: **n.** vibrissa; (**pl.** vibrissae) : **a.** vibrissal
  having, esp. if large: **a.** nasute
  hooked type: **a.** aduncous; aquiline
  turned up: **n.** *nez retroussé;* **a.** retrousse
  well-developed: **a.** nasute

NOT *too much:* **a. or adv.** *non troppo*

NOTABLE (or NOTED) : **a.** celebrated; distinguished; eminent; illustrious; important; impressive; majestic; memorable; memorious; noteworthy; observable; prominent; remarkable; renowned; salient; signal; significant; striking; supereminent

NOTCH: **v.** denticulate; serrate; **n.** denticulation; serration; **a.** NOTCHED: dentate; denticulate(d); dentiform; serrate(d); serrulate

NOTE(S), *collection of:* **n.** adversaria; scrapiana
    marginal: see **under** "marginal"
    personal: **n.pl.** anecdotes; personalia
    things worthy of: **n.pl.** notabilia
    varied: **a.** miscellanea; scrapiana
    well: **adv.** *nota bene* (abb. *n.b.*)
    worthy of: **adv.** *notatu dignum*

NOTEBOOK, *looseleaf:* **n.** cahier
    student's: **n.** *index rerum*

NOTED: *see* "notable"

NOTHING: *from or out of:* **a. or adv.** *ex nihilo*
    out of comes (nothing): **adv.** *de nihilo nihil; ex nihilo nihil fit*
    thing amounting to: **n.** bagatelle; nihility; nonentity; nullity; triviality; (**pl.** trivia)
    to come to: **v.** *n'aboutir à rien*

NOTHINGNESS: (**see** "trifle") **n.** annihilation; bagatelle; cipher; naught; nihility; nonentity; nullity; oblivion; triviality; (**pl.** trivia); vacuity; vacuum

NOTICE: (**see** "heed") **v.** recognize; **n.** advertence; announcement; apprehension; attention; awareness; cognizance; conspicuity; conspicuousness; knowledge; observation; prominence
    take particular: **adv.** *nota bene* (**abb.** n.b.)

NOTICEABLE: **a.** arresting; conspicuous; manifest; observable; obvious; palpable; perceptible; prominent; salient; signal

NOTION: (**see** "idea") **n.** apprehension; bibelot; conception; inclination; inkling; knickknack; understanding; vagary; whimsicality; **a.** NOTIONAL: crotchety; imaginary; theoretical; unreal; visionary; whimsical

NOTORIOUS: (**see** "notable") **a.** arrant; celebrated; discreditable; disreputable; ignominious; inglorious; unmitigated; villainous

NOTWITHSTANDING: **prep.** *malgré; mauger;* maugre; *quand même;* **adv.** howbeit; nevertheless; *nonobstante*

NOUN, *made fr. common name:* **n.** antonomasia; **a.** antonomastic
    verbal: **n.** gerund

NOURISHING: **a.** alible; alimental; alimentative; invigorating; nutural; nutritious; nutritory; nutritive; strengthening
    not: **a.** inalimental; innutrious

NOURISHMENT: (**see** "food") **n.** aliment(ation); collation; forage; nutriment; pabulum; sustenance
    derived parasitically fr. others: **a.** paratrophic
    healthy or good: **n.** eutrophy; **a.** eutrophic
    lacking in: **a.** atrophic; distrophic; inalimental; innutrious; oligotrophic; **n.** atrophy; dystrophia; dystrophy

NOVEL: *see* "new"; **n.** NOVELTY: innovation; neoteric; newness
    developing character fr. child to adulthood: **n.** entwicklungsroman
    about early development or spiritual education of main character: **n.** Bildungsroman
    leading character in: **n.** agonist
    philosophical type: **n.** *roman à thèse*
    w/ real persons, events, etc. disguised: **n.** *roman à clef*

NOVICE: (**see** "beginner" **and** "learner") **n.** neophyte; neoteric; tyro

NOW: **adv.** *in praesenti*
    and always: ora e sempre
    for then: **adv.** *nunc pro tunc;* **a.** *ex post facto*
    or never: **adv.** *nunc aut nunquam*

NOWHERE, *state or quality of being:* **n.** nullibicity; nullibiety

NUDE: *see* "naked"; **n.** NUDISM: Adamitism; gymnosophy; naturalism; **n.** NUDIST: Adamite; gymnosophist

NULL: **a.** invalid; nonexistent; nugatory; *nullius juris;* void; **n.** NULLITY: nihility; **v.** NULLIFY: abolish; abrogate; invalidate; negate; rescind; stultify; **n.** NULLIFICATION: invalidation; stultification; vitiation

NUMB: **see** "blunt"

NUMBER: **n.** aggregate; legion; magnitude; multitude; myriad; quantity
    indefinitely large: **n.** legion; myriad
    large: **n.** hecatomb; manifold; multeity; multifariousness; multiplicity; **a.** manifold; multifarious; myriad

NUMBERLESS: (**see** "unlimited") **a.** innumerable; innumerous; **n.** innumerability

NUMEROUS: (**see** "many") **a.** manifold; multifarious; multiplex; multitudinous; myriad; plentious; plentiful; populous; **n.**

NUMEROUSNESS: manifold; multeity; multiplicity; numerosity; plurality

NUN: **n.** cenobite; recluse; religious; sanctimonial; **a.** cenobitic; **n.** cenobitism

NUTRITION: (**see** "food" **and** "nourishment") **n.** diatetics; **a.** NUTRITIOUS: **see** "nourishing"
    fundamental, involving metabolic change in tissues: **n.** metabolism; trophism
    healthy or good: **n.** eutrophy
    science of: **n.** dietetics; trophology

NUTS, *bearing:* **a.** nuciferous
    living on: **a.** nucivorous

NUTSHELL, *in a:* **adv.** *in nuce*

O

OATH: (see "curse") n. adjuration; affirmation; attestation; blasphemy; execration; expletive; imprecation; malediction
being bound by: a. objurgative; n. objurgation
breaking of: n. perjury; a. perjur(i)ous
pert. to: a. juratory
united by common: n. adjuration; conjuration

OBEDIENT: a. acquiescent; amenable; biddable; compliant; deferential; docile; malleable; obeisant; obsequious; submissive; tractable; n. OBEDIENCE: compliance; conformity; deference; docility; submission
to be servilely or humbly: v. genuflect; kow-tow

OBESE: (see "stout") a. corpulent; orbicular; portly; pyknic; rotund; n. OBESITY: adiposis; adiposity; avoirdupois; corpulence; embonpoint; pinguidity; plumpness; portliness; pursiness; steatosis; stoutness

OBJECT: (see "protest") v. cavil; demur; expostulate; remonstrate; n. (see "aim") intention; materiality; objective
mental rather than real: n. numenon
of human effort or workmanship: n. artefact; artifact; (n.pl. *fructus industriales*); a. artefactitious; artifactitious

OBJECTION: n. exception; protest(ation); remonstrance; remonstration; scruple; a. OBJECTIONABLE: (see "offensive") disagreeable; distasteful; inappropriate; inexpedient; loathsome; nauseous; noisome; obnoxious; rebarbative; reprehensible; repugnant; repulsive; revolting, unpleasing

OBJECTIVE: (see "intent") n. aspiration; *quaesitum;* a. material; postival

OBLIGATION: n. encumbrance; liability; onus; responsibility; a. OBLIGATED: behooving; imperative; incumbent; pledged; a. OBLIGATORY: *de rigueur;* imperative; incumbent; mandatory; prerequisite
ethics or science of moral: n. deontology; a. deontological
imposing mutual: a. synal(l)agmatic
rel. to: a. deontic; obligatory

OBLIGED, *much:* adv. *bien obligé*

OBLIGING: a. amiable; cooperative; obligatory
manner: n. *prévénance*
not: a. *désobligeant*

OBLIQUE: (see "devious") a. duplicitous; evasive; indirect; louche; perverse; sinister

OBLIVION: n. forgetfulnes; lethe; limbo; obliviscence; nirvana; a. OBLIVIOUS: (see "unaware") lethean; oblivial; nirvanic

OBNOXIOUS: see "objectionable"

OBSCENE: (see "lewd") a. ithyphallic; lascivious; pornographic
books, pictures, etc.: n. erotica; esoterica; facetiae; pornography
cult of the: n. aischrolatreia
language, excessive or uncontrollable use of: n. coprolalia

OBSCENITY: n. coprolalia; coprology; pornography; scatology; vulgarism; vulgarity
fondness for or preoccupation w/: n. coprophilia; scatology; a. cloacal; coprophilous; scatologic(al)
study of: n. coprology; pornography
worship of: n. aischrolatreia

OBSCURE: (see "vague") v. adumbrate; becloud; bedim; obfuscate; obnebulate;

221

obnubilate; a. abstruse; ambiguous; ambivalent; cabalistic; caliginous; crepuscular; cryptic(al); Delphian; Delphic; enigmatic(al); equivocal; fuliginous; incomprehensible; inscrutable; obfuscatory; recondite; transcendent; unfathomable; **n.** OBSCURITY: (**see** "confusion") abstrusity; ambiguity; ambivalence; fuliginosity; inconspicuousness; obfuscation; oblivion; obscuration; opacity; profundity; seclusion; turbidity
  area: **n.** limbo; penumbra; twilight zone
  literary style: **n.** obscuranti(ci)sm

OBSERVABLE: (**see** "noticeable") **a.** detectable; discernible; **a.** OBSERVANT: alert; attentive; heedful; mindful; (on the) *qui vive;* perceptive; percipient; regardful
  fact or event: **n.** phenomenon; (**pl.** phenomena); **a.** phenomenal

OBSERVATION: **n.** descant; observance; reflection; utterance
  based on one's: **a.** autoptic
  if under suspicion: **n.** surveillance; **a.** surveillant
  keenness of: **n.** acumen; percipience; percipiency; perspicacity; perspicuity; **a.** acuminous; percipient; perspicacious

OBSERVE: (**see** "commemorate" **and** "see") **v.** celebrate; solemnize; witness
  unable or unwilling to: **a.** astigmatic(al); purblind; myopic; **n.** astigmatism; myopia

OBSESSION: **n.** compulsion; *idée fixe;* impulse; preoccupation; mania

OBSOLETE: **a.** antediluvian; antiquated; archaic; outmoded; *passé;* rudimentary; timeworn; vestigial
  become by lapse of time: **v.** obsolesce; superannuate; **n.** depletion; obsolescence; superannuation
  becoming: **a.** obsolescent; **n.** depletion; obsolescence; **v.** obsolesce

OBSTINATE: (**see** "stubborn") **a.** *entêté;* pertinacious; pervicacious; tenacious; unpliable; unrepentant; unyielding; **n.** OBSTINACY: (**see** "stubbornness") adamancy; asininity; contumely; inveteracy; persistence; pertinacity; pervicaciousness; pervicacity; tenacity

OBSTRUCT: **v.** barricade; encumber; impede; incommode; occlude; oppilate; re-

tard; **n.** OBSTRUCTION: (**see** "impasse") barrier; embolus; impediment; (**pl.** impedimenta); obstacle; oppilation; stenosis; strangulation; **a.** OBSTRUCTIVE: impedimental; impedimentive; impeditive; obstruent; occlusive; oppilative; stenotic

OBTAIN: **see** "get"

OBVIOUS: **a.** conspicuous; evident; literal; manifest; palpable; patent; prominent; unambiguous; unequivocal; **n.** OBVIOUSNESS: conspicuity; conspicuousness; manifestness; patency
  beyond or below what is: **a.** subintelligential; subliminal

OCCASIONAL: **a.** episodic(al); incidental; infrequent; sporadic
  state of being: **n.** infrequency; occasionality; sporadicity

OCCUPANCY: **n.** incumbency; (in)habitation; occupation; residency; tenancy; tenure; **n.** OCCUPANT: incumbent; inhabitant; tenant; **a.** OCCUPATIONAL: employmental; habitudinal; industrial; professional; vocational

OCCUPIED *mentally:* **a.** abstracted; versant

OCCURRENCE: **n.** circumstance; episode; incident
  unexpected or embarrassing: (**see** "accident") **n.** contretemps

OCCURRING *at same time:* **a.** coetaneous; coeval; coincident(al); coinstantaneous; coinciding; concomitant; concurrent; contemporaneous; contemporary; coordinant; harmonious; synchronic(al); synchronous; synchronistic(al); unanimous; **n.** coetaneity; concurrency; contemporaneity; simultaneity; synchronicity; synchrony; unanimity
  later: **a.** subsequent(ial); supervenient; **n.** supervenience; supervention; **v.** supervene

OCEAN(S): (**see** "sea") **n.** brine; deep
  beyond the: **see under** "sea"
  inhabiting depths of: **a.** bathyal(ic); bathybic; bathypelagic; bathysmal; benthic; benthopelagic; suboceanic
  pert. to: **a.** marine; maritime; oceanic; pelagic; thalassic

to deep part of: **a.** bathyal(ic); bathybic; bathypelagic; bathysmal
study of: **n.** oceanography; thalassography

ODD: (**see** "unrealistic") **a.** anomalous; atypical; azygous; bizarre; capricious; eccentric; fantastic(al); grotesque; haphazard; idiosyncratic; inexplicable; nondescript; occasional; *outré;* singular; vagarious; whimsical; **n.** ODDITY: (**see** "peculiarity") bizarrerie; caprice; curiosity; eccentricity; fantasticality; grotesquerie; h(a)ecceity; idiosyncrasy; particularity; quiddity; singularity; vagary; whim(sicality)
at (odds): **see** "unharmonious"
character: **n.** *drôle de corps*

ODOR: **n.** aroma(ticity); cachet; effluvium; emanation; estimation; fragrance; redolence; repute
disagreeable or noxious: **n.** aromaticity; effluvium; (**pl.** effluvia); mephitis; nidor; **a.** (**see** "stinking") effluvial; fetid; malodorous; mephitic; nidorous; noisome; odiferous
giving off: **a.** aromatic; odoriferous; odorous; olent; redolent

ODORLESS: **a.** inodorous; scentless

OF *course:* **adv.** *bien entendu*
this day: **a.** hodiernal

OFF-COLOR: **a.** dubious; *risqué*

OFFENSE: **n.** affront; delict(um); delinquency; dudgeon; felony; malfeasance; malum; misdemeanor; misfeasance; pique; resentment; transgression; trespass; **v.** OFFEND: affront; pique; transgress; trespass; **a.** OFFENSIVE: (**see** "attack" **and** "objectionable") blatant; defamatory; displeasing; distasteful; execrable; fetid; invidious; loathsome; noisome; (ob)noxious; obtrusive; odious; reprehensible; repugnant; repulsive; ribald(rous); ridiculous; unsavory; verminous; **n.** OFFENSIVENESS: blatancy; objectionability; repugnance; repugnancy; unsavoriness
caught in act of committing: **adv.** (in) *flagrante delicto;* red-handed
minor: **n.** culpa; delinquency; misdemeanor; peccadillo; veniality; **n.** delinquent; misdemeanant
none intended: **adv.** *absit invidia*
opening position for: **n.** *en garde*
slight: **see** *"minor"* **above**

OFFENDED *easily:* **a.** squeamish; umbrageous; **n.** squeamishness

OFFER: **v.** proffer; tender

OFFERING *of thanksgiving, sacrifice, etc.:* **n.** oblation

OFFHAND: (**see** "impromptu") **a.** *ad lib(itum);* autoschediastic; *brevi manu;* casual; extemporaneous; extemporary; extempore; improvisatorial; improvisatory; improviso; impulsive; informal; spontaneous; unceremonious; unconventional; unpremeditated; unstudied; **adv.** *currente calamo*
something done (offhand): **n.** autoschediasm; improvisation

OFFICE *attire or vestments:* **n.** pontificalibus
by virtue of: **n.** or **a.** *ex cathedra;* **a.** *ex officio;* functional; perquisite; *virtute officii*
functions of: **n.** officialdom; **a.** (ad)ministerial; administrative
-holder(s): **n.** functionaire; functionary; incumbency; incumbent; officialdom; officiality
investing into: **n.** inauguration; installation; investiture
no longer in, or power ended: **a.** emeritus; *functus officio;* superannuated
of honor or profit: **n.** preferment
power or function going with: **n.** attribution; perquisite

OFFICIAL(S): **a.** accredited; authoritative; authorized; cathedral; sanctioned; **n.** functionary; functionary; incumbency; incumbent; officialdom; officiary
language of: **n.** federalese; officialese
pedantic: **n.** bureaucrat; mandarin; pedantocrat
state of being: **a.** authoritative; **n.** officialism; officiality

OFFICIOUS: **see** "meddlesome"

OFFSET: **v.** checkmate; compensate; counteract; counterbalance; counterpoise; countervail; reimburse

OFFSHOOT: **n.** digression; outgrowth; ramification; ramus; tangent; **a.** tangent(i)al

OFFSPRING: **n.** descendant(s); issue; posterity; progeniture; progeny; (s)cion
   having two at birth: **a.** biparous
   incapacity for producing: **a.** barrenness; sterility
   love of: **n.** philoprogeneity; philoprogenitiveness; storge; **a.** philoprogenitive
   producing female: **a.** thelygenic; thelytokous
   producing male: **a.** androgenous
   production of: **a.** philoprogenitive

OGLE, *amorous:* **n.** oeillade

OIL, *bearing or producing:* **a.** oleaginous; oleiferous

OILY: (**see** "elusive") **a.** deceitful; lardaceous; lubric(i)ous; oleaginous; pinguid; saponaceous; servile; suave; unctuous; **n.** OILINESS: lubricity; plasticity; saponaceousness; unctuosity

OINTMENT: **see** "salve"

OLD: (**see** "ancient") **a.** aboriginal; antebellum; antediluvial; antediluvian; antemundant; antiquated; antique; archaic; archaistic; decrepit; grandfatherly; immemorial; ogygian; paleolithic; paleozoic; *passé;* patriarchal; preadamite; prehistoric; prelapsarian; primeval; primitive; protohistoric; troglodytic; venerable; **adv.** *ab antiquo*
   -age: **n.** anecdotage; autumn of life; caducity; decrepitude; dotage; evening of life; senectitude; senility
      decay from: **n.** consenescence
      growing or onset of: **n.** senescence; **a.** senescent; **v.** senesce
      pert. to: **a.** caducous; gerontal; gerontic; senile
      study of: **n.** geriatrics; gerontology; nostology
   -fashioned: **a.** antebellum; antediluvian; antiquated; archaic; archaistic; conservative; dated; decadent; *démodé;* demoded; fuddy-duddy; Neanderthal; obsolescent; obsolete; old hat; outmoded; *passé;* reactionary; troglodytic; *vieux jeu;* **n.** ancientry; antiquation; decadence; obsolescence
      ideas: **n.** fogyism
      person or thing: **n.** antediluvian; antequarian; fogram; fogrum; fuddy-duddy; mossback; stick-in-the-mud; ultraconservative

   love of what is (*old*): **n.** archaeolatry; archai(ci)sm
   men children twice: bis pueri senes
   order: **n.** *ancien regime*
   person: **n.** antediluvian; antequarian; cidevant; dotard; fogram; fogrum; graybeard; Methuselah; patriarch; preadamite; veteran
      esp. over 100: **n.** centenarian; macrobian
   preference for what is (*old*): **n.** archaeolatry; archai(ci)sm
   story: **n.** *crambe repetita*
   -womanish: **a.** anile; **n.** anility
   world, rel. to: **a.** gerontogeous
   worship of what is: **n.** archaism; archaeolatry

OLDEST *example of some category:* **n.** dean; doyen (**fem.** doyenne)
   person of class or group: **n.** dean; doyen; (**fem.** doyenne); patriarch

OMEN: **n.** augury; auspice; divination; foretoken; handwriting on the wall; harbinger; portent; precursor; presage; presentiment; **a.** OMINOUS: augural; augurous; fateful; gravid; imminent; inauspicious; menacing; portentous; premonitory; sinister; unpropitious
   favorable: **n.** *omen faustum*
   may there be no evil (*omen*): **n.** *absit omen*
   of good: **a.** auspicious; *de bon augure*

OMISSION: (**see** "failure") **n.** delinquency; exclusion; misfeasance; neglect; preterition; pretermission
   in rhetoric or grammar: **n.** ellipsis; paral(e)ipsis (**or** paralepsis)

OMIT: **v.** exclude; forbear; ignore; neglect; overlook
   as letter or vowel: **v.** elide; **n.** elision

OMITTED *parts of work, printed as supplement:* **n.pl.** paralipomena

ONCE: **a.** bygone; elapsed; quondam; **adv.** erewhile; whilom
   at: (**see** "prompt") **a.** instantaneous; momentaneous; *tout de suite*
   for all: **adv.** *semel pro semper*

ONE-AND-ONE-HALF *as great, or ratio of:* **a.** sesquialteral

ONE-HUNDRED-AND-FIFTY, *pert. to, or 150th anniversary:* **a. or n.** sesquicentennial

ONE-HUNDRED *fold:* **v. or a.** centuplicate; **a.** centuple
  years, period of: **n.** centenary; centennial; **a.** centenary
  years, person of: **n. or a.** centenarian; n. macrobian

ONENESS: **n.** omneity; unanimity; unicity; uniquity; unity

ONESELF, *in spite of:* **adv.** *malgré soi*

ONE-SIDED: **a.** excentric(al); *ex parte;* factionary; partisan; self-serving; unilateral

ONE-THOUSAND, *group of, or period of 1000 yrs.:* **n.** chiliad; millennium

ONE *year old:* **a.** annotinous

OOZE: **v.** extravasate; osmose; transudate; transude; **n.** extravasation; transudation; **a.** osmotic; transudative

OPAQUE: **a.** adiaphorous; fuliginous; impervious; nubiferous; obscure; unintelligible

OPEN: **v.** extend; inaugurate; introduce; unfold; unveil; **a.** (**see** "free") accessible; dehiscent; exoteric; frank; gaping; liable; manifest; notorious; patent; patulous; undisguised; undissembling; unfeigned; unobstructed; unrestricted; **adv.** OPENLY: *ex professo;* unconcealed; unreservedly; **n.** OPENNESS: artlessness; *naïveté;* patency; unobstructedness
  air: **a. or adv.** *à la belle étiole; al fresco;* hypaethral; *sub Jove;* upaithric
  to attack or assault: **a.** vulnerable; **n.** vulnerability
  -worked: **a.** *à jour; ajouré; ajourisé*

OPENING: (**see** "outlet") aperture; breach; *débouché;* fenestration; foramen; gambit; hiatus; inauguration; opportunity; orifice; os; **a.** inauguratory; initiatory; orificial
  absence or closing of an: **n.** atresia; imperforation; stenosis; **a.** imperforate
  as of career: **n.** debut; debutant(e); inauguration; investiture
  of body: **n.** aperture; fistula; foramen; meatus; orifice; os; sinus

of speech or treatise: **n.** exordium; prologue
of symphony or mus. composition: **see under** "music"

OPERATE, *as by hand:* **v.** manipulate; **n.** manipulation; **a.** manipulable; manipulatable; manipulatory

OPERATING: **a.** functional; operational; physiologic(al); **n.** OPERATION: functioning; processus
  not: **a.** afunctional; defunct; quiescent

OPINION(S): (**see** "belief") **n.** conclusion; consensus; conviction; diagnosis; impression; judgment; persuasion; sentiment
  collection of, on a subject: **n.** symposium
  difference of: (**see** "controversy") **n.** brannigan
  express an: **v.** editorialize; opine; pontificate
  fond of one's own: **a.** philodoxical; **n.** philodox
  formal statement of: **n.** dictum; judgment
  general: **n.** consensus; unanimity; **a.** consentaneous; consentient; unanimous
  in defiance of general: **adv. or a.** *contra mundum*
  in my: **adv.** *à mon avis; me judice*
  so many men, so many (opinions): *quot homines, tot sententiae*
  unity of: **n.** consentience; solidarity; unanimity

OPINIONATED: (**see** "stubborn") **a.** autotheistic; bigoted; conceited; doctrinaire; doctrinal; dogmatic; officious; *opiniâtre;* philodoxical; pontifical; pragmatic(al); prejudiced; sophomoric; vainglorious
  person: **n.** dogmatist; philodox; **a.** dogmatic; philodoxical

OPPONENT: **n.** adversary; antagonist; assailant; competitor; defendant; disputant
  attacking rather than issue: **adv.** *ad hominem;* **n.** *(argumentum) ad hominem*

OPPORTUNITY: (**see** "chance") **n.** conjuncture; occasion; **a.** OPPORTUNE: (**see** "pertinent") advantageous; *à propos;* auspicious; expedient; miraculous; propitious; providential; seasonable; tempestive; timely
  grasp the: **n.** *carpe diem*
  makes the thief: occasio facit furem

OPPOSE: **v.** antagonize; confront; contravene; counteract; countervail; militate; thwart; withstand
  by argument: **v.** impugn; oppugn; **n.** impugnation; oppugnation
  directly: **v.** contrapose; polarize; **n.** contraposition; polarity; polarization
  inclined to: **a.** argumentative; militant; oppositious; oppositive; pugnacious
  w/ equal weight: **v.** counteract; counterbalance; counterpoise; countervail; **a.** oppositious; oppositive

OPPOSED (or OPPOSING): (**see** "contrary") **a.** adversative; adverse; antagonistic; antipathetic(al); antonymous; argumentative; contralateral; contrariant; militant; oppositional; oppositious; oppositive; pugnacious
  determinedly: **a.** oppositious

OPPOSITE: **a.** antagonistic; antipathetic(al); antipodal; antipodean; antipodic; antithetic(al); antonymic; antonymous; contradictory; converse; diametrical; incompatible; **prep.** vis-à-vis; **n.** antipod (**pl.** antipodes); antithesis; antonym; complement; counterpart
  directly: **a.** antipodal; antipodean; antithetic(al); diametrical; inverse
  gather or concentrate at (opp.) extremes or poles: **v.** polarize; **n.** polarity; polarization
  looking or acting in (opp.) ways: **a.** double-dealing; duplicitous; Janus-faced; Janus-like
  position directly: **n.** antithesis; contraposition; polarity; polarization; **v.** contrapose; polarize; **a.** antithetic(al)
  state of being: **n.** antipodes; antithesis; contrariety; contrawise; **a.** antipodean; diametrical
  tendency: **n.** ambitendency; ambivalence
  to: **adv.** *ex adverso; ex adversum*

OPPOSITION: **n.** antagonism; antipathy; confrontation; contraposition; contrariety; contravention; disaffinity; hostility; oppugnation; recalcitration; refractoriness; repugnance; **a.** oppositious; oppositive; **adv.** *au contraire*
  having natural: **a.** antipathetic(al)
  one engaged in: **n.** antipathist; opponent
  to traditions, etc.: **n.** disestablishmentarianism; **a.** oppositious; oppositive

OPPRESS: **v.** dragoon; overburden; persecute; tyrannize; **a.** OPPRESSIVE: exacting; grievous; onerous; Tarquinian; tyrannic(al); tyrannous; **n.** OPPRESSION: tyranny

OPTICAL *effect or illusion:* **n.** *deceptio visus; fata morgana; ignis fatuus;* mirage; phantasmagoria; phantasmagory; **a.** illusional; phantasmagoric(al); kaleidoscopic(al)

OPTIMISTIC: **a.** confident; eupeptic; euphoric; expectant; heartening; hopeful; Micawberish; Pollyann(a)ish; promising; roseate; sanguine; sanguinic; **n.** OPTIMISM: (**see** "hopefulness") euphoria; Micawberism; Pollyann(a)ism; sanguinity

OPTIONAL: **a.** alternative; discretional; discriminative; elective; facultative; preferential; voluntary

ORAL: **a.** buccal; nuncupative; parol(e); phonetic; tacit; *viva voce;* vocal; **adv.** *ore tenus*
  instruction: **n.** catechism; catachresis; **a.** catechetic(al); catechistic; **v.** catechize

ORATION: **n.** declamation; **n.** ORATOR: Demosthenes; rhetor(ician); spellbinder; (**fem.** oratrix); **a.** ORATORICAL: Ciceronian; Demosthenean; Demosthenic; declamatory; rhetorical

ORBIT, *point farthest out:* **n.** apogee
  point nearest in: **n.** perigee

ORDEAL, *trial by:* **n.** *dei judicium*

ORDER: (**see** "arrangement") **n.** adjuration; caveat; command; concinnity; cosmos; curriculum; direction; discipline; disposition; eutaxy; fiat; formation; harmonization; harmony; husbandry; injunction; mandate; mandatum; ordinance; precedence; precept; protocol; regime; requisition; symmetry; uniformity; **v. see** "arrange"
  according to time: **n.** chronology; **a.** calendric(al); chronologic(al)
  arranged in: **a.** alphabetical; categorical; chronological; consecutive; *en règle; en suit;* methodical; ordinal; pragmatic; regimental; sequacious; sequential; seriatim; successional; systematic; **adv.** *par ordre alphabetique;* **n.** consecution; regimentation; sequence; sequent; seriality
  authoritative: **n.** decretal; fiat; injunc-

tion; mandate; mandatum; ordinance; **a.** mandatory
   good: **n.** concinnity; economy; eutaxy; husbandry
   in: **see** "arranged in" **above**
   lack of: **see** "confusion"
   not in: **a.** inconsecutive; inconsequent; inordinate
   of rank, bring into: **v.** coordinate; **n.** co-ordination

ORDERLY: (**see** "peaceful" **and** "rule, according to") **a.** alphabetical; compatible; congruent; congruous; consonant; harmonious; methodic(al); methodological; parliamentary; programmatic; rational; shipshape; systematic
   arrangement: **n.** concinnity; eutaxy; syntax; **a.** Apollonian; concinnate; concinnous
   system: **n.** cosmos

ORDINARY: (**see** "commonplace") **a.** administrative; average; conventional; indifferent; inferior; habitual; mediocre; middling; nomic; nominal; second-rate; uncosmic; uneventful; **n.** mediocrity

ORE, *rich vein of:* **n.** bonanza; El Dorado

ORGANIC: **a.** constitutional; functional; fundamental; inherent; physiological; structural; systemic
   life, laws of: **n.** organonomy

ORGANISM: **n.** organization; system
   very small: **n.** animalcule; animalculum; (**pl.** animalcula(e))

ORGANIZATION: **n.** administration; arrangement; constitution; cosmos; establishment; hierarchization; regimentation; stratification; structure; system(ization); **v.** ORGANIZE: (**see** "arrange") mobilize; orchestrate; **n.** ORGANIZER: impresario

ORGANS, *internal body:* **n.pl.** viscera; **a.** splanchnic; visceral

ORGY: **n.** bacchanal(ia); carousal; saturnalia; **a.** ORGIASTIC: bacchanal(ian); bacchantic; Dionysiac(al); Dionysian; saturnalian

ORIENTAL: **a.** Byzantine; Levantine; ortative
   materials, as lit., artistic or archaeologic: **n.** Orientalia

ORIGIN(S): (**see** "beginning" **and** "source") **n.** ancestry; causation; derivation; etiology; genesis; inauguration; inchoation; nascency; incipience; parentage; primordium; (**pl.** primordia); provenance; provenience
   beginning to form: **a.** aborning; embryonic; nascent; parturient; **n.** nascency
   doctrine of: **n.** archology
   fr. the: **adv.** ab incunabulis; ab initio; **a.** primordial
   having common: **a.** monogen(et)ic; monogenistic
   having more than one source of: **a.** polygenetic
   identity of: **n.** isogeny; **a.** isogenous
   of known: **a.** phenerogen(et)ic
   of unknown: **a.** cryptogenic; idiopathic
   pert. to: **a.** embryonic; genetic; inaugural; inceptive; inchoate; inchoative; nascent; rudimental; rudimentary
   place of: **n.** natale solum; provenance
   source and (origin): **n.** fons et origo
   spontaneous: **n.** idiogenesis; **a.** idiogen(et)ic
   study of: **n.** etiology; **a.** etiological

ORIGINAL: **a.** aboriginal; authentic; causative; fontal; generative; genetic; germinal; germinative; inceptive; inventive; naissant; neoteric; primitive; primogenial; primogenital; primordial; pristine; protogenic; prototypal; seminal; spermatic(al); underivative; **n.** (**see** "native") ectype; neoteric
   daringly: **a.** Promethean
   growth or tissue: **n.** naissance
   not: (**see** "counterfeit") **a.** derivative; unoriginal

ORIGINALITY: **n.** ingenuity; ingenuosity; inventiveness

ORIGINATING *at various places or times:* **a.** polygenetic
   spontaneously: **see under** "origin"

ORNAMENT: **v.** (**see** "adorn") embellish; **n.** adornment; embellishment; exornation; garniture; ornamentation; **a.** ORNAMENTAL: (**see** "ornate") festooned; spangled; tasselled

ORNATE: (**see** "showy") **a.** arabesque; aureate; aurelent; aurelian; clinquant; baronial; baroque; bombastic; flamboyant; florid; grandiloquent; magniloquent; orotund; ostentatious; resplendent; rococo; sumptuous

ORNERY: see "contrary"

OSTENTATIOUS: see "ornate"

OSTRICH(ES), *pert. to:* **a.** struthian;
struthious
 resembling: **a.** struthi(oni)form

OTHER *persons, centering interest or attention on:* **a.** allocentric
 *things being equal: cetera desunt; ceteris
paribus*
 with many (*others*): **adv.** *cum multis
aliis*

OTHERNESS: **n.** alterity; diversity

OUT-and-out: (see "absolute") **a.** arrant;
complete; confirmed; consummate; downright; notorious; shameless; sheer; thoroughgoing; unmitigated; unqualified; utter
 of action: (see "retired") **adv.** *hors de
combat*
 -of-date: (see "old-fashioned") **a.** antediluvian; archaic; archaistic; decadent;
démodé; demoded; effete; *fin-de-siècle;*
moribund; Neanderthal; neolithic; obsolete; outmoded; *passé;* troglodytic;
vieux jeu
 of many, one: e pluribus unum
 of the mouths of babes: ex ore infantum
 of this world: **a.** untramundane

OUTBURST: (see "outpouring") **n.** ebullition; eruption; fantod; fusillade; paroxysm; spate; **a.** ebullient; paroxysmal

OUTCAST: **n.** abject; castaway; expatriate; Ishmael; leper; offscouring; pariah;
reprobate; **a.** abject; expatriate; Ishmael-
itish; reprobative
 status of being: **n.** pariahdom; pariahism

OUTCOME: **n.** conclusion; consequence;
consummation; dénouement; emanation;
exitus; progeny; residual; residuum; **a.**
consequential; consummative; residual
 possible: **n.** eventuality; possibility;
probability

OUTCRY: (see "uproar") **n.** bruit;
clamor; conclamation; vociferation
 making loud: **a.** blatant; boisterous;
clamorous; vociferous
 of multitude or many: **n.** conclamation;
a. conclamant

OUTDOOR(S): **a.** *al fresco;* extraforane-
ous; hypoethial; hypaethral; upaithric;
adv. *al fresco*

OUTFIT: **v.** accouter; accoutre; caparison;
n. armamentarium; equipage; equipment;
(**pl.** accoutrements; caparisons; paraphernalia; regalia; trappings)

OUTGROWTH: (see "consequence") **n.**
ramification

OUTLET: (see "opening") **n.** aperture;
egress; orifice; os; **a.** orificial
 as for goods or trade: **n.** *débouché*
 as of river or stream: **n.** debouchment

OUTLINE: (see "summary") **v.** adumbrate; delineate; diagram; **n.** abridgement; adumbration; *aperçu;* circumference; compendium; configuration; conformation; conspectus; contour; delineation;
diagram; portrayal; prospectus; schema;
silhouette; synopsis
 faint: **n.** adumbration
 form, in: **a.** diagrammatic(al); schematic

OUTLOOK: (see "view") **n.** configuration; expectation; mentality; panorama;
perspective; perspectivity; prognosis;
prognostication; prospect
 limited in: **a.** cloistral; egocentric; parochial; provincial; sectarian

OUTMODED: (see "out-of-date") **a.** obsolete; troglodytic; **n.** obsoleteness; obso-
letism
 or discarded status: **n.** desuètude

OUT-OF-DATE: see **under** "out"

OUTPOURING: (see "outburst") **n.** debouchment; *épanchement*
 unusually large, as of words: **n.** spate

OUTRAGE: **n.** affront; dishonor; indecency; indignity; infamy; *lèse majesty;*
a. OUTRAGEOUS: abhorrent; arrant;
atrocious; extravagant; fantastic; flagrant; heinous; infamous; monstrous; notorious; unconscionable

OUTSET, *from:* (see "beginning") **adv.**
ab initio; ab initium; ab ovo; **a.** aboriginal; primordial; **n.** primordium

OUTSIDE, *coming fr. the:* **a.** adventitious; exogenous; extraneous; extrinsic; **n.** extraneity; invection
growing or developing from: **a.** exogenous
regular duties or work: **a.** extracurricular; supererogatory; **n.** extracurriculum
surface: **n.** externality; perimeter; periphery; **a.** peripheral

OUTSIDER: **n.** auslander; exoteric; Ishmael; layman; tramontane

OUTSTANDING: (**see** "excelling" **and** "noted") **a.** conspicuous; noticeable; paramount; pending; prominent; salient; signal; significant; significative; stellar; (super)eminent; supreme; unresolved; **n.** conspicuity; predominance; predominancy; saliency; signality
item of a group: **n.** *pièce de résistance*

OUTWARD *form or appearance:* **n.** configuration; physicality; physiognomy; semblance; silhouette

OUTWEIGH: **v.** preponderate; surpass; **a.** precedental; preponderant; **n.** preponderance

OUTWIT: **v.** circumvent; frustrate; victimize; **n.** circumvention

OVAL: **a.** curvilinear; elliptic(al); nummiform; nummular; ovate; ovoid; spherical; spheroidal

OVER: **see** "finished" **and** "excessive"

OVERACTING (**or** OVERACTED): **n.** histrionics; theatrics; **a.** histrionic; theatrical

OVERBEARING: (**see** "haughty") **a.** arbitrary; arrogant; autocratic; cavalier; compelling; despotic; dictatorial; dogmatic; domineering; imperative; imperious; insupportable; lordly; masterful; preponderating; supercilious

OVERCOME: **v.** conquer; demolish; domineer; overpower; overwhelm; subdue; surmount; vanquish
incapable of being: **a.** insubvertible; insuperable; insurmountable; invincible; inviolable; invulnerable; sacrosanct; unconquerable; **n.** insuperability; invulnerability

OVERCONFIDENT: **a.** overweening; presumptuous; **n.** OVERCONFIDENCE: **see** "presumption"

OVERDECORATED: (**or** OVERDRESSED): **a.** bedizened; **n.** bedizenment; **v.** bedizen
man who is (overdressed): **n.** Beau Brummel

OVERDO: **v.** cloy; satiate; supererogate

OVEREAT: **v.** gormandize; **n. see** "gluttony"

OVERFLOWING: **a.** abundant; copious; cornucopian; inundatory; redounding; redundant; scaturient; superabundant; torrential; **n.** cornucopia; deluge; inundation; profusion; redundance; redundancy; spate; superabundance

OVERINDULGENCE (*any activity*): **n.** orgy; satiation; satiety; **a.** orgiastic

OVERLAPPING: **a.** jugate

OVERLOOK: **v.** condone; disregard; ignore; pretermit; superintend; **n.** condonation; pretermission; surveillance

OVERNICE: **a.** euphemistic; fastidious; fastigial; meticulous; nice Nelly; per(s)-nickety; prudish; scrupulous; squeamish; **n.** OVERNICETY: correctitude; fastidiousness; fastidium; finicality; meticulosity; per(s)nicketiness; scrupulosity

OVERPOWERING: (**see** "overwhelming") **a.** copious; torrential

OVERSHADOW: **v.** adumbrate; eclipse; **n.** adumbration; eclipse; **a.** adumbral

OVERSTATEMENT: **n.** embellishment; exaggeration; hyperbole; ornamentation; **a.** hyperbolic(al)

OVERTHROW: **v.** demolish; dethrone; dislodge; exterminate; overturn; unhorse; vanquish; **n.** bouleversement; *coup d'état;* débâcle; deféasance; labefaction
incapable of: **see under** "overcome"

OVERTURNING: **a.** anatreptic; refuting

OVERWHELM: (**see** "defeat") **v.** confound; deluge; demolish; inundate; submerge; vanquish; **a.** OVERWHELM-ING: deluginous; devastating; ineffable; inundatory; murderous; **n.** flood tide; ineffability; inundation

OWL(S), *rel. to or like:* **a.** strigine

OWN: **v.** acknowledge; concede

OWNERSHIP: **n.** proprietary; proprietor-ship; **a.** proprietary
   pride in or consciousness of: **a.** proprie-torial; proprietous

OXYGEN *deficiency:* **n.** anoxemia; cyano-sis; **a.** anoxemic; cyanotic

P

PACE, *at equal:* **a. or adv.** *pari passu*

PACIFY: (**see** "appease") **v.** ameliorate;
assuage; conciliate; mitigate; mollify;
placate; propitiate; reconcile; tranquilize;
n. PACIFICATION: amelioration; conciliation; mitigation; tranquilization; **a.**
PACIFICATORY: (**see** "peaceful")
conciliatory; irenic(al); pacifistic; placative; propitiative

PAGE (*of book*), *rel. to:* **a.** paginal
to number: **v.** paginate; **n.** pagination

PAIN: **n.** affliction; agony; anguish; distress; dolor; lancination; martyrdom; paroxysm; penance; punishment; throe; torment; travail
agent to destroy or deaden: **n.** analgesic;
anesthetic; anodyne; hypnotic; opiate; **a.**
analgesic; anodynic; hypnotic
capacity to endure: **n.** forbearance; longanimity; sufferance; tolerance
causing: **a.** afflictive; dolorific
fear of: **n.** algophobia
flashing: **a.** fulgurant; fulgurating; fulgurous; lancinating
high sensitivity to: **n.** hyperalgesia; hy-
peralgia; **a.** hyperalgesic
incapable of: **a.** impassible; insentient;
n. impassibility; insentience
intense: **n.** agony; travail; **v.** travail
lessened sensitivity to: **n.** analgesia; anesthesia; hypalgesia; **a.** analgesic; hypalgesic
lessening: **a.** assuasive; lenitive; mitigatory; obtundent; palliative; palliatory; **n.**
lenity
loss of: **n.** anesthesia; **a.** anesthetic
mental, or of mental origin: **n.** dysphoria; psychalgesia; **a.** dysphoric
of labor (*childbirth*): **n. or v.** travail
piercing: see "flashing" above
pleasure in inflicting: **n.** algophilia; sadism; **a.** algophilic; sadistic; **n.** algophilist;
sadist

in inflicting or receiving: **n.** algophilia; **a.** algophilic
in receiving: **n.** algophilia; masochism; **a.** algophilic; masochistic; **n.** algophilist; masochist
rectal: **n.** proctalgia
rel. to or causing: **a.** algedonic; algetic;
algogenic
relieving: (**see** "lessening" **above**) **a.**
alleviatory; narcotic; opiate; opiatic; palliative; palliatory; remedial
sensitivity to: **n.** (hyper)algesia

PAINFUL: **a.** afflictive; agonal; dolorific;
distressing; excruciating; irksome; tor-
minous; tortuous; troublesome; vexatious
route or series of experiences: **n.** *via
dolorosa*
to touch: **a.** hyperalgesic; hyperesthetic;
hypersensitive

PAINTING *of genre or still-life, or of mean
or sordid subjects:* **n.** rhyparography; **a.**
rhyparographic

PAIR(S): **v.** conjugate; **n.** conjugation;
counterpart(s); duality; dyad; partnership; **a.** PAIRED: bigeminal; binary; duplex; dyadic; jumelle
growing in: **a.** didymous

PALE: **a.** achromic; anemic; ashen; cadaverous; etiolated; ghastly; ischemic;
livid; pallid; **n.** etiolation; ghastliness;
ischemia; lividity; pallidity

PALLIATE: **see** "lessen"

PALMIST: **n.** chirognomist; chiromancer;
n. PALMISTRY: chirognomy; chiro-
mancy

PAMPER: (**see** "caress") **v.** mollycoddle

PAMPHLET: (**see** "manual") **n.** brochure; monograph; treatise

231

PANTING: **n.** anhelation; dyspnea; hyperpnea; palpitation

PAPER: **see** "essay"
resembling: **a.** papyraceous

PAR: (**see** "equality") **n.** normality; parity
under: (**see** "inferior") **a.** suboptimal; substandard

PARABLE *in form, or expressed by:* **a.** parabolic(al); **v.** parabolize

PARADISE: **n.** Abraham's bosom; Eden; elysium; Nirvana; oblivion; utopia; **a.** PARADISIAC(AL): Edenic; elysian; nirvanic; utopian

PARAGON *of excellence or beauty:* **n.** phoenix

PARALLEL: **a.** analogous; companion; concurrent; correlative; correspondent; equidistant; paradromic; **n.** *alter ego;* analog(ue); correlative; counterpart
to make: **v.** collimate; parallelize; **n.** collimation; parallelization

PARAPHRASE: **n.** *oratio obliqua;* recapitulation; restatement

PARASITE: **n.** saphrophyte; sponger; sycophant; today; **a.** PARASITIC(AL): saphrophytic; sycophantic(al); **v.** sycophantize

PARDON: **v.** absolve; acquit; condone; excuse; remit; **n.** absolution; acquittal; amnesty; condonation; indulgence; remission; **a.** PARDONABLE: **see** "excusable"
me: **n.** *pardonnez-moi*

PARENT(S): **n.** ancestor; author; genitor; (**fem.** genetrix; **pl.** genetrices); originator; producer; progenitor
acting as, or being in place of: **adv.** *in loco parentis*
murder of, also murderer: **n.** parenticide; parricide; **a.** parricidal; parricidious
rel. bet. child and: **a.** filial; parental
transmitting characteristics of both: **a.** amphigonic; amphigonous

PARENTAL *love or affection:* **n.** philoprogenitiveness; storge
power, subject to: **a.** unemancipated

PARENTHETIC(AL): **a.** ejaculatory; episodic(al); incidental; interjaculatory; interjectional; interjectural; interlocutory; tangential; **adv.** *par parenthèse*
remark(s): **n.** dictum; digression; *gratis dictum; obiter dictum;* scholium; tangent; (**pl.** *obiter dicta; scholia*)
speech: **n.** interlocution; **a.** interlocutory

PARISH, *pert. to:* **a.** parochial

PARK, *wooded:* **n.** arboretum

PARODY: **n.** burlesque; caricature; lampoon; satire; travesty
in nature of: **a.** parodistic; satirical

PART(S): **n.** component; constituent; element; fragment; integral; ingredient; integrant; moiety; particularity; quantum; (**pl.** quanta); sector; segment; **a.** componental; constituent; integral; **v. see** "divide"
complex aggregation of: **n.** complexus
divided into many: **a.** multipartite; polychotomous; polytomous
into three: **a.** trichotomous; tripartite; **n.** trichotomy; tripartition; triplex
into two: **a.** bifid; bifurcated; bipartite; dichotomous; **n.** dichotomy
from the (part) one may recognize the whole: ex pede Herculem; ex ungue leonem
necessary: **n.** component; constituent; essentiality

PARTED: **a.** bifid; bifurcated; cloven; dichotomous; estranged; partite

PARTIAL: (**see** "incomplete") **a.** biased; fractionary; fragmental; fragmentary; predisposed; prejudiced; segmented

PARTIALITY: (**see** "bias") **n.** partisanship; predilection
on acct. of: **adv.** *propter affectum*
undue or invidious: **n.** chauvinism

PARTICIPANT: **n.** antagonist; combatant; (**pl.** *dramatis personae*)

PARTICULAR: (**see** "careful") **a.** captious; fastidious; finical; scrupulous; **n.** characteristic; particularity
state or fact of being: **n.** particularity; scrupulosity

PARTING: (**see** "separation") **n.** cleavage; disjunction; dismemberment; disso-

lution; disunion; estrangement; sundering
word: (**see** "farewell") **n.** envoi

PARTISAN: (**see** "follower") **n.** advocate; aficionado; factionary; sectarian; sympathizer; **a.** denominational; factionary; sectarian

PARTNER: **a.** associate; coadjutor; colleague; confederate; confrere; consort; partaker; participant; **n.** PARTNERSHIP: accomplicity; alliance; association; participation
    in crime: **n.** accomplice; *particeps criminis; socius criminis*

PARTY: (**see** "celebration") **n.** potlatch

PASS: **v.** admit; authorize; exceed; intromit; terminate; **n.** (**see** "permit") crisis; intromission; predicament
    (*palm off as genuine*) : **v.** foist
    permission to: **n.** *passe partout;* passport; visa

PASSAGE, *in or during:* **adv.** *in transitu*

PASSION: (**see** "zeal") **n.** ardor; *béquin;* enthusiasm; evangelism; fervor; infatuation; martyrdom; suffering; torridity; transport
    abnormal sexual: **n.** erogeneity; eroticism; erotomania

PASSIONATE: **a.** ardent; bacchanalian; bacchic; Dionysian; ebullient; evangelistic; faustian; fervent; impassioned; impetuous; intense; orgiastic; precipitate; sultry; torrid; vehement
    protest or cry: **n.** *cri de (or du) coeur*
    violently: **a.** sulfurous; sulphurous; voluptuous

PASSIVE: (**see** "patient") **a.** inactive; inert; inexcitable; invertebrate; negative; obedient; quiescent; receptive; stoical; submissive; supine; unresisting; unresponsive; **n.** PASSIVENESS: inactivity; passivity; stoicism; submissiveness

PASSOVER, *pert. to:* **a.** paschal

PASSWORD: **n.** countersign; *mot de passe; mot d'ordre; mot du guet; passe parole;* sesame; shibboleth; watchword

PAST, *influence of, as controlling or restricting the present:* **n.** mortmain

longing for: **n.** nostalgia; **a.** nostalgic
person or thing of: **n.** antediluvian; antequarian; cidevant; mossback; patriarch
surveying the: **n.** memoir(s) ; reflection; reminiscence; retrospection

PASTE, *make into:* **v.** levigate

PASTIME: **n.** passetemps

PASTORAL: (**see** "rural") **a.** Arcadian; bucolic; geoponic; georgic; idyllic; innocent; picturesque; rustic; Theocritean

PATH, *the beaten is the safe: via trita, via tuta*

PATIENCE: **n.** composure; endurance; equanimity; forbearance; fortitude; imperturbability; indulgence; leniency; lenity; longanimity; long-suffering; perseverance; resignation; submission; sufferance; toleration; **a.** PATIENT: (**see** "forbearing") bovine; composed; charitable; dispassionate; enduring; imperturbable; longanimous; philosophic(al) ; resigned; sedate; stoical; temperate; tolerant; unimpassioned
    something which exhausts: **n.** abradant; irritant; provocation

PATRIOT, *fanatical:* **n.** chauvinist; flagwaver; jingoist; patrioteer; superpatriot; superzealot

PATRIOTISM: **n.** *amor patriae*
    display of, or writings and speeches on: **n.pl.** patriotics
    extreme or fanatical: **n.** chauvinism; ethnocentrism; jingoism; spread-eagleism; super-patriotism

PATRONIZING *manner or behavior:* **n.** condescendence; condescension

PATTERN: (**see** "model") **n.** archetype; *beau idéal;* characteristic; configuration; conformation; exemplar; exemplum; modality; orthodoxy; paradigm; paragon; precedent; prototype; stereotype; syndrome; yardstick
    having but one structural: **a.** monomorphic; monomorphous

PAUNCH: **see** "abdomen"

PAUSE: **v.** intermit; **n.** armistice; c(a)esura; cessation; *entr'acte;* hiatus; inter-

mission; interregnum; moratorium; respite; **a.** cessative
as in speech: **n.** hiatus; **a.** hiatal

PAWN: **v.** hypothecate; (im)pignorate; pledge; **n.** hypothecation; impignoration

PAY: **v.** compensate; indemnify; liquidate; recompense; reimburse; remunerate; satisfy; **n. see** "payment" **and** "salary"

PAYMENT: (**see** "compensation") **n.** defrayal; honorarium; liquidation; remittance; remuneration; retribution
where no set fee: **n.** honorarium

PEA, *resembling in size or shape:* **a.** pisiform

PEACE: (**see** "calmness") **n.** nirvana; pacification; quiescence; (re)conciliation; repose; serenity; tranquility
(*be*) *with you:* **n.** *pax vobiscum; sholom aleichim*
go in: **adv.** *vade in pace*
goddess of: **n.** Irene; Minerva; Pax
offer or gesture of: **n.** olive branch
promoting: (**see** "peaceful") **a.** irenic; pacific; peaceable; **n.** peaceability
rest in: **adv.** *requiescat in pace* (**abb.** R.I.P.)

PEACEFUL: (**see** "calm") **a.** affable; amiable; appeasing; conciliatory; (con)-genial; halcyon; harmonious; henotic; irenic(al); neighborly; nirvanic; oasitic; pacific(atory); pacifistic; pastoral; quiescent; serene; tempean; tranquil; unaggressive; unagitated; undisturbed; **n.** PEACEFULNESS: amiability; pacification; placability; serenity; tranquility; tranquilization

PEACE-MAKER: **n.** conciliator; intercessor; mediator; placater
blessed are the (*peacemakers*): *beati pacifici*

PEACOCK, *of or resembling:* **a.** pavonian; pavonine

PEAK: (**see** "acme") **n.** apogee; climax; culmination; flood tide; maximum; meridian; pinnacle; summit; ultimate; zenith; **a.** apogeal; apogean; apogeic; maximum; supernal; zenithal

PEARL-*bearing:* **a.** margaritiferous

PEARLY: **a.** iridescent; lustrous; margaritaceous; nacreous; opalescent

PECULIAR: (**see** "odd") **a.** aberrant; anomalous; atypical; bizarre; characteristic; eccentric; grotesque; heterogeneous; idiocratic; idiosyncratic; *outré;* unconventional; whimsical; **n.** PECULIARITY: (**see** "oddity" **and** "whim") bizarrerie; caprice; characteristic; eccentricity; haecceity; idiasm; idiocrasy; idiosyncrasy; individuality; particularity; quiddity; quirk; singularity; uniquity; vagary; whimsicality
to a particular group or person: **a.** idiomatic(al)
to the individual: **a.** idiopathic; innate

PEDESTAL, *place upon a:* **see** "deify" **and** "exalt"

PEEL: **v.** decorticate; desquamate; excoriate; exfoliate; exuviate; **a.** PEELING: deciduous; desquamative; desquamatory; exfoliative; exuviative; **n.** decortication; desquamation; ecdysis; excoriation; exfoliation; exuviation

PEEPER: **n.** peeping Tom; scopophiliac; *voyeur;* **a.** PEEPING: scopophilic; voyeuristic; **n.** scopophilia; voyeurism

PEERLESS: **a.** immutable; incomparable; incommensurable; majestic; matchless; *ne plus ultra;* optimum; paramount; preeminent; sovereign; (super)eminent; superlative; superexcellent; unequaled; unsurpassable
person or thing: **n.** nonpareil; nonesuch; paragon; phoenix

PEERS, *before one's:* **a. or adv.** *coram paribus*
by one's own: **adv.** *per pares*

PEEVISH: (**see** "gloomy") **a.** atrabilarious; atrabiliar; atrabilious; caustic; choleric; fretful; irascible; irritable; petulant; querulous; restive; splenetic; testy; waspish; **n.** PEEVISHNESS: (**see** "crankiness") distemper; irascibility; petulance; pique; protervity; querulousness
person: **n.** atrabilarian; curmudgeon

PEN *name:* **see under** "name"
slip of the: **n.** *lapsus calami*
with running: **adv.** *currente calamo*

PENAL: **a.** castigatory; corrective; disciplinary; expiatory; penitentiary; punitive; reformative; reformatory; retributive; retributory; **v.** PENALIZE: (see "punish") amerce

PENALTY: (see "punishment") **n.** amercement; chastisement; expiation; penance; retribution
>*appeal to:* **n. or adv.** *(argumentum) ad baculum*
>*deserved:* **n.** comeuppance; condignity; deserts; **a.** condign
>*pay the:* **v.** atone; expiate
>*required or done under:* **a.** penal; punitive; subpoenal

PENDING: **a.** abeyant; imminent; impending; *in fieri;* pendent (**or** pendant); pendular; pendulous; provisional; undecided; undetermined; **n.** PENDENCY: abeyance; abeyancy; imminence; imminency; pendulation; pendulosity; suspension

PENETRATE: **v.** impenetrate; permeate

PENETRATED, *capable of being:* **a.** penetrable; permeable; pervious
>*incapable of being:* **a.** impenetrable; impermeable; imperforate; imperviable; impervious
>*thoroughly:* **a.** permeated

PENETRATING: (see "keen") **a.** astute; discerning; incisive; osmotic; penetrative; perforating; permeable; piquant; poignant; sagacious; trenchant

PENITENCE: (see "regret") **n.** attrition; compunction; contrition; remorse; repentance; **a.** PENITENT: contrite; remorseful; repentant

PENITENTIAL *suffering:* **n.** satispassion

PENMAN: **n.** calligrapher; chirographer; **n.** PENMANSHIP: calligraphy; chirography; **a.** calligraphic; chirographic

PENNILESS: (see "poor") **a.** bankrupt; impecunious; indigent; *sans le sou;* **n.** PENNILESSNESS: bankruptcy; impecuniosity; insolvency; mendicancy

PENSIVE: **a.** cogitable; cogitabund; cogitative; contemplative; meditative; reflective

PEOPLE(S): (see "person") **n.** commonalty; *homo sapiens;* mankind; multitude; nation; populace; race; throng
>*common:* **n.pl.** commonalty; demos; *hoi polloi; le bas peuple;* lumpen proletariat; multitude; pleb(e)ian; populace; population; *profanum vulgus;* proletariat; *vulgus ignobile;* **a.** lumpen; plebeian; proletarian; proletariat(e)
>*considered boobs:* **n.pl.** booboisie
>*dregs of the:* **n.pl.** *faex populi*
>*formed of or inhabited by many:* **a.** polyethnic
>*group of varied:* **n.** menagerie
>*high class:* see "nobility"
>*humble:* (see "common" **above**) **n.pl.** *gens de peu*
>*in general:* **n.** commonalty; *hoi polloi;* masses; multitude
>*lower class:* see "rabble"
>*middle class:* **n.** bourgeois(ie)
>*of fashion:* **n.pl.** *gens du monde*
>*of rank:* **n.pl.** *gens de condition*
>*pert. to:* **a.** demotic; ethnic; popular
>*pert. to all:* **a.** cosmopolitan; pandemic; universal; **n.** pandemia
>*primitive, study of:* **n.** agriology; anthropology
>*relating to or peculiar to a:* **a.** gentilitial; gentilitious
>*to please the:* **adv.** *(argumentum) ad captandum (vulgus)*
>*upper class:* see "nobility"
>*voice of the:* **n.** *vox populi* (**abb.** vox pop.)
>*wish to be fooled: populus vult decipe*

PERCEIVABLE (**or** PERCEPTIBLE): **a.** cognizable; cognoscible; cognoscitative; comprehensible; discernible; intelligible; observable; palpable; recognizable; tangible
>*barely:* **a.** liminal
>*not:* **a.** subliminal
>*readily:* **a.** translucent
>*to senses:* **a.** corporeal; discernible; palpable; patent; sensible; tangible; **n.** corporeality; corporeity; sensibility; tangibility

PERCEIVE, *having power or capacity to:* **a.** (ap)percipient; perspicacious; **n.** cognizance; percipience; percipiency; perspicacity
>*instrument or apparatus for (perceiving):* **n.** sensorium
>*unable or unwilling to:* **a.** astigmatic(al); insentient; myopic; strabismic; **n.**

astigmatism; insentience; myopia; strabismus

PERCEPTION: (see "knowledge") **n.** apprehension; cognizance; comprehension; consciousness; discernment; insight; observation; percipience; (re)cognition; sensibility
   below: **a.** subliminal; **n.** sublimination
   gifted w/: **a.** (ap)percipient; clairvoyant; prehensile; telepathic
   imaginary or unreal: **n.** delusion; *fata morgana;* hallucination; hallucinosis; *ignis fatuus;* illusion; phantasmagoria; will-of-the-wisp; **a.** delusive; hallucinatory; illusive; phantasmagoric(al)
   keen: **n.** acumen; clairvoyance; cryptesthesia; hyperesthesia; percipience; perspicacity; sagacity; **a.** clairvoyant; hyperesthetic; percipient; sagacious
   lacking in: **a.** astigmatic(al); insentient; myopic; strabismic
   of distant objects, events, etc.: **n.** clairvoyance; extra sensory perception; telegnosis; telepathy; telesthesia
   of what not normally perceptible: **n.** clairsentience; clairvoyance; extra sensory perception; telegnosis; **a.** clairsentient; clairvoyant

PERCEPTIVE: **a.** cognitive; cognitional; knowing; observant; penetrating; percipient; perspicacious; sensible; sensitive; sentient; trenchant
   not: (see "stupid") **a.** imperceptive; impercipient; **n.** impercipience

PERFECT: (see "flawless") **a.** accurate; consummate; exemplary; expert; immaculate; inerrable; inerrant; inerratic; infallible; integral; inviolate; plenary; proficient; saintly
   incapable of being made: **a.** imperfectible; **n.** imperfectibility
   more than: **a.** pluperfect; superlative
   to make: **v.** perfectivize; **n.** perfectivization

PERFECTION: **n.** accomplishment; *beau idéal;* completion; consummation; excellence; exemplarity; expertise; finality; immaculacy; impeccability; indefectibility; inerrancy; infallibility; integrality; maturity; perfectibilism; perfectibility; proficiency; saintliness; virtuosity; wholeness; **n.** PERFECTIONIST: perfectibilist; perfectibili(tari)an; *précieuse;* precisian; precisionist; purist

   highest: **n.** *cordon bleu; nec plus supra; nec plus ultra;* supermundane; supernaculum
   symbol of: **n.** *cordon bleu;* exemplarity; *grand prix*
   tendency to fall short of: **n.** defectibility

PERFORMER: see "actor" **and** "doer"

PERFUMED: see "scented"

PERHAPS: **a. or adv.** peradventure

PERIL: (see "danger") **n.** Charybdis; hazard; insecurity; instability; jeopardy; **a.** PERILOUS: destructive; explosive; icarian; jeopardous; malignant; parlous
   at his own: **adv.** *suo periculo*

PERIOD(S): **n.** cycle; eon; epoch; era; *siècle*
   for indefinite: **a.** *sine die;* **adv.** *ad infinitum;* **n.** infinity
   division into: **n.** periodization
   latent or incubation: **n.** deliquescence; dormancy; latency; quiescence
   of great happiness or prosperity: **n.** golden age; millennium
   of long duration: **n.** millennium; saeculum
   of success or achievement: **n.** fluorescence
   recurring at indefinite: **a.** cyclic(al)

PERIODIC(AL): **a.** cyclic(al); etesian; intermittent; recurrent; rhythmical

PERIPHERAL: (see "external") **a.** circumferential; distal; marginal; peripheric

PERISHABLE: (see "fleeting") **a.** caducous; deciduous; ephemeral; evanescent; fugacious; mortal; transitory; volatile; **n.** PERISHABLENESS: caducity; evanescence; fugacity; perishability; transience; volatility

PERMANENT: (see "eternal" **and** "lasting") **a.** immarcescible; immutable; imperishable; indefaceable; indelible; indestructable; indissoluble; ineffaceable; ineradicable; inextirpable; invariable; irreversible; irrevocable; (per)durable; perdurant; unalterable; **n.** PERMANENCE (**or** PERMANENCY) durability; indissolubility; ineffaceability; perdurance; persistence

PERMISSION : **n.** authorization; sanction; sufferance; tolerance; toleration; **a.** PERMISSIVE : authorized; elective; empowering; enabling; facultative; indulgent; lawful; legitimate; licit; official; optional; sanctioned; sanctionative; tolerant; undemanding
  involving or implying: **a.** authoritative; sanctionative; tolerant
  to depart: **n.** *congé*
  with: **adv.** *avec permission*

PERMIT : **v.** acquiesce; authorize; concede; countenance; empower; franchise; sanction; tolerate; **n.** franchise, *laissez-passer;* license; permittance
  graciously: **v.** vouchsafe

PERMITTED : (**see** "permissive") **a.** allowed; licit; permissible
  beyond what is: **adv.** *ultra licitum; ultra vires*
  not: **a.** impermissible; **n.** impermissibility
  within what is: **adv.** *intra vires*

PERPENDICULAR, *state of being:* **n.** perpendicularity

PERPETUAL : (**see** "permanent") **a.** immortal; incessant; persistent; sempiternal; unceasing; undying; **v.** PERPETUATE : (**see** "endure") eternalize; immortalize; preserve; **n.** PERPETUATION : eternalization; immortalization; perpetuality; perpetuity
  motion: **n.** *moto perpetuo; perpetum mobile*
  state of being: **n.** perpetuality; perpetualness; perpetuation; perpetuity

PERPLEX : (**see** "bewilder") **v.** complicate; confuse; disconcert; embrangle; entangle; interweave; **a.** PERPLEXED : anxious; bewildered; disconcerted; distracted; distraught; nonplus(s)ed; **n.** PERPLEXITY : conglomeration; cruciality; *cul-de-sac;* dilemma; embarassment; embranglement; embroilment; entanglement; exigency; imbroglio; impasse; labyrinth; morass; plight; predicament; puzzlement; quandary

PERPLEXING : (**see** "puzzling") **a.** bewildering; disconcerting; enigmatic(al); inexplicable
  situation or position: **see** "perplexity"

PERSECUTE : **v.** afflict; dragoon; oppress; torment; tyrannize; **n.** PERSECUTOR : sadist; Torquemada; tyrant; **n.** PERSECUTION : oppression; torment; tyranny

PERSIST : **v.** perpetuate; persevere; sustain; **a.** PERSISTENT : (**see** "stubborn") demanding; determined; enduring; importunate; indefatigable; indomitable; lingering; obstinate; perpetual; pressing; solicitous; tenacious; **n. see** "stubbornness"

PERSON(S) : (**see** "man" **and** "people") **n.** existent; personality; propositus; specimen; subject; (**pl.** *dramatis personae*)
  affected and snobbish: **n.pl.** *gens à chichis;* **n.** *poseur;* (**fem.** *poseuse*)
  aggressive: **n.** arrivist(e); pusher
  among other: **adv.** *inter alios*
  bad: (**see** "base" **below**) **n.** *enfant terrible*
  bald-headed: **n.** pilgarlic
  base and despicable: **n.** barbarian; Beelzebub; brutalitarian; caitiff; malefactor; Mephistopheles; miscreant; renegade; reprobate; ribald; rogue; sadist; scapegrace
  bigoted: **see** "narrow-minded" **below**
  bold and saucy: **n.** malapert; picaroon
  bragging or blustering: **n.** braggart; rodomontade; swashbuckler
  careless: **n.** pococurante; superficialist
  charitable: **n.** almoner; *amicus humani generis;* charitarian; eleemosynar; humanitarian; philanthropist; Samaritan
  clever and cultivated: **n.** *bel esprit*
  clumsy: **n.** stumblebum
  coarse: **see** "vulgar" **below**
  common: (**see** "rabble") **n.** bourgeois(ie); commonality; *hoi polloi;* plebeian; *roturier*
  compassionate: **see** "charitable" **above**
  contrary or inconsistent: **n.** paradox
  conventional: **see under** "conventional"
  cowardly: **n.** dastard; poltroon; recreant
  crabby: **n.** crotcheteer; curmudgeon
  creative: **n.** Prometheus; **a.** Promethean
  crude: **n.** buffoon; grobian; rustic
  cultivated: **n.** *bel esprit;* literatus
  degraded and contemptible: **n.** lumpenproletariat
  determined: **n.** *esprit fort;* Trojan
  distinguished in his field: **n.** Brahmin; *cordon bleu;* laureate; paladin; pantheon
  domineering: **n.** autocrat; Napoleon; tyrant
  dull, stupid or clownish: **n.** Abderite;

237

Babbitt; Boeotian; bromide; buffoon; dullard; flibbertigibbet; goose; grobian; harlequin; Juke; Merry Andrew; nincompoop; pachyderm; scaramouche
eccentric: **n.** beatnik: Bohemian; zealot
esteemed: (see "of high rank" **below**) **n.** pantheon
frivolous: n. or a. flibbertigibbet; futilitarian
functioning as a (as corpn., state, etc.): **n.** *universitas personarum*
generous: see "charitable" **above**
gigantic: see "giant"
gloomy: **n.** cynic; dismal Jimmie; gloomy Gus; pessimist
good-natured: **n.** *bon diable; bon naturel*
greedy: (see "self-centered" **below**) **n.** glutton; mercenary
hater of new things or ideas: **n.** misoneist; **a.** misoneistic
of wisdom or knowledge: **n.** anti-intellectualist; misopher; misophist
high in class or field: (see "of high rank" **below**) **n.** pantheon
ignorant: **n.** am haarez; analphabet; ignoramus; Philistine; sciolist
ill-disciplined, turbulent: **n.** bashibazouk; *enfant terrible*
important: **n.** bashaw; celebrity; colossus; cynosure; grandee; luminary; magnate; mogul; notability; notoriety; panjandrum; poo(h)bah; potentate; sachem; sagamore; tycoon
in (person): **adv.** *in propria persona*
inconsistent or contrary: n. paradox
indecisive: **n.** invertebrate; milksop; milquetoast
insensitive: **n.** pachyderm
insignificant: **n.** pipsqueak
insincere: **n.** charlatan; mountebank; *poseur;* (**fem.** *poseuse*); pretender
insolent: **n.** jackanapes; malapert
intellectual: (see "intellectual(s)") **n.** *bel esprit*
irresponsible: **n.** apostate; charlatan; *enfant terrible;* maverick; mountebank; pretender
irritable: **n.** atrabilarian; crotcheteer; curmudgeon; Tartar
large: see "giant"
lazy or idle: **n.** faineant
leading: (see "important" **above**) **n.** luminary
learned: (see "intellectual[s]") **n.** academe; academician; *bel esprit;* Brahmin; erudite; *homo multarum literarum;* illuminato; philologist; polyhistor; polymath; pundit; rhetorician; savant;

scholar; sophist; (**pl.** illuminata; intelligentsia; literati)
legal: **n.** corporation; *homo legalis*
lewd: **see** "libertine"
liberal: **n.** charitarian; eleemosynar; humanitarian; latitudinarian; libertarian; philanthropist
literary: **see under** "literary"
living high and well: **n.** *bon vivant; bon viveur; sybarite*
low: **n.** groundling(s); *polisson;* vulgarian
materialistic: **n.** Babbitt; Gradgrind; Philistine
mean: **see** "base and despicable" **above**
mentally defective but brilliant in some field: **n.** idiot savant
miserly: **n.** curmudgeon; Scrooge
modern: **n.** moderne; neoteric
mysterious: **n.** enigma; paradox; sphinx
narrow-minded: **n.** bigot; lilliputian; pedant; Philistine; quidnunc; sectarian
of great size or power: **n.** colossus; gargantua; titan
of high rank, respect or importance: **n.** aristocrat; bashaw; Brahmin; eminentissimo; luminary; magnifico; mahatma; minion; *nec plus ultra;* nonesuch; paladin; panjandrum; paradigm; paragon; patrician; (**pl.** aristoi)
of humble origin: **n.** *filius terrae*
of letters: **n.** *homme de lettres; literateur; literato; literatus;* (**pl.** *gens de lettres; literati*)
of little importance: **n.** mediocrity; nihility; nonentity; reprobate
of low rank or repute: (see "rabble") **n.** *polisson;* vulgarian
of oustanding quality, or firm in course or object: **n.** paladin; paradigm; protagonist
offensive or pernicious: **n.** cocatrice
old: (**see under** "old") **n.** macrobian
opinionated: **n.** dogmatist; philodox; sectarian
overly precise in lang.: **n.** *précieuse; précieux;* purist
peerless: **n.** nonesuch; nonpareil; paragon; phoenix
pernicious: **n.** cocatrice
plucky: **n.** Trojan
pompous: **n.** Aldibrontiphoscophornio; panjandrum
powerful or wealthy: **n.** Croesus; leviathan; mogul; plutocrat; potentate; powerhouse; titan; tycoon
practical: **n.** practician; pragmatist; materialist; utilitarian

precise or punctilious: **n.** perfectibilist; perfectibilitarian; *précieuse; précieux;* precisian; precisionist

presumptuous: **n.** coxcomb; fantastico; jackanapes

prominent: (see "important" **above**) **n.** celebrity; luminary; notability; notoriety

quarrelsome: **n.** rantipole; termagant

ragged: **n.** ragamuffin; tatterdemalion

rascally: **see** "base and despicable" **above**

rash: **n.** hotspur

rowdy: **n.** yahoo

saintly and righteous: **n.** zaddik

saucy and bold: **n.** malapert; picaroon

self-centered: **n.** autotheist; egocentric; egocentrist; ego(t)ist; *flâneur;* (**fem.** *flâneuse*) ; hedonist; iotacist; misanthropist; narcissist; solipsist; sycophant; sybarite

self-important: **n.** megalomaniac; **a.** autotheistic

sensuous: **see under** "sensuous"

shiftless: **n.** prodigal; vagabond; (**pl.** flotsam and jetsam)

silly: (see "dull, stupid or clownish" **above**) **n.** *gobe-mouche*

simple: **n.** Abderite; *bon enfant;* nincompoop

skillful: **see** "expert"

small: **see** "dwarf"

small-minded: **see** *"narrow-minded"* **above**

snobbish and affected: **n.** poseur; (**fem.** *poseuse*) ; (**pl.** *gens à chichis*)

something carried about the (person): **n.** *vade mecum*

strict: **n.** disciplinarian; martinet; Pharisee; precisian; rigorist; ritualist; sabbatarian

strong-minded: **n.** *esprit fort;* Trojan

stubborn: **n.** intransige(a)nt; recalcitrant

stupid: **see** "dull, stupid or clownish" **above**

swaggering: **n.** braggadocio; rodomontade

talkative: **n.** blatherskite; popinjay

timid: **n.** invertebrate; milksop; milquetoast; nervous Nellie

turbulent, ill-disciplined: **n.** bashibazouk; *enfant terrible*

unconventional: **n.** beatnik; Bohemian; heretic; heterodox; solecist

uncouth: **see** "vulgar" **below**

unique: **n.** nonpareil; nonesuch; paragon; phoenix; uniquity

unusual: **n.** *rara avis*

unwelcome: **n.** *persona non grata*

vagrant: **n.** itinerant; peregrine; peripatetic; vagabond: (**pl.** flotsam and jetsam)

vain: **n.** coxcomb; dandiprat; jackanapes; macaroni; popinjay

visionary. **n.** altitudinarian; doctrinaire; dogmatist; idealist; ideologist; ideologue; theorist; utopian

vulgar or coarse: **n.** Babbitt; Falstaff; grobian; libertine; plebeian; plugugly; reprobate; vulgarian; yahoo

wasteful: **n.** prodigal; profligate; spendthrift; wastrel

weak: (see "indecisive" **above**) **n.** invertebrate; valetudinarian

wealthy: **n.** Croesus; leviathan; Midas; mogul; plutocrat; tycoon

welcome or acceptable: **n.** *persona grata; persona gratissimo;* (**pl.** *personae gratissimae*)

wicked: **see** "base and despicable" **above**

wise: **n.** mahatma; Nestor; patriarch; sage; Solomon

with fine mind: **n.** *bel esprit*

with undefined status: **n.** hybrid; maverick; mongrel

witty: **n.** Aristophanes; *bel esprit; homme d'esprit*

working-class: **n.** bourgeois(ie) ; proletarian; proletariat

worthless: **see** "rogue"

worthy: (see "of high rank" **above**) **n.** mahatma; paradigm

PERSONAL *anecdotes, notes, belongings, etc.:* **n.pl.** personalia

effects, most valued: **n.pl.** lares and penates

feelings or attitudes, based on: **a.** attitudinal

history: **see** "autobiography"

property: **n.** personalty; (**pl.** personalia)

remove (personal) from: **v.** depersonalize; impersonalize; **n.** depersonalization; impersonalization

PERSONALITY: **n.** disposition; egoity; individuality; personeity; temperament

split: **n.** schizophrenia; schizophreniac; schizophrenic

PERSONALLY: **adv.** *in propria persona*

PERSONATION: **n.** anthropomorphism; anthropomorphization; embodiment; impersonation; incarnation; personification; prosopopeia; **a.** anthropomorphic; anthropomorphous; personificative

of animals, as in art or lit.: v. anthropomorphize; zoomorphize; n. anthropomorphism; zoomorphism
speech or lit. for rhetorical purposes: n. apostrophe; prosopopeia; a. apostrophic

PERSONIFY: v. anthropomorphize; apostrophize; embody; incarnate; zoomorphize

PERSPIRATION: n. diaphoresis; excreta; exudation; sudation; sudor; transpiration; (pl. egesta); v. PERSPIRE: egest; excrete; transpire
absence of: n. anhidrosis; anhydrosis
agent or drug checking: n. an(h)idrotic; anhydrotic; antiperspirant
agent or drug, etc., producing: n. diaphoretic; sudorific
excessive: n. hidrosis; hyperhidrosis; polyhidrosis
foul-smelling: n. bromidrosis; kakidrosis
lack of or deficiency in: n. adiaphoresis; anhidrosis; anhydrosis
pert. to: a. diaphoretic; egestive; excrementious; sudoriferous; sudorific

PERSUADE: (see "allure") v. exhortate; expostulate; a. PERSUASIVE: (see "encouraging") exhortative; expostulatory

PERTINENT: a. *ad rem;* applicable; apposite; appropriate; apropos; categorical; commensurate; congruent; felicitous; germane; material; opportune; proportional; proportionate; relevant; n. PERTINENCE: aproposity; pertinency; relevance; relevancy
not: a. *à propos de rien;* inapposite; inappropriate; irrelevant
to present matter: adv. *ad rem*

PERVERSE: see "contrary"

PESSIMISM: n. melancholia; miserabilism; weltschmerz; n. PESSIMIST: cynic; dismal Jimmie

PET: see "caress" and "favorite"
name: n. hypocorism; hypocoristic; *petit nom*

PETITION: (see "prayer") n. complaint; entreaty; obsecration; solicitation; supplication; a. PETITIONARY: beseeching; supplicative; supplicatory; n. PETITIONER: applicant; candidate; orator; (fem. oratrix); postulant; supplicant

PETTY: (see "childish" and "trifling") a. contemptible; frivolous; ignoble; insignificant; lilliputian; meager; paltry; parochial; pettifogging; picayune; picayunish; scurvey; shabby; subordinate; trivial; unimportant; n. PETTINESS: parochialism; parochiality; parvanimity; triviality

PETULANT: see "irritable"

PHANTASY: see "fantasy"

PHASE(S): (see "aspect") n. facet; transition
having many: a. multiphasic; polyphasic

PHENOMENA, *science dealing w/:* n. phenomenology
secondary: n.pl. epiphenomena; n. epiphenomenon; a. epiphenomenal
state of being (phenomenal): n. phenomenality; a. phenomenological

PHILANTHROPIST: see "person, charitable"

PHILOSOPHER, *keep silent and be counted a: sile, et philosophus esto*
natural: n. physiologizer; physiologue

PHILOSOPHY: (see "doctrine") n. credo; *scientia scientiarum*
pretender or dabbler in: n. philosophaster
spurious or pretended: n. philosophastry; sciosophy; a. philosophastering

PHOTOGRAPHIC: a. photogenic

PHRASE(S): (see "word") n. diction
in formal and not always sincere: a. phraseological; n. lexiphanicism

PHRASEOLOGY: n. diction; parlance; syntax
pretentious: n. lexiphanicism

PHYSICAL: (see "natural") a. corpor(e)al; material(istic); palpable; physiological; ponderable; somatic; tangible; n. corporeality; corporeity; materiality; physicality; substantiality
beyond the: see "supernatural"
form or construction: n. constitution; habitus; physique
predominance of the: n. physicality
skill or energy, pert. to or requiring:

a. manual; muscular; physical
 treatment: n. physiatrics; physical medicine (or therapy); physiotherapy
  specialist in: n. physiatrist; physiotherapist

PHYSICIAN, *disease or disorder produced by or by treatment:* a. iatrogenic; medicamentous
 pert. to: a. Aesculapian; iatric(al)
 stock in trade of: n. armamentarium; *materia medica;* (pl. armamentaria; instrumentaria)

PHYSIQUE: n. constitution; habitus; physicality

PIANO, *display of expertness in playing:* n. expertise; virtuosity; (pl. pianistics)
 female player: n. pianiste
 pert. to: a. pianistic

PICTURE: v. delineate; depict(ure); illustrate; photograph; portray; represent; n. configuration; delineation; iconography; illustration; portraiture; similitude
 composite: n. collage; (photo)montage
 writing(s): n.pl. curiologics; hieroglyphics; a. curiologic(al); hieroglyphic(al)

PIECEMEAL: a. aliquot; fractional; fractionary; fragmentary; *par pièces*

PIERCE: v. impale; lancinate; penetrate; perforate; puncture; transfix

PIGEON(S), *of or rel. to:* a. peristeronic

PILE: n. accumulation; agglomeration; aggregation; congeries
 up: v. (ac)cumulate; agglomerate; pyramid; a. cumulative

PILLAGE: v. despoil; devastate; plunder; n. brigandage; depredation; (de)spoliation; rapine

PIMPLY: a. papuliferous; papulose; n. papule

PINCH: v. compress; constrict; impinge; vellicate; n. exigency; impingement; juncture; predicament; vellication; vicissitude

PIOUS: a. consecrated; devotional; devout; religious; reverent; sanctified
 excessively or falsely: a. hypocritical;

religiose; sanctimonious; n. odor of sanctity; piosity; religiosity; sanctimoniousness
 fraud: n. *fraus pia*
 not: (see "disbeliever") a. adiaphorous; aporetic; blasphemous; impious; irreligious; sacreligious

PIRATE: n. buccaneer; corsair; freebooter; picaroon; privateer; a. piratical
 flag: n. Jolly Roger

PIT: n. lacuna; a. PITTED: lacunal; lacunar

PITCH (*tar*), *of or like:* a. piceous

PITFALL: n. artifice; inveiglement; maelstrom; stratagem; subterfuge; temptation

PITH: see "heart" and "embodiment"; a. PITHY: (see "terse") aphoristic; apothegmatic; cogent; concentrated; epigrammatic(al); gnomic(al); laconic(al); sententious; vigorous

PITY: n. charity; commiseration; compassion; condolence; empathy; remorse; sympathy; a. PITIABLE: commiserable; squalid; a. PITIFUL: abject; commiserable; contemptible; despicable; lamentable; pathetic; squalid; touching; a. PITILESS: despiteful; dispiteous; impiteous; implacable; inexorable; malicious; merciless; relentless; revengeful; ruthless; unfeeling
 appeal(ing) to: adv. or n. (*argumentum*) *ad misericordiam*
 mock, person regarded w/: n. pilgarlic

PLACE(S): n. locale; locus; (pl. loci); status; situ(s); situation
 cited or quoted, at: adv. *loco citato* (abb. *loc. cit.*)
 in its: adv. *in situ*
 in the first: adv. imprimis
 in the proper or natural: adv. *in loco; in situ*
 name: n. toponym; a. toponymic(al)
 of torment or martyrdom: n. Golgotha; *via dolorosa*
 out of: a. ill-timed; inappropriate; *mal à propos;* malapropos

PLAGUE: n. abomination; affliction; calamity; harassment; infestation; outbreak; pestilence: a. calamitous; pestilential; pestilentious

PLAIN: (see "clear" and "simple") a. candid; ingenious; literal; manifest; nondescript; perspicacious; transparent; unadorned; unalluring; unattractive; uncosmetized; undisguised; undramatic; unembellished; unembroidered; unobstructed; unprepossessing; unpretentious; unspectacular; unvariegated; unvarnished
    in neatness: adv. *simplex munditiis*
    in (plain) words or lang.: adv. *nudis verbis;* a. or adv. *en clair*

PLAN(S): v. calculate; cogitate; conspire; contemplate; contrive; ideate; preconceive; precogitate; prefigure; premeditate; scheme; n. conspiracy; formula; intrigue; preconception; project; regimen; schema; (pl. schemata); a. calculatory; formulaic; premeditative; schematic
    abstract: n. architectonics
    orderly: n. architectonics; cosmos; syntax; a. architectonic; syntactic(al)

PLANNED *progress:* n. conservation; husbandry; telesia; telesis

PLANT(S), *and animals, development of:* n. biology; a. biological
    and animal life, regional: n. biota; flora and fauna
    and domestic animals, science of propagation: n. thremmatology
    and plant life, regional: n. flora
    -eating: a. herbivorous; phytiverous; phytophagous; phytophilous; vegetarian
    -eating animal: n. herbivore; (pl. herbivora); vegetarian
    fond of: a. phytophilous
    growing in solution: n. hydroponics
    pert. to: a. botanical; herbaceous; herbal; phytologic(al)
    science of distribution of: n. biogeography; phytogeography
    specialist: n. botanist; herbologist; phytologist
    study of: n. botany; herbology; phytology
    worship of or undue fondness for: n. phytolatry

PLASTIC: (see "pliant") a. adaptable; creative; ductile; fictile; formative; governable; impressionable; labile; malleable; manageable; mutable; pluripotent; sculptural; n. PLASTICITY: creativity; ductility; elasticity; impressionability; malleability

PLATFORM: n. dais; *haut pas;* lectern; lyceum; podium; rostrum

PLAUSIBLE: (see "probable") a. colorable; credible; specious; n. PLAUSIBILITY: credibility
    but not genuine: a. specious; n. speciosity

PLAY: (see "drama") n. *pièce de théâtre;* n.pl. PLAYERS: (see "actor(s)") *corps dramatique; dramatis personae*
    subtle: n. artifice; finesse; maneuver; stratagem

PLAYFUL: (see "frolicsome") a. convivial; facetious; frivolous; impish; jocose; jocular; jovial; roguish; sportive; n. PLAYFULNESS: (see "banter") archness; jocosity; jocularity; joviality; roguery; roguishness; sportiveness

PLAYWRIGHT: n. dramatist; dramaturge; a. dramaturgic

PLEA: (see "entreaty") n. advocation; allegation; blandishment; contention; pretext; supplication; n. PLEADER: advocate; intercessor; paraclete; supplicant

PLEAD: see "beg"

PLEASANT: (see "pleasing") a. idyllic; n. PLEASANTNESS: amity; bonhom(m)ie; harmonization; harmony; n. PLEASANTRY: facetiosity; facetiousness; jocularity; *plaisanterie*
    idleness: n. *dolce far niente*
    in sound or tone: (see "harmonious") a. euphonic(al); euphonious; sonorous; n. euphony; harmonics; harmony
    make: v. edulcorate

PLEASE: (see "satisfy") v. delectate; exhilarate; gratify; titillate; tit(t)ivate; a. *s'il vous plaît*
    as you: adv. *al piacere*
    hard to: a. captious; fastidious; hypercritical; implacable; inexorable; insatiable; meticulous; scrupulous; unappeasable
    willingness or disposition to: n. amiability; complaisance; a. amiable; complaisant

PLEASING: (see "agreeable") a. amiable; comely; compatible; consonant; delectable; ecstatic; elysian; empyrean; felici-

tous; harmonious; idyllic; ingratiating; ingratiatory; palatable; prepossessing; **n.** harmonization; titillatation; tit(t)ivation
delusions or hallucinations: **n.** amenomania
for sake of: **adv.** *ad captandum*
in appearance: **a.** captivating; comely; enchanting; pellucid; personable; ravishing
to ear: see "harmonious"

PLEASURE(S): **n.** cakes and ale; delectation; diversion; fruition; inclination; oblectation; titil(l)ation; tit(t)ivation; **a.** PLEASURABLE: (see "pleasing") delectable; hedonistic(al); sybaritic(al)
and pain, rel. to either or both: **a.** algedonic
at: **adv.** *a beneplacito; ad arbitrium; ad lib(itum)*; *al piacere; à volonté*
doctrine of: **n.** Cyreniacism hedonism; sybaritism; **a.** Cyrenaic; hedonistic(al); sybaritic(al); **n.** Cyrenaic; hedonist; Sybarite
enjoy those of the moment: **n.** *carpe diem;* **adv.** *carpe diem; in horam vivere*
everyone has his own: sua cuique voluptas
from being mistreated, hurt or dominated: **n.** algophilia; masochism; **a.** algophilic; masochistic; **n.** algophilist; masochist
given to: **a.** apolaustic; hedonic; hedonistic(al); sybaritic(al)
in administering physical or mental pain or cruelty: **n.** algophilia; sadism; **a.** algophilic; sadistic; **n.** algophilist; sadist
insensitiveness to: **n.** anesthesia; anhedonia; hypesthesia; hypnosis
one fond of: **n.** Cyrenaic epicure; hedonist; libertine; sybarite; tragalist; *viveur;* voluptuary
pert. to or to nature of: **a.** eudaemonic; eudemonia; hedonic(al)
sensual: **n.pl.** *voluptates corporis;* **a.** amatory; Anacreontic; convivial
small: **n.pl.** *menus plaisirs*
to each his own: cuique voluptas sui; sua cuique voluptas
with: **adv.** *avec plaisir*

PLEAT(ED): **v.** plicate; **a.** plicate(d)

PLEDGE: **v.** guarantee; hypothecate; (im)pignorate; plight; **n.** collateral; guarantee; hypothecation; (im)pignoration; surety; **a.** impignorative
as security: **v.** hypothecate

for performance: **n.** collateral; recognizance
living: **n.** *vivum vadium*
of love: **n.** betrothal; *gage d'amour;* plight

PLENTY: (see "abundance") **n.** affluence; amplitude; copiousness; copiosity; opulence; plen(t)itude; plethora; profusion; repletion; spate; **a.** PLENTIFUL: (see "abundant") abounding; ample; copious; cornucopian; exuberant; opulent; plentitudinous; plenteous; plethoric; replete; superabundant
horn of: **n.** *corne d'abondance;* cornucopia; **a.** cornucopian

PLIANT: (see "plastic") **a.** adaptable; amenable; ductile; fictile; flexible; governable; malleable; manageable; susceptible; tractable; yielding

PLIGHT: (see "predicament") **n.** dilemma; *mauvais pas;* quandary

PLOT: (see "conspiracy") **n.** cabal; conspiration; intrigue; junta; machination; scenario; stratagem; **a.** cabalistic; conspirative; conspiratorial; **n.** conspirator
secretly: **v.** conspire; machinate; **n.** cabal; conspiration; machination

PLUCK: **v.** velicate; **n.** determination; resolution; vellication
person with: **n.** Trojan

PLUG: **v.** occlude; **n.** embolus; occlusion; pledget; tamp(i)on

PLUMP: **a.** corpulent; distended; portly; rotund; **n.** corpulency; portliness; rotundity

PLUNDER: **v.** depredate; despoil; maraud; pillage; ransack; spoliate; **n.** depredation; (de)spoiliation; plunderage; rapine

POCKETBOOK, *appeal(ing) to the:* **n.** or **adv.** *(argumentum) ad crumenam*

POEM: see "poetry"
birthday: **n.** genethliacon
bucolic: **n.** eclogue; idyll; pastoral
initial letters in alphabetical order: **n.** abecedarius
medieval love: **n.** madrigal

POET, *distinguished:* **n.** laureate
is born, not made: poëta nascitur, non fit

poor or inferior: **n.** balladmonger; poetaster; versemonger
would-be: **n.** *poète manqué*

POETIC(AL): **a.** idealized; lyric; Pegasean; poematic
inspiration: **n.** pegasus
license: **n.** *licentia vatum*
quality or expression: **n.** poeticality
rage: **n.** *furor poeticus*

POETRY: see "verse"
art of: **n.** *ars poetica;* metrification; versification
dabbling in: **n.** balladmongering; poetastering; poetastery
muse of: **n.** Calliope (*epic*); Erato (*amatory and lyric*)
pert. to: **a.** bardic; lyric; melic; metrical; poetical
pert. to art of: **a.** Parnassian
second-rate: **n.** crambo

POINT(S): (see "gist") **n.** characteristic; locality; *locus;* (**pl.** *loci*); proposition; thesis
-by-point: **a.** alphabetical; categoric(al); seriatim
fine (as distinction): **n.** nuance; quiddity; subtlety; tenuosity
having or rel. to two: **a.** bipunctate; bipunct(u)al
highest or farthest: **n.** apogee; solstice; ultima Thule
lowest: **n.** nadir; perigee
pert. to: **a.** apical; cacuminal; cacuminous
to the: **adv.** *ad rem*
vantage: see "vantage point"

POINTED: **a.** aciculate(d); acuminate; apicular; apiculated; epigrammatic; incisive; poignant; pungent; spicate; spicigerous; stimulating; stimulative; zestful

POINTLESS: **a.** hebetudinous; impertinent; incongruous; irrelevant; obtuse; **n.** POINTLESSNESS: hebetude; ineffectuality; irrelevancy

POISE: **v.** balance; librate; stabilize; **n.** adroitness; aplomb; bearing; carriage; composure; dexterity; equilibrium; equipoise; imperturbability; libration; nonchalance; perpendicularity; posture; *savoir-faire; sang-froid;* self-possession; serenity; tranquility; **a.** libratory

POISON: **v.** corrupt; pollute; toxify; **n.** (see "pollution") bane; malignancy; pestilence; pestilency; toxicity; toxin; venenation; venom; virulence; **a.** POISONOUS: (see "deadly") baneful; deleterious; loathsome; malevolent; malignant; mortal; nauseating; (ob)noxious; pernicious; septic; toxiferous; venomous; viperous; virulent
antidote against: **n.** or **a.** alexipharmic; prophylaxis; **n.** mithridate; mithridatum; prophylaxis

POLISHED: (see "polite") **a.** cavalier; courteous; couth; cultivated; diplomatic; elegant; politic; refined; *soigné(e);* suave; tactful; urbane; **n.** POLISH: artistry; consummation; courtliness; diplomacy; elegance; finesse; gloss; luster; preciosity; refinement; suavity; urbanity
affectedly: **a.** *précieuse; précieux;* **n.** preciosity
brilliantly: **a.** vernicose
literary style: **a.** Addisonian

POLITENESS: (see "polish") **n.** affability; civility; comity; complaisance; courtesy; courtliness; decorum; deferentiality; diplomacy; *prévenance;* suaveness; suavity; urbanity; **a.** POLITE: (see "courteous" and "polished") affable; cavalier; ceremonial; Chesterfieldian; complaisant; courtly; decorous; deferential; diplomatic; gracious; politic; sophisticated; suave; tactful
esp. if excessive: **n.** decorousness; politesse
expression of: **n.** euphemism
formal and cultivated: **n.** diplomacy; politesse
lack of: **n.** angularity; incivility; inurbanity; rusticity; uncourtliness

POLITICAL *boss w/ military following:* **n.** caudillo
favor: **n.** nepotism; patronage
party, aristocratic, or supporting authority: **n.** Ghibelline(s)
opposing authority: **n.** Guelf(s); (or Guelph[s])
organization: **n.** polity
power or authority; **n.** temporality
stumping or electioneering: **n.** hustings
to make: **v.** politici(ali)ze; **n.** politicalization; politicization

POLITICIAN: **n.** courtier; statesman
petty or contemptible: **n.** politicaster; **a.** unstatesmanlike

POLITICS, *bring within realm of:* **v.** politici(ali)ze; **n.** politicalization; politicization
discuss or discourse upon: **v.** politicize; **n.** politicization
power: **n.** *machtpolitik*
practical: **n.** *realpolitik*

POLLUTION: (**see** "poison") **n.** adulteration; contamination; corruption; defilement; desecration; impurity; profanation; uncleanliness

POMPOUS: (**see** "bombastic") **a.** consequential; fatuous; fustian; grandiose; imposing; magisterial; ostentatious; pretentious; supercilious; theatrical; turgid; **n.** POMP: *coup de théâtre;* grandeur; magnificence; pomposity; pretense; ostentation; ritual; vainglory
as of speech or writing(s): **a.** bombastic; grandiloquent; orotund; rubescent; **n.** grandiloquence; orotundity; pomposity; rubescence
excessively: **n.** pomposity; **v.** pontificate
official or person: (**see under** "person") **n.** panjandrum

PONDER: **v.** deliberate; (ex)cogitate; meditate; perpend; ruminate; **n.** cogitation; rumination; **a.** cogitative; meditative; ruminative

PONDS, *thriving in:* **a.** tychopotamic

POOR: **a.** bankrupt; despicable; destitute; hardscrabble; humble; impecunious; impoverished; inadequate; indigent; insolvent; meager; moneyless; necessitous; portionless; poverty-stricken; resourceless; shoddy; squalid; straitened; undesirable; unfavorable; **n.** (**see** "poverty") immiserization; impecuniosity; impecunity; impoverishment; indigence; indigency; mendicancy; pauperization
act of making: **n.** immiserization; impoverishment; pauperization; **v.** pauperize
devil or wretch: **n.** *pauvre diable*
in midst of great wealth: magna inter opes inops
to make: **v.** depauperate; impoverish; pauperize

POORLY *conceived:* **a.** malentendu
constructed, as lit. work: **a.** incondite

POPE, *pert. to:* **a.** episcopal; papal; pontifical

POPULACE, *appeal(ing) to the:* **n. or adv.** (*argumentum*) *ad populum*

POPULAR: (**see** "prevalent") **a.** accepted; approved; demotic; enchorial; exoteric; fashionable; modish; plebeian; prevailing; prevalent; proletarian; vulgar
favor: **n.** *aura popularis*

POPULATION(S) *area of greatest density:* **n.** ecumene
science or study of: **n.** demography; larithmics

POPULOUS: **a.** multitudinous

PORCH, *for carriages:* **n.** *porte cochère*

PORNOGRAPHY: **n.pl.** curiosa; erotica; esoterica; facetiae

PORTENT: (**see** "foretell") **v.** augur; auspicate; presage; **a.** auspicatory; foreboding; presageful: **n.** (**see** "omen") presentiment

PORTION: (**see** "amount" **and** "part") **n.** inheritance; quantum; (**pl.** quanta); quota

PORTRAY: **v.** delineate; depict; represent

POSE: **v.** attitudinize; baffle; **n.** (**see** "posture" **and** "staginess") affectation; attitude; attitudinization; mannerism; masquerade; theatricality
for effect: **v.** attitudinize; **n.** attitudinarian; *poseur;* (**fem.** *poseuse*)
in dancing: **n.** plastique

POSITION: (**see** "office") **n.** attitude; employment; *métier;* posture; ubiety; vocation
awareness or sense of: **n.** kinesthesia; orientation; proprioception; **a.** kinesthetic; proprioceptive
favorable: **n.** coign (of vantage)
having same relative: **a.** homologous; **n.** homologue

POSITIVE: **a.** absolute; affirmative; arbitrary; categorical; concrete; decisive; definitive; dogmatic; emphatic; indisputable; opinionated; philodoxic(al); preemptory; self-assured; substantive; thetic(al); unconditional; unequivocal; **n.** absolute; concretum; unconditionality

POSSIBILITY: **n.** contingency; dynamis; eventuality; feasibility; potentia; potential(ity); practicability; virtuality
to actuality: **adv.** *a posse ad esse*

POSSIBLE: **a.** achievable; conceivable; executable; implicit; *in posse;* latent; potential; practicable; practical; promising; superable; surmountable; undeveloped; **adv.** *in posse;* peradventure; potentially
to make: **v.** possibilitate

POSTCARD *collector:* **n.** deltiologist; **n.** deltiology

POSTER: **n.** affiche; broadside; bulletin; placard

POSTERIOR: **see** "behind"; **adv.** POSTERIORLY: cauded; posteriad

POSTPONE: **v.** defer; forbear; procrastinate; prorogue; protract; respite; **n.** POSTPONEMENT: (**see** "delay") **n.** deferment; procrastination; prorogation; respite
in law: **v.** continue; **n.** continuance

POSTURE: (**see** "pose") **n.** attitude; attudination
erect: **n.** orthograde; orthostatic

POTATOES, *served or prepared w/* **a.** parmentier; *parmentière*

POTENT: (**see** "strong") **a.** cogent; convincing; dynamic; puissant

POTENTIAL: **see** "possible"; **adv.** POTENTIALLY: *in posse; prima facie*

POUCH, *shaped like:* **a.** bursiculate; bursiform; saccate; scrotiform

POULTICE: **n.** fomentation

POUND: **v.** malleate; **n.** malleation

POUR *out:* **v.** disembogue

POVERTY: **n.** dearth; destitution; impecuniosity; inadequacy; indigence; mendicancy; paucity; pauperism; penury; privation; *res angusta domi;* scarcity; squalor; tenuity

POWDERY: **a.** friable; pulverous; pulverulent

POWER: (**see** "authority" **and** "rule") **n.** ascendency; capacity; cogency; control; domain; dominion; *dynamis;* dynamism; faculty; influence; potency; potentiality; prerogative; puissance; regency; superiority; supremacy
behind scenes: **n.** *éminence grise;* gray eminence
beyond permissive: **adv.** ultra licitum; ultra vires
creative or decisive (as institution, idea or person): **n.** demiurge; **a.** demiurgeous; demiurgic
full discretionary: **n.** *carte blanche;* plenipotentiary; **a.** plenary; plenipotent(ial); plenipotentiary
in acting or attempting to act: **n.** nisus
of office, etc.: **n.** attribution; jurisdiction; **a.** attributive; jurisdictional; jurisdictive
range or limit of: **n.** jurisdiction
supernatural, or of supposed divine origin: **n.** charism(a); **a.** charismatic
supreme or regal: **n.** diadem; imperium; sovereignty
to command admiration or esteem: **n.** prestige; **a.** prestigious
to do many things: **a.** multipotent; omnipotent; **n.** omnipotence; omnipotency
tyrannical: **n.** Moloch
unlimited: (**see** "full discretionary" **above**) **n.** absolutism; authoritarian(ism); omnipotence; omnipotency; **a.** authoritarian; omnipotent; plutocratic; tyrannical; tyrannous
within permitted: **adv.** intra vires

POWERFUL: (**see** "strong") **a.** almighty; authoritarian; cogent; dominant; dynamic; forceful; forte; Herculean; influential; leonine; (multi)potent; plutocratic; prepotent; puissant; substantious; tyrannical; tyrannous
all-: **see** "almighty"
group: **n.** powerhouse
in battle or arms: **a.** armipotent
make more: **v.** augment; potentiate
person: **n.** Croesus; leviathan; mogul; plutocrat; potentate; tycoon

POWERLESS: (**see** "helpless") **a.** *brutum fulmen;* impotent; impuissant; nugatory; sterile; **n.** POWERLESSNESS: impotency; impuissance; sterility

PRACTICAL: **a.** banausic; empirical; existential; feasible; functional; materialistic; practicable; pragmatic(al); profi-

cient; unromantic; unsentimental; utile; utilitarian
person: **n.** materialist; practician; pragmatist; utilitarian
thinker: **n.** Aristotelian; **n.** Aristotelianism; **a.** Aristotelian

PRACTICE, *correctness of:* **n.** orthopraxy
distinguished fr. theory: **n.** praxis
makes perfect: fit fabricando faber

PRAISE: **v.** adulate; applaud; approbate; celebrate; commend(ate); compliment; emblazon; extol; hosanna; laureate; lionize; paen; pean; rhapsodize; **n.** accolade; acclamation; adulation; approbation; ascription; blandishment; elegy; emblazonment; encomium; eulogy; hosanna; laudation; lionization; panegyric; plaudit; rhapsody; (**pl.** *baise-mains*); **a.** PRAISING: see "eulogistic"
be to God: laus Deo
deserved: **see** "praiseworthy"
eager or hungry for: **a.** esurient; **n.** captation; esurience
excessive or offensive: **n.** fulsomeness; panegyric; **a.** fulsome; panegryic(al)
expression of: **n.** approbation; commendation; plaudit; **a.** approbative; commendative; commendatory
high: **n:** dithyramb; encomium; eulogium; eulogy; extol(l)ment; panegyric; **v.** eulogize; panegyrize; **a.** commendative; commendatory; complimentary; encomiastic; eulogistic; panegyrical
hymn of: **n.** canticle; doxology; magnificat; paen; pean; *te deum;* theody
one who (praises): **n.** encomiast; eulogist; extoller; laudator; laureate; panegyrist; rhapsodist
shout of: **n.** hallelujah; hosanna
to God: **n.** ascription; doxology; *laus Deo*
with: **a. or adv.** *cum laude*
with great or high: **a. or adv.** *magna cum laude*
with greatest or highest: **a. or adv.** *summa cum laude*

PRAISEWORTHY: **a.** approbatory; commendable; commendatory; complimentary; credible; creditable; encomiastic(al); estimable; eulogistic(al); exemplary; honorific; laudable; laudative; laudatory; meritorious; panegyric(al); (super)eminent; **n.** PRAISEWORTHINESS: commendability; creditability; estimability; exemplarity; laudability
not: **a.** illaudable

PRANK(S): (**see** "frolic") **n.** caper; capriccio; dido; *échappée;* escapade; *espièglerie;* marlock; vagary; whimsicality
comic: **n.** harlequinade
reckless: **n.** escapade

PRAY: **v.** beseech; entreat; implore; importune; invocate; invoke; solicit; supplicate
and work: ora et labora
for us: ora pro nobis

PRAYER: **n.** *absit omen;* adjuration; benediction; conjuration; entreaty; imploration; imprecation; invocation; litany; obsecration; orison; petition; solicitation; supplication; **a.** PRAYING (or PRAYERFUL): invocative; invocatory; precative; precatory; supplicatory
for mercy: **n.** Miserere

PREACHER: **see** "clergyman"

PRECAUTION, *from excessive:* **adv.** *ex abundante cautela*

PRECEDENT(S), *uphold:* **n.** *res adjudicata; stare decisis*

PRECIOUS: (**see** "valuable") **a.** alembicated

PRECISE: (**see** "exact") **a.** ceremonious; conscientious; definite; definitive; determinative; discriminating; explicit; fastidious; immaculate; impeccable; implicit; mathematical; meticulous; minute; minutious; minutose; orthodox; painstaking; punctilious; puritanical; rigorous; scrupulous; slavish; specific; unequivocal; **n.** PRECISION: ceremony; correctitude; definitude; exactitude; exactness: literality; minuteness; scrupulosity; veracity
person, esp. in morals or religion: **n.** precisian; sabbatarian
very: **a.** scrupulous; slavish

PRECONCEIVED *opinion:* **n.** ideation; *parti pris;* predilection; prejudice

PREDATORY: **a.** harpactophagous; predaceous; predacious; predative; rapacious; **n.** predacity; rapacity

PREDESTINATION: **n.** determinism; fatalism; foreknowledge; foreordination; necessarianism

PREDETERMINATION: **n.** *parti pris;* prejudgment; prejudication

PREDICAMENT: (**see** "perplexity") **n.** *cul-de-sac;* cruciality; (horns of a) dilemma; imbroglio; impasse; quandary; **a.** PREDICAMENTAL: dilemmatic; nonplussed

PREDICT: (**see** "foretell") **v.** adumbrate; forecast; presage; predicate; prognosticate; **a.** PREDICTABLE: calculable; prognosticable; **a.** PREDICTING (or PREDICTIVE): foreboding; haruspical; ominous; prognostic; prophetic; **n.** PREDICTION: forecast; haruspication; haruspicy; prognosis; prognostication; prophecy; vaticination; **n.** PREDICTOR: forecaster; haruspex; Nostradamus; prognosticator; soothsayer
    on basis of known facts: **v.** triangulate; **n.** triangulation

PREDISPOSITION: (**see** "tendency") **n.** diathesis; inclination; predilection
    to disease: **n.** diathesis

PREDOMINATE: **see** "prevail"

PREEMINENTLY: **adv.** *par excellence*

PREFACE: (**see** "introduction") **n.** *avant-propos;* exordium; foreword; isagoge; preamble; prelude; proem; programma; prolegomenon; (**pl.** prolegomena); prologue; prolusion; protasis; **a.** PREFACTORY: prefactorial; preliminary; prolegomenous; premonitory
    literary: **n.** isagoge

PREFERENCE: (**see** "prejudice") **n.** alternative; antecedence; discrimination; inclination; precedence; predilection; predisposition; priority

PREGNANCY: **n.** fecundity; fetation; gravidation; gravidity; gestation; meaningfulness
    vomiting of: **n.** *hyperemesis gravidarum*

PREGNANT: **a.** *enceinte;* fecund; germinal; gravid; meaningful; parous; significant; weighty
    with ideas, etc.: **a.** tumefacient; tumescent

PREJUDGMENT: **see** "predetermination"

PREJUDICE: (**see** "preference") **n.** bigotry; insularism; insularity; jaundice; partiality; *parti pris;* predilection; prepossession; sectionalism; **a.** PREJUDICED: (**see** "biased" **and** "narrow") bigoted; determined; insular; insulated; partial; prejudicial
    appeal(ing) to: **n.** or **adv.** (*argumentum*) *ad hominem*
    without: **adv.** *sine praejudicio*

PRELIMINARY: (**see** "introductory") **a.** antecedent; imperative; indispensable; liminary; precedential; precursive; precursory; prefactory; prefatorial; premonitory; **n.** **see** "prerequisite"
    discussion: **n.** pourparler
    knowledge: **n.** praecognitum
    matter: **n.** *avant-propos*

PRELUDE: (**see** "preface") **n.** overture; prolusion; **a.** prolusory

PREMATURE: **a.** anticipatory; inopportune; precipitate; precocious; prevenient; unseasonable; untimely

PREPARATORY: (**see** "introductory" **and** "preliminary") **a.** antecedent; prefatorial
    instruction: **n.** propaedeutics; **a.** propaedeutic(al)

PREPARE: (**see** "make") **v.** admonish; caution; confect; counsel; facilitate; precondition; **n.** PREPARATION: concoction; conditioning; confection; purveyance

PREPARED: (**see** "ready") **a.** admonished; *en garde;* expugnatory; preconditioned
    always: **n.** or **adv.** *semper paratus*
    for all things (or *ready for anything*): *in omnia paratus*
    for either event: in utrumque paratus

PREREQUISITE: **n.** condition precedent; essentiality; indispensability; postulate; *sine qua non;* **a.** **see** "preliminary"

PRESCRIBED: **a.** arbitrary; prescriptive; recommended; thetic(al)

PRESENT: **a.** contemporary; immediate; instant; **n.** (**see** "gratuity") *status quo;* temporality
    all-: (**see** under "all") **a.** multipresent; omnipresent; ubiquitous
    for the: **adv.** pro nunc
    I am: **adv.** *ad sum*
    time: **n.** nonce

PRESERVATION: (see "conservation") n. guardianship; immortalization; maintenance; perpetuation

PRESSING: (see "clamorous" and "urgent") a. critical; exigent; imminent; impending; imperative; important; insistent; poignant; threatening

PRESSURE: n. constraint; exaction; exigency; imminency; insistence; ponderosity

PRESTIGE: n. ascendency; authority; cachet; influence; reputation; repute; (super)eminence; a. prestigious; reputable
having great: (see "eminent") a. illustrious; influential; prestigious

PRESUME: (see "presuppose") v. anticipate; assume; postulate; a. PRESUMED: (see "probable") circumstantial; presumable; presumptive: n. PRESUMPTION: arrogance; audacity; circumstantiality; effrontery; expectation: *outrecuidance*

PRESUMPTUOUS: (see "pretentious") a. arrogant; audacious; Icarian; imperious; impertinent; insolent; overweening
person: n. jackanapes

PRESUPPOSE: (see "presume") v. assume; posit; postulate; n. PRESUPPOSITION: postulate; postulation; prolepsis

PRETEND: v. beseem; counterfeit; dissemble; simulate; a. PRETENDED: (see "affected") affectional; barmecidal; beseeming; hypocritical; ostensible; ostensive; quasi; self-styled; simulated; so-called; *soi-disant*
to be sick: v. malinger; n. malingering; pathomimesis; n. malingerer

PRETENDER: n. affecter; charlatan; claimant; counterfeit; deceiver; hypocrite; imposter; mountebank; *poseur;* (fem. *poseuse*); pretendant; quacksalver; Tartuf(f)e; *tricheur;* (fem. *tricheuse*)
to knowledge or scholarship: n. sciolist; a. sciolistic; sciolous; n. sciolism

PRETENSE: (see "pomp") n. affectation; (dis)simulation; fabrication; hypocrisy; persiflage; postiche; pretention; pretex; semblance; simulacrum; subterfuge
almost transparent: n. charade

PRETENTIOUS: (see "showy") a. affectational; ambitious; bombastic; faustian; ostentatious; pharisaical; pompous; self-important; sonorous; n. PRETENTIOUSNESS: blague; bombast; flummery; humbug; ostentation; pomposity
official: n. panjandrum

PREVAIL: (see "conquer") v. actuate; (pre)dominate; preponderate; n. PREVALENCE: ascendency; circulation; currency; predominance; predomination; regnance; regnancy; a. PREVAILING: (see "popular") ascendant; current; demotic; enchorial; epidemic; indigenous; (pre)dominant; prevalent; regnal; regnant; victorious

PREVENT: v. anticipate; circumvent; forestall; intercept; obviate; preclude; restrain; n. PREVENTION: alexeteric; circumvention; prevent(at)ive; prophylactic; prophylaxis; a. PREVENTING: circumventive; preventative; preventive; prophylactic

PREVIOUS: a. antecedent; anterior; preceding; premature
condition: n. precedent; *status quo ante*

PREYING *or living on other animals:* (see "predatory") a. predaceous; predacious; predative; rapacious; n. predacity; predation; predatoriness; predatism; rapaciousness; rapacity; n. predator

PRICE, *at any or regardless of:* adv. *à tout prix; coûte que coûte*

PRICELESS: (see "costly") a. impayable; incalculable; inestimable; invaluable; matchless

PRICKLY: (see "spinous" and "spiny") a. acanthoid; acanthous; echinate; horrent; muricate

PRIDE: n. *amour propre;* arrogance; conceit; ego(t)ism; *esprit de corps;* exaltation; haughtiness; hauteur; hubris; pomposity; self-esteem; self-exaltation; vainglory; vanity; a. PRIDEFUL: (see "haughty") fastuous; n. PRIDEFULNESS: see "self-importance"
disdainful: n. haughtiness; hauteur; hubris
of group or organization: n. *esprit de corps*
overweening: n. hubris

PRIEST : **n.** cleric; ecclesiastic; hierophant; **n.** PRIESTHOOD: clericality; eccliasticism; priestianity (*usu.* disparagingly); sacerdocy; **a.** PRIESTLY: Aaronic; ecclesiastic; hieratical; hierophantic; levitical; sacertot(ic)al
functions of: **n.** clericature; priestcraft; (**pl.** spiritualities)

PRIM : see "prissy"; **n.** PRIMNESS: decorousness; preciosity; priggishness; sanctimony; squeamishness

PRIMARY : (**see** "basic") **a.** constitutional; fundamental; idiopathic; primitive

PRIME *of life:* **n.** *fleur de l'âge; les belles années*

PRIMER : **n.** abecedarium; (**pl.** abecedaria) ; hornbook

PRIMITIVE : **a.** aboriginal; antiquated; archaic; autochthonal; autochthonic; autochthonous; elemental; fundamental; indigenous; native; prehistoric; primeval; primogenial; primordial; rudimentary; **n.** aboriginal; aborigine; primitiveness; primitivism; primitivity
people, study of: **n.** agriology

PRINCIPAL : **see** "chief"

PRINCIPLE(S) : **n.** *alpha and omega;* axiom; canon; doctrine; foundation; philosophy; principium; (**pl.** principia); (quint)essence; theorem; theory
basic: **n.** doctrine; fundament; postulate; tenet
having high: **a.** magnanimous; rectitudinous; righteous
statement of: **n.** canon; constitution; decalogue; declaration; *Magna C(h)arta*
system of: **n.** organon
vital: **n.** *anima bruta; anima mundi; élan vital*

PRINCIPLED, *overly:* **a.** rectitudinous; religiose; sanctimonious

PRINTED *on both sides of paper:* **a.** opisthographic(al)
on one side only: **a.** anopisthographic

PRIOR : (**see** "preliminary") **a.** antecedent; anterior; preceding; precursory

PRIORITY : **n.** antecedence; anteriority; precedence; preference; preeminence;

preferment; prerogative; primacy; seniority; superiority; supremacy
having: **a.** antecedaneous; precedent(ial); preferential

PRISON : **n.** bastil(l)e; limbo; **n.** PRISONER: *detenu;* (**fem.** *detenué*)

PRISSY : (**see** "affected") **a.** demure; fastidious; priggish; prudish; squeamish; schoolteacherish

PRIVACY : **n.** hermitage; isolation; penetralia; sanctuary; secrecy; seclusion; solitude
place of utmost: **n.** *sanctum sanctorum*

PRIVATE : **a.** auricular; confidential; covert; delitescent; esoteric; personal; privy; restricted; sequestered; **adv.** PRIVATELY: *à deux; à huis clos; à la derobée;* backstage; confidentially; covertly; *entre nous; inter nos;* privatim; privily
in: (**see** "secretly") **adv.** *à deux; à huis clos;* covertly; *entre nous; in camerâ; inter nos; in petto; sub rosa*
knowledge: **n.** privity; (**pl.** esoterica)
state of being: **n.** insularity; interiority
to make: **v.** interiorize; **n.** interiorization

PRIVATION : (**see** "poverty") **n.** deprivation; destitution; hardship; penury; squalor
causing: **a.** privative

PRIVILEGE : **n.** dispensation; franchise; immunity; license; patent; prerogative; **a.** PRIVILEGED: immune; prerogative
prior or exclusive: **n.** franchise; immunity; precedence; prerogative

PRIZE, *highest or first:* **n.** *cordon bleu; grand prix*
pert. to winner of: **a.** laureate

PROBABLE : **a.** apparent; circumstantial; credible; ostensible; plausible; presumable; presumptive; *prima facie;* promising; verisimilar

PROBATION, *period or state of:* **n.** novitiate; postulancy; **a.** probationary

PROBATIONER : **n.** acousmatic; novice; novitiate; recruit; trainee

PROBING : **a.** inquisitorial

PROBLEM : (see "difficulty") n. bugbear; enigma; perplexity; proposition
many-sided: n. hydra

PROCEDURE : (see "method") n. accouterment; approach; method(ology); *modus operandi;* protocol; technique
code of, or of conduct: n. protocol

PROCEEDING : n. *démarche;* maneuver; negotiation; transaction

PROCLAIM : v. announce; annunciate; asseverate; manifest; nuncupate; predicate; promulgate; n. PROCLAMATION : see "edict"

PROCLIVITY : see "inclination"

PRODIGY : see "child, gifted"

PRODUCE : v. accomplish; beget; engender; fabricate; generate; manufacture; originate; procreate; propagate; a. PRODUCING : generative; procreant; procreative
abundantly: (see "fruitful") a. feracious
at point or in process of (producing): a. aborning; in production; parturient
live beings: a. proligerous; viviparous; n. viviparity; viviparousness

PRODUCED *by human skill or effort:* a. (arti) factitious; n. artifact; (pl. *fructus industriales*)
by natural methods: n.pl. *fructus naturales*
capable of being: a. manufacturable; producible; productible

PRODUCT(S) : n. composition; consequence; manifestation; performance; progeny
man-made or industrial: n.pl. *fructus industriales;* a. (arti) factitious
natural: n.pl. *fructus naturales*

PRODUCTIVE : a. causative; constructive; creative; exuberant; fructiferous; fructuous; generative; imaginative; originative; procreative; profitable; uberous; n. PRODUCTIVENESS : creativity; fecundity; productivity; prolificity; uberty

PROFANE : (see "irreverent") v. blaspheme; desecrate; pollute; a. blasphemous; impious; mundane; sacrilegious; secular; sulfurous; sulphurous; temporal;

n. PROFANITY : blasphemy; desecration; profanation; sacrilege

PROFESSION : see "work"

PROFESSIONAL *jealousy:* n. *jalousie de métier*

PROFICIENCY : (see "ability" and "perfection") n. accomplishment; adeptness; competence; competency; deterity; expertise; expertness; mastery; virtuosity; a. PROFICIENT : accomplished; adept; *au fait;* consummate; dextrous; masterly; skillful

PROFILE : (see "outline") n. configuration; silhouette

PROFIT : (see "gain") n. increment; ophelimity; a. PROFITABLE : expedient; fructiferous; fructuous; fruitful; lucrative; remunerative

PROFLIGATE : see "lewd"

PROFUSE : (see "lavish") a. abundant; bountiful; copious; exuberant; prodigal; rampant; replete; superabundant; n. PROFUSION : (see "abundance") affluence; copiosity; extravagance; lavishness; opulence; plethora; prodigality; sumptuosity

PROGRAM : n. agendum; (pl. agenda); catalog(ue); exhibition; prospectus; schedule; syllabus; (pl. syllabi)

PROGRESS : n. evolution; movement; progression; progressivism
planned: see "planned"

PROGRESSIVE : (see "modern") a. categoric(al); consecutive; sequential; serial; successive

PROHIBIT : (see "ban") v. enjoin; inhibit; interdict; preclude; taboo; n. PROHIBITION : forbiddance; inhibition; injunction; interdiction; interdictum; outlawry; preclusion; proscription; a. PROHIBITIVE : inhibitory; interdictive; interdictory; proscriptive; verboten

PROJECTING : a. beetling; conspicuous; gibbous; prominent; protuberant; salient; v. PROJECT : extrapolate; n. enterprise; extrapolation; protuberance

abnormally: **a.** prognathous
part: **n.** ramus; **(pl.** rami)

PROLIFIC: **(see** "fertile" **and** "fruitful")
a. fecund; philoprogenitive; propagative;
reproductive; **n.** PROLIFICITY: fecundity; philoprogeneity
to make: **v.** prolificate

PROLOGUE: **see** "introduction"

PROLONG: **v.** lengthen; postpone; prorogue; protract; **a.** PROLONGED: profuse; protracted; protractive; prolix; repetitious; sostenente; sostenuto; sostinente;
sustaining; **n.** PROLONGATION: prolixity; prorogation; sustentation; sustention

PROMINENCE: **(see** "superiority") **n.**
celebrity; conspicuity; conspicuousness;
eminence; prestige; protuberance; salience; saliency; **a.** PROMINENT: **(see**
"eminent" **and** "notable") aquiline; blatant; celebrated; conspicuous; notorious;
protuberant; salient; stellar

PROMISE: **v. or n.** covenant; pledge;
plight
for promise: **n.** mutuality; *quid pro quo;*
reciprocity
land of (promised land): **n.** Canaan

PROMOTION: **(see** "advancement") **n.**
advertising; enhancement; preferment; **n.**
PROMOTER: abettor; entrepreneur;
(fem: entrepreneuse); encourager; impressario

PROMPT: **v.** actuate; animate; encourage;
a. celeritous; expeditious; mercurial;
punctual; telegraphic; **n.** PROMPTNESS: **(see** "speed") alacrity; celerity;
expedition; promptitude; punctuality

PRONGS, *having two:* **a.** bidentate; bidigitate(d); **n.** bidigitation

PRONOUNCEMENT: **see** "edict"

PRONUNCIATION: **(see** "speech") **n.**
articulation
bad **n.** cacoepy; cacology; **a.** cacoepistic
correct: **n.** orthoepy; phonology; **a.**
orthoepic(al); orthoepistic; **n.** orthoepist
distinct, as in separation of syllables: **n.**
incisiveness; syllabification; **a.** syllabic
standard, also study of: **n.** orthoepy;

a. orthoepic(al); orthoepistic; **n.** orthoepist

PRONOUNCING *clearly:* **a.** enunciative;
incisive; **n.** incisiveness; syllabification; **v.**
syllabicate; syllabify

PROOF: **n.** attestation; certification; corroboration; demonstration; documentation; evidence; verification
burden of: **n.** onus *(probandi)*
capable of: **a.** apodictic(al); demonstrable; **n.** demonstrability
incapable of: **a.** undemonstrable; unverifiable

PROOFREAD: **v.** collate; **n.** authentication; collation

PROPAGANDA: **n.** agitprop

PROPER: **(see** "suitable") **a.** accepted;
appropriate; à propos; *au fait;* comely;
comme il faut; condign; conventional;
decorous; felicitous; kosher; lawful; legitimate; licit; opportune; orthodox;
seemly
stickler for what is: **n.** proprietarian;
rigorist
what is considered: **see** "proprieties"

PROPERTIED *class:* **n.** proprietariat; **a.**
proprietarian

PROPERTY: **(see** "attribute") **n.** essence;
estate; resource(s); substance
given for support: **n.** ap(p)anage
inherited fr. father: **n.** patrimony; **a.**
patrimonial
personal: **n.** chattels; personalty; **(pl.**
personalia)
transfer of title: **v.** bequeath; convey;
demise; devise; **n.** conveyance

PROPHECY: **n.** divination; foretelling;
haruspication; omen; portent; prediction;
prognostication; pythonism; **a. see** "foretelling"

PROPHESY: **(see** "foretell") **v.** auspicate;
hariolate; prognosticate; vaticinate
art of (prophesying): **n. or a.** mantic

PROPHET: **n.** augur; Deborah; haruspex;
mantic; Nostradamus; oracle; predictor;
prognosticator; soothsayer; vaticinator
of misfortune or disaster: **n.** Cassandra;
Jeremiah; **a.** Cassandran

PROPHETIC(AL) : **a**: adumbrated; anticipative; apocalyptic(al) ; augural; cabalistic; divinatory; fatidic(al) ; incantatory; interpretive; ominous; oracular; phylacteric; portentious; presageful; prognosticative; pythonic; revelatory; sibylline; talismatic

PROPORTION: **n.** commensurability; commensuration; harmony; percentage; ration; symmetry; **a.** PROPORTIONATE: aliquot; commensurable; commensurate; corresponding

PROPOSITION: (**see** "assumption") **n.** hypothesis; philospheme; postulate; postulatum; (**pl.** *postulata*)
   assumed for argument: **n.** *obligatum:* (**pl.** *obligata*)

PROPRIETIES, *social:* **n.pl.** *agrémen(t)s;* amenities; conventionalities; decora; (*les*) *convenances;* urbanities
   stickler for: **n.** proprietarian; rigorist

PROPRIETY: **n.** *agrémen(t)s;* amenity; appropriatcness; aproposity; decorum; *bienséance;* grace; pertinence; pertinency; relevance; relevancy; suitability; **a.** appropriate; à propos; decorous; pertinent; relevant
   departure or deviation fr.: **n.** aberrance; aberrant; aberration; **a.** aberrant; aberrational; aberrative
   strict adherence to: **n.** correctitude; rigorism; scrupulosity; **n.** proprietarian; rigorist

PROSAIC: **a.** commonplace; down-to-earth; humdrum; jejune; literal(istic) ; matter-of-fact; monotonous; prolix; *terre à terre;* terrestrial; unimaginative; unleavened; **n.** prosaism

PROSCRIBE: **see** "ban"

PROSE, *writer of:* **n.** prosaist; prosateur

PROSPECT: (**see** "outlook") **n.** anticipation; expectation; foresight; futurity; panorama; perspective; prognosis; purview; vision; vista

PROSPERITY: **n.** *bonne fortune;* **a.** PROSPEROUS: (**see** "flourishing") affluent; auspicious; halcyon; propitious
   has many friends: felicitas multos habet amicos
   opposite of: **n.** illth

PROSTITUTE: **n.** courtesan; debauchee; demimondaine; demimonde; doxy; *fille de joie;* harlot; hetria; huzzy; *nymphe du pavé; petite dame;* quean; strumpet; trollop
   higher rank: **n.** courtesan; courtezan
   lover of (prostitutes): **n.** philopornist
   of or rel. to, or having traits of: **a.** meretricious
   part-time: **n.** grisette

PROSTITUTION: **n.** corruption; debasement; harlotry; promiscuity
   of talents: **n.** venality

PROSTRATION: **n.** abashment; collapse; prosternation; stupefaction; submissiveness

PROTECTION: **n.** aegis; armament; auspice(s) ; bastion; bulwark; custody; guardianship; indemnity; palladium; patronage; preservation; prophylactic; prophylaxis; redoubt; sanctuary; tutelage; umbrella; **a.** PROTECTIVE: custodial; maternal(istic) ; paternal(istic) ; preservative; prophylactic; sheltering; tutelary; tutorial; **n.** PROTECTOR: (**see** "champion") chaperone; custodian; guardian; guarantor
   means of: **n.** armament; muniment

PROTEST: (**see** "complain") **v.** deprecate; expostulate; inveigh; oppugn; remonstrate; **n.** (**see** "complaint") protestation; remonstrance; remonstration; **a.** remonstrative
   one who makes: **n.** complainant; oppugner; protestant; remonstrator

PROTUBERANCE: **n.** gibbosity; protuberancy; protrusion; salience; saliency; **a.** PROTUBERANT: bulbous; conspicuous; gibbose; gibbous; obtrusive; prominent; salient

PROUD: **a.** arrogant; bombastic; contemptuous; disdainful; ego(t)istical; elated; exultant; haughty; hubristic; imperious; orgilous; orgulous; overweening; presumptuous; prideful; scornful; supercilious; **n.** see "pride"
   boastfully: **a.** hubristic; vainglorious

PROVED (or PROVEN): see "established"; **v.** PROVE: circumstantiate; confirm; demonstrate; establish; manifest; verify; **a.** PROVING: confirmative; confirmatory; demonstrative

253

able to be: **a.** apodictic(al) ; indisputable
something which is (proved): **n.** probatum ; (**pl.** probata)
that which was to be: quod erat demonstrandum (**abb.** q.e.d.)
unable to be: **a.** anapodictic

PROVERB(S) : (**see** "maxim") **n.** apothegm ; gnome ; parable ; **a.** apothegmatic(al) ; gnomic(al)
student of: **n.** par(o)emiologist
study of: **n.** paroemiology
writer of: **n.** paremiographer ; paroemiographer

PROVIDE : **see** "prepare"

PROVIDENCE, *with favoring:* **adv.** *benigno numine*

PROVISION(S) *for journey or travel:* **n.** viaticum ; (**pl.** viatica)

PROVISIONAL : **a.** *ad hoc;* circumstantial ; conditional ; contingent ; interim ; temporary ; tentative

PROVOKE : (**see** "aggravate") **v.** exacerbate ; excite ; perturb ; pique ; quicken ; stimulate

PROWL *lecherously:* **n. or v.** caterwaul

PRUDENCE : **n.** calculation ; canniness ; cautiousness ; circumspection ; discretion ; forethought ; frugality ; judiciousness ; moderation ; providence ; restraint ; sophrosyne ; temperance ; vigilance ; **a.** PRUDENT : **see** "careful"

PRUDISH : (**see** "prissy") **a.** lily-white ; nice-Nellie ; priggish ; puribund ; squeamish ; PRUDERY : Comstockery ; Grundyism ; priggishness ; puribundity ; squeamishness

PRYING : **a.** curious ; inquisitorial
observer: **n.** quidnunc ; scopophiliac ; *voyeur;* **a.** scopophilic ; voyeuristic

PSYCHIC : **see** "mental" **and** "supernatural"

PUBERTY, not having reached : **n.** impuberty ; **a.** impubic ; prepubertal
of or happening at: **a.** hebetic ; pubertal ; pubescent
rites at attaining: **see under** "adulthood"

PUBIC *hair:* **n.** byssus ; escutcheon
hair, site of: **n.** *mons veneris* (**fem.**) pubic triangle

PUBLIC : (**see** "popular") **a.** exoteric ; **n.** commonalty ; community ; populace ; population
belonging to the: **a.** *publici juris*
declaration or report: **n.** manifesto ; white paper
for good of the: **adv.** *pro bono publico*
in: **a. or adv.** *coram populo; coram publico*
office, mania for holding: **n.** empleomania
officer: **n.** fonctionnaire
speaking, rel. to: **a.** demegoric
use, seize for: **see under** "seize"

PUBLICATION : (**see** "disclosure") **n.** divulgation ; proclamation ; promulgation

PUBLICITY : **n.** ballyhoo ; dissemination ; exploitation ; promulgation ; propaganda

PUBLICIZE (**or** PUBLISH) : **v.** circulate ; delate ; disseminate ; exploit ; herald ; nuncupate ; proclaim ; promote ; promulgate ; pronunciate ; ventilate

PUBLISHED *after author's death:* **a.** posthumous

PULP : **n.** cellulose ; magma ; **a.** PULPY : macerated ; magmatic ; pultaceous

PULSATE : **v.** oscillate ; palpitate ; pulse ; vibrate ; **a.** PULSATIVE : palpitant ; pulsatile ; pulsatory ; throbbing ; **n.** PULSATION : ictus ; oscillation ; palmus ; palpitation ; undulation

PULVERIZE : **v.** annihilate ; comminute ; contriturate ; demolish ; disintegrate ; levigate ; triturate ; **n.** PULVERIZATION : comminution ; trituration

PUN : **n.** adnomination ; assonance ; calembour ; equivoke ; equivoque ; *jeu de mots;* paradigm ; paronomasia ; *turlupinade*

PUNISH : **v.** admonish ; castigate ; chasten ; chastize ; discipline ; flagellate ; penalize ; retaliate ; **a.** PUNISHING : castigatory ; corrective ; disciplinary ; expiatory ; flagellant ; penal ; penitentiary ; punitive ; retaliatory ; retributory ; retributive ; vindicative ; vindicatory
by fine: **v.** amerce ; **n.** amercement

PUNISHMENT: **n.** admonition; amercement; castigation; chastenment; chastisement; correction; discipline; expiation; Nemesis; penalty; penance; punition; purgatory; retaliation; retribution; vindication
   enforcer of: **n.** disciplinarian; martinet; Nemesis; rigorist
   freedom from: **n.** immunity; impunity
   just: **n.** comeuppance; Nemesis
   lessening of: **n.** commutation; leniency; mitigation; **v.** commute; mitigate; reprieve
   liability to: **n.** penality; **a.** penalizable
   not subject to or capable of: **a.** immune; indisciplinable; **n.** immunity; indiscipline
   pert. to or having nature of: **a.** castigatory; disciplinal; disciplinary; disciplinatory; punitive; punitory; retributive; vindicatory
   self, pert. to: **a.** intropunitive; self-condemnatory
   strong and severe: **n.** peine forte et dure
   study of: **n.** penology; **a.** penological; **n.** penologist
   voluntary, as token of repentence: **n.** penance; **a.** penitential

PUNNING, *act or practice of:* **n.** adnomination; paronomasia

PUPIL: **n.** abecedarian; alphabetarian; apostle; catechumen; disciple; neophyte; novice; probationer; *protégé,* (**fem.** *protégée*); scholar
   pert. to: **a.** abecedarian; apostolic; catechumenal; catechumenical; scholarly; scholastic

PURCHASES, *insane desire to make:* **n.** oniomania; **n.** oniomaniac

PURE: **a.** absolute; (arch)angelic; artless; chaste; cherubic; classic(al); crystalline; devout; guileless; hermetic(al); immaculate; imputrescible; incorrupt(ed); incorruptible; innocent; intemerate; inviolable; inviolate; *pur et simple;* seraphic; sheer; spotless; sterile; sublime; unadulterated; unalloyed; uncorrupted; uncorruptible; undefiled; unmixed; unsoiled; unstained; unsullied; untainted; untouched; upright; vestal; virgin
   unqualifiedly: **a.** archangelic; *pur et simple;* simon-pure

PURGE: **v.** absterge; defecate; deterge; eliminate; **n.** abstersion; catharsis; cathartic; laxative; purgation; purgative

PURIFICATION: **n.** ablution; abreaction; alembication; catharsis; defecation; depuration; epuration; lustration; purgation; **a.** PURIFICATORY: expiatory; purgatorial
   by ceremony: **n.** lustration; **a.** lustral; **v.** lustrate

PURIFY: **v.** alembicate; chasten; defecate; depurate; edulcorate; epurate; exorcise; lustrate
   by washing: **v.** elutriate; **n.** elutriation
   something which (purifies): **n.** purificant

PURITY: **n.** chastity; cleanliness; continence; immaculacy; incorruptibility; inviolability; sacredness; sanctity; sanctitude; virtue
   exaggerated: (**see** "religious, overly")
   n. Comstockery; pudency; pudibundity; pudicity; puritanism; **a.** PURITANICAL: lily-white; priggish; prudish; puribund; sanctimonious
   those who claim or profess: **n.** (the) unco guid

PURPLE, *clad in:* **a.** porporate
   to become or make: **v.** empurple; **a.** empurpled

PURPLISH: **a.** porphyrous; purpureal; purpurean; purpurescent; purpureous; purpurine

PURPOSE: (**see** "destiny" and "intention") **n.** ambition; aspiration; *causa finalis;* design; determination; function; intendment; philosophy; purport; resolution; significance
   aside from the: **adv.** *hors de propos*
   for what?: **adv.** *cui bono?*
   fulfilled and no longer valid: **adv.** *functus officio*
   having many: **a.** multiphasic; multipurpose; multivious
   without definite: **see** "purposeless"

PURPOSEFUL: (**see** "intentional") **a.** directional; functional; purposive; teleological; telic

PURPOSELESS: **a.** aimless; amorphous; dysteleological; meaningless; purportless; random; undirected; unpremeditated

PURSE, *appeal(ing) to the:* **n. or adv.** *(argumentum) ad crumenam*

PURSUIT: (see "quest") **n.** activity; *métier;* occupation; ploy; prosecution; **a.** persequent

PUS: **n.** suppuration; **a.** suppurative
discharge: **v.** maturate; suppurate
of, like or containing: **a.** puriform; purulent; suppurative; **n.** maturation; purulence; purulency

PUSHER: **n.** arrivst(e); parvenu; **n.** arrivism

PUSHING: **a.** aggressive; arrogant; bumptious; presumptuous

PUZZLE: **see** "bewilder" **and** "mystery"
key to the: **n.** *le mot de l'enigme*

PUZZLING: **a.** ambiguous; ambivalent; bewildering; cabalistic; cryptic; enigmatic(al); equivocal; impenetrable; incomprehensible; inexplicable; inscrutable; mysterious; occult; paradoxical; perplexing; sphinxlike; undecipherable; unfathomable

PYRAMID, *pert. to or having shape of:* **a.** pyramidal; **n.** zigguart

Q

QUACK: (see "pretender") **n.** Cagliostro; charlatan; empiric; humbug; imposter; medicaster; mountebank; quacksalver

QUAINT: (see "odd") **a.** antique; bizarre; eccentric; exotic; grotesque; *outré;* rococo; singular; whimsical; **n.** see "oddity" and "peculiarity"

QUALIFY: **v.** capacitate; habilitate; **n.** QUALIFICATION: (see "capacity") capacitation; expertise; expertness; habilitation; hability; virtuosity; **a.** QUALIFIED: (see "capable") accomplished; certified; competent; conditional; consummate; eligible; licensed; registered; restricted; **a.** QUALIFYING: (see "limiting") adjectival; adjective; qualificatory

QUALITY: (see "attribute") **n.** character-(istic); property; resonance; timbre
  having different (qualities): **a.** heterogeneous; heteroousian; heterousian; **n.** heterogeneity
  something of superior: **n.** *nec plus supra; nec plus ultra;* nonesuch; nonpareil; supernaculum

QUANTITY, *having to do with:* **a.** quantitative; **n.** amplitude; magnitude; quantum; (**pl.** quanta)
  large: **n.** hecatomb; legion; multitude; spate
  very small in: **a.** diminutive; homeopathic; miniscular; miniscule; minuscule

QUARREL: (see "breach") **n.** altercation; *démêlé;* dissention; embroglio; fracas; melee; ruction; wrangle
  lover's: **n.pl.** *amatium irae*
  noisily: **v.** or **n.** caterwaul ;**n.** ruction
  riotous: **n.** donnybrook

QUARRELSOME: **a.** *acariâtre;* argumentative; bellicose; belligerent; boisterous; cantankerous; choleric; combative; contentious; discordant; disputable; disputatious; dissentient; dissentious; dissident; fractious; gladiatorial; perverse; pugna-cious; querulous; refractory; ructious; termagant(ish); turbulent; **n.** QUARRELSOMENESS: *acariâtre;* bellicosity; belligerency; pugnacity; turbulence

QUEER: see "odd"

QUEST: **n.** desideratum; emprise; expedition; (Holy) grail; inquisition; odyssey; perlustration; perscrutation; pursuit; reconnaissance; reconnoiter; safari; venture

QUESTION: **v.** catechize; inquisit; **n.** QUESTIONER: inquisitor
  and answer method of discussion: **n.** dialectics; **a.** dialectic(al)
  of instruction: **n.** catechesis; catechism; **v.** catechize; **a.** catechetic(al); catechistic; Socratean; Socratic
  begging the: **n.** *petitio principii*
  beyond: **a.** impregnable; indubitable; invulnerable; undoubtable; unquestionable
  bringing into: **n.** impugnment; **v.** impugn
  handbook of (questions): **n.** catechism
  in rhetoric, as when speaker asks question to answer it: **n.** prosopopoeia; rhetorical question; sermocination
  not open to: (see "beyond" above) **a.** axiomatic; incontestable; incontrovertible; indisputable; indubitable; unassailable; undoubted; **n.** matter of breviary
  open to: see "questionable"
  subject to. **a.** impugnable

QUESTIONABLE: (see "doubtful" and "vague") **a.** ambiguous; contentious; controversial; controvertible; cryptic; debatable; disputable; disputatious; disreputable; dubious; dubitable; equivocal; hypothetical; indeterminate; obscure; occult; paradoxical; polemical; problematical; provisional; shady; suspicious; uncertain; unreliable; unsafe
  something which is: **n.** ambiguity; equivocality; equivocation
  state of being: **n.** ambiguity; dubiosity; equivocality; equivocacy; equivocity

257

QUESTIONING, *close:* **n.** catechesis; catechism; catechization; inquisition; **v.** catechize; **a.** catechistic(al); inquisitorial
   to bring forth ideas or memories: **n.** maieutics; **a.** maietuic(al); Socratic

QUIBBLE: **v.** bicker; carp; cavil; equivocate; **a.** QUIBBLING: captious; carping; causistic; sophistical; sophomoric; specious; **n.** chicanery; equivocation; scrupulosity; sophistry; speciosity

QUIBBLER: **n.** *advocatus diaboli* (devil's advocate); carper; caviler; equivocator

QUICK: **a.** animated; celeritous; expeditious; facile; impetuous; instantaneous; mercurial; nimble; telegraphic; **adv.** *tout de suite*
   -tempered: (**see** "contentious" **and** "fiery") **a.** choleric; iracund; irascible

-witted: **a.** astucious; astute; mercurial; perspicacious; scintillescent

QUICKNESS: **n.** alacrity; celerity; expedition; facilitation; facility; instantaneity
   mental: **n.** acumen; astucity; nous; perspicacity; sagacity

QUIET: (**see** "calm") **a.** dormant; pacific; quiescent; secluded; tranquil; **v.** allay; pacify; repress; tranquilize; **n.** QUIET (**or** QUIETNESS): dormancy; quiescence; quietude; repose; tranquility
   that which produces: **n.** nepenthe; opiate; sedative; tranquilizer

QUIT: **see** "resign"

QUIVER: (**see** "throb") **n.** motitation

QUOTATIONS, *disjointed:* **n.pl.** *disjecta membra*

R

RABBIT: **n.** coney; cuniculus; hare; lagomorph

RABBLE: **n.** canaille; commonalty; demos; *faex populi; hoi polloi;* horde; *ignoble vulgus; lumpen proletariat;* populace; *profanum vulgus;* proletariat; masses; multitude; rifraff; varletry **a.** lumpen; plebeian; proletarian; proletariat(e)
   -rouser: **n.** demagogue; ochlocrat; **a.** demogogic(al); ochlocratic
   wretched: **n.pl.** *miserabile vulgus*

RACE(S): (**see** "people") **n.** genus; paternity; pedigree; phylum; sept
   as a center: **a.** ethnocentric; **n.** ethnocentrism
   human: **see** "man" **and** "mankind"
   mixed: **n.** hybrid(ization); **a.** hybrid; **v.** hybridize
   mixing of: **n.** hybridization; mestization; miscegenation
   pert. to: **a.** ethnic; ethnologic
   segregation: **n.** apartheid
   study of: **n.** anthropology; ethnology; raciology; **a.** anthropologic(al); ethnologic(al);
      of degeneration: **n.** dysgenics
      of distribution: **n.** anthropogeography; ethnogeography
      of origin and development: **n.** anthropogenesis; anthropogeny; **a.** anthropogenetic
      of primitive: **n.** agriology

RACIAL: **a.** cultural; ethnic(al); gentilic; phyletic; phylogen(et)ic; tribal
   extermination: **n.** genocide; **a.** genocidal
   history (plant or animal): **n.** phylogensis; phylogeny; **a.** phylogen(et)ic

RADIANT: (**see** "brilliant") **a.** auroral; aurorean; blithe; divergent; ecstatic; lambent; luminous; resplendent; scintillescent; **n.** RADIANCE: effulgency; resplendency; scintillation; **v.** RADIATE: diffuse; disseminate; effulge

RADICAL: (**see** "rebel") **n.** firebrand; Jacobin; revolutionary; sansculotte; septembrist; ultraist; Young Turk; **a.** drastic; extreme; heretical; heterodox; Jacobinic; revolutionary; sansculottic; sansculottish; thoroughgoing; unconventional; unorthodox
   to uphold (radical) principles: **v.** sansculottize

RADICALISM: **n.** heresy; heterodoxy; Jacobinism; radicality; sansculotterie; sansculottism; ultraism

RAGE: (**see** "anger") **n.** dudgeon; fashion; fervor; frenzy; enthusiasm; paroxysm; pique; **a.** RAGING: (**see** "violent") berserk; blustering; cyclonic; frenzied; fulminating; furibund; infuriated; maniac(al); paroxysmal; rampant
   being in sudden: **a.** fulminating; fulminous; **v.** fulminate
   poetic: **n.** *furor poeticus*

RAGGED *person:* **n.** ragamuffin; tatterdemalion

RAID: **v.** maraud; **n.** foray; incursion; inroad; **a.** incursionary

RAILLERY: (**see** "mockery") **n.** asteism; badinage; persiflage; pleasantry

RAIN: **v.** precipitate; **n.** precipitate; precipitation; **a.** pluvian; pluvious
   abundant: **n.** pluviosity; **a.** pluviose
   ga(u)ge: **n.** udometer
   pert. to: **a.** pluvial; pluvian; pluvious
   study of: **n.** ombrology
   thriving in: **a.** ombrophilous

RAINBOW, *resembling:* **a.** iridian

RAISE: **v.** aggrandize; elevate; enhance; ennoble; escalate; exalt; extol; intensify; levitate; sublimate; transcend; **n.** advancement; elevation; enhancement; ennoble-

ment; escalation; promotion; transcendency
  tending to: **a.** elevatory; transcendent

RAKE: **n.** debauchee; lecher; libertine; lothario; profligate; rakehell; *roué;* **a.** libertine; profligate; rakehell

RAMBLE: (**see** "wander") **v.** meander; perambulate; peregrinate; **n.** perambulation; peregrination; ploy; **a.** RAMBLING: circuitous; desultory; devious; discursive; meandering; parenthetical; perambulatory; peregrine; peripatetic; **n.** meandering; perambulation; peregrination
  alone: **a. or n.** solivagant
  in speech, thought or writing: **n.** circumbendibus; circumlocution; **n.pl.** circumambages; **a.** circumambagious

RANDOM: **a.** desultory; fortuitous; haphazard; indiscriminate; purposeless; stochastic
  at: **adv.** *à l'abandon; à tort et à travers;* stochastically

RANGE: (**see** "outlook" **and** "prospect") **n.** calendar; catalog(ue); category; compass; diapason; excursion; gamut; gradation; incidence; jurisdiction; latitude; lexicon; orbit; purview; spectrum; **a.** categoric(al); jurisdictional; latitudinal; latitudinous
  continuous: **n.** spectrum
  of sight or understanding: **n.** panorama; purview

RANK: (**see** "grade") **n.** array; distinction; formation; precedence; prestige; rating; **a.** exuberant; flagrant; indecent; luxuriant; luxurious; rampant; rancid
  equal for all: **n.** pantisocracy
  equal in: see "equal"
  lowering in: **a.** *declassé;* declensional; declinitory; **n.** declension; declination; subordination; **v.** declass; subordinate
  of highest: **n.** top-drawer; top-flight
  of lower: **a.** *déclassé* (**fem.** *déclassée*); junior; puisne; subaltern(ate); subordinate; **n.** juniority; subordinate
  on acct. of or respect for: **adv.** *propter honoris respectum*
  people of: (**see** "elite") **n.pl.** *gens de condition;* **n.** aristocratism; patriciate; (**pl.** aristoi)
  superior in: **n.** antecedence; precedence; seniority; **a.** antecedent; precedent; superordinate

RAPID: (**see** "quick") **a.** agile; cursory; desultory; expeditious; meteoric; superficial
  gallop or dash, in a: **n. or a.** tantivy

RAPIDLY *shifting:* **a.** kaleidoscopic; oscillatory; phantasmagoric(al)

RAPTURE: **n.** ecstasy; elation; enthusiasm; euphoria; exaltation; paroxysm; raptus; transport; **a.** RAPTUROUS: (**see** "elated") delirious; ecstatic; frenzied; orgiastic; paroxysmal; **v.** ecstasiate; ecstasize
  frenzied: **n.** delirium; orgasm; paroxysm
  greatest: **n.** seventh heaven
  state of spiritual: **n.** raptus

RARE: **a.** estimable; exotic; incomparable; infrequent; novel; paranormal; *recherché;* supernacular; tenuous; uncommon; unexampled; unique; unparalleled; unprecedented; **n.** RARENESS: attenuation; rarefaction; subtilization; tenuity

RARITY: **n.** anomaly; extravaganza; infrequency; phenomenality; prodigality; prodigy; *rara avis;* scarcity; tenuity; *tulipe noir*
  extreme: **n.** *cygne noir*

RASCAL: (**see** "rogue") **n.** miscreant; rakehell; rapscallion; reprobate; ribald; scalawag; scaramouche; villain; **a.** RASCALLY: villainous
  conduct of: **n.** rascality; scalawaggery

RASH: (**see** "reckless") **a.** (ad)venturous; audacious; *écervelé;* hare-brained; headstrong; heady; Icarian; ill-advised; impetuous; imprudent; impulsive; inconsiderate; madcap; precipitate; presumptuous; temerarious; unadvised; **n.** RASHNESS: assumption; audacity; effrontery; impetuosity; presumption; temerity

RATE: (**see** "classify") **n.** incidence; proportion; velocity
  at equal: **a. or adv.** *pari passu*

RATIFICATION, *formal, as by seal:* **n.** obsignation

RATIFY: see "affirm"

RATING: see "rank"

RATION: see "apportion"

RATIONAL: **a.** Apollonian; Apollon(ist)ic; Cartesian; cognitive; consequential; defensible; intellective; intellectual; intelligent; judicious; philosophical; reasonable; restrained; sapient; sensible; tenable

RATTLE: **v.** agitate; crepitate; discompose; disconcert; **n.** crepitation; **a.** crepitant

RAVAGE: **v.** denudate; deplumate; depauperate; deracinate; despoil; devastate; extirpate; impoverish; pillage; spoliate; **n.** denudation; deplumation; depradation; deracination; despoilment; despoliation; devastation; rapine; spoliation

RAVE: **v.** fulminate; **a.** RAVING: beserk; delirious; frenzied; fulminating; maniac(al)

RAVEN, *like or pert. to:* **a.** corvine

RAVENOUS: (**see** "gluttonous") *a.* lupine; rapacious; voracious

RAVISH: **see** "defile"

RAW: **a.** inclement; undigested; unevaluated; unprocessed; unseasoned
   as to food: **a.** *au naturel*
   flesh, eating of: **n.** omophagia; **a.** omophagic; omophagous

REACTIONARY: **see** "conservative"

REACTIVATE: (**see** "revive") **v.** recrudesce; revivify; **a.** recrudescent; revivescent; **n.** REACTIVATION: recrudescence; recrudescency; resuscitation; revivification

REACTOR: **n.** activator; catalyst; **a.** catalytic

READ *and write, able to:* **a.** literate; **n.** literacy
   inability to: **n.** alexia; illiteracy

READABLE: **a.** comprehensible; decipherable; legible; scrutable; understandable

READING *beforehand, or a previous:* **n.** pr(a)election
   or having read everything: **a.** omniligent; omnivorous

reversal of words, etc. in: **n.** strephosymbolia
systematic or habitual: **n.** frequentation

READY: **a.** available; compliant; convenient; dextrous; *en garde;* expectant; expeditious; facile; operational; opportune; preconditioned; prepared; resourceful; unhesitating; **n.** READINESS: alacrity; aptitude; facility; promptitude
   for anything: **adv.** *in omnia paratus*
   for attack: **a.** *en garde;* expugnatory; operational

REAL: (**see** "actual") **a.** authentic; *bona fide;* definitive; demonstrable; inherent; intrinsic; legitimate; objective; official; postival; substantive; veritable; **a.** REALISTIC: (**see** "practical") Cartesian; unromantic; unsentimental
   assume to be or treat as: **v.** hypostatise; hypostatize

REALITY: **n.** actuality; entity; existent; objectivity; verity
   appearing to have: **a.** verisimilar; verisimilous; **n.** verisimilitude; verisimility
   doctrine of no: **n.** nihilism; **a.** nihilistic
   escape fr. by fantasy: **n.** autism; escapism; identification; **a.** autistic; escapist
   having, after existence of particulars: **a.** *post rem; post res*
     before existence of particulars: **a.** *ante rem; ante res*
   regard as: **v.** hypostatise; hypostatize
   science dealing w/ nature of: **n.** ontology; **n.** ontologist; **a.** ontological

REALLY!: **int.** *ma foi!*

REALM: **see** "region"

REAR: **v.** construct; elevate; originate; produce; **n.** (**see** "rump") posterior
   in the: **adv. or a.** *en arrière;* **a.** posterior

REARRANGE: **v.** permutate; refurbish; **n.** REARRANGEMENT: permutation; refurbishment

REASON: (**see** "think") **v.** expostulate; intellectualize; ratiocinate; rationalize; **n.** (**see** "reasoning") argument; intellect; intuition; justification; noesis; nous; ratiocination; rationale; rationality; understanding
   against: **v.** oppugn; **n.** oppugnation; **a.** alogical; argumentative; disputatious
   all the more: raison de plus

appeal to: **n.** argumentation; argumentum
by a stronger: **a.** *a fortiori*
by formal logic: **v.** ratiocinate; **a.** ratiocinative; **n.** ratiocination
creature of: **n.** *ens rationis*
falsely: **v.** paralogize; **a.** paralogistic; specious; **n.** paralogism; speciosity
for being or existing: **n.** *raison d'être*
life governed by: **n.** eudaemonia; sophrosyne; **a.** eudaemonic(al)
of state (diplomatic): **n.** *raison d'état*
"pure": (see "innate intelligence") **n.** noesis
with: **v.** expostulate; **n.** expostulation

REASONABLE: (**see** "rational") **a.** acceptable; defensible; judicious; justifiable; legitimate; moderate; rationalistic; tenable; **n.** justifiability; legitimacy; rationality
part: **n.** *pars rationabilis*

REASONER: **n.** dialectitian; dialectologist; logician; ratiocinator; rationalist

REASONING: (**see** "argument") **n.** argumentation; dialectics; intellection; ratiocination; **a.** ratiocinative
contrary to logic: (**see under** "logic") **n.** paralogism; **a.** paralogistic
deductive: **n.** syllogism; synthesis; **a.** *a priori;* aprioristic; intuitive; syllogistic(al)
equivocal or specious: **see** "subtle, etc." **below**
from general to particular: **see** "deductive" **above**
from particular to general: **see** "inductive" **below**
in a circle: **n.** *circulus in probando*
inductive: **n.** empiricism; epigogue; **a.** *a posteriori;* aprioristic; empirical
intuitive: **n.** *a priori;* apriority; **a.** aprioristic
irrational: **n.** alogism; **a.** alogistic
logical or sophisticated: **n.** ergotism
mode of: **n.** *modus ponens; modus tollens*
presumptive: **see** "deductive" **above**
subtle, tricky or specious: **n.** casuistry; sophism; sophistry; syllogism; **a.** casuistic
w/o exam. or analysis: **a. or adv.** *a priori;* **a.** aprioristic; intuitive; presumptive

REBEL: (**see** "radical") **n.** anarch(ist); dissident; frondeur; insurgent; malcontent; mutineer; sansculotte; septembrist; **v. see** "oppose"

REBELLION: **n.** contumacy; insurrection; mutiny; putsch; sedition; **a.** REBELLIOUS: (see "stubborn") anarchic(al); disaffected; fractious; insurgent; insurrectionary; malcontent; mutinous; perverse; refractory; seditious
one who stirs up: **n.** firebrand; incendiary

REBIRTH: (**see** "revival") **n.** reincarnation; renascence; renaissance; revivification
of soul (doctrine): **n.** metempsychosis; reincarnation; transmigration
something which undergoes: **n.** phoenix

REBORN: **a.** redivivius; regenerated; reincarnated; renascent; revivified

REBOUND: **v.** carom; recoil; reecho; resile; repercuss; reverberate; richochet; **n.** carom; resilience; resiliency; richochet; **a.** resilient; reverberative
on the: **adv.** *à rebours*

REBUKE: **v.** admonish; animadvert; berate; castigate; objurgate; reprehend; reprimand; reprove; vituperate; **n.** admonishment; animadversion; castigation; objurgation; reproof; **a.** REBUKING: admonishing; admonitory; castigatory; objugatory; reprehensive
deserved: **n.** comeuppance; deserts

RECALL: **v.** recollect; reminisce; **n.** (**see** "recollection') reminiscence; **a.** reminiscent(ial)

RECANT: **see** "renounce"

RECEDE: **v.** countermarch; depreciate; dwindle; regress; retrocede; retrograde; **n. see** "recession"

RECEIVE: (**see** "admit") acquire; entertain; intromit
willingness to: **n.** receptivity; sentience; sentiency; susceptibility; **a.** receptive; susceptible

RECEIVER: **n.** bailee; conservator; donee; receptionist; receptor; **a. or n.** recipient

RECEIVING: **a.** recipient; **n.** reception; recipience; recipiency
within, act of: **n.** admittance; intromission; introsusception; intussusception

RECENT: (see "new") **a.** advanced; contemporary; modern(e); neoteric

RECEPTION: **n.** acceptance; admission; collation; conversazione; intromission; reaction; soiree

RECEPTIVE: **a.** acceptant; susceptible; susceptive; **n.** receptivity; susceptibility

RECESS: **n.** armistice; continuance; *entr'acte;* hiatus; interim; intermission; respite

RECESSION: **n.** abatement; declension; decrescence; diminution; retreat; retrocession; withdrawal

RECIPROCAL: see "mutual"

RECKLESS: (see "bold") **a.** audacious; foolhardy; harum-scarum; heedless; hotspur; Icarian; improvident; imprudent; incautious; irresponsible; precipitate; prodigal; *sans attention;* scatterbrain; temerarious; **n.** RECKLESSNESS: audacity; daredeviltry; improvidence; imprudence; prodigality; temerariousness; temerity
   courage: **n.** bravado; derring-do

RECLINING: **n.** accumbency; anaclysis; decubation; decubitus; decumbency; recumbency; reclination; **a.** decumbent; recumbent

RECLUSE: **n.** anchoret; anchorite; ascetic; cenobite; eremite; solitudinarian
   esp. religious: **n.** anchorite; eremite; Essene; **a.** anchoristic; cloistered; eremitic(al)

RECOGNITION: **n.** acknowledgment; apperception; discernment; identification; salutation; **a.** apperceptionistic; identificatory; recognitive; recognitory

RECOGNIZED, *capable of being:* **a.** cognoscible; cognoscitive; (re)cognizable; **n.** identifiability; recognizability
   incapable of being: **a.** incognito; incognizable; incognoscible; indiscernible; **n.** incognoscibility; indiscernibility

RECOIL: (see "rebound") **v.** reecho; reverberate; richochet; **n.** reverberation; richochet

RECOLLECTION: **n.** anamenesis; memoir; remembrance; reminiscence; **a.** reminiscent(ial)

RECOMPENSE: **v.** compensate; reimburse; remunerate; requite; **n.** (see "salary") compensation; emolument; guerdon; indemnification; indemnity; quittance; reimbursement; remuneration; requital; retribution

RECONCILE: (see "appease") **v.** harmonize; propitiate; (re)conciliate; syncretize; synchronize; **a.** RECONCILIATORY: conciliatory; syncretistic; **n.** RECONCILIATION: (see "harmony") (e)irenicon; rapprochment; reconcilement; syncretism
   having power or tendency to: **a.** henotic; irenic; reconcilable; (re)conciliatory; **n.** reconcilability

RECORD(S): **v.** enscroll; **n.** agendum; (**pl.** agenda); archive; calendar; chronicle; compendium; dossier; lexicon; transcript(ion)
   study of to determine authenticity, meaning, etc.: **n.** philology
   written, of facts or proceedings: **n.** procès-verbal; (**pl.** procès-verbaux)

RECOVER, *as loss or health:* **v.** recup(erate); retrieve
   unable to: **a.** irretrievable; irreversible; irrevocable

RECOVERY: **n.** reacquisition; recoverance; recuperation; retrieval; retrievement
   period of: **n.** convalescence; puerperium; recuperation; **a.** convalescent; recuperative

RECREATION: see "entertainment"

RECUR: **v.** perseverate; reappear; (re)iterate; **n.** RECURRENCE: periodicity; perseveration; recurrency; (re)iteration; **a.** RECURRING: perennial; periodic; (re)iterative; revenant
   tune, phrase, etc. which (recurs): **n.** leitmotif; leitmotiv

RED, *becoming:* **a.** rubescent; **n.** rubescence; **v.** empurple
   -haired, **a.** hirsutorfous; rufous; xanthous; **n.** pyrrhotism

-handed, caught: **adv.** (in) *flagrante delicto*
paint with: **v.** miniate; rubify; rubricate

REDDISH (or REDDENED): **a.** (e)rubescent; incarmined; incarnadine; rubicund; rubious; rufescent; rutilant; **n.** REDDISHNESS: (e)rubescence; rubicundity; rufosity
glow, having: **a.** rubescent; rutilant
-yellow: **a.** fulvous; xanthous

REDNESS *of skin:* **n.** erythema; hyperemia; rubefaction; **a.** erythematous; hyperemic; rubescent; rubicund

REDUCE: **see** "lessen"
by half: (see "halved") **v.** bisect; dimidiate; **a.** bisected; dimidiate; **n.** dimidiation

REDUCTION: (see "lessening") **n.** abridgement; conquest; declension; decrement; demotion; depreciation; diminution; minimization; mitigation; subjugation
to absurdity: **n.** *reductio ad absurdum*
argument by this method: **n.** apagoge; **a.** apagogic(al)
to lower level: **n.** denigration; minimization; pejoration; plebification; vulgarization; **v.** denigrate; minify; minimize; pejorate; plebeianize; vulgarize

REDUNDANCY: **n.** circumlocution; copiosity; macrology; overabundance; periphrasis; pleonasm; profusion; prolixity; superabundance; supererogation; superfluity; tautology; verbiage; verboseness; verbosity; **a.** REDUNDANT: *de trop;* exuberant; immaterial; pleonastic; prolix; superabundant; supererogative; supererogatory; superfluous; tautological; tautologous; verbose

RE-ECHO: **v.** reverberate; **a.** reverberant; reverberative; reverberatory; **n.** reverberation

REED, *of or like:* **a.** arundinaceous

REESTABLISHMENT: (see "restoration") **n.** apocatastasis; reacquisition; recuperation
of friendship or relation: **n.** rapprochement

REFERABLE: **a.** ascribable; assignable; attributable; imputable; pertinent; referential; **adv.** anent; *in re*

REFERENCE(S): **n.** bibliography; testimonial (s); **n.pl.** compendia
book: (see "manual") **n.** *index rerum;* promptuary; *vade mecum*
exact: **n.** chapter and verse
for: **adv.** *ad referendum*
used for: **a.** referential

REFINE: **v.** alembicate; chasten; civilize; cultivate; debarbarize; defecate; depurate; educate; elevate; expurgate; rarefy; spiritualize; subtilize
something which (refines) or transmutes: **n.** alembic

REFINED: (see "polished") **a.** alembicated; cultivated; fastidious; *recherché*
extremely or affectedly: **a.** *précieuse; précieux;* **n.** preciosity

REFINEMENT: (see "elegance" **and** "polish") **n.** alembication; artistry; civilization; cultivation; discrimination; finesse; gentility; humanization; perfectionment; rarefaction; subtlety
characterized by exquisite: **a.** spirituel(le)
lacking in: **a.** gauche; incondite; maladroit; unpolished; **n.** gaucherie
over-: **n.** alembication; preciosity; **a.** *précieuse; précieux*

REFLECT: (see "re-echo" **and** "rebound") **v.** contemplate; deliberate; (ex)cogitate; ideate; mirror; perpend; philosophize; ponder; ratiocinate; ruminate; **n.** REFLECTION: (see "thought") aspersion; cogitation; consideration; ideation; imputation; meditation; perpension; ratiocination; **a.** REFLECTIVE: (see "meditative") cogitative; deliberative; ratiocinative; ruminant
light or sound: **v.** reverberate; **a.** reverberative; reverberatory; **n.** reverberation

REFLECTED *light, pert. to:* **a.** catoptric(al)

REFORM: **v.** chasten; convert; rectify; remodel; **n.** REFORMATION: conversion; emendation; redemption; renovation
capable of: (see "correctible") **a.** corrigible; docile; reformable; tractable; **n.** corrigibility; docility; tractability

REFRESHMENT(S): **n.** collation; reanimation; recreation; regeneration; reinvigoration; revivification; stimulation; **v.** REFRESH: recreate; refocillate; rein-

vigorate; replenish; revivify; **a.** RE-FRESHING: fragrant; heartening; oasitic
place of: **n.** oasis; **a.** oasitic

REFUGE: **see** "sanctuary"

REFUND: **v.** reimburse; restitute; **n.** reimbursement; restitution

REFUSAL: **n.** abnegation; declension; declination; denegation; disclaimer; rejection; **a.** declensional; declinatory; **v.** REFUSE: decline; reject; renege; **n.** debris; detritus; offal; offscouring(s); (**pl.** (d)ejecta; rejecta; (r)ejectamenta)

REFUTATION: **n.** confutation; disproof; elenchus; **a.** REFUTING: anatreptic; elenc(h)tic; refutative
incapable of: **a.** irrefrangable; irrefrangible; irrefutable

REGAL: (**see** "kingly") **a.** imperial; imposing
female, pert. to: **a.** junoesque; statuesque

REGARD: (**see** "admiration") **n.** estimation; *estime*

REGENERATION, *as of tissue:* **n.** neogenesis; **a.** neogenetic

REGION(S): (**see** "kingdom") **n.** domain; dominion; environment; hemisphere; jurisdiction; locale; milieu; purlieu; realm; terrain
description of: **n.** periegesis
native to, or occurring in several: **n.** polydemic

REGRESS: **v.** recidivate; retrograde; retrogress; **n.** REGRESSION: recidivation; retrogression; retrogradation; **a.** recidivous; retrograde; retrogressive

REGRET: (**see** "bewail") **v.** deplore; lament; repine; **n.** attrition; compassion; compunction; contrition; lamentation; penitence; qualm; remorse; scruple; **a.** REGRETFUL: compunctious; contrite; deplorable; deprecative; lamentable; penitent; remorseful; repining; rueful; **a.** REGRETTABLE: **see** "deplorable"
without: **a.** impenitent; **n.** impenitence

REGULAR: (**see** "authorized") **a.** methodical; metronomic(al); official; orderly;

orthodox; rhythmic(al), symmetrical; synchronous; **n.** REGULARITY: periodicity; synchroneity

REGULATE: **see** "guide"

REGULATED, *capable of being:* **a.** modificative; modificatory; modulatory; normative; **n.** modificability; modulability

REGULATION: **see** "rule"

REGULATOR: **see** "controller"

REHASH: **a.** or **n.** *réchauffé;* **v.** refurbish; renovate; summarize

REJECT: **v.** abjure; decline; dismiss; forsake; forswear; ostracize; repudiate; **a.** REJECTING: rejectable; rejectaneous; rejectitious; renunciatory
incapable of being (rejected): **a.** irrecusable

REJECTION: **n.** abdication; banishment; denigation; disavowal; disclaimer; disclamation; ostracism; relegation; repudiation; renunciation
not subject to: **a.** irrecusable
of customary beliefs: **n.** nihilism; **a.** nihilistic

REJOICING: **n.** exuberation; exultation; festivity; jubilation; **a.** carnivalesque; exuberant; exultant; jubilant

RELAPSE: **v.** backslide; recidivate; retrocess; retrogress; **n.** declination; palindromia; recidivation; recidivism; regression; retrocession; **a.** palindromic; recidivant; recidivous; regressive; retrocessive

RELATE: **see** "tell"

RELATED: (**see** "akin") **a.** affiliated; analogous; ancillary; applicable; apposite; auxiliary; cognate; congeneric; congenerous; consanguineous; correlative; germane; leagued; material; pertinent; satellite
by family or blood: **a.** or **n.** agnate; cognate; **a.** cognatic; consanguineous
closely: **a.** affinitive; **n.** affinity
naturally: **a.** correlate; **n.** correlation
on mother's side: **a.** or **n.** cognate; **a.** matrilateral; matrilineal; matrilinear; **n.** cognatus; (**pl.** cognati); matrilineage
thru male: **n.** agnate; agnation; **a.** ag-

natic; patrilineal; patrilinear; **n.** patrilineage

RELATION: **n.** agnate; cognate; congener; connection; kindred; kinsman; narration; pertinence
  standing in same: **a.** homonymous

RELATIONSHIP: **n.** affinity; agnation; cognation; consanguinity; kinship; liaison; relativity
  blood: **n.** cognate; (**pl.** cognati); cognatus; consanguinity; syngenesis; **a.** cognate; consanguineous
  close spacial: **n.** juxtaposition; **a.** juxtapositional

RELATIVE: **see** "applicable" **and** "relation"

RELAXATION: (**see** "entertainment") **n.** abatement; cessation; detachment; *détente;* disengagement; diversion; laxation; recreation; remission; repose
  carefree: **n.** *dolce far niente;* **a.** *dégagé*

RELEVANT: **a.** *ad rem;* applicable; apposite; appropriate; apropos; cognate; competent; congruous; germane; pertinent; material; **n.** RELEVANCE: applicability; aproposity; homogeneity; relevance; materiality
  not: **a.** *à propos de rien;* impertinent; inappropriate; irrelevant

RELIABLE: **see** "dependable"; **n.** RELIABILITY: authenticity; credence; dependability; trustworthiness

RELIEF: **n.** alleviation; assuagement; *bon secours;* deliverance; succor
  incapable of: **a.** implacable; intractable; **n.** implacability; intractability
  that which brings: **n.** alleviant; anesthetic; antidote; nepenthe; opiate; palliative

RELIEVE: (**see** "ease") **a.** alleviate; assuage; deliver; diminish; lessen; mitigate; succor; unburden

RELIEVED, *not, or not capable of being:* (**see** "incurable") **a.** implacable; intractable; unassuaged; unmitigated

RELIGION(S): **n.** clericalism; creed; denomination; devoutness; faith; persuasion; sanctity; sect; theology

asst. in ceremonies: **n.** acolyte
  belief in established: **n.** orthodoxy; **a.** orthodox
  believer in all: **n.** omnist
  bitterness or controversy over: **n.** *odium theologicum*
  disbeliever in: (**see** "disbeliever") **n.** freethinker; latitudinarian
  excessive devotion to: **n.** ecclesiolatry; religiosity; theomania; theopathy
  indifference or apathy to: **n.** adiaphoria; adiaphorism; agnosticism; **a.** adiaphoric; adiaphorous; agnostic; **n. or a.** Laodicean; **n.** adiaphorist; agnostic
  knowledge or beliefs of: **n.** hierology
  lukewarm in: **n. or a.** Laodicean
  pert. to: **a.** clerical; ecclesiastic(al); hierarchic(al)
  practice, correctness of: **n.** orthopraxy
  reconciliation or union of conflicting beliefs: **n.** syncretism; **a.** syncretic; syncretistic; **v.** syncretize

RELIGIOUS: **a.** benedictional; devout; orthodox; pious; sanctified; spiritual
  elite: **n.pl.** *perfecti*
  overly: **a.** pietistic(al); religiose; sacrosanct; sanctimonious; theopathetic; **n.** ecclesiolatry; piosity; religiosity; sanctimony; theomania; theopathy
  not: (**see** "ungodly") **a.** heathenish; impious; laic(al); pagan; secular; worldly

RELINQUISH: **see** "renounce"
  capable of being (*relinquished*): **a.** abdicable

RELISH: **n.** appetite; gratification; gusto; inclination; savor; zest

RELUCTANT: (**see** "indisposed") **a.** averse; recalcitrant; unwilling; **adv.** *à contre coeur*

REMAINS: (**see** "sediment") **n.** *caput mortuum;* magma; residue; residuum; vestige; vestigium; (**pl.** debris; detritus; remnants; residua; vestigia); **n.** REMAINDER: remnant; residual; (**pl.** residua); residue; residuum; **a.** residual; residuary; vestigial
  worthless: **n.** *caput mortuum*

REMAKING, *as lit, or mus. work:* **n.** rifacimento

REMARK(S): **see** "expression"
  commonplace or trite: **n.** bromide;

cliche; platitude; **a.** banal; bromidic; platitudinal; platitudinous
   concluding: (**see** "farewell") **n.** envoi; valediction
   derogatory: **n.** aspersion; innuendo; insinuation
   foolish: **see under** "foolish"
   gratuitous: **n.** *gratis dictum;* (**pl.** *dicta*)
   idle: **n.** insipidity; vaporing(s)
   incidental: **n.** interjection; *obiter dictum;* parenthesis; (**pl.** parentheses); **a.** parenthetical
   sharp, rude or cutting: **n.** causticity; mordacity; spinosity
   shrewd: **n.** sagacity; witticism
   side or offhand, as by judge: **n.** (*obiter*) *dictum*

REMEDIAL: **a.** curative; lenitive; medicamentive; panacean; remediable; reparable; restorative; salubrious; salutary; salutiferous; sanable; sanatory; therapeutic(al)

REMEDY: **n.** antidote; corrective; elixir; embrocation; medicament; nostrum; panacea; palliative; pharmacon; prescription; reparation; restorative; specific; therapeutic(s); therapy
   act or process of (*remedying*): **n.** remediation
   capable of: **see** "remedial"
   favorite or quack: **n.** catholicon; elixir; nostrum; panacea; placebo
   incapable of: **a.** intractable; irremediable; irreparable; uncorrectable
   secret: **n.** arcanum; elixir
   useful in several diseases, etc.: **n.** polychrest; **a.** polychrestic
   worse than disease: aegrescit mendendo; aegrescitque mendendo

REMEMBERING: **n.** anamnesis; reminiscence; **a.** anamnestic; reminiscent(ial); **v.** REMEMBER: recall; recollect; reminisce; **a.** REMEMBERED: commemorated; memoried; memorized
   not worth: **a.** unmemorable
   things worth: **n.pl.** memorabilia

REMEMBRANCE: (**see** "reminder") **n.** commendation; memento; memorial; reminiscence; souvenir; token
   in everlasting: **adv.** *memoria in aeterna*
   prayer: **n.** anamnesis

REMINDER: **n.** amulet; memento; memorandum; phylactery; remembrancer

REMINISCENCE(S): (**see** "remembrance") **n.** anamnesis; feuilleton; **a.** anamnestic
   noteworthy: **n.pl.** memorabilia

REMISSION: **n.** delinquency; deliverance; dereliction; forgiveness; misfeasance; pardon; relaxation; **a.** REMISS: delinquent; derelict; dilatory; inattentive; misfeasant; neglectful; negligent
   gradual, as fever: **n.** lysis

REMORSE: **n.** compunction; contrition; penitence; repentance; self-reproach; **a.** REMORSEFUL: (**see** "regretful") contrite; penitent; repentant

REMOTE: (**see** "isolated") **a.** alien; antipodean; distant; forane; inaccessible; segregated; separated; secluded; tramontane; transmontane; ultramundane; ultimate
   control: **n.** *actio ad distans*
   more: **a.** ulterior
   place or thing: **n.** ultima Thule

REMOVE: **v.** abstract; depose; dislodge; eliminate; eradicate; resect; sequester; supersede; transfer; **n.** REMOVAL: ablation; abstraction; deprivation; elimination; eradication; expurgation; separation; sequestration; supersedence; supersedure; supersession; transference
   by cutting: **v.** ablate; excide; excise; extirpate; resect
   by shelling or husking: **v.** enucleate; **n.** enucleation
   parts of book: **v.** bowdlerize; expurgate; **n.** bowdlerization; emasculation; expurgation

RENEW: (**see** "renovate") **v.** reawaken; reestablish; refurbish; reinvigorate; restore

RENOUNCE: **v.** abandon; abjure; abrogate; apostatize; disclaim; forswear; recant; renunicate; repudiate; rescind; retract; **a.** RENUNCIATORY: abjuratory; **n.** RENUNCIATION: abjuration; abnegation; abrogation; apostasy; disclaimer; recantation; recission; repudiation

RENOVATE: (**see** "renew") **v.** recondition; refurbish; regenerate; repristinate; **n.** RENOVATION: refurbishment; regeneration; repristination

REPAIR: (**see** "renovate") **n.** reconditioning; renovation; reparation; restoration
   capable of: **see** "remedial"

REPARATION: (see "restoration") n. atonement; indemnification; propiation; recompense; requital; restitution; retribution
honorable: n. *amende honorable*

REPAY: v. compensate; reciprocate; recompense; refund; remunerate; requite; retaliate

REPEAL: (see "cancel") v. abrogate; rescind; revoke; n. abrogation; recision; rescission; revocation; a. rescissory; revocatory

REPEAT: see under "repetition"

REPENTANCE: n. contrition; penitence; remorse; a. REPENTANT: contrite; penitent; remorseful
not (repentant): a. or n. impenitent

REPETITION: n. alliteration; anaphora; battology; ingemination; perseverance; reduplication; reiteration; replication; reproduction; verbigeration; v. REPEAT: battologize; ingeminate; perseverate; recapitulate; redouble; reduplicate; (re)-iterate; replicate; n. REPEATER: recidivist; repetent; a. REPEATING: alliterative; battological; frequentive; reduplicative; (re)iterative; repetitious; replicate; a. REPETITIOUS: alliterational; alliterative; echoic; frequentive; imitative; monotonous; perseverant; (re)iterative; repetitional; repetitive; stereotyped; stereotypical
in outline: n. recapitulation; summarization; v. recapitulate; summarize
mania for: n. cataphasia; echololia; onomatomania; verbigeration
needless, in diff. words: n. pleonasm; redundancy; tautology; a. pleonastic; tautologic(al); tautologous; v. tautologize
of actions of others (pathological): n. echomimia; echopraxia
of letters or words, unintentional: n. dittography
of same sound(s): n. tautophony; a. tautophonic; tautophonous
of word in sentence: n. anadiplosis
of words, senseless: n. echolalia; onomatomania; verbigeration; verbomania
of words, unnecessarily: n. battology; a. battological; v. battologize
of words or sentences, endlessly or meaninglessly: n. verbigeration; v. verbigerate

sound or phrase at beg. of each sentence: n. anaphora
stress by: v. ingeminate; n. ingemination
tedious: n. verbigeration; a. repetitious; repetitive

REPLACE: v. substitute; a. substitutionary; substitutive; n. see "removal"

REPLY: (see "answer") v. rejoin; replicate; *réplique;* resound; n. rejoinder; repartee; replication; reverberation
clever or witty: n. repartee
in writing: n. rescription; a. rescriptive
please: repondez s'il vous plaît (abb. R.S.V.P.)

REPORT: n. account; cahier; character; communiqué; fame; narration; reputation; repute; a. reportorial

REPOSE: (see "sleep") n. composure; *dolce far niente; en famille;* (re)laxation; (re)quiescence; respite; tranquility

REPRESENTATIVE: n. ambassador; champion; delegate; deputy; diplomat; representant; specimen; substitute; surrogate; a. emblematic(al); symbolic(al); typical; typifying; v. REPRESENT: delineate; depict; emblematize; exemplify; personate; portray; symbolize; typify
confidential: n. *alter ego*

REPRIMAND: see "rebuke"

REPROACH: (see "scold") v. chasten; reprimand; n. accusation; *bar sinister;* castigation; discredit; disgrace; ignominy; opprobrium; rebuke; reprehension; reproof
above: a. inviolable; inviolate; invulnerable; sacrosanct; unassailable

REPRODUCTION: n. counterpart; duplicate; duplication; ectype; gestation; reconstruction; regeneration; a. REPRODUCTIVE: gestational; gestative; progenitive; n. reproductivity
by bringing forth live beings: n. parturition; viviparity; a. parturient; viviparous
by budding: n. gemmation; protogenesis
by cross-fertilization: n. allogamy; a. allogamous
by eggs: see under "egg"
by union of male and female: n. amphig-

268

ony; gamogenesis; syngamy; syngenesis; **a.** amphigonous; gamogenetic; syngamic; syngamous; syngenetic
　of original: **n.** duplicate; ectype; **a.** ectypal
　period of: **n.** gestation; **a.** gestational
　pert. to: **a.** reproductive; seminal
　science of: **n.** genesiology
　sexless: **n.** abiogenesis; accrementation; agamogenesis; autogenesis; fission; gemmation; parthenogenesis; protogenesis; **a.** abiogenetic; autogenetic; gemmative
　sexual: see "by union of male and female" **above**
　w/o male: **n.** parthenogenesis; **a.** parthenogenetic

REPROVE: see "rebuke" **and** "reproach"; **a.** REPROVING: admonitory; castigatory; chastening

REPTILE(S): (see "snake") **n.** amphibian; groveling; ophidian
　pert. to: **a.** ophidian; reptant; reptilian; serpentiform; serpentine
　resembling: **a.** ophidian; reptilian; reptiloid; serpentiform
　specialist in study of: **n.** herpetologist; ophiologist
　study of: **n.** herpetology; ophiology; **a.** herpetologic(al)

REPUDIATION: **n.** disaffirmance; disaffirmation; disclamation; reunuciation; **a.** REPUDIATIVE: disclamatory; renunciative; **v.** REPUDIATE: abjure; abrogate; disaffirm; disavow; disclaim; renunciate

REPUGNANT: (see "hateful") **a.** incompatible; inconsistent; loathsome; objectionable; repulsive

REPULSIVE: (see "hateful") **a.** abominable; despicable; fulsome; grisly; repugnant; sordid; squalid; unsavory; **n.** REPULSIVITY: despicability; repugnancy; squalidity; squalor

REPUTATION: (see "fame") **n.** character; distinction; estimation; odor; renown; prestige; **a.** REPUTABLE: (see "famous" **and** "respectable") prestigious
　injury to: **n.** aspersion; calumny; defamation; libel; slander; vilification; **a.** defamatory; libelous; slanderous
　of slightly respectable: **a.** subreputable
　person(s) of doubtful: (see "rascal")

n. rapscallion; villain; (**fem.** courtesan; demimondaine)

REPUTE: see "reputation"

REQUEST: (see "pray") **v.** importune; **n.** application; requisition; rogation; solicitation; supplication
　expressing a: **a.** requisitorial; supplicatory

REQUIRED: (see "imperative") **a.** coercive; compelling; compulsory; deontic; *de rigueur;* essential; indispensable; mandatory; obligatory; (pre)requisite; **n.** REQUIREMENT: condition precedent; essentiality; indispensibility; precondition; (pre)requisite; prius; *sine qua non*
　by fashion, etiquette, or custom: **a.** de *règle; de rigueur*
　do more than: **v.** supererogate; **a.** supererogative; supererogatory; **n.** supererogation

RESCUE: (see "aid") **v.** emancipate; liberate; redeem; **n.** deliverance; emancipation; liberation; redemption
　one who (rescues) fr. tyranny and injustice: **n.** pimpernel
　to the!: **int.** *au secours!*

RESEMBLANCE: **n.** affinity; analogy; approximation; assonance; counterpart; equivalence; facsimile; image; parallelism; parity; representation; similarity; simile; similitude; simulacrum; uniformity; verisimilitude; verisimility
　lack of: **n.** dissimilitude; heterogeneity
　partial: **n.** analogy; homology; **a.** analogical; analogous; homologous

RESENTMENT: (see "anger") **n.** animosity; dudgeon; indignation; irascibility; jaundice; pique; prejudice; vexation; umbrage; **a.** RESENTFUL: belligerent; umbrageous

RESERVATION: see "condition"

RESERVED: **a.** apathetic; detached; distant; egocentric; incommunicable; incommunicative; indrawn; phlegmatic(al); phlegmatous; restrained; retarded; retentive; reticent; taciturn; unapproachable; uncommunicative; undemonstrative; unsociable; withdrawn; **n.** RESERVE: apathy; detachment; forbearance; restraint; retardation; reticence; self-control; self-restraint; taciturnity; unsociability

RESIDE, *or establish residence:* v. domicile; domiciliate; n. domiciliation

RESIDENT: a. denizen; domicile; *habitué;* inhabitant; inhabitress; occupant; a. RESIDENTIARY: immanent; indwelling; residential; n. RESIDENCE: inhabitance; inhabitancy; inhabitation; occupancy
   of place of birth: (see "native") n. sedens; (**pl.** sedentes)

RESIDENTIAL *section, fashionable:* n. Belgravia; a. Belgravian

RESIDUE: see "remains"

RESIGNATION: n. abandonment; abdication; acquittance; defeatism; disaffiliation; disassociation; humility; obedience; obeisance; passivity; relinquishment; renunciation; retirement; submission; v. RESIGN: abdicate; disaffiliate; disassociate

RESIST: see "fight"; a. RESISTANT: (see "stubborn") incompliant; recalcitrant
   capacity to: n. resistance; resistivity

RESISTANCE, *point or place of least:* n. *locus minoris resistentiae*

RESONANT: a. orotund; plangent; sonorant; son(or)iferous; sonorous; tympanic; vibrant; n. RESONANCE: orotundity; plangency; sonority

RESORT, *last:* n. *dernier ressort; pis aller; ultima ratio*

RESOURCE: n. expediency; expedient; makeshift; stratagem

RESPECT: (see "honor") v. admire; esteem; n. approbation; deference; deferentiality; devotion; devoir; fealty; homage; izzat; obeisance; obsequiousness; obsequity; prestige; veneration; (**pl.** *baisemains*)
   act of: n. devoir; genuflection; obeisance; obsequity
   as a token of: a. or adv. *honoris causa*
   deserving of: (see "praiseworthy") a. estimable; venerable
   expressive of: a. commendatory; complimentary; deferential; reverential; venerative
   showing: (see "respectful") a. honorific

RESPECTABLE (or RESPECTED): (see "honorable") a. creditable; estimable; presentable; prestigious; reputable; venerable; n. RESPECTABILITY: creditability; estimability; reputability; prestige
   not: a. disreputable
   persons doubtfully: see **under** "reputation"

RESPECTFUL: a. amenable; decorous; deferent(ial); dutiful; obeisant; reputable; reverential; tractable
   not: see "sassy"

RESPONSE: (see "answer") n. antiphon; reaction; retort; reverberation; a. RESPONSIVE: amenable; antiphonal; reactive; sensible; tractable
   heightened: n. hyperesthesia; a. hyperesthetic

RESPONSIBLE: a. accountable; amenable; answerable; (re)liable; solvent; trustworthy; n. RESPONSIBILITY: accountability; amenability; obligation; onus; (re)liability; solvency; trustworthiness

REST: (see "repose" **and** "sleep") n. immobility; immobilization; a. RESTING: dormant; inactive; incumbent; latent; quiescent; sessile
   at: adv. *in situ;* a. dormant; latent; quiescent; sessile; n. dormancy; tranquility
   in peace: adv. *requiescat in pace* (**abb.** R.I.P.)
   place or state of: n. Canaan; nirvana
   recurring period of: n. diastole; a. diastolic; sabbatical
   something to induce: n. anesthesia; anesthetic; opiate; sedative; tranquilizer

RESTITUTION: (see "restoration") n. apocatastasis; indemnification; indemnity; reparation; reinstatement

RESTLESS: a. agitato; anxious; disobedient; erethic; fitful; obstinate; rebellious; restive; riotous; spasmodic; unceasing; n. RESTLESSNESS: (see "uneasiness") agitation; disquietude; dyspathy; dysphoria; inquietude

RESTORATION: n. instauration; reanimation; reconstruction; redemption; reestablishment; refurbishment; rehabilita-

tion; reimbursement; reinstitution; reinvigoration; rejuvenation; rejuvanescence; reparation; repristination; restitution; resurgence; resurgency; resuscitation; revitalization; revivescence; revivification; v. RESTORE: reanimate; reawaken; reconstruct; rehabilitate; reinstate; reinstitute; reinvigorate; rejuvenate; repristinate; restitute; resuscitate; revivify; a. RESTORED: reconditioned; redivivus; refurbished; reinvigorated; rejuvenated
capable of: a. reparable; restitutive; resuscitative; n. revivability; revivescent
of harmony or concord: n. rapprochement
of or to previous status: n. *restitutio in integrum; status quo (ante)*
something which undergoes: n. phoenix

RESTORATIVE: see "cure," "curable," and "remedy"

RESTORING: a. analeptic; invigorating; rejuvenating; rejuvenescent; resuscitative; roborant; tonic

RESTRAINT: (see "prudence") n. circumspection; coertion; confinement; constraint; discipline; durance; duress; embargo; hindrance; inhibition; interdiction; manacle; monopoly; repression; restriction; retention; sanction; shackle; v. RESTRAIN: circumscribe; constrain; demarcate; discipline; enslave; fetter; hamper; inhibit; manacle; repress; restrict; shackle; a. RESTRAINED (or RESTRAINING): Apollonian; Apollonic; Apollonistic; circumscribed; disciplined; harmonious; inhibitory; rational; restrictive; retentive; unemancipated
place of: n. limbo
revolt against or defiance of: n. titanism

RESTRICT: (see "restrain") v. delimit(ate); fetter; hamper; circumscribe; discipline

RESTRICTED *in outlook:* a. cloisteral; cloistered; insulated; parochial; provincial; truncated
in scope: a. abbreviated; abridged; circumscribed; circumscriptive; parochial; peninsular; provincial; truncated

RESTRICTION: (see "restraint") n. circumspection; coercion; (de)limitation; immanence; sanction
under: adv. *sub modo*

RESULT: see "consequence"
complex operation or sequence: n. denouement
justifies deed: exitus acta probat

RÉSUMÉ: n. abridgement; abstract; compendium; epitome; recapitulation; summary; syllabus; synopsis

RETAINER(S), *body of:* n. adherents; claque; clique; cortege; minions; retinue
loyal or hired: see "mercenary"

RETALIATION, *law of:* n. *lex talionis*

RETALIATORY *maneuver:* n. repartee; ripost(e)

RETARDED: a. impeded; inhibited; repressed; v. see "delay"

RETENTIVENESS: n. retentivity; tenacity

RETICENT: a. brachysyllabic; laconic; reserved; taciturn

RETIRED: (see "inactive") a. cloisteral; cloistered; emeritus; otiose; reserved; sequestered; withdrawn; adv. *en retraite; hors de combat;* a. RETIRING: see "shy" and "humble"; v. RETIRE: retreat; withdraw; n. RETIREMENT: insularity; otiosity; *otium cum dignitate;* sedentation
and no longer having power: n. or a. cidevant; emeritus·
but retaining rank and title: a. or n. emeritus
for age or infirmity: n. invalidation; superannuation; a. superannuated

RETRACE: v. perseverate; recall; recollect; reiterate; reminisce

RETRACTION: n. disavowal; recantation; withdrawal
formal, or poem or song about: n. palinode

RETREAT: (see "sanctuary") n. asylum; hermitage; recession; redoubt; retrocession; withdrawal
disorganized: n. *sauve qui peut*
in: adv. *en retraite*

RETRIBUTION: (see "punishment") n. nemesis

also one who inflicts: **n.** nemesis
goddess of: **n.** Nemesis

RETROACTIVE: **a. or adv.** *ex post facto;*
nunc pro tunc

RETURN(S) : **v.** reciprocate; recompense;
requite; **a.** reciprocative; **n.** reciprocation;
reciprocity; recursion; restoration
give or do in: **v.** reciprocate; requite;
n. reciprocation; requital
in: **adv.** *en revanche*
injury for injury, like for like, etc.: **v.**
retaliate; **a.** retaliatory; retributory; **n.** retaliation; retribution
order to: **v. or n.** remand
person who, after long absence: **n.**
Enoch Arden; prodigal (son); revenant;
Rip van Winkle
to former cond. or situation: **n.** reparation; restitution; *status quo ante*
to previous place or cond.: **n.** apocatastasis; *status quo ante*

REUNITING, *act of:* **n.** reunition

REVEAL: **v.** disburden; disclose; divulge;
evince; manifest; unmask; **a.** REVELA-
TORY (or REVEALING): epiphanic;
heuristic; revelative; **n.** REVELATION:
disclosure; divulgence; epiphany; revealment

REVEL: (**see** "carouse") **v.** roister; royster; wassail; **a.** REVELROUS: (**see**
"gay") roistering; roisterous; **n.** REV-
ELRY: conviviality; ecstasy; saturnalia;
wassail

REVELATION: **n.** apocalypse; disclosure;
divulgence; *exposé;* oracle; revealment;
a. REVELATIVE: apocalyptic; epiphanic; revelatory
psychic: **n.** (the) numinous

REVENGE: **v.** requite; retaliate; **n.** nemesis; requital; retaliation; retribution; *re-*
vanche; vengeance; vindication; vindica-
tiveness; **a.** REVENGEFUL: punitive;
retaliative; retaliatory; retributive; retributory; *revanchist;* vindicative; viperish;
vituperative

REVERE: (**see** "honor") **v.** esteem; reverence; venerate; worship; **n.** REVER-
ENCE: veneration; **a.** REVERENT:
(**see** "religious") reverential

REVERSAL: **n.** about-face; bouleversement; *culbuter;* inversion; metathesis;
mutation; transposition; *volte-face;* **adv.**
conversely; *vice versa*
of opinions, attitude, etc.: **n.** *volte-face*
of words, letters, etc. as in reading: **n.**
strephosymbolia; **a.** strephosymbolic
sudden or unexpected: **n.** anticlimax;
bathos; peripet(e)ia; peripety; **a.** anti-
climactic(al); bathetic

REVERSION *to primitive type:* **n.** atavism;
mutation; **a.** atavistic

REVIEW: **see** "survey"

REVISE: **v.** rearrange; redact; renovate;
a. REVISIONAL: revisionary; **n.** RE-
VISION: recension; redaction

REVISER *of manuscripts:* **n.** diaskeuast;
redactor

REVIVE: **v.** reanimate; reawaken; refocillate; reinspirit; reinvigorate; repristinate;
resurge; resuscitate; (re)vivify; revital-
ize; vivificate; **a.** REVIVING: redivivus;
renascent; revivescent; **n.** REVIVAL:
anabiosis; recrudescence; renaissance; renascence; repristination; restoration; resurrection; (re)vivification; risorgimento

REVOKE: **v.** abrogate; countermand; nullify; recant; rescind; vitiate; withdraw;
n. REVOCATION: counteraction; countermand; nullification; recantation; recission; repeal; reversal; vitiation; withdrawal

REVOLTING: (**see** "disgusting") **a.** bilious; choleric; despicable; fulsome; irascible; loathsome; nauseating; noisome;
offensive; repugnant; repulsive; revellent;
revulsive

REVOLUTION (or REVOLT): (**see**
"riot") **n.** anarchy; *coup d'état;* insubordination; insurgency; insurrection; sedition;
a. REVOLUTIONARY: see "radical"

REVOLVE: **v.** circumduct; circumgyrate;
vertiginate; **n.** circumduction; circumgyration; **a.** vertiginous

REWARD: **v.** guerdon; recompense; remunerate; requite; **n.** guerdon; honorarium; indemnity; recompense; requital;
retribution

REWORD *and shorten:* **v. or n.** paraphrase; **a.** paraphrastic(al)

RHETORIC, *master or teacher of:* **n.** rhetor(ician)

RHETORICAL: (**see** "bombastic") **a.** Ciceronian; declamatory; Demosthenean; Demosthenic; eloquent; epideictic; forensic; grandiloquent; rubescent
flourish: **n.** circumgyration

RHINOCEROS: **n.** pachyderm

RHYTHM: **n.** cadence; ictus; melody; meter; periodicity; **a.** RHYTHMIC(AL); cadenced; cadential
abnormal or faulty: **n.** ar(r)hythmia; asynchronism; cacophony; dysrhythmia; **a.** ar(r)hythmic(al); asynchronous; cacophonic; cacophonous; immetrical; unmetrical
absence of: **n.** ar(r)hythmia; arrhythmicity

RICE, *feeding on:* **a.** oryzivorous

RICH: **a.** abundant; affluent; daedalian; daedal(ic); lavish; lucull(i)an; luxuriant; luxurious; opulent; plentiful; redolent; resourceful; sumptuous
govt. by: **n.** plutocracy
man: **n.** Croesus; *homme de fortune;* nabob
newly: **n.** *nouveau riche; parvenu;* roturier
person of plebeian origin: **n.** roturier

RICHES: (**see** "wealth") **n.** abundance; affluence; fortune; luxuriance; opulence; sumptuosity
as object of worship, or personified: **n.** mammon
embarrassment of: **n.** *embarras de richesses*
worship or undue love of: **n.** plutolatry; plutomania

RICKETY: (**see** "flimsy") **a.** rachitic; tenuous; tremulous

RID: (**see** "free") **v.** delete; disabuse; disencumber; eradicate; extricate; purge; relinquish; unburden
as a burden: **v.** disencumber; extricate
of mistake or error: **v.** disabuse

RIDDLE: **n.** ambiguity; charade; conundrum; enigma; intricacy; labyrinth; para-

dox; perplexity; quandary; rebus; sphinx; **a.** enigmatic(al)
key to: **n.** *le mot de l'enigme*

RIDGE: **n.** ruga; (**pl.** rugae); rugosity; RIDGED: corrugated; rugose

RIDICULE: **v.** deride; lampoon; satirize; **n.** asteism; derision; irony; lampoon; pasquinade; raillery; ridiculosity; satire; **a.** derisible; derisive; satirical

RIDICULOUS: **a.** bizarre; derisible; derisive; eccentric; extravagant; farcical; grotesque; ludicrous; *outré;* preposterous; risible
make: **v.** stultify; **n.** ridiculosity; stultification
perfectly: **adv.** *d'un ridicule achevé*

RIDING *academy:* **n.** *haute école;* manège

RIG: **v.** manipulate

RIGHT: **n.** appanage; franchise; immunity; perquisite; prerogative; **a.** (*see* "appropriate") dextral; equitable; legitimate; orthodox
-angled: **a.** orthogonal
as a matter of: **a. or adv.** *ex debito justitiae*
away: **adv.** *tout de suite*
by what?: **adv.** *quo jure?*
deviation or departure fr.: **n.** aberration; aberrance; **a.** aberrational; aberrative; aberrant
for the purpose: (**see** "timely") **a.** advantageous; opportune
hand: **n.** major hand; *mano destra*
-handedness: **n.** dextrality
of elder or superior: **n.** *droit et* (**or** *du*) *seigneur;* primogeniture
of first night (of feudal lord to deflower bride): **n.** *droit et* (**or** *du*) *seigneur; jus prima noctis*
prior or exclusive: **a. or n.** prerogative; **n.** seniority
strict legal: **n.** *strictum jus; summum jus*
to or on the (*right*): **a.** dexter; dextral; droite; **adv.** dextrad

RIGHTEOUS: **a.** equitable; magnanimous; principled; rectitudinous; upright; **n.** RIGHTEOUSNESS: **n.** dharma; probity; rectitude; uprightness
overly: **a.** religiose; sanctimonious; **n.** religiosity; sanctimoniousness; sanctimony; scrupulosity

RIGID: (see "strict") **a.** austere; immalleable; inclement; inelastic; inexorable; inflexible; rigorous; scrupulous; stringent; unshakable; unyielding; **n.** RIGIDITY: austerity; inclemency; inflexibility; rigidification; rigorism; severity; strenuosity

RIGOR: **n.** ardor; austerity; inclemency; rigidity; scrupulosity; severity; strenuosity; **a.** RIGOROUS: (see "harsh") asperous; austere; drastic; inclement; inexorable; preemptory; Procrustean; strenuous

RIND: (see "skin") **n.** integument

RING: **v.** circumnavigate; encircle; surround; **n.** annulation; encirclement; sonority; tintinnabulation; **a.** RINGED: annular; annulate; annulose; circumferential
    of or like: **a.** annular; armillary
    -shaped: **a.** annular; cingular; circinate

RINGING *or jingling sound, as of bells:* **n.** tintinnabulation; **a.** tintinnabular(y); tintinnabulous

RIOT: (see "revolution") *émeute;* pandemonium; turmoil; welter

RIOTOUS: **a.** abundant; agitated; exuberant; incendiary; inflammatory; mutinous; pandemoniac(al); profuse; seditious; tumultary; tumultuous; turbulent; ungovernable; unmanageable; unrestrained; unsubmissive
    affair: **n.** *attroupement;* donny-brook; insurrection; pandemonium; riotry

RIPEN: see "develop"

RISE: (see "advance") **n.** ascension; escalation
    in air: **v.** levitate; **n.** levitation
    tendency to: **n.** assurgency; **a.** ascensive; ascentional; assurgent

RISING, *as of sun or moon:* **a.** ortive

RISK: see "peril"; **a.** RISKY: (see "dangerous") explosive; hazardous; jeopardous; ominous; parlous; precarious; venturesome; **n.** RISKINESS: jeopardy; perilousness; precariousness

RISQUÉ: **a.** off-color; salacious; scabrous

RITUAL (or RITE): **n.** ceremonialism; ceremony; formality; procedure; protocol; liturgy; **a.** RITUALISTIC: ceremonious; ceremonial; **v.** ritualize
    on attaining adulthood: **see under** "adulthood"
    quality: **n.** rituality

RIVAL: **v.** emulate; **a.** antagonistic; competing; competitive; contesting; rivalrous; **n.** antagonist; competitor; opponent

RIVER(S), *adapted to life in:* **a.** autopotamic
    bank(s), of or pert. to: **a.** riparian; riparious
    bet. or enclosed by: **a.** interamnian; mesopotamian; **n.** mesopotamia
    description of: **n.** potamography; **a.** potamographic
    going up to spawn: **a.** anadromous
    in Hell: **n.** Acheron; Styx
    pert. to: **a.** potamic
    study of: **n.** potamology; **a.** potamological; **n.** potamologist

RIVIERA, *French:* **n.** Côte d'Azur

ROAD(S), *having many:* **a.** multivious
    main or principal: **n.** camino real; turnpike
    painful or difficult: **n.** via doloroso
    pert. to: **a.** viatic(al)

ROAMING: (see "roving") **a.** discursive; itinerant; meandering; migratory; nomadic; (per)ambulatory; peripatetic; prodigal; vagrant; vagarious

ROB: **v.** burglarize; depredate; despoil; plunder; rifle; spoliate; **a.** ROBBING: larcenous; predaceous; predacious; predatory; **n.** ROBBERY: burglary; depredation; (de)spoliation; larceny; pillage; piracy; predacity

ROBUST: **a.** athletic; brawny; lusty; muscular; robustious; robustuous; stalwart; virile; **n.** ROBUSTNESS: lustihood; lustiness; robusticity
    rudely: **a.** boisterous; robustious; robustuous

ROCK(S), *composed or inscribed on:* **a.** rupestral; rupestrian
    inhabiting or growing among: **a.** petricolous; saxicolous; saxigenous
    living among, inhabiting or growing on:

a. rupicoline ; rupicolous
   of or like: **a.** petrous
   study or science of: **n.** geology ; petrology ; **a.** geologic(al) ; petrologic ; **n.** geologist ; petrologist

ROD, *appeal(ing) to the:* **adv. or n.** (*argumentum*) *ad baculum*
   divining by: **n.** dowsing ; rhabdomancy
   pert. to punishment w/: **a.** baculin
   -shaped: **a.** baculiform

ROGUE : **n.** caitiff ; gamin ; (**fem.** gamine) ; knave ; malefactor ; miscreant ; picaro(on) ; rapscallion ; renegade ; reprobate ; ribald ; scant-o-grace ; scalawag ; scapegrace ; scaramouche ; scoundrel ; vagabond ; *vaurien;* **a.** ROGUISH : arch ; *espiègle;* mischievous ; picaresque ; puckish ; unprincipled ; waggish ; **n.** ROGUISHNESS : *espièglerie;* gaminerie ; rascality ; roguery ; scalawaggery ; waggishness
   pert. to: **a.** picaresque ; roguish ; **n.** roguery

ROILY : **a.** turbid ; turbulent ; **n.** turbidity ; turbulence

ROLLING : **a.** lurching ; resounding ; reverberating ; undulant ; undulate(d) ; undulating
   inward: **a.** involuted ; **n.** involution

ROMANTIC : (**see** "idealistic") **a.** cavalier ; chimerical ; enticing ; exotic ; fanciful ; glamorous ; imaginative ; melodramatic ; picturesque ; quixotic ; Romanesque ; sentimental ; unrealistic ; utopian ; visionary
   episode: **n.** idyll
   style: **a. or n.** Gothic

ROOF, *shaped like:* **a.** tectiform

ROOFLESS : **a.** *alfresco;* homeless ; hypaethral ; upaithric

ROOMY : **a.** ample ; baronial ; capacious ; cavernous ; commodious

ROOT *out:* **v.** deracinate ; eradicate ; exterminate ; extirpate ; **n.** deracination ; extirpation
   out, inability to: **a.** ineradicable ; inextirpable

ROOTED *deeply:* **a.** chronic ; confirmed ; ingrained ; inveterate ; radicated

ROPE *walker:* **n.** funambulist

ROSTER : **n.** agendum ; (**pl.** agenda) ; catalog(ue) ; register ; rota

ROSY : **a.** auroral ; aurorean ; blooming ; *couleur de rose;* optimistic ; radiant ; rosaceous ; roseate ; sanguine

ROT : **v.** corrupt : decay ; decompose ; degenerate ; deteriorate ; putrefy ; putresce ; **n.** corruption ; degeneration ; gangrene ; mortification ; necrosis ; putrescence ; **a.** ROTTING (or ROTTEN) ; abominable ; carious ; decomposed ; fetid ; necrotic ; putrefied ; putrescent ; termitic
   incapable of (rotting): **a.** imputrescible ; **n.** imputrescibility
   pert. to: **a.** putrefactive ; saprogenic ; saprogeneous

ROTATE : **v.** alternate ; circulate ; circumduct ; (circum)gyrate ; circumvolve ; oscillate ; pirouette ; revolve ; vertiginate ; **a.** ROTATING : gyrating ; rotary ; vertiginous
   around axis: **v.** circumduct ; circumgyrate ; **n.** circumduction ; circumgyration

ROUGH : **a.** asperate ; asperous ; boisterous ; hispidulous ; hispidulate ; inclement ; robust(i)ous ; scabrous ; tartarly ; unpolished ; **n.** ROUGHNESS : asperity ; hispidity ; inclemency ; robusticity ; scabrousness
   (bold): **a.** harageous ; robust(i)ous
   (bristly): **a.** hispid ; **n.** hispidity

ROUND : (**see** "circular") **a.** annular ; convex ; cylindrical ; gibbose ; gibbous ; globular ; orbicular ; rotund ; spherical ; spheroid(al) ; spheriform ; **n.** ROUNDNESS : circularity ; globosity ; orbicularity ; rotundity ; spheroidicity

ROUNDABOUT : (**see** "devious") **a.** ambagious ; ambient ; anfractuous ; circuitous ; labyrinthian ; labyrinthine ; serpentine ; **n.** anfractuosity ; circuity ; circumbendibus ; circumlocution : indirection
   in expression or writing: **n.** circularity ; *circuitous verborum;* circumbendibus ; circumlocution ; periphrasis ; **a.** circumlocutious ; circumlocutory ; periphrastic

ROUSE : **see** "incite"

ROUT : **n.** debacle ; *sauve qui peut*

ROUTE, *painful or difficult:* **n.** *via dolorosa*

ROUTINE: (**see** "habit") **a.** administrative; customary; formal; functional; mechanical; ordinary; perfunctory; periodic; *pro forma;* usual
    one who insists on: **n.** routineer

ROVING: (**see** "roaming") **a.** ambulatory; arrant; desultory; digressive; discursive; itinerant; migratory; nomadic; peregrine; Peripatetic; vagrant; **n.** ambulation; nomadism; peregrination; peregrinism; peregrinity; vagrancy

ROYAL: (**see** "kingly") **a.** basilic(al)
    possessing (royal) privileges: **a.** palatine
    symbol of (royalty) : **n.** diadem

RUBBISH: (**see** "debris") **n.** detritus; offal; scoria; (**pl.** scoriae); trumpery; (**pl.** (r)ejectamenta)

RUDDY: **a.** rubescent; rubicund; rufescent; **n.** rubefaction; rubescence; rufescence

RUDE: (**see** "abrupt," "bold" **and** "uncouth") **a.** abusive; awkward; barbarous; contumelious; dedecorous; discourteous; disrespectful; impudent; indecorous; inurbane; unceremonious; uncourtly; ungracious; unmannered; **n.** RUDENESS: barbarism; contumely; disrespect; impudence; incivility

RUDIMENTARY: **a.** abecedarian; abecedary; abortive; contingent; elementary; embryonic; fragmental; germinal; imperfect(ed); inchoate; inchoative; incipient; incomplete; nascent; potential; undeveloped; vestigial

RUIN: (**see** "decay") **n.** annihilation; bankruptcy; catastrophe; collapse; dilapidation; havoc; labefaction; perdition; undoing; **a.** RUINED: *flambé;* hopeless; kaput; perdue; **a.** RUINOUS: baneful; cataclysmic(al); catastrophic(al); damnatory; destructive; disastrous; malignant; pernicious
    sudden and great: **n.** cataclysm; catastrophe; holocaust; **a.** cataclysmic(al); catastrophic(al)

RUINS: (**see** "rubbish") **n.** debris; détritus

RULE(S): **v.** administer; determine; govern; predominate; preponderate; **n.** administration; authority; criterion; (**pl.** criteria); covenant; discipline; dominion; imperative; method(ology); precedent; precept; predomination; principle; protocol; regency; regime; regimen; *règlement;* regnancy; regula; reign; technique; theorem
    absolute: **n.** tyrannis; tyranny; **v.** tyrannize; **a.** tyrannic(al); tyrannous
    according to: **a.** consuetudinary; conventional; *de rigueur; de règle;* programmatic; ritualistic; **adv.** *ad amussim; ad usum; ex more; secundum artem; secundum regulam*
    according to the: **adv.** *selon les règles*
    basic set of: **n.** constitution; decalogue; *Magna C(h)arta*
    by pedantic system, as school, etc.: **n.** pedantocracy; **n.** pedantocrat
    conforming to: (**see** *"according to"* **above**) **a.** conventional; exemplary; orthodox; **n.** conventionality; normalcy; normality; orthodoxy
    equally by all: **n.** pantisocracy; **a.** pantisocratic(al)
    individual: **n.** autocracy; monarchy; monocracy
    joint: **n.** condominium; synarchy; **a.** condominate
    of majority: **n.** arithmocracy
    rel. or pert. to: **a.** administrative; normative; reglementary; regulatory
    strict enforcer of: **n.** disciplinarian; martinet; precisian; rigorist; sabbatarian
    subject to another's **a.** heteronomous; **n.** heteronomy
    system of: **n.** discipline; organon
    undivided: **n.** monocracy

RULER: (**see** "king") **n.** dictator; potentate
    almighty: **n.** pantocrator

RULING: **a.** administrative; current; determinative; executive; precedential; predominant; predominating; regnal; regnant; reigning; **n. see** "decision"

RUMINANT: **n.** bovine; (**pl.** bovidae); **a.** bovine; bovid; meditative

RUMINATE: **see** "think"

RUMOR: **n.** canard; hearsay; notoriety; roorback; scuttlebutt

noisy: **n.** *fama clamosa*
vague: **n.** *on-dit*

RUMP: **n.** *derrière;* gluteus; podex; posterior; **a.** pygal

RUN-*down:* **a.** depleted; dilapidated; exhausted; squalid; tatterdemalian

RUNNING: **a.** continuous; cursive; linear
adapted to: **a.** cursorial
in opp. direction(s): **a.** countercourant; countercurrent

RURAL: (**see** "pastoral") **a.** agrarian; agrestic; Arcadian; bucolic; campestral; churlish; countrified; geoponic; georgic; idyllic; peasant; provincial; rustic; sylvan; villatic
feature, characteristic, etc.: **n.** pastorality; peasantry; provincialism; rurality; rusticism; rusticity

RUSH, *overwhelming:* **n.** avalanche; spate; **a.** Gaderine; precipitous

RUSHING: **a.** impetuous; precipitate; precipitous; torrential; **n.** exigency; impetuosity; precipitation
precipitously forward: **a.** Gaderine

RUST-*colored:* **a.** aeruginous; ferruginous; rubiginous
on copper or brass, accumulation of: **n.** aerugo; patina; verdigris

RUSTIC: (**see** "rural") **n.** bumpkin; hayseed; peasant; yokel
characteristic(s), as speech, habit or custom: **n.** provincialism; rurality; rusticism; rusticity

RUSTLING: **see** "murmuring"

RUTHLESS: **a.** barbaric; pitiless; Procrustean; relentless; revengeful; savage; unsparing

S

SABBATH, *act of keeping:* **n.** sabbatization; **v.** sabbatize
  pert. to: **a.** dominical; sabbatarian
  strict observance of: **n.** sabbatism; **a.** sabbatarian
  one who advocates: **n.** sabbatarian

SACRED: (**see** "divine") **a.** consecrated; dedicated; hallowed; inviolable; inviolate; numinous; sacramental; sacramentary; sacrosanct; sainted; sanctified; **n.** SACREDNESS: sacramentality; (sacro)-sanctity; sanctification; sanctitude
  thing(s) considered, as relic: **n.** halidom(e); (**pl.** sacramentalia)

SACRIFICE: **v.** immolate; **n.** deprivation; immolation; oblation; sacrification
  anything regarded as great: **n.** moloch
  of many: **n.** hecatomb
  offer as: **v.** immolate; **n.** immolation; sacrification
  pert. to: **a.** sacrificatory; sacrificial
  ritual slaughter for: **n.** mactation
  something offered as: **n.** oblation; sacrification

SACRILEGE: **n.** blasphemy; desecration; profanation; **a.** SACRILEGIOUS: blasphemous; hypocritical; impious; irreverent; profane

SAD: (**see** "sorrowful") **a.** dejected; *désolé;* despondent; disconsolate; distressing; doleful; dolent(e); dolentissimo; dolorific; doloroso; dolorous; elegaic; forlorn; funereal; funebr(i)ous; inconsolable; lachrymal; lachrymatory; lachrymose; lamentable; lamented; lugubrious; melancholic; melancholious; melancholy; morbid; mournful; pathetic; pensoroso; plaintive; sepulchral; somber; sombrous; triste; unfestive; wretched; **n.** SADNESS: dejection; depression; dreariment; forlornity; gloominess; languishment; lugubrosity; melancholia; melancholy; *tristesse;* (**pl.** doldrums; lachrymals; megrims)
  person (man): **n.** *il pensioroso*

story or complaint: **n.** jeremiad; lamentation; (**pl.** pathetics)

SAFE: (**see** "certain") **a.** impregnable; invulnerable; unassailable; unconquerable

SAFEGUARD: (**see** "protection") **n.** palladium

SAFETY: **n.** *anchora salutis; ex abundanti cautela;* refuge; sanctuary
  place of: **see** "stronghold"

SAGE: **n.** Nestor; philosopher; pundit; savant; Solomon; **a.** (**see** "wise") acuminous; discerning; judicious; Nestorian; perspicacious; profound; prudent; sagacious; sapient; Solomonic

SAILOR(S): **n.** matelot; (**pl.** *gens de mer*)

SAINTLY: (**see** "sacred") **a.** angelic; beatific; pietistic; seraphic
  person: **n.** seraph; zaddik

SAINTS *and angels, homage to:* **n.** dulia
  catalog(ue) of, or lives of: **n.** hagiography; hagiology; **n.** hagiographer; hagiographist; **a.** hagiographic(al)
  reverence for or worship of: **n.** dulia; hagiolatry; hierolatry

SALARY: (**see** "recompense") **n.** compensation; emolument; honorarium; remuneration; stipend(ium); **a.** remunerative; stipendiary

SALE: **n.** vendition; **a.** SALABLE: marketable; mercenary; merchantable; venal; vendible

SALIVA, *excessive flow of:* **n.** ptyalism; salivation

SALLOW: **a.** etiolated; icteric; ischemic; jaundiced

SALT, *containing or producing:* **a.** saliferous; saline; **n.** salinity
  with grain of: **adv.** *cum grano salis*

SALUTE: **v.** congratulate; **n.** allocution; salutation; **a.** salutatory
with rifles (*mil.*) : **n.** *feu de joie*

SALVATION: **n.** absolution; atonement; deliverance; extrication; liberation; manumission; nirvana; preservation; redemption; regeneration; reprieve
anchor of (*or of safety*): **n.** *anchora salutis*
pert. to: **a.** soterial; soteriological; **n.** soteriology

SALVE: **n.** cerate; inunction; ointment; unction; unguent

SAME: (**see** "alike") **a.** adequate; commensurate; congruent; equiponderant; equipotent; equipotential; equivalent; identical; isonomous; synonymous; tantamount; **n.** SAMENESS: (**see** "equality") analogy; congruency; equiponderation; equivalence; identicality; parity
always the: **adv.** *semper idem* (**fem.** *eadem*)
condition, in: **adv.** *in statu quo;* **n.** *status quo*
nature or quality: **a.** cognate; consubstantial; homogeneous; **n.** consubstantiality; homogeneity
place, in the: **adv.** *ibidem* (**abb.** *ibid.*)
race, class, genus, etc.: **n.** congener; **a.** congeneric; congenerous
the: **adv.** *idem* (**abb.** *id*)
time, occurring at: (**see** "occurring") **a.** coexisting; contemporaneous; isochronous; synchronic(al); synchronous; **adv.** or **a.** *pari passu;* **n.** coetaneity; concurrency; contemporaneity; simultaneity; simultaneousness; synchroneity; synchronicity; synchrony; unanimity

SAMPLE: (**see** "pattern") archetype; *beau idéal;* exemplar; exemplification; microcosm; prototype; replica; specimen

SANCTION: **v.** approbate; countenance; encourage; ratify; vouchsafe; **n.** approbation; countenance; dispensation; imprimatur; indulgence; ratification; suffrage; sufferance; **a.** SANCTIONED: authorized; conventional; legitimate; institutive; official; orthodox
sign or mark of: **n.** cachet; hallmark; imprimatur

SANCTITY: **n.** godliness; inviolability; sacredness; saintliness

appearance of: **n.** odor of sanctity; piosity; religiosity; sanctimoniousness; sanctimony; **a.** holier-than-thou; Pecksniffian; pharisaic(al); pietistic(al); religiose; sanctimonious; self-righteous
persons who profess strict: **n.pl.** (the) *unco guid*

SANCTUARY: **n.** adytum; *anchora salutis; anchora spei;* asylum; haven; hospice; oasis; penetral(e); sanctum; *sanctum sanctorum;* **a.** oasitic
(*as inner room*): **n.** adytum; sanctum; *sanctum sanctorum*
shelter by: **v.** sanctuarize

SAND, *growing in:* **a.** ammophilous
living or burrowing in: **a.** arenicolous
of or like (*sandy*): **a.** acervulus; arenaceous; sabulous

SANE: (**see** "legally competent") **a.** competent; *compos mentis;* logical; lucid; *mens sana;* rational; **n.** SANITY: competence; lucidity; rationality

SANITARY: **a.** hygienic; sterile
act or process of making: **n.** sanification; sterilization; **v.** autoclave; sanify; sanitize; sterilize

SARCASM: (**see** "satire") **n.** aspersion; cynicism; derision; invective; irony; **a.** SARCASTIC: (**see** "abusive") acidulous; acrimonious; Archilochian; caustic; cynical; incisive; ironical; mordant; mordacious; sardonic; satiric(al); sulfurous; sulphurous; trenchant; virulent; vitriolic

SARDONIC: **see** "cynical"
grin: **n.** *risus sardonicus*

SASSY (or SAUCY): (**see** "abusive") **a.** contemptuous; contumelious; despicable; disdainful; impertinent; impudent; insolent; irreverent; malapert; officious; **n.** SASSINESS (or SAUCINESS): contemptibility; contumely; impertinence; impudence; insolence; procacity; protervity

SATAN, *get thee hence!:* **int.** *apage Satanas!*

SATIRE: **n.** cynicism; diatribe; irony; lampoon; pasquinade; philippic; sarcasm; sardonicism; Sotadic
good-natured: **n.** raillery
marked by coarse and extravagant: **a.**

Pantagruelian; **n.** Pantagruelism
one who engages in: **n.** *farceur;* (**fem.** *farceuse*) ; Pantagruelist; railleur; satirist
usu. w/ political implications: **n.** pasquinade

SATIRIC(AL) : (**see** "sarcastic") **a.** ironic(al) ; Juvenalian; sardonic(al) ; Swiftian
coarsely: **a.** hudibrastic

SATIRIST : **n.** *farceur;* (**fem.** *farceuse*) ;
Pantagruelist; railleur; sillographer

SATISFACTION : **n.** atonement; complacency; contentment; gratification; indemnification; oblectation; reconciliation; repletion; restitution; satiability; satiation; satiety; **v.** SATISFY: (**see** "please") appease; atone; convince; fulfill; gratify; indemnify; reconcile; satiate
capable of: **a.** satiable
hard to: (**see under** "please") **a.** insatiable
incapable of: **a.** implacable; inexorable; insatiable; unappeasable; **n.** insatiability

SATURATION : **n.** impregnation; interpenetration; permeation; satiation; satiety; surfeit; **v.** SATURATE: imbue; impregnate; infuse; interpenetrate; permeate; pervade
liquid: **n.** imbibition

SAUCY : **see** "sassy"

SAVAGE : (**see** "wild") **a.** barbarous; feral; ferocious; heathenish; inhuman; pagan; relentless; uncivilized; untamed; **n.** barbarian; primitive; **n.** SAVAGENESS: barbarity; ferity; primitivity

SAVIO(U)R : **n.** benefactor; deliverer; emancipator; liberator; Messiah; redeemer; **a.** messianic

SAVORY : (**see** "appetizing") **a.** ambrosial; delectable; edifying; flavorous; gustable; gustatory; nectareous; palatable; piquant; savorous; toothsome

SAWDUST, *resembling:* **a.** scobicular; scobiform

SAW-EDGED : **a.** denticulate; serrate(d) serrulate(d)

SAYING : (**see** "maxim") **n.** dictum; saw; witticism

clever: **n.** *bijouterie; bon mot;* epigram; witticism
gratuitous: **n.** *gratis dictum; obiter dictum*
it goes w/o: **adv.** *il va sans dire*
that goes w/o: **adv.** *cela va sans dire*
trite or commonplace: **n.** banality; bromide; cliché; platitude; shibboleth; stereotype; **a.** banal; bromidic; hackneyed; platitudinal; stereotyped; stereotypical
wise or witty: (**see** "witticism") **n.** apothegm; gnome; maxim; **a.** apothegmatic(al) ; gnomic(al) ; sentient

SCABBY : **a.** desquamative; scabrous; *n.* scabrousness

SCALE : **n.** despumation; desquamation; diapason; exfoliation; furfuration; gamut; incrustation; lamina; proportion; ramentum; **n.** SCALINESS: scabrousness; squamation; squamosity; **a.** SCALY: paleiform; scabrous; squamous
off (peel): **v.** desquamate; exfoliate; **a.** desquamative; exfoliative

SCAMP : (**see** "rogue") **n.** *mauvais sujet* (black sheep) ; *polisson;* rapscallion; scalawag; scaramouche

SCANDAL : **n.** aspersion; defamation; infamy; obloquy
current: **n.** *fama clamosa*

SCANDALOUS : **a.** atrocious; disreputable; flagitious; flagrant; heinous; infamous; malodorous; notorious; outrageous; villainous
details (report, history, biography, etc. which stresses) : **n.** *chronique scandaleuse*

SCANTY : **a.** exiguous; infinitesimal; parsimonious; **n.** SCANTINESS: (**see** "scarcity") exiguity; frugality; parcity; paucity; stringency

SCAR : **v.** cicatrize; disfigure; scarify; **n.** cicatrix; cicatrization; ulosis

SCARCITY : **n.** dearth; deficiency; exiguity; famine; inadequacy; insufficiency; parcity; paucity; rareness; rarity; stringency; uncommonness

SCARE : **v.** affright; agrise; cow; intimidate; panic; petrify; terrorize

SCARECROW: **n.** bugaboo; *homme de paille;* ragamuffin; tatterdemalian; **a.** tatterdemalian

SCATHING: (**see** "sarcastic") **a.** caustic; corrosive; mordant; sulfurous; sulphurous; truculent; virulent; vitriolic; vituperative; **n.** causticity; corrosiveness; mordancy; vituperation

SCATTER: (**see** "spread") **v.** decentralize; derange; dispel; disperse; disseminate; dissipate; diverge; diversify; intersperse; promulgate; **a.** SCATTERED: discrete; disunited; infrequent; interspersed; isolated; sporadic; vagrant; **n.** SCATTERING: diaspora; diffusion; disbursion; dispersion; dissemination; distribution; promulgation; scatteration; sporadicity

SCENE, *changing or complex, as in a dream:* **n.** phantasmagoria; phantasmagory; **a.** kaleidoscopic; phantasmagoric(al)
    unlimited: **n.** panorama; **a.** panoramic

SCENT: **n.** aroma; aura; bouquet; cachet; effluvium; (**pl.** effluvia); essence; fragrance; redolence; **a.** SCENTED: aromatic; fragrant; odiferous; odorous; perfumed; pungent; redolent

SCHEDULE: **n.** agendum; (**pl.** agenda); curriculum; inventory; program(me); prospectus; regime; tariff

SCHEME: (**see** "plot") **v.** contemplate; contrive; machinate; premeditate; **n.** cabal; cadre; hypothesis; machination; stratagem; strategy; **a.** (**see** "shrewd") schematic; stratagematic
    abstract: **n.** architectonics; hypothesis
    as with evil intent: **v.** machinate; **n.** machination

SCHOLAR: (**see** "person of letters") **n.** academician; academist; literato; *literatus;* (**pl.** *literati*); pedant; philomath; pundit; savant
    universal: **n.** polyhistor; polymath

SCHOLARLY: (**see** "learned") **a.** academic; erudite; philomathic(al); scholastic; **n.** SCHOLARLINESS (**or** SCHOLARSHIP): erudition
    person: (**see** "scholar") **n.** littérateur; (**pl.** intelligentsia; literati)

SCHOOL, *graduate of:* **n.** alumnus; (**pl.** alumni)
    leader of (*as painters, writers, etc.*): **n.** *chef d'école;* coryphaeus; dean
    life or environment: **n.** academia
    one's own: **n.** *alma mater*
    pert. to: **a.** academic; scholastic(al); collegiate; **n.** scholasticism

SCHOOLFELLOW: **n.** condisciple

SCIENTIFIC *club:* **n.** athena(e)um

SCOFFER: **n.** Abderite

SCOLD: (**see** "censure") **v.** berate; castigate; excoriate; lambaste; objurgate; upbraid; vilify; vituperate; **a.** SCOLDING: castigatory; termagant(ish); vituperative

SCOPE: **n.** ambit; compass; comprehensiveness; diapason; gamut; jurisdiction; latitude; lexicon; panorama; purview; spectrum; **a.** SCOPIC: comprehensive; jurisdictional; latitudinal; latitudinous; panoramic

SCORCHED, *or discolored as if by scorching:* **a.** ustulate

SCORN: (**see** "contempt") **n.** asteism; contumely; derision; disdain; opprobrium; **a.** SCORNFUL: contemptuous; derisible; derisive; despicable; disdainful; haughty; supercilious
    meriting: **a.** contemptible; despicable; disdainful; opprobrious

SCORNFULNESS: **n.** arrogance; condescension; contemptibility; derision; despicability; disdain; hauteur

SCOTSMAN: **n.** Caledonian

SCOUNDREL: (**see** "rogue") **n.** knave; miscreant; rapscallion; reprobate; varlet

SCOUT: **v.** explore; reconnoiter; **n.** exploration; reconnoiter; reconnaissance

SCOUTING *party:* **n.** reconnaissance

SCRAPE: (**see** "predicament") **n.** dilemma; *mauvais pas;* quandary

SCRATCH: **v.** abrade; cicatrize; scarify; score; obliterate; **n.** abradant; cicatrix; cicatrization

SCREAM: **v.** caterwaul; protest; vociferate; **n.** caterwaul; clamor; protestation; vociferation; **a.** SCREAMING: clamorous; stentorian; vociferous

SCRIBBLING: **n.** cacography; griffonage; hieroglyphic(s); *pattes de mouche*
on walls, etc.: **n.** graffito; (**pl.** graffiti)

SCRIBE: **n.** amanuensis; scrivner

SCRUPLE: (**see** "peculiarity") **n.** compunction; hesitation; penitence, qualm, scrupulosity; suspicion; **a.** SCRUPULOUS: (**see** "precise") compunctious; conscientious; fastidious; meticulous; painstaking; precise; punctilious; rabbinic(al); **n.** SCRUPULOUSNESS: meticulosity; punctiliousness; scrupulosity

SCULPTURED *human figure or face, fantastic, as in architectural support:* **n.** antic; caryatid; telamon

SCUM: **n.** despumation; desquamation; offscouring(s)

SEA(S), *beyond the:* **a.** *outre mer;* transmarine; transmarinus; ultramarine
inhabiting, or floating on open: **a.** pelagic
living in: **a.** maricolous
living in or pert. to deep: **a.** bathybic; bathypelagic; bathysmal; benthopelagic
open, or freedom of the: **n.** *mare liberum*
pert. to: **a.** marine; maritime; naval; oceanic; thalassic
pert. to open: **a.** oceanic; pelagic
study of: **n.** oceanography; thalassography
the high: **n.** *altum mare*

SEAL *of approval:* **n.** cachet; imprimatur
under: **adv.** *sub pede sigilli*

SEAM: **n.** cicatrix; cicatrization; commisure; juncture; raphe; suture; synchrondrosis

SEAMAN: **n.** matelot; (**pl.** *gens de mer*)

SEARCH: **v.** expiscate; explore; investigate; perlustrate; scrutinize; **n.** expiscation; exploration; inquiry; inquisition; perlustration; reconnaissance; safari; scrutiny; **a.** SEARCHING: expiscatory; inquisitive; inquisitorial; inquisitory; scrutinous; **n.** SEARCHER: disquisitor; inquisitor; investigator; querist; researcher

SEASHORE, *pert. to:* **a.** littoral

SEASICKNESS: **n.** *mal de mer;* naupathia; *nausea marina; nausea navalis*

SEASON: **see** "accustom"; **a.** SEASONABLE: (**see** "timely") auspicious; convenient; expedient; opportune; propitious
out of: **n.** *hors de saison*

SEATED: **see** "sitting"

SECEDER(S): **n.** Adullamite; cave of Adullam; schismatic; schismatist; secessionist

SECLUDE: (**see** "hide") **v.** cache; isolate; protect; secrete; sequester; **a.** SECLUDED: ascetic; cloisteral; cloistered; deserted; desolate; enisled; hermitic; isolated; monastic; seclusive; secreted; sequestered; unfrequented; withdrawn; **n.** SECLUSION: detachment; isolation; retirement; sequestration; solitude
oneself: **v.** immure; **n.** immurement

SECOND *in order (as brightness of star):* **a.** *beta*
person, use of in speaking: **n.** tuism
son, right of inheritance: **n.** secundogeniture
to none: **a.** *nulli secundus*

SECONDARY: **a.** accessorial; accessory; ancillary; auxiliary; collateral; consequential; derivational; derivative; epiphenomenal; subaltern(ate); subordinate; subservient; subsidiary; substandard; tangential; tributary

SECRET(S): (**see** "hidden") **a.** abstruse; acroamatic; *à huis clos;* apocryphal; arcane; auricular; cabalistic; clandestine; concealed; confidential; covert; cryptic(al); cryptogenic; epoptic; enigmatic(al); esoteric; furtive; hugger-mugger; mysterious; occult; privy; recondite; sibylline; stealthy; surreptitious; undivulged; unrevealed; veiled; **n.** arcanum; (**pl.** arcana; apocrypha; esoterica); **adv.**
SECRETLY: *à huis clos; en sourdine; à porte close;* confidentially; covertly; *in camera; in pectore; in petto; januis clausis; sub rosa; sub silento;* **n.** SECRECY: clandestinity; confidentiality
agent: **n.** *agent provocateur*
agreement: **n.** cabal; collusion; **a.** cabalistic; collusive; collusory

bet. two persons: **n.** privity; **a.** privy
court, deliberative body or proceedings:
n. star chamber; **a.** star-chamber
  doctrine(s): **n.** cabalism; **n.pl.** cabala;
a. cabalistic
  extremely: **a.** super secret; top-drawer
  in: **see** "secretly"
  love affair: **n.** amour; intrigue; liaison
  matter(s): **n.** cabal; (**pl.** cabala); **a.**
cabalistic
  meeting: **n.** assignation; conclave; rendezvous; tryst
  name: **n.** cryptonym; **a.** cryptonymous
  not: **a.** exoteric; manifest; notorious;
patent
  place: **n.** adytum; penetrale; rendezvous; *sanctum sanctorum;* tryst
  plot: **n.** cabal; (**pl.** cabala); conspiracy;
intrigue; machination; **a.** cabalistic; conspiratorial; conspirative
  political association: **n.** Carbonari
  religious rights: **n.pl.** Eleusinian mysteries
  society: **n.** Mafia
  state (secrets): **n.pl.** *arcana imperii*
  teachings or things: **n.pl.** acroamata;
acroamatics; acousmatics; arcana; ca-
balas; esoterica; **a.** acroamatic; cabalistic
  thing(s) kept: **n.** penetrale; (**pl.** penetralia)
  ultimate: **n.** *arcanum arcanorum*
  ways of action: **n.** ambage(s)

SECT, *narrow-minded attachment to:* **n.**
sectarianism

SECTIONAL: **a.** disjunctive; multipartite;
provincial; provisional

SECULAR: **a.** civil; laic; mundane; nonclerical; profane; **n.** secularity; **v.** SECU-
LARIZE: temporalize

SECURE: **a.** *à couvert;* dependable; impregnable; inalienable; inviolable; invulnerable; trustworthy; **n.** SECURITY:
confidence; guaranty; impregnability; in-
alienability; invulnerability; pledge; protection; stability

SEDENTARY: **a.** sedent; sessile

SEDIMENT: (**see** "remains") **n.** alluvium;
deposit; hypostasis; precipitate; recrement; residuum; sedimentation; scoria;
(**pl.** scoriae)

SEDUCE: (**see** "allure") **v.** corrupt; debauch; entice; **a.** SEDUCTIVE: **see** "alluring"; **n.** SEDUCTION: debauchery;
debauchment; seducement

SEDUCER, *female;* **n.** Circe; seductress;
succubus; vampire

SEE: **v.** ascertain; comprehend; descry; discern; perceive; understand
  and believe: vide et crede
  we shall: nous verrons

SEED(S), *feeding on:* **a.** granivorous;
seminivorous
  of, containing or like: **a.** seminal

SEEKING: **a.** appetent; **n.** appetency; desideration

SEEMING: **a.** apparent; ostensible; ostensive; quasi; semblable; virtual
  to be true or real: **a.** verisimilar; **n.**
verisimilitude; verisimility

SEEMLY: (**see** "proper") **a.** appropriate;
comely; decorous; handsome

SEGREGATE: (**see** "isolate") **v.** ghettoize;
a. SEGREGATED: **see** "isolated"; **n.**
SEGREGATION: **see** "isolation"
  capable of being (segregated): **a.** seg-
regable; segregative

SEIZE: **v.** afflict; appropriate; arrogate;
commandeer; confiscate; preempt; sequester; **n.** SEIZURE: confiscation;
manucapture; orgasm; paroxysm; preemption; **a.** SEIZING: confiscatory
  by public authority: **v.** appropriate; confiscate; sequester; **n.** *eminent domain;* im-
pressment; sequestration

SELECTED *from various authors:* **n.** anthology; chrestomathy; (**pl.** analecta)
  from various sources: **n.** eclecticism; **a.**
eclectic
  passages: **n.pl.** analecta; analects; collectanea

SELECTIVE: **a.** eclectic; discriminative;
n. SELECTIVITY; discrimination; eclecticism

SELF: **n.** ego; psyche
  -assured: **a.** confident; sophomoric
  -centered (or self-conceited): **a.** autotheistic; egocentric; egocentristic(al)
ego(t)istic(al); individualistic; introver-
sive; **n.** (**see** "selfishness") autism; ego-

centricity; ego(t)ism; iotacism; *outrecuidance;* solipsism

-condemnatory: **a.** compunctious; intropunitive; penitent; remorseful; self-accusatory

-consciousness: **n.** apperception; **a.** apperceptionistic

-contained: **a.** autonomous

-contradictory: **a.** antinomic; paradoxical; **n.** paradox

-control: (**see** "calmness" **and** "poise") **n.** abnegation; abstinence; aplomb; ascesis; asceticism; automat(i)on; continence; perpendicularity; temperance; **a.** ascetic; automatic; automatous; mechanical; self-contained; temperate

defense, in: **adv.** *se defendendo*

-denial: **n.** abnegation; abstinence; ascesis; asceticism; humility; self-abnegation; **a.** abstemious; abstentious; abstinent; ascetic; monastic

-derived or originated, quality of: **n.** aseitas; aseity

-educated, one who is: **n.** autodidact; **a.** autodidactic

-evident: **a.** aphoristic; axiomatic; hypothetico-deductive; indubitable; manifest; patent; postulational; prima facie; *res ipsa loquitur*

examination: **n.** introspection

excessive interest in: **n.** egocentrism; narcissism; **a.** autotheistic; egocentristic-(al); narcissistic; narcistic

-existent entity: **n.** substantive

-generated: **a.** autogenic; autogenous; endogenous

-governed: **a.** autonomic; autonomous

-gratification: **n.** onanism; sybartism

-humiliation: **n.** abnegation; ascesis; asceticism; **v.** abnegate

identification w/ another (self): **n.** empathy; escapism; identification; **a.** empath(et)ic; escapist; heteropathic

-importance: **n.** conceit; consequentiality; illuminism; pomposity; pursiness; **a.** arrogant; assertive; assertoric; autotheistic; consequential; insufferable; pompous; pontifical; pretentious; pursey

air of: **n.** consequentiality; flatulence; pomposity; pontificality; pursiness

-important person: **n.** bashaw; bigwig; megalomaniac; panjandrum; pasha; philodox

-inclusive: **adv.** *per se;* **n.** perseity

-indulgent: **a.** apolaustic; gluttonous; hedonistic; intemperate; sybaritic

interest in: (**see** "self-centered" **above**) **n.** introversion

-knowledge: **n.** autognosis; **a.** autognostic

-love: (**see** "selfishness") **n.** *amour de soi;* amour; autophilia; egocentricity; egocentrism; narcissism; **a.** egocentric; narcissan; narcissistic; narcistic; **n.** autophiliac; egocentrist; narcissist

manifestation of (self): **n.** heautophany

-originated or derived: **n.** aseity; **a.** autogenic; autogenous; endogenous

other, or another (self): **n.** *alter ego; alteregoism; alter idem;* **a.** alteregoistic

-possession: (**see** "calmness" **and** "poise") **n.** perpendicularity

-respect: **n.** *amour-propre*

-restraint: **n.** abnegation; abstinence; continence; moderation; sobriety; sophrosyne; temperance; **a.** abstemious; abstentious; abstinent; continent; temperate

-righteous: **a.** hypocritical; pharisaic(al); pietistic(al); rectitudinous; sanctimonious; **n. see** "hypocrisy"

-satisfied: **a.** complacent; vainglorious

second (self): **see** "other" **above**

-seeker: **n.** cormorant; hedonist; sybarite; sycophant

-styled: **a.** *soi-disant*

-sufficiency: **n.** aseitas; aseity; confidence; perseity; resourcefulness; smugness

-taught, one who is: **n.** autodidact; **a.** autodidactic

theory that nothing exists or is real but the (self): **n.** solipsism

-tormenter: **n.** heautontimorumenos

-worship: **n.** autotheism; **a.** autotheistic(al)

SELFHOOD: **n.** individualization; ipseity; personality; proprium

SELFISH: (**see** "self-centered") **a.** *aleni appetens;* asocial; egocentric(al); ego-(t)istic(al); gluttonous; intemperate; narcissan; narcis(sis)tic; self-serving; **n.** SELFISHNESS: (**see** "self-love") asociality; autism; *après nous* (or *moi*) *le déluge;* egocentricity; egoism; hedonism; introversion; iotacism; *outrecuidance;* selfhood; self-satisfaction; solipsism

interests, appeal(ing) to: **n. or adv.** (*argumentum*) *ad hominem*

person: **n.** egocentric; egocentrist; ego-(t)ist; hedonist; iotacist; misanthropist; narcissist; solipsist; sycophant

SELLING *or buying of church office or preferment:* **n.** simony

SEND *back:* **v.** or **a.** remand

SENILE : (**see** "aged") **a.** anecdotal ; caducous ; decrepit ; senescent ; superannuated ; venerable ; **n.** SENILITY : (anec)dotage ; anility ; caducity ; senescence ; superannuation
   study of the: **n.** geriatrics ; nostology

SENIOR *member:* **n.** dean ; doyen ; (**fem.** doyenne)
   state of being: **n.** precedence ; precedency ; seniority

SENIORITY : **see** "priority"

SENSATION : **n.** esthesia ; perception ; phenomenality ; sensibility
   concomitant: **n.** syn(a)esthesia ; **a.** synesthetic ; **n.** synesthete
   conveying: **a.** sensiferous
   distorted or abnormal: **n.** paralgesia ; **a.** paralgesic
   having: **a.** sensate
   lacking: **a.** inanimate ; insensate ; insentient
   loss or reduction of: **n.** anesthesia ; hypalgesia ; **a.** anesthetic ; hypalgesic
   producing: **a.** sensific ; sensiferous

SENSATIONAL : **a.** arresting ; extraordinary ; melodramatic ; phenomenal ; sensationary ; spectacular

SENSE(S), *as of word or phrase:* **n.** connotation ; denotation ; intendment ; purport ; signification
   common: **n.** *bon sens;* prudence ; sophrosyne
   in a bad: **adv.** *sensu malo*
   in proper: **adv.** *in sano sensu*
   involving more than one: **a.** synesthetic
   muscular (as movement): **n.** kinesthesia ; proprioception ; **a.** kinesthetic ; proprioceptive
   perceptible to the: **a.** sensate ; sensible
   perception or apprehension: **n.** Anschauung
   pert. to: **a.** sensorial ; sensory ; sensual ; sensuous
   remote from common: **a.** stratospheric(al)
   transcending: **a.** supersensory ; supersensual

SENSED, *what is:* **n.pl.** sensibilia

SENSELESS : (**see** "nonsensical" **and** "pointless") **a.** fatuous ; insensate ; irrational ; irrelevant

   talk: **n.** Choctaw ; galimatias ; gallimaufry ; gibberish ; jargon ; stultiloquence ; **a.** stultiloquent(ial)

SENSIBLE : (**see** "aware") **a.** cognizant ; conscious ; judicious ; perspicacious ; philosophic(al) ; politic ; prudent ; rational ; sagacious ; sapient

SENSITIVE : **a.** allergic ; fastidious ; hyperesthetic ; impressible ; impressionable ; leiodermatous ; sentient ; susceptible
   highly, as skin or to pain: **a.** hyperalgesic ; hyperesthesic ; **n.** hyperalgesia ; hyperesthesia
   low (sensitivity): **n.** hypesthesia ; **a.** hypesthetic ; insensitivity

SENSUAL : (**see** "sensuous") **a.** Apician ; carnal ; epicurean ; epithumetic ; irreligious ; lurid ; materialistic ; scabrous ; sensualistic ; sultry ; sybaritic ; *voluptuaire;* voluptuary ; *voluptueux;* voluptuous ; **n.** SENSUALITY : carnality ; concupiscence ; sensualism ; sensuosity ; sensuousness ; sybaritism ; *volupté* voluptuosity ; voluptuousness ; worldliness
   appetite: **n.** concupiscence ; **a.** concupiscent ; concupiscible
   pleasures: **n.pl.** *voluptates corporis*

SENSUOUS : **a.** anacreontic ; Bacchic ; Dionysian ; epicurean ; faustian ; hedonic ; hedonistic ; orgiastic ; sensualistic ; sybaritic(al) ; voluptuous ; **n. see** "sensuality"
   person: **n.** epicure ; hedonist ; libertine ; sybarite ; voluptuary ; voluptueux

SENTENCE, *ambiguous:* **n.** amphibology ; **a.** amphibiological ; amphibolous
   breaking of thought in: **n.** aposiopesis ; **a.** aposiopetic
   change in structure before completion: **n.** anacoluthon ; (**pl.** anacoluthia)
   construction or structure, science of: **n.** syntax
   contrast of thoughts in: **n.** antithesis ; **a.** antithetic(al)
   reading same backward as forward: **n.** palindrome
   reversal or inversion of regular order: **n.** anastrophe
   stopping in middle of: **n.** abscission
   violation of structure in: **n.** anacoluthon ; **a.** anacoluthic

SENTIMENTAL : **a.** bathetic ; maudlin ; mawkish ; (melo)dramatic ; romantic ; **n.** SENTIMENTALISM : bathos ; maudlin-

ism; mawkishness; romanticism
song: n. strephonade
value: n. *pretium affectionis*
weakly: a. cloying; conciliatory; insipid; ma dlin; mawkish; namby-pamby; nauseating; wishy-washy

SEPARATE: (see "divide") v. abstract; compartmentalize; demarcate; departmentalize; disassociate; disaffiliate; discriminate; dissect; dislocate; dissociate; divaricate; diverge; exclude; fractionalize; ghettoize; isolate; segregate; sequester; sunder; a. SEPARATE(D): (see "distinct") compartmentalized; departmentalized; detached; discrete; disengaged; distinguished; individual; secluded; solitary; unaffiliated; unassociated; n. SEPARATENESS: detachment; disjointure; disjunction; distinctness; individuality; sejunction; severality; a. SEPARATING: (see "divisive") centrifugal; demarcative; disjunctive; dissociative; schismatic(al)
for special purpose: v. sequester; n. sequestration
from environment: v. deracinate; n. deracination
into parts: v. atomize; disjoin(t); dissect; divaricate; subdivide; n. disjunction; divarication
portions: n.pl. *disjecta membra*
unable to: a. indiscerptible; indissociable; indissoluble; indivisible; inextricable; infractible; inseparable; inseverable; inviolable

SEPARATION: (see "parting") n. demarcation; detachment; diremption; disarticulation; discerption; discharge; disjointure; disjunction; disjunctivity; dissociation; distinction; divarication; divergence; divorcement; estrangement; resignation; schism; seclusion; segregation; sejunction; sequestration
of substances: n. dialysis; dissolution; a. dialytic
violent: n. divulsion

SEQUENCE: (see "series") n. concatenation; consecution; sequacity; succession
in: a. alphabetical; categorical; chronological; consecutive; *en suite;* numerical; ordinal; sequacious; sequential; n. concatenation; sequacity; seriality
in continuous: n. spectrum
regular: n. causality

SERENE: (see "calm") a. halcyon; limpid; tranquil; unperturbed; n. SERENITY: (see "composure") equanimity; imperturbability; imperturbation; limpidity; *sang-froid;* tranquility

SERF: n. *ascriptus glebae;* colonus; helot; peon; villein; n. SERFDOM: bondage; helotism; helotry; peonage; servitude; subjection; thralldom

SERIAL: (see "sequence") a. chronologic(al); adv. *seriatim;* n. seriality
novel in form of: n. feuilleton

SERIES, *arrange in:* v. alphabetize; categorize; concatenate; hierarchize; serialize; stratify; n. alphabetization; categorization; concatenation; hierarchization; seriality; stratification
continuing, of scenes or events: n. feuilleton; panorama; phantasmagoria
in a: see under "sequence"
of miseries, disasters, marital exploits, etc.: n. iliad; *via doloroso*
unite in: (see "arrange in" above) a. or v. concatenate; n. concatenation

SERIOUSNESS: n. gravity; sedateness; seriosity; sobriety; solemnity; a. SERIOUS: consequential; critical; formidable; earnest; emphatic; grievous; humorless; momentous; sedate; *sérieux;* serioso; significant; unmirthful; adv. *au sérieux*
in all: adv. *au grand sérieux*
lack of: (see "frivolity") n. levity

SERMON: n. discourse; dissertation; exhortation; homily; lecture; preachment; a. homiletic; sermonic
knowledge or study of (sermons): n. homiletics; sermonology

SERRATED: a. denticulated

SERVANT(S): (see "serf") n. menial; servitor; servitress; a. menial; servitorial

SERVILE: (see "compliant") a. abject; cringing; deferential; fawning; imitative; menial; obsequious; parasitical; sequacious; servient; slavish; subordinate; subservient; sycophantic; toadyish; tractable; n. SERVILITY: deference; obsequiousness; obsequity; subservience:; subserviency; sycophancy; toadyism

SERVITUDE: see "serfdom"

SET: (see "clique") **n.** battery; series
against: **v.** contrapose; **n.** contraposition
apart: (see "separate") **v.** demarcate;
discriminate; enisle; segregate; sequester;
a. demarcative; **n.** demarcation; sequestration
   in a: **a.** *en suite*
   in place or position: **v.** posit
   right: **v.** disabuse

SETTING: (see "environment") **n.** locale;
milieu; *mise-en-scène*

SETTLE: **v.** colonize; determine; establish; liquidate; resolve
   as bet. contestants: **v.** intercede; interpose; mediate

SETTLED: (see "stable") **a.** immutable;
liquidated; *res judicata;* sedentary; sessile; steadfast; unswerving
   in habits, practices, prejudices, etc.: **a.**
inveterate; **n.** sedentation
   that which can be: **a.** resoluble; **n.** resolubility

SETTLEMENT: **n.** accommodation; adaptation; colonization; compromise; disposition; habitation; harmonization; installation; liquidation; reconciliation; sedentation; understanding
   final: **n.** liquidation; quietus

SEVEN: **n.** hebdomad; heptad; septenary
   composed of, or occurring every 7 days:
a. hebdomadal; **n.** hebdomad
   consisting of or including, 7-fold or 7-times as great: **a.** septuple; **n.** septuplicate
   lasting or occurring every 7 years: **a.**
septennial; **n.** septennium
   ruling body of: **n.** septemvirate; **a.** septemviral
   the number, group of, or consisting of 7:
n. hebdomad; heptad; septenary; **a.** hebdomadal; septenary; septennium
   years, period of: **n.** septennate; septennium; **a.** septennial

SEVENTY, *or bet. 70 and 80:* **a.** septuagenary; **n.** septuagenarian

SEVER: **v.** disarticulate; disengage; dissociate; divorce; **n.** SEVERANCE: disarticulation; disengagement; dissociation; dissolution; divorcement

SEVERAL, *comb. of into whole:* **n.** polysynthesis

SEVERE: (see "harsh") **a.** arduous; ascetic; atrocious; austere; crucial; exacting; flagrant; heinous; grievous; inclement; inexorable; inflexible; lamentable; obdurate; rigorous; stringent; tyrannical; uncharitable; unrelenting; vehement; **n.**
SEVERITY: austerity; harshness; inclemency; rigor; stringency; vehemence
   inhumanly: **a.** Draconian; Procrustean
   state of becoming progressively: **n.** ingravescence; **a.** ingravescent

SEX: **n.** gender
   attraction to either: **n.** amphigenous; bisexual; **n.** amphieroticism; bisexuality
   double or doubtful: **n.** androgyny; hermaphrodite; **a.** androgynous; hermaphroditic
   indicating neither, or common to both:
a. epicene
   male and fem. as different individuals:
n. dioecism; **a.** dioecious
   male and fem. in one: **n.** androgyne;
androgyneity; androgyny; hermaphrodite; hermaphroditism; monoecism; monoecy; **a.** androgynous; hermaphroditic;
mon(o)ecious
   organs: **n.pl.** externalia; genitalia; pudenda; naturalia
      female: **n.** *vulva;* (**pl.** muliebria); pudenda
      male: **n.** see "male generative organ"
   pert. to both: **a.** ambisexual; ambosexual; androgynous; bisexual; epicene
   pert. to or having desire for opp.: **a.** or
n. hetersexual; **n.** alleroti(ci)sm; heteroti(ci)sm
   pert. to or having desire for same: **a.** or
n. homosexual; uranist; urning; **n.** homoeroti(ci)sm; homosexuality; uranism; **a.**
homoerotic
   *state or period of development when
child becomes interested in opp.:* **n.**
altrigenderism

SEXINESS: **n.** erotogenicity; ero(to)geneity; erotogenesis; voluptuousness; voluptuosity

SEXLESS: **a.** asexual; castrate(d); neuter; **n.** asexuality; asexualization

SEXUAL *activity, abstinence fr.:* **n.** chastity; continence; **a.** chaste; continent; virginal
   craving, excessive or unreasonable: **n.**
erogeneity; erotogenesis; erotomania

female: **n.** andromania; nymphomania; **n.** nymphomaniac
  male: **n.** gynecomania; satyriasis
desire: **n.** *ardor veneris;* erogeneity; ero(to)genesis; erotogeneity; erogeny; eroti(ci)sm; **a.** erogenic; erogenous
  abnormal: (**see** "craving" **above**) **n.** aidiomantia; aphrodisia; erotomania; erotopathy; **a.** aphrodisiac
  arousing or increasing, or drug or agent to increase: **n.** *or* **a.** aphrodisiac; n. erotogenesis
  inclination or capacity: **n.** lustihood; potency
  intercourse: **n.** carnal knowledge; coition; coitus; copulation; concubitus; pareunia; venery
    inability to perform: **n.** impotence; impotency; *impotentia coeundi*
  interest in others: **n.** alleroti(ci)sm; heteroti(ci)sm; **n.** *or* **a.** heterosexual
    in same (sex): **n.** homosexuality; uranism; **n.** *or* **a.** homosexual; uranist; urning
    in self: **n.** autoeroti(ci)sm; onanism
  love, inclined or pert. to: **a.** amative; amatory; amorous; passionate
  matters, abnormal preoccupation w/: **n.** erogeneity; eroticism; erotomania
  organs: **see under** "sex"
  perversion: **n.** homosexuality; uranism; **n.** homosexual; uranist; urning
  pleasure by hurting or mistreating: **n.** algolagnia; sadism; **a.** sadistic; **n.** sadist
    fr. receiving pain or mistreatment: **n.** algolagnia; masochism; **a.** masochistic
    fr. watching: **n.** scopophilia; voyeurism; **a.** scopophilic; voyeuristic; **n.** scopophiliac; voyeur
  pleasures, indulging in: **n.** venery; **a.** venereal
  practices, preference for unusual; **n.** paraphilia; paraphiliac
  reproduction: (**see under** "reproduction") **a.** syngamic
  urge (instinct): **n.** libido; passion

SEXUALLY *stimulating:* **a.** aphrodisiac; ero(to)genic; erogenous; erotic; **n.** aphrodisiac; erogenesis; erogeneity; erotogenesis; erotogenicity
  books, pictures, etc.: **n.pl.** *erotica;* faceliae; pornography

SEXY: (**see** "sexiness") **a.** bawdy; erogenous; erotic; voluptuary

SHABBY: (**see** "contemptible" **and** "untidy") **a.** despicable; deteriorated; dilapi-

dated; dishonorable; paltry; sordid; squalid; tatterdemalian; threadbare; unfair; **n.** SHABBINESS: squalidity

SHACKLED: **see** "restrained"

SHADE: **v.** inumbrate; **n.** adumbration; obscurity; nuance; (pen)umbra; protection; umbrage; umbrella; **a.** **see** "shady"
  of difference in tone, color or meaning: **n.** nuance
  thriving in: **a.** sciophilous

SHADOW: **v.** adumbrate; inumbrate; **n.** adumbration; aura; (pen)umbra; umbrage
  -boxing: **n.** sciamachy
  dispelling: **a.** scialytic
  having or casting a long: **a.** macroscian
  projecting: **n.** skiagraphy
  veiled in, or use in painting: **n.** chiaroscuro; sfumato; tenebrism

SHADOWY: **a.** adumbral; fleeting; imaginary; penumbral; tenebrous; unsubstantial
  area: **n.** penumbra; twilight zone

SHADY: (**see** "suspicious") **a.** devious; disreputable; dubious; *louche;* penumbral; questionable; uncertain; unethical; unreliable
  (giving shade): **a.** adumbral; umbrageous; umbriferous
  place: **n.** frescade

SHAGGY: **a.** hirsutal; hirsute; unkempt; **n.** hirsutism

SHAKESPEARE, *supporting of as author of plays:* **n.** *or* **a.** Stratfordian
  worship of or undue fondness for: **n.** bardolatry; **n.** bardolatrist

SHAKING: **a.** quavering; tremorous; tremulous; **n.** quaver; tremblement; tremor; tremulation

SHALLOW: (**see** "artificial") **a.** cursory; frivolous; inane; incondite; magazinish; sophomoric; specious; superficial; tenuous; trifling; trivial; **n.** SHALLOWNESS: (**see** "emptiness") inanity; speciosity; superficiality; tenuosity; triviality

SHAM: **v.** counterfeit; simulate; travesty; **a.** (**see** "bogus") adulterated; apocryphal; artificial; Brummagem; dissimulative; factitious; postiche; pseudo; simulated; spurious; **n.** affectation; deceitfulness; decep-

tion; dissemblance; dissimulation; hypocrisy; imposture; legerdemain; pretense; simulacrum; travesty
fight: **n.** sciamachy

SHAME: (**see** "disgrace") **v.** abash; discomfit; disconcert; discountenance; dishonor; **n.** abashment; chagrin; discomfiture; dishonor; ignominy; infamy; humiliation; mortification; opprobrium; reproach; stigma; **a.** SHAMEFUL: (**see** "disgraceful") degrading; ignominious; indecent; infamous; inglorious; outrageous; **a.** SHAMELESS: (**see** "brazen") arrant; degrading; immodest; outrageous; unabashed; unblushing; unmitigated; **a. or adv.** *sans pudeur* **n.** SHAMELESSNESS: (**see** "brass") immodesty; impudicity
false: **n.** *malus pudor; mauvaise honte;* prudery
feeling of: **n.** abashment; embarrassment
for (shame!): **int.** *fi! pro(h) pudor!* (or) *fi donc!*

SHAPE: (**see** "form" **and** "outline") **n.** configuration; conformation; construction; profile; silhouette; **a.** SHAPELESS: amorphous; heterogeneous; misshapen; **a.** SHAPELY: curvaceous; sculpturesque; statuesque; symmetrical; **a.** SHAPING: determinative; formative
having a single, or but one: **a.** monomorphic; monomorphous
having similar or identical: **a.** homeomorphic; isomorphic

SHARE: **v.** apportion; partake; participate
incapable of being (shared): **a.** impartible; imparticipable
indefinite: **n.** moiety

SHARP, *as biting to smell or taste:* **a.** acrid; piquant; poignant; pungent
-cornered: **a.** angular; angulous; **a.** angularity
remark: **n.** mordacity; sarcasm; spinosity
-sighted: **a.** hawkeyed; lyncean

SHAVING: **n.** pogonotomy

SHED, *as skin:* **v.** desquamate; exfoliate; exuviate; slough; **a.** SHEDDING: desquamative; exfoliative; **n.** desquamation; ecdysis; exfoliation; exuviation

SHEDDING, *as leaves:* **a.** deciduate; deciduous; exfoliative

SHEEN: **n.** brightness; brilliance; fluorescence; fulguration; glossiness; illumination; luminosity; luster; nitidity; phosphorescence; radiance; refulgence; refulgency; scintillation

SHEER: **a.** absolute; diaphanous; precipitous; utter; unmitigated; unmixed
assertion: **n.** *gratis dictum*

SHEET, *roll or compress in:* **v.** laminate

SHELL, *of turtle, etc.:* **n.** carapace
out, remove by: **v.** enucleate; **n.** enucleation

SHELTER: **v.** embosom; **n.** asylum; coverture; protection; retreat; sanctuary; sanctum; **a. see** "secure"
temporary: **n.** bivouac

SHEPHERDESS: **n.** Amaryllis

SHERIFF'S *deputies:* **n.** posse (comitatus)

SHIELD: (**see** "shelter") **n.** aegis; escutcheon
of Zeus or Athena: **n.** (a)egis
shaped like: **a.** clypeate; clypeiform; scutate

SHIFT, *as in disease:* **v.** metastasize; **n.** metabasis; metastasis; **a.** metastatic

SHIFTING: **a.** inefficient; vagabond; vagrant
person: **n.** prodigal; vagabond; (**pl.** flotsam and jetsam)

SHIFTY: (**see** "unreliable") **a.** elusive; evasive; fickle; lubricious; oleaginous; resourceful; unstable; **n.** lubricity; **a.** SHIFTLESS: **see** "idle" **and** "lazy"

SHIN: **n.** antecnemion; cnemis; tibia

SHINING: **a.** effulgent; lucent; lustrous; nitid; phosphorescent; radiant; refulgent; resplendent; rutilant; splendorous; **v.** SHINE: effulge; irradiate; phosphoresce; rutilate; scintillate; **n. see** "sheen"
most brightly: **a.** prefulgent; **n.** prefulgence; prefulgency

SHIP(S), *pert. to:* **a.** nautical; naval
shaped like or resembling: **a.** navicular
wreckage from: **n.** flotsam and jetsam

SHIRK: **v.** malinger; **n.** SHIRKER: *embusqué;* malingerer

SHOCKED, *easily:* **a.** squeamish; **n.** squeamishness

SHOCKING: (see "deplorable" **and** "vulgar") **a.** appalling; dedecorous; degrading; humiliating; *infra dignitatem;* opprobrious; percussive

SHODDY: **see** "cheap"

SHOEMAKER, *let not the . . . leave his last: ultra crepidam ne sutor*

SHOOT, *as of plant:* **n.** (s)cion

SHORE, *region along:* **n.** or **a.** littoral

SHORT (or SHORTENED): (see "abrupt" **and** "terse") **a.** abbreviated; compendious; curtailed; decurtate; diminished; diminutive; ephemeral; expeditious; fugitive; inadequate; instantaneous; insufficient; momentaneous; summary; transitory; truncated
   in: **adv.** basically; essentially; fundamentally
   lit. or mus. piece: **n.** morceau
   -lived: **a.** deciduous; ephemeral; transient; transitory; **n.** ephemerid; ephemeron; transient
   -sighted: **a.** astigmatic; myopic; purblind; strabismic; **n.** astigmatism; brachymetropia; myopia; strabismus
   syllables, rel to or composed of: **a.** brachysyllabic; **n.** brachysyllabicism
   -winded: **a.** dyspn(o)eic; pursy; **n.** dyspn(o)ea; pursiness

SHORTCOMING: (see "defect") **n.** deficiency; dereliction; foible; imperfection; remission

SHORTEN, *as a word:* **v.** abbreviate; abridge; apocopate; elide; syncopate; **n.** abbreviation; aph(a)eresis; apocopation; elision; syncopation

SHORTENING: (see "abridgement") **n.** abbreviation; apocopation; curtailment; retrenchment; truncation
   as of lit. work: **n.** abridgement; epitome; *résumé;* synopsis

SHOUT: (see "scream") **v.** vociferate; **n.** vociferation; **a.** vociferous

   of multitude or many: **n.** conclamation; **a.** conclamant
   of praise: **n.** hallelujah; hosanna
   or thunder forth denunciations: **v.** fulminate; **n.** fulmination; **a.** fulminous
   together w/ joy: **v.** conjubílate; **n.** conjubilation; **a.** conjubilant

SHOW: **see** "demonstrate"
   gorgeous or ornate: **n.** extravaganza; floridity; ostentation; pageantry; pomposity; pontificality; pretentiousness
   serving to: **a.** demonstrative; revelatory

SHOWY: (see "ornate") **a.** actorish; actressy; agonistic; baronial; baroque; bedizened; blatant; Brummagem; carnivalesque; circusy; claptrap; clinquant; dramatic(al); dramaturgic(al); extravagant; fastuous; flamboyant; garish; grandiloquent; grandiose; orgillous; orgulous; orotund; ostentatious; pretentious; prismatic; rococo; sonorous; specious; splendid; splendorous; theatrical; thespian; tessellated; **n.** SHOWINESS: (see "gaudiness") acrobatics; acrobatism; affectation; attitudinization; blatancy; cabotinage; floridity; histrionism; orotundity; ostentation; pageantry; pomposity; pontificality; Sardoodledom; speciosity; theatricality; trumpery
   and elaborate in style: **a.** rhetoric(al); rococo; rubescent
   but worthless: **n.** trumpery
   something which is: **n.** bric-a-brac; furbelow; trumpery
   to make: **v.** gaudify; glamorize; theatricalize

SHREWD: **a.** acuminous; artful; astute; calculating; canny; circumspect; diplomatic; discerning; heady; parlous; penetrating; perspicacious; politic; reflective; sagacious; stratagematic; suave; **n.** SHREWDNESS: acumen; callidity; canniness; comprehension; discrimination; perspicacity; sagacity

SHRILL: **a.** calliopean; penetrating; strident; stridulous; **n.** SHRILLNESS: stridor; stridulation

SHRINE: **n.** adytum; mausoleum; reliquary; sanctorium; sanctuary; *sanctum sanctorum*

SHRINK: **v.** atrophy; contract; diminish; recoil; retract; telescope: **a. see** "shrunken" *ability or tendency to:* **n.** contractibility; contractility

SHROUD: **n.** cerement; winding-sheet

SHRUB(S): **n.** arboret; boscage; foliage; **a.** arboresque; frutescent
   pert. to art of trimming and shaping: **a.** topiary
   trimmed and shaped: **n.** topiary

SHRUNKEN: **a.** atrophic; atrophied; wizened

SHUDDER: **n.** frisson; quake; tremor; tremulation; vibration

SHUN: (**see** "avoid") **v.** disdain; eschew; evade; **n.** avoidance; eschewal; evasion

SHY: (**see** "bashful") **a.** cautious; circumspect; constrained; daphnean; demure; diffident; distrustful; pavid; modest; reclusive; shamefaced; solitary; suspicious; timorous; verecund; unassuming; **n.** SHYNESS: bashfulness; coyness; diffidence; timidity; verecundity
   away from: **v. or n.** demur

SICK (or SICKLY): (**see** "diseased") **a.** *à la mort;* aeger; amort; cachetic; chagrined; disgusted; indisposed; infirm; maladive; morbific; morbose; queasy; unhealthy; unwholesome; valetudinarian; valetudinary; wretched; **a.** SICKEN: deteriorate; nauseate
   as result of intemperance: **n.** crapulence; **a.** crapulent; crapulous
   man's dream: **n.** *aegri somnia*
   near point of dying: **a.** *in articulo mortis;* in extremis; fey; moribund
   pretend to be: **v.** malinger; **n.** malingerer; malingering; pathomimesis

SICKENING: **a.** cloying; insipid; mawkish; nauseating; nauseous
   to point of being: **adv.** *ad nauseam*

SICKLE, *shaped like:* **a.** falciform

SICKNESS: see "disease"
   sudden fit of: **n.** paroxysm; qualm; seizure

SIDE, *affecting or appearing on same:* **a.** homolateral; ipsilateral; unilateral
   -by-side: (**see** "parallel") **adv.** paradromic; *pari passu*

to set or place: **v.** collocate; juxtapose; **n.** collocation; juxtaposition; **a.** juxtapositional
   having many (*sides*): **a.** multilateral; multiphasic; polygonal
   hear the other: audi alteram partem
   on opposite: **a.** contralateral; heteronymous; oppositious; **adv.** *ex adverso; ex adversum*
   pert. to both (*sides*): **a.** ambilateral; bilateral; bipartisan; bipartite
      to many: **a.** multilateral; multiphasic; polygonal
      to one: **a.** homolateral; homonymous; ipsilateral; unilateral

SIGH: **v.** suspirate; **n.** suspiration; **a.** suspirous

SIGHT: see "vision"
   at first: **adv.** *d'abord; au premier abord;* **a.** *prima facie*

SIGN(S): (**see** "warning") **n.** adumbration; augury; criterion; divination; emblem; escutcheon; gesture; indication; indicia; indicium; manifestation; portent; signum; symptom; vestige; **a.** augural; emblematic; indicial; portentous; signific; symptomatic
   advance or warning: **n.** adumbration; harbinger; symptom
   behold the: ecce signum
   by this (*sign*) *thou wilt conquer: in hoc signo vinces*
   language: **n.** dactylology; *lingua franca*
   of disease: **n.** semeiotics; stigma; (**pl.** stigmata); symptom(atology); syndrome; **a.** emblematic; pathognominic(al); semeiotic; symptomatic(al)
   study of: **n.** semantics; semasiology; sem(e)iology; symptomatology; **n.** semeiologist

SIGNATURE: **n.** autograph; signum; **a.** autographic(al)
   flourish at end of: **n.** paraph
   made for another: **n.** allograph
   without: **a.** anonymous; pseudonymous

SIGNIFICANT: see "important"

SILENCE: **n.** inarticulation; muteness; obmutescence; quiescence; quietude; taciturnity; tranquility
   gives consent: chi tace acconsenti; qui tacet consentit
   under or in: **adv.** *sub rosa; sub silento*

SILENT: **a.** brachysyllabic; inarticulate; inaudible; incommunicable; incomunicative; laconic; quiescent; reserved; retentive; reticent; silentious; speechless; tacit; taciturn; tranquil; uncommunicative; **adv.** *nil decit*
> *actor:* **n.** pantomimist; *persona muta*
> *becoming or keeping:* **n.** muteness; obmutescence; reticence; taciturnity; **a.** obmutescent; reticent; taciturn
> *habitually:* **a.** reticent; silentious; taciturn
> *keep (silent) and be counted a philosopher: sile, et philosophus esto*
> *singing or speaking (moving lips):* **n.** mussitation

SILKY: **a.** sericeous

SILLY: (see "foolish") **a.** anserine; anserous; asinine; fatuous; inane; frivolous; preposterous; puerile; ridiculous; vertiginous; **n.** SILLINESS: (see "absurdity") asininity; fatuity; frivolity; inanition; inanity; *niaiserie;* puerility; ridiculosity
> *person:* **n.** Abderite; flibbertigibbet; goose; nincompoop; simpleton

SILVER, *like or pert. to:* **a.** argentine; argentous
> *ore-bearing:* **a.** argentiferous

SIMILAR: (see "comparable") **a.** analogical; analogous; congruent; duplicate; equivalent; homogenous; homologous; homonymous; parallel; semblable; synonymous
> *in a (similar) case:* **adv.** *in pari materia*
> *in function but diff. in structure:* **a.** analogical; **n.** analogue
> *in structure and function:* **a.** homologous
> *something which is:* **n.** analog(ue); duplicate; homolog(ue); parallel

SIMPLE: (see "easy") **a.** artless; asinine; candid; credulous; fatuous; guileless; humble; idyllic; ignorant; incomplex; incomplicate; inelaborate; ingenuous; naïve; non-pontifical; primitive; unadorned; uncomplicated; uncompounded; unembellished; unillusioned; unsophisticated; untutored; unvarnished
> *(easy to understand):* **a.** limpid; pellucid; translucent
> *elegance, of:* **adv.** *simplex munditiis*
> *(foolish):* **a.** anserine; asinine; fatuous
> *person:* see "simpleton"

SIMPLETON: **n.** Abderite; *bon enfant;* goose; nincompoop

SIMPLICITY: **n.** artlessness; austerity; clarity; guilelessness; humility; ingenuousness; intelligibility; *naïveté;* primitivity
> *elegant in:* **adv.** *simplex munditiis*
> *natural or childlike:* **n.** artlessness; guilelessness; humility; *naïveté;* unsophistication
> *rustic:* **a.** bucolic; idyllic; pastoral; Theocritean

SIMPLIFY: **v.** clarify; informalize; streamline
> *over-:* **a.** simplistic; **n.** simplism

SIMULATED: (see "artificial" **and** "assumed") **a.** counterfeit; derivative; factitious; imitated; **v.** SIMULATE: **see** "counterfeit"

SIMULTANEOUS: **see** "at same time"

SIN: **v.** transgress; **n.** delict; depravity; immorality; iniquity; misdemeanor; peccancy; transgression; wickedness
> *capable of or liable to:* **a.** peccable; **n.** peccability
> *forgiveness of:* **n.** absolution; **a.** absolutory
> *minor or petty:* **n.** peccadillo; veniality
> *not capable of or liable to:* (**see** "sinless") : **a.** impeccable
> *that which may be forgiven:* **a.** venial

SINCERE: (see "innocent") **a.** artless; *bona fide;* candid; genuine; guileless; heartfelt; ingenuous; unaffected; unfeigned; wholehearted; **adv.** *ex animo;* **n.** SINCERITY: *bona fides; bonne foi;* candor; innocence; integrity; probity; veracity

SINFUL: (see "wicked") **a.** culpable; depraved; flagitious; heinous; iniquitous; nefarious; piacular; unregenerate(d); unrepentant
> *beings to obtain blessedness, doctrine:* **n.** apocatastasis

SING: **v. or n.** descant

SINGER: **n.** cantor; chanteur; (**fem.** chanteuse); descanter
> *cabaret:* **n.** chansonnier

SINGING, *at pleasure:* **adv.** *a capriccio*
  coach: **n.** repititeur
  florid: **n.pl.** melismatics; **n.** coloratura; obbligato
  pert. to: **a.** canorous; cantabile; cantatory; melodious
  suitable for: **a.** lyric; melic; melodic
  the same old song: cantilenam enadem canis
  w/o music: **adv.** *a capella*
  w/o music and solo: **a.** monophonic; monophonous
  w/o sound, as in moving lips (pretended) : **n.** mussitation

SINGLE: **a.** azygous; celibate; discrete; individual; particular; separate; solitary; unique; unwedded
  state of being: **n.** celibacy

SINGULAR: see "odd"; **n.** SINGULARITY: (**see** "peculiarity") haecceity; individuality; particularity; specificity

SINK *or swim: aut vincere aut mori*

SINLESS: (**see** "innocent") **a.** immaculate; impeccable; impeccant; inculpable; **n.** SINLESSNESS: immaculacy; impeccability; impeccancy

SINNING, *capable of:* **n.** peccability

SISTER (*or brother*), *pert. to:* **a. or n.** sibling
  pert. to (sister only) : **a.** sibling; sisterly; sororial

SITTING: **a.** sedent(ary); situated; **adv.** *in situ*

SITUATION: **n.** (con)juncture; predicament; locality; status
  bad: (**see** "predicament") **n.** *mauvais pas*
  perplexed or awkward: **n.** dilemma; plight; predicament; quandary; **a.** dilemmatic; predicamental

SIX-*fold:* **a.** sextuple
  group of: **n.** hexad; **a.** hexadic; senary; sextuple
  months, pert. to or occurring every: **a.** semestral; **n.** semester
  -sided or angled figure: **n.** hexagon; **a.** hexagonal; sexagonal; sexangular
  times as much or folded or duplicated 6 times: **a. or v.** sextuple

  years, lasting, coming every, or 6-year event, etc.: **n. or a.** sex(t)ennial

SIXTY, *pert. to number:* **a.** sexagenary
  years, being bet. 60 or 70 or pert. to such person or period: **n. or a.** sexagenarian

SIZE: **n.** amplitude; caliber; dimension; enormity; magnitude; volume
  person or thing of great: **n.** gargantua; titan

SKELETON, *like:* **a.** cadaverous; skeletonic
  organization: **n.** cadre; nucleus

SKEPTICAL: **a.** aporetic; *cum grano salis;* dissident; distrustful; dubious; dubitable; incredulous; negativistic; negatory; Pyrrhonian; Pyrrhonic; recusant; **n.** SKEPTIC: (**see** "disbeliever") agnostic; apikores (**or** apikoros); (**pl.** apikorsim) ; aporetic; giaor; latitudinarian; nullifidian; pyrrhonist; zetetic; **n.** SKEPTICISM: (**see** "doubt") agnosticism; dogmatism; dubiety; dubiosity; dubitation; incredulity; negativism; negativity; Pyrrhonism; skepsis

SKETCH: (**see** "outline") **n.** adumbration; *aperçu;* compendium; delineation; portrayal; **a.** SKETCHY: adumbral; diagrammatic(al) ; superficial
  short literary: **n.** feuilleton; vignette

SKILL(S): (**see** "art") **n.** adeptness; adroitness; (ambi)dexterity; aptitude; artifice; competence; efficiency; expertise; expertness; hability; ingeniosity; ingenuity; inventiveness; *savoir-faire;* technique; virtuosity; **a.** SKILLED: see "expert"
  expert or specialized: **n.** expertise; virtuosos; virtuosity
  in part. occupation or field: **n.** armamentarium; expertise; repertoire; repertory; technique(s) ; virtuosity
  special or mysterious surrounding a calling, etc.: **n.** mystique; virtuosity

SKILLFUL: **a.** accomplished; adept; adroit; (ambi)dextrous; consummate; daedalian; daedal(ic) ; facile; habile; ingenious; inventive; masterful; masterly; proficient; scient(al) ; subtle; versatile; **n.** SKILLFULNESS: **n.** accomplishment; adeptness; adroitness; consumma-

tion; dexterity; expertise; proficiency; virtuosity
   feat: **n.** legerdemain; *passe-passe;* prestidigitation; *tour de force*
   in statecraft: **a.** politic

SKIM : **v.** despumate

SKIN : **n.** cutis; epidermis; integument; pelage
   bluish discoloration of: **n.** cyanosis; ecchymosis; purpura; **a.** cyanotic; ecchymotic; purpureal; purpureous
   flabby: **n.** *cutis pendula*
   having brown or blackish: **a.** melanous
   having dark or swarthy: **a.** melanochrous
   of animal (hairy): **n.** pelage
   pert. to: **a.** cutaneous; cuticular; (epi)-dermal; integumental
   redness of: **n.** erythema; **a.** erythematic; erythemic; erythematous
   shedding of: **n.** desquamation; ecdysis; exfoliation; exuviation; **v.** exuviate; molt
   tenderness of: **n.** hyperalgesia; hyperesthesia; **a.** hyperalgesic; hyperesthesic
   thick, having: **a.** pachydermatous; pachydermic; **n.** callosity; pachydermia
   thin, having: **a.** leptodermous

SKINNY : **a.** cadaverous; malnourished; skeletonic; tabescent; **n.** SKINNINESS: see "malnutrition"

SKIRMISH : **n.** engagement; recontre; tilt; tournament; velitation

SKIRTING : **a.** circumferential; peripheral

SKULL, *openings or soft parts in infant's:* **n.** fontanel(le)
   thick: **n.** pachycephalia; pachycephaly; **a.** pachycephalous

SKY: (see "atmosphere") **n.** empyrean; firmament; welkin
   -blue: **a.** cerulean
   of, from or being in the: **a.** celestial; empyreal; firmamental; supernal
   open to the: **a.** alfresco; hypaethral; upaithric

SLACK *period, as in business:* **n.pl.** depression; doldrums; recession

SLACKER: see "shirker"; **n.** SLACK-(ENING) : abatement; detente; moderation; (re)laxation; retardation

SLACKNESS *toward duty:* **n.** laches; misfeasance

SLANDER: **v.** calumniate; defame; denigrate; derogate; disparage; malign; revile; traduce; vilify; vituperate; **n.** aspersion; calumniation; calumny; *coup de bec;* execration; libel; malediction; traducement; traduction

SLANDEROUS : **a.** calumnial; calumnious; defamatory; libelous; vilifying
   report: **n.** calumniation; *chronique scandaleuse; fama clamosa*

SLANG: **n.** argot; cant; colloquialism; dialect; jargon; Koine; lingo; *lingua franca;* patois; vulgarism

SLAUGHTER, *great or wholesale:* **n.** aceldama; armageddon; hecatomb; holocaust

SLAUGHTERHOUSE: **n.** abattoir

SLAVE(S) : (see "serf") **n.** mancipium; **n.** SLAVERY: helotism; helotry; peonage; servitude; subjection; thraldom; vassalage
   female: **n.** odalisk; odalisque
   recently freed: **n.pl.** *hesterni quirites*
   willing and devoted: **n.** *âme damnée*

SLEEP: **n.** dormancy; hibernation; hypnosis; quiescence; repose; slumber; somnolence
   abnormal or disordered: **n.** somnipathy
   deity of: **n.** Hypnos; Morpheus; Somnus
   drug or agent for: **n.** hypnotic; narcotic; opiate; soporific
   during day: **n.** diurnation
   inducing or causing: **a.** dormitive; hypnotic; lethargic; somnifacient; somniferous; somnorific; soporiferous; soporific; **n.** hypnotic; hypnotoxin; morpheus; narcotic; opiate; soporific
   study of: **n.** hypnology
   talker in: **n.** somniloquist
   talking in, also words said: **n.** somniloquy
   uncontrollable desire for: **n.** narcolepsy; **a.** narcoleptic
   unnaturally deep: **n.** coma; sopor; stupor; **a.** comatose; soporous; stuporous
   walker in: **n.** noctambulist; somnambule; somnambulist
   walking in: **n.** noctambulation; somnambulation; **a.** noctambulistic; noctambulous; somnambulant; somnambulistic; somnambulous

SLEEPING: (see "asleep") : a. comatose; dormant; latent; quiescent; a. SLEEPLESS: insomnious; n. SLEEPLESSNESS: insomnia; insomnolence; insomnolency; a. SLEEPY: comatose; hypnotic; lethargic; phlegmatic; oscitant; somnolent; soporiferous; soporific

SLENDER: a. acicular; aciculate(d); gracile; lissome; lithe(some); *soigné(e)*; svelt(e); tenuous; n. SLENDERNESS: gracility; lissomness; lithesomness; tenuity

SLIGHT: v. disparage; disregard; disrespect; n. denigration; detraction; disparagement; a. cursory; imperceptible; inconsiderable; insignificant; nominal; paltry; superficial; trivial
   importance or value, thing of: n. bagatelle; nihility; *peu de chose;* triviality; (pl. inconsequentia; trivia)
   -of-hand: (see "magic") n. conjuration; escamotage; legerdemain; prestidigitation; manipulation; n. conjurer; conjuror; prestidigitator

SLIM: see "slender"

SLIMY: a. glutinous; offensive; mucilaginous; oleaginous; saponaceous; unctuous; viscid; viscous

SLIP: see "relapse"
   of memory: n. *lapsus memoriae*
   of the pen: n. *lapsus calami*
   of the tongue: n. *lapsus linguae;* parapraxia

SLIPPERY: (see "slimy") a. elusive; lubricious; treacherous; unreliable; n. SLIPPERINESS: lubricity; unctuosity

SLOGAN: n. catchword; maxim; password; shibboleth; watchword

SLOPE: n. acclivity; declension; declination; declivity; gradient; inclination; a. SLOPING: acclivitous; declensional; declinatory; declivitous; oblique
   downward: n. declivity; a. declivitous
   of a mountain, or general of a country: n. inclination; versant
   steep: n. perpendicularity; a. perpendicular; precipitous
   upward: n. acclivity; a. acclivitous

SLOPPY: (see "slovenly") a. dishevel(1)ed; effusive; gushing; tatterdemalian; unkempt; n. SLOPPINESS: dishevelment

SLOTH: (see "inaction") n. acedia; adynamia; inertia; lassitude; lethargy; otiosity; slothfulness; sluggishness; supinity; torpidity

SLOVENLY: (see "sloppy" and "untidy") a. raunchy; slatternly; unkempt

SLOW: v. decelerate; slacken; a. (see "sluggish") apathetic; bovine; comatose; deliberate; dilatory; languescent; languid; languorous; lentago; lentissimo; lethargic; listless; lumbering; phlegmatic; tedious; torpid; unenergetic; unprogressive; adv. lentado; lentamente; lentissimo; n. SLOWNESS: (see "sloth") inertia; lassitude; lethargy; log(g)iness; retardation; tediosity; torpidity
   cautiously: n. cunctation
   in perceiving or understanding: a. purblind
   moderately: adv. andante
   (plodding): a. elephantine
   very: adv. lentissimo
   -witted: a. adenoid(al); cretinous; lumbering; moronic; stolid; n. moron; nincompoop

SLUGGISH: (see "slow") a. adynamic; apathetic; indolent; inert; languescent; languorous; lethargic; listless; slothful; stagnant; supine; tardigrade; torpid; n. SLUGGISHNESS: (see "slowness") inertia; lethargy; listlessness; log(g)iness; torpidity

SLUMP: n. depression; doldrum(s); repression

SLUR: (see "slander") v. asperse; denigrate; disparage; n. aspersion; calumny; defamation; denigration; disparagement; innuendo; insinuation; vilification
   as omission of letter or vowel: v. elide; n. elision

SLY: (see "sneaky" and "stealthy") a. artful; cunning; diplomatic; duplicitous; furtive; guileful; hugger-mugger; ingenuous; insidious; roguish; *rusé(e)*; serpentine; sinuous; strategic; subtle; adv. *en tapinois*
   on the: see "secretly"

SMALL: (see "little") a. diminutive; inappreciable; infinitesimal; insignificant;

lilliputian; microscopic; miniature; minikin; miniscular; miniscule; minute; petite; ultramicroscopic; **n.** SMALLNESS: (**see** "insignificance") infinitesimality; minitude; parvanimity; parvitude
> *amount or portion:* **n.** modicum; moiety
> *as to space:* **a.** hampering; incommodious
> *compared to expectation:* **a.** subnominal; suboptional
> *in body:* **a.** microsomatic.; microsomatous
> *in viewpoint:* **see** "narrow-minded"
> *indefinitely or insignificantly:* **a.** atomic; inappreciable; infinitesimal; microscopic; **n.** infinitesimality
> *matter:* **n.** nihility; *peu de chose*
> *-minded:* **a.** liliputian; parvanimitous; **n.** parvanimity
> *number:* **n.** dearth; paucity
> *quantity:* **n.** iota
> *scale, on a:* **a.** miniscular; miniscule; **adv.** *in petto*
> *very, or very small thing:* **n.** lilliputian; miniscule; parvitude; **a.** atomic; infinitesimal; microscopic; miniscular; miniscule; minute; submicroscopic; ultramicroscopic

SMALLER *than required:* **a.** subminimal; suboptimal

SMART: (**see** "intelligent") **a.** adroit; astute; natty; *soigné(e)*; spruce; svelt(e)

SMELL: (**see** "scent") **n.** aroma; atmosphere; aura; bouquet; effluvium; (**pl.** effluvia); olfaction; osmesis; osphresis; redolence
> *absence or loss of:* **n.** anosmia
> *having delicate sense of:* **n.** hyperosmia; macrosmatic; nasute
> *offensive* (**see** "stinking") **a.** mephitic; noisome; noxious; pestilential
> *perceiving by:* **n.** olfaction; osmesis
> *pert. to sense of:* **a.** olfactory; osphretic
> *stimulating to sense of:* **a.** osmagogue

SMILE, *sardonic:* **n.** *risus sardonicus*
> *wearing or offered with a:* **a.** subrident

SMILING: **a.** subrident; subrisive

SMOOTH: (**see** "easy") **v.** edulcorate; facilitate; palliate; polish; tranquilize; **a.** amiable; courteous; frictionless; glabrate; glabrescent; glabrous; levigate; oleaginous; saponaceous; unctuous; uninterrupted; velutinous; **adv.** *sans à coups;*

n. SMOOTHNESS: lubricity; polish; saponaceousness; unctuosity
> *as in music:* **a.** dolce; dolcissimo; legato
> *like marble:* **a.** marmoreal; marmorean
> *-skinned:* **a.** glabrous; leiodermatous
> (*sweet-sounding*): **a.** mellifluent; mellifluous; mellisonant; melodic; sonorous
> *-talking:* **a.** mellifluent; mellifluous; oleaginous; sonorous; unctuous

SMUG: **a.** bourgeoise; complacent; egocentric; pedantic; pretentious; priggish; self-inflated; self-satisfied; **n.** SMUGNESS: complacency; egocentricity; pedanticism; self-satisfaction

SNAKE(S): (**see** "reptile") **n.** groveling; ophidian; reptilian; serpent
> *in the grass:* **n.** *anguis in herbâ*
> *like in form or motion:* **a.** anguiform; anguinal; anguine(ous); ophidian; reptilian; serpentiform; serpentine; sinuous
> *poisonous:* **n.pl.** thantophidia
> *study of:* **n.** herpetology; ophiology; **n.** herpetologist; ophiologist
> *worship of or undue fondness for:* **n.** ophiolatry

SNAP (*easy job*): **n.** sinecure; *un (bon) fromage*

SNARE: (**see** "trick") **n.** cajolement; enticement; inveiglement; pitfall

SNEAKY: (**see** "sly") **a.** cowardly; duplicitous; furtive; Janus-faced; ophidian; perfidious; reptilian; serpentine; sinuous; stealthy; treacherous; two-faced

SNEERING: **a.** cynical; derisive; ironical; sarcastic; sardonic; **n.** cynicism; derision; irony; sarcasm; sardonism

SNEEZE: **n.** sternutation; **a.** ptarmic(al); sternutative; sternutatory
> *something which causes:* **n.** ptarmic

SNOB: **n.** arriviste; *nouveau riche;* parvenu; pedant; **n.** SNOBBERY (or SNOBBISHNESS) arrogance; *chichi;* hauteur; haughtiness; pedantry; **a.** SNOBBISH: *chichi;* haughty; pedantic

SNORE: **n.** rhonchus; stertor; **a.** rhonchial; stertorous

SNOUT: see "nose"

SNOW, *pert. to or growing in or under:*
a. nival ; niveous
  situated or occurring under: **a.** sub-nivean

SNOWY : **a.** niveous

SO-*called:* **a.** pretended ; quasi ; *soi-disant*
  much the better: **adv.** *tant mieux*
  much the worse: **adv.** *tant pis*

SOAKING, *soften by:* **v.** macerate ; **n.** maceration

SOAP, *convert into:* **v.** saponify ; **n.** saponification
  resembling: **a.** saponaceous

SOBER : (**see** "calm") **a.** abstemious ; abstentious ; ascetic ; continent ; dispassionate ; moderate ; self-controlled ; temperate ; **n.** SOBERNESS : ascesis ; asceticism ; continence ; temperance

SOCIABLE : **a.** affable ; amadelphous ; companionable ; convivial ; hospitable ; gregarious ; jovial : **n.** SOCIABILITY : affability ; conviviality ; cordiality ; gregariousness ; joviality ; sociality

SOCIAL *circle or set:* **n.** clique ; coterie
  error or blunder: (**see** "impropriety")
n. *faux pas; gaffe;* solecism
  proprieties: **see** "proprieties"
  propriety, strict observance of: **n.** correctitude ; scrupulosity
  register: **n.** *libro d'oro*
  sympathy: **n.** philia
  usage(s), etc.: **n.** *agrémens;* (**pl.** *agréments*) ; amenities ; convenances ; *savoir vivre;* (the) proprieties
      person who prescribes rules or is authority on: **n.** *arbiter elegantiarum (or elegantiae)*
      sanctioned by: **a.** conventional ; **n.** conventionality

SOCIALIZATION, *process of:* **n.** acculturation ; **a.** acculturational ; acculturative

SOCIETY : (**see** "association") **n.** companionship ; ethnos ; monde ; **a.** societal ; sociogenic
  betterment of by improving health conds., etc.: **n.** meliorism
  dangerous to: **a.** pernicious ; pestiferous ; pestilent(ial)

  fear of or aversion to: **n.** anthropophobia ; apanthropia ; apanthropy
  high, fashionable or refined: **n.** *beau(x̂) monde(s) ;* *bon ton; haut monde; grand monde*
  observance of usages of fashionable: **n.** *savoir vivre*
  religious or charitable: **n.** confraternity ; confraternization ; **a.** eleemosynary
  world of fashionable: **n.** *le beau monde;* (*le*) *monde*

SOCRATIC *method of questioning:* **n.** maieutics ; Socraticism ; Socratic induction ; **a.** maieutic(al)

SOFT, *very (mus.)* : **a.** pianissimo

SOFTENING : **a.** emollient ; emulsive ; lenitive ; mitigatory ; **v.** SOFTEN : assuage ; edulcorate ; intenerate ; palliate ; macerate ; mitigate ; mollify
  by soaking: **n.** maceration ; **v.** macerate
  or tending to soften: **a.** mollescent ; **n.** mollescence

SOIL, *bound to, one who is:* **n.** *adscriptus glebae*
  management: **n.** agronomics ; agronomy ; **n.** agronomist
  of or arising fr. the: **a.** telluric ; terrestrial
  of or pert. to science of: **a.** pedologic(al)
  pert. to or affected by: **a.** edaphic
  son of the: **n.** *fillius terrae*
  study of: **n.** *agrology;* pedology ; **n.** agrologist

SOLDIERLY : **a.** heroic ; martial ; military

SOLEMN : (**see** "formal") **a.** awe-inspiring ; ceremonial ; ceremonious ; dispassionate ; funereal ; imposing ; impressive ; memorable ; momentous ; ritualistic ; sedate ; sermonic ; somber ; **n.** SOLEMNITY : ceremony ; reverence ; sedateness

SOLICITOUS : (**see** "diligent") **a.** assiduous ; **n.** assiduity ; solicitude

SOLID : (**see** "compact") **a.** concentrated ; massive ; monolithic ; ponderable ; substantial ; unanimous
  process of making or state of being: **n.** calculus ; concretion ; concretization ; gelation ; solidification ; **a.** concretionary

SOLITARY : (**see** "secluded") **a.** desolate ; hermitic ; individual ; isolated ; ivory-towered; reclusive; sequestered; solitudinarian

SOLO *voice w/o accompaniment:* **a.** monophonic; monophonous

SOLUTION: **n.** dénouement; explanation
artificial or strained, or out of ordinary:
n. *deus ex machinâ*
capable of: **a.** resoluble; **n.** resolubility
to riddle or puzzle: **n.** *le mot de l'enigme*

SOMETIME: **a.** erstwhile; formerly; occasional; quondam

SOMEWHAT: **adv.** *un peu*

SON *or daughter:* **n.** or **a.** sibling
pert. to: **a.** filial; sibling

SONG(S): **n.** aria; arietta; canticle; canzona; canzone; chanson; descant; lyric; madrigal; melisma; rondo; roundelay
collection of: **n.** chansonnier; repertoire
cradle-: **n.** berceuse
light and graceful: **n.** canzonet
-like: **a.** ariose; canorous; cantabile; lyric; melic
morning: **n.** aubade
of praise: **n.** anthem; canticle; doxology; hymn; magnificat; paen; *te deum*
pert. to: **a.** lyric; melic
sentimental: **n.** strephonade
swan: **n.** *chant du cygne*
w/ alternation of voices: **n.** antiphony; **a.** antiphonal; antiphonic
-writing: **n.** melopoeia; **a.** melopoe(t)ic

SONGFUL: **a.** lyric(al); melodic; **n.** lyricism

SOOT, *of or like:* **a.** fuliginous; **n.** fuliginosity

SOOTHING: (**see** "bland") **a.** anodynic; anodynous; anodyne; antiphlogistic; assuasive; calmative; conciliatory; conciliative; demulcent; dulcent; emollient; hesychastic; lenitive; mitigatory; nepenthean; palliative; placative; placatory; sedative; tranquilizing; **n.** assuagement; conciliation; lenity; placation; **v.** SOOTHE: (**see** "appease") allay; alleviate; assuage; conciliate; pacify; palliate; placate; mollify; reconcile; tranquilize
agent or drug to (*soothe*): **n.** antiphlogistic; balm of Gilead; calmative;

demulcent; emollient; nepenthe; opiate; placebo; tranquilizer; unction

SOOTHSAYER: (**see** "prophet") **n.** auspex; Chaldean; diviner; haruspex; prognosticator; pythonist; **a.** divinatory; haruspical; prognosticative

SOP: (**see** "bribe") **n.** concession; placebo

SOPHISTICATED: **a.** alembicated; *blasé;* knowledg(e)able, knowing; precocious; subtle; world-weary

SORCERY: (**see** "magic") **n.** conjuration; diablerie; diabolism; enchantment; exorcism; incantation; necromancy; sortilege; thaumaturgy; theurgy; witchcraft; **n.** SORCERER: alchemist; conjurer; conjuror; haruspex; necromancer; sortileger; thaumaturge; thaumaturgist; warlock

SORE: **n.** affliction; lesion
bed-: **n.** decubitus (ulcer)
excretion(s) from: **n.** acatharsia; maturation; purulence; purulency; **a.** purulent
water discharge: **n.** ichor; serum

SORROW: **n.** commiseration; compassion; compunction; dolor; lamentation; penitence; remorse; sympathy; *tristesse;* **a.** SORROWFUL: (**see** "sad") commiserable; compassionate; contrite; *désolé;* doleful; dolent(e); dolentissimo; doloroso; dolorous; lamentable; lamented; mournful; penitent; pitiable; plaintive; rueful
causing: **a.** luctiferous
forgetfulness of, drug or agent for: **n.** euphoriant; nepenthe; **a.** euphoric; nepenthean

SORRY: **a.** contemptible; contrite; despicable; insignificant; lamentable; mournful; paltry; penitent; regretful
not: **a.** impenitent

SORT: **v.** alphabetize; arrange; catalogue; categorize; classify; collate; collocate; compartmentalize; concinnate; dispose; distribute; orchestrate; segregate; systematize; tabulate; **n.** character; disposition; quality

SO-SO: **a.** intermediate; mediocre; middling; passable; tolerable; **adv.** *comme ci comme ça; couci-couça;* tolerable; **n.** mediocrity

SOUL(S): **n.** pneuma; psyche; quint(essence)
  divine: **n.** *anima divina*
  of the world: **n.** *anima mundi*
  one who denies that exists in space: **n.** nullibist; nullifidian
  the brute: **n.** *anima bruta*
  transmigration of, theory: **n.** metempsychosis; reincarnation; transmigration
  world of the: **n.** pneuma

SOUND(S), *confusion of:* (**see** "confusion") **n.** Babelism; Babelization; **v.** Babelize
  harsh or discordant: **n.** cacophony; discordance; dissonance; **a.** cacophonic; cacophonous; discordant; disharmonious; dissonant; immelodious; ineuphonious; strident; unharmonious
  loud and piercing: **a.** calliopean
  mania for repeating: **n.** echolalia; onomatomania; verbigeration
  mind in sound body: mens sana in corpore sano
  mind, not of: **a.** incompetent; *non compos (mentis)*
  mind, of: **a.** competent; *compos mentis*
  morbid fear of: **n.** phonophobia
  multiplication of, as echo: **n.** polyphony; reverberation; **a.** echoic; polyphonic; polyphonous
  outburst of: **n.** diapason
  pert. to: **a.** acoustic; phonetic; sonant; sonic; **n.** phonology; sonics
  pert. to single or single sound path: **a.** monophonic; monophonous
  producing: **a.** articulate; phonetic; sonant; soniferous; sonorant; sonorous; **n.** articulation; sonification
  ringing or jingling as of bells: **n.** tintinnabulation; **a.** tintinnabular(y)
  sameness of: **n.** homophony; monotony; **a.** homophonic; homophonous; monotonous; unisonous
  science of: **n.** acoustics; phonetics; phonology; sonics
  seeming to come fr. elsewhere: **a.** ventriloquistic; ventrilquous
  similarity of: **n.** assonance; homeophony; **a.** homeophonic; homeophonous
  word derived fr.: **n.** echoic (word); onomatope; onomatopoeia; **a.** echoic; onomatopoe(t)ic

SOUNDNESS: **n.** integrality; integrity; levelheadedness; solidarity; solidity; solvency

SOUR: **v.** acidify; ferment; **a.** (**see** "acid") acerb(ic); acetose; acidulent; acidulous; cynical; embittered; infestive; mirthless; querulous; vinegary; **n.** SOURNESS: acerbity; acidification; infestivity; mirthlessness
  -tempered: **a.** acidulent; acidulous; austere; morose

SOURCE(S): (**see** "origin") **n.** bibliography; derivation; etiology; fountain(head); genesis; incipience; provenance; provenience; wellspring
  and origin: **n.** *fons et origo*
  consisting of a: **a.** seminal
  from another: **a. or adv.** *aliunde*
  having many, or more than one: **a.** polygenetic; polyphyletic
  of information: **n.** bibliography

SOUTHERN (or SOUTHERLY): **a.** austral; meridional; **n.** meridionality

SOUVENIR: **n.** bibelot; keepsake; memento; recollection; remembrance

SOVEREIGNTY: **n.** authority; autonomy; dominion; empery; independence; jurisdiction
  emblems, insignia or prerogatives of: **n.** regalia; regality
  joint: **n.** condominium

SPACE: **n.** capacity; expanse; firmament; hiatus; interstice; interval; lacuna; **a.** SPATIAL: hiatal; spacial
  filled with matter: **n.** plenum; **a.** gravid; plenum
  for life, growth, activity, etc.: **n.** lebensraum
  lacking: **a.** incapacious
  navigation: **n.** astrogation
  pert. to, happening or existing in: **a.** hiatal; lacunal; lacunar; spacial; spatial
  state of being located in, or of being spatial: **n.** spatiality; ubiety
  vacant: **n.** vacuum

SPACIOUS: **a.** baronial; capacious; cavernous; commodious; comprehensive; copious; expansive; scopious; voluminous

SPANGLED: **a.** caparisoned; clinquant

SPARK (or SPARKLE): **v.** coruscate; scintillate; **n.** coruscation; scintilla(tion); **a.** rutilant; scintillesce(nt)

SPASM: **n.** agitation; clonicity; clonus; convulsion; orgasm; paroxysm; seizure; tetany; throe; tonus; **a.** SPASMODIC(AL): clonic; convulsive; intermittent; paroxysmal; spasmatic; spastic

SPEAK: (**see** "talk") **v.** articulate; converse; enunciate; intonate; labialize; phonate; pronounce; utter; verbalize; vocalize; **n. see** "speech"
   at length: (**see** "wordliness") **v.** harangue; perorate
   disinclined to: (**see** "reserved") **a.** incommunicative; inconversable; laconic; obmutescent; retentive; reticent; taciturn
     emphatically: **a.** lexical; **n.** lexicality
     extravagantly: **v.** rhapsodize
     indistinctly or disconnected: **v.** maunder
     in flowing or rhetorical lang.: **v.** (per)orate; rhapsodize; **n.** (per)oration
     in short syllables: **a.** brachysyllabic; monosyllabic; telegraphic
     unable to: (**see** "muteness") **a.** aphonetic; aphonic; inarticulate

SPEAKER: (**see** "orator") **n.** annunciator; chairman; collucator; *conférencier;* conversationalist
   elegant: **n.** rhetorician

SPEAKING: (**see** "speech") **n.** articulation; enunciation; phonation; vocalization
   at length: **see** "wordiness"
   indirect or roundabout: **n.** circumambage(s); circumlocution; periphrasis; **a.** circuitous; circumlocutory; periphrastic
     mania for: **n.** *furor loquendi*
     pert. to: **a.** elocutionary; enunciative; exophasic; phonetic; vocal
     public, pert. to: **a.** demegoric; oratori(c)al; **n.** elocution
     thru closed or partly-closed teeth: **n.** dentiloquy
     thru nose: **v.** nasalize; **n.** nasality
     to self (inaudible): **n.** endophasia
     unbounded, fondness for: **n.** *studium immane loquendi*
     way of: **n.** *façon de parler*
     with heavy stress: **a.** labial; lexical

SPECIALIZED *skill:* **n.** expertise; technique; virtuosity

SPECIALTY: **n.** forte; *métier;* particularity

SPECIFIC: **a.** categorical; definitive; determinative; explicit; express; peculiar; specificative; unequivocal

purpose, for a: **adv.** *ad hoc; pro tempore*
quality or state of being: **n.** specificality; specification; specificity

SPECIOUS *reasoning:* **n.** casuistry; sophism; sophistry; speciosity; syllogism; **a.** casuistical; sophistical; syllogistic(al)

SPECTACLE: **n.** drama; exhibition; extravaganza; pageant(ry); spectacular

SPECULATE: **v.** conjecture; hypothesize; philosophize; surmise; theorize; **n.** SPECULATION: conjecture; hypothesis; surmise; theoretics
   in psychological terms or ideas: **v.** psychologize

SPEECH: (**see** "language," "speaking," and "talk") **n.** allocution; articulation; colloquy; confabulation; conversation; declamation; dialogue; diction; discourse; disquisition; (e)locution; enunciation; exophasia; glottology; harangue; linguistics; oration; parlance; peroration; phonation; phraseology; pronunciation; recitation; recitative; vocalization
   artificial, affected or excessive eloquence of: **n.** bombast; euphuism; grandiloquence; **a.** bombastic; declamatory; euphuistic(al); rhetorical; rubescent
   authoritative: **n.** allocution; (ex)hortation; **a.** (ex)hortative; (ex)hortatory
   boastful: **n.** kompology; rodomontade
   brevity of: **see under** "brevity"
   common or informal: (**see under** "language") **n.** colloquialism; patois; vernacular; vulgate
   conciseness of: (**see under** "brevity") **n.** brachylogy; syllabification
   defects, pert. to: **a.** phoniatric
   disordered: **n.** idoglossia; idiolalia; lalopathy; pararthria
   eloquent: **see** "grandiose" **below**
   empty, stilted, etc.: **n.** balderdash; flatulence; gasconade; kompology
   exactness in: **n.** incisiveness; syllabification
   figure of: **n.** apostrophe; hyperbole; metaphor; metonymy; litotes; simile; synecdoche; tralatition; trope; **a.** synecdochic(al); tropological
     use of: **n.** tropology; **a.** tropological
   flowery or rhetorical: **n.** peroration; **v.** perorate
   fluency of: **n.** *copia verborum;* eloquence; facundity; grandiloquence; loquaciousness; loquacity; mellifluence

fondness for: **n.** *stadium immane loquendi*

foolish: **see under** "language"

grandiose: (**see** "bombast") **n.** grandiloquence; magniloquence; rubescence; **a.** grandiloquent; magniloquent; mercurial; rubescent

high-flown or pompous: (**see** "bombast") **n.** altiloquence; grandiloquence; grandiosity; kompology; pomposity; **a.** altiloquent; grandiloquent; pompous

honeyed: **a.** mellifluent; mellifluous; mellisonant

illiterate or substandard: **n.** Choctaw; vulgate; **a.** grammarless

imitative: **n.** onomatopoea; **a.** echoic; mimetic; onomatopoe(t)ic

indirect or roundabout: **see under** "speaking"

internal or inaudible (to self): **n.** endophasia

lightness or gaiety of: **n.** levity

local or individual: **n.** colloquialism; patois; provincialism; vernacular; villagism; **a.** colloquial; idiomatic; vernacular

long, monopolizing conversations: **n.** monologue

long, w/ little sense: **n.** macrology; pleonasm; **a.** pleonastic

loss of power of: **n.** aphonia; obmutescence; **a.** aphonic; obmutescent

mania for: **n.** *furor loquendi*

nonsense: (**see** "foolish" **under** "language") **n.** Choctaw; gibberish; jaberwock(y); jargon

pause in: **n.** hiatus

pert. to: **a.** glottologic(al); linguistic; lingual; phonetic

rambling: **a.** peripatetic

rustic: **n.** ruralism; rusticism; **a.** ruralistic

solo: **n.** monologue; soliloquy

specialist in: **n.** glottologist; linguist; phoneticist

study of: **n.** glottology; linguistics; phonetics; phonology

substandard, use of: **see under** "language"

that puts one asleep: **n.** *discours assoupissant*

thru body motions, signs, etc.: **n.pl.** kinesics; **n.** *lingua franca;* **a.** *kinesic*

to self: **n.** endophasia; soliloquy

uncontrolled in: **a.** rampageous; rampant; **n.** *furor loquendi;* onomatomania; verbomania

unintelligible: **see** "jargon"

uttered or vocalized: **n.** *exophasia*

vocalized: **n.** exophasia; **a.** exophasic

warning or advisory w/ authority: **n.** allocution

windiness or emptiness of: (**see** "empty" **above**): **n.** bombast; flatulence

SPEED (or SPEEDINESS): (**see** "haste") **n.** acceleration; alacrity; *aussitôt dit, aussitôt fait;* celerity; deftness; dispatch; expedition; promptitude; velocity; **a.** SPEEDY: (**see** "fast") adept; alacritous; celeritous; expeditious; expeditive; posthaste; velocious

at full or breakneck: **adv.** *à corps perdu; à toute allure;* Gaderine; precipitous

reduce: **v.** decelerate; **n.** deceleration

SPELL, *magic:* (**see** "charm") **n.** conjuration; enchantment; evocation; incantation

SPELLING *correct or as subject or style or way of:* **n.** orthography

diff. from current way: **n.** heterography

in letters or characters of another lang.: **n.** metagraphy; transliteration; **v.** transliterate; **a.** transliterative

SPHERE: **n.** domain; dominion; jurisdiction; *métier;* milieu; province; purview; spheroid; theater; **a.** SPHERICAL: cylindrical; discoid; globate; globose; globular; orbicular; (o)rotund; spheriform; spheroidal; spheroidical

form of: **n.** sphericity; spheroidicity; **a.** spheroidal

SPIKED: **a.** spicate; spicigerous

SPINE: **n.** acantha; chine; rachis; spicule; spinosity; vertebra

near or beside the: **a.** juxtaspinal; paraspinal

pert. to: **a.** spondylic; vertebral

SPINELESS: (**see** "spiritless") **a.** invertebrate; **n.** invertebracy

SPINY (or SPINOUS): (**see** "prickly") **a.** acanthaceous; acanthological; acanthous; acicular; aciculate(d); spicose; spicular; spiculate; spiculiferous; spiculose; spinose

SPIRAL: (**see** "coiled") **a.** cochleate; (con)voluted; helical; helicoid(al); volute; whorled; **n.** convolution; helix; spirality; volute

SPIRIT(S) : (see "ghost" and "soul") **n.** animus; ardor; *brio;* character; courage; *élan; esprit; esprit de corps;* mettle; nous; phantasm(ata) ; pneuma; vigor; vivacity; (**pl.** lemures)
evil: **n.** cacod(a)emon
guiding: **n.** muse; numen
high: **n.** animation; ebullience; enthusiasm; euphoria; exhilaration; exuberance; intoxication; invigoration; optimism; **a.** ebullient; euphoric; exuberant; flamboyant; heady; intoxicated
low in: (see "sad") **a.** vaporish; **n.pl.** doldrums; megrims
of a place or locality: **n.** *genius loci*
of natural objects(s) or phenomena, belief: **n.** numen
of the time: **n.** zeitgeist
presiding: **n.** numen
with: (see "spirited") **adv.** *con spirito*
world of the: **n.** pneuma

SPIRITED: (see "brisk") **a.** animated; assiduous; energetic; enterprising; forceful; mettlesome; spiritful; vigorous; vivacious; zealous; zestful; **adv.** *avec ardeur; con anima; con brio; con spirito;* **n.** SPIRITEDNESS: see "briskness"

SPIRITLESS: **a.** adenoid(al) ; amort; apathetic; arenaceous; dejected; depressed; desiccated; dispirited; exanimate; feckless; inanimate; invertebrate; lackadaisical; lackluster; languescent; languorous; lethargic; listless; pusillanimous; unenthusiastic

SPIRITUAL: **a.** angelic; celestial; ethereal; incorporeal; intellectual; psychic(al) ; religious; supermundane; supernatural; supersensible; supersensory; supersensual; **n.** SPIRITUALITY: ethereality; incorporeality; incorporeity; interiority
ideals, pert. to: **a.** anagogic(al)
make: **v.** apotheosize; canonize; celestialize; deify; etherealize; spiritualize; **n.** apotheosis; deification; spiritualization
rapture, state of: **n.** raptus
torpor or apathy: **n.** acedia

SPITE, *out of:* **adv.** *par dépit*

SPITEFUL: (see "abusive") **a.** dispiteous; malevolent; malicious; malignant; rancorous; splenetic(al) ; venomous; vindicative; **n.** SPITEFULNESS: malevolence; maliciousness; malignancy; venom; venosity

SPLENDID: **a.** aurelian; bravissimo; effulgent; gorgeous; lustrous; magnificent; opulent; refulgent; splendaceous; splendacious; splendiferous; sublime; sumptuous; superb; **n.** SPLENDOR: *éclat;* effulgence; luster; magnificence; pomp; sublimity; sumptuosity; sumptuousness

SPLIT: **a.** bifid; bifurcate(d) ; bipartite; bipartisan; bisected; cleft; cloven; dichotomous; dimidate; schismatic(al) ; **n.** bifurcation; cleavage; divarication; dichotomy; dissidence; disunion; diversity; fission; fracture; **adv.** *à cheval*
(*burst open*) : **v.** dehise; **n.** dehiscence; **a.** dehiscent
on issues: **adv.** *à cheval*
-personality: **n.** schizophrenia; **a.** schizophrenic; **n.** schizoid; schizophrene; schizophreni(a)c

SPOIL: **v.** corrupt: defile; pervert; putrefy; putresce; vitiate; **n.** pillage
not subject to (spoiling) : **a.** imputrescible

SPOKEN: see "oral"
word cannot be recalled: nescit vox missa reverti

SPOKESMAN: **n.** advocate; chairman; hierophant; prolocutor; protagonist

SPONGING: **a.** parasitic(al) ; predatory; sycophantic; **n.** commensalism; parasitism; predation; symbiont; symbiosis

SPONSORSHIP: (see "protection") **n.** (a)egis; auspice(s) ; guardianship; patronage; protectorship; tutelage

SPONTANEOUS: (see "natural" and "off-hand") **a.** automatic; impulsive; indigenous; unpremeditated; **n.** impulsivity; spontaneity
generation: **n.** abiogenesis; autogenesis; **a.** abiogenetic(al)
not: (see "artificial") **a.** factitious
origin, of: **a.** idiogenetic; idiopathic; **n.** idiogenesis
state of being: **n.** automaticity; automatism; impusivity; spontaneity

SPORT: **n.** *bon vivant;* diversion; divertissement; mutation; recreation; **a.** divertive; recreational; sportful; sportive

SPOT: **n.** macula(tion) macule; stigma

SPOTLESS: (see "clean") **a.** blameless; immaculate; irreproachable; unblemished; unsullied; untarnished

SPOTTED: **a.** maculate; macular; maculose; mottled; piebald; punctate(d); puncticular; punctiform; sullied; tarnished; variegated; **n.** maculation; puncticulation; variegation
like a leopard: **a.** pardine

SPRAY: **v.** atomize; nebulize

SPREAD: (see "radiate" **and** "scatter") **v.** circulate; diffuse; dilate; disperse; disseminate; diversify; (inter)penetrate; (ir)radiate; proliferate; promulgate; propagate; publish
out or branch: **v.** decentralize; divaricate; **n.** decentralization; divarication; proliferation; ramification

SPREADING: **a.** expanded; patulous; serpiginous; **n.** circulation; diaspora; diffusion; dispersion; dissemination; diversification; diversity; irradiation; proliferation; promulgation; propagation
in all directions: **a.** radial; radiating
(standing open): **a.** patulous; **n.** patulousness

SPREE: **n.** bacchanal; bender; brannigan; orgy

SPRIGHTLY: (see "gay") **a.** animated; balletic; blithe(ful); effervescent; exuberant; frolicsome; jaunty; perky; roguish; spirited; sportive; vivacious; zestful; **n.** SPRIGHTLINESS: (see "gaiety") *allégresse;* buoyancy; exuberance; lightheartedness; vivacity; zest

SPRING(TIME): **n.** *le printemps;* primavera; **a.** primaveral; vernal
beginning of: **n.** vernal equinox

SPROUT: **v.** burgeon; germinate; pullulate; **a.** burgeoning; pullulant; **n.** burgeoning; pullulation

SPRUCE: *up:* **v.** tit(t)ivate; **n.** tit(t)ivation

SPUR: (see "stimulus") **n.** calcar; calcarium; **v.** see "stimulate"

SPURIOUS: (see "counterfeit") **a.** adulterine; apocryphal; inauthentic; meretricious; pinchback; specious

argument: **n.** casuistry; philosophism; pilpul; sophism; sophistry; speciosity; **a.** casuistic; sophistical; specious
as of writing(s): **n.pl.** apocrypha; pseudepigrapha; **a.** apocryphal; pseudepigraphic(al); pseudepigraphous

SQUABBLE: **see** "controversy"

SQUALID: **a.** contemptible; feculent; ordurous; scabrous; sordid; **n.** scabrousness; squalidity

SQUEAKY: **a.** strident; stridulate; stridulous

SQUEAMISH: (see "prissy") **a.** fastidious; hypercritical; nauseated; sanctimonious; scrupulous

SQUINT: **n.** esotropia; exotropia; *louchement;* strabismus; **a.** SQUINTING: louche; strabismic

STAB: **v.** impale; lancinate

STABILITY: **n.** constancy; equilibrium; permanence; permanency; *status quo;* steadfastness; steadiness; **a.** STABLE: (see "steady") immutable; inexpungable; irreversible; irrevocable
internal, social or psychological (or tending to maintain): **n.** homeostasis

STAFF *officers:* **n.** cadre

STAGE, *front part of:* **n.** proscenium
manager: **n.** impresario; regisseur
setting: **n.** *mise-en-scène*
trick: **n.** *jeu de théâtre;* legerdemain; prestidigitation; *tour de force*

STAGED: (see "showy") **a.** contrived; histrionic; manipulated; (melo)dramatic; operated; theatric(al); **n.** STAGINESS: (see "showiness") melodrama; sardoodledom; theatricality
situation or effect(s): **n.** acrobatics; cabotinage; *deus ex machinâ;* histrionics; histrionism; melodramatics; sardoodledom; theatricality; theatrics

STAGGER: **v.** titubate; welter; **n.** titubation; **a.** titubant

STAGNATION: **n.** quiescence; sluggishness; stasis; torpidity; torpor

STAGY: **see** "showy"

STAIN: **n.** *bar sinister;* macula(tion); stigma; tarnish
without: **adv.** *sans tache;* **a.** immaculate; virtuous

STALE: (**see** "dull") **a.** banal; commonplace; hackneyed; jejune; stereotyped; threadbare; trite; vapid; **n.** banality; jejunity; vapidity
become by lapse of time: **v.** obsolesce; superannuate; **n.** obsolescence; superannuation

STAMP *collecting or collector:* **n.** philately; **n.** philatelist; **a.** philatelic

STAND *by decided cases:* **n.** precedent; *res adjudicata; stare decisis*

STANDARD(S): **n.** *beau idéal;* canon; criterion; (pl criteria); emblem; gauge; gonfalon; modality; touchstone; yardstick; **a.** (**see** "uniform") classic; emblematic; prime; recognized; typical
accepted: **n.pl.** canons of propriety; civilities; convenances; conventions; criteria; (the) amenities; (the) proprieties
below normal: **a.** raunchy; subnormal; suboptimal
conforming to: (**see** "proper") **a.** canonical; consuetudinary; conventional; *de rigueur; en règle;* ethical; exemplary; orthodox; sanctioned; traditional
for distinguishing: **n.** criterion; (**pl.** criteria); differentia(e); differentiation
not conforming to: **see** "improper"

STANDARDIZE: **v.** calibrate; gauge; **n.** calibration

STANDING: (**see** "status") **n.** antecedence; perpendicular; precedence; prestige; statant; stature; status; vertical

STAR(S): **n.** asterisk; *étoile;* luminary; pentacle; **a.** STARRY: (**see** "visionary") astral; sidereal; stellar; stellate
as symbol of Judaism: **n.** Magen (**or** Morgen) David; Shield of David; Star of David
covered w/ or resembling: **a.** stellar; stellate; stelliform
group or patch of: **n.** asterism; constellation; galaxy; nebula; **a.** asterismal; constellational; constellatory
having: **a.** astiferous

one fond of (*star*) *lore:* **n.** astrophile
pert. to or like: **a.** asterial; astral; stellar; stellate; stelliform
set among or turn into: **v.** stellify; **n.** instellation: stellification
study of: **n.** astronomy; uranology
to the, thru difficulties: ad astra per aspera
worship of: **n.** astrolatry

STARCHY: **a.** amyloid; farinaceous

STARLINGS, *flock of:* **n.** murmuration

START: **see** "begin"

STARTING *point:* **n.** commencement; *terminus (ad quem)*

STARTLING: **a.** awe-inspiring; bizarre; electrifying; galvanic

STATE: **n.** body politic; civitas; commonalty; commonweal(th); dilemma; plight; posture; predicament; situation; status; (the) *res publica*
economic planning and control: **n.** *dirigisme*
highly centralized, advocacy of: **n.** statolatry
lack of planning and control by: **n.** laissez faire; laissez-faireism
secrets: **n.pl.** *arcana imperli*
worship of the: **n.** statolatry

STATELY: (**see** "dignified") **a.** august; baronial; ceremonious; courtly; eminent; haughty; imposing; magnificent; majestic; marmoreal; palatial; pompous; Praxitelean; regal; sculpturesque; statuesque; togated; unapproachable
esp. if exaggerated: **a.** pompous; pontifical; portentous
female, pert. to: **a.** Junoesque

STATEMENT: **n.** allegation; assertion; asseveration; constantation; declaration; dictum; presentation; profession; recital; recitation; verbality; **a.** assertative; assertoric; assertorial
dogmatic, or w/o confirmation: **n.** dixit
gratuitous: **n.** *gratis dictum; obiter dictum*
positive: **n.** asseveration; **v.** asseverate; aver

STATESMAN: **n.** *homme d'état*

STATUE, *like:* **a.** Junoesque; marmoreal; Praxitelean; sculpturesque; statuesque

STATUS: **n.** posture; prestige; recognition; situation; standing; stature
high: **n.** cachet; eminence; prestige; **a.** eminent; illustrious; prestigious
inferior in: **a.** subalternate
lowering of: **v.** denigrate; minimize; pejorate; plebify; vulgarize; **n.** declension; degradation; demotion; denigration; pejoration; plebification,; vulgarization; **a.** *déclassé;* declensional; declinatory; denigratory; pejorative

STEADY (or STEADFAST): (**see** "constant," "cool" and "firm") **a.** continual; dependable; disciplined; equable; immutable; incessant; irreversible; irrevocable; persistent; reliable; resolute; undeviating; unfaltering; unflinching; unhesitating; uninterrupted; unremittant; unremitting; **n.** **see** "stability"
(*stable*): **a.** equable; stabile; **v.** stabilize; **n.** equability; equanimity; stability

STEAL: **v.** abstract; burglarize; defalcate; embezzle; extort; extract; filch; misapply; misappropriate; peculate; pilfer; purloin; **n.** STEALING: abstraction; defalcation; embezzlement; extraction; larceny; misappropriation; peculation; **a.** burglarious; larcenous; thieving; thievish
abnormal impulse to: **n.** kleptomania; **n.** kleptomaniac; **a.** kleptomaniac(al)
lit. work, etc.: **v.** plagiarize; **n.** piracy; plagiarism; **a** plagiaristic; **n.** plagiarist
one who (*steals*): **n.** burglar; defalcator; embezzler; larcenist; peculator

STEALTHY: **a.** cabalistic; clandestine; duplicitous; furtive; Machiavellian; secretive; serpentine; sinuous; surreptitious; **adv.** *à la dérobée; en tapinois*

STEEP: **a.** acclivitous; arduous; declivitous; exorbitant; perpendicular; precipitous

STEMLESS: **a.** acaulescent; acauline; **n.** acaulescence

STENCH: (**see** "stink") **n.** mephitis; **a.** malodorous; mephitic; noisome; noxious

STEP(S): **n.** *démarche;* echelon; maneuver; plateau
by: **adv.** *per gradus*
first: **n.** *le premier pas*
w/o intermediary (*by single bound*): **adv. or a.** *per saltum*

STERN: (**see** "severe" **and** "strict") **a.** (a) stringent; austere; exacting; inexorable; inflexible; inhospitable; resolute; rigorous; scrupulous; uncompromising; uninviting

STEW: **n.** olla podrida; potpourri; ragout

STICK: **v.** (ag) glutinate; adhere; cohere; conglutinate; **n.** agglutination; conglutination; **n.** STICKINESS: glutinosity; tenacity; viscosity; **a.** STICKING (or STICKY) adherent; adherescent; adhesive; agglutinant; glutinous; mucilaginous; tenacious; viscid; viscous; **n.** adherence; agglutination; conglutination

"STICKS" (*back country*): **n.** hinterland; **n. or a.** up-country

STICK-TO-ITIVENESS: **n.** importunity; perseverance; pertinacity; steadfastness; tenacity

STIFF: **see** "inflexible"

STIFFENED, *as a joint:* **a.** ankylosed; ankylotic; **n.** ankylosis

STIGMA: (**see** "disgrace") **n.** *bar sinister*

STILL: **a.** dormant; halcyon; immobile; impassive; inactive; inarticulate; inoperative; obmutescent; quiescent; silentious; stationary; tranquil; unperturbed; **n.** STILLNESS: immobility; lifelessness; quiescence; quietude; serenity; tranquility
standing (*still*): **a.** languishing; **v.** languish; **n.** languishment

STIMULATION: (**see** "incentive" **and** "incitement") **n.** piquancy; provocation; refreshment; (re) invigoration; stimulant; titillation; tit(t) ivation; **v.** STIMULATE: animate; foment; incite; innervate; inspirit; instigate; provoke; titillate; tit(t) ivate; **a.** STIMULATING (or STIMULATIVE): (**see** "brisk") accelerative; animating; aspirational; catalytic; galvanic; heartening; incisive; inspirational; inspiriting; piquant; poignant; promptive; provocative; psychogogic; pungent; stimulogenous; titillating; tit(t) ivating
developing as a consequence of: **a.** stimulatory; stimulogenous

STIMULATOR: **n.** accelerant; accentuator; agitator; catalyst; catalytic; flagellant;

gadfly; incendiary; precipitator; propulsor; synergist

STIMULUS: **n.** catalyst; catalytic; fillip; incendiary; incentive; provocation

STINGING: **a.** acrimonious; caustic; incisive; mordant; penetrating; piquant; poignant

STINGY: **a.** avaricious; cheeseparing; curmudgeonly; extortionate; miserly; niggardly; parsimonious; penny-pinching; penurious; tight-fisted; ungenerous; **n.** STINGINESS: avarice; parsimony; penury

STINK: **n.** effluvium; (**pl.** effluvia); fetor; mephitis; nidor; putridity; stench; **a.** STINKING: effluvial; fetid; fulsome; gravolent; malodorant; malodorous; mephitic; nidorous; noisome; (ob)noxious; pestilent(ial); putrid; undeodorized

STIR: **see** "incite" **and** "stimulate"

STOCK, *single ancestral, of or developed fr.:* **a.** monophyletic

STOIC(AL): **a.** dispassionate; impassive; imperturbable; indifferent; philosophic(al); phlegmatic; resolute; spartanic; stolid; undemonstrative; Zenonian

STOLID: (**see** "stubborn") **a.** anserine; asinine; bovine; brutish; **n.** STOLIDITY: asininity; bovinity; impassiveness; imperturbation; indifference; phlegm

STOOP-SHOULDERED: **a.** gibbose; gibbous; kyphotic; **n.** gibbosity; gibbousness; kyphosis

STONE(S), *consisting of or pert. to one:* **a.** monolithic
 leave no (stone) unturned: omnem movere lapidem
 pelt w/ or kill by: **v.** lapidate; **n.** lapidation
 precious, cutter or polisher of: **n.** lapidarist
 precious, pert. to: **a.** lapidary
 rel. to: **a.** lapideous; lithic; petrous
 rolling gathers no moss: saxum volutum non obducitur musco
 turn into: **v.** calcify; lapidify; lithify; petrify; **n.** calcification; lapidification; petrification; **a.** petrescent; petrefactive

STOP: (**see** "discontinue") **v.** arrest; cease; checkmate; circumvent; thwart; **n.** STOPPAGE: armistice; cessation; obstruction; obturation; oppilation; stasis
 cause to: **v.** arrest; surcease
 for a time: **v.** intermit; **n.** armistice; hiatus; intermission
 up: **v.** obstruct; occlude; oppilate; **n.** obturation; occlusion; oppilation

STOPPING: **a.** cessative; oppilative; **n.** arrestation; arrestment; quiescence
 in middle of sentence: **n.** abscission

STORAGE *place:* **n.** ambry; argosy; arsenal; cache; depository; entrepot; larder; magazine; repertorium; repertory; repository; storehouse

STORE: **v.** accumulate; cache; secrete; **n.** accumulation; budget; repertoire; repository
 up: **v.** thesaurize; **n.** thesaurization

STOREHOUSE: **see** "storage place"

STORK, *pert. to the:* **a.** pelargic

STORM: **v.** besiege; bombard; fulminate; **n.** agitation; disturbance; monsoon; tempest; turbulence; vortex; **a.** STORMY. cyclonic; fulminous; inclement; passionate; procellous; tempestical; tempestuous; turbulent; **n.** STORMINESS: inclemency; tempestivity; tempestuousness; turbulence; turbulency

STORY: **n.** anecdote; chronicle; epic; falsehood; lexicon; narration; narrative; romance; saga
 add fictitious details to: **v.** confabulate; embellish; fantasticate; **n.** confabulation; embellishment
 continued, or in installments: **n.** feuilleton
 doleful: **n.** jeremiad; lamentation
 false and scandalous, as in politics: **n.** canard; roorback
 long: **n.** epic (*poem*); heroic (*poem*); iliad
 of house, chief: **n.** bel étage
 old: **n.** crambe repetita
 scandalous: **n.** chronique scandaleuse; roorback
 several in one: **n.** polymythy
 teller of (stories): **n.** narrator; (ra)-conteur; (**fem.** (re)conteuse)

STOUT: (**see** "obese") **a.** corpulent; courageous; forceful; hearty; implacable;

liparous; lusty; orbicular; plentitudinous; plethoric; portly; powerful; pursy; replete; resolute; robust; rotund; valiant; vigorous; **n.** STOUTNESS: corpulence; embonpoint; firmness; fortitude; plethora; ponderosity; portliness; pursiness; robusticity

STRADDLE (or STRADDLING), *as line or issue:* **adv.** *à cheval*

STRAIGHT: (**see** "straightforward"): **a.** direct; undiluted; uninterrupted; unmixed; unmodified; perpendicular; vertical; **n.** perpendicularity; verticality

STRAIGHT LINE, *bring into:* **v.** collimate; **n.** collimation
    lying in: **a.** collinear

STRAIGHTFORWARD: (**see** "simple") **a.** artless; candid; clear-cut; ingenuous; naïve; outspoken; precise; undeviating; **n.** candidness; ingenuosity; ingenuousness; probity; rectitude; scrupulosity

STRAINED: **see** "far-fetched"

STRANGE: (**see** "unusual") **a.** alien; anomalous; atypic(al); bizarre; eccentric; exceptional; exotic; extraordinary; fantastic; foreign; glamorous; grotesque; outlandish; *outré;* picturesque; preternatural; singular; tramontane; unaccountable; unaccustomed; uncanny; unfamiliar; unfrequented; unique
    hater of anything (strange) or new: **see under** "new"
    something which is: **see** "curiosity"

STRANGENESS: **n.** bizzarerie; grotesquerie

STRANGER(S): **n.** auslander; foreigner; inconnu; *novus homo;* outlander; tramontane
    entertainment of: **n.** xenodochy
    fear of: **n.** xenophobia
    hatred of: **n.** misoxeny; xenophobia; **n.** misoxene; xenophobe

STRAW, *like or resembling (straw-colored)*: **a.** stramineous
    -man: **n.** *homme de paille*

STRAYING: (**see** "deviation") **n.** divagation; divergence; **v.** STRAY: deviate; di-

gress; divagate; divaricate; meander; **n.** maverick; straggler; waif
    fr. truth or correct course: **n.** aberrance; aberrancy; aberration; **n.** aberrant; **a.** aberrational; aberrative; aberrant

STREAKED: **a.** linear(istic); lineate; **n.** lineation

STREAM(S), *adapted to life in:* **a.** autopotamic
    lying bet. two: **a.** interfluvial; **n.** mesopotamia

STRENGTH: (**see** "strong") **n.** brawn; concentration; doughtiness; durability; fortitude; intensity; lustihood; permanency; potency; robusticity; stamina; sthenia; strenuosity; vigor; virility; vitality
    bodily: **n.** brawn; lustihood; physique; robusticity; thews
    established in position of: **a.** castellated; ensconced; fortified
    from on high: *vigueur de dessus*
    loss or lessening of: **n.** adynamia; asthenia; **a.** adynamic; asthenic
    of or by own: **adv.** (*ex*) *propria vigore*
    place of: **see** "stronghold"
    pregnant with: **a.** Dionysian

STRENGTHEN: (**see** "support") **v.** anneal; augment; buttress; confirm; corroborate; encourage; enhance; fortify; hearten; intensify; invigorate; lace; reinforce; sustain; **a.** STRENGTHENING: (**see** "bracing") corroborative; corroboratory; roborant
    as character, conduct, etc.: **v.** chasten; **n.** chastenment

STRENUOUS: **a.** arduous; Herculean; onerous; rigorous; vigorous; **n.** strenuosity

STRESS: **v.** accent(uate); emphasize; **n.** **see** "accent" **and** "pressure"
    period of great: **n.** convulsion
    physical or mental: **n.** trauma(tism); **a.** traumatic; **v.** traumatize

STRETCHING, *as when drowsy or on awakening:* **n.** pandiculation

STRICT: (**see** "stern") **a.** austere; conscientious; Draconian; inclement; inexorable; inquisitorial; intransigent; obdurate; onerous; orthodox; pharisaical; precise; puritanical; rigorist(ic); rigorous; ruthless; scrupulous; Spartanic; stringent; tyrannical; uncompromising; unsparing; unyielding; **n.** STRICTNESS: austerity; correctitude; intransige(a)nce; obduracy; preciseness; precisianism; puritanism; rigidity; rigorism; scrupulosity; stringency; tyranny

enforcer of discipline or rules: **n.** ascetic; disciplinarian; martinet; Pharisee; *precisian;* rigorist

extremely: **a.** rhadamanthine; rigoristic

in customs, religion or morality: **a.** puritanic(al); sabbatarian; **n.** precisian; precisionist; rigorist; sabbatarian

in living: **a.** ascetic; cenobitic(al); **n.** asceticism; ascesis; ascetic; cenobite

person who is rigidly: **n.** disciplinarian; martinet; Pharisee; precisian; rigorist; ritualist; sabbatarian

STRIDE: **see** "step"

with a giant's: **adv.** *à pas de géant*

STRIFE: (**see** "fight") **n.** *concours;* contention; dissension; warfare

breeds strife: lis litem generat

excuse or cause for: **n.** *casus belli*

one fond of: **n.** stormy petrel

one who stirs up: **n.** incendiary; mutineer

STRIKING: **a.** conspicuous; eminent; extraordinary; impressive; noticeable; notorious; percussive; prominent; remarkable; salient

STRIP: **v.** decorticate; defoliate; denudate; denude; deplume; disembellish; dismantle; divest; ransack; **a.** STRIPPING: denudative; **n.** decortication; denudation; desquamation; dismantlement; divestiture; ecdysis; excoriation; exfoliation

as of leaves: **v.** defoliate; **n.** defoliation; **a.** defoliative

or peel, as of skin: **v.** desquamate; excoriate; **n.** desquamation; excoriation

STRIPED: **see** "streaked"

STRIPTEASER: **n.** ecdysiast; stripteuse

STRIVING: **a.** conative; **n.** conation; conatus; **v.** STRIVE: contend; contest; endeavor

creatively: **a.** Dionysian

STROKE: **n.** coup; ictus

finishing: **n.** *coup de grâce*

master: **n.** *coup de maître; tour de force*

of apoplexy: **n.** cerebral accident (**or** insult)

result of: **n.** hemiplegia

of state: **n.** *coup d'état*

STROLL: **v.** perambulate; promenade; **n.** deambulation; perambulation; promenade; **a.** circumforaneous; deambulatory; perambulatory; promenading

STRONG: **a.** Achillean; adamantine; Atalantean; brawny; castellated; cogent; Cyclopean; Dionysian; doughty; emphatic; Herculean; impregnable; indomitable; invincible; potent; puissant; robust(ious); Samsonesque; Samsonian; stalwart; sthenic; tenacious; urgent; vigorous

man: **n.** gladiator; Hercules; Samson

point, person's: **n.** forte

right of the (strongest): **n.** *le droit du plus fort*

STRONGHOLD: **n.** bastion; blockhouse; breastwork; citadel; fastness; Gibraltar; redan; redoubt

STRUCTURE: **n.** anatomy; architecture; cadre; configuration; conformation; fabrication; lineament; organization; skeleton; texture; **a.** STRUCTURAL: constitutional; edificial; skeletonic

having similar or identical: **a.** homologous; isomorphic; isomorphous

of irregular or unusual: **a.** heteromorphic; heteromorphous; **n.** heteromorphosis

or position, having same relative: **a.** homologous

STRUGGLE: (**see** "fight") **n.** agon; collucation; contention; endeavor; warfare; **a.** agonistic; contending; contentious

STUB, *check or receipt:* **n.** counterfoil

STUBBORN: (**see** "obstinate") **a.** absonant; adamant(ine); cantankerous; contemptuous; contumacious; contumelious; crotchety; defiant; determined; disdainful; disobedient; dogged; *entêté;* fractious; implacable; incompliant; indocile; indurate; indurative; inductible; inexorable; inflexible; insubordinate; intractable; intransigent; inveterate; irreconcilable; monolithic; mulish; oppositious; persistent; pertinacious; perverse; pervicacious; pigheaded; preemptory; rebellious; re-

calcitrant; refractory; renitent; resistant; restive; stiff-necked; tenacious; unalterable; uncompromising; unreconcilable; unreconstructed; unregenerate(d); unrepentant; unswerving; untoward; willful; **n.** STUBBORNNESS: (**see** "obstinacy") adamancy; contumely; crotchiness; determination; incompliance; incompliancy; intractability; intransigeance; noncompliance; obduracy; persistency; pertinacity; pigheadedness; recalcitrance
   person: **n.** intransigeant; recalcitrant

STUDENT: (**see** "pupil") **n.** disciple; scholar; scholastic; undergraduate
   fellow-: **n.** condisciple

STUDIO, *artist's:* **n.** atelier

STUDY: (**see** "ponder") **v.** lucubrate; **n.** abstraction; concentration; contemplation; investigation; lucubration; meditation; reflection
   fondness for: **n.** *attachement à l'étude*
   place for: **n.** atelier; phrontistery

STUFF, *ever the same old:* **n.** *cantilenam enadem canis; crambe repetita*

STUFFED: **a.** copious; replete; sated; satiated; surfeited; **n.** copiosity; satiety

STUN: **v.** flabbergast; paralyze; perplex; stupefy; **n.** stupefaction; **n.** torporific

STUNT, *special or spectacular:* **n.** acrobatics; derring-do; forte; prestidigitation; *tour de force*

STUPID: **a.** Abderian; anserine; anserous; asinine; baboonish; Boeotian; bovine; brutish; crass; doltish; fatuous; hebetate; idiotic; imperceptive; inane; loutish; oafish; obtuse; opaque; oscitant; moronic; purblind; unimaginative; vacuous; **a.** STUPIDITY: absurdity; baboonery; *balourdise; bêtise;* crassitude; fatuity; hebetation; hebetude; impercipience; inanity; insipience; moronity; obtusity; oscitancy; stupidness
   cause to appear: **v.** stultify; stultification
   person: **n.** Abderite; Boeotian; Juke; nincompoop

STUPOR: **n.** asphyxia; catalepsy; coma; hypnosis; insensibility; lethargy; narcosis; stupefaction; torpor; **a.** STUPOROUS: cataleptic; comatose; hypnotic; lethargic; stupefactive

STURDY (**see** "strong") **a.** lusty; roborant; robust(ious); stalwart; yeomanly

STY (*eye*): **n.** hordeolum

STYLE: **see** "fashion"
   high-flown: **n.** *un style ampoulé*
   imposing or impressive in: **see** "pretentious" **and** "showy"
   literary: **see under** "literary"
   passing out of: **a.** archaic; *démodé; fin-de-siècle;* obsolescent; *passé*

STYLISH: **a.** *à la mode; bon ton;* fashionable; jaunty; modish; *recherché; soigné(e);* well-groomed; **n.** STYLISHNESS: *bon ton; dernier cri;* fashionableness
   elegantly: **a.** *soigné;* (**fem.** *soignée*)

SUAVITY: **n.** amenity; diplomacy; unctuosity; urbanity; **a.** SUAVE: (**see** "oily") diplomatic; gracious; modish; oleaginous; politic; unctuous; urbane
   lack of: **n.** angularity; barbarism; insuavity; inurbanity; rusticity

SUBDUE: **v.** conquer; overwhelm; quash; subjugate; surmount; vanquish

SUBJECT(S): **v.** enthral(1); **n.** liege; propositus; *protégé;* subordinate; **a.** accountable; susceptible
   dealing w/ wide range of: **a.** polygraphic
   foreign to the: **see under** "foreign"
   on the same, or w/ single: **a.** monographic; **adv.** *in pari materia*

SUBJECTIVE: **a.** emotional; intellectual; pectoral; psychic; psychological; psychosomatic

SUBLIME: (**see** "supreme") **a.** eminent; empyreal; exalted; magnanimous; magnificent; majestic; transcendent; **n.** SUBLIMITY: eminence; exaltation; magnanimity; magnificence; majesty
   to ridiculous: **n.** bathos; anticlimax; **a.** bathetic; anticlimactic(al)

SUBMISSIVE: (**see** "subservient") **a.** amenable; deferential; genuflectory; humble; menial; obedient; penitent; slavish; tractable; yielding; **n.** SUBMISSIVENESS: acquiescence; amenability; deferentiality; genuflection; genuflexion; inertia; obsequiousness; obsequity; servility; tractability
   overly: **a.** cringing; deferential; fawn-

ing; humble; menial; obsequious; servile; slavish

SUBNORMAL: **a.** subminimal; suboptional; substandard

SUBORDINATE: (**see** "assistant") **n.** ancilla(ry); auxiliary; minion; parergon; *protégé;* satellite; subaltern(ant); subalternation; subalternity; subordination; subserviency; **a.** SUBORDINATE(D): ancillary; auxiliary; satellite; satellitic; secondary; servile; subalternate; submissive; subservient; tangential
loyal or hired: **see** "mercenary"
official: **n.** satrap
something which is: **n.** ancilla; parergon; (**pl.** parerga)

SUBSEQUENT: see "after"

SUBSERVIENT: (**see** "submissive") **a.** menial; ministerial; obeisant; subalternate; subordinate; subsidiary; truckling; unemancipated

SUBSIDIARY: (**see** "accessory") **a.** derivitive; segmental; segmentary; succursal; supplemental; tangential; tributary; **n.** assistant; tributary

SUBSTANCE: **n.** corporality; corporeity; essence; materiality; resource(s); substantia
give (substance) or substantive character to: **v.** substantify; **n.** substantification
having some (substance) or essence: **a.** coessential; consubstantial; **n.** consubstantiality
in the (substance) of the matter: **adv.** *in medias res*
lacking: (**see** "unreal") **a.** disembodied; insubstantial; **n.** disembodiment; insubstantiality
pert. to or having to do w/: **a.** hypostatic(al)

SUBSTANTIAL: **a.** abundant; corporeal; essential; formidable; fundamental; material; plenteous; plentiful; ponderable; substantious; **n.** SUBSTANTIALITY; corporeality; corporeity; materiality; physicality

SUBSTITUTE: **v.** commute; exchange; **n.** commutation; expedient; *faute de mieux;* Hobson's choice; *quid pro quo;* under-

study; **a.** SUBSTITUTED: substitutional; substitutionary; substitutive; succedaneous; **n.** SUBSTITUTION: exchange; surrogation; vicariousness
for another: **n.** *locum tenens;* succedaneum; surrogate

SUBTLE: **a.** alembicated; crafty; elusive; imperceptible; ingenious; insidious; intangible; skillful; sophisticated; wily

SUBURB(S): **n.** *banlieue(x)*; environ(s); *faubourg;* purlieu(s); suburbia
being in, or pert. to: **a.** suburbicarian
social life, manners, customs, etc. of: **n.** suburbia

SUCCESS, *accidental:* **n.** *succès de circonstance*
brilliant: **n.** éclat
due to scandalous conduct or by conn. w/ scandal: **n.** *succès de scandale*
extraordinary: **n.** *succès fou*
indifferent: **n.** *succès d'estime*

SUCCESSION: **n.** alternance; alternation; consecution; progression; sequacity; sequence; subsequence; **a.** SUCCESSIVE: alphabetical; categorical; consecutive; hereditary; repetitive; sequacious; seriate; (sub)sequential; succedent

SUCH *is life:* **adv.** *sic eunt fata hominum*

SUCKING: **a.** paratrophic
adapted for: **a.** suctorial
period of in young: **n.** lactation

SUDDEN: (**see** "abrupt") **a.** imminent; precipitate; subitaneous; **adv.** *à l'improviste*
change, movement or development: **n.** saltation
disappearance of symptoms: **n.** delitescence
stroke, political: **n.** *coup d'état*
utterance: **n.** ejaculation; exclamation; interjection

SUFFER: **v.** agonize; allow; brook; endure; experience; languish; permit; tolerate

SUFFERING: **n.** agony; languishment; resignation; tribulation
incapable of: **a.** impassible; **n.** impassibility
penitential: **n.** satispassion

place or state of: (**see** "hell") **n.** Gethsemane; inferno; purgatory

relieving or lessening: **v.** alleviate; palliate; **a.** alleviatory; palliatory

voluntary, as token of repentence: **n.** penance; satispassion

SUFFICIENT: (**see** "adequate") **a.** commensurate; equipollent; equiponderant; resourceful; **n.** SUFFICIENCY: **see** "adequacy"

to make: **v.** adequate; **a.** adequative; **n.** adequation; *quantum sufficit* (**abb.** q.s.)

SUFFOCATE: **v.** asphyxiate; **n.** asphyxiation

SUGAR, *producing or containing:* **a.** sacchariferous; saccharogenic

SUGGESTION: **n.** connotation; implication; innuendo; insinuation; insinuendo; overtone; **v.** SUGGEST: adumbrate; allude; connote; insinuate; intimate; prompt; **a.** SUGGESTIVE: connotative; insinuative; meaningful; provocative; reminiscent; *risqué;* seminal; significant

false: **n.** *suggestio falsi*

(trace) : **n.** *soupçon*

used to influence another: **n.** heterosuggestion

SUICIDE: **n.** *felo-de-se*

mania for: **n.** thantomania

SUITABLE: (**see** "pertinent" and "proper") **a.** adequate; appropriate; apropos; comely; comportable; condign; congruent; congruous; consonant; convenient; creditable; decorous; expedient; felicitous; idoneous; opportune; plausible; semblable; **n.** SUITABILITY: (**see** "fitness") appropriateness; aproposity; creditability; expediency; idoneity; plausibility; propriety

not: (**see** "improper") **adv.** *à propos de rien*

SULLEN: (**see** "stubborn") **a.** irascible; melancholy; morose; peevish; saturnine; splenetic; unsociable; **n.** SULLENNESS: (**see** "moody condition") irascibility; melancholy; moodiness; morosity; saturninity

SULTRY, *as of air:* **a.** miasmic; sulfurous; sulphurous

SUM: **n.** aggregate; complement; epitome; quantity; recapituation; result(ant); substance; summation

up: **v.** recapitulate; summarize; **a.** recapitulative; recapitulatory; summatory; **n.** recapitulation; summation

SUMMARIZE: **v.** epitomize; recapitulate; synopsize; **a.** recapitulative; recapitulatory; summarizable; summative; **n.** SUMMARY: abbreviation; abridgement; breviary; breviate; compendium; conspectus; epitome; pandect; *précis;* prospectus; recapitulation; *résumé;* schema; summarization; summation; syllabus; synopsis; truncation

SUMMER, *spend the:* **v.** estivate; **n.** estivation

SUMMIT: (**see** "acme") **n.** apogee; climax; consummation; crown; culmination; meridian; pinnacle; zenith

SUMMON: **v.** convene; convoke; muster; **n.** SUMMONING: convocation; evocation; invocation; muster

SUN, *at greatest distance fr. equator:* **n.** solstice (*Dec. and June*)

crosses equator: **n.** autumnal equinox (**Sept.**); vernal equinox (**Mar.**)

fear of or of sunlight: **n.** heliophobia

nothing new under: **n.** *nihil sub sole novi*

point most distant from: **n.** aphelion

point nearest to: **n.** perihelion

-stroke: **n.** calenture; *coup de soleil;* heliosis; siriasis

worship of: **n.** heliolatry

SUNBATHE: **v. or n.** apricate

SUNDAY: **see** "sabbath"

SUNLIGHT, *one sensitive to:* **n.** heliophobe; photophobe; **a.** heliophobic; photophobic; heliophobia; photophobia

treatment by: **n.** heliotherapy

SUNRISE (*or sunset*) *glow:* **n.** alpenglow

song: **n.** aubade

SUPERFICIAL: (**see** "shallow") **a.** casual; cursory; desultory; incondite; sophomoric; specious; tenuous; **n.** SUPERFICIALITY: inanity; speciosity; tenuosity; triviality

appearance: **n.** externality; (**pl.** superficies)

knowledge: **n.** sciolism; **a.** sciolistic; **n.** sciolist

SUPERFLUOUS: (see "extravagant") **a.** *de trop;* nonessential; prodigal; profuse; recrementious; recrementitious; redundant; superabundant; supernumerary; supererogatory; **n.** SUPERFLUITY: extravagance; prodigality; superabundance; supererogation; superfluity; superflux
do what is: pisces natare docere (to teach fishes to swim)

SUPERIOR: **a.** haughty; magisterial; magintrational; meritorious; palmy; paramount; predominant; preeminent; prepotent; supercilious; supereminent; supernal; supernatural; superordinary; superordinate; unsurpassed; **n. see** "superiority"
in rank: **n.** antecedence; precedence; seniority; unsurpassed; **a.** antecedent; precedent; superordinate
manner, in or w/ a: **a. or adv.** *de haut en bas;* **a.** supercilious
that which is: **n.** magnifico; *nec plus supra; nec plus ultra;* supereminence; supernaculum
to be: **v.** predominate; preponderate; **a.** paramount; predominant; supernal

SUPERIORITY: **n.** conspicuity; haughtiness; meliority; (pre)eminence; predominance; predomination; preponderance; preponderation; prominence; superciliousness; transcendence; worthiness
in race, culture, group, etc., belief in: **n.** chauvinism; ethnocentrism; sociocentrism
personal, belief or claim of intellectual or cultural: **n.** illuminism; illuminist

SUPERLATIVE: (see "choice" **and** "supreme") **a.** consummate; exaggerated; excessive; incomparable; peerless; pluperfect; prepotent; transcendent; **n.** supereminence; supernaculum

SUPERNATURAL: **a.** extraphysical; extrasensory; hyperphysical; incorporeal; metaphysical; miracular; miraculous; numinous; paraphysical; parapsychological; preternatural; psychic; superhuman; supermundane; transcendent(al); **n.** extraphysicality; incorporeality; incorporeity; supermundanity; transcendentality; transcendence
effects, etc.: **n.** phantasmagoria; **a.** phantasmagoric(al)
power, claimed: **n.** charism(a); **a.** charismatic
semi-: **a.** metempirical

study of the: **n.** metaphysics; parapsychology

SUPERSEDE: **see** "remove"

SUPERVISE: **v.** chaperone; invigilate; proctor; scrutinize; survey; **a.** SUPERVISORY: supervisorial; surveillant; **n.** SUPERVISOR: chaperone; director; proctor; superintendent; surveillant; **n.** SUPERVISION: chaperonage; invigilation; oversight; proctorship; superintendence; surveillance

SUPPLE: **a.** complacent; compliant; gracile; lissom(e); lithe(some); obsequious; submissive; **n.** SUPPLENESS: gracility; lissomeness

SUPPLEMENT: **n.** addendum; (**pl.** addenda); additament; postscript; **a.** SUPPLEMENTAL or SUPPLEMENTARY): (see "contributory") accessorial; accessory; addititious; adjuvant; adjunctive; adminicular; adscititious; ancillary; auxiliary; complemental; complementary; corollary; corroborative; succenturiate; supervenient; tangential
containing things passed over: **n.** paralipomena
containing data as basis for critical study: **n.** *apparatus criticus*

SUPPLICATION: (see "prayer") **n.** entreaty; obsecration; petition; rogation; solicitation

SUPPLY (or SUPPLIES), *abundant:* (see "abundance") **n.** affluence; copiosity; reservoir; spate
as for troops: **n.pl.** armamentaria; impedimenta; *matériel*
for journey or trip: **n.** viaticum

SUPPORT: **v.** abet; advocate; bolster; buttress; champion; corroborate; countenance; espouse; maintain; patronize; sanction; **n.** (see "assistance") abetment; adminicle; advocacy; alimentation; auxiliary; clientele; corroboration; patronage; sponsorship; sustentation; sustention; **a.** SUPPORTIVE (or SUPPORTING): adminicular; alimentative; auxiliary; corroborative; corroboratory; sustenacular; sustentative; tangential
for cause, etc.: **n.** advocacy; espousal; **v.** advocate; espouse
serving to: **a.** sustentacular

313

SUPPORTER: (see "follower") n. abettor; adherent; advocate; aficionado; (fem. aficionada); cohort; colleague; constituent; patron; votary
of unrighteous cause or course: n. *advocatus diaboli*

SUPPOSE: v. conceive; conjecture; divine; postulate; presume; speculate; surmise; theorize; a. SUPPOSED: academic; alleged; conjectural; deemed; hypothetical; presumptive; putative; reputed; suppositional; suppositi(ti)ous; suppositive; theoretic(al); adv. *ex hypothesi*

SUPPOSITION: n. assumption; conception; conjecturality; conjecture; divination; hypothesis; postulation; postulatum; speculation; surmise; theory
based on: a. hypothetical; supposititious; theoretic(al)
logical: n. hypothesis; philosophy; theory

SUPPRESS: v. annihilate; extinguish; inhibit; overpower; overwhelm; quash; quell; repress; subdue; a. SUPPRESSIVE: inhibitory; n. SUPPRESSION: inhibition; repression

SUPPRESSED *emotions, relief of by talking:* n. abreaction; catharsis

SUPREMACY: n. ascendancy; ascendency;; domination; dominion; eminence; precedence; preeminence; preeminency; preponderance; primacy; priority; sovereignty; suzerainty

SUPREME: (see "sublime") a. celestial; crucial; eminent; *hors concours;* inimitable; incomparable; matchless; nonpareil; olympian; outstanding; palmy; paramount; peerless; predominant; preeminent; preponderant; *sans pareil;* stellar; signal; significant; supereminent; superlative; sovereign; transcendent; vital
Being: n. *Ens Entium*
homage: n. latria
jurisdiction: n. *jus gladii* (right of the sword)

SURE: (see "certain") a. authentic; enduring; indubitable; ineluctable; inevitable; secure; unfaltering; adv. *à coup sûr;* n. SURENESS: (see "certainty") indubitability; ineluctability; inevitability

SURETY: n. adpromissor; assurance; certainty; guaranty; recognizance

SURFACE: n. exterior(ity); facet; periphery; veneer
feature(s): n. lineament(s); mien; topography
floating on the: a. supernatant
outer: n. externality; periphery; superficies

SURGICAL *removal:* n. ablation; abscission; enucleation; resection; v. ablate; abscise; enucleate; excise; resect
union, two hollow parts: n. anastomosis; a. anastomotic

SURLY: (see "sullen") a. acrimonious; boorish; churlish; crabbed; haughty; morose; sullen
person: n. curmudgeon

SURMISE: (see "suppose") v. conjecture; deduce; extrapolate; hypothesize; imagine; infer; theorize; n. conjecture; deduction; extrapolation; hypothesis; inference; peradventure; presumption; suspicion

SURNAME: n. cognomen(ation); *nom de famille;* patronym(ic); a. patronymic; surnominal

SURPASS: v. eclipse; preponderate; outstrip; overstep; surmount; transcend; n. preponderance; a. SURPASSING: excelling; preponderating; transcendent

SURPRISE: (see "astonish") v. amaze; astound; electrify; a. see "baffle"
attack or move: n. *coup d'état; coup de main*

SURRENDER: v. abandon; abnegate; capitulate; relinquish; n. abandonment; capitulation; cessation; compliance; dedition; resignation; a. capitulatory
one who does: n. capitulant; capitulator

SURROUNDING(S): n. alentours; ambient; circumfusion; circumjacencies; circumvention; confines; entourage; environment; environs; milieu; *mise-en-scène;* periphery; a. circumambient; circumferential; circumjacent; circumvallate; encapsulated; encompassing
in strange: a. *dépaysé*
space or area: n. environment; externality; periphery; (pl. environs)

SURVEY: **v.** appraise; estimate; evaluate; perlustrate; **n.** conspectus; examination; perlustration; prospectus; recension; reconnaissance; scrutiny; surveillance
comprehensive: **n.** panorama; **a.** panoramic

SURVIVAL: **n.** continuation; survivance
from another period: **n.** relict
incapable of: **a.** inviable; **n.** inviability

SURVIVE *or perish: aut vincere aut mori*

SUSCEPTIBLE: (**see** "sensitive") **a.** impressible; prone; tendentious; **n.** SUSCEPTIBILITY: impressibility; impressionability; predilection; sensitivity; tendentiousness

SUSPEND: **v.** adjourn; discontinue; intermit; interrupt; postpone; pretermit
indefinitely: **n.** *sine die*

SUSPENSION: **n.** abeyance; abeyancy; armistice; cessation; intermission; moratorium; pendulosity; pretermission
of activity or payment: **n.** armistice; moratorium

SUSPICIOUS: **a.** accusatory; distrustful; dubious; equivocal; incredulous; incriminatory; *louche;* querulant; querulent(ial); questionable; umbrageous; **n.** dubiety; incredulity; skepticism
person, pathologically: **n.** paranoi(a)c; paranoid; **a.** paranoid

SUSTAIN: **see** "support" **and** "prolong"; **n.** SUSTENANCE: (**see** "food") aliment(ation); nutriment; refreshments; **n.** SUSTENTION: maintenance; sustentation; **a.** SUSTAINING: sustentative; sustenacular

SWAGGER: **v.** hector; swashbuckle; **n.** arrogance; bravado; cockiness; fanfaronade; flamboyance; gasconade; panache; rodomontade; **n.** SWAGGERER: braggadocio; bravado; gasconade; rodomontade; swashbuckler; **a.** SWAGGERING: jaunty; swashbuckling

SWALLOWING, *act of:* **n.** deglutition; ingurgitation

SWAMP: **v.** deluge; engulf; inundate; overwhelm; **n.** morass; quagmire; slough;

a. SWAMPY: deluginous; fenny; paludal; paludous; palustral; uliginose
living or growing in (swamps): **a.** palustrine; uliginous

SWAN, *curved like neck of:* **a.** cygneous
song: **n.** *chant du cygne*

SWASTIKA: **n.** gammadion; gammation; hakenkreuz; tetraskelion; (**pl.** tetraskelia **or** tetraskelions)

SWAY: (**see** "hang **and** "influence") **n.** ascendency; dominance; dominion; oscillation; sovereignty
ability to: **n.** puissance

SWEAR: (**see** "curse") **v.** adjure; affirm; anathematize; asseverate; depone; depose; pledge; testify
falsely: **v.** perjure; **n.** perjury

SWEARING: **n.** adjuration; affirmation; asseveration; blasphemy; deposition; profanity; testimony
together: **n.** conjuration

SWEAT: **see** "perspire"

SWEEPING: **see** "absolute"

SWEET, *as innocent:* **a.** cherubic; engaging; personable; winsome
soft, as music: **a.** dolce; dolcissimo
soothing: **a.** dulcet
sugary: **a.** honeyed; nectareous; saccharine; treacly

SWEETHEART: **n.** *bonne amie;* chéri(e); dulcinea; inamorato; (**fem.** inamorata); valentine
country: **n.** amaryllis

SWEETNESS: **n.** amiability; saccharinity

SWELL: **v.** dilate; distend; inflate; intumesce; protrude; tumefy; **a. see** "swollen"

SWELLING: **n.** inflation; (in)tumescence; nodosity; protuberance; protuberation; tumefaction; tumidity; turgescence; turgor; undulation; **a.** nodal; nodose; nodular; overweening; tumefactive; (in)-tumescent; turgescent
as music: **n.** crescendo; undulation; **a.** undulatory; undulous
in volume: **a. or n.** crescendo

subsidence of: **n.** detumescence; deturgescence; **a.** detumescent; deturgescent

SWIFT: **a.** celeritous; expeditious; mercurial; meteoric; precipitous; quicksilver; summary; telegraphic; **n.** SWIFTNESS: acceleration; alacrity; celerity; expedition

SWIMMER, *girl or woman:* **n.** naiad
male or female: **n.** natator

SWIMMING: **a.** natant; natatory; **n.** natation
pert. to or adapted for: **a.** natatorial; natatory
pool, esp. inside: **n.** natatorium

SWINDLE: **see** "cheat"; **n.** SWINDLER: charlatan; *chevalier d'industrie;* cozener; embezzler; imposter; mountebank; quacksalver

SWINE, *pert. to:* **a.** porcine; suoid; swinish

SWING: **v.** fluctuate; oscillate; pendulate; suspend; undulate; **a.** fluctuating; oscillating; pedant; pendular; pendulous; undulating; **n.** SWINGING: oscillation; pendulation; pendulosity; undulation

SWOLLEN: **a.** bulbous; distended; dropsical; edematous; gravid; hypertrophied; incrassate; (in)tumescent; pompous; protuberant; tumefacient; tumefactive; tumid; turgescent; turgid

SWORD: **n.** cutlass; estoc; foil; rapier; saber
right of the: **n.** *jus gladii*
streamer or ribbon for: **n.** cicisbeo
trust not to a boy: ne puero gladium

SYLLABLE(S), *dropping of first:* **n.** aphaereasis; aph(a)eresis
dropping of last: **n.** apocopation; apocope; **v.** apocopate
dropping one or more sounds or letters from middle of word: **n.** syncope
having more than two: **a.** polysyllabic(al)
having one: **a.** monosyllabic(al)
last but one: **n.** penult(ima); **a.** penultimate
last but two: **n.** antepenult(ima); **a.** penultimate
short, pert. to or composed of: **a.** brachysyllabic(al)

to form or divide into: **v.** syllabify; **n.** syllabification
word of many: **n.** plurisyllable; polysyllable; sesquipedalian

SYMBOL(S): **n.** attribute; emblem; ensign; ideogram; logogram; **v.** SYMBOLIZE: allegorize; emblematize; typify; **n.** SYMBOLIZATION: typification
inspiring devotion: **n.** oriflamme
magical: **n.** pentacle; pentagram
mysterious: **n.** or **a.** hieroglyphic; **n.** mystique
science of: **n.** symbolics; symbology
used as word, as %: **n.** ideogram; logogram; **a.** ideogrammatic; ideogram(m)ic; logogrammatic
worship of: **n.** symbololatry

SYMBOLIC(AL): **a.** allegorical; emblematic(al); hieroglyphic; figurative; metaphoric(al); pathognomonic; representative; schematic
banner or standard: **n.** labrum
invested w/ (symbolical) significance: **a.** fetichistic

SYMPATHETIC: (**see** "kind") **a.** altruistic; compassionate; condolatory; congenial; empathetic; infectious; Samaritan; simpatico
relationship: **n.** empathy; *en rapport*

SYMPATHY: **n.** altropathy; altruism; benevolence; clemency; commiseration; compassion; condolence; empathy; tendresse
feeling of: **n.** compassion; empathy; identification; pathos; simpatico
in: (**see** "sympathetic") **a.** empath(et)ic; *en rapport*
lack of: **n.** antipathy; dyspathy; **a.** unsympathetic

SYMPHONY, *small or w/ fewer instruments:* **n.** sinfonietta

SYMPTOM(S): (**see** "clew") criterion; (**pl.** criteria); indication
comb. of, characteristic of disease or condition: **n.** syndrome
decline of, in disease: **n.** catastasis; lysis
pert. to: **a.** diagnostic; pathognomonic; semeiotic; symptomatic
sudden disappearance of: **n.** crisis; delitescence
warning: **n.** prodrome; **a.** prodromal

SYNONYMS, *express variously by means of:* v. synonymize; n. synonymization
list or study of: n. synonymicon; synonymics; synonymy
pert. to: a. synonymatic; synonymic; synonymous

SYNOPSIS: (see "summary") n. abridgement; epitome; v. SYNOPSIZE: (see "abbreviate") epitomize

SYSTEM: (see "organization") n. arrangement; economy; network; organism; regime(n); syntax
complete and orderly: n. cosmos

SYSTEMATIC: a. cosmic; methodical; orderly; regular; symmetrical; taxonomic(al)
in arrangement or construction: a. architectonic; n. regime(n)

T

TABLE *companion:* **n.** commensal
  good talker at (table philosopher): **n.**
deipnosophist
  pert. to or happening at: **a.** mensal
  talks, collection of: **n.** ana

TABOO (or TABU): **n.** convention; embargo; interdiction; prohibition; proscription; restraint; superstition; **a.** contraband; ineffable; inviolate; prohibited; proscribed; proscriptive

TACT: **n.** acumen; address; aptness; delicacy; delicatesse; diplomacy; discrimination; discernment; discretion; finesse; perspicacity; poise; prudence; refinement; *savoir-faire;* sensitivity; **a.** TACTFUL: adroit; consummate; diplomatic; discriminating; fitting; perspicacious; prudent; sensitive; suave

TACTLESS: **a.** gauche; impolite; impolitic; inapt; inconsiderate; indiscreet; inept; maladroit; undiplomatic; untactful; **n.** TACTLESSNESS: gaucheness; indiscretion; ineptitude; maladroitness
  act: **n.** gaucherie; indiscretion; ineptitude

TAIL: **n.** cauda; caudal appendage
  having or pert. to: **a.** caudal; caudate
  having long: **a.** macrurous
  having short: **a.** brevicaudate
  remove: **v.** decaudate
  shaped like: **a.** caudiform
  toward the: **a.** caudad

TAILLESS: **a.** acaudal; acaudate; anurous; ecaudate

TAILOR(S), *master:* **n.** *maestro-sastre*
  pert. to or to work of: **a.** sartorial

TAINT: **v.** contaminate; corrupt; debase; defile; deprave; pollute; tarnish; **n.** blemish; cloud; contamination; corruption; defilement; macula(tion); pollution; reproach; vitiation

TAKE *by force:* **v.** accroach; appropriate; assume; confiscate; sequester; usurp; **n.** appropriation; confiscation; sequestration; usurpation; **a.** confiscatory; usurpative; usurpatory
  by govt. action: **v.** appropriate; commandeer; confiscate; preempt; sequester; **n.** eminent domain; preemption; sequestration; **a.** confiscatory; preemptive
  for one's own: (**see** "steal") **v.** appropriate; embezzle; purloin; spheterize

TALE, *folk:* **n.** fabula; (**pl.** fabulae)
  unbelievable: **n.** Munchausenism

TALENT(S): **n.** accomplishment(s); adeptness; adroitness; aptitude; capacity; dexterity; endowment; expertise; genius; hability; ingeniosity; inventiveness; virtuosity
  comic: **n.** *vis comica*
  divine or supernatural: **n.** charism(a); **a.** charismatic

TALK: (**see** "speak" **and** "speech") **n.** articulation; babblement; colloquy; communication; confabulation; conversation; descant; discourse; discussion; lecture; palaver; parlance; **v.** articulate; communicate; confabulate; converse; descant; discourse; palaver
  and nothing else: vox et praeterea nihil
  boasting or blustering: **n.** bravado; gasconade; kompology
  by use of hands: **v.** gesticulate; **n.** dactylology; gesticulation; **a.** gesticulatory
  by use of one syllable: **n.** monosyllabicity; monosyllabism; **a.** monosyllabic(al)
  clever: **n.** asteism; banter; persiflage; witticism
  familiarly together: **v.** confabulate; **n.** confabulation
  idle: **n.** *caquet*
  inclined or liking to: (**see** "talkative") **a.** conversable; conversant
  indirect: **n.** ambage; circumlocution; **a.** ambagious; circuitous; circumlocutory
  informal, light: **n.** badinage; bavardage; causerie

informally: v. confabulate; n. confabulation

in sleep: (see under "sleep") n. somniloquy; n. somniloquist

intimate or private bet. two: n. tête-à-tête

loud: see under "loud"

mania for (talking): n. furor loquenti

meaningless or nonsense: n. Choctaw; galimatias; gibberish; stultiloquence; stultiloquy

meeting for: n. conversazione

not liking to: (see "silent") a. laconic; reticent; tactiturn; trenchant; n. obmutescent; reticence; tactiturnity

pert. to: a. colloquial; conversational; discursive

relieving emotions by: n. abreaction; catharsis; a. abreactive; cathartic

senseless or silly: see "meaningless" above

"small": n. asteism; badinage; causerie; persiflage

together: v. confabulate; n. confabulation; powwow

to oneself: n. monologue; soliloquy

　inaudible: n. endophasia

use of hands in (talking): see "by use of hands" above

TALKATIVE: (see "wordy") a. articulate; babblative; communicative; conversable; discursive; fluent; garrulous; logorrheic; (multi)loquacious; multiloquent; verbose; vocative; vociferous; voluble

person: n. blatherskite; popinjay

TALKATIVENESS: n. flux de bouche (or paroles); garrulity; garrulousness; loquaciousness; loquacity; multiloquence; volubility

abnormal: n. flux de bouche (or paroles); furor loquenti; logomania; logorrhea; verbomania

TALKER: n. colloquist; confabulator; conversationalist

fluent or witty: n. causeur; (fem. causeuse); raconteur; (fem. raconteuse)

TALL: a. altitudinous; statuesque; towering

TAME(D): a. amenable; benign(ant); cultivated; docile; domestic(ated); domitae naturae; tractable; n. TAMENESS: complaisance; docility; domesticality; domesticity; tractability; tractableness

TAMPER: v. manipulate; a. manipulable; manipulatory

TAN, *light:* a. café au lait

TANGIBLE: see "material"

TAPERING: a. acuminate; lanceolar; lanceolate(d)

TAR, *of or like:* a. piceous

TARDY: (see "slow") a. comatose; dilatory; lethargic; procrastinative; remiss

TARNISH: (see "darken") n. debasement; deterioration

on bronze or copper: n. aerugo; patina; verdigris

TASK: n. assignment; devoir; enterprise; onus; undertaking

insurmountable: n. pile Pelion on Ossa; a. Sisyphean

onerous, unpleasant or unavoidable: n. corvée

TASKMASTER, *cruel:* (see "disciplinarian") n. Simon Legree

TASTE: (see "appetite") n. degustation; inclination; penchant; predilection; preference; sapidity; v. degustate; a. TASTELESS: banal; inartistic; insipid; uninteresting; unleavened; unsavory; vapid; n. TASTELESSNESS: insipidity; a. TASTY (or TASTEFUL); (see "appetizing") (a)esthetic(al); artistic; discriminating

abnormal or perverted: n. allotriogeustia; allotriophagia; allotriophagy; geophagy; parageusia; pica

act or sense of: n. (de)gustation; a. gustatory

agreeable: see "appetizing"

bad: n. cacogeusia; mauvais goût; parageusia; a. egregious; execrable

blunting of: n. hypogeusia

everyone to own: chacun à son goût; de gustibus non est disputandum

increased sense of: n. hypergeusia; hypergeusesthesia

judge or arbiter of good: n. arbiter elegantiae (or elegantarum)

no accounting for: see "everyone to own" above

showing good: a. (a)esthetic(al); discriminating; n. (a)esthetics

person of low: **n.** groundling
pert. to: **a.** gustatory
pleasing to: **see** "appetizing"
testing by: **v.** degustate; **n.** degustation

TATTLETALE: **n.** quidnunc

TAUGHT, *capable of being:* **see** "teachable"

TAVERN: **see** "inn"

TAWDRY: **see** "cheap"

TAWNY: **a.** *café au lait;* fulvous

TAX, *poll:* **n.** capitation; **a.** capitation; *per capita*

TEACH: **v.** discipline; disseminate; educate; enlighten; exhort; exposit; expound; inculcate; indoctrinate; tutor; **a.** TEACHABLE: disciplined; docible; docile; educa(ta)ble; governable; instructible; manipul(at)able; tractable; **n.** docility; tractability
he who (teaches) learns: qui docet discit
not (teachable): **a.** indocile; intractable; uneduca(ta)ble; unteachable
things which injure (teach): quae nocent docent

TEACHER(S): **n.** didact; didacticist; docent; doctor; educator; guru; instructor; maestro; mentor; pedagog(ue); preceptor; scholastic
chief (headmaster): **n.** archididascalos; archididasculus; **a.** archididascalian; archididascaline
not on regular faculty: **n.** docent
pert. to or to teaching: **a.** didactic(al); educational; instructional; instructorial; pedagogic(al); preceptorial; professorial; propaedeutic(al); sermonic; tutelary; tutorial
who rules strictly: **n.** disciplinarian; pedantocrat; *precisian;* rigorist

TEACHING(S): **n.** didacticism; didactics; instruction; pedagogics; pedagogism; pedagogy; propaedeutics; tuition; tutelage
bad or perverse: **n.** cacodoxy; heterodoxy
college or univ.: **n.** professordom; professoriat(e)
pert. to: **see under** "teacher"
secret or abstruse: **n.pl.** acousmata; acroamatics; arcana; esoterica
theory or art of: **n.** didacticism; paedeutics; pedagogy
we learn by: docendo discimus

TEAR: **v.** dilacerate; disarticulate; discerp; disjoin; dismember; lacerate; lancinate; laniate; rupture; **n.** disarticulation; discerption; dismemberment; divulsion; laceration; rupture

TEARFUL: **a.** lachrymal; lachrymatory; lachrymose; maudlin; mawkish

TEARS, *burst into:* **n.** *fondre en larmes*

TEDIOUS: **see** "tiresome"
passage, as in a book, play or music: **n.** longueur

TEEM: **v.** burgeon; pullulate; **n.** burgeoning; pullulation

TEETH, *gnashing of (involuntary):* **n.** bruxomania
having: **a.** dentate; denticulate(d); denticular; dentulous
having large: **a.** macrodont;
having small: **a.** denticulate(d)
not having: **a.** edentate; edentulate; edentulous
speaking thru closed or partly closed: **n.** dentiloquy

TELL: **v.** acquaint; annunciate; articulate; asseverate; communicate; disclose; divulge; enunciate; narrate; unbosom
shudder to: horresco referens
too horrible to: **adv.** *horribile dictu*
wonderful to: **adv.** *mirable dictu*

TEMPER, *sharpness of:* **n.** acerbity; asperity; **a.** acerbic; asperous; vinegary

TEMPERAMENT: (**see** "humor") **n.** constitution; crasis; disposition; personality; propensity; **a.** TEMPERAMENTAL: capricious; mercurial; quicksilver; volatile; **n.** mercurality; quicksilver; volatility
steady in: **a.** equable; equanimous; phlegmatic; undemonstrative; **n.** composure; equability; equanimity; phlegm; *sang-froid*

TEMPERANCE: **n.** abnegation; mediocrity; moderation; restraint; self-control; sobriety; sophrosyne
a virtue is: est modus in rebus

TEMPERATE: (**see** "calm") **a.** abstemious; Apollonian; Apollon(ist)ic; continent; moderate; self-controlled; sober; **n.**

TEMPERATENESS: abstention; abstinence; moderation; sobriety

TEMPERATURE, *abnormally high body:* n. hyperpyrexia
    having equality of: a. isothermal; synthermal

TEMPORARY: (see "fleeting") a. *ad hoc; ad interim;* conditional; deciduous; ephemeral; ephemerous; episodic(al); evanescent; impermanent; interm(istic); mundane; provisional; temporal; tentative; topical; transient; transitory; transitional; adv. *ad hoc; ad interim; pro tem(pore)*; n. TEMPORARINESS: ephemerality; impermanence; impermanency; temporality; topicality
    agreement: n. *modus vivendi*
    delay: n. armistice; continuance; moratorium

TEMPTATION: n. allurement; enticement; seduction; v. TEMPT: allure; entice; persuade; provoke; seduce; a. TEMPTING: enticing; provocative; seductive; sirenic(al)
    susceptible to: a. gullible; peccable; seducible

TEN *persons, group of:* n. decemvir(ate)
    -sided: a. decagonal; n. decagon
    -thousand: n. millennium; myriad
    years, occurring every: a. or n. decennial
        period of: n. decade; decennary; decenniad; decennium; a. decennial

TENACIOUS: (see "stubborn") a. adhesive; cohesive; obstinate; retentive; viscous
    of purpose: n. tenacity; *tenax propositi*

TENDENCY: n. conatus; direction; disposition; inclination; nisus; predilection; (pre)disposition; proclivity; propensity; susceptibility; temperament; a. tendentious
    congenital or constitutional: n. diathesis; innate; predisposition; propensity
    natural: n. conatus; diathesis; nisus
    to act in opp. ways or directions: n. ambitendency; ambivalence; a. ambivalent

TENDER: (see "merciful") a. affectionate; benevolent; clement; compassionate; hyperalgesic; solicitous; sympathetic; adv. *amoroso; con amore*
    feeling: (see "sympathy") n. empathy; tendresse

to make: (see "soften") v. intenerate; tenderize

TENDERNESS, *as of skin:* n. hyperalgesia; hyperesthesia; a. hyperalgesic; hyperesthetic

TENDING *in favor of point of view:* (see "prejudiced") a. tendential; tendentious; n. predilection

TENSE: a. frenetic; hectic; high-strung; tonic

TENSION, *pert. to or characterized by:* a. tonic; n. tonicity
    state of: n. fanteeg; fantigue; tautness; tonicity

TENTH *anniversary:* n. decennial
    kill every (tenth): v. decimate; n. decimation

TERM(S): (see "name") n. condition; duration; semester; tenure
    idea w/o exact: n. anonym(e)
    in express: adv. *expressis verbis*
    list of: see under "word"
    technical, science of defining: n. orismology; a. orismological

TERMINAL (or TERMINATION): (see "conclusion" and "ending") a. ultimate

TERMINOLOGY: n. nomenclature; orismology; a. TERMINOLOGICAL: orismological

TERRIBLE: a. apocalytic(al); appalling; awesome; formidable; ghastly; horrific; portentious; redoubtable

TERRITORY: n. demesne; dominion; empire; imperium; jurisdiction; terrain; terrene; topography
    necessary for expansion, etc.: n. lebensraum
    not claimed by any nation: n. terra nullius
    within a territory: n. enclave; *imperium in imperio*

TERROR: n. apprehension; *bête noir;* bugbear; consternation; scourge; v. TERRIFY: affright; agrise; appal(l); petrify; a. TERRIFYING: Gorgonian; gorgonesque; hideous

TERSE: (see "concise") **a.** abbreviated; aphoristic; axiomatic; brachysyllabic; compact; compendious; epigrammatic(al); laconic(al); poignant; pointed; postulational; sententious; succinct; tacitean; telegrammatic; telegraphic; trenchant
   as in speaking: **a.** brachysyllabic; laconic(al); monoyllablic; succinct; **n.** monosyllabicity; monosyllabism

TEST(S): **n.** analysis; audition; criterion; (**pl.** criteria); norm; **a.** analytical
   of ability, imposed on inexperienced or ignorant: **n.** *pons asinorum*
    serving to: **a.** exploratory; probative; probatory; substantiating

TESTICLES, *removal of:* see "castrate"

TESTIFY: (see "swear") **v.** affirm; depone; depose; **n.** TESTIMONY: allegation; attestation; declaration; deposition; evidence

THANK *you:* **n.** *danke schön; gracias; merci*

THANKLESS: see "ungrateful"

THANKS *to God:* **n.** *Deo gratias*

THANKSGIVING, *hymn of:* **n.** doxology; magnificat; *te deum*

THAT *is:* **adv.** *id est* (**abb.** *i.e.*)
   is to say: **adv.** *c'est-à-dire*

THAT'S *war:* **adv.** *c'est la guerre*

THAW: **v.** deliquesce; **n.** deliquescence; **a.** deliquescent

THEATRE, *art of the:* **n.pl.** dramatics; histrionics; theatricals; theatrics

THEATRICAL: (see "showy") **a.** artificial; dramaturgic(al); histrionic; (melo)dramatic; meretricious; operatic; pompous; stag(e)y; thespian
   hit: **n.** *coup de théâtre*
   situation or effect: **n.pl.** histrionics; (melo)dramatics; theatricalities; theatrics; **n.** cabotinage; histrionism; sardoodledom; theatricality

THEFT: see "stealing"
   literary: **n.** piracy; plagiarism; **v.** plagiarize; **a.** piratical; plagiaristic

THEME, *dominant recurring:* **n.** leitmotif; leitmotiv
   having but one dominant: **a.** monothematic
   underlying, or symbolic meaning: **n.** mythos; (**pl.** mythoi)

THEMSELVES, *among or between:* **a.** or **adv.** *inter se*

THEORETIC(AL): (see "academic") **a.** conjectural; contemplative; fictitious; hypothetical; impractical; platonic; postulatory; presumptive; putative; quodlibetic(al); speculative; supposititious; suppositional; **adv.** *ex hypothesi;* **n.** THEORIST: doctrinaire; dogmatist; idealogist; idealogue; theoretician; theorician; visionary; **v.** THEORIZE: hypothesize; philosophize; postulate; speculate; **n.** THEORY: conjecture; doctrine; dogma; fundament; hypothesis; philosopheme; (pre)supposition; postulate; postulatum; speculation; surmise; (**pl.** postulata; theoretics)

THEY *say:* **adv.** *on-dit*

THICK: (see "stupid") **a.** coagulated; consolidated; inspissate(d)
   -skinned: **a.** callous; insensate; insensitive; pachydermatous

THICKET: **n.** boscage; chaparral; coppice; copse; covert

THIEF: **n.** burglar; depredator; embezzler; felon; larcener; larcenist; peculator; picaroon; pilferer; **a.** THIEVISH: burglarious; furtive; larcenous; mercurial; stealthy
   opportunity makes the: occasio facit furem

THIGH, *pert. to:* **a.** crural

THIN: **a.** attenuated; cadaverous; emaciated; macilent; malnourished; skeletal; skeletonic; tenuous; **n.** THINNESS: macilency; malnourishment; malnutrition; tenuity
   watery: **a.** ichorous

THING(S), *among other:* **adv.** *inter alia*
   belonging to no one: **n.** *res nullius*
   concerning all: de omnibus rebus
   done: **n.** *fait accompli; res geste*

regard as a: **v.** hypostatize; materialize; reify; **n.** hypostatization; reification

speaks for itself: **n.** *res ipsa loquitur*

to do (customary): **adv.** *de rigueur; en règle*

worthless: **n.** ambsace; flummadiddle; nihility

THINK: **v.** cerebrate; conceive; conceptualize; conjecture; contemplate; deliberate; (ex) cogitate; hypothesize; ideate; intellectualize; lucubrate; meditate; opine; ponder; rationalize; reflect; ruminate; speculate; **n. see** "thought"

beforehand: **v.** precogitate; premeditate; **a.** precognitive; premeditative

carefully: **v.** excogitate; **n.** excogitation

I (think) therefore I am: cogito ergo sum

inability to: **a.** incogitable; incogitative

that which does: **n.** *res cogitans*

THINKABLE: **a.** cogitable

THINKER: **n.** contemplater; philosopher; speculator; theorist

THINKING: (**see** "thought") **a.** cogitative; conceptualistic; contemplative; meditative; ruminant; ruminative

contrary to logic: **a.** alogical; dereistic; **n.** alogism; dereism

fallacy in: **n.** idolum; (**pl.** idola); illogicality; paradoxicality; *petitio principii*

due to human factors, as lang.: **n.pl.** idols of the forum; idols of the market

due to peculiarities and prejudices: **n.pl.** idols of the cave

false form of: **n.** idolum

place for: **n.** phrontistery

practical: **a.** Aristotelian; **n.** Aristotelianism

way of: **n.** ideology; philosophy

THINNER: **n.** solvent

THIRD, *also in rank, order or formation:* **a.** tertiary

day, every, or occurring every: **a.** tertian

party of ambiguous status: **n.** *tertium quid*

THIRST, *intense or excessive:* **n.** anadipsia; dipsomania; polydipsia

THIRTEEN, *morbid fear of number:* **n.** triadaidekaphobia

THORNY: **see** "spiny"

THOROUGHGOING: **see** "absolute" **and** "out-and-out"

THOROUGH(LY): **a.** complete; consummate; perscrutative; **adv.** *à fond; au pied de la lettre*

THOUGHT: (**see** "think") **n.** cerebration; cogitation; conception; conceptualization; consideration; contemplation; deliberation; ideation; intellection; lucubration; meditation; mentation; perception; ponderation; recollection; reflection; rumination; sentiment; speculation; supposition

absence or want of: **n.** incogitancy; **a.** incogitant; incogitative; unmindful

being lost in: (**see** "daydream") **n.** reverie

creative, capacity for: **n.** ideaphoria

expressed in lit. form: **n.** *pensée*

having appearance of deep: **a.** cogitabund

in deep: **a.** cogitabund; meditative; pensive

lost in: **a.** abstracted; bemused; **n.** abstraction; bemusement; reverie

one given to lofty: **a. or n.** altitudinarian

process of: (**see** "mental activity") **n.** mentation

"pure": **n.** noesis; **a.** noetic

rel. to: **a.** cogitative; contemplative; dianoetic; intellectual; meditative; ruminative

science or fundamental laws of: **n.** stoichiology

system or rules of: **n.** organon

transference of (claimed): **n.** telepathy; **a.** mentiferous; telepathic

THOUGHTFUL: (**see** "wise") **a.** calculative; circumspect; cogitative; considerate; contemplative; deliberative; engrossed; heedful; introspective; meditative; mindful; penetrating; pensive; philosophic(al); provident; prudent; reflective; sagacious; speculative; studious

THOUGHTLESS: **a.** abstracted; frivolous; hoity-toity; heedless; improvident; imprudent; inattentive; incogitable; incogitant; incogitative; inconsiderate; indeliberate; insensate; unmindful: **n.** THOUGHTLESSNESS: frivolity; improvidence; imprudence; incogitability;

incogitance; incogitancy
  act: étourderie; impropriety

THOUSAND, *or thousand years or anniversary:* **n.** chiliad; millennial; millenniary; millennium; **a.** millenarian; millenary
  years, pert. to: **a.** chiliadal; chiliastic; millenarian; millennial
  years, period of: **n.** chiliad; millenary; millennium

THOUSANDTH: **n. or a.** millesimal

THRASH: **v.** flog; flourish; lambaste; vanquish

THREAD, *like a:* **a.** capillaceous; capilliform; filamentous; filar
  of a novel, tune, etc.: **n.** leitmotif; leitmotiv
  suspended by, or strung upon a: **a.** filipendulous

THREADBARE: **a.** banal; deteriorated; hackneyed; jejune; stale; stereotyped; tatterdemalion; trite; vapid; **n.** banality; jejunity; vapidity

THREAT: **n.** anathema; commination; denunciation; minacity; sword of Damocles; **v.** THREATEN: comminate; hector; menace; portend
  by way of: **a. or adv.** *in terrorem*
  empty: **n.** *brutum fulmen*

THREATENING: (**see** "pressing") **a.** comminatory; denunciatory; fateful; imminent; inauspicious; menacing; minacious; minatorial; minatory; ominous; prognostic; portentous; sinister
  evil or harm: **a.** apocalyptic(al); ominous; portentous; sinister; sinistrous
  force: **n.** Four Horsemen (of the Apocalypse)

THREE: **see** "third"
  bet. or shared by: **adv.** *à trois*
  consisting of or based on: **a.** ternate; ternary
  corners or angles, having: **a.** triangular; trigonal; trigonous
  -fold: **a.** ternary; trinal; trinary; trinitarian; triple; **n. or v.** triplicate; **n.** triplication
  group or set of: **n.** ternion; triad; trilogy; trinity; trio; triplet; triplicity

household of, one the lover of one of spouses: **n.** *ménage à trois*
  hundred, anniv. or celebration: **n.** tercentenary; **a.** tercentenary; tercentennial
  liberal arts: **n.** trivium
  parts, divide into or having: **a.** trichotomic; trichotomous; tripartite; **n.** trichotomy; tripartition; triplex; **v.** trisect
  -sided: **a.** pyramidal; triangular; trilateral
  years, celebration or event, or period of: **n.** triennium
    happening every or lasting: **a.** triennial

THRESHOLD, *as of consciousness, pert. to:* **a.** liminal
  at the: **adv.** *in limine*
  below the: **a.** subliminal

THRIFT: **n.** conservation; economy; frugality; husbandry; parcity; providence; prudence; **a.** THRIFTY: frugal; provident; prudent; **a.** THRIFTLESS: (**see** "wasteful") improvident; imprudent; lavish; prodigal; **n.** improvidence; imprudence; prodigality

THRILL: **n.** enthrallment; frisson

THRIVE: **see** "flourish"

THROAT: **n.** gorge
  "lump in": **n.** *globus hystericus*

THROB: **v.** oscillate; palpitate; pulsate; undulate; **n.** ictus; oscillation; palmus; palpitation; pulsation; undulation; **a.** palpitant; pulsatile; pulsating; pulsatory

THRONG: **see** "multitude"

THROUGH *right and wrong: per fas et nefas*

THROUGHOUT: **adv.** completely; passim

"THROWBACK": **n.** atavism; mutation; **a.** atavistic

THRUST: **n.** intrusion
  verbal: **n.** repartee; ripost(e); *touché*

THRUSTING *away:* **n.** abstrusion

THUMB, *lacking a:* **a.** epollicate
  or its equivalent: **n.** pollex

THUNDER *and lightning, of or like:* **a.** fulmin(e)ous; tonitruant; sulfureous; sulphureous
　fear of: **n.** tonitruphobia

THUNDERING: **a.** foudroyant; fulminating; fulmin(e)ous; thunderous; tonitruant; tonitruous

THUS: **adv.** sic
　ever to tyrants (motto of Va.): *sic semper tyrannis*
　go to the fates of men: *sic enut fata hominum*
　passes the glory of the world: *sic transit gloria mundi*

THYROID *deficiency:* **n.** hypothyroidism; cretinism; myxedema

TICKET: **n.** *carte d'entrée;* voucher

TICKLE: **v.** provoke; stimulate; titillate; tit(t)ivate; **n.** titillation; tit(t)ivation

TIDBIT: **n.** *bonne bouche;* kickshaw; morceau; morsel

TIDY: (**see** "neat") **a.** *soigné(e)* ; spruce; **n.** nattiness

TIE: **n.** ligation; ligature; linchpin; nexus; stalemate

TIME(S), *arranged in order of:* **a.** calendric(al); chronological; **n.** chronology
　at same: **see under** "same"
　at the right: **adv.** *dextro tempore*
　at this or at present: **adv.** *hoc tempore; in praesenti*
　behind the: (**see** "old-fashioned") **a. or n.** ultraconservative
　being: **n.** nonce
　　for the: **adv.** *ad hoc; pro tempore*
　beyond: **a.** supertemporal
　computing by tree rings: **n.** dendrochronology
　duration, position or extension in: **n.** temporality
　error of: **see** "chronological error"
　extending over long period of: **a.** longitudinal; **n.** perpetuity
　flies: **n.** *hora fugit; tempus fugit*
　from olden: **adv.** *ab antiquo*
　gone by: **n.pl.** *tempi passati*
　lasting for long or indefinite: **a.** *ad infinitum;* aeonial; aeonian; aeonic
　measuring of: **n.** chronometry

　method of reckoning and measuring: **n.** chrononomy
　occurring at same: **see** "occurring" **and** "same"
　one must yield to the: *tempori parendum*
　parley so as to gain: **v.** temporize; **n.** temporization
　person or thing out of, or of historical order: **n.** anachronism; **a.** anachronistic
　place in definite (time)relation: **v.** temporalize
　reveals the truth: *veritatem dies asperit*
　uncovers all things: *tempus omnia revelat*
　unlimited: **n.** infinity; perpetuity; timelessness

TIMELESS: (**see** "everlasting") **a.** dateless; eternal; in perpetuity; intemporal; interminable; **n.** TIMELESSNESS: indefinitude; infinity; perpetuality; perpetuity

TIMELY: **a.** advantageous; apposite; appropriate; auspicious; expedient; opportune; propitious; providential; relevant; seasonable; tempestive

TIMEPIECE(S): **n:** chronometer; horologue; sundial
　dealer in: **n.** horologist
　description of, or art of making: **n.** horo(lo)graphy; horology
　water: **n.** clepsydra

TIMES, *one must yield to the:* *tempori parendum*

TIMID: **a.** cowardly; craven; effeminate; humble; irresolute; pavid; pusillanimous; timorous; tremulous; **n.** TIMIDITY: inferiority complex; pusillanimity
　make: **see** "intimidate"

TIN, *containing:* **a.** stanniferous
　pert. to: **a.** stannic; stannous

TINGE: **v.** affect; imbue; impregnate; tincture; **n. see** "shade"

TINGLE: **v.** stimulate; **n.** frisson

TINSEL: **n. or a.** clinquant

TINY: **see** "small"

TIP: **n.** baksheesh; doceur; gratuity; insinuation; lagniappe; perquisite; pourboire; terminus; trinkgeld

TIPPLER, *fellow:* **n.** compotator

TIRADE: **n.** fulmination; invective; philippic

TIRED: **see** "fatigued"

TIRELESS: **a.** indefatigable; sustained; unflagging; **n.** indefatigability

TIRESOME: (**see** "dull") **a.** bromidic; exhausting; monotonous; tedious; **n.** TIRESOMENESS: exhaustion; monotony

TITLE: (**see** "name") **n.** appellation; appellative; denomination; designation; honorific; ownership; rubric
    act of calling or addressing by: **n.** compellation
    bearing the, or in title only: **a.** titular(y); **n.** titularity
    evidence which defends: **n.** muniment
    transfer of: **v.** abalienate; convey; **n.** abalienation; conveyance

TO *be rather than to seem: esse quam videri*
    be sure: **adv.** *bien entendu*
    this extent: **adv.** *quod hoc*

TOASTMASTER: **n.** *arbiter bibendi;* ceremoniarius; officiator

TOBACCO *smoke, hater of:* **n.** misocapnist; **a.** misocapnic

TODAY *king, tomorrow nothing: aujourd'hui roi, demain rien*

TOE (**or** finger): **n.** dactyl; digit; phalanx
    like: **a.** digiform; digit; phalanx
    major or large: **n.** hallux

TOGETHER: **adv.** (con)jointly; mutually; *pari passu;* reciprocally; *tête-à-tête; vis-à-vis*
    all: (**see** "unanimous") **adv.** *en banc; en masse;* holus-bolus
    belonging or going: **a.** companionate
    coming: **n.** concourse; concursion; confluence; congress(ion); rapprochement; unanimity
    done or existing: (**see** "at same time") **a.** conjoined; conjoint; unanimous; unisonant; unisonous

TOGETHERNESS: **n.** concentricity; cooperation; mutuality; omneity; oneness; simultaneity; solidarity; unanimity

TOIL: **v. or n.** travail
    unending, pert. to: **a.** Sisyphean

TOKEN: **see** "symbol"

TOLERANT: (**see** "peaceable") **a.** agnostic(al); benign(ant); benevolent; broadminded; enduring; forbearing; indulgent; latitudinarian; magnanimous; placable; submissive; tractable; undogmatic; **n.** TOLERANCE (**or** TOLERATION): allowance; benevolence; fortitude; habituation; indulgence; *laissez faire;* latitudinarianism; license; magnanimity; stamina; sufferance

TOMB: **see** "grave"
    empty, as monument: **n.** cenotaph

TOMBOY: **n.** gamine; *garçon manqué;* hoyden; **a.** TOMBOYISH: gamine; hoydenish

TONE: **n.** accent; pitch; resiliency; timbre; tonicity; tonus
    high and thin (mus.): **a.** sfogato
    lack of muscular: **n.** hypokinesia; myasthenia; myatonia
    quality of: **n.** timbre; tonality
    vary in: **v.** modulate; **n.** modulability

TONGUE: (**see** "language") **n.** glossa; (**pl.** glossae)
    pert. to or produced by, as certain sounds: **a.** glossal; lingual
    shaped like: **a.** linguiform; lingulate
    slip of the: **n.** *lapsus linguae*
    speaking in unknown (tongues): **n.** glossolalia

TONIC: **n.** catalyst; fillip; roborant; **a.** bracing; invigorating; refreshing; roborant

TOO *much, or too many:* **a.** *de trop;* excessive; redundant; replete; superabundant; supererogatory; supernumerary

TOOLS, *ability to use:* **a.** chrestic
    and materials necessary to work: **n.** armentarium; (**pl.** armamentaria); *matériel*
    of another, willing and devoted: (**see** "mercenary") **n.** *âme damnée;* minion

TOOTH-*shaped:* **a.** dentate; denticulate(d); dentiform; serrate(d)

TOP: (see "apex") n. apogee; climax; consummation; crown; culmination; maximum; meridian; pinnacle; summit; zenith
pert. to: a. apical; cacuminal; cacuminous; climactic; consummate; meridian

TOPIC(S): n. gambit; theme (pl. themata); a. TOPICAL: current; thematic; timely
index of: n. *index rerum*

TORMENT: v. afflict; agonize; dragoon; excruciate; harrow; lacerate; persecute; plague; tantalize; n. affliction; agony; calamity; distress; (ex)cruciation; plague; persecution; purgatory; scourge; visitation
place or state of: (see "hell") n. golgotha; inferno

TORPID: a. apathetic; comatose; dormant; hypnotic; lackadaisical; lethargic; phlegmatic(al); pococurante; nonchalant; somnolent; stolid

TORTOISE: n. or a. chelonian; n. terrapin
pert. to or resembling: a. chelonian; testudinal; testudinarious
shell: n. carapace

TORTURE: see "torment"

TORTUOUS: see "devious"

TOSS *about:* v. or n. welter

TOTAL: (see "all" and "sum") a. absolute; out-and-out; summatory; thoroughgoing; utter; adv. *in toto; tout à fait;* n. aggregate; recapitulation; summarization; n. TOTALITY: entirety; integrality; omneity; mutuality; unanimity; universality
expression, as of work of art: n. *tout ensemble*

TOTTER: see "stagger"

TOUCH: n. (see "touching") modicum; palpation; scintilla; smattering; *soupçon;* tincture; trace; vestige
closely: v. impinge; osculate; a. osculant; n. impingement
diminished sense of: n. hypesthesia; a. hypesthetic
do not: noli me tangere
examine by: v. palpate; n. palpation

increased sense of: n. hyperesthesia; a. hyperesthetic
loss of power to recognize by: n. astereognosis
not perceivable by: a. impalpable
perceivable by or pert. to: a. palpable; tactic; tactile; tactual; tangible; n. palpability; tactility
up: v. adorn; embellish; ornament; refurbish

TOUCHING: a. attingent; concerning; co(n)terminous; contiguous; pathetic; tactual; tangent(ial); n. contact; contingence; continuity; palpation; tactation; taction; tangency
light on subject: a. lambent; tangential

TOUCHY: a. choleric; irascible; precarious

TOUGH: (see "stubborn") a. aggressive; crustaceous; forceful; hardy; inured; rowdyish; ruffianly; tenacious; threatening; n. TOUGHNESS: hardihood; tenacity

TOUR: n. circuit; excursion; expedition; itineration; peregrination; pilgrimage; promenade; safari

TOWERING: see "tall"

TOWN (*or city*): n. municipality
citizen of: n. burgher; oppidan; urbanite
officers: n.pl. *corps de ville*
pert. to: a. municipal; oppidan; urban(istic)

TOWNSMAN: n. burgher; oppidan; urbanite
characteristic of: a. bourgeois; urbanistic

TOY: v. philander; n. bauble; geegaw; kickshaw; knick-knack

TRACE: v. delineate; n. (see "touch") scintilla; vestige; vestigium; (pl. vestigia) a. delineative; vestigial
as of vestigial organ or part, or mark or sign of something that once existed: n. vestige; vestigium; a. vestigial

TRADE: v. barter; negotiate; traffic; n. clientele; commerce; commutation; merchandise; *métier;* occupation; patronage; profession; transaction

TRADITION : **n.** convention ; custom ; folk-lore ; **a.** TRADITIONAL : (**see** "conventional") ancestral ; characteristic ; customary ; legendary ; orthodox (ical) ; prescriptive ; tralatitious ; unwritten ; venerated ; veteran
   breaker of: **n.** iconoclast ; **a.** iconoclastic
   worship or veneration of, pert. to: **a.** filiopietistic

TRAGEDY, *muse of:* **n.** Melpomene
   pert. to or characteristic of: **a.** calamitous ; cothurnal ; tragic (al)

TRAGIC(AL) : **a.** calamitous ; deplorable ; lamentable ; woeful
   make: **v.** tragedize

TRAIT : (**see** "peculiarity") **n.** h(a)ecceitas ; h(a)ecceity ; particularity

TRAITOR : **n.** apostate ; Judas (Iscariot) ; Modred ; renegade ; tergiversator ; turncoat ; **a.** TRAITOROUS : (**see** "treacherous") faithless ; iscariotic (al) ; perfidious ; treasonable

TRANCE : **n.** coma ; hypnosis ; stupor
   of joy: **n.** ecstasy ; raptus

TRANSFORM : **v.** convert ; metamorphose ; renovate ; transfigure ; transmogrify ; transmutate ; transmute ; **a.** TRANSFORMATIVE ; permutative ; metamorphic ; metamorphous ; transmutative ; **n.** TRANSFORMATION : conversion ; metamorphosis ; permutation ; renovation ; transfiguration ; transmogrification ; transmutation

TRANSIENT : (**see** "fleeting") **a.** deciduous ; ephemeral ; ephemerous ; evanescent ; fugitive ; impermanent ; momentary ; preterient ; temporary ; transitory ; **n.** TRANSIENCY : ephemerality ; evanescence ; fugacity ; temporality ; transitoriness

TRANSIENTS : **n.pl.** flotsam and jetsam

TRANSITORY : (**see** "transient") **a.** evanescent ; transitional
   quality: **see** "transiency"

TRANSLATE *in letters or characters of another lang.:* **v.** transliterate ; **n.** metagraphy ; transliteration
   loosely: **v. or n.** paraphrase ; **a.** paraphrastic (al)

TRANSLATION : **n.** conversion ; rendition ; transformation ; transition ; transmutation

TRANSMIGRATION : **n.** metempsychosis ; reincarnation

TRANSMISSION : **n.** conductance ; conduction ; conveyance

TRANSPARENT : **a.** amorphous ; crystalline ; diaphanous ; hyaline ; intelligible ; limpid, luminous, pellucid ; perspicacious ; translucent ; transpicuous ; vitreous ; vitrescent ; **n.** TRANSPARENCY : (**see** "clearness") crystallinity ; diaphaneity ; limpidity ; perspicacity ; translucence ; translucency ; transpicuity ; vitrescence
   made so by wetting: **a.** hydrophanous

TRANSPLANTED *fr. native land or environment:* **a.** heterochthonous

TRANSPOSITION *of letters, words, etc., as in reading or writing:* **n.** metathesis ; strephosymbolia

TRAP : **v.** incarcerate ; **n.** incarceration ; inveiglement ; pitfall

TRASH : (**see** "refuse") **n.** balderdash ; debris ; detritus ; fatras ; flummaddiddle ; (**pl.** dejecta ; (r)ejectamanta) : **a.** TRASHY : **see** "cheap"

TRAVEL : (**see** "tour") **v.** itinerate ; journey ; peregrinate ; safari ; traverse ; **n.** excursion ; expedition ; itineration ; peregrination ; pilgrimage ; safari
   daily or regular: **v.** commute ; **n.** commutation
   expenses, also provisions: **n.** viaticum
   urge to: **n.** wanderlust

TRAVELER(S) : **n.** itinerant ; peregrinator ; viator ; wayfarer
   on particular quest: **n.** argonaut
   refuge for: (**see** "inn") **n.** caravansary ; hospice ; hostelry ; xenodochium

TRAVELING : **a.** ambulatory ; discursive ; errant ; itinerant ; locomotive ; nomadic ; perambulatory ; peripatetic ; portable
   companion: **n.** compagnon de voyage

TREACHERY : (**see** "treason") **n.** duplicity ; fides Punica (or Punica fides) (Punic faith) ; perfidy ; *tracasserie;* triplicity ; **a.** TREACHEROUS : arrant ; duplicitous; faithless; infamous; insidious; iscariotic(al); malignant; perfidious; Punic; rascally; traitorous; unscrupulous; venomous; viperish

TREASON: **n.** betrayal; duplicity; *lese majesty;* perfidy; prodition; treachery

TREASURE, *hidden:* **n.** cache
　up: **v.** thesaurize; **n.** thesaurization

TREASURER: **n.** bursar; chamberlain; exchequer; quaestor

TREAT: **v.** administer; negotiate; regale; **n.** (see "delicacy") *bonne bouche*
　difficult to (cure): **a.** intractable; irremediable; irreparable; refractory

TREATISE: see "essay"
　comprehensive: **n.** catholicon; encyclopedia
　covering entire subject. **n.** pandect
　explanatory: **n.** exegesis; **a.** exegetic(al)
　formal: **n.** disquisition
　further explanatory: **n.** epexegesis; **a.** epexegetic(al)
　on single subject: **n.** monograph
　rudimentary or basic: **n.** abecedarium; (**pl.** abecedaria); hornbook; primer

TREATMENT: (see "remedy") **n.** medicament(s); medication; therapeusis; therapeutics; therapy; **a.** therapeutic(al)
　grows worse w/ the: **adv:** *aegrescitque mendendo*
　one who administers: **n.** therapist
　science of: **n.** iatreusiology; iatrics; therapeutics; therapy

TREE(S), *culture of:* **n.** arboriculture; silviculture; sylviculture
　feeding on: **a.** dendrophagous
　growth or grove of: **n.** arboretum; boscage; copse
　like or pert. to: **a.** arboraceous; arboreal; arbor(e)ous; arborescent; arboresque; arboriform; dendriform; dendroid
　living in or on: **a.** arboreal; dendrophagous; dendrophilous
　place where grown: **n.** arboretum
　rings, computing time by: **n.** dendrochronology
　shaped like or resembling: **a.** arboriform; dendriform; dendroid
　study of: **n.** dendrology; silvics; silviculture; sylvics; **n.** dendrologist

TREMBLE: (**see** "throb") **v.** agitate; quaver; quiver; tremulate; vibrate; **a.** TREMBLING: quavering, tremorous; tremulous; **n.** agitation; tremblement; tremor; tremulation

TRENCH, *shallow:* **n.** scorbicula

TRESPASS: **v.** encroach; impinge; infringe; invade; **n.** encroachment; impingement; infringement; misfeasance; transgression; **n.** TRESPASSER: encroacher; misfeasor; transgressor

TRIAL: **n.** affliction; calvary; *crucis experimentum;* demonstration; endeavor; experiment; ordeal; tribulation; visitation
　-and-error method: **n.** empiricism; **a.** empiric; experimental; factual; observational
　by ordeal: **n.** *dei judicium*
　liable for or subject to: **a.** justiciable
　pert. to: **a.** empiric(al); judiciary

TRIANGULAR: **a.** deltoid(al); pyramidal

TRIBE, *as a center:* **n.** ethnocentrism; **a.** ethnocentric
　life of: **n.** tribalism
　subdivision of: **n.** clan; phratry; **a.** phratric

TRIBUTE: see "praise"

TRICK: (see "artifice") **v.** cajole; cozen; defraud; inveigle; manipulate; victimize; **n.** expedient; maneuver; manipulation; prestidigitation; stratagem; subterfuge; **n.** TRICKERY: (see "deception") artifice; charlatanry; chicanery; cozenage; defraudation; duplicity; escamotage; finesse; fourberie; hanky-panky; hocus-pocus; inveiglement; legerdemain; maneuver; montebankery; pettifoggery; phonus-bolonus; prestidigitation; roguishness; skullduggery; stratagem; subterfuge; subtlety; wile; **a.** TRICKY: (see "dishonest") artful; captious; circuitous; disingenuous; duplicitous; ingenious; ingenuous; insidious; intricate; stratagemic(al); subtle; tortuous; unreliable
　skillful: see **under** "skillful"

TRIFLE(S): (see "nothingness") **n.** bagatelle; bauble; flotsam and jetsam; flummadiddle; folderol; geegaw; inconsequence; inconsequentia; kickshaw; nihility; *nugae (canorae);* particle; *peu de*

chose; quelque-chose; triviality
silly: **n.** *niaiserie*
very great in: maximus in minimus

TRIFLER: **n.** boulevardier; *flaneur;* (**fem.** *flaneuse*)

TRIFLING: (**see** "trivial") **a.** banal; commonplace; contemptible; decipient; frivolous; hackneyed; immoment(ous); inconsequential; insignificant; namby-pamby; negligible; nugacious; nugatory; paltry; pettifogging; picayune; picayunish; puerile; ridiculous; trivial; wishy-washy; **n.** TRIFLINGNESS: desipience; desipiency; negligibility; triviality
point or particular: **n.** minutia; (**pl.** minutiae); nugacity; quiddity; subtlety; triviality; (**pl.** inconsequentia; trivia)

TRINKET(S): **n.** bagatelle; bauble; bibelot; bijou(terie); geegaw; kickshaw; *objet d'art; peu de chose; quelque-chose*

TRIP: (**see** "travel") **n.** expedition; peregrination; safari
record or outline of: **n.** itinerary

TRIPLE: **v.** triplicate; **a.** ternate; ternary; threefold; treble; trichotomus; trinal; trine; trinitarian

TRITE: (**see** "commonplace") **a.** banal; bromidic; hackneyed; pedestrian; platitudinous; stereotyped; stereotypical; threadbare; **n.** TRITENESS: banality; bathos; pedestrianism
saying: (**see under** "saying") **n.** banality; bromide; *cliché;* platitude; stereotype

TRIUMPH: **see** "conquest"

TRIUMPHANT: **a.** elated; exultant; jubilant; triumphal; victorious

TRIVIAL: (**see** "petty" **and** "trifling") **a.** inconsequential; inconsiderable; mediocre; nugacious; **n.** TRIVIALITY: banality; inconsequenticality; insignificality; nugacity; (**pl.** inconsequentia; marginalia; minutiae; trivia)

TROOPS, *science of moving, supplying and quartering:* **n.** logistics; **a.** logistic(al)

TROUBLE(S): **v.** discommode; perplex; **n.** adversity; annoyance; chagrin; coil; encumbrance; hindrance; obstruction; per-

plexity; uneasiness; vexation; **a.** TROUBLED: agitated; solicitous; stormy; troublous; turbulent; vexatious
harbinger of, or one fond of: **n.** stormy petrel
not worth the: non est tanti
prolific source of: **n.** Pandora's box

TROUBLESOME: (**see** "inconvenient") **a.** arduous; boisterous; discommodious; distressing; disturbing; Herculean; infestive; laborious; lamentable; obstreperous; pestiferous; pestilent(ial); recalcitrant; refractory; turbulent; unruly; vexatious
person: **n.** *enfant terrible;* stormy petrel

TRUE: (**see** "truth") **a.** accurate; inherent; intrinsic; legitimate; official; orthodox; unassailable; unfeigned; veracious; veritable
accept as: **v.** nostrificate; **n.** fideism
considered as (not denied or proved otherwise): **a. or adv.** *pro confesso*
necessarily: **a.** apodictic(al); indisputable

TRUISM: (**see** "maxim") **n.** axiom; banality; bromide; *cliché;* platitude; postulate

TRUST: (**see** "confidence") **n.** assurance; credence; dependence; reliance; monopoly
betrayal of: **n.** duplicity; perfidy; traitorism; **a.** duplicitous; perfidious; traitorous
breach of: **n.** *trahison des clercs*
implicit: **n.** *uberrima fides*
not overmuch to appearance: nimium ne credi colori
not the face: ne fronti credi

TRUSTWORTHY: **see** "dependable"

TRUTH: (**see** "certainty") **n.** accuracy; actuality; certitude; fidelity; precision; probity; veracity; verisimilitude; verity; (**pl.** verities); *vraisemblance;* **a.** TRUTHFUL: accurate; candid; sincere; trustworthy; veracious; veridical; **n.** TRUTHFULNESS: accuracy; veracity; vericacity; veridicality
according to: **adv.** *secundum veritatem*
conquers: veritas vincit
conquers all things: vincit omnia veritas
denial of any basis for: **n.** nihilism; **a.** nihilistic
departing fr.: **a.** (ab)errant; aberrational; aberrative; **n.** aberrance; abberation; inveracity

engenders hatred: veritas odium parit
eternal (truths): **n.pl.** (the) eternities; (the) verities
having appearance of: **a.** verisimilar; verisimilous; **n.** verisimilarity; verisimilitude
in: **adv.** *en vérité*
in wine (when intoxicated): in vino veritas
lover of: **n.** philalethist
naked: **n.** *nuda veritas*
nothing is so lovely as: rien n'est plus beau que le vrai
of or pert. to: **a.** alethic; gnomic; veracious
suppression of: **n.** *suppressio veri*
w/o fear: vérité sans peur

TRY: (**see** "endeavor") **v.** essay; **a.** TRYING: annoying; arduous; exacting; irritating; rigorous; strenuous
anything once: ein mal, kein mal

TUBERCULOSIS, *pulmonary:* **n.** phthisis; **a.** phthisic(al); tubercular; tuberculous

TUFTED: **a.** cespitose; comose

TUMOR: see "growth"

TUMULT: (**see** "commotion") **n.** agitation; Babelism; bouleversement; brouhaha; disturbance; paroxysm; rabblement; *Sturm und Drang;* welter; **a.** TUMULTUOUS: see "turbulent"

TUNE: **v.** syntonize; **n.** intonation; melisma; sonance; syntonization; **a.** TUNEFUL: (**see** "melodious") chantant
in: **a.** assonant; *d'accord; en rapport;* harmonious; homophonous; melodious; rhythmic(al); symphonious; syntonic; syntonous; unisonant
out of: **a.** absonant; asynchronistic; asynchronous; cacophonous; discordant; disharmonious; dissonant; inharmonious; unharmonious

TURBULENT: (**see** "noisy") **a.** termagant; tumultuous

TURMOIL: (**see** "commotion" **and** "tumult") **n.** *Sturm und Drang*

TURN: (**see** "rotate") **v.** gyrate; pirouette; slue

TURNING: **n.** about-face; flexure; gyration; reversal; *volte-face;* **a.** flexuous; serpentine

aside: **n.** declination; deflection; deviation; divergence; ricochet; veering; **a.** declinatory; divergent
involved or marked by: **a.** rotary; vertiginous
point: **n.** climax; crisis; fulcrum

TURNED *up, as a nose:* **a.** retroussé; **n.** *nez retroussé*

TURTLE: **n. or a.** chelonian
shell: **n.** carapace

TWELFTH: **a.** duodecimal

TWELVE, *based on number:* **a.** duodenary
occurring once in 12 years: **a.** duodecennial
pert. to: **a.** duodecimal; duodenary

TWILIGHT: **n.** crepuscule
pert. to or appearing at: **a.** crepuscular; vespertilian; vespertine

TWIN(S): **n.** *alter ego;* counterpart; sibling(s); **a.** binary; didymous; dioscuric; duplicate; dyadic; gemel; jumelle; parallel
-like: **a.** bigeminal
product of one ovum: **n. or a.** enzymotic; identical; monovular
product of two ova: **n. or a.** biovular; dizygotic; fraternal

TWINKLING: **a.** scintillating; scintillescent; **n.** scintillization; **v.** TWINKLE: scintillate
of an eye: **n.** *clin d'oeil*

TWIRL (or TWIST): **v.** contort; gyrate; gnarl; intort; vertiginate; **n.** convolution; sinuosity; tortuosity; twistification; **a.** (con)volute; intorted; meandering serpentine; sinuous; tortile; tortuous; vertiginous

TWITCH: **v.** vellicate; **n.** fasciculation; tic; vellication

TWO, *between:* **a.** *à deux*
consisting of: **a.** duel(istic)
conversation by: **n.** duologue
divide into: **v.** bifurcate; bisect; dichotomize; halve; **a.** bifurcate(d); bipartient; bipartisan; bipartite; bisected; dichotomic; dichotomous; distichous; **n.** bifurcation; dichotomy; diremption
-faced: (**see** "double-dealing") **a.** duplicitous; Janus-faced; Janus-like

-fold: **a.** bigeminal; binal; binary; bipartisan; bipartite; didymous; duplicate(d); twifold; **n.** duality; duplexity; duplicity

govt. by: **n.** diarchy; diumvirate; duumvirate; dyarchy

having (two) lives, natures, positions, qualities, etc.: **a.** amphibian; amphibious

having (two) shapes or bodies: **a.** twiformed

heads better than one: due teste valgano più che una sola, nemo solus satis sapit

-hoofed: **a.** bifid; bisulcate; **n.** bifidity

insanity of (two, as hus. and wife): **n.** *folie à deux*

parties, shared by: **a.** bilateral; bipartisan; bipartite; **n.** bipartisanism; bipartisanship

parts, divided into or having: **see** "divide into" **above**

position held jointly by: **n.** diumvirate; duumvirate; **n.** duumvir

-sided: **a.** bilateral; bipartisan; syngal-(l)agamatic; **n.** bilaterality; duality

-toned or colored: **a.** dichromatic

units regarded as one: **n.** dyad; **a.** dyadic

TYPE: (**see** "model") **n.** description; exemplar; exemplum; ilk; kidney; nature; representation; species; stripe

conforming to: **see** "rule" **and** "typical"

perfect: **n.** *beau idéal; nec plus supra*

to act as: **v.** exemplify; typify; **n.** exemplification; typification

TYPICAL: **a.** classic; emblematic; exemplary; prefigurative; quintessential; symbolic(al); typic; **n.** TYPICALITY: exemplarity; quintessentiality; typification

TYRANNY: **n.** absolutism; autocracy; despotism; oppression; **a.** TYRANNOUS: **see** "oppressive"

TYRANT(S): (**see** "dictator") **n.** autocrat; commissar; despot; martinet

petty: **n.** martinet; satrap

thus ever to (motto of Va.): **sic semper tyrannis**

U

UGLY: (see "unappealing") **a.** inaesthetic; unbeautious; uncomely; uncosmeticised
something which is: **n.** hideosity
to make: **v.** plebify; uglify; **n.** plebification; uglification

ULTERIOR: **a.** latent; remote
motive: **n.** *arrière pensée*

UNABRIDGED: **a.** comprehensive; cyclopedic(al); *in extenso;* unexpurgated

UNAFRAID: (see "bold") **a.** unapprehensive

UNADULTERATED: (see "pure") **a.** simon-pure

UNALTERABLE: see "unchangeable"

UNANIMOUS: **a.** concordant; consentient; harmonious; unisonant; unisonous; **adv.** UNANIMOUSLY: *nemine contradicente* (**abb.** nem con.); *nemine dissentiente; una voce; unanime;* **n.** UNANIMITY: concordance; consension; consentience; harmony

UNAPPEALING: (see "ugly") **a.** impersonable; inaesthetic; insipid; somber; subfusc(ous); unbeauteous

UNAPPEASABLE: see "appeased, incapable of being"

UNATTACHED: (see "isolated") **a.** celibate; discrete; uncommitted.
to any party or faction: **n.** or **a.** maverick; recalcitrant

UNATTAINABLE *goal, seemingly or nearly so:* **n.** ultima Thule

UNATTEMPTED: (see "untried") **a.** unessayed; untested

UNATTRACTIVE: see "unappealing"

UNAUTHORIZED: (see "unofficial") **a.** apocryphal; contraband; counterfeit; illegal; proscriptive; spurious; unapproved; unauthoritative; unsanctioned

UNAVOIDABLE: (see "certain") **a.** accidental; indubitable; inevitable; unpremeditated
accident: **n.** act of God; *casus fortitus; force majeure; vis major*

UNAWARE: **a.** incognizant; nescient; oblivious; unconscious; **n.** UNAWARENESS: incognizance; incognoscibility

UNBALANCE: **n.** astasia; disequilibration; disequilibrium; imbalance; instability

UNBEARABLE: see "unendurable"

UNBEATABLE: (see "unconquerable") **a.** invincible; unexcelled; unsurpassable

UNBECOMING: **a.** demeritorious; dishonorable; disreputable; immodest; impertinent; improper; inappropriate; incongruous; indecent; indecorous; unseemly; unsuitable; untoward

UNBELIEVABLE: **a.** improbable; incredible; incredulous; preposterous; prodigious; **adv.** *ab absurdo;* **n.** incredibility

UNBELIEVER: (see "disbeliever" **and** "heretic") **n.** atheist; latitudinarian; miscreant; nihilist; skeptic; **a.** UNBELIEVING: aporetic; heretical; heterodox; incredulous; skeptical; unorthodox

UNBEND: **v.** condescend; slacken; vouchsafe
on occasion, to: desipere in loco

UNBRANDED: **a.** or **n.** maverick

UNBREAKABLE: **a.** adamant(ine); immarcescible (**or** immarcescible); immutable; imperishable; indestructible; infrangible; inviolable; inviolate; invulnerable; irrefragable

335

UNBRIDLED: (see "unrestrained") a. crapulous; incontinent; intemperate; rampageous; rampant; unchecked; ungoverned

UNBROKEN: a. contiguous; continuous; intact; inviolate(d); uninterrupted; unsubsided; unsubdued; untamed; n. contiguity; continuity
series or succession: n. continuity; continuum

UNCALLED *for:* (see "unbecoming") a. gratuitous; impertinent; inappropriate; indecorous; unmerited; unnecessary; unseemly; n. impertinency; impropriety; indecorousness; indecorum; unseemliness

UNCERTAIN: (see "vague") a. *ambigendi locus;* ambiguous; ambivalent; amphibolic; contingent; dubious; dubitable; enigmatical; equivocal; flickering; impredictable; improbable; inconclusive; indefinite; indefinitive; irregular; nebulous; penumbral; precarious; problematic(al); questionable; unformalized; unmathematical; vacillary; variable; visionary
middle ground: n. penumbra

UNCERTAINTY: (see "doubt") n. ambiguity; ambivalence; dubiety; dubiosity; dubitation; fluctuation; incertitude; indefinability; indefinitude; indetermination; inexactitude; precariousness; skepticism
of meaning: n. ambiguity; amphibologism; a. ambiguous; amphibolic(al); amphibolous
of occurrence: n. contingency; fortuitousness; fortuity; a. contingent; fortuitous
state of being in: n. (horns of a) dilemma; predicament; quandary; a. dilemmatic; predicamental
state of, as to whether thing is true: n. dubiosity; *non liquet*

UNCHANGEABLE: (see "absolute", "fixed" and "stubborn") a. adamant(ine); immutable; implacable; imprescriptible; inalienable; incommutable; inconvertible; indomitable; inexorable; intractable; invariable; irreversible; irrevocable; monolithic; permanent; unalterable; a. UNCHANGED: intact; pristine; sedentary; sessile; static; stationary; unaltered; unexpurgated; unretouched; n. staticism; *status quo*

UNCHANGING: (see "fixed" and "eternal") a. changeless; consistent; constant;

immarcescible; indomitable; intractable; invariable; static

UNCHECKED: (see "unrestrained") a. unextirpated

UNCIVILIZED: a. barbaric; barbarous; discourteous; *ferae naturae;* feral; Gothic; inhuman; primitive; savage; uncultivated; uncultured; n. barbarity; ferity; inhumanity; primitivity

UNCLASSIFIABLE: a. acategorical; amorphous; heterogeneous

UNCLE, *pert. to maternal:* a. avunculocal
pert. to or like: a. avuncular; n. avuncularity

UNCLEANLINESS: n. acatharsia; feculence; immundity; maculacy; squalor; a. UNCLEAN: (see "dirty" and "filthy") excrementious; immund; impure; maculate(d); putrid
abnormal attraction to: n. mysophilia
abnormal fear of or distaste for: n. mysophobia

UNCLEAR: see "ambiguous" and "vague"

UNCOMMON: (see "rare") a. exceptional; outstanding; *recherché*

UNCOMMUNICATIVE: a. laconic; obmutescent; reserved; reticent; tactiturn; n. obmutescence; reticence; taciturnity

UNCOMPLIMENTARY: a. antagonistic; derogatory; disparaging; dyslogistic

UNCOMPROMISING: a. inflexible; intractable; intransigent; recalcitrant; unyielding; n. intransigence; recalcitrance

UNCONCERN: (see "apathy" and "indifference") n. insouciance; nonchalance; a. UNCONCERNED: (see "apathetic" and "calm") indifferent; insouciant; lackadaisical; phlegmatic; pococurante; unsolicitous

UNCONDITIONAL: (see "absolute") a. plenary; n. unconditionality

UNCONFORMING: *see* "unconventional"

UNCONGENIAL: a. asocial; discordant; incompatible; incongruous; inharmonious;

ungregarious; unsociable; **n.** UNCON-GENIALITY: asocialism; asociality; incompatibility; unsociability

UNCONQUERABLE: **a.** Achillean; impregnable; indefeasible; indomitable; inexpugnable; insurmountable; intractable; invincible; invulnerable; irrepressible; undefeatable; unsurpassable; unswerving; unyielding; **n.** UNCONQUERABILITY: impregnability; indomitability; inexpugnability; invincibility; invulnerability

UNCONSCIOUS: (see "unaware") **a.** comatose; insensible; **n.** UNCONSCIOUSNESS: coma; insensibility; narcosis

UNCONTROLLED: (see "unbridled" **and** "unrestrained") **a.** irrepressible; rampant; unbounded; unchecked; ungoverned; **n.** rampancy; unrestraint

UNCONVENTIONAL: **a.** Bohemian; *dégagé; eccentric;* heretical; heterodox; *outré;* uncultured; unorthodox; **n.** UNCONVENTIONALITY: Bohemianism; heterodoxy; unorthodoxy
　　action or behavior: **n.** heresy; heterodoxy; solecism; transgression
　　person: **see under** "person"

UNCOOKED: **adv.** *au naturel*

UNCOUTH: (see "rude") **a.** agrestic; baboonish; barbarous; clownish; incondite; indecorous; plebeian; provincial; rustic; unbeseeming; unchivalrous; uncourtly; uncultivated; **n.** babbittry; baboonery; indecorum; rusticity

UNCOVERED: **see** "naked"
　　(*unroofed*): **a.** *al fresco;* hypaethral; upaithric

UNCULTIVATED: **see** "uncouth"

UNDAMAGED: (see "whole") **a.** unscarred; unscathed

UNDAUNTED: **a.** undiscouraged; undismayed

UNDECEIVE: **v.** disabuse

UNDECIDED: **a.** abeyant; ambivalent; inconstant; irresolute; pendant; pendent; pending; under advisement; undetermined;

unresolved; unsettled; vacillating; volatile; wavering

UNDEFILED: (see "pure") **a.** immaculate; intemerate; inviolate; uncorrupted; unpolluted; unstained; untainted

UNDEMONSTRABLE (or UNDEMONSTRATIVE): (see "indifferent") **a.** anapodictic; apathetic; laconic(al); nonchalant; phlegmatic; phlegmatous; reserved; restrained; stoic(al); stolid

UNDENIABLE: **a.** incontestable; incontrovertible; indisputable; indubitable; unquestionable; **n.** indisputability; indubitability

UNDER: **adv.** inferior; nether; subalternate; subjacent; subordinate; substrative
　　state of being: **n.** inferior; infraposition; subalternity; subordination
　　to place (under or beneath): **v.** infrapose; infraposition

UNDERGROUND: **a.** submundane; subterranean; subterrestrial
　　pert. to: **a.** chthonian; subterranean

UNDERHAND: **a.** chicane; clandestine; devious; disingenuous; duplicitous; furtive; huggermugger; Machiavellian; oblique; sinister; stealthy; surreptitious; wily; **n.** UNDERHANDEDNESS: chicanery; clandestinity; duplicity; sinisterity; stealth; surreption

UNDERLYING: **a.** fundamental; implicit; subjacent; substantive; substratal; substrative; subtending; **n. see** "base"

UNDERSTAND, *ability to:* **n.** acumen; comprehensibility; impenetrability; perspicacity
　　difficult to: **a.** abstruse; impalpable; impenetrable; inscrutable; obscure; opaque; recondite; tenebrific; tenebrous; tenuous; unfathomable; **n.** abstrusity; impenetrability; opacity; tenebrosity; (**pl.** impalpables)
　　easy to: **a.** limpid; perspicacious; translucent
　　one who does: **n.** appercipient

UNDERSTANDABLE: **see** "clear"

UNDERSTANDING: (see "insight" **and** "reason") **n.** apperception; apprehension;

discernment; empathy; entente; implication; intelligence; intuition; perception; perspicacity; signification; **a.** apperceptive; appercipient; empathetic; empathic; intuitive; sympathetic
beyond ordinary: **a.** abstruse; arcane; cabalistic; recondite; profound; **n.** abstruseness; abstrusity; profundity
exercising or implying: **a.** intelligential
friendly: **n.** *entente cordiale*
lack of: **n.** anoesia; anoesis; incomprehensibility; incomprehension; **a.** anoetic
science or study of: **n.** noology
slow in: (**see** "stupid") **a.** astigmatic(al); pedestrian; purblind
where not specifically expressed: **n.** subaudition; subintelligitur

UNDERSTATEMENT: **n.** litotes; meiosis

UNDERSTOOD: **a.** assumed; connotative; implicate; implicit; implied; tacit
by intuition: **a.** intuitive; noumenal; **n.** noumenon
capable of being: (**see** "clear") **a.** comprehensive; exoteric; intelligible; limpid; **n.** comprehensibility; intelligibility
condemn what is not: damnat quod non intelligunt
not capable of being: (**see** "vague") **a.** impenetrable; incomprehensible; indecipherable; inscrutable; undecipherable; unfathomable; unintelligible
well: **adv.** *bien entendu*

UNDERTONE, *in an:* **a. or adv.** *sotto voce*

UNDERVALUE: **v.** depreciate; misprize

UNDERWORLD, *pert. to:* **a.** chthonian; plutonian; plutonic; subterranean

UNDESERVED (or UNDESERVING: (**see** "unworthy") **a.** unearned; unjustified; unmerited; unwarranted

UNDESIRABLE: **a.** egregious; flagrant; inappropriate; inexpedient; inopportune; objectionable; unenviable
highly: **a.** cancerous; leprous; malignant; sarcomatous; scabrous

UNDETERMINED: **see** "unfathomed"

UNDEVELOPED: (**see** "crude") **a.** embryonic; immature; incipient; latent; nascent; primitive; primordial; quiescent; rudimentary; vestigial

UNDIGNIFIED: **a.** *infra dignitatem* (**abb.** infra dig.)

UNDIPLOMATIC: **see** "tactless"

UNDISCIPLINED: (**see** "aimless" **and** "unrestrained") **a.** haphazard; tumultuary

UNDISCOURAGED: **see** "undaunted"

UNDISCLOSED *thought or intention:* **n.** *arrière pensée*

UNDIVIDED: (**see** "whole") **a.** impartible; imparticipable; impartite

UNDOING: (**see** "ruin") **n.** defeasance; destruction; labefaction

UNDOUBTED: **see** "unquestionable"

UNDRESSED, *partly:* **a.** deshabille; dishabille; *en déshabilé*

UNDULY: **adv.** excessively; overweening

UNDYING: (**see** "permanent") **a.** amaranthine; immarcescible; immarcessible; immortal; immutable; indestructible; perpetual

UNEARTHLY: (**see** "heavenly") **a.** miraculous; preternatural; supernatural; unworldly

UNEASINESS: (**see** "anxiety") **n.** agitation; compunction; disquiet(ude); dyspathy; dysphoria; inquietude; instability; malaise; penitence; queasiness; remorse; restlessness; scruple; **a.** UNEASY: (**see** "restless") dysphoric; erethic; **adv.** *gêné*
mental: **n.** psychalgia
physical: **n.** dysphoria; malaise

UNEDUCATED: **see** "ignorant" **and** "illiterate"

UNEMOTIONAL: **see** "calm"

UNEMPLOYED: **see** "idle"

UNENDURABLE: **a.** insufferable; insupportable; intolerable; unbearable; unbrookable; **a.** UNENDURING: (**see** "transient") caducous; deciduous; ephemeral; transitory

UNENFORCEABLE *agreement or pact:* **n.** *nudum pactum*

UNENLIGHTENED: (see "ignorant") **a.** benighted; uninformed; uninstructed

UNEQUAL: (see "unjust") **a.** disparate; disproportionate; dissimilar; inadequate; incommensurate; inegalitarian; inequalitarian; inequitable; irregular; variable

UNEQUALED: **a.** incommensurable; incomparable; matchless; *nec plus ultra;* nonpareil; peerless; transcendent; unparagoned; unparalleled; unprecedented; unrivaled; unsurpassed; untranscended; **n.** UNEQUALITY: see "inequality"
or unrivaled: **a.** or **adv.** *hors concours person or thing which is:* **n.** *nec plus ultra;* nonesuch; nonpareil; paragon

UNESSENTIAL: (see "nonessential") **a.** dispensable; supererogatory; unimportant
small decorative: **n.** grace note

UNEVEN: (see "erratic") **a.** asperate; asperous; asymmetric(al); disparate; dissymetric(al); inadequate; inequitable; irregular; spasmodic; unsymmetric(al)

UNEXPECTED: (see "accidental" **and** "sudden") **a.** supervenient; unannounced; unanticipated; unforeseen; unheralded

UNEXPLAINED: **a.** inscrutable; insoluble; irresolute; unresolved

UNEXPLORED: **a.** uncharted; undetermined; unfathomed; uninvestigated; unplumbed
territory or field of knowledge: **n.** *terra incognita*

UNEXPRESSED: **a.** implicit; implied; inarticulate; tacit; unspoken; unuttered

UNFADING: (see "permanent" **and** "undying") **a.** amaranthine; immarcescible; immortal

UNFAIR: **a.** disproportionate; excessive; inequitable; prejudiced

UNFAITHFULNESS: **n.** apostasy; disloyalty; improbity; infidelity; perfidy; treachery

UNFAMILIAR: (see "strange") **a.** exotic; inconversant; unaccustomed; uncanny

UNFATHOMED: **a.** immense; undetermined; unsounded

UNFAVORABLE: (see "undesirable") **a.** derogatory; detrimental; disadvantageous; dyslogistic; ill-omened; inauspicious; inclement; ominous; portentous; sinister; sinistrous; unpropitious

UNFEELING: (see "stoical") a. analgesic; apathetic; impassible; impenitent; impervious; impiteous; implacable; incompassionate; indurate; indurative; insensate; insentient; insensitive; obdurate; unaffectionate; uncompassionate; unemotional; unresponsive; unsusceptible; **n.** (see "callousness") insensibility

UNFERMENTED: **a.** azymous

UNFIT: (see "improper" **and** "unsuitable") **a.** unexemplary
to be mentioned: (see "unspeakable") **a.** nefandous

UNFITNESS, *total and absurd:* **n.** *asinus ad lyram* (ass at the lyre)

UNFORGIVABLE: **a.** inexcusable; inexpiable; irremissible; unpardonable

UNFORGIVING: **a.** impenitent; implacable; relentless

UNFORESEEABLE: (see "unexpected") **a.** incalculable

UNFORTUNATE: **a.** calamitous; deplorable; hapless; infelicitous; inopportune; lamentable; unpropitious; unsuitable; unsuccessful; untoward
it's most: **adv.** *c'est un grand malheur*

UNFRIENDLY: (see "hostile") **a.** asocial; disaffected; frosty; inhospitable; inimical; uncongenial; unfavorable; ungregarious; unsympathetic; **n.** inhospitality

UNFRUITFUL: see "barren'"

UNGAINLY: **a.** angulous; **n.** angularity; ungainliness

UNGODLY: **a.** blasphemous; desecrating; heathenish; impious; irreligious; pagan; profane; sacrilegious; unholy; **n.** UNGODLINESS: blasphemy; impiety; irreligiosity
to make: **v.** heathenize; paganize; vulgarize

UNGRATEFUL: **a.** thankless; ungracious

UNHAPPINESS: (see "sadness") **n.** anhedonia; dysphoria; infelicity; melancholy; misfortune; wretchedness; **a.** UNHAPPY: (see "mournful") anhedonic; disconsolate; dysphoric; infelicitous; melancholy; miserable; unfortunate; wretched
chronic: **n.** anhedonia
productive of: **a.** infelicific

UNHARMONIOUS: (see "disharmonious") **a.** cacophonic; cacophonous; discordant; disputatious; dissentient; dissentious; dissident; dissonant

UNHEALTHY (or UNHEALTHFUL): (see "unwholesome") **a.** inimical; insalubrious; insalutary; insanitary; morbid; noxious; pathological; pernicious; septic; **n.** insalubrity; morbidity

UNHOLY: (see "ungodly" **and** "wicked") **a.** unconsecrated; unhallowed

UNHONORED: **a.** unacknowledged; unesteemed; unlaureated; unrespected; unsung

UNIDENTIFIED: **a.** incognito; (**fem.** incognita); unrecognized

UNIFIED: see "united"; **a.** UNIFYING: afferent; cementatory; centralizing; centripetal; consolidating; integrative

UNIFORM: (see "comparable") **a.** consistent; constant; equable; equiform; harmonious; homogenous; invariable; isogenous; monolithic; symmetrical; synonymous; unanimous; unchanging; undifferentiated; **n.** UNIFORMITY: equability; equanimity; homogeneity; isogeny; monolithism; monotony; (re)semblance; similitude; unanimity
as dress or clothing: **n.** panoply

UNIMAGINATIVE: (see "prosaic") **a.** frigid; insipid; monotonous; pedantic; pedestrian; pointless; practical; unleavened

UNIMPORTANT: (see "trifling" and "trivial") **a.** dispensable; inconsequential; insignificant; insubstantial; irrelevant; minor-league; unessential; unimpressive; **n.** UNIMPORTANCE: see "insignificance"
matter, or unnecessary details: **n.** minutia; (**pl.** inconsequentia; inconsequenti-alities; infinitesimalities; minutiae; trivia-(lities)
matters, being interested in: **a.** finical; meticulous; minutiose; minutious; picayune; picayunish; rabbinic(al)

UNINSPIRED: (see "dull") **a.** pedestrian; prosaic

UNINTELLIGENT: see "stupid"; **a.** UNINTELLIGIBLE: abstruse; incomprehensible; unfathomable

UNINTENTIONAL: (see "accidental") **a.** inadvertent; unpremeditated; **n.** inadvertence; inadvertency

UNINTERESTED: **a.** apathetic; inattentive; incurious; indifferent; lackadaisic(al); languid; languorous

UNINTERESTING: (see "dull") **a.** banal; bromidic; commonplace; immature; insipid; jejune; prosaic(al); sterile; vapid: **n.** banality; insipidity; jejunity; sterility; vapidity

UNION: (see "unite") **n.** accouplement; agglutination; alliance; amalgamation; anastomosis; association; coadunation; coalescence; coalition; colligation; (con)-federation; confluence; conjugation; conjunction; (con)juncture; consolidation; consortion; fusion; integration; lamination; *rapprochement;* suture; syncretism; synchrondrosis; synoecism; unanimity; unition
in strength: **adv.** *juncta juvant; vis unita fortior*
of blood vessels or channels: **n.** anastomosis; **a.** anastomotic
of cells or parts: **n.** coalescence; concrescence
of govt. or territory: **n.** anschluss
political or economic: **n.** anschluss

UNIQUE: (see "rare") **a.** eccentric; exceptional; nonpareil; *sui generis;* uncommon; unequaled; unexampled; unprecedented; **n.** UNIQUENESS: phoenixity; unicity; uniquity
person or thing: **n.** nonpareil; nonesuch; *rara avis;* uniquity
pert. to, involving or dealing w/ the: **a.** idiographic

UNISON, *being in:* **a.** unanimous; unisonant; unisonous; **n.** unanimity

UNIT: **n.** entity; existent; monad; **a.** UNITARY: integrative; monadic; monadological; monistic

UNITE: (**see** "union") **v.** agglutinate; amalgamate; associate; centralize; coadunate; coagment; colligate; (con)catenate; concur; conjugate; consolidate; cooperate; federate; incorporate; inosculate; laminate; recapitulate; syncretize; synoecize
   by adhesion: **v. or a.** conglutinate; **n.** conglutination
   having power or tendency to: **a.** henotic; irenic
   one who (unites): **n.** concatenator; integrationist; syncretist

UNITED: **a.** amalgamative; coadunate; coadunative; conjugate; conjugative; integrated; syncretic; syncretistic
   in fellowship: **a.** consociate; integrative
   in opn. or view: **a.** concordant; consentaneous; consentient; harmonious; unanimous; **adv.** *una voce;* **n.** concordance; consentience; harmony; solidarity; totality; unanimity; unification

UNITY: **n.** allness; harmony; integration; omneity; oneness; singleness; solidarity; syncretism; totality; unanimity; unification
   of opn., purpose, feeling, etc.: **see under** "united"

UNIVERSAL: **a.** catholic; cosmopolitan; ecumenical; encyclopedical; epidemic; (macro)cosmic; pandemic; panharmonic; peregrine; transcendental; **n.** UNIVERSALITY: catholicity
   language: **n.** Esperanto; pasigraphy
   principle: **n.** logos
   solvent: **n.** menstruum
   solvent, supposed (in alchemy): **n.** alkahest; **a.** alkahestic
   wisdom or knowledge: **n.** pansophism; pansophy; **a.** pansophic(al)

UNIVERSE: **n.** cosmos; firmament; macrocosm(os); **a.** (macro)cosmic
   as orderly system, or pert. to: **n.** cosmos; **a.** cosmic
   on small scale: **n.** microcosm; **a.** microcosmic(al)
   science or study of: **n.** cosmography; cosmology; universology; **a.** cosmologic(al)

   theory of origin: **n.** cosmogeny; cosmogony; **a.** cosmogenetic
   worship of: **n.** cosmolatry; cosmotheism; pantheism

UNJUST: **a.** inequal; inequitable; unequal; unwarranted; wrongful

UNJUSTIFIED: **a.** gratuitous; iniquitous; injudicious; unwarranted

UNKIND: (**see** "cruel") **a.** *désobligeant;* disobliging; disgracious; inconsiderate; ungracious; ungrateful; **n.** UNKINDNESS: inconsideration; ingratitude; ungratefulness

UNKNOWABLE: **a.** imponderable; (**pl.** imponderabilia); incogitable; incomprehensible
   object, as soul: **n.** noumenon; **a.** noumenal

UNKNOWN: **a.** imponderable; (**pl.** imponderabilia); incalculable; inglorious; uncharted
   cause, pert. to: **a.** agnogenic; idiopathic
   everything (unknown) is thought to be magnificent: omne ignotum pro magnifico
   origin, of: **a.** cryptogenic; idiopathic; phanterogen(et)ic
   person: (**see** "stranger") **n.** inconnu
   place: **n.** Weissnichtwo
   the: **n.** *l'inconnu;* (**pl.** imponderabilia; imponderables)

UNLADYLIKE: **a.** gamine; hoydenish; tomboyish
   behavior: **n.** gaminerie; hoydenism; rowdyism; tomboyishness

UNLAWFUL: (**see** "illegal") **a.** *bar sinister;* illegitimate; illicit; irregular; malfeasant
   act: (**see** "crime") **n.** malfeasance; misdemeanor

UNLEAVENED: **a.** azymous; banal; pedestrian; tedious; trite; unimaginative

UNLIKE: (**see** "dissimilar") **a.** anomalous; antipathic; disparate; heterogeneous; incongruous; **n.** UNLIKENESS: disparity; heterogeneity; incongruity

UNLIKELY: (**see** "doubtful") **a.** dubious; dubitable; implausible; improbable; incredible; **n.** dubiety; dubiousness; implausibility; improbability; unlikelihood

UNLIMITED: (see "free" and "vast") a. boundless; immeasurable; immeasurate; imponderable; infinite; innumerable; plenipotent(ial); plenipotentiary; unconfined; unimpeded; untrammeled
  power to transact business: a. plenipotent(ial)
  time: n. boundlessness; infinity; perpetuity

UNLOAD: (see "rid") v. disburden; disencumber; disgorge

UNLUCKY: (see "disastrous") a. hapless; ill-omened; ill-starred; inauspicious; infaust; inopportune; unfortunate; unpropitious; untoward
  day: n. *dies infastus* (or *infaustus*); (pl. *nefasti dies*)

UNMANAGEABLE: (see "stubborn" and "unruly") a. recalcitrant; n. recalcitrance

UNMARRIED: a. celebate; n. celibacy; celibate
  born of (unmarried) woman: a. parthenic; parthenian; n. *bar sinister*

UNMERCIFUL: see "merciless"

UNMERITED: a. indign; undeserved; unearned

UNMINDFUL: (see "careless") a. abstracted; forgetful; inattentive; neglectful; oblivious; ungrateful

UNMISTAKABLE: (see "clear") a. decisive; definitive; manifest; obvious; patent

UNMIXABLE: a. immiscible; incompatible; n. immiscibility; incompatibility

UNMOVABLE: (see "stubborn") a. apathetic; inexorable; obstinate; recalcitrant; resolute; unbudgeable

UNMUSICAL: a. arrhythmic(al); cacophonic; cacophonous; discordant; inharmonious; unharmonious; n. cacophony, discordance

UNNAMED: a. anonymous; incognito; innominate; pseudonymous; undubbed; unidentified; unspecified; n. anonymity; pseudonymity

UNNECESSARY: a. gratuitous; inessential; needless; n. inessentiality
  to make: v. obviate; n. obviation

UNOBSERVANT: a. astigmatic; inattentive; incurious

UNOFFICIAL: a. contraband; informal; officious; offstage; unauthorized; unorthodox

UNORIGINAL: (see "counterfeit") a. derivative; unimaginative

UNORTHODOX: (see "radical") a. heretical; heterodox; unconventional; n. UNORTHODOXY: heterodoxy; unconventionality
  labeling as: n. mark of the beast

UNPAIRED: a. azygous; unmatched

UNPARALLELED: (see "exceptional") a. epochal; nonpareil; unequaled; unsurpassed

UNPARDONABLE: a. inexcusable; inexpiable; irremissible; unforgivable

UNPIERCED: a. imperforate; intact; unpenetrated

UNPLEASING (or UNPLEASANT): (*see* "disagreeable") a. bilious; plutonian; plutonic; unpalatable; n. UNPLEASANTNESS: (see "disagreement") disamenity

UNPOLISHED: (see "coarse" and "uncouth") a. agrestic; gauche; inurbane; uncivilized; unrefined

UNPREDICTABLE: (see "erratic") a. ambivalent; capricious; chameleonic; fickle; incalculable; vagarious

UNPREJUDICED: a. cosmopolitan; equitable; impartial; unbiased

UNPREMEDITATED: (see "accidental") a. *a brevi manu;* extemporaneous; headlong; impromptu; undesigned; unintentional

UNPREPAREDNESS, *in state of:* n. *illotis manibus*

UNPROFITABLE: **a.** frustaneous; infructuous; inutile; sterile; unremunerative; unrewarding; **n.** inutility

UNPROVED: **a.** undocumented; unestablished; unsubstantiated
theory, proposition, etc.: **n.** hypothesis; theorem

UNPUBLISHED *material:* **n.** ineditum; (**pl.** inedita)

UNPUNISHED: **a.** unatoned; unchastened; unchastised; unexpiated

UNQUALIFIED: (**see** "absolute" **and** "incompetent" **a.** disbarred; disqualified; plenary; ineligible; unreserved; unrestricted

UNQUESTIONABLE: (**see** "certain") **a.** implicit; indisputable; indubitable; undisputable; **n.** indubitability

UNREAL(ISTIC): **a.** affected; artificial; barmecidal; baroque; chimerical; delusive; disembodied; fantastic; fictitious; grotesque; histrionic; illusive; illusory; illusional; imaginary; impalpable; imperceptible; incorporeal; insubstantial; intangible; (melo) dramatic; paper-mache; *papier-mâché;* phantasmagoric(al); phantasmal; phantom; platonic; staged; unsubstantial; Utopian; visionary; **a. or n.** Gothic; **n.** UNREALISM: aeriality; ideality; unsubstantiality

UNREASONABLE: (**see** "illogical" **and** "stubborn") **a.** absonant; fatuous; inappropriate; incongruous; inordinate; irrational; paralogical; paralogistic; preposterous; unconscionable; **n.** UNREASONABLENESS: illogicality; incoherence; irrationality; unsoundness

UNREASONED: **see** "thinking"

UNREFINED: (**see** "coarse") **a.** barbaric; earthy; inelegant; troglodytic

UNRELATED: **a.** accidental; arbitrary; discrete; disjointed; dissociate(d); extraneous; extrinsic; heterogenous; impertinent; inapplicable; inapposite; incidental; intercalary; irrelevant; parenthetical; tangential

UNRELIABLE: (**see** "tricky") **a.** contradictuous; duplicitous; feckless; shiftless; unconscionable; undependable; unprincipled; unscrupulous; untrustworthy; villainous; **n.** UNRELIABILITY: duplicity; unconscionability; unscrupulosity

UNRESERVED: **see** "unrestrained"

UNRESPECTABLE: **see** "disrespectable"

UNREST: **see** "disquiet"

UNRESTRAINED: (**see** "free," "lawless" **and** "uncontrolled") **a.** bizarre; exaggerated; extravagant; flamboyant; immoderate; impertinent; incontinent; indiscriminate; inordinate; intemperate; limitless; *outré;* prodigal; promiscuous; rampant; spontaneous; tumultuary; uncontrolled; uncurbed; undampened; undisciplined; unlicensed; unreserved; wanton; **adv.** *abandonnement; con abbandono; con alcuna licenza*

UNRESTRICTED: (**see** "open" **and** "unrestrained") **a.** plenary; plenipotent(ial)

UNREVEALED: (**see** "hidden") **adv.** *in pectore; in petto*

UNREWARDING: **see** "unprofitable"

UNRIVALED: **a.** incomparable; peerless; nonpareil; unparalleled

UNRULY: (**see** "stubborn") **a.** boisterous; headstrong; intractable; mutinous; obstinate; rampageous; rampant; recalcitrant; recusant; refractory; turbulent; unbridled; undisciplined; ungovernable; wanton; willful

UNSAID: **see** "unspoken"

UNSATISFIED: **a.** insatiated; unfulfilled
desire: **n.** insatiability; insatiety

UNSEASONABLE: (**see** "untimely") **a.** inexpedient; inopportune; **adv.** malapropos

UNSEEMLY: (**see** "unbecoming") **a.** inappropriate; indecent; indecorous; solecistic; unbecoming; unseasonable
something which is: **n.** barbarism; impropriety; solecism

UNSELFISH: (see "generous") a. altruistic; charitable; chivalrous; magnanimous; philanthropic; n. UNSELFISHNESS: (see "generosity") altropathy; altruism; magnanimity; philanthropy

UNSETTLED: a. abeyant; deranged; erratic; itinerant; pendant; pendent; nomadic; unstable; vagrant; n. instability; itinerancy; vagrancy

UNSHAKABLE: (see "firm") a. adamant; impregnable; inflexible

UNSIGNED: a. anonymous; pseudonymous; unidentified

UNSKILLFUL: (see "inexperienced") a. amateurish; gauche; inapt; inept; maladroit; unartful; n. UNSKILLFULNESS: gaucherie; inaptitude; maladroitness

UNSOCIABLE: a. antisocial; asocial; detached; discordant; incompatible; inharmonious; inhospitable; insociable; moronic; reserved; solitary; solitudinarian; troglodytic; uncompanionable; uncongenial; ungregarious; withdrawn; n. UNSOCIABILITY: see "reserve"

UNSOLVABLE: a. inextricable; inscrutable; insoluble; unexcogitable

UNSPARING: a. inexorable; procrustean; profuse; relentless; ruthless; adv. *à outrance*

UNSPEAKABLE: a. execrable; ineffable; indescribable; indicible; inenarrable; inexpressible; nefandous; unmentionable; unutterable; utterless; adv. *horrible dictu;* n. ineffability

UNSPOKEN: a. inarticulate; obmutescent; tacit; unarticulated; uncommunicated; unexpressed; unsaid; unuttered; unverbalized

UNSTABLE: (see "unsteady") a. astatic; ataxic; fickle; inconstant; labile; mercurial; mutable; protean; titubant; vacillating; variable; vertiginous; volatile; voluable; n. astasis; astaticism; ataxia; lability; volatility; volubility

UNSTOPPABLE: a. inextinguishable; insatiable; unextinguishable; unquenchable

UNSUBSTANTIAL: (see "unreal") a. aerial; diaphanous; ethereal; filigree; imaginary; shadowy; visionary; n. UNSUBSTANTIALITY: aeriality; diaphaneity; ethereality; shadowiness

UNSUCCESSFUL: a. *manqué*

UNSUITABLE (or UNSUITED): (see "untimely") a. *à propos de rien;* discordant; impertinent; inapplicable; inappropriate; inapt; incompatible; incongruent; incongruous; inept; infelicitous; inharmonious; unbecoming; unmeet; unseemly; n. UNSUITABILITY: inaptitude; inconcinnity; incongruity; infelicity; maladroitness; maladjustment; misalliance

UNSUPPORTED: a. unbuttressed; undocumented

UNSURPASSED: see "unequaled"

UNSYMPATHETIC: a. ill-disposed

UNTAMED: (see "wild") a. barbarous; *ferae naturae;* feral; rambunctious; unfettered; unsubdued; n. barbarity; ferity; ferocity

UNTEACHABLE: a. indocile; intractable; n. indocility; intractability

UNTHINKABLE: (see "unspeakable") a. extraordinary; incogitable; inconceivable; incredible; unimaginable

UNTHINKING: a. heedless; inattentive; incogitant; inconsiderate; unmindful; unmotivated; unphilosophic(al); n. incogitability

UNTIDY: a. dishevel(l)ed; slovenly; tatterdemalian; unfastidious; unkempt; n. UNTIDINESS: dishevelment
  or confused place: n. Bedlam; mare's nest

UNTIMELY: a. inappropriate; inauspicious; inconvenient; inexpedient; inopportune; intempestive; premature; unfavorable; unpropitious; unpunctual; unseasonable

UNTIRING: a. everlasting; indefatigable; sustained; tireless; unflagging; unwearying; n. indefatigability

UNTOLD: **a.** boundless; immeasurable; incalculable; innumerable; unrevealed

UNTOUCHABLE: **a.** inviolable; invulnerable; sacrosanct; **n.** inviolability; invulnerability; sacrosanctity

UNTRAINED: **a.** illiterate; nescient; uncultivated; uneducated; untutored

UNTRIED: (**see** "unattempted") **a.** callow; immature; inexperienced; unexpert; unfledged

UNTRUE: **a.** disloyal; fabulous; fictitious; mendacious; mythological; spurious; supposititious; unfaithful; **n.** UNTRUTHFUL: **see** "false" **and** "truth, departing from"; **n.** UNTRUTHFULNESS: dishonesty; inaccuracy; inveracity; mendacity
    though characteristic or appropriate: **a.** *ben trovato*

UNTRUSTWORTHY: (**see** "dishonest" **and** "uncertain") **a.** disingenuous

UNUNITED: **a.** disarticulated; disassembled; discrete; disunited

UNUSABLE: (**see** "useless") **a.** afunctionable; afunctional; inutile; **n.** inutility

UNUSUAL: (**see** "odd" **and** "strange") **a.** anomalistic; anomalous; bizarre; exceptional; exotic; extraordinary; fantastic; grotesque; irregular; *outré;* paranormal; peculiar; phenomenal; *recherché;* remarkable; singular
    experience: **n.** escapade
    person: **n.** *rara avis*
    structurally: **a.** ectopic; heteromorphic; heteromorphous; **n.** heteromorphosis
    thing: **n.** extravaganza; *rara avis;* unusuality

UNUTTERABLE: (**see** "unspeakable") **a.** indescribable; ineffable; inexpressible

UNVARYING: (**see** "dull") **a.** constant; monotonous; unchanging; uniform

UNWANTED: **a.** *de trop;* nonessential; superfluous; undesirable

UNWARLIKE: **see** "peaceful"

UNWELCOME: **a.** *de trop; non grata;* unacceptable
    person: **n.** *persona non grata*

UNWHOLESOME: (**see** "unhealthy") **a.** deleterious; inimical; insalubrious; malignant; morbid; pathological; pernicious

UNWIELDLY: (**see** "bulky") **a.** awkward; cumbrous; cumbersome; elephantine; hippopotamian; hippopotamic; ponderous; ungainly

UNWILLING: (**see** "indisposed" **and** "involuntary") **a.** a(d)verse; reluctant; **n.** UNWILLINGNESS: aversion; disinclination; nolition; repugnance; reluctance; reluctancy; reluctation
    or willing: **adv.** *nolens volens*

UNWISE: (**see** "senseless") **a.** ill-advised; impolitic; imprudent; indiscreet; inexpedient; injudicious; untimely

UNWORTHY: (**see** "base" **and** "undeserving") **a.** indign; inglorious; derogatory; despicable; unmeet; worthless

UNWRITTEN: **a.** customary; nuncupative; tacit; traditional
    law: **n.** *jus commune; lex non scripta*

UNYIELDING: (**see** "rigid" **and** "stubborn") **a.** adamant(ine); immalleable; impregnable; indomitable; inductile; inflexible; intractable; obstinate; perseverant; persistent; pertinacious; recalcitrant; resolute; tenacious; unalterable; unassailable; uncompromising; unshakable

UPHEAVAL: **n.** cataclysm; convulsion; labefaction; orogeny; overthrow; **a.** cataclysmal; cataclysmic(al)

UPKEEP: **n.** maintenance; sustentation; **a.** sustentative

UPLIFTING: **a.** inspirational; inspirative; inspiriting; instigative

UPPISH: **see** "proud"

UPRIGHT: **a.** chivalrous; conscientious; honorable; perpendicular; punctilious; rectitudinous; scrupulous; vertical; **n.** UPRIGHTNESS: integrity; perpendicularity; probity; rectitude; scrupulosity; verticality

UPRISING: **n.** *coup d'état;* insurgence; insurgency; insurrection; mutiny
tending to: **a.** insurgescence; mutinous

UPROAR: (**see** "clamor") **n.** Babelism; Bedlam; brouhaha; callithump; furore; hubbub; pandemonium
great: **n.** charivari; conclamation; pandemonium; tintamar(re); **a.** callithumpian; pandemoniac(al)

UPROOT: **v.** deracinate; eradicate; exterminate; extirpate; **n.** deracination; extirpation; **a.** UPROOTED: (**see** "displaced"); lumpen

UPSET: **v.** capsize; discompose; disconcert; disparage; overthrow; overturn; subvert; **n.** bouleversement

UPSIDE *down:* **a.** *sens dessus dessous;* topsy-turvy; **n.** topsy-turvydom; topsy-turviness

UPSTART: **n.** *arrivist(e); hesterni quirites;* Johnny-come-lately; *novus homo; nouveau riche; parvenu;* pip-squeak
social: **n.** *arrivist(e); parvenu*

UP-TO-DATE: **see** "modern"

UPWARD, *moving or tending:* **a.** anabatic; ascensional; ascensive; assurgent; **n.** assurgency; escalation

URGE: **see** "beseech"

URGENCY: **n.** criticality; exigency; imminence; importunity; instancy; **a.** URGENT: compelling; critical; exigent; imminent; impending; imperative; imperious; importunate; insentient; menacing; momentous; necessitous; persistent; poignant; solicitous; straitened; vehement; vital

URINATE: **v.** micturate; void; **n.** miction; micturition

USABLE: (**see** "practical") **a.** feasible; functional; instrumental; practicable; utile
not: **see** "useless"

USAGE(S): **n.** consuetude; custom; mores; prescription; tradition; utility; **a.** consuetudinal; traditional

according to: **adv.** consuetudinally; customarily; *secundum usum*
fashionable, observance of: **n.** *savoir vivre*

USE(S): **n.** applicability; application; deployment; disposition; employment; exercitation; utility; utilization
something having many: **n.** polychresty
to own advantage: **n.** embezzlement; exploitation; (mis)appropriation
unethical: **n.** exploitation
up: **v.** deplete; impoverish; **n.** impoverishment

USEFUL: **a.** advantageous; beneficial; efficacious; expedient; feasible; functional; materialistic; opportune; practicable; remunerative; utilitarian; yeoman; **n.** USEFULNESS: efficacy; feasibility; functionality; practicability; utility
things, learning of: **n.** chrestomathy; **a.** chrestomathic(al)

USELESS: **a.** afunctional; futile; ineffectual; inefficacious; inefficient; inutile; nugatory; otiose; unavailing; unserviceable; **n.** USELESSNESS: *hors de combat;* ineffectuality; inutility; otiosity

USER: **a.** beneficiary; consumer

USUAL: **a.** accustomed; commonplace; conventional; customary; habitual; ordinary; prevalent; prevailing; traditional; wonted; **n.** USUALNESS: conventionality; prevalence; tradition
as: **adv.** *à l'ordinaire; comme à l'ordinaire; comme d'ordinaire*

UTILITY: **see** "usefulness"

UTMOST *degree:* **n.** fare-thee-well; fare-you-well; uttermost
extent: **adv.** *à fond*
to the: **adv.** *à outrance*

UTTER: (**see** "speak") **v.** articulate; phonate; pronounce; **a.** (**see** "complete") consummate; incarnate; preemptory; pluperfect; sheer; unqualified; unspeakable; uttermost; **n.** UTTERANCE: articulation; descant; expression; observation

UTTERED, *capable of being:* **a.** effable

V

VACANT: (see "void") untenanted; vacuous

VACILLATING: see "wavering"

VAGABOND: (see "rogue") n. Bohemian; gypsy; nomad; truant; wastrel; a. VAGABONDISH: Bohemian; nomadic; picaresque

VAGRANT: (see "roving") a. circumforaneous; itinerant; peregrine; peripatetic; n. (see "vagabond") itinerant; peregrine; Peripatetic; (pl. flotsam and jetsam)

VAGUE: (see "abstract" and "indecisive") a. acategorical; aerial; ambiguous; amorphous; amphibolic; amphibological; cryptic; doubtful; dubious; dubitable; elusive; equivocal; illogical; imprecise; inconcrete; indefinable; indefinite; indescribable; indeterminate; indistinct; insubstantial; intangible; nubilous; obscure; sibylline; unexplicit; vaporous; adv. in nubibus; n. VAGUENESS: dubiety; dubiosity; insubstantiality; vaporosity
  suggestion: (see "trace") n. nuance; soupçon; umbrage

VAIN: a. abortive; dogmatic; ego(t)istical; flatulent; fruitless; frustaneous; hubristic; nugatory; officious; ostentatious; otiose; pedantic; pompous; pragmatic(al); pretentious; vainglorious; n. see "vanity"
  person: n. coxcomb; dandiprat; dogmatist; jackanapes; macaroni; popinjay
  threat: n. fulmen brutum

VALIANT: (see "bold" and "brave") a. chivalric; chivalrous; intrepid; noteworthy; stout-hearted; valorous; n. see "valor"

VALIDITY, accept or give full to: v. nostrificate; n. nostrification
  without: a. null and void; nullius juris

VALOR: n. arete; chivalry; gallantry; intrepidity; a. see "valiant"

VALUABLE: a. classic; (in)estimable; meritorious; priceless; treasured

VALUE(S), according to: adv. ad valorem
  based on or involving intrinsic or fundamental: a. axiological
  based on sentiment or whim: n. pretium affectionis
  having same relative in position or structure: a. analogous; homologous
  least possible: n. ambsace; nihility; triviality; (pl. trivia)
  lowering in: see under "lower"
  making moral obligations dependent on: a. axiological
  of little or slight, thing of: n. ambsace; bagatelle; continental; corpus vile; (pl. corpus villa); nihil(ity); sou markee
  of no: a. fustian
  theory or study of: n. axiology; a. axiological

VALUELESS: see "worthless"

VAMPIRE: n. Dracula; extortioner; lamia; sorceress; succubus

VANISHING: (see "fleeting") a. diaphanous; ephemeral; ethereal; evanescent; unsubstantial; n. diaphaneity; ethereality; evanescence; unsubstantiality

VANITY: n. amour-propre; arrogance; ego(t)ism; flatulence; hollowness; hubris; ostentation; otiosity; pomposity; vainglory
  all is: omnia vanitas
  of vanities: n. vanitas vanitatum

VANTAGE point: n. coign (of vantage); pou sto

VAPOR: see "cloud"
  changing readily to: a. volatile; n. volatility
  disagreeable: n. effluvium; (pl. effluvia); miasma; a. effluvial; miasmic
  heavy, as from swamps: n. miasma; a. miasmatic; miasmic

VARIABLE: (see "changeable") a. alterable: (am)bivalent; capricious; chamele-

onic; fickle; inconstant; irresolute; mercurial; mutable; quicksilver; vagrant
exceedingly: **a.** protean

VARIATION: **n.** alternation; diversification; modification; (per)mutation; variance
allowed fr. standard: **n.** tolerance
in form: **n.** multiformity; mutation; polymorph; sport; **a.** allotropic; polymorphic; polymorphous
slight: **n.** nuance

VARIED: **a.** diversified; manifold; mosaic; multifarious; multiform
quality or state: **n.** heterogeneity; miscellaneity

VARIEGATED: **a.** chimeral; diversified; heterogeneous; iridescent; kaleidoscopic; mosaic; motley; parti-colored; opalescent; prismatic; tessellate(d); **n.** VARIEGATION: diversification; heterogeneity; iridescence; mosaic; tessellation

VARIETIES, *composed of or containing all:* **a.** omnigenous
of all: **a.** heterogeneous; omnifarious

VARIETY: **n.** assortment; diversification; diversity; genre; genus; heterogeneity; medley; melange; multifariousness; multiformity; stock; strain; versatility
having infinite or great: **a.** kaleidoscopic
of great: **a.** heterogeneous; manifold; multifarious; multiple; multiplex; multiplicitous; protean

VARIOUS *parts, in* (*of a book*): **adv.** *passim*
sources, drawn or derived from: **a.** eclectic; variorum
things: **n.pl.** miscellanea; varia

VARY: **see** "diversify"; **a.** VARYING: **see** "unstable"

VAST: (**see** "huge") **a.** boundless; colossal; comprehensive; cosmic; cyclopean; elephantine; Gargantuan; grandiose; herculean; immeasurable; imponderable; infinite; magnitudinous; titanic; unlimited; **n.** VASTITUDE: collosality; comprehensiveness; immeasurability; immensity; indefinitude; infinitude; magnitude; vastity

VAULT: **n.** concameration; fornix; **a.** concamerated

VEGETABLES, *cultivation and marketing of:* **n.** olericulture
garden: **n.** potagerie(s)

VEGETATION, *feeding on:* **a.** herbivorous; phytophagous; vegetarian; **n.** herbivore: (**pl.** herbivora); vegetarian
goddess of: **n.** Ceres; Flora
of or characteristic of growing: **a.** verdant; verdurous; **n.** verdancy

VEILED: (*in shadow*): **n.** chiaroscuro; sfumato; tenbrism; **a.** penumbral; tenebrous

VELVETY: **a.** velutinous

VENAL: **see** "mercenary"

VENERABLE: (**see** "ancient") **a.** patriarchal; respected; reverential

VENEREAL: **a.** aphrodisiac; Cytherean

VENGEANCE: **n.** Nemesis; reprisal; retaliation; retribution
goddess of: **n.** Fury; Nemesis
inflictor of: **n.** Nemesis

VENT: **n.** aperture; orifice; **a.** orificial

VENTURE: **n.** enterprise; jeopardy; speculation; **a.** VENTURESOME: **see** "adventurous"

VENUS, *votary of, or pert. to:* **a.** or **n.** Cytherean

VERB, *change into:* **v.** verbify; **n.** verification

VERBAL: (**see** "oral") **adv.** *ore tenus*
description: **see under** "description"
statement or formulation: **n.** verbality
thrust: **n.** repartee; ripost(e)

VERIFIED: (**see** "established") **a.** documented
capable of being: **a.** confirmable; verifiable; verificatory; **n.** verificability

VERSATILE: **a.** ambidextrous; inconstant; polygraphic; **n.** VERSATILITY: ambidexterity

VERSE: (**see** "poetry") **n.** metrification; versification
obscene piece of: **n.** ithyphallic

witty, light or ironic: **n.** limerick; *vers de société*

VERTICAL: (**see** "erect") **a.** perpendicular; **n.** VERTICALITY: perpendicularity

VERY *good or well:* **adv.** *très bien*
great in trifles: maximus in minimus
nature of the case, by the: **adv.** *ipso facto*
words, the: **n.** *ipissima verba*

VETERAN: **n.** grognard; oldster; patriarch; stager; **a. see** "venerable"

VEX: (**see** "annoy") **v.** afflict; pique; **n.** VEXATION: affliction; chagrin; displeasure; impatience; irritation; mortification; pique; **a.** VEXATIOUS: (**see** "annoying") afflictive; choleric; disordered; impatient; pestilent; petulant; restive

VIBRATE: **v.** oscillate; palpitate; quaver; tremulate; undulate; **a.** VIBRATORY: oscillant; tremulant; tremulous; undulant; undulatory

VICE: **see** "wickedness"

VICIOUS: (**see** "wicked") **a.** egregious; feral; flagitious; flagrant; iniquitous; villainous; **n.** VICIOUSNESS: barbarity; egregiousness; ferity; flagitiousness; flagrancy; iniquity; villainy

VICTORY: (**see** "conquest" **and** "defeat") **n.** achievement; ascendancy; mastery; prevailment; subjugation; supremacy; triumph
at great loss or sacrifice: **n.** Cadmean (victory); Pyrrhic (victory)
celebrating: **a.** epinician
hymn or ode in honor of: **n.** epinicion; **a.** epicinian
in name only: **see** "at great loss" **above**
sign of (vee): **n.** bidigitation

VIEW: (**see** "opinion" **and** "outlook") **n.** panorama; perspective; perspectivity; prospect; scrutiny; survey; vista
affording a general: **a.** panoramic; synoptic
or survey, quick: **n.** *coup d'oeil*
unlimited: **n.** panorama; **a.** panoptic; panoramic

VIEWPOINT: (**see** "scope") **n.** frame of reference

VIGILANT: (**see** "aware") **a.** Cerberean; circumspect; watchful

VIGOR: **n.** ardor; *élan;* gusto; impetuosity; lustiness; stamina; tonicity; verve; vivacity; zest; **a.** VIGOROUS: (**see** "bracing") animated; *con spirito;* cyclonic(al); dynamic(al); energetic; flourishing; forceful; puissant; spirited; strenuous; torrential; vehement; virile; **adv.** *con anima; con brio; con spirito*
deprive of: **v.** debilitate; devitalize; emasculate; enervate; **n.** enervation
given to great: **a.** cyclonic(al); dynamic; robustious; **n.** dynamism; robusticity
lacking in: **see under** "vitality"

VILE: (**see** "bad" **and** "wicked") **a.** abominable; contemptible; degenerate; despicable; egregious; flagitious; flagrant; infamous; ignominious; odious; profligate; putrid; sordid; vicious; vulturine; vulturous; **n.** (**see** "abuse") VILENESS: abomination; despicability; putridity

VILIFY: **see** "slander"

VILLAGE: **n.** microcosm; settlement; **a.** microcosmic(al); villagic; villageous

VILLAIN: (**see** "rogue" **and** "traitor") **n.** miscreant; profligate; rapscallion; **n.** VILLAINY: miscreancy; wickedness; **a.** VILLAINOUS: miscreant; rapscallion; unconscionable; unprincipled; unscrupulous

VINDICATION: **n.** compurgation; exoneration; justification; revenge; substantiation; **v.** VINDICATE: absolve; exculpate; exonerate; justify; substantiate

VINEGAR, *like:* **a.** acetous; acidulant; acidulous; vinegary

VIOLATE: (**see** "defile") **v.** contravene; desecrate; impinge; transgress; **a.** VIOLATIVE: transgressive; violational; **n.** VIOLATION: contravention; desecration; encroachment; impingement; infraction; infringement; misdeed; profanation; ravishment; transgression; trespass
not capable of (violation): **a.** inviolable; invulnerable; irrefrangable; irrefrangible

VIOLENT: (**see** "raging") **a.** impetuous; maniac(al); rampant; tempestuous; torrential; turbulent; vehement; **n.** VIO-

LENCE: barbarity; ferocity; fervor; fury; impetuosity; impetuousness; mania; passion; rampancy; tempestuousness; turbulency; vehemence

VIOLIN, *resembling in outline:* **a.** pandurate; panduriform

VIRGIN(S): **n.** *virgio intacta;* **a.** undefiled; unspoiled; unsullied; untapped
  demi- or "technical": **n.** demi-vierge
  for, and for boys: virginibus puerisque
  pert. or belonging to: **a.** parthenian; parthenic
  worship of: **n.** parthenolatry

VIRGINITY, *deprive of:* **v.** devirginate; devirginize; **n.** devirgination; **n.** devirginator

VIRTUE: **n.** arete; chastity; dharma; fidelity; integrity; morality; probity; rectitude; sanctity; uprightness; **a.** VIRTUOUS: exemplary; meritorious; rectitudinous; righteous; seraphic; virginal
  false assumption of: **n.** hypocrisy; piosity; religiosity; **a.** hypocritical; religiose
  four cardinal (virtues): **n.** fortitude; justice; prudence; temperance
  goddess of: **n.** Fides
  honor is reward of: virtutis praemium
  is strongest shield: aegis fortissima virtus
  rejoices in trial: gaudet tentamine virus
  "science of": **n.** aretaics

VIRULENCE, *lessening of:* **n.** abatement; attenuation

VISIBLE: **a.** apparent; discernible; manifest; obvious; patent; perceptible; **adv.** *à vue; d'oeil; ad oculos*
  to naked eye: **a.** macroscopic; **adv.** *nudis oculis*

VISION: (**see** "prospect") **n.** apparition; discernment; foresight; hallucination; illusion; percipience; perception; perspicacity
  acuteness of: see "keenness of" below
  blurred: **n.** astigmatism; **a.** astigmatic(al)
  defective: **n.** amblyopia
  double: **n.** diplopia; **a.** diplopic
  fallacy in: **n.** fantasy; illusion; mirage; phantasm(agory); phantom; poltergeist; specter; wraith; **a.** phantasmagoric(al); spectral

faulty: see "blurred" **above**
keenness of: **n.** *acuité visuelle;* oxyblepsia; visual acuity; **a.** lynx-eyed
universal (all-seeing): **n.** omnividence

VISIONARY: **a.** aerial; airy-fairy; chimerical; doctrinaire; dogmatic(al); dreamy; idealistic; impractical; irresponsible; ivory-tower; laputan; notional; platonic; platonistic; poetic(al); quixotic(al); romantic; starry-eyed; theoretical; translunary; unsubstantial; Utopian; **n.** (see "dreamer") doctrinaire; dogmatist; enthusiast; ideologist; ideologue; theorist

VISIT: **n.** sojourn(ment); visitation
  esp. brief or temp.: **v.** sojourn; **n.** sojournment; **n.** sojourner

VISITING *card:* **n.** *carte de visite*
  often or habitually: **n.** frequentation; habituation; **v.** frequent; habituate

VISITOR: **n.** sojourner; visitant

VISUALIZE: (**see** "imagine") **v.** envision; foresee; perceive

VITAL: (**see** "important") **a.** animated; energetic; fatal; fundamental; indispensable; mortal; pivotal
  force: **n.** *anima bruta; anima mundi; élan vital*
  statistics, science of: **n.** demography

VITALITY: **see** *"vigor"*
  drain of: **v.** desiccate; devitalize; enervate
  lack of: **n.** abiotrophy; adynamia; **a.** abiotrophic; adynamic; desiccated

VIVID: **a.** eidetic; picturesque; piquant; poignant; trenchant

VOCALIZE: **v.** articulate; enunciate; phonate; pronounce; **n.** VOCALIZATION: articulation; enunciation; phonation; **a.** see "voiced"

VOCATIONAL: **a.** banausic; employmental; materialistic; professional

VOICE, *clearness or distinctness of:* **n.** lamphrophonia
  characteristic of: **n.** timbre
  deep, heavy bass: **n.** *basso profundo*
  effeminate: **a.** gynecophonous
  high: **n.** *haute voix*

in a clear and distinct: **see under** "pronunciation"
   in a low: **a. or adv.** *sotto-voce*
   loss of: **n.** aphonia; obmutescence
   of God: **n.** *vox Dei*
   of one crying in wilderness: vox clamantis in deserto
   of the people: **n.** *vox populi* (**abb.** vox pop.)
   secret: **n.** *vox clandestina*
   with one: **adv.** *una voce*

VOICED: **a.** articulated; enunciated; phonated; phonetic; sonant; sonic; vocalized

VOCIFEROUS: **see** "loud"

VOID: (**see** "null") **a.** nugatory; *nullis juris;* vacuous; **n.** vacuum
   make: **v.** abrogate; delete; negate; nullify; quash; repeal

VOLUME: (**see** "capacity") **n.** amplitude; loudness; magnitude; **a.** VOLUMINOUS: (**see** "huge") bouffant(e); multitudinous

VOLUPTUOUS: **see** "sensuous"

VOMIT: **v.** disgorge; regurgitate; **n.** disgorgement; emesis; regurgitation

VOMITING: **n.** (hyper)emesis; **a.** emetic; regurgitating

drug or agent for: **n.** emetic
   of pregnancy: **n.** hyperemesis; *hyperemesis gravidarum*

VOTE: (**or** VOTING): **n.** franchise; plebiscite (**or** plebescite); referendum; suffrage; **a.** plebiscitary; plebiscitic: **n.** VOTER(S): constituency; constituent

VOW: **n.** profession
   of chastity: **n.** *votum castitatis*
   pert. to or consecrated by: **a.** votary

VOWEL, *having more than one:* **a.** plurivocalic
   immediately preceding a: **a.** antevocalic; prevocalic

VULGAR: (**see** "common" **and** "lewd") **a.** earthy; Falstaffian; Hogarthian; ignoble; irreverent; obscene; plebeian; Rabelaisian; ribald(rous); scurrile; scurrilous; sordid; unrefined; **n.** VULGARITY: commonness; pleb(e)ianism; ribaldry; scurrility; vulgarization
   person: **see under** "person"
   to make: **v.** heathenize; paganize; plebeianize; vulgarize

VULTURE, *of or characteristic of:* **a.** vulturine; vulturous

W

WAG: see "wit"

WAGE: **n.** compensation; emolument; honorarium; remuneration; stipend(ium); **a.** stipendiary
earner(s) **n.** bourgeois; proletarian; proletariat; **a.** bourgeois; proletarian

WAGGISH: (see "humorous") **a.** espiegle; frolicsome; **n.** WAGGISHNESS: *espieglerie;* roguery; roguishness

WAIL: **v.** caterwaul; deplore; lament; ululate; **n.** caterwaul; lamentation; ululation; **a.** WAILING: plangorous; ululant

WAIST, *having slender:* **a.** waspish

WAITER, *head:* **n.** *maître d'hôtel*

WALK: **v.** pedestrianize; (per)ambulate; peregrinate; traverse; **n.** promenade; peregrination
about and around: **v.** circumambulate; deambulate; promenade; **n.** circumambulation; deambulation; promenade; **a.** circumambulatory; deambulatory; perambulatory
inability to fr. muscular incoordination: **n.** astasia-abasia; astasis; ataxia
thru, around or about: **v.** perambulate; **a.** perambulatory; **n.** perambulation

WALKING: **a.** ambulant; *à pied;* (de)ambulatory; itinerant; pedestrian; Peripatetic; **n.** deambulation; (per)ambulation; peregrination; peripateticism
adapted for: **a.** gressorial
alone: **n. or a.** solivagant
fr. place to place: **n. or a.** itinerant; Peripatetic
in sleep: see under "sleep"
pert. to ability for: **a** ambulatorial
upright or vertical: **n. or a.** orthograde; orthostatic; plantigrade
w/ body horizontal, as most animals: **a.** pronograde

WALL *in:* **v.** immure; **n.** immurement
pert. to: **a.** mural; parietal

WALLOW(ING): **v.** flounder; welter; **n.** volutation

WAND, *divination by:* **n.** rhabdomancy

WANDER: **v.** circumambulate; deviate; divagate; expatiate; itinerate; meander; perambulate; peregrinate; **n.** circumambulation; divagation; itineration; perambulation; peregrination
aimlessly or idly: **v.** meander; **n.** meandering
at leisure; **v.** circumambulate; **a.** circumambulatory; **n.** circumambulation
tendency to: **n.** itinerancy; peregrinism; peregrinity
urge to: **n.** dromomania; wanderlust

WANDERER: **n.** itinerant; Odysseus; peregrinator; peregrine; vagabond
solitary: **n. or a.** solivagant

WANDERING: (see "straying") **a.** circumambulatory; errant; erring; itinerant; meandering; migratory; nomadic; Odyssean; Peripatetic; vagabond(ish); vagarious; vagrant; **n.** circumambulation; divagation; errantry; expatiation; fugitivity; odyssey; peregrination; peregrinity; vagabondage; vagabondism
alone: **a.** solivagant
extended, incl. intellectual, etc.: **n.** odyssey; **a.** Odyssean; peregrinate
fr, place to place: **a.** circumforaneous; itinerant; Odyssean; peregrinic; vagrant
intellectual or spiritual: **n.** odyssey; **a.** Odyssean
one topic to another: **a.** desultory; digressive; discursive; pleonastic

WANING: **a.** decrescent; declinatory; **n.** (see "recession") abatement; declension; declination; decrescence; diminution

WANT: (see "need") **v.** desiderate; necessitate; require; **n.** dearth; deficiency; desideratum; destitution; exigency; indigence; (pl. desiderata; desideria); **a.** WANTING: deficient; desiderative; destitute; lacking; necessitous

353

WANTON : see "lustful" **and** "extravagant"

WAR(S) (or WARFARE) : **n.** hostility
after the: **a.** postbellum
before the (as Civil): **a.** antebellum
between: **a.** interbella; interbellum
deadly or lethal: **n.** *bellum lethale*
doctrine opposed to: **n.** pacifism; **a.** pacifistic
during the: **adv.** *flagrante bello*
equipment for: **n.** *apparatus belli;* armamentarium; (**pl.** armamentaria); armament(s); *matériel*
excuse or cause for: **n.** *casus belli*
hating of: **a.** misopolemical
-horse: **n.** *cheval de bataille*
laws are silent in time of: silent legis inter arma
paper (war): **n.** *guerre de plume*
stratagem of: **n.** *ruse de guerre*
such is, or that is: **adv.** *c'est la guerre*
to the death: **n.** *guerre à mort; guerre à outrance*
widespread or annihilative: **n.** armageddon; holocaust

WAREHOUSE : (**see** "storage place") **n.** *entrepôt*

WARINESS : see "prudence"

WARLIKE : (**see** "hostile") **a.** agonistic; amazonian; armigerous; bellicose; belligerent; disputatious; martial; militant; oppugnant; Spartan(ic) unpacific

WARM : **a.** ardent; calid; enthusiastic; **a.** WARMING : calefacient; calefactory; calescent; **n.** calefaction; calescence
-blooded: **a.** endothermic
growing: **a.** incalescent
-up: **n.** prologue; prolusion; **a.** prolusory

WARMED-*over:* **n.** or **a.** *réchauffé*
-over cabbage (old story): **n.** *crambe repetita*

WARMTH : (**see** "heat") **n.** ardency; ardor; calor; cordiality; fervor; hospitality; graciosity; graciousness; empressement; passion; temperature
excess: **n.** empressement; hyperpyrexia
producing or promoting: **a.** euthermic
sense or sensation of: **n.** thalposis; **a.** thalpotic

WARNING : **n.** (ad)monition; augury; caveat; (ex)hortation; homily; omen; premonition; presentiment; tocsin; **a.** (ad)monitorial; (ad)monitory; (ex)hortative; (ex)hortatory; homiletic; ominous; premonitory; **v.** WARN : admonish; caution; counsel; exhort; precondition; sermonize
against touching or interference: **n.** *noli me tangere*
as a (or by way of): **adv.** *in terrorem*
of death: **n.** *memento mori*
serving as a: **a.** deterrent; (ex)hortative; (ex)hortatory; monitory; sematic
symptom: **n.** prodrome; **a.** pathognomonic(al); prodromal

WART : **n.** ecphyma; excrescence; papilloma; verruca vulgaris
resembling: **a.** verrucose; verrucous

WASHING : **n.** ablution; lavage; lavation; **a.** ablutionary; **v.** WASH : (**see** "clean") deterge; erode; mundify
religious ceremonial: **n.** ablution; lavabo; maundy; nipter

WASTE(S) : **v.** despoil; devastate; dissipate; emaciate; exhaust; pillage; **n.** debris; decrement; depreciation; detritus; dilapidation; diminution; dross; excrement; prodigality; recrement; scoria; sordor; wilderness; (**pl.** (d)ejecta; egesta; excreta; rejecta[menta])
away, as by fasting or disease: **v.** atrophy; macerate; **a.** atrophic; atrophied; emaciated; tabescent; **n.** atrophy; emaciation; tabefaction; tabescence
giving off: **a.** depurant; emunctory; excretory
pert. to: **a.** excremental; excrementious; recrementitious
products: **n.** carrion; offal; offscourings
to lay: **v.** denudate; depauperate; depredate; deracinate; despoil; pillage

WASTEFUL : **a.** extravagant; improvident; imprudent; lavish; prodigal; profligate; thriftless; **n.** WASTEFULNESS : extravagance; improvidence; lavishness; prodigality; profligacy; superfluity
person: **n.** prodigal; profligate; spendthrift; wastrel

WATCH : **v.** chaperone; invigilate; proctor; supervise; survey; **n.** chaperonage; invigilation; scrutiny; surveillance; **a.** WATCHFUL : (**see** "aware") alert; Cerberean; surveillant; vigilant; wide-awake
on the: **adv.** *aux aguets*

WATCHER: **n.** Cerberus; chaperone; custodian; surveillant; watchdog
   sexual: **n.** scopophiliac; *voyeur*

WATCHMAKER *or repairman:* **n.** horologist; **n.** horology

WATCHWORD: **see** "password"

WATER(S), *absorbing:* **a.** bibulous; hydrophilic; hygroscopic; osmotic; **n.** bibulosity; deliquescence; osmosis
   animal that sheds: **n.** hydrophobe
   being in shallow: **a.** adlittoral
   containing (watery): **a.** hydrated; hydrous; ichorous; serous
   conveying or supplying: **a.** aquiferous
   cultivating plants, etc. in: **n.** aquiculture; hydroponics
   destitute of, or not containing: **a.** anhydrous; desiccated
   living in fresh: **a.** helolimnic
   living in, or on land: **a.** amphibious; **n.** amphibian
   moving, living or active in: **a.** lotic
   needing minimal amt. of: **a.** xerophilous
   nymph: **n.** naiad
   of the world: **n.** seven seas
   one adverse to: **n.** hydrophobe
   pure: **n.** *aqua pura*
   rel. to: **a.** aquatic
   still, rel. to or living in: **a.** lentic
   swimming or floating in or on: **a.** natant; natatory
   thriving in both flowing and still: **a.** eupotamic
      in flowing only: **a.** autopotamic
      in salt (water): **a.** halophilic
      in stagnant: **a.** stagnicolous
      in still only: **a.** tychopotamic
   to remove: **v.** dehydrate; desiccate; distil; evaporate; inspissate; sublimate
   treatment by: **n.** balneotherapy; balneotherapeutics; hydrotherapy
   under: **a.** subaqueous; submarine; suboceanic
   without: **a.** anhydrous; dehydrated; desiccated; inspissated; sublimated

WATERPROOF: **a.** repellant

WATERY: **a.** humid; hydrated; hydrous; ichorous; serous; **n.** WATERINESS: aquosity; humectation; humidity

WAVE(S): **v.** brandish; oscillate; undulate; **a. see** "wavy"

   sound of breaking: **n.** plangency; **a.** plangent

WAVER(ING): **v.** fluctuate; hesitate; oscillate; vacillate; **n.** indecision; irresolution; oscillation; vacillation; **a.** ambivalent; desultory; fitful; inconclusive; indecisive; intermittent; irresolute; pendulous; spasmodic; vacillating

WAVY (or WAVING): **a.** flexuating; flexuous; ondoyant; oundy; undulating; undulant

WAX, *ear:* **n.** cerumen; **a.** ceruminous
   producing: **a.** ceriferous

WAY(S), *having many:* **a.** multivious
   in his own: more suo
   of life or living: **n.** *modus vivendi*
   on the: **adv.** *chemin faisant*
   painful or sorrowful: **n.** *via dolorosa*

WAYLAY: **v.** ambush; **n.** ambuscade; ambush(ment)

WAYWARD *act or tendency:* **n.** caprice; capriciousness; erraticism; peccadillo; venality

WEAK (or WEAKENED): **a.** adynamic; anile; asthenic; attenuated; debilitated; decrepit; devitalized; effete; enervated; enfeebled; etiolated; feckless; fragile; impotent; impuissant; ineffective; infirm; invertebrate; irresolute; maladive; milk-and-water; phthisic(al); sapless; unfortified; unsupported; vacillating; valetudinarian; vulnerable; wavering; wishy-washy
   of mind: **n. or adv.** *impos animi;* **n.** imbecility
   morally: **a.** maladive
   person: **see under** "person"
   point: **n.** Achilles' heel; *locus minoris resistentiae;* vulnerability

WEAKEN: **v.** attenuate; debilitate; denude; denudate; devitalize; disable; emasculate; enervate; enfeeble; exhaust; incapacitate; undermine; unman; unnerve

WEAKENING: **a.** debilitating; devitalizing; enervating; **n.** attenuation
   as of moral principles or civil authority; **n.** labefaction
   gradual: **n.** attrition; erosion

WEAKNESS: (see "defect") n. adynamia; asthenia; atony; attenuation; cowardice; cowardliness; debilitation; debility; decrepitude; devitalization; effeminacy; enervation; *faiblesse;* foible; hypodynamia; imbecility; impotence; impuissance; inability; inanition; incapacity; languor; languishment; lassitude; marasmus; pusillanimity; tenuity; vulnerability
  body: n. adynamia; asthenia; a. adynamic; asthenic
  muscular: n. hypokinesia; hypokinesis; myasthenia; a. myasthenic
  of mind: see under "weak"
  point or place of: n. Achilles' heel; *locus minoris resistentiae;* vulnerability
  small, as of character: n. foible

WEALTH: n. abundance; affluence; luxuriance; luxury; opulence; profusion; prosperity; substance
  as evil or personified: n. mammon
  delusions of, or mad pursuit of: n. plutomania
  devoted to: a. mammonish; n. mammonist
  of, pert. to, or occupied in gaining: a. chrematistic
  opposite of: n. illth; poverty
  place or source of great: n. bonanza; El Dorado
  study of: n. chrematistics
  theory of as measured in money: n. chrematistics
  worship of: n. plutolatory; plutomania

WEALTHY: (see "rich") a. abundant; affluent; luxuriant; luxurious; opulent; profuse
  person: n. Croesus; leviathan; plutocrat; tycoon
  person who favors the: n. plutogogue; n. plutogogery

WEANING: n. ablactation

WEAR *and tear:* n. attrition; detrition; erosion

WEARINESS: (see "fatigue") n. boredom; ennui; languishment; lassitude; lethargy; monotony; tedium; adv. *ad nauseam*
  of life: n. *taedium vitae*

WEATHER *conditions, pert. to:* a. meteorologic(al); synoptic(al)

forecasting: n. aeromancy; meteorology; prognostication; a. synoptic(al)
  harshness of: n. asperity; inclemency; a. inclement
  science of: n. climatology; meteorology; a. meteorologic(al)
  study of effects on living beings: n. biometeorology; a. biometeorologic(al)

WEDDING: see "marriage"
  pert. to: a. epithalmic(al); hymeneal; nuptial
  song or poem: n. epithalamion; epithalamium; prothalamion; hymenal

WEDGE-*shaped:* a. cuneate; cuneatic; cuneiform

WEEK: n. hebdomad; a. hebdomadal

WEEP: see "cry"

WEIGH *in the mind:* n. perpension; v. perpend
  well the end: adv. *avise la fin*

WEIGHED, *capable of being:* a. ponderable
  not capable of being: a. imponderable

WEIGHT: n. avoirdupois; consequence; gravity; importance; influence; ponderance; ponderosity; prestige
  greater in: a. preponderant; n. preponderance
  having little: a. imponderable
  loss of: see "emaciation"
  of equal: a. equiponderant; isonomous
  pert. to or estimated in terms of: a. ponderal

WEIGHTY: a. burdensome; corpulent; cumbersome; cumbrous; gravid; grievous; important; influential; momentous; onerous; ponderable; ponderous; significant; solemn; n. WEIGHTINESS: ponderability; ponderosity

WEIRD: a. bizarre; cabalistic; eerie; eldri(t)ch; grotesque; incantatory; mysterious; supernatural; talismanic; uncanny; unearthly; n. bizarrerie; grotesquerie

WELCOME: n. *accueil; bienvenue;* salutation; a. delectable; felicitous; salutatory; salutiferous
  one who is: n. *persona grata; persona gratissimo;* (pl. *personae gratissimae*)
  one who is not: n. *persona non grata*

WELFARE, *harmful to, or to society:* **a.** *contra bonos mores*

WELL *and good:* **adv.** *à la bonne heure*
   -being: **n.** eudaemonia; euphoria; **a.** eudaemonic(al); euphoric; euphorious
      feeling of: **n.** euphoria
   -bred or mannered: **a.** *bien elevé(e)*
   done!: **adv.** *à la bonne heure;* bravissimo; bravo
      groomed: **a.** modish; *soigné* (**fem.** *soignée*)
   -known: **a.** celebrated; classic; eminent; proverbial; notorious

WELL, *as source of water, pert. to:* **a.** phreatic

WELSH *singing festival:* **n.** eisteddfod

WEST: **n. or a.** Occident

WESTERN: **a.** Hesperian; Occidental
   inhabitant: **n.** Hesperian; Occidental

WETNESS: **n.** aquosity; humectation; humidity

WETTING, *made transparent by:* **a.** hydrophanous

WHALE(S), *pert. to:* **a.** cetacean; cetaceous; **n.** cetacean

WHAT *will be, will be: che sarà sarà*

WHEAT, *of or like:* **a.** farinaceous; frumentaceous

WHEEDLE: **v.** cajole; flatter; **n.** cajolery; cajolement

WHEEL(S), *of or pert. to:* **a.** rotal; rotary

WHEN *all is said and done: en fin de compte*

WHERE (*mentioned*) *above:* **adv.** *ubi supra* (**abb.** u.s.)

WHERENESS: **n.** ubiety

WHICH *is.* **adv.** *quod est* (**abb.** q.e.)
   see: **adv.** *quod vide* (**abb.** q.v.)

WHILE, *not worth:* **adv.** *non est tanti*

WHIM(S): **n.** bizarrerie; caprice; chimera; eccentricity; fancy; fantasque; haec-ceity; idiosyncrasy; megrim(s); oddity; peculiarity; quiddity; quirk; singularity; vagary; whimsicality; **a.** WHIMSICAL: capricious; captious; crotchety; fanciful; fantastic; impish; notional; puckish; roguish; vagarious; **n.** WHIMSICALNESS: caprice; chimera; puckishness; roguery; vagary; whimsicality

WHIP: **v.** castigate; chastise; flagellate; fustigate

WHIRL: **v.** pirouette; vertiginate; **a.** vertiginous; **n.** bustle; commotion

WHIRLPOOL: **n.** charybdis; gurge; maelstrom; riptide; vortex; **a.** vertiginous
   large and violent: **n.** maelstrom

WHISKEY: **n.** *spiritus frumenti*

WHISPER: **v.** siffilate; **n.** sussurus; *vox clandestina;* **a.** WHISPERING: **see** "murmuring"
   in a: **a. or adv.** *sotto voce*

WHISTLE: **v.** siffle; **n.** siffleur

WHITE, *from heat:* **a.** candent; candescent; **n.** candescence
   like marble: **a.** marmoreal
   turning: **a.** albescent; canescent; etiolated; **n.** canescence; etiolation

WHO *goes there?:* **n.** *qui va là?; qui vive?*
   guards the guards?: **n.** *quis custodiet ipsos custodes?*

WHOLE: (**see** "entire") **n.** integer; integral; solidium; totality; **a.** *en bloc; en masse;* impartite; intact; maiden; unbroken; undivided; unimpaired; unmarred; unmotivated; **adv.** WHOLLY: *de fond; de haut en bas; en comble;* **n.** WHOLENESS: (**see** "totality") integrality; integrity
   affording a gen. view of: **a.** panoramic; synoptic
   as a: **adv.** *en masse; in toto*
   form into a: **v.** synthesize; **n.** synthesis

WHOLESOME: **a.** beneficial; curative; healthful; remedial; restorative; salubrious; salutary; salutiferous; **n.** WHOLESOMENESS: salubrity; salutariness

WHOOPING *cough:* **n.** pertussis; **a.** pertussal

WICKED: (see "base" and "evil") **a.** abhorrent; abominable; atrocious; Babylonian; devilish; diabolic(al); dissolute; execrable; flagitious; flagrant; ghoulish; heinous; hellish; infamous; iniquitous; intractable; licentious; malignant; Mephistophelian; nefarious; nefast; notorious; odious; piacular; sacrilegious; satanic; saturnine; scandalous; vicious; villainous; viperish; viperous; **n.** WICKEDNESS: (see "evil") abomination; Belial; diablerie; enormity; flagitiousness; infamy; iniquity; rascality; sinfulness; turpitude
    no rest for the: nemo malus felix
    (*not pious*): **a.** blasphemous; impious; irreligious; profane; sacrilegious
    person: **n.** Beelzebub; caitiff; Mephistopheles

WIDE: (see "intensive") **a.** expansive; extensive; illimitable; magnitudinous; **n.** see "width"
    in range of knowledge: **a.** bibliognostic; cyclopedic; omniscient; pansophic(al)
    open: **a.** distended; patulous
    -spread: **a.** catholic; epidemic; far-reaching; peregrine; peregrinic; predominant; prevalent; regnal; regnant; universal; **n.** catholicity; ecumenicity; prevalence; regnancy; universality

WIDOW: **n.** relict

WIDTH: **n.** amplitude; comprehension; expansiveness; expansivity; fullness; liberality; magnitude; spaciousness

WIFE: (see "wives") **n.** consort; *femme couverte;* spouse; *ux(or)*
    dear: **n.** *cara sposa*
    doting or fond of, or submissive to: **a.** uxorious; **n.** uxoriousness
    faithful: **n.** Penelope
    having but one at a time: **n.** monogamy; monogyny; **a.** monogamous; monogynous
        two or more at a time: **n.** polygamy; polygyny; **a.** polygamous; polygynous
    located or centered around family of the: **a.** matrilocal
    murder of by hus.: **n.** uxorcide
    of, befitting or characteristic of: **a.** uxorial

WILD: (see "reckless") **a.** barbaric; barbarous; beserk; boisterous; brutal; corybantic; dissolute; extravagant; fantastic; feral; heathenish; impassioned; inordinate; insane; licentious; maniac(al);

pagan; riotous; savage; tempestuous; turbulent; uncivilized; uncultivated; undisciplined; undomesticated; ungovernable; unruly; unsubdued; untamed; **n.** WILDNESS: barbarity; ferity; mania; turbulence; wilderness
    by nature: **a.** *ferae naturae*
    emotionally: **a.** berserk; corybantic; dithyrambic; frantic; frenetic(al); frenzied; hysterical; impassioned; insane; maniac(al); phrenetic(al)
        (*growing in fields, etc.*): **a.** agrestic
    nature, having: **a.** *ferae naturae*

WILE: (see "whimsicality") **n.** artifice; machination; stratagem

WILL: **v.** bequeath; demise; devise; **n.** determination; disposition; inclination; intention; resolution; testament; volition
    act or exercise of: **n.** volition; **a.** volitional
    adverse action of: **n.** nolition
    against one's (will) or consent: **adv.** *in invitum*
    at: **adv.** *a capriccio; ad arbitrium; à discrétion*
    freedom of (doctrine): **n.** libertarianism; **a. or n.** libertarian
    having made none, or not disposed by: **a.** intestate
    -power, loss of: **n.** abulia
    with good: **adv.** *de bonne volonté*

WILLING: (see "compliant") **a.** acceptant; acquiescent; amenable; voluntary; **adv.** WILLINGLY: *de bonne grâce; de bonne volonté; ex animo*
    and able: **adv.** *volens et potens*
    or unwilling: **adv.** *nolens volens*

WILLINGNESS: **n.** amenability; tractability
    to receive: **n.** receptivity; **a.** receptive

WILLY-NILLY: **a.** *nolens volens;* **adv.** *bon gré; mal gré; nolens volens*

WILY: see "cunning"

WIND(S), *fertilized by:* **a.** anemophilous
    measuring velocity: **n.** anemography; anemology; anemometry
    puff of: **n.** flatus
    sound of: **a.** aeolian; aeolic
    study of: **n.** anemology; **n.** anemologist
    treatise on: **n.** anemography; anemology

WIND(ING) : (see "devious") **v.** intort; meander; undulate; wreathe; **a.** anfractuous; circuitous; flexuous; meandering; meandrous; serpentine; sinuate; sinuous; tortuous; **n.** anfractuosity; flexuosity; intorsion; sinuation; torsion
path, course or action: **n.** anfractuosity; sinuosity

WINDOW(S) : **n.** aperture; fenestration; (**pl.** fenestra)
situated bet.: **a.** interfenestral
throwing or being thrown thru: **n.** defenestration

WINE, *god of:* **n.** Bacchus
lover or connoisseur of: **n.** oenophile; oenophilist
of or pert. to: **a.** vinic; vinous
maker of, or merchant: **n.** vinter
pert. to making: **a.** oenopoetic
science of, or of making: **n.** (o)enology
steward: **n.** sommelier
truth in (in intoxication): **n.** *in vino veritas*

WINEBIBBER : **n.** oenophilist

WING(S), *having:* **a.** aliferous
having two: **a.** bipentate; dipterous
pert. to or resembling: **a.** pteric
-shaped: **a.** aliform

WINK : **v.** nictate; nictitate; **n.** nictitation

WINTER, *pert. to (wintery):* **a.** boreal; brumal; heimal; hibernal
spend the, or become dormant in: **v.** hibernate; **n.** hibernation; **a.** hibernatant

WISDOM : **n.** acumen; discernment; discretion; discrimination; judgment; judicality; knowledge; perspicacity; prudence; rationality; sagacity; sageness; sanity; sapience; sapiency; subtlety
divine: **n.** Sophia; **a.** Sophian
goddess of: **n.** Minerva
hater of: **n.** misosopher; misosophist; **n.** misosophy
human: **n.** anthroposophy; **a.** anthroposophic(al)
marked by great: **a.** Nestorian; Solomonian; Solomonic
pert. to or having great: **a.** sagacious; sapient(ial); sophistic(al)
rel. to **a.** paladian

WISE : (see "sage") **a.** acuminous; cognizant; circumspect; discerning; discreet;
discriminating; equitable; erudite; judgmatic(al); judicious; Nestorian; oracular; orphic; perspicacious; politic; profound; sagacious; sapient(ial); Solomonian; Solomonic
and pithy: **a.** aphoristic; apothegmatic; gnomic(al); gnomonic; **n.** see "witticism"
moderation: **n.** continence; prudence; sophrosyne
no one sufficiently by himself: nemo solus satis sapit
person: (see "intellectual") **n.** Nestor(ian); patriarch; sage; Solomon
saying: see "maxim" **and** "witticism"

WISECRACKING *spirit:* **n.** gaminerie

WISH *or desire, expressing:* **a.** benedictive; optative; precative
slight: **n.** velleity

WIT(S) : **n.** acumen; alertness; coruscation; drollery; facetiosity; facetiousness; irony; jocularity; *nugae canorae;* persiflage; repartee; *sal Atticus;* sarcasm; whimsicality; **n.** Aristophanes; *bel esprit; causeur; farceur;* (**fem.** *farceuse*); *homme d'esprit; persifleur*
biting: **n.** causticity; mordacity; sarcasm; spinosity
display flashes of: **v.** coruscate; **n.** coruscation; pyrotechnics
end, at his: au bout de son latin
light: **n.** badinage; bavardage; causerie; repartee
sallies or flashes of: **n.pl.** coruscations; *feux d'artifice;* pyrotechnics

WITCH : **n.** Circe; enchantress; lamia; necromancer; pythoness; sibyl; sorceress; vampire; **n.** WITCHCRAFT : necromancy; sorcery; **n.** necromancer; sorcerer

WITCHES, *midnight assembly of:* **n.** sabbat

WITH *all one's might:* **adv.** *à toute force*
certainty: **adv.** *à coup sûr*
equal pace: **a. or adv.** *pari passu*
grain of salt: **adv.** *cum grano salis*
great praise: **adv.** *magna cum laude*
greatest praise or highest honors: **adv.** *summa cum laude*
honor(s) or praise: **adv.** *cum laude*
many others: cum multis aliis
one voice: **adv.** una voce; unisonal; unisonous
pleasure: **adv.** *avec plaisir*
running pen: **adv.** *currente calamo*

WITHDRAW: **v.** abjure; recede; relinquish; retract; retreat; revoke; subduct; **n.** WITHDRAWAL: detachment; insularity; retraction; revocation; revulsion; subduction; **a.** WITHDRAWN: **see** "secluded"

WITHER: **v.** atrophy; decline; paralyze; senesce; wizen; **n.** WITHERING: annihilation; devastation; senescence; tabescence

WITHIN, *from or existing:* **adv.** *ab intra;* **a.** autogenous; endogenous; indwelling
   originating or developing fr.: **a.** autogenous; endogenous; esoteric

WITHOUT *a day (being set):* **a. or adv.** *sine die*
   care or worry: **adv.** *sans souci; sine cura;* **a.** *dégagé*
   definite plan or method: **a.** desultory
   delay: **adv.** *sine mora; tout de suite*
   doubt: **adv.** assuredly; indisputably; indubitable; *sans doute; sine dubio;* undoubtedly
   embarrassment or constraint: **adv.** *sans gêne;* unconstrainedly
   envy: **adv.** *sine invidia*
   equal: **adv.** *sans pareil*
   fail: **adv.** *à coup sûr*
   from: **adv.** *ab extra;* **a.** advenient; adventitious; exogeneous; extraneous; extrinsic
   hatred: **adv.** *sine odio*
   issue: **adv.** *sine prole*
   prejudice: **adv.** *sine praejudicio*
   this: **adv.** *abseque hoc*

WITHSTAND: **v.** brook; contest; endure; oppose; resist

WITNESS, *call to:* **v.** obtest; **n.** obtestation
   in: **adv.** *in testimonium*

WITTICISM: (**see** "maxim") **n.** aphorism; apothegm; bijouterie; *bon mot;* coruscation; epigram; *jeu d'esprit; jeu de mots;* jocosity; *mot pour rire;* truism; *turlupinade;* (**pl.** *facetiae*)

WITTY: **a.** Aristophanic; epigrammatic(al); facetious; jocose; jocular; laconic; mercurial; scintillescent; scintillating; **n.** WITTINESS: facetiosity; jocosity; *plaisanterie*
   person: **see under** "wit"
   sprightly: **a.** spirituel(le)

   to be: **v.** coruscate; scintillate
   writer: **n.** epigrammatist; satirist
   writing(s): **n.pl.** *facetiae*

WIVES: **see** "wife"
   having but one, or having more than one: **see under** "wife"
   or husband(s), having two or more at same time: **n.** polygamy; **a.** polygamous

WIZARD: **see** "magician"

WOE: **n.** affliction; anguish; dolor; heartache; tribulation
   tale of: **n.** jeremiad; lamentation; threnode; threnody; **a.** lamentable; threnodic
   to the conquered: vae victis

WOLF-*like:* **a.** lupine
   mental cond. or belief that person has turned into: **n.** loup-garou; lycanthropy; werewolf; **n.** lycanthrope

WOMAN (or WOMEN): (**see** "lady") **n.** femineity; feminity; womankind
   abnormal fear of: **n.** gynephobia
   adviser or companion: **n.** Egeria
   apartment for: **n.** gynaeceum; seraglio; thalamus; zenana
   bold, brazen, impudent or immoral: **n.** quean
   club for: **n.** sorority; sorosis
   enchanting: **n.** charmeuse; Circe; enchantress; *femme fatale;* sorceress
   exclusion from public: **n.** purdah
   "fallen": **n.** *femme perdue*
   fascinating: **see** "seductive" **below**
   fashionable: **n.** *femme du monde;* mondaine; sophisticate
   flighty or silly: **n.** flibbertigibbet
   fond of: **a.** philogynous; **n.** philogyny; **n.** philogynist
   frenzied, raving or distressed: **n.** maenad; **a.** maenadic
   frivolous, young: **n.** coquette; soubrette
   govt. by: **n.** gynarchy; gynecocracy; matriarchy
   hater, hatred or distrust of: **n.** misogyne; misogynist; **n.** misogynism; misogyny; **a.** misogynic; misogynous
   having borne more than one child: **n.** multipara; **a.** multiparous
   having borne no child: **n.** nullipara; **a.** nonparous; nulliparous
   head of house: **n.** chatelaine; materfamilias; matriarch; **a.** matriarchal
   idealization or worship of: **n.** Mariol-

atry; philogyny; **a.** Mariolatrous; philogenous

ill-tempered: **n.** shrew; termagant; virago; vixen; Xanthippe; **a.** shrewish; termagantish; viraginous; vixenish

Jewish, attaining age 13, also rite: **n.** bat(h) **or** *bas mitzvah*

kept: **n.** demimondaine

learned and literary, esp. if pedantic and undomestic: **n.** bluestocking; *femme savante*

little: **n.** microgyne; *petite dame*

look for the: **adv.** *cherchez la femme*

loud: **n.** rounceval; shrew; termagant; virago

love or fondness for: **n.** philogyny; **n.** philogynist

lover of married: **n.** cicisbeo

married: **n.** *femme couverte*

masculine-like: **n.** Amazon; amazonism; hermaphrodite; hermaphroditism; gynander; gynandry; **a.** amazonian; gynandrous; hermaphroditic; mannish; unwomanish

of erudition: **n.** *femme savante*

of fashionable society: **see** "fashionable" **above**

of high rank: **n.** *grande dame*

of loose morals: **n.** nymph; nymphet (young)

of questionable reputation: **n.** coquette; courtesan; demimondaine; demimonde; quean

of the house(hold): **see** "head of house" **above**

of the street: (**see** "prostitute") **n.** *nymphe du pavé*

of the world: **n.** *femme du monde;* mondaine; sophisticate

old and imposing, or dominant: **n.** dowager; matriarch

old or cantankerous: **n.** beldam(e); crone; gammer; grimalkin; harridan

old, state of being: **n.** anility; **a.** anile

pregnant for first time, or borne but one child: **n.** primipara; **a.** primiparous

pure and chaste: **n.** vestal (virgin)

raging: **n.** beldam(e); shrew; virago

rel. to or characteristic of: **a.** distaff; muliebral; **n.** muliebriety

rooms or apts. for: **see** "apartment for" **above**

scolding: **see** "loud" **above**

seductive: **n.** charmeuse; Circe; enchantress; *femme fatale;* intrig(u)ante; Lorelei; siren; sorceress; succubus

separate quarters: **see** "apartment for" **above**

separation or exclusion of: **n.** purdah

shameless: **n.** huzzy; Jezebel; quean; trollop

small: **see** "little" **above**

society: **see** "fashionable" **above**

stately old: **n.** dowager; matriarch

treacherous: **n.** Delilah

unmarried: **n.** *femme seule*

untidy or slovenly: **n.** gorgon; grimalkin; slattern; trollop

young, inexperienced and unworldly: **n.** ingenue; soubrette

if flighty or silly: **n.** flibbertigibbet

wise: **n.** *femme savante*

worldly or sophisticated: **n.** bluestocking; *femme du monde; flaneuse;* mondaine; sophisticate

worship of: **see** "idealization" **above**

WOMANHOOD: **n.** feminality; femineity; femininity; muliebrity; (**pl.** feminie)

goddess of: **n.** Juno

Jewish, attaining age 13: **see under** "woman"

WONDER *at nothing: nil admirari*

WONDERFUL: **a.** admirable; astonishing; astounding; extraordinary; ineffable; marvelous; miraculous; mirific; phenomenal; stupendous; surprising; wondrous

to see: **adv.** *mirabile visu*

to tell: **adv.** *mirabile dictu*

WONDERS, *year of:* **n.** *annus mirabilis*

WOOD(S), *inhabiting:* **a.** nemoral; silvicolous

pert. to: **a.** ligneous; nemoral; sylvan; sylvatic; sylvestran

resembling: **a.** ligneous; lignescent; xyloid

WOODED: **a.** arboraceous; arboreal; arboreous; arborescent; **a.** WOODY: ligneous; lignescent; xyloid

place: **n.** arboretum

WOOLLY: **a.** flocculent; lanate; laniferous; lanigerous

WORD(S): (**see** "name") **n.** lexicon; thesaurus; vocabulary

abundant flow of: (**see** "wordiness") **n.** affluence; *copia verborum;* facundity; loquaciousness; loquacity

adaption of foreign to English: **v.** anglicise; anglicize; **n.** anglicization

addition of letter(s) to: **n.** prosthesis

ambiguous use of: **n.** amphibolism; amphibology; verbal fallacy

arbitrary or capricious coinage of; **n.** logodaedaly

at a loss for: **a.** nonplussed

backward same as forward: **n.** palindrome

-blindness: **n.** alexia

blunder: **see** "mischance or misuse" below

-book: **n.** calepin; dictionary; glossary; gradus; lexicon; nomenclature; onomasticon; synonymicon; terminology; thesaurus; vocabulary

burning (words): **n.** *ardentia verba*

choice or pattern of: **n.** diction; phraseology

coinage of, arbitrary: **n.** logodaedaly

compound, separation of: **n.** tmesis

consisting of one: **a.** monepic

contradictory or incongruous in effect (as "kind cruelty"): **n.** oxymoron

defining, art or practice of: **n.** lexicography; **a.** lexicographic

degeneration in meaning of: **n.** bastardization; corruption; pejoration

derivation: **n.** etymology; lexicology; provenance; semantics

derived fr. another in another lang.: **n.** paronym; **a.** paronymous

derived fr. sound(s): **n.** onomatope; onomatopoea; **a.** echoic; onomatopoe(t)ic

disparaging one for usual, also word so used: **n.** dysphemism

dispute over or about: **n.** logomachy

distortion of sense of, also one who does: (**see** "punning") **n.** verbicide

drop first letter or syllable of: **n.** aph(a)eresis

drop last letter or syllable of: **n.** apocopation; apocope; elision; **e.** apocopate; elide

drop middle or internal letter or sound: **n.** syncope

empty or idle: **n.pl.** *paroles en l'air*

enough: **n.** *satis verborum*

exact or appropriate (the right): **n.** *mot juste*

excess use of: **see** "wordiness"

expert: **n.** etymologist; lexicographer; morphologist; philologist; phonemicist; semanticist

expressing a definite image or idea: **n.** semanteme

few, in a: **adv.** *en abrégé; paucis verbis*

for a symbol, as %: **n.** logogram

-for-word: **a.** *ad verbum;* literal(istic);

literatim; mot à mot; textual; unvarnished; *verbatim; verbatim et literatim*

-for-word-and-letter-for-letter: **a.** *verbatim et literatim*

formed for an occasion: **n.** nonce (word)

formed fr. first letters, as A.W.O.L.: **n.** acronym; **a.** acronymic

formed fr. word in another lang.: **n.** paronym; **a.** paronymous

foul: **n.pl.** *gros mot*

four-letter: **n.** tetragram

game: **n.** anagrams; logomachy

having few syllables: **a.** brachysyllabic

having many syllables: **a.** polysyllabic(al); sesquipedalian(istic)

having more than one meaning: **n.** polysemant; **a.** polysemantic; polysemous

having one meaning only: **a. or n.** univocal

history or course of development of: **n.** phylogenesis; phylogeny; **n.** phylogenist

honeyed: **n.pl.** *paroles mielleuses;* **a. see** "honeyed"

idea w/ no exact (word) for: **n.** anonym(e)

idle: **see** "empty" above

imitative of sound(s): **see** "derived fr. sound(s)" **above**

in a few: **adv.** *en abrégé; paucis verbis*

in express: **adv.** *expressis verbis*

in plain: **adv.** *nudis verbis;* **a. or adv.** *en clair*

in so many: **adv.** *(in) totidem verbis*

in these (or in the same): **adv.** *in haec verba*

index of: **n.** *index verborum*

last syllable of: **n.** ultima

last syllable but one: **n.** penult; penultima(te); **a.** penultimate

last syllable but two: **n.** antepenult; **a.** antepenultimate

list of: **n.** lexicon; nomenclature; onomasticon; synonymicon; terminology; vocabulary

literal meaning acc. to origin: **n.** etymon

long: **n.** polysyllable; sesquipedalian; (**pl.** *sesquipedalia verba*) **a.** multisyllabic; polysyllabic(al); sesquipedalian(istic)

use of: **n.** polysyllabism; sesquipedalianism: sesquipedality

loss of one or more sounds in middle in pronouncing: **n.** syncope; **a.** syncopal

loss of ability to remember: **n.** aphasia; **a.** aphasic

loss of vowel at beginning: **n.** aphesis

loss of vowel or letter at end: **n.** apocopation; apocope; **v.** apocopate *made for the time or occasion:* **n.** nonce (word)

mania for repeating certain: **n.** echolalia; onomatomania; verbomania

meaning: **n.** etymology

    study of: **n.** semantics; semasiology; semology; significs

    where changed for worse: **see** "degeneration" **above**

mischoice or misuse of: **n.** cacology; catachresis; impropriety; malaprop(ism); solecism; spoonerism; **a.** catachrestic(al); **n.** malaprop; spoonerism

new, or new meaning for old: **n.** neologism; neoterism; **v.** neologize; **a.** neological; neologistic

next to last syllable: **n.** penult; penultima(te) **a.** penultimate

obsession w/: **n.** onomatomania; verboonomatomania; verbomania; **n.** verboonomatomaniac; verbomaniac

of honor: **n.** *parole d'honneur*

of many syllables: **a.** multisyllabic; polysyllabic

of mouth: **adv.** *ore tenus; viva voce*

of one syllable: **n.** monosyllable; **a.** monosyllabic(al)

of opposite meaning: **n.** antonym; **a.** antonymous

omission of sound in: **n.** apocopation; elision; haplology; **v.** apocopate; elide

opp. or diff. fr. meaning for emphasis: **n.** trope; tropology; **a.** tropologic(al)

opp. to meaning as in humor: **n.** antiphrasis; **a.** antiphrastic

parting: (**see** "farewell") **n.** envoi; valediction

pass-, watch-, or catchword: **n.** shibboleth

pert. to: **a.** lexical; verbal; vocabular

pert. to meaning: **a.** semasiological; semantic(al)

play on: (**see** "pun") **n.** equivoque; *jeu de mots*

pretentious use of recondite: **n.** lexiphanticism; **a.** lexiphantic

reading same backward as forward: **n.** palindrome

repeat endlessly and meaninglessly: **v.** verbigerate; **n.** echolalia; verbigeration

repetition for emphasis or effect: **n.** alliteration; iteration; ploce

repetition of, in sentence: **n.** anadiplosis; echolalia; onomatomania; verbigeration

repetition, senseless: **n.** cataphasia; echolalia; onomatomania; verbigeration

repetition, unnecessary: **n.** battolology; **a.** battological; **v.** battologize

ridiculous misuse of: **n.** malapropism

same backward as forward: **n.** palindrome

same pronunciation as another but diff. meaning: **n.** homonym

same spelling as another but diff. meaning and pronunciation: **n.** heteronym

science of origin and development: **n.** etymology; onomastics; onomatology; phylogeny; **a.** etymological; onomasiologic(al)

senseless repetition or meaningless jumble of: **n.** Babelism; cataphasia; echolalia; onomatomania; verbigeration

sentence expressed by a: **n.** polysynthesism; **a.** holophrastic

serving to fill out sentence or line: **n.** expletive

sharp: **n.pl.** *paroles aigres;* **n.** mordacity; spinosity

spell or represent in letters or characters of another lang.: **v.** transliterate; **n.** metography; transliteration

spelled or pronounced alike but diff. in meaning: **n.** homograph; homonym; homophone *(as sea and see)*

spoken (word) cannot be recalled: nescit vox missa reverti

student of: **see** "expert" **above**

study of: **n.** etymology; semantics; semasiology; semology; significs

study of form and structure of: **n.** morphology; phonetics

study of origin and development: **see** "science" **above**

substandard: **n.** barbarism; bastardization; colloquialism; patois

symbol used to represent, as %: **n.** ideogram; logogram; **a.** ideogrammatic; ideogram(m)ic; logogrammatic

the right: **n.** *mot juste*

the very: **n.** *ipissima verba*

to a: **adv.** *ad verbum*

to blows: **adv.** *a verbis ad verba*

to wise is sufficient: verbum sapient satis est (abb. *verbum sap.*)

transposition of, or of letters in: **n.** metathesis; strephosymbolia

transposition of sounds: **n.** spoonerism; **v.** spoonerize

unacceptable use of: **see** "misuse of" **above**

unconscious use of other than intended: **n.** heterophemy; *lapsus linguae*

uncontrollable obsession for: **see** "obsession with" **above**

unsound reasoning by ambiguous use of: amphibologism; amphibology; verbal fallacy

use of equivocal or ambiguous: **n.** amphibologism; amphibilogy; officialese; parsiology
    of long: **see under** "long" **above**
    of many where few would do: **n.** circumlocution; periphrasis; **a.** periphrastic
    of too many: **see** "wordiness" **and** "wordy"
    of wrong for context: **n.** catachresis; **a.** catachrestic(al)
    opp. to meaning as in humor: **n.** antiphrasis; **a.** antiphrastic
    opp. to or diff. fr. meaning for emphasis: **n.** trope; tropology; **a.** tropologic(al)
    worship of: **n.** grammatolatry
    written: **n.pl.** *literae scriptae*

WORDBOOK: **see under** "word"
    in specialized field: **n.** nomenclature; onomasticon

WORDINESS: **n.** affluence; catalogia; circumlocution; *copia verborum;* diffusion; fecundity; garrulity; logorrhea; loquacity; loquaciousness; macrology; officialese; periphrasis; pleonasm; prolixity; redundancy; tautology; verbality; verbiage; verbalism; verbigeration; verbomania; verbosity; voluminosity

WORDY: (**see** "talkative") **a.** circumlocutious; circumlocutory; copious; diffuse; garrulous; logorrheic; palaverous; pleonastic; profuse; prolix; protracted; redundant; repetitious; tautological; verbose

WORK: **n.** accomplishment; employment; exertion; *métier;* moil; occupation; production; profession
    able to do any kind of: **a.** panurgic
    additional: **n.** supererogation; **a.** supererogatory
    as musical or literary: **n.** oeuvre; opus
      major: **n.** *chef d'oeuvre; magnus opus; meisterwerk; pièce de résistance*
      minor: **n.** opuscule; opusculum
    fear of or aversion to: **n.** ergasiophobia; ergophobia
    love of or great desire to: **n.** ergasiomania; ergomania; ergophilia
    -over: **see** "rehash"
    pert. to: **a.** employmental; industrial; occupational; vocative; vocational
    subordinate or accessory: **n.** parergon; (**pl.** parerga)

WORKED-*over:* **n.** or **a.** *réchauffé;* **a.** refurbished; renovated

WORKING *class:* **n.** proletarian; proletariat; **a.** proletarian
    hard and steady: **a.** sedulous; **n.** sedulity

WORKMANSHIP: (**see** "skill") **n.** artisanship; artistry; craftsmanship; expertise; virtuosity

WORKSHOP: **n.** atelier

WORLD: (**see** "earth") **n.** creation; humanity; macrocosm; mankind; sphere
    against the (in defiance of opn.): **a.** or **adv.** *contra mundum*
    all the: **adv.** *tout le monde*
    ancient or primeval: **n.** foreworld
    before creation of: **a.** antemundane; premundane
    belief that tends to become better: **n.** meliorism
    citizen of: **n.** cosmopolitan; cosmopolite; *homme du monde*
    -creating: **a.** cosmopoietic
    denying reality of temporal: **a.** acosmic; **n.** acosmism
    end of: **n.** götterdämmerung
    extending or lying beyond the: **a.** extramundane; transmundane
    fashionable: **n.** *le beau monde; (le) monde*
    in its entirety: **n.** macrocosm; **a.** macrocosmic
    learned, the: **n.** *le monde savant*
    little: **n.** microcosm; **a.** microcosmic(al)
    lower, of or rel. to: **a.** chthonian; plutonian; plutonic; subterranean
    man of the: **n.** boulevardier; cosmopolitan; cosmopolite; *homme du monde*
    of the dead: **n.** netherworld
    of this: **see** "worldly"
    on small scale: **n.** microcosm; **a.** microcosmic(al)
    out of this, or not of this: **a.** extramundane; extraterrestrial; supermundane; transmundane
    pert. to: **a.** cosmic; cosmopolitan; global; mundane; planetary; subcelestial; terrestrial; universal
    private: **n.** autocosm; **a.** autocosmic
    transcending the: **a.** extramundane; supermundane; supernatural; transmundane
    under-: **n.** or **a.** chthonian; subterranean; subterrestrial; **n.** subterrene
    view or outlook: **n.** weltanschauung
    vital force: **n.** *anima mundi; élan vital*

way of the: **n.** *l'usage du monde*
-weariness: **n.** ennui; **a.** *fin-de-siècle*
-wide: **a.** cosmopolitan; ecumenic(al); global; pandemic; peregrinic; planetary; terrestrial; universal(ized); **n.** ecumenicity; pandemia; universality
   wishes to be fooled: mundus vult decepi
   within this: **a.** intramundane

WORLDLY: (**see** "sensuous") **a.** carnal; fashionable; global; hedonic; intramundane; laic; lustful; luxurious; mondain(e); mortal; mundane; profane; secular; sensual; sensuous; sophisticated; subastral; subcelestial; sublunary; temporal; terrene; terrestrial; uncelestial; universal; unspiritual; **n.** WORLDLINESS: carnality; mundacity; mundanity; secularism; secularity; sensuality; temporality; universality
   activities or troubles: **n.** coil; moil; (**pl.** temporalities)
   not: **see** "heavenly" **and** "unearthly"

WORM-*eaten:* **a.** vermiculate; vermoulu
   infested w/ (worms): **a.** verminous; **n.** verminosis
   resembling: **a.** vermicular; vermiculate; vermiform

WORN *by constant use:* **a.** hackneyed; stereotyped; threadbare; trite; vapid; **n.** attrition; erosion
   -out: **a.** decrepit; dilapidated; effete; **n.** decrepitude; dilapidation

WORRY: (**see** "annoyance") **v.** disconcert; harass; importune; tantalize; torment; **n.** complication; fantod(s); harassment; nightmare; vexation; **a.** WORRYING: (**see** "concerned") apprehensive; disconcerted; distressed; perplexed

WORSE, *so much the:* **adv.** *tant pis*
   state of becoming progressively: **n.** ingravescence; **a.** ingravescent
   to make: **v.** bastardize; denigrate; disimprove; exacerbate; minify; pejorate; tragedize; **a.** denigrative; exacerbative; pejorative; **n.** denigration; disimprovement; exacerbation; pejoration
   to worse, from: **adv.** *de pis en pis*

WORSEN: **v.** decline; degenerate; deteriorate; exacerbate; retrograde; retrogress; **a.** WORSENING: exacerbative; retrogressive; retrograde; **n.** declination; deterioration; exacerbation; retrogression

WORSHIP: **v.** adore; adulate; observe; venerate; **n.** adoration; adulation; devotion; dulia; hierurgy; homage; liturgy; observation; veneration; **n.** WORSHIPER: adulator; congregant; devotee
   due to God alone: **n.** latria
   erotic, as of articles of female clothing: **n.** fetichism; **a.** fetichistic
   of ancestors: **n.** ancestor cult; manism; **a.** filopietistic; manistic
   of Bible: **n.** Bibliolatry
   of books: **n.** bibliolatry; bibliomania; **a.** bibliolatrous; **n.** bibliolater; bibliomaniac
   of church or church matters: **n.** ecclesiolatry
   of dead: **n.** necrolatry; **a.** necrolatrous
   of devil(s): **n.** demonolatry; **n.** diabolist
   of dogs: **n.** cynolatry; **n.** cynolatrist
   of foreign or unsanctioned gods: **n.** allotheism
   of idols: **n.** iconolatry; idolatry
   of letters or words: **n.** grammatolatry
   of man: **n.** anthropolatry
   of many gods: **n.** polytheism
   of money: **n.** amor nummi; mammonism; plutolatry; plutomania
   of nature or natural forces: **n.** pantheism; physiolatry; priapism; **a.** pantheistic; physiolatrous; **n.** pantheist; physiolater
   of obscenity: **n.** aischrolatreia
   of old, or what is old: **n.** archeolatry; archai(ci)sm
   of one god: **n.** henotheism; monolatry; monotheism; **a.** monolatrous; monotheistic(al)
   of religion: **n.** ecclesiolatry
   of riches: see "of money" **above**
   of saints or sacred things: (see "saints") **n.** hierolatry
   of self: **n.** autotheism; **a.** auththeistic(al)
   of Shakespeare and/or his works: **n.** bardolatry
   of snakes: **n.** ophiolatry
   of spirits of deceased: see "of ancestors" **above**
   of state or govt.: **n.** statolatry
   of sun: **n.** heliolatry
   of symbols: **n.** symbololatry
   of virgin(s): **n.** Mariolatry; parthenolatry
   of wealth: see "of money" **above**
   of woman or women: **n.** Mariolatry; philogyny
   of words or letters: **n.** grammatolatry
   place of: **n.** adoratory

religious, pert. to: **a.** hierurgical; liturgical; ritualistic; rubrical

WORST, *at the:* **adv.** *au pis aller*
govt. by (worst) men: **n.** kakistocracy

WORTH: **n.** appreciation; estimation; excellence; integrity; importance; merit; morality; nobleness; rectitude; sincerity; stability; usefulness
man of: **n.** *homme de bien;* (**pl.** *gens de condition*)

WORTHLESS: **a.** contemptible; despicable; fustian; impotent; incompetent; ineffectual; insignificant; inutile; nugatory; paltry; profligate; stramineous; unproductive; valueless; **n.** WORTHLESS-NESS: floccinaucinihilipilification
object: **n.** ambsace; nihil(ity)
part of anything: (**see** "waste") **n.** *caput mortuum;* dross; recrement; scoria
person: **see** "rogue"
thing: (**see** "waste") **n.** ambsace; *corpus vile;* (**pl.** *corpus villa*); flummadiddle; nihil(ity); (**pl.** flotsam and jetsam)

WORTHY: **a.** chivalrous; commendable; condign; creditable; estimable; exemplary; heroic; honorable; laudable; meritorious
of note: **adv.** *notatu dignum*

WOUND: (**see** "sore") **v.** lacerate; traumatize; **n.** contusion; laceration; lesion; trauma(tism); traumatization; vulnus; **a.** traumatic; vulnerary
incurable: **n.** *immedicable vulnus*

WRANGLE: (**see** "argue") **v.** ergotize

WRATH: (**see** "anger") **n.** animosity; exasperation; indignation; resentment; **a.** WRATHFUL: (**see** "angry") Achillean
day of: **n.** *dies irae*

WREATHE: **v.** intort; **a.** intorted

WRECKAGE, *ship's:* **n.pl.** flotsam and jetsam

WRETCHED: (**see** "deplorable") **a.** abominable; abysmal; calamitous; contemptible; damnable; despicable; detestable; execrable; lamentable; miserable; odious; paltry; squalid

WRINKLE: **n.** corrugation; rugosity; **a.** corrugated; rugate; rugose

WRITE *extravagantly:* **v.** rhapsodize
having strong desire to: **a.** scripturient; **n.** *cacoëthes scribendi; furor scribendi*

WRITER: (**see** "author") **n.** communicator; contributor; correspondent; essayist; litterateur; novelist; prosaist; prosateur; satirist; **a.** contributorial
bearing name of: **a.** onomatous; onymous
complete works of: **n.pl.** *opera omnia*
elegant: **n.** belletrist; bellelettrist; rhetorician; **a.** Addisonian; bellet(t)ristic; Ovidian; rhetorical
insignificant anonymous: **n.** anonymuncule
man using woman's name: **n.** pseudogyny
modern: **n.** neoteric
not bearing name of: **a.** anonymous; pseudonymous
of prose: **n.** prosaist; prosateur
of satires: **n.** satirist; sillographer
professional: **n.** litterateur
witty: **n.** epigrammatist; satirist; sillographer
woman using man's name: **n.** pseudandry

WRITER'S *cramp:* **n.** chirospasm

WRITING(S): **n.** *belles lettres;* communication; literature; scrivening(s)
abstruse: **n.pl.** esoterica; esoterics; hermetics; **n.** hermeti(ci)sm
ancient: **a.** or **n.** cuneiform; hieroglyphic(s)
at length: **see** "wordiness"
collection of: **n.** corpus; (**pl.** collectanea; corpora); syntagm(a)
of varied: **n.** miscellanea; variorum
conversational style: **n.** causerie; journalese
disputatious or controversial: **n.** polemic(s); **a.** polemic(al)
doubtful authenticity: **n.pl.** apocrypha; **a.** apocryphal
erased, found beneath later writing: **n.** or **a.** palimpsest
excess refinement in: **n.** literaryism
false and spurious: **n.pl.** anagignoskomena; apocrypha; pseudepigraph(a); pseudograph(a); **a.** apocryphal; pseudepigraphic(al); pseudepigraphous
falsely attributed to Biblical characters: **n.pl.** pseudepigrapha
fine: **n.pl.** *belles lettres;* **a.** bellet(t)ristic
hand: **see** "handwriting"
high-flown or pompous: (**see** "bom-

bast") **n.** fustian; gasconade; grandilo-quence; grandiosity; lexiphanticism; pomposity; **a.** bombastic; fustian; grandilo-quent; rubescent

made for another: **n.** allograph

mania for: **n.** *cacoëthes scribendi; furor scribendi*

newspaper or magazine style of: **n.** journalese; **a.** magazinish

obscene: **n.** *erotica; esoterica; facetiae;* ithyphallic (verse); pornography

of early church fathers, or of any church, cult or system: **n.pl.** patristics; **a.** patristic

of words not having certain letters: **n.** lipogram

omission in, inadvertent, as of letter or syllable: **n.** lipography; **a.** lipogrammatic; **n.** lipogrammatism

on both sides of paper: **a.** opisthographic

on one side of paper: **a.** anopisthographic

on many subjects, or wide range of: **a.** polygraphic; **n.** polygraph

on single subject: **a.** monographic; **n.** monograph

on walls, etc.: **n.** graffito; (**pl.** graffiti)

ornate and artificial style: **n.** gongorism; mandarinism; rubescence

overly recondite, derivative, or artificial: **a.** alexandrian

pert. to: **a.** bellet(t)ristic; epistolary; graphic; scriptory; scriptorial; textual

picture: **n.pl.** curiologics; hieroglyphics

praising something, exaltedly: **n.** dithyramb

pretentious: **see** "high-flown" **above**

reply in: **n.** rescription; **a.** rescriptive

ribald or coarsely witty: **n.pl.** *facetiae;* a Rabelaisian

style of: **see under** "literary"

superficial or shallow, pert. to: **a.** magazinish

systematic collection of: **n.** syntagm(a)

vividness in: **a.** Addisonian; Ovidian

witty or clever: (**see** "witticism") **n.** *jeu d'esprit;* (**pl.** *facetiae*)

WRITTEN **above:** **a.** superscribed; **n.** antescript; superscription

afterwards: **n.** postscript (**abb.** p.s.)

as: **adv.** *ad lit(t)eram;* sic

before or above: **n.** antescript; superscription; **a.** superscribed

in handwriting of author: **n.** holograph; **a.** holographic(al); onomastic

minutely: **a.** micrographic

on both back and front: **a.** opisthographic

on one side only: **a.** anopisthographic

WRONG: **n.** delict; delinquency; iniquity; malefaction; malfeasance; misdemeanor; misfeasance; transgression; turpitude; venality; villainy; violation; **a.** erroneous; immoral; inappropriate; inequitable; venal; villainous

avenger of: **a.** Nemesis; retributor; *vindex injuriae*

because prohibited or unlawful: **adv. or n.** *malum prohibitum*

civil: **n.** tort

in itself or inherently: **adv. or n.** *malum in se*

of or by reason of a: **adv. or a.** *ex delicto*

-side-out: **adv.** *à rebours*

way: **adv.** *à rebours*

WRONGFUL: **see** "unjust"

Y

YAWN: **v.** dehise; oscitate; **n.** dehiscence; oscitance; oscitation; **a.** YAWNING: cavernous; gaping; oscitant; patulous

YEAR, *great:* **n.** *annus magnus*
 in the course of the (years): **adv.** *volventibus annis*
 of relief for travel, education, etc.: **n.** sabbatical; Shemittah; **a.** sabbatical
 of wonders: **n.** *annus mirabilis*
 school: **n.** *année scolaire*

YEARLY: **see** "annual"

YEARN(ING) **see** "long" **and** "desire"

YELLOW(ISH): **a.** flavescent; flavous; fulvid; fulvous; luteous; lutescent; xanthic; xanthous

YESTERDAY, *pert. to:* **a.** hesternal

YIELDING: **a.** adaptable; amenable; capitulatory; (com)pliant; ductile; malleable; plastic; submissive; susceptible; tractable; **n.** capitulation; cession; complaisance; compliance; resignation; submission; succumbence; succumbency; surrender; **v.** YIELD: capitulate; submit; succumb; surrender
 in judgment or opn.: **n.** deference; **a.** deferential

YOUNG: (see "youthful") **a.** adolescent; immature; impubic; inconabular; inexperienced; juvenile; puisne; vernal
 bearing or bringing forth living: **a.** parturient; proligerous; viviparous; **n.** parturition; viviparity
 bringing forth by eggs: **a.** oviparous; ovoviparous; **n.** oviparity; ovoviparity

bringing forth, or about to: **a.** aborning; parturient; **n.** parturition
 lit. works designed for: **n.pl.** juvenilia
  made by (writings, drawings, scratchings, etc.): **n.pl.** juvenilia
 man: **n.** ephebe; ephebus; (**pl.** ephebi); yo(u)nker; **a.** ephebic
 people, rich and fashionable ("gilded youth"): **n.pl.** *jeunesse dorée*
 person: **n.** juvenile; minor; adolescent
 state of being: **n.** adolescence; juniority; juvenescence; minority; nonage; puberty
  to make again: **v.** reinvigorate; rejuvenate; rejuvenesce; **n.** reinvigoration; rejuvenation; rejuvenescence; renaissance; **a.** rejuvenescent
 woman: **n.** ingénue; soubrette
  actress who plays this part: **n.** ingénue
  unsophisticated: **n.** debutant(e); ingénue
 writings, drawings, scratchings, etc. of: **n.pl.** juvenilia

YOUNGER: **a.** junior; puisne; **n.** cadet; puisne
 status of being: **n.** juniority; minority

YOUTH, *gawky:* **n.** hobbledehoy (**or** hobbletehoy)
 "gilded:" **n.pl.** *jeunesse dorée*
 goddess of: **n.** Hebe
 period of: **n.** adolescence; juniority; *le bel âge;* minority; nonage; puberty

YOUTHFUL: (see "young") **a.** adolescent; callow; hebetic; juvenile; maiden(ly); nealogic; neanic; puerile; vernal; virginal
 growing: **v.** juvenesce; **a.** juvenescent; **n.** juvenescence
 state of being: **n.** juvenescence

Z

ZEAL: **n.** ardor; assiduity; calenture; devotion; diligence; eagerness; enthusiasm; fanaticism; fervidity; fervor; fidelity; gusto; intensity; loyalty; passion; rabidity; sedulity; vehemence; verve; vigor; zest

   excess of: **n.** fanaticism; zealotry

ZEALOUS: **a.** animated; ardent; assiduous; devoted; diligent; eager; evangelis-

tic; fanatic(al); fervent; fervid; impassioned; intense; perfervid; rabid; sedulous; vehement; vivacious; zestful; **n.** animation; ardency; assiduity; devotion; diligence; eagerness; evangelism; vivacity; zest; zestfulness

ZENITH: **see** "acme"

ZEST: **see** "vigor" **and** "zeal"

371